USING AND NOT USING THE PAST AFTER THE CAROLINGIAN EMPIRE

Using and Not Using the Past after the Carolingian Empire offers a new take on European history from c.900 to c.1050, examining the 'post-Carolingian' period in its own right and presenting it as a time of creative experimentation with new forms of authority and legitimacy.

In the late eighth century, the Frankish king Charlemagne put together a new empire. Less than a century later, that empire had collapsed. The story of Europe following the end of the Carolingian Empire has often been presented as a tragedy: a time of turbulence and disintegration, out of which the new, recognizably medieval kingdoms of Europe emerged. This collection offers a different perspective. Taking a transnational approach, the authors contemplate the new social and political order that emerged in tenth- and eleventh-century Europe and examine how those shaping this new order saw themselves in relation to the past. Each chapter explores how the past was used creatively by actors in the regions of the former Carolingian Empire to search for political, legal, and social legitimacy in a turbulent new political order.

Advancing the debates on the uses of the past in the early Middle Ages and prompting reconsideration of the narratives that have traditionally dominated modern writing on this period, *Using and Not Using the Past after the Carolingian Empire* is ideal for students and scholars of tenth- and eleventh-century European history.

Sarah Greer is a post-doctoral fellow at the University of St Andrews. Her research explores the relationships between memory and power in the long tenth century.

Alice Hicklin is a post-doctoral fellow at the Freie Universität Berlin. Her research compares legal and diplomatic practices throughout western Europe in the early middle ages.

Stefan Esders is professor of Late Antique and Early Medieval History at the Freie Universität Berlin, specializing in legal history. He has recently co-edited *East and West in the Early Middle Ages: The Merovingian Kingdoms in Mediterranean Perspective* (2019) with Yaniv Fox, Yitzhak Hen, and Laury Sarti.

USING AND NOT USING THE PAST AFTER THE CAROLINGIAN EMPIRE

C. 900–C.1050

Edited by

Sarah Greer,
Alice Hicklin, and
Stefan Esders

LONDON AND NEW YORK

First published 2020
by Routledge
2 Park Square, Milton Park, Abingdon, Oxon OX14 4RN

and by Routledge
52 Vanderbilt Avenue, New York, NY 10017

Routledge is an imprint of the Taylor & Francis Group, an informa business

© 2020 selection and editorial matter, Sarah Greer, Alice Hicklin and Stefan Esders; individual chapters, the contributors

The right of Sarah Greer, Alice Hicklin and Stefan Esders to be identified as the authors of the editorial material, and of the authors for their individual chapters, has been asserted in accordance with sections 77 and 78 of the Copyright, Designs and Patents Act 1988.

All rights reserved. No part of this book may be reprinted or reproduced or utilised in any form or by any electronic, mechanical, or other means, now known or hereafter invented, including photocopying and recording, or in any information storage or retrieval system, without permission in writing from the publishers.

Trademark notice: Product or corporate names may be trademarks or registered trademarks, and are used only for identification and explanation without intent to infringe.

British Library Cataloguing-in-Publication Data
A catalogue record for this book is available from the British Library

Library of Congress Cataloging-in-Publication Data
Names: Greer, Sarah (Researcher), editor. | Hicklin, Alice, editor. |
Esders, Stefan, editor.
Title: Using and not using the past after the Carolingian Empire, c.
900–c.1050 / edited by Sarah Greer, Alice Hicklin and Stefan Esders.
Description: New York : Routledge, 2019. | Includes bibliographical
references and index. | Identifiers: LCCN 2019032634 (print) | LCCN 2019032635 (ebook) | ISBN
9780367002510 (hardback) | ISBN 9780367002527 (paperback) | ISBN 9780429400551 (ebook)
Subjects: LCSH: Europe--Politics and government--476-1492. |
Europe--History--476-1492--Historiography. | Middle
Ages--Historiography.
Classification: LCC D116 .U76 2019 (print) | LCC D116 (ebook) | DDC
940.1/44--dc23
LC record available at https://lccn.loc.gov/2019032634
LC ebook record available at https://lccn.loc.gov/2019032635

ISBN: 978-0-367-00251-0 (hbk)
ISBN: 978-0-367-00252-7 (pbk)
ISBN: 978-0-429-40055-1 (ebk)

Typeset in Bembo
by Swales & Willis, Exeter, Devon, UK

Printed and bound by CPI Group (UK) Ltd, Croydon, CR0 4YY

CONTENTS

List of Illustrations	*vii*
Notes on contributors	*ix*

1 Introduction *Sarah Greer and Alice Hicklin*	1

PART I
Past Narratives   **13**

2	The future of history after empire *Geoffrey Koziol*	15
3	Remembering troubled pasts: episcopal deposition and succession in Flodoard's *History of the Church of Rheims* *Edward Roberts*	36
4	In the shadow of Rome: after empire in the late-tenth-century chronicle of Benedict of Monte Soratte *Maya Maskarinec*	56
5	Infiltrating the local past: supra-regional players in local hagiography from Trier in the ninth and tenth centuries *Lenneke van Raaij*	77
6	After the fall: lives of texts and lives of modern scholars in the historiography of the post-Carolingian world *Stuart Airlie*	94

vi Contents

PART II
Inscribing Memories 109

7 How Carolingian was early medieval Catalonia? 111
Matthias M. Tischler

8 Orchestrating harmony: litanies, queens, and discord in the
Carolingian and Ottonian empires 134
Megan Welton

9 Models of marriage charters in a notebook of Ademar of
Chabannes (ninth- to eleventh-century) 154
Philippe Depreux

10 All in the family: creating a Carolingian genealogy in the
eleventh century 166
Sarah Greer

11 'Charles's stirrups hang down from Conrad's saddle':
reminiscences of Carolingian oath practice under
Conrad II (1024–1039) 189
Stefan Esders

PART III
Recalling Communities 201

12 Notions of belonging. Some observations on solidarity
in the late- and post-Carolingian world 203
Maximilian Diesenberger

13 Bishops, canon law, and the politics of belonging in
post-Carolingian Italy, c. 930–c. 960 221
Jelle Wassenaar

14 Migrant masters and their books. Italian scholars and
knowledge transfer in post-Carolingian Europe 241
Giorgia Vocino

15 The dignity of our bodies and the salvation of our souls.
Scandal, purity, and the pursuit of unity in late tenth-century
monasticism 262
Steven Vanderputten

16 Law and liturgy: excommunication records, 900–1050 282
Sarah Hamilton

Index 303

ILLUSTRATIONS

Figures

4.1 Monte Soratte as viewed from Rome (Photo by author)	57
4.2 Vat. Chigi. F.IV.75, fol. 40r (courtesy of the Biblioteca Apostolica Vaticana, with all rights reserved)	60
4.3 Reused architectural elements in the church of S. Andrea (Photos by author)	61
10.1 © The British Library Board, British Library, Arundel MS 390, f. 133r	172
10.2 Diagram of the Arundel 390 Table (created by author)	182

Map

4.1 Monte Soratte and its environs (Map created by Gordie Thompson)	58

Table

5.1 Hagiographical works of local patrons of Trier until the first half of the eleventh century (created by author)	80

NOTES ON CONTRIBUTORS

Stuart Airlie is senior lecturer in Medieval History at the University of Glasgow. His research focuses on early medieval political culture. He is the author of *Power and Its Problems in Carolingian Europe* (2012). He is currently completing a book on Carolingian dynastic hegemony as well as one on religious critiques of rulership from 400–1100.

Philippe Depreux is professor of Medieval History at the University of Hamburg. He has published numerous works on early and high medieval political life, written norms, and social and cultural networks. He has recently co-edited *La productivité d'une crise: le règne de Louis le Pieux (814–840) et la transformation de l'Empire carolingien* (2018) with Stefan Esders.

Maximilian Diesenberger is the head of division of Historical Identity Research at the Institute for Medieval Research, Austrian Academy of Sciences. His research interests include medieval identity formation and social cohesion. He is currently finishing a book about morality, pastoral care, and the perception of foreign peoples at the beginning of the tenth century.

Stefan Esders is professor of Late Antique and Early Medieval History at the Freie Universität Berlin, specializing in legal history. He has recently co-edited *East and West in the Early Middle Ages: The Merovingian Kingdoms in Mediterranean Perspective* (2019) with Yaniv Fox, Yitzhak Hen, and Laury Sarti.

Sarah Greer is a post-doctoral fellow at the University of St Andrews. Her research explores the relationships between memory and power in the long tenth century. Her first book, *Commemorating Power: Writing and Rewriting the Past at Gandersheim and Quedlinburg*, is forthcoming from Oxford University Press.

x Notes on contributors

Sarah Hamilton is professor of medieval history at the University of Exeter. She works on social and religious history in the Latin West in the tenth and eleventh centuries. She is currently preparing a co-authored book with Simon MacLean on tenth-century Western Europe and has recently co-edited *Understanding Medieval Liturgy: Essays in Interpretation* (2016) with Helen Gittos.

Geoffrey Koziol is professor of History at the University of California, Berkeley. His research focuses primarily on West Frankish and proto-French history from the ninth through the early twelfth centuries, particularly those points where political and religious discourses intersect. His most recent book is *The Peace of God* (2018).

Maya Maskarinec is an assistant professor of history at the University of Southern California and the author of *City of Saints: Rebuilding Rome in the Early Middle Ages* (2018). Her research interests focus on the city of Rome and include urban history, hagiography and historiography, legal history, and the afterlife of Rome's Christian and classical heritage.

Edward Roberts is lecturer in Early Medieval History at the University of Kent. He specializes in Carolingian and Ottonian Europe, with particular interests in historiography, bishops, and legal culture. His first book, *Flodoard of Rheims and the Writing of History in the Tenth Century*, was published in 2019.

Matthias M. Tischler received his PhD from Heidelberg (1998) and completed his Habilitation in Dresden (2008/2009). Since 2017 he has been a senior research professor at ICREA, Barcelona. His comparative studies raise questions about the geographical, linguistic, religious, cultural, and mental borders of the multi-layered legacy in the centres and peripheries of medieval worlds. He is the founder and editor-in-chief of the *Journal of Transcultural Medieval Studies* (from 2014) and the book series *Transcultural Medieval Studies* (from 2019).

Steven Vanderputten is a full professor in the History of the early and high Middle Ages at Ghent University. His research is mainly involved with the study of the institutional development, societal embedding, and culture of religious communities between c. 800 and 1200, with a particular focus on monastic groups. His monographs include *Monastic Reform as Process: Realities and Representations in Medieval Flanders, 900–1100* (2013) and *Dark Age Nunneries: The Ambiguous Identity of Female Monasticism*, 800–1050 (2018).

Lenneke van Raaij obtained her research master degree in medieval history at Utrecht University in 2016. She is currently completing her PhD thesis at the University of Exeter, in which she explores the uses of liturgy in constructing local pasts. Her fields of interests include manuscript studies and religious and intellectual culture of the early and high Middle Ages.

Notes on contributors **xi**

Giorgia Vocino is currently a research fellow at the Institut de Recherche et d'Histoire des Textes (IRHT-CNRS). Her research interests include intellectual history, the history of education and hagiographical writing in early medieval Italy.

Jelle Wassenaar is a PhD student at the Institute of Medieval Research at the Austrian Academy of Sciences. He is currently writing a dissertation on the construction of diocesan and episcopal group identities in tenth-century Europe.

Megan Welton is currently a post-doctoral research fellow at Utrecht University. Her research focuses on early medieval political culture in the Anglo-Saxon, Carolingian, and Ottonian realms, with a particular interest in early medieval queenship.

1

INTRODUCTION

*Sarah Greer and Alice Hicklin**

The vision of the figure of Charlemagne, who established an empire of almost a million square kilometres reaching from the frontiers of modern Hungary to the Atlantic, and from the English Channel to central Italy and Catalonia, has been a heady one for those who came after him. In the year 1000, the Roman Emperor Otto III returned to the German heartlands of his empire after a grand tour around his kingdom. He was finally drawn to a site laden with imperial significance: the Carolingian palace complex of Aachen, where the remains of his predecessor Charlemagne had been laid to rest in the cathedral after his death some 186 years earlier. Remarkably the exact location of the emperor's body had been lost to posterity, and consequently Otto ordered that the ground of the cathedral should be ripped up, so that he could look upon the body of his great predecessor. The excavations eventually uncovered the site, and the emperor, accompanied by members of his imperial court, came face to face with his predecessor. According to contemporary reports, the body of Charlemagne was found sitting upright on a royal throne in a crypt below the cathedral, wearing a golden crown and holding a sceptre. Otto reverently removed relics from Charlemagne's body – though all the sources disagree on exactly what these relics were – before reburying him with the greatest honour within the church.[1] This millennial unveiling of one emperor by another reverberated throughout the empire and beyond. What Otto specifically hoped to achieve or convey with his exhumation of Charlemagne is disputed, but its symbolism is nevertheless clear: almost 200 years after Charlemagne's death, the lure of aligning his own empire with the memory of the first post-Roman western

---

* The research for this chapter was funded by the 'After Empire: Using and Not Using the Past in the Crisis of the Carolingian World, c.900–1050' HERA project, receiving funding from the European Union's Horizon 2020 research and innovation programme under grant agreement no. 649307.

emperor brought Otto to Aachen and to the feet of Charlemagne. The Carolingian past, personified by its eponymous and most successful ruler, exerted a gravitational pull on those who came after.[2]

The power of Charlemagne as a political symbol has endured. Remembered from the time of his death to the present day, Charlemagne is linked to a vision of a coherent political entity for the territories that once lay within his empire, and was celebrated on the 1,200th anniversary of his death in 2014 as the 'father of Europe', *pater Europae*.[3] Earlier in the twentieth century, Charlemagne's empire functioned as a point of reference – and perhaps inspiration – for the architects of the European Union as they embarked on the ambitious project of constructing a post-national, post-war Europe in the 1940s and 1950s.[4] Even now, the yearly Charlemagne Prize in Aachen is awarded to those who have served the cause of European unity.[5] Charlemagne's conquests of different areas of Europe that had fractured politically with the collapse of Roman imperial power in the west in the fifth century have long fascinated historians, and these, along with the extensive administrative and ecclesiastic reform programmes begun in his reign and the remarkable flourishing of intellectual life at his court and those of his descendants, have been the subject of an immense body of scholarship.[6]

In contrast, European history after the middle ninth century was for many years often cast as the nadir to Charlemagne's zenith, and as a period of decline preceding the seismic political and cultural changes brought about in the later eleventh century.[7] The eventual fragmentation of the empire in the tenth century was seen as the tragic result of the failures of Charlemagne's descendants, epitomized by the battle of Fontenoy in 841, when Charlemagne's grandsons' territorial disputes escalated into what is widely considered to be the bloodiest battle of the Carolingian era.[8] Over the course of the ninth century the raids of Scandinavian warbands on the coasts and rivers of western Europe, Britain and Ireland destabilized existing power structures to a greater and greater extent, as on the Continent contemporaries lamented the inability of the later Carolingian rulers to assuage their suffering. Iberian and North African warbands drawn from the Islamic caliphates had a similarly transformative effect on the regions they targeted in the Mediterranean: churches were destroyed, outposts built, and alliances made. By the end of the ninth century Magyar raids on the eastern edges of the Carolingian Empire proved debilitating to marcher lords there and in northern Italy; these raids would grow in intensity until the middle of the tenth century. This narrative of Carolingian woes, crowned by the untimely deaths of a number of Carolingian princes, came to a head as the empire splintered into regional kingdoms – East Francia, Lombardy, Burgundy, Lotharingia, Provence, West Francia, and Catalonia – whose magnates famously – according to a contemporary chronicler – elected new kings 'from their own guts'.[9]

The splintering of western Europe into different kingdoms meant that each territory charted its own trajectory of rulership over the following century and a half. East Francia saw the rise of a new Saxon dynasty, the Ottonians, who eventually conquered Lotharingia and Lombardy and claimed hegemony over the surrounding territories of Burgundy and Provence as well as principalities to the east of the Elbe. The new German-Italian Empire that was thus formed over the tenth century went on to be ruled by the Salians, an offshoot of the Ottonian family who had established themselves in the Middle Rhine region, from 1024 through the rest of the eleventh century. While Lombardy ended the tenth century as part of this empire, the immediate post-Carolingian period saw northern Italy riven by internal conflict over who should rule; competing Italian kings and their supporters battled for dominance, which opened the opportunity for external figures to repeatedly interfere in Italian affairs and eventually lay claim to the Italian throne. Southern Italy remained a febrile area for much of the period as well, held by the Byzantine emperors who faced challenges both from the Saxon Roman emperors and the Islamic caliphate, before the watershed change of the Norman Conquest of Sicily in the mid-eleventh century.

The West Frankish kingdom, on the other hand, cannot truly be described as 'post-Carolingian' until 987. In the century following the deposition and death of Charles the Fat, West Francia saw a legitimate line of Carolingian kings take the throne. However, their position was far from assured; several non-Carolingian kings were drawn from the Robertian/Capetian dynasty over the late ninth and tenth centuries and Carolingian kings needed to manoeuvre with increasing care around the claims of this family as well as other magnates to rule over large areas of the West Frankish kingdom. The Capetians eventually claimed the throne of West Francia definitively in 987, albeit in the face of considerable resistance from the last generation of Carolingian heirs. In contrast, Catalonia, which lay sandwiched between southern West Francia and the Islamic territory of al-Andalus on the periphery of the Carolingian Empire, had a very different experience as Carolingian and even Frankish power in the region dwindled. Local magnates, such as the counts of Barcelona, stepped forward to claim authority in the tenth-century power vacuum.

Another form of Carolingian periphery can be seen in Anglo-Saxon England; while it was never formally part of the Carolingian Empire, it was enmeshed in the institutional and personal networks of the Carolingian realm and retained close links with the Continent. The tenth century saw the successors of King Alfred in Wessex push back against the viking presence that had swept through the various Anglo-Saxon kingdoms in the ninth century, claiming rulership over a newly created 'English' kingdom. The renewal of viking raids in the late tenth century, however, culminated in a second conquest in the early eleventh century and the accession of Scandinavian kings to the throne. Though the exiled son of Æthelred II, Edward the Confessor, eventually returned the line of Alfred to power, his death without issue ended the line, with the Norman Conquest following months later.

This explosion of new dynasties and territories that sprawled across the former empire and beyond its borders have long been the subject of fervent scrutiny. For earlier historians, influenced by the rise of nationalism in nineteenth-century Europe, the tenth century was the era commonly pinpointed for the origins of the countries that would later become modern nation-states. These origin narratives are prominent in Germany, France, and England, but are visible too in Poland, Norway, Iceland, Denmark, Wales, Scotland, and beyond. Though each of these origin stories differ, the identification of the tenth century as the point of national genesis has nonetheless shaped the overall vision of this period. The long tenth century has thus been seen as a period of chaos and turbulence, from which, eventually, the founding figures of these new nations were able to bring order and stability, creating the structures that would underpin the more recognizable kingdoms of the later eleventh and twelfth centuries. In order for this kind of triumphalist national origin story to function, the tenth century must necessarily lie in the shadows, with its political order characterized as the debris resulting from the collapse of the Carolingian Empire.[10] Fortunately, more recent approaches have moved away from these flawed accounts, recognizing instead the fluidity of this period and the resulting political experimentation. The creation of these new kingdoms is now seen in the light of the uncertainty and various experiments in rulership and government within the tenth century, rather than as part of an inevitable drive towards the nations of modernity.

Yet, while few would still subscribe wholeheartedly to these nationalist views, the legacy of these approaches endures in modern scholarship on the long tenth century. There remains a tendency to consider each territory individually and thus to push narratives of exceptionalism for each. As a result, systematic comparisons of the different regions of tenth- and eleventh-century Europe have been somewhat discouraged. Arguably, the current corpus of scholarship taken as a whole divides the kingdoms of the post-Carolingian Empire more sharply than those living in the tenth century did. Ironically, however, the tendency towards nationalistic scholarship has also encouraged us to view local phenomena as pan-European trends: the kingdoms and principalities of tenth- and eleventh-century Europe are thus at once homogeneous and exceptional.

If the Carolingian Empire is one book-end to the gloomy world of the long tenth century, then the other is provided by the apparently wholesale societal changes that shaped the later eleventh century. The new, 'medieval' order that characterized the twelfth century has cast a shadow that obscures almost entirely the preceding 150 years, turning them, as one commentator observed, into 'a medieval Middle Ages'.[11] Again, the attention of scholars on individual territories has led to the development of different focal points and debates, which have occasionally been applied across all of Europe, despite their rather localized origins. In France, famously, the year 1000 has long been identified as a turning point between the post-Roman world of the Early Middle Ages and the world of the High Middle Ages,[12] a battleground for debates over whether a so-called 'Feudal Revolution' rapidly changed the nature of western European society.[13] Georges Duby and those who followed him focused less attention on the collapse of the Carolingian Empire than on the new forms of lordship that rose up around the turn of the millennium, when local rulers began appropriating power from royal hands.[14] The tenth century played an integral part in such discussions, being closely examined for evidence of when and where the seeds of this later social order were planted.[15]

In Germany, the long tenth century has been overshadowed by the Investiture Contest, a series of convulsions between secular and ecclesiastical powers at the highest level that reshaped kingly and papal authorities and their interactions and brought the 'Early Middle Ages' to their end.[16] The transformation of the Church that began in earnest in the second half of the eleventh century from the impetus of Gregory VII (leading to them being referred to as the 'Gregorian Reforms') drew on ideas that had already taken root in monasteries throughout Europe in the tenth century. In the German Empire, however, the timing of this new reform movement in the later eleventh century offered an opportunity for those who were becoming increasingly frustrated with the Salian dynasty to legitimize new non-Salian rulers. The conjunction of this reform movement with a civil war in Saxony and the rise of several 'anti-kings' sparked a crisis which threatened the basis of the Salian emperors' legitimacy; accordingly, the long tenth century is viewed as a prelude to this fundamental clash between secular and ecclesiastical rulers in the Empire.[17]

In Italy, the collapse of independent power in the long tenth century is seen as heralding the rise of the city-states of twelfth-century northern Italy. With the fragmentation of the Italian peninsula into different areas under the control of external forces, the resulting power vacuums created by absent rulers are thought to have allowed new polities to emerge which were defined by their local nature. This build-up of local, urban power is thus viewed in the light of a collapse of public order in Italy in the tenth century and then linked to the concurrent revival of Roman law in Italy in the later eleventh century and the emergence of a cadre of professional lawyers – with a resulting shift in the nature of Italian documentary culture.[18] In Catalonia, again, the vision of a breakdown of public order in the late tenth/early eleventh century is implicated in ideas of an increasingly feudalized society;[19] and in England, the tenth century's successes were snuffed out by the Norman Conquest of 1066 and the radical restructuring of society which followed.[20] Whether the focus has been on the east or the west, northern Europe or the Mediterranean, looking at the tenth century as the prelude for what lay beyond it in the later eleventh century has led to the impression that the period stretching between 888 and 1050 presents little more than an interval between the lost order of the Carolingian era and the new, more recognizably 'medieval' order of the long twelfth century.

Important work has nevertheless begun to change our view. There has been a shift in favour of interpreting the period under consideration on the Continent on its own terms and with sensitivity to the interconnectedness of its regions. This scholarship, largely but not exclusively produced within the last thirty years, has shown the potential of the sources to shine light onto a period often shrouded in obscurity. From assessments of individual kings or dynasties to considerations of reform movements, monasticism, diplomacy or documentary culture, little by little the tenth and early eleventh centuries emerge from their reputation as the poor relation to what came before and after, showing themselves to be deserving of serious consideration in their own right.[21]

Across continental Europe, the scale and orientation of polities underwent a seismic shift: kingdoms shrank, principalities grew, and power shifted away from the traditional heartlands of the Carolingians towards new areas. Regions that had been peripheries of the former empire, such as Saxony and Catalonia, now found themselves the centres of new polities. Even the idea of 'Frankishness' that had dominated the empire now broke open into different identities, some new and some far older, whether 'Normans', 'Saxons' or 'Lotharingians'. There was a notable diversification of political authority: in addition to new kings, emperors, and dynasties, local figures of authority asserted themselves, from the emergence of sub-regnal 'dukes' in various kingdoms to the apparently commensurate increase in episcopal authority. Power in areas that had once tended towards administrative centralization – such as West Francia and northern Italy – splintered, while the West-Saxon dynasty of Anglo-Saxon England, ruling over a kingdom newly constructed in the wake of Scandinavian conquest, borrowed heavily from past Carolingian models of power as a means to centralize authority and rejuvenate its literary and cultural milieu.

The Carolingian Empire's heyday may well have ushered in a 'renaissance' of knowledge, art and culture, but the tenth and earlier eleventh centuries saw intellectual breathing space develop as an inevitable outcome of the fragmentation of power. The long tenth century thus offers us the chance to look closely at how authority and legitimacy were consciously constructed in a new political order, and how these constructs reflected, manipulated and rejected the past. At all turns, contemporary writers evinced a need to validate, justify and critique the new forms of authority that rose and sometimes fell within their lifetimes, often with reference to what had come before. As previous consensus on the natures of authority and legitimate power vanished, debate (and disagreement) on these topics intensified. Secular rulers, bishops, abbots, abbesses and their *familiae*, clerics and laypeople all attempted to comprehend the changes that they were experiencing by situating them in ideological frameworks that they already possessed. In particular, they turned to the past in order to comment on the present, a reflection of anxieties about the ever-changing present. Innovations and new ways of ruling, writing or governing might be cloaked in references to the past in order to provide the veneer of respectability and historical precedent for new ideas; equally, the past could be a yardstick against which contemporaries and their actions were measured (and then beaten with, should they fall short). In this era of exceptional change, the past became an increasingly powerful tool to comment on the present.

Historians have not failed to notice the sudden changes to the volume and types of historical sources available after the Carolingian Empire's decline. The many narrative histories that illuminate the Carolingian world, long perceived as characteristic of the Carolingian intellectual project through their connections to royal and imperial court culture, had all ended by the early tenth century.[22] Yet the decline in the first half of the tenth century of this style of history-writing did not leave a void. Across Europe, we witness the growing reification of the past in diverse texts. While long-form historical narratives dwindled, they continued to be read and copied, and after 950 there is a clear revival of this type of historical record, in both traditional and new forms. In England and on the Continent hagiographical texts that commemorated living or recently-deceased holy men and women became an increasingly important medium for relating the past, where before hagiographers tended to focus on saints at considerable historical remove; *Gesta* of bishops, too, surged in popularity. The relationships of new histories to the Carolingian past were complex: some new histories were cast as continuations of ninth-century texts, while others showed little interest in Carolingian history and events, and instead focused more intently on their authors' here-and-now.

Innovations and developments in the field of liturgy can also show us new ways of using the past. These are often at first glance more subtle than those of narrative sources but nevertheless highly revealing, as their authors and compilers consciously manipulated Carolingian models to create new ways of commemorating their communities and celebrating their faith. New genres appeared, such as the pontifical, a collection of rites and texts relating to the office of the bishop, and an important witness to the construction of episcopal authority. Changing attitudes to governance present complex regional and normative interactions with the past in documentary culture: the enormous corpus of Carolingian capitularies, diplomas and charters remained a powerful source of legal authority that were copied, revised and manipulated across the former empire and beyond. At the same time the way kingdoms were governed appears to have radically changed: the application of laws and legal norms changed significantly in response to present needs and practices. Agencies came to rely less on the production of new texts, indicating some kind of rupture with what went before, but also used the past to develop different strategies to justify and support legal claims and normative measures in their present world. Falsified documents attributed to Carolingian rulers offer us insight into when and why Carolingian legitimacy may have been wanted or needed and how the past could be used for present effect, as do invocations of the names of previous kings and their legal decisions in contemporary documents.

The 'crisis' of the Carolingian world therefore produced an abundance of texts and authors who tried to understand the present and forecast or shape the future through reference to the past, even if their forms and functions appear at first glance more inscrutable to the historian of early medieval Europe. Those behind the writing and copying of texts simultaneously viewed their present as marked by uncertainty and change, and used the past with increasing creativity and liberty. Understanding how these two interlocking impulses flowed through narratives and texts of the tenth and earlier eleventh centuries offers us a way to comprehend the period on its own terms more fully. This, of course, is not to view the tenth and eleventh centuries through the lens of the Carolingian era, but instead to try to recalibrate our understanding of this period through looking at how tenth- and eleventh-century individuals themselves thought about their present in relation to their past, whether that meant their immediate predecessors, the Carolingians, or further back still, to Merovingian, Lombard, Roman or Greek precedents.

The following volume uses these contradictory and multivalent conceptions of the past as a way to open up lived experiences without resorting to national or teleological perspectives. The various contributors to this collection explore how insecurity around social, political and religious authority in the period after the collapse of the Carolingian Empire drove creative uses of the past across Europe. The chapters of this collection cover a wide geographical remit, including the former territories of the Carolingian Empire, but also looking east and south to its borders on the Slavic march and in Spain, and north-west to Anglo-Saxon England, a society with deep debts to Carolingian ideas about power and authority in the period under scrutiny. A transnational approach to this period, in which historic and contemporary 'frontier' and heartland regions are perceived to be of equal importance, helps us move beyond traditional narratives of national origins associated with tenth-century Europe. The following presentation of cases ranging from France to Germany, Italy to Flanders, and England to Catalonia, offers a comparative view of history after the Carolingian Empire which serves to break the isolation of these different regional histories.

Our first section, 'Past Narratives', explores the writing of texts explicitly concerned with history, considering how different authors approached the past under the new political realities of the long tenth century. In his contribution, Geoffrey Koziol argues that the evaporation of the Carolingian Empire as a framework for presenting past and present events reoriented historiographical texts in the tenth century. New structures needed to be introduced to fill the gap, with those springing up from ecclesiastical genres finding particular favour in shaping new memories of the past. The three subsequent case studies offered by Maya Maskarinec, Edward Roberts and Lenneke van Raaij tackle this same question in fine detail. Maskarinec examines how an Italian monk offered monastic history as an encouraging alternative to the sad lament of imperial history in Rome. As Roberts shows, Flodoard of Reims also tried to find hope for the future in the stories of the past in his careful presentation of the troubled history of the archbishops of Reims. The timelessness of saintly history provided hagiographic authors in Trier another way to respond to the changing political world around them, which van Raaij outlines in her contribution. Stuart Airlie concludes the section by contemplating our own ongoing attempts to find new structures to understand the past as medieval historians, drawing out how the genre of biography has shaped our view of the long tenth century, and how biographies of medievalists, as well as those of medieval texts, can help us better understand our own perceptions of this period.

From this focus on historically-minded texts, we turn to texts that engaged in the past in other, subtler ways in the section 'Inscribing Memory'. Here, our contributors examine the impact of past exemplars and ideas on various genres of text created after the end of the Carolingian Empire, whether that was through adopting or adapting the wording of past documents or creating new texts or manuscripts that visually imitated Carolingian models. Matthias M. Tischler reveals how border regions like Catalonia created their own expressions of 'Carolingian-ness', which evolved in response to localized pressures; these could look rather different from the 'Carolingian-ness' of the Frankish heartlands. The development of Catalan manuscript culture of the ninth to eleventh century provides a case study of this process, featuring the development of a hybrid Visigothic-Caroline minuscule. The visual memories held within manuscripts are also explored by Megan Welton in her study of the role of Carolingian and Ottonian royal women in royal liturgy: we can see the hints of discord and dissenting voices over time in manuscripts where queens' names were written down, erased, or replaced. Liturgy promoted a timeless image of the queen's role in the kingdom, but these sources reveal the tensions that liturgical rites were attempting to quell. This attempt to impose harmony is also seen in Philippe Depreux's examination of the wedding charters recorded by Ademar of Chabannes: the use of Carolingian models for these contemporary texts reveals how the past could be drawn on to provide further stability for acts in the present. The final two contributions both examine the explicit attempts of the Salian dynasty to imitate the Carolingians in two different genres. Sarah Greer focuses on the creation of new genealogical tables that sprang up in the tenth and eleventh century, arguing that one unusual royal genealogy can only be understood when set in the context of the Salian court's intense interest in the Carolingians. This interest was also expressed in the obvious modelling of Salian oaths on Carolingian forms, as Stefan Esders outlines; he argues that this was a deliberate decision on the part of the Salian rulers, revealing the conscious shaping of their rulership in imitation of non-Ottonian past practices.

The final section of the volume, 'Recalling Communities', moves away from specific texts to think more broadly about how the past was used to define communities and communal identity in a period where identities were suddenly in flux. The idea of solidarity, unsurprisingly, became an increasing concern to authors in the tenth and eleventh century as they faced the fluid nature of the new political order. Both Max Diesenberger and Jelle Wassenaar address how authors defined and historicized solidarity and what their aims were in promoting these ideas; Diesenberger provides an overview of the development of the rhetoric of solidarity from the late Carolingian era through to the post-Carolingian kingdoms, while Wassenaar provides a targeted case study, exploring the discussions of solidarity in the tenth-century Italian episcopacy. Giorgia Vocino continues the focus on the Italian episcopate, but provides another facet of their community and identity by exploring the networks of masters and students that shaped the Italian intellectual elite. She notes these networks predated the tenth century, providing some continuity after the collapse of Carolingian power and the rise of new polities while also offering opportunities for Italy to develop its distinctive intellectual culture of the eleventh century. The final two chapters turn to examples where the past was being used to shape religious communities through exclusion. Steven Vanderputten addresses the discourses on monastic purity that spread across Europe through the tenth century, emphasizing how authors relied on time-honoured rhetorical traditions to shape their criticism of contemporary communities. In contrast, Sarah Hamilton describes the innovation of a new form of text, the recording of excommunication practices, which only emerged in post-Carolingian Europe. However, Hamilton

10 Sarah Greer and Alice Hicklin

shows the underlying foundation of ninth-century legislation on these new texts; they were at the same time both innovative and traditional.

Each of our authors draws out how individuals in the long tenth century perceived their present by exploring their depictions of political, legal and social legitimacy in reconstructed versions of the past. Rather than simply treating this period as the sad aftermath of the collapsed Carolingian project, or as the turbulent period that preceded a new social order, this collection of essays considers the tenth and earlier eleventh centuries in their own right, revealing a complex, fluid world where definitions of authority and legitimacy were constantly negotiated.

Notes

1 Thietmar of Merseburg, *Chronicon* 4.47, in Robert Holtzmann (ed.), Scriptores rerum Germanicarum in usum separatim editi 9 (Berlin: Monumenta Germaniae Historica, 1935), p. 184ff; *Chronicon Novaliciense* c. 32, in Gian Carlo Alessio (ed.), *Cronaca di Novalesa* (Torino: Einaudi, 1982), p. 182; Ademar of Chabannes, *Chronicon* 3.31 in P. Bourgain with R. Landes and G. Pon (eds.), *Ademari Cabannensis Chronicon* (Turnhout: Brepols, 1999), p. 153; Johann Friedrich Böhmer *et al.*, *Regesta Imperii II: Sachsisches Haus, 919–1024. 3. Abt.: Die Regesten des Kaiserreiches unter Otto III. (980) 983–1002* (Graz: Böhlau), p. 760.
2 For more on Charlemagne as a model for later rulers, see the commentary and references in Jennifer R. Davis, *Charlemagne's Practice of Empire* (Cambridge: Cambridge University Press, 2015), p. 433.
3 On Charlemagne as *pater Europae*, see *Epos Karolus Magnus et Leo Papa*, in *Poetae Latini aevi Carolini* 1 ed. by Ernst Dümmler (Berlin: Monumenta Germaniae Historica, 1881), p. 94, line 504.
4 Desmond Dinan, 'The Historiography of European Integration' in idem (ed.) *Origins and Evolution of the European Union* (Oxford: Oxford University Press, 2014), pp. 345–75 at p. 349.
5 www.karlspreis.de.
6 The literature on Charlemagne and his reign is too vast to outline in full here. Work on his rule continues apace, sparked in part by the 1,200th anniversary of Charlemagne's death in 2014. A small selection of these recent titles includes: Davis, *Charlemagne's Practice of Empire*; Steffen Patzold, *Ich und Karl der Große: das Leben des Höflings Einhard* (Stuttgart: Klett-Cotta, 2014); Frank Pohle, (ed.), *Karl der Grosse, Charlemagne. Orte der Macht* (Dresden: Sandstein, 2014); Barbara Segelken, (ed.), *Kaiser und Kalifen. Karl der Große und die Mächte am Mittelmeer um 800* (Darmstadt: P. von Zabern, 2014); Philippe Depreux, (ed.), *Charlemagne: du royaume à l'empire* (Chaponnay: Achéodunum, 2014); Johannes Fried, *Karl der Grosse: Gewalt und Glaube. Eine Biographie* (Munich: C.H. Beck, 2013); trans. by Peter Lewis as *Charlemagne* (Cambridge, MA: Harvard University Press, 2016); Anne Latowsky, *Emperor of the World: Charlemagne and the Construction of Imperial Authority, 800–1229* (Ithaca: Cornell University Press, 2013); Bernard S. Bachrach, *Charlemagne's Early Campaigns (768–777): a Diplomatic and Military Analysis* (Leiden: Brill, 2013); Wilfried Hartmann, *Karl der Große* (Stuttgart: Kohlhammer, 2010); Rosamond McKitterick, *Charlemagne: the Formation of a European Identity* (Cambridge: Cambridge University Press, 2008).
7 Marc Bloch, *La société féodale*, 2 vols., (Paris: Albin Michel, 1939); trans. by L. A. Manyon as *Feudal Society*, 2 vols., (Chicago: University of Chicago Press, 1961).
8 See, for example, Edward Gibbon, *History of the Decline and Fall of the Roman Empire*, 2 vols., (2nd ed., Chicago: Encyclopedia Brittanica Inc., 1990), vol. 2, p. 213.
9 Regino of Prüm, *Chronicon*, 888, in *Scriptores rerum Germanicarum in usum scholarum separatim editi* 50 ed. by Friedrich Kurze, (Hanover: Monumenta Germaniae Historica,

1890), p. 129, translated in Simon MacLean (ed.), *History and Politics in Late Carolingian and Ottonian Europe: The Chronicle of Regino of Prüm and Adalbert of Magdeburg* (Manchester: Manchester University Press, 2009), p. 199.

10 For a superb introduction to this historiography, see Timothy Reuter, 'Introduction: Reading the Tenth Century', in idem (ed.), *New Cambridge Medieval History, Volume Three, c. 900–c. 1024* (Cambridge: Cambridge University Press), pp. 1–24.

11 Conrad Leyser, 'Introduction: England and the Continent', in *England and the Continent in the Tenth Century: Studies in Honour of Wilhelm Levison (1876–1947)* (Turnhout: Brepols, 2011), pp. 1–16, at p. 10. On the problematic nature of the term 'medieval' altogether, see Timothy Reuter, 'Medieval: Another Tyrannous Construct?', *The Medieval Journal* 1 (1998), 1–25. On issues of periodisation see especially Kathleen Davis, *Periodization and Sovereignty: How Ideas of Feudalism and Secularization Govern the Politics of Time* (Philadelphia: University of Pennsylvania Press, 2008).

12 Timothy Reuter, 'Debating the Feudal Revolution', in Janet L. Nelson (ed.), *Medieval Polities and Modern Mentalities* (Cambridge: Cambridge University Press, 2006), p. 79.

13 The literature on this topic is extensive; some major works include: Bloch, *La société féodale*; Jean-François Lemarignier, *Le gouvernement royal aux premiers temps capétiens (987–1108)* (Paris: Picard, 1965); Georges Duby, *Les trois ordres, ou l'imaginaire du féodalisme* (Paris: Gallimard, 1978); Dominique Barthélemy, 'La mutation féodale a-t-elle eu lieu? Note critique', *Annales E. S. C.* 47 (1992), 767–77; Cinzio Violante & Johannes Fried (eds.), *Il secolo XI: una svolta?* (Bologne: Il Mulino, 1993); Susan Reynolds, *Fiefs and Vassals* (Oxford: Oxford University Press, 1994). On the debates in historiography see: Dominique Barthélemy & Stephen D. White, 'The "Feudal Revolution"', *Past and Present* 152 (1996), 196–223; Timothy Reuter and Chris Wickham, 'Debate: The "Feudal Revolution"', *Past & Present* 155 (1997), 177–208.

14 Georges Duby, *La société aux XIe et XIIe siècles dans la région mâconnaise* (Paris: Armand Colin, 1953); Jean-Pierre Poly and Éric Bournazel, *La mutation féodale, X^e–XIIe siècles* (Paris: Presses Universitaires de France, 1980); Robert Fossier, *Enfance de l'Europe. X^e–XIIe siècles: aspects économiques et sociaux* (Paris: Presses Universitaires de France, 1982).

15 For challenges to Duby's vision, see, for example, Dominique Barthélemy, *La mutation de l'an mil, a-t-elle eu lieu?: servage et chevalerie dans la France des Xe et XIIe siècles* (Paris: Fayard, 1997); Charles West, *Reframing the Feudal Revolution: Political and Social Transformation between the Marne and Moselle, c. 800–c. 1100* (Cambridge: Cambridge University Press, 2013).

16 Again, the literature on this is vast. See Gerd Tellenbach, *Libertas: Kirche und Weltordnung im Zeitalter des Investiturstreites* (Stuttgart: Kohlhammer, 1932); trans. by Ralph Francis Bennett as *Church, State and Christian Society at the Time of the Investiture Contest* (Oxford: Blackwell, 1940); Josef Fleckenstein, (ed.), *Investiturstreit und Reichsverfassung* (Sigmaringen: Jan Thorbecke, 1973); Horst Fuhrmann, *Germany in the High Middle Ages, c. 1050–1200* (trans. by Timothy Reuter, Cambridge: Cambridge University Press, 1986); Uta-Renate Blumenthal, *The Investiture Controversy: Church and Monarchy from the Ninth to the Twelfth Century* (Philadelphia: University of Pennsylvania Press, 1988); H. E. J. Cowdrey, *Pope Gregory VII 1073–1085* (Oxford: Clarendon Press, 1998); Hartmut Hoffmann, 'Canossa – eine Wende?' *Deutsches Archiv* 66 (2010), 535–69.

17 Some good general introductions are: Gerd Tellenbach, *Die Westliche Kirche vom 10. bis frühen 12. Jahrhundert* (Göttingen: Vandenhoeck & Ruprecht, 1988); trans. by Timothy Reuter as *The Western Church from the Tenth to the Early Twelfth Century* (Cambridge: Cambridge University Press, 1993); Timothy Reuter, 'Pre-Gregorian Mentalities', *The Journal of Ecclesiastical History* 45 (1994), 465–74; Giles Constable, *The Reformation of the Twelfth Century* (Cambridge: Cambridge University Press, 1996); Phyllis G. Jestice, *Wayward Monks and the Religious Revolution of the Eleventh Century* (Leiden: Brill, 1997).

18 Paul Fournier, 'Un tournant de l'histoire du droit: 1060–1140', *Nouvelle revue historique de droit français et étranger* 41 (1917), 129–80; Harold J. Berman, *Law and Revolution: the Formation of the Western Legal Tradition* (Cambridge, MA: Harvard University Press, 1983); Peter Landau, 'Wandel und Kontinuität im kanonischen Recht bei Gratian', in Jürgen

Miethke & Klaus Schreiner (eds.), *Sozialer Wandel im Mittelalter: Wahrnehmungsformen, Erklärungsmuster, Regelungsmechanismen* (Sigmaringen: Jan Thorbecke, 1994), pp. 215–33; Constable, *The Reformation of the Twelfth Century*. On Italian city-states: Renato Bordone and Jörg Jarnut (eds), *L'evoluzione delle città italiane nell' XI secolo* (Bologna: Il Mulino, 1988); Daniel Philip Waley and Trevor Dean, (eds.), *The Italian City Republics* (4th ed., London: Routledge, 2009); Chris Wickham, *Sleepwalking into a New World: The Emergence of Italian City Communes in the Twelfth Century* (Princeton: Princeton University Press, 2015). On southern Italy, see Graham Loud, 'Continuity and Change in Norman Italy: the Campania in the Eleventh and Twelfth Centuries', *Journal of Medieval History* 22.4 (1996), 313–43; idem., *The Age of Robert Guiscard. Southern Italy and the Norman Conquest* (Harlow: Routledge, 2000).

19 Pierre Bonnassie, *La Catalogne du milieu du Xe à la fin du XIe siècle: croissance et mutations d'une société* 2 vols., (Toulouse: Association des Publications de l'Université de Toulouse-Le Mirail, 1975–6); Thomas N. Bisson, 'Feudalism in Twelfth-Century Catalonia', *Publications de l'École Française de Rome* 44 (1980), 173–92; Josep M. Salrach, 'El procés de feudalització (ségles III–XII)', in Pierre Vilar (ed.), *Historia de Catalunya* II (Barcelona: Edicions 62, 1987); Roger Collins, *Early Medieval Spain: Unity in Diversity, 400–1000* (2nd ed., London: Palgrave Macmillan, 1995).

20 On the appearance of the Early Common Law, see now John Hudson, *The Formation of English Common Law: Law and Society in England from the Norman Conquest to Magna Carta* (London: Routledge, 2017).

21 See Karl Leyser, *Medieval Germany and its Neighbours, 900–1250* (London: Hambledon Press, 1982); Heinrich Fichtenau, *Lebensordnung des 10. Jahrhunderts: Studien über Denkart und Existenz im einstigen Karolingerreich* (Stuttgart: Hiersemann, 1984); trans. by Patrick Geary as *Living in the Tenth Century: Mentalities and Social Orders* (Chicago: University of Chicago Press, 1991); Reuter (ed.), *The New Cambridge Medieval History,* Volume 3; Gerd Althoff and Hagen Keller, *Die Zeit der späten Karolinger und der Ottonen: Krisen und Konsolidierungen 888–1024* (Stuttgart: Klett-Cotta, 2008); Jonathan Jarrett, *Rulers and Ruled in Frontier Catalonia, 880–1010* (London: Boydell, 2010); Ludger Körntgen and Dominic Wassenhoven, *Patterns of Episcopal Power: Bishops in Tenth- and Eleventh-Century Western Europe* (Berlin and Boston: De Gruyter, 2011); Gerd Althoff, *Die Macht der Rituale: Symbolik und Herrschaft im Mittelalter* (2nd ed., Darmstadt: Wissenschaftliche Buchgesellschaft, 2013); Graham Loud, 'Southern Italy and the Eastern and Western Empires, c. 900–1050', *Journal of Medieval History* 38.1 (2012), 1–19; Simon MacLean, *Ottonian Queenship* (Oxford: Oxford University Press, 2017).

22 See commentary in Rosamond McKitterick, *The Frankish Kingdoms under the Carolingians, 751–987* (London: Longman, 1983), pp. 305–6.

PART I
Past narratives

2

THE FUTURE OF HISTORY AFTER EMPIRE

Geoffrey Koziol

Histories written in the reigns of Pippin and Charlemagne were triumphalist grand narratives that chronicled the successes of the Franks and their Carolingian rulers. Histories written under Louis the Pious had fewer triumphs to celebrate; yet what Mayke de Jong has argued about polemics written during Louis's reign applies equally to histories: they were deeply engaged in debates about the Carolingian empire. To a large extent this remained the case under Louis's sons: even when Nithard and Hincmar wrote to criticize kings and magnates, they still wrote in the belief that the Carolingian enterprise mattered historically.[1] So when the dynasty and the empire failed, what did those who wrote history think history was about? What had become the *purpose* of history? What framework now gave history coherence? And the problem was not just the purpose and coherence of the *events* of history. The growing separateness of the Carolingian kingdoms also created a narratological problem about how to *write* history coherently. For example, Ado of Vienne had managed to write a short chronicle that provided a clear, coherent, summary narrative from the Creation to the death of Lothar I in 855. Even his highly abbreviated account of Lothar II's troubles is coherent, if partisan. But in the brief sections he and his continuator wrote about subsequent events, the narrative falls apart entirely, while the continuation ends in an incomprehensible jumble.[2] The same applies to the end of Regino of Prüm's *Chronicle*, if to a lesser extent. Its entries for its last thirteen years largely focus on Arnulf and Zwentibald but sometimes dash into Italy and the West Frankish kingdom for particular events, interrupted by the sudden irruption of Huns onto the scene and their equally sudden disappearance; and always events seem to end in failures or, worse, massacres.[3] Arnulf subdues Italy and is crowned emperor only to die, leading to a civil war between Louis the Blind and Berengar, one battle following another until Berengar captured Louis by treachery and had him blinded. 'And so', Regino comments, 'at last Berengar acquired the kingdom of Italy, bloodstained by many slaughters'.[4]

16   Geoffrey Koziol

Then there is the assassination of Fulk of Reims, and Odo's execution of Walcher, and the treacherous murder of Eberhard by the son of Gerulf, to say nothing of the uprising against Zwentibald and Zwentibald's death. Not least there was the Babenburg feud that arose over what Regino calls 'the smallest and most trivial matter'. Again quoting Regino, it, too, ended 'in mutual slaughter. A countless number on each side perished by the sword, hands and feet were lopped off, and the regions subjected to them were completely devastated by plunder and burning'.[5]

Stuart Airlie has written eloquently on some of the issues that underlay these aspects of Regino's *Chronicle*. In his words, the *Chronicle* shows that Regino

> was thinking what was nearly unthinkable for the actors in his text, namely, that the crisis of the system of Carolingian dynastic hegemony ... revealed that this system, even at its height, was just another transient historical arrangement.[6]

To this lucid statement one might only add that the problem was not just a failure of Carolingian dynastic leadership. It was a failure of the entire Carolingian programme for the creation of a Christian society, and the failure of an assumption that the course of history had been leading towards the Carolingian empire so that it might create such a society. It might also be suggested that one reason the great wealth of Carolingian historical writing ends in the later ninth century — leaving Regino nearly alone in undertaking a major historiographical enterprise – was precisely this problem: the purpose of history – history understood both as events and as the recording of events – had become opaque.

This realization raises a central question that must be addressed by anyone who would understand 'the transformation of the Carolingian world': how did contemporaries deal with this new opacity of history? How did they think about the unthinkable?

To continue with Regino, the best known aspect of his paradigm for understanding historical failure was his repeated emphasis on *fortuna*. The wheel of fortune rises and falls, carrying rulers with it – and by extension not only rulers but their kingdoms and empires as well.[7] It is also well known that although Regino was writing a kind of universal chronicle, he differed markedly from other Carolingian practitioners of the genre like Ado of Vienne and Frechulf of Lisieux, for he did not go back to Adam but began with Augustus and the foundation of the Roman empire.[8] One possible reason was that to make his point Regino did not need the succession of four world empires or the six ages of man, because those models of succession implied that history was *going* someplace, that the present was the culmination of the past. But Regino was no longer sure that history was going anywhere at all.[9] His view of history was what Hayden White would have called 'satirical': just one damn thing after another, in fact the same damn thing after another.[10] Moreover, since Regino's real purpose was to understand the historical place of the Carolingian empire, and since the Carolingian empire was imagined as a prolongation of the Roman empire, Regino could make his point simply by beginning with Augustus. Indeed, omitting the three empires prior to the Roman clarified the issues immensely. For the Assyrian, Persian, and Greek empires had risen and fallen before Christ's birth and the redemption of humankind, whereas the story of the Roman empire was the story of Christ's birth, humanity's redemption, and the creation of a Christian empire under Christian emperors.[11] Thus, Rome's failure established a different imperial model: history could become the story of the impossibility of a truly Christian empire.

In writing his history of Rome Regino relied on just a handful of works. The most important of them was Bede's *De ratione temporum*, specifically, the Eusebian-type chronicle that makes up Chapter 66 of *De ratione*.[12] But even though Regino closely followed Bede's sequence of events, he radically abbreviated Bede's accounts. The result was to give Regino's version of Roman imperial history a much different cast than Bede's. One sees this in the way Regino's *Chronicle* opens: in the forty-second year of Caesar Octavian, Jesus Christ, the son of God, was born, his birth proclaimed by angels and visited by shepherds.[13] What Regino left out was Bede's Eusebian framing of the event: in Bede's account, Christ was born the very 'year in which the movements of all the peoples throughout the world were held in check, and "by God's decree Caesar established genuine and unshakeable peace"'.[14] In other words, Bede followed a typical Christian historiographical model which went back to Melitus of Sardis that required the Roman empire for God's unfolding, providential historical plan. Regino completely ignored the model, and with it, discarded the empire's foundation as a linchpin of a knowable providential plan for history.

Or take the two historians' accounts of the reigns of Vespasian and Titus. Bede notes the emperors' suppression of the Jewish revolt, their conquest of Judea, and Titus's destruction of the Temple. But he also speaks of what he calls Vespasian's 'great deeds' (*magnorum operum*) which included not only his conquest of Britain but also his building of the Colossus of Rome – 107 feet high, a fact which Bede took from Jerome. And from Eutropius Bede took his description of Titus as 'a man so admirable in all forms of virtue that he could be called the love and delight of humankind.'[15] None of this praise is in Regino. Instead, he provides the dates of Vespasian's rule, states that 'the kingdom of Judea was overthrown and the temple destroyed by Titus', then adds: 'It was during his reign that Bishop Apollinaris, sent to Ravenna by the blessed Peter, was martyred'.[16]

Granted, Regino is providing an epitome of Bede's epitome, so his accounts are always much briefer than Bede's. Yet for that very reason his distinctive pattern is always much more obvious. Emperors do nothing in Regino's narrative but provide occasions to highlight the glories of martyrs. Over and over, Regino simply gives the dates of imperial reigns, then writes immediately of the martyrdoms that occurred under them. Thus, in writing of Marcus Aurelius and Commodus, Bede mentions their unusual joint rule, their victories against the Parthians, and a plague that struck Italy and Rome. He notes Marcus Aurelius's establishment of his son as emperor. He writes that during Marcus's reign Melitus of Sardis sent his apology for Christianity to the emperor, and the king of Britain wrote to Pope Eleutherius

18   Geoffrey Koziol

asking to become a Christian, and Bishops Apollinarus of Hieropolis and Dionysius of Corinth lived. Folded into this mass of information documenting the steady expansion of Christianity, and without any particular emphasis, Bede adds that there was a persecution in Asia in which Polycarp and Pionius were martyred and that 'in Gaul as well many gloriously shed their blood for Christ'.[17] Though it is based on Bede, Regino's account is entirely different. He gives a simple statement that Marcus Aurelius ruled with Commodus for nineteen years and one month, then writes: 'In these times and those mentioned above the following were martyred'. He now names twenty-six individual martyrs, adding that there were, in addition, fifty unnamed martyrs in Armenia and forty-eight from Lyon, to say nothing of the seven sons of Felicity.[18]

Regino does this consistently. He ignores the virtues of emperors and the great successes of the empire, leaving only a bloody trail of martyrs. Just as interesting, this continues to be the pattern after Constantine. Bede, of course, lavishes attention on Eusebius's great hero, writing of Constantine's conversion; the council of Nicaea; the emperor's building of basilicas in Rome and elsewhere in honour of the Cross, Peter and Paul, John the Baptist, and various martyrs; the emperor's desire to establish a great new capital named after him; and finally his order that pagan temples be closed, adding that he executed this order 'without killing anyone'.[19] Regino omits nearly all of this. Instead, he focuses his attention on Pope Sylvester, even asserting that the council of Nicaea was summoned at *his* direction, not Constantine's, and strongly implying that although the cross of Christ was found during Constantine's reign it was *not* found by his mother Helena.[20] And far from Constantine's conversion representing a culminating moment of Christian triumph, it simply inaugurated a different kind of persecution under Christian emperors and new martyrs under Constantine's sons and later Julian.[21] Then begins an entirely new set of travails: the Huns attacking the Goths, who waste Thrace; Goths, Vandals and Alans attacking Italy and Gaul; the Goths sacking Rome; Vandals, Alans and Goths devastating Africa; and the Vandals finally capturing Carthage.[22]

So in Regino, the unification of the world under the Roman empire changed nothing. The conversion of Constantine changed nothing. The only constant in Christian history is that every success is followed by failure, and there is *always* persecution and martyrdom.

Seen in this light, another characteristic of Regino's *Chronicle* may take on a different meaning than it is usually given. For the decades between the death of Charles Martel and the death of Charlemagne Regino simply copied out the *Royal Frankish Annals* (*RFA*), nearly verbatim. These annals are, of course, the epitome of Carolingian triumphalist history. But Regino sandwiched them between two very different kinds of historical narratives – his history of the Roman empire and that of the contemporary Carolingian empire – and in the latter as in the former, triumph is invariably followed by or accompanied by martyrdom, dissension, and failure. This placement of the *Royal Frankish Annals* between two histories of imperial failure almost demands that a reader interpret the *Annals'* grand narrative differently,

The future of history after empire **19**

not as a turning point of history but as only another transient moment when the wheel of fortune lifted the Franks to the heights before their inevitable fall.

Regino's distinctly untriumphalist interpretation of Christian empire renders one of his rare changes to the *RFA* exceptionally significant. He added an interesting fable about Carloman, the brother of Pippin the Short who resigned as mayor of the palace to become a monk at Monte Cassino. The fable depicts Carloman as a perfect monk, perfect especially in humility, as he undertook the most self-abasing tasks without complaint, even patiently suffering insult and physical abuse without ever revealing his true identity. In this tale, when Carloman had first knocked on the door of the monastery and was brought into the abbot's presence, he immediately fell to the ground, 'declaring that he was a murderer and guilty of all sorts of crimes, and he begged for mercy and asked for a place of penance'.[23] Presumably, the crimes and murders requiring penance were some discreet or garbled reference to his massacre of Alamans at Cannstatt. Regino seems to allude to it earlier, though the allusion is too broad to be certain (and in any case, it came verbatim from the *RFA*). But what is important is that for Regino Carloman, not Pippin, was the exemplary figure of the dynasty, for after doing what kings did by conquering and killing, he sought a life of penitential atonement – as a monk.[24]

Recently, Charles West has argued that Regino's understanding and writing of history were shaped by what he had read. Although one can only agree, the most important influences on Regino may not have been those West identifies: the *Royal Frankish Annals* and the materials on Lothar II's divorce collected by Adventius of Metz.[25] The most important influences were surely Bede's *De ratione temporum* and, alongside it, Justin's *Epitome* of Pompeius Trogus's *Philippic History*.[26] The former gave him a brief, accepted, completely orthodox account of Roman imperial history. The latter gave him a model for an explicitly un-Providential historical narrative. Reading Bede through the prism of Justin, Regino was able to write a history of the Roman empire that could serve as a prototype for a different history of the Carolingian empire. For his additions and subtractions to Bede's 'Greater Chronicle' turned his own history into an illustration of the ultimate failure of worldly political power and the inevitable sinfulness of those who wield such power. And much more than in Bede's chronicle, in Regino's history the Church appears most resplendent in the suffering of its martyrs and confessors.

Regino's recasting of Bede's account of Roman imperial history raises an important point. As Rosamond McKitterick has reminded us, the history of the Roman empire and its intertwining with the history of the Church remained the touchstone for Carolingian historical writing throughout the entirety of the ninth century.[27] This does not mean, however, that chroniclers drew the same lessons from Roman history or described the relationship of Church and empire in the same way. To understand just how differently Roman imperial history had been read earlier in the century, one might compare Regino's treatment with that of Frechulf of Lisieux's *Histories*.[28] Admittedly, the two works are not exactly comparable. Where Regino began with Augustus, Frechulf began with Adam and followed Eusebius and Orosius in adopting the schema of the four world empires, the very schema Regino's focus on Rome allowed him to ignore. And where Regino continued his Roman imperial history to its Carolingian prolongation in his own day, Frechulf ended his history in the early seventh century, with Franks and Lombards destroying the last remnants of the western Roman empire and the Roman pontiff formally recognized as the head of the universal church.[29] Yet the two works overlap in treating the beginnings of the Roman empire, and here their treatments are strikingly divergent. For in pronounced contrast to Regino, Frechulf's Augustan Rome is a grand construction, preordained by God the Father for the birth of His Son. Borrowing heavily from Eusebius, Orosius and others, Frechulf does describe the glories of the martyrs and the wisdom of the 'doctors' of the early church. But Eusebius and Orosius had also treated Roman imperial power, since it was a building-block of God's providential history. Frechulf adopted these stories also.[30] Above all, when writing of the early Roman emperors he quoted the *Epitome de Caesaribus* of Pseudo-Aurelius Victor, doing nothing to mask that work's proudly secular outlook, since pagan political virtues and vices were equally Christian virtues and vices. Thus, Frechulf's sections on Augustus offer a lengthy catalogue, taken from the *Epitome*, of the first Roman emperor's great military deeds and administrative reforms. Frechulf also insists on Augustus's virtues: he refused the title of 'lord', believing it unfitting for a ruler of free men; he was faithful in friendship; he was a lover of poetry and eloquent himself; he was a careful lawgiver and a great builder of monuments. The specifically Christian element Frechulf adds to the *Epitome* is a criticism of Augustus's lasciviousness (illustrated by his divorcing his wife Scribonia).[31] The same emphases are found in Frechulf's treatment of Augustus's successors, again largely borrowed from the *Epitome* (though Orosius had told many of the same stories). For example, although Tiberius was eloquent and knowledgeable in letters he did not inspire trust, for 'he pretended to want what he did not and … seemed gracious to those he actually hated'. Over time, he became increasingly intolerant of opposition and caused the deaths of senators, prefects, and even his own sons.[32] Caligula was nothing but a lewd tyrant, committing incest with his own sisters, demanding that he be worshipped as a god, and killing members of the nobility before being killed by his own palace guard.[33] Claudius obeyed only his belly and his lust while allowing himself to be commanded by his wives and freedmen.[34] Nero was even worse, not just lustful but wanton and greedy, and so depraved that he set Rome on fire just for the spectacle of seeing the city burn.[35] Models of imperial virtues return with Vespasian and his son Titus, who conquered Jerusalem and razed its walls and the Temple, then celebrated a triumph at Rome the likes of which had not been seen in the 320 triumphs staged since the city's founding, for this was a triumph not merely over foreign peoples but over the enemies of God. Having brought peace to the entire world, Vespasian then had the gates of the temple of Janus closed for only the sixth time in Rome's history. Vespasian's particular political achievements were much like those of Augustus: he pacified rather than punished enemies, repaired Rome's buildings, restored the empire's cities, and built and strengthened its roads. As for

Titus, during his youth it was feared that he might follow Nero onto the path of tyranny. Instead, he came to surpass his father in virtue and ruled with clemency, liberality, honour, and contempt of wealth. He thereby gained 'immortal glory' as 'the delight and love of humanity'.[36]

The contrast with Regino could not be clearer. In Frechulf's narrative of Roman history, not only is the empire's establishment under Augustus foreordained by God as the historical moment for Christ's Incarnation – a centuries-old topos of Christian historiography which Regino pointedly ignored – but the fate of the empire depends on the virtues and vices of its rulers. 'Fortune' had nothing to do with it.

Why these differences? It is not a matter of genre. For one thing, Frechulf was writing what is usually called a universal history (indeed, it is a classic example of the type), and it is often thought that Regino was writing a species of one, simply one more limited in time and space.[37] In any case, scholars are today much less prone to seeing hard and fast distinctions in historiographical genres, having recognized not only how many historical works combined elements of what were once thought to have been different genres, but also how purposively authors deviated from antecedent histories.[38] In fact, Regino's *Chronicle* is a prime instance of this, for his deviations from exemplary universal histories (whether Eusebius-Jerome, Orosius, or Bede) are best seen as conscious choices made to heighten his implicit comparison of the fates of the Roman and Carolingian empires. Whatever genre we assign Regino's *Chronicle*, the fact remains that both Regino and Frechulf used the early history of the Roman empire to set out their themes, both used that history to imply a historical interpretation of the Carolingian empire, and both were equally interested in moral readings of history and in the direction of history. Accordingly, the most significant finding that emerges from their comparison is that precisely where the coverage of their histories overlapped, their moral readings and their understanding of the direction of history differed most greatly. The reason for the difference is not that Frechulf was a bishop, and therefore a secular cleric, whereas Regino was a monk, for Frechulf had evidently been educated at Fulda, and his *Histories* were most widely read and annotated by monks at Sankt Gallen and Reichenau.[39] A more important reason for the difference is signalled by the two authors' respective dedications. The *Chronicle* was dedicated to Bishop Adalbero of Augsburg at a time when Regino had been effectively deposed from his abbacy at Prüm and was in exile. Since Adalbero was both godfather and tutor of the young reigning king, Louis the Child, Regino may have hoped the bishop could help restore him to favour. Yet the circumstances of Regino's disfavour point to the very problem the later portions of his chronicle document: an increase in conflicts over power played out regionally between aristocratic alliances, as there ceased to be any stable royal 'court' that channelled patronage.[40] In contrast, Frechulf dedicated the first part of his *Histories* to Helisachar, one of Louis the Pious's most favoured palatines.[41] He dedicated the second book – the part that contains his Roman imperial history – to Judith, Louis the Pious's empress and mother of the young Charles the Bald, with the explicit request that Judith use the *Histories* as a 'mirror'

22 Geoffrey Koziol

for her son, so that Charles might commit to memory the deeds of emperors, the triumphs of saints, and the teachings of doctors, and from them learn what to strive for and what to avoid.[42] Frechulf's *Histories* were therefore a mirror for a prince, produced by a bishop with close contacts at court, who was sent on embassies for the court, and who wrote for leading members of the court, for the empress of that court, and for the benefit of a future king.

The fact that Regino wrote in disgrace could be one reason he was so attuned to the theme of martyrdom, for the famous passage in the *Chronicle* mentioning his deposition as abbot of Prüm has the unmistakably aggrieved tone of someone who himself felt persecuted.[43] And Frechulf's attention to the lives of Roman emperors surely owes something to the fact that he was ultimately writing for a young prince who would someday be king. This may be why his *Histories* are chock-full of the kinds of stories that might appeal to a boy – stories about sieges and triumphs and sex. It is certainly why he dwelt on the importance of the virtues and vices of Roman emperors: he was trying to impress upon Charles the importance of a ruler's personal virtue and vice for his future fame or infamy.

Nevertheless, the most obvious reason for the differences in the two chronicles is surely the most important one. Regino wrote around 908, when the Carolingian empire was a thing of the past – and Regino's awareness that it was past is evident from his chronicle's most famous passage, on the fragmentation of the empire in 888.[44] In contrast, Frechulf wrote in the late 820s, at the zenith of Carolingian power, under a dynasty imbued with the belief that Rome had died only to be reborn as a better, wholly Christian empire. Yet the obviousness of this difference can obscure another that was ultimately critical to the future of medieval historiography. Frechulf could combine secular and ecclesiastical narrative because for him, the church and the empire were the same thing.[45] In this regard, too, his understanding of history was not dissimilar to Eusebius's, Orosius's, and Bede's. But it also applied to history one of the most important guiding principles of the first part of Louis the Pious's reign, which found its best illustration in Jonas of Orléans' well-known recasting of Gelasius's *Duo quippe*. In Gelasius's original formulation, the sacred authority of the pontiffs and the royal power ruled the 'world'. In Jonas's reformulation – articulated at the very moment that Frechulf was submitting his *Histories* to Judith – they shared rule of the 'church'.[46] Regino's more pessimistic view of secular politics required him to re-extract *ecclesia* from *regnum*, creating space for a history of the church that was separate from the history of secular power, a history in which secular power and secular power struggles often worked *against* the church's mission, a history in which bishops and monks, like the martyrs and confessors before them, had an obligation to resist secular powers when those powers oppressed them. Given these differences, it is not surprising that in addition to writing his *Histories* Frechulf compiled a new, improved edition of Vegetius's *De re militari*, which he composed for and dedicated to Charles the Bald.[47] Nor is it surprising that besides the *Chronicle*, the work for which Regino is best known is the *Libri duo de synodalibus causis et ecclesiasticae disicplinae*, a compilation of strictly ecclesiastical canons that establishes the church within its own separate

The future of history after empire **23**

governmental sphere, a sphere ruled exclusively by churchmen and exclusively by church laws.[48]

In other words, when the Carolingian dynasty failed in its historic mission, writers of history like Regino were not really cast adrift without any historical framework for understanding the present in terms of the past. But the historical framework that was left to them was a kind of ecclesiastical history that described the church and the world as fundamentally separate entities in perennial potential conflict. In this history, the age of martyrs and confessors had never ended.

If we place it within this momentous paradigmatic shift, then Regino's *Chronicle* no longer appears quite so solitary, for we find something very similar in another genre of contemporary historiography, *gesta abbatum* and *gesta episcoporum*.

The first Carolingian-era works that look something like such *gesta* were every bit as triumphalist as other histories. And just as Frechulf's *Histories* correlated the history of the church and the history of empires, so in these *gesta* the history of individual churches and the acts of their eighth- and early ninth-century prelates were always placed within the framework of the Carolingian dynasty and empire. To take just the most obvious example, in his *Liber de episcopis Mettensibus*, Paul the Deacon so ties the fate of the Carolingians to the see of Metz that he makes them descendants of Bishop Arnulf of Metz via Arnulf's son Ansegisel.[49] In Paul's history another bishop of Metz, Chrodegang, was the former referendary of Charles Martel, and 'especially chosen by Pippin and the whole assembly of the Franks' to escort Pope Stephen II to Gaul.[50] This, of course, was the papal visit that resulted in the first *pacis foedus* between the new Frankish king and the vicar of St. Peter and culminated in the pope's consecration of Pippin, his wife, and their two sons.[51] In the reign of Louis the Pious, a *gesta abbatum* was begun at Fontenelle. Like Paul, its author used genealogy to link the monastery to the Carolingian dynasty: in this case, Arnulf of Metz's son Anchises (that is, Ansegisus) remains the father of Pippin, 'most glorious duke of the Franks', but now Pippin's brother Waltchisus is introduced as the father of Wandregisilus, Fontenelle's founder.[52] And the bond between monastery and dynasty remained close, for the abbots of Fontenelle whose deeds the *Gesta* recounts include Charles Martel's nephew Hugh; Pippin the Short's godfather Raginfrid; the great courtier and biographer of Charlemagne Einhard; and Ansegis, perennial *missus* of Louis the Pious and compiler of royal capitularies.[53] Of Abbot Gervold, chaplain to Pippin's queen Bertrada, the author notes that Charlemagne sent him as legate to the Greek emperor and appointed him receiver of payments from the empire's northern coastal emporia.[54] In the author's recounting Fontenelle was central to Charles Martel's victories over the Neustrian mayor of the palace Raganfrid and the duke of the Frisians Radbod.[55] So closely does he conjoin the monastery's history and the history of the ruling family that he often interrupts his narrative of Fontnelle's local past to recount the far-flung victories of the rising dynasty, borrowing from the Carolingians' own house chronicle, the *Annales Mettenses priores*.[56] And while he laments the monastery's loss of estates and revenues that abbots appointed by the kings leased out to the kings' men, he only blames the abbots, never the kings themselves. In fact, when faced

24 Geoffrey Koziol

with abbots whom the *Gesta* calls not 'rectors' but 'tyrants', the monks' remedy always lies with the Carolingian rulers.[57]

The *Actus pontificum Cenomanensis in urbe degentium* is the next extant *gesta*. It is also one of the most problematic, since so much of its narrative is invention, so many of its embedded charters forgeries. The text is so difficult that historians have not even been able to agree on the stages of the collection's compilation or their dates. Still, there is general agreement that the extant version was completed between 855 and 863. There is also agreement that the invention and forgeries were mobilized to advance a clearly discernable theme – the inalienability of church property – whose treatment announces that we have entered a historiographical world very different from that of both earlier *gesta* and earlier histories and annals.[58] To be sure, the Carolingian dynasty features prominently in the narrative. For example, the longest chapter of the *Actus* focuses on the tyrannical control of the bishopric of Le Mans by the local *dux* Rotgar, his son Charivius, and their illegitimate episcopal appointee, Rotgar's son Gauziolenus. Their tyranny was said to have begun under the last Merovingian ruler, Childeric III. It was ended only by the first Carolingian kings, Pippin and Charlemagne, who intervened repeatedly and actively to restore canonical order to the see.[59] Nevertheless, the attitude of the author (or authors, for though the themes of the *Actus* are so unified that they reveal a single mind, the episcopal narratives and diplomatic apparatus are so complex that they could only have been executed by a team) are notably ambivalent. Although the *Actus* dates the tyranny of Rotgarius, Charivius, and Gauziolenus to the reign of Childeric III, every ninth-century reader of histories and hagiographies would have known that their policies were those of Charles Martel, who is conspicuously not mentioned at all. And Pippin's actions in ending the tyranny were of markedly mixed success, for while he appointed a new bishop (Herlemund), he did not end Gauziolenus's position as bishop. Even after Gauziolenus had Herlemund blinded, Pippin refused to have him deposed. Instead, he appointed what turned out to be the first in a series of three chorbishops to execute episcopal functions. When Gauziolenus died, episcopal properties were again siphoned off by Gauziolenus's *vicedominus* Abraham, who not only distributed them to his lay and clerical followers but also bribed Charlemagne to grant them to Abraham's men as benefices. Charlemagne did so, 'deluded by human greed', giving out monasteries, churches, *vici*, and villas that were intended to support the clergy and poor. When Charlemagne was finally alerted to the ensuing poverty of the bishopric and its clergy, he still did not fully restore the lost properties. Rather, he allowed their current holders to continue to possess them for their lifetimes, on condition of paying census to the church with the properties returning to the church on their deaths. Learning of the accusations against the next bishop, Joseph, Charlemagne was 'very angry', yet in the end he did nothing because the charges could not be proved. Not until Joseph defected from the royal army and assembly did Charlemagne have him deposed, leaving Joseph's successor Franco as poor as his predecessors.[60] Only now did Charlemagne act to right the wrongs he himself had consented to, asking Franco to name the properties that should be restored to the church. But once Franco named them Charlemagne refused to restore them, on the grounds that the men who held the properties were travelling with him to Rome, so the properties could not be returned to the church. He asked Franco to name another property instead. Franco asked for the monastery of Saint-Calais. This was approved after an inquest into the bishops' title to it, and confirmed by a precept issued at Rome itself by the newly crowned emperor.[61]

The *Actus*'s treatment of the Carolingians reveals them to be not heroes but deeply flawed rulers. They allow themselves to be duped by gifts. They compromise the rights of the church rather than doing what is right. They are as much the cause of the see's problems as its saviours. Never does the *Actus* represent the new dynasty as a turn towards a new historical moment. Quite the contrary: borrowing from an account of the translation of Scholastica (sister of Benedict of Nursia) written a little earlier at Le Mans, the *Actus* praises Dagobert's son Clovis II far more lavishly than it does Pippin or Charlemagne: Clovis was

> a man most noble in everything, and most astute in the administration of what pertained to *res publica*. For he was esteemed on account of his outstanding virtues, offering assent to the petitions of the servants of God not just readily but devotedly. And so, it was in his time that many monasteries were built throughout his kingdom and noteworthy religious deeds flourished.[62]

The ambivalent role of the Carolingians in the *Actus* is closely connected with a different framing of history itself. The difference is most clearly seen in the very first chapter, dealing with the foundation of the church of Le Mans under its first bishop, Julian. According to the *Actus*, the foundation occurred at the beginning of the Roman empire, but Roman emperors had nothing to do with it – the empire is not even mentioned. Rather, it was a quasi-apostolic foundation, Julian being one of the seventy disciples ordained by the apostles. He was personally instructed and consecrated bishop by Peter's successor Clement, who sent him to preach in the Gauls as one of the companions of Dionysius and his *socii*, who were martyred at Paris. Arriving at Le Mans, Julian found the people adoring idols, worshipping demons, and venerating mountains, groves, and stones. Yet the people listened to him. The *princeps* of the place (Defensor) invited him to preach before him. When Julian worked a miracle Defensor humbled himself before the bishop. Julian made the sign of the cross over Defensor, they embraced and kissed, and a multitude was baptized as a result of the bishop's sermon. Defensor then gave Julian his own house to use as a church and ordered the people to come to Julian, listen to his preaching, and obey his orders, while the *princeps* and his *optimates* bestowed gold, silver, and vestments on the church and endowed it with whatever property they had in the city and its suburb. The *princeps* himself gave other villas he possessed, asking the bishop to build churches and establish priests and ministers in them to instruct and baptize those people who could not come to the city.[63]

Stories about origins and foundations often announce the main themes of *gesta* and histories, and so it is in the *Actus*. The reason neither Merovingian nor

26 Geoffrey Koziol

Carolingian rulers are specially singled out for any historic mission is because they simply iterate the exemplary role of Defensor. Whether pagan or Christian, Merovingian or Carolingian, *principes* are introduced in the history to show their support of bishops, who are the real leaders of a Christian society comprised of clergy, people and nobles acting together. Again and again the *Actus* shows us the people and nobles (*populus*, *optimates*) gathered around their bishop, devoted to him, and supporting him with their donations. And over and over, it is the people who act at key moments in the *Actus*. 'With one voice and one heart', the people elected Julian's companion Pavacius to succeed Julian as bishop.[64] The clergy and people later elected Victurius II bishop.[65] After a period without a bishop, 'the city and the people of that diocese, inspired by the lord', welcomed Domnolus to Le Mans, 'and all the princes of the region and the priests, clerics, and nobles of the diocese beseeched him to take the city under his rule'. Though unwilling, Domnolus finally assented, 'forced by the clergy and people'.[66] When faced with the tyranny of Rotgar and Charivius,

> the people, seeing themselves deceived (*illusum*) by them, began to ask that they be given a pontiff who might instruct and fortify them with divine words and exercise the episcopal ministry, since without a bishop they could scarcely be good Christians or be saved.[67]

For the authors of the *Actus*, the church is really 'the clergy and people' working together under *principes* but led spiritually by bishops, whose churches benefit from the largesse of people and *optimates*. In this regard, the church of Le Mans is simply a microcosm of the wider church, and kings are simply *principes* writ large. This is the reason intersections with the Carolingians are incidental, not essential, to the identity of the church of Le Mans. It is also the reason the *Actus* repeatedly places the history of the church of Le Mans within the history of the wider church, both Roman and Frankish. This pattern, too, is established in the very first chapter, which identifies Julian as one of Christ's seventy disciples and has him being sent out by Peter's successor Clement to the Gauls as a companion to none other than Dionysius of Paris.[68] The second and third bishops, Turibius and Pavacius, were also ordained by Clement, who sent them as Julian's companions.[69] Bishop Liborius was buried by Martin of Tours, who had been forewarned of Liborius's death by a divine vision.[70] By divine inspiration Martin also recognized Victurius as Liborius's successor, presenting him with his own staff and personally leading him into Le Mans.[71] Martin also instructed Victurius's son (likewise named Victurius) and personally ordained him in Tours.[72] Victurius II's successor was Principius, whom the *Actus* turns into the brother of Remigius of Reims.[73] Bishop Domnolus founded a monastery and had it dedicated by Germanus of Paris, who subscribed Domnolus's foundation charter. Germanus also taught and ordained Domnolus's successor Bertichramnus.[74] At every opportunity the *Actus* seems to eschew offering a history of the Franks and their great deeds and heroic kings, offering instead a history of the Frankish church as a college of legendary, sainted bishops.

The next important *gesta episcoporum* was composed only a decade or so after the *Actus*, between 873 and 875, when two canons of the cathedral chapter of Auxerre began to compile what is known as the *Gesta pontificum Autissiodorensium*.[75] The authors had remarkably few diplomatic sources at hand on which to base their history of the church of Auxerre. They did, however, have hagiography, particularly for the earliest period. Save for Constantius's fifth-century life of Germanus, most of these works had been compiled in the late sixth and early seventh centuries. Factually and chronologically impossible, their stories were concocted, in part, to give the church of Auxerre a depth of sacred history it did not have.[76] Yet the authors of the Auxerre *Gesta* mobilized them with skill and imagination to create a history very different from the *Gesta* of Fontenelle but not all that dissimilar from the *Actus* of Le Mans.[77] Here, too, the authors established the pattern at the very outset, in the section devoted to Auxerre's first bishop, Peregrinus.[78] The authors knew very little about this obviously invented figure. Accounts of Peregrinus in relevant martyrologies are very brief and not terribly specific, while the saint's *passio* is singularly lacking in detail.[79] The *Gesta* itself says that Christians at Auxerre requested Pope Sixtus to send someone to revivify a faith weakened by persecution. In response, Sixtus ordained Peregrinus as bishop and sent with him a priest, an archdeacon, and a lector, all of whom are named. These men then travelled to Lyon via Marseille and began to preach as soon as they reached Auxerre. Peregrinus built a small church and had such success that soon the cult of the pagan gods disappeared from the city. Peregrinus then extended his preaching into the neighbouring *vici*, until he confronted a large crowd of pagans assembled for the worship of Jupiter and was beheaded.

So Peregrinus was the first bishop, a martyr, and the founder of the church of Auxerre, and he was first and foremost a preacher of the word of God, sent by the pope himself at the direct request of the faithful of the city. Because this was too little on which to build a stirring foundation legend of the church of Auxerre, the canons fleshed it out with details from passions and *vitae* of famous Burgundian saints, including those of Columba, Andochius, Benignus, and Symphorian. In this way, the passion of Auxerre's first bishop became integrated into the history of the Christian faith in the Gauls since the time of Peter's successor Pope Clement who – according to the *Gesta* – had earlier sent as evangelists Savinian, bishop of Sens; Dionysius, bishop of Paris; Ursinus, bishop of Bourges; Martial, bishop of Limoges; Saturninus, bishop of Toulouse; and Memmius, bishop of Châlons. Then the authors introduce the persecutions of the Roman emperor Aurelian, which spread to Gaul and to Auxerre, where they were implemented by a particularly harsh antagonist named Alexander. To illustrate his savagery the authors cite the martyrdom of Priscus in the vicinity of Auxerre (a legend transmitted locally by earlier hagiography), and thereafter the martyrdoms of Benignus, Andochius, Thyrsus, and Symphorian. These persecutions nearly wiped out Christianity in the Auxerrois, leading the most faithful of the remaining Christians to ask Sixtus to send someone to re-evangelize the region, which resulted in the mission of Peregrinus.

28   Geoffrey Koziol

What may be most interesting about this opening section of the *Gesta pontificum Autissidorensium* is the way it places the foundation of the church of Auxerre within a Roman history, but a Roman history in which empire stands for nothing but persecution, and empire is opposed by the bishops of Rome, leading the battle for Christianity. Like the *Actus*, it is also very much a history of the Gauls and their Christianization, with a scarcely known martyr placed by juxtaposition in the company of the great founding bishops of the Gallic sees, who were themselves the titular saints of some of the oldest, greatest monasteries in the ninth-century West Frankish kingdom.[80]

Having announced the motif of martyrdom in their foundation legend of the see, in subsequent chapters the authors of the *Gesta* return to it whenever they can. The third bishop, for example, Valerius, was not himself martyred, but his episcopate is dated by reference to the emperors Diocletian and Maximian and the martyrdom of three Roman pontiffs by these emperors.[81] Nothing whatsoever was known of the ninth bishop, Fraternus, except that he received 'the crown of martyrdom from the barbarians'.[82] Little was known of the eleventh bishop Ursus except that he died during the Roman pontificate of John, the authors noting that John was martyred by 'the heretical king' Theoderic.[83] Nothing was known of the seventeenth bishop, Romanus, but 'it is said' that he was martyred by decapitation in the time of the martyred Pope John.[84] As to the twenty-second bishop, Vigilius, he was martyred by the mayor of the palace (*princeps palatii*) Waratto, the author adding that in this Waratto followed the example of his predecessor Ebroin, who had martyred Leodegar, bishop of Autun.[85] Treticus, the twenty-fourth bishop, was killed by his archdeacon, Ragenfred, and so 'ended his life in martyrdom', being buried in the church of the martyr St. Eusebius. Above the bench where he was murdered while asleep, his successors built an oratory for his memory and veneration, the location being much honoured by the faithful.[86] Above all there was Hainmarus, whose enemies accused him of treason before Pippin, 'the king'. He escaped from prison and fled on horseback. Realizing he could not outride his pursuers, 'he extended his arms in the manner of a cross, his eyes raised to heaven, and beseeched divine grace', before being run through with lances. 'It is said' that he was buried on the very spot of his death. To this day, the authors wrote, the altar of the church of Auxerre has a gold-gilt cross showing his 'martyrdom'.[87] Even bishops who are not killed can still, when possible, be likened to martyrs: when Charles Martel diverted the property of the church of Auxerre, Bishop Aidulf 'suffered almost to death' on account of the 'humiliation' of his church, to the point that he became paralysed and lost the use of his limbs, and could no longer act as bishop.[88]

Martyrdom is an ostinato sounding throughout the *Gesta* of the bishops of Auxerre. Just as important is what does not sound at all: any note of Roman, Frankish, or Carolingian providential triumphalism. As we have seen, apart from serving to date pontificates, Roman emperors and their provincial officials are introduced exclusively as persecutors. Neither is the conversion of Clovis mentioned, nor Pippin's elevation as king; and Charlemagne's imperial coronation is mentioned only to note that Bishop Aaron accompanied him to Rome for the occasion, and at that time received a monastery at Auxerre.[89] As to other events involving the Franks and their kings, the longest account involves the above-mentioned killing of Hainmarus. It is a bizarre farrago, placed against the background of the Carolingians' campaigns against Odo of Aquitaine, only the campaigns are said to have occurred under Pippin, not Charles Martel, and the author manages to introduce a daughter of Odo who is supposed to have married the king of Saragossa. The only act ascribed to Charles Martel himself is his seizure of the church's property, which was given over to 'the lordship of seculars'.[90] Otherwise, one of the rare allusions to Frankish history occurs in the *gesta* of Bishop Savaric. In his time, 'the Franks were fighting among themselves and engaging in many civil wars', including a battle in the forest of Cuise, where 'they fell upon each other and killed each other with the greatest slaughter'. Savaric, the bishop, actively engaged in the killing; for he had 'little by little fallen from the status of his order, and avidly gave himself up secular concerns more than episcopal'. So at Cuise, he led troops on Lyon, trying to 'subdue it by iron', but was instead killed 'by a divine blow'.[91]

The *Actus pontificum Cenomanensis*, written in the late 850s and early 860s, and the *Gesta pontificum Autissidorensium*, written in the early 870s, already share a surprising amount with Regino of Prüm's *Chronicle*. There is no Carolingian triumphalism. The Carolingian empire is not a rebirth of Roman imperial authority as part of God's providential plan for the fulfilment of Christian history. The acts of Roman emperors are not exemplary tales told to educate Carolingian princes to do good and avoid evil. History has become a tale of persecution, warfare, and turmoil without any promise of a more just, more Christian political society in the future. The very frame of history has changed from empire to church, where the church is an apostolic foundation led by bishops and nourished by the blood of martyrs.

How did this happen? And why did it seem to happen first in two opposite ends of the West Frankish kingdom, and nearly at the same time? That, of course, is the $64,000 question, too complex to resolve here. But three interrelated factors will surely form part of any answer.

First, the period when this new historiography was developing immediately followed the sudden proliferation of a very different kind of historical text: the historical martyrology. Initiated in England by Bede, the genre luxuriated on the Continent during the first half of the ninth century, particularly at Lyon and Vienne, before reaching its fullest realization with Usuard's compilation, made at Saint-Germain-des-Prés between c. 850 and c. 865.[92] Usuard's work quickly became the most widespread martyrology of all. Importantly, Usuard incorporated information about the recent martyrs of Córdoba, which he had personally gathered during a remarkable journey in 858.[93] In other words, the lesson Usuard brought back from Spain which his work helped propagate was that martyrs were not just heroes of the ancient church; the contemporary church was also a church of martyrs. Second, ever since 825 the Carolingian episcopacy had been developing a greater sense of a collective identity and, vis-à-vis kings, even autonomy. This sense was especially pronounced among the West Frankish and Lotharingian episcopate during the reign of Charles the Bald. Thus, it is conciliar acta from these regions that are most insistent on bishops exercising a *ministerium* complementary to but independent of kings, and on the need for rulers to heed bishops.[94] And it was primarily West Frankish and Lotharingian bishops who issued and circulated the episcopal capitularies that promoted the authority of bishops in administering dioceses, reasserted the centrality of episcopal capitals in diocesan sacraments and liturgies, and took over the responsibility of applying the principles of the Carolingian reform locally.[95] Third, and above all, it was the West Frankish church especially – bishops, regular abbots, and secular clergy and monks alike – that was most preoccupied with the protection of ecclesiastical property. This assertion of the sacrosanctity of church property was a direct response to Charles the Bald's appointment of powerful laymen and bishops to abbacies in politically and militarily sensitive areas, allowing these titular abbots to divert monastic properties to support their military functions. Charles's military actions against vikings and Bretons also allowed the leaders of his armies to demand requisitions in labour and kind from residents of ecclesiastical estates. Criticism of such policies was rife. The best known examples were tracts by Archbishop Hincmar of Reims, notably his *De raptoribus* and his collection of capitularies on military exactions, but Hincmar was not the only critic. The kingdom's bishops made increasingly strident complaints about the diversion of ecclesiastical property in councils at Beauvais, Meaux, and Paris in 845 and 846. And though Charles largely rejected their demands, in subsequent years he did award an exceedingly large number of royal charters to monasteries and a few cathedral chapters guaranteeing the convents' rights to renders and revenues from a defined number of estates. It was the price of getting the convents' acceptance of his abbatial and episcopal appointments.[96]

These three developments were instrumental in re-extracting from the *regnum* an *ecclesia* with its own interests – and its own history. Not surprisingly, then, all three feature prominently in the *gesta* of Le Mans and Auxerre. Thus, as already mentioned, the *Gesta pontificum Autissidorensium* was written as a history of martyred bishops. Indeed, the connection between this *Gesta* and martyrologies is demonstrable. For on his return trip from Córdoba Usuard stayed at Saint-Germain of Auxerre, where an important version of his martyrology was adapted.[97] Martyrdom is much less a feature of the *Actus pontificum Cenomanensis*. On the other hand, the issue of church property is everywhere. Indeed, the spark that triggered the project of which the *Actus* forms the largest part was precisely this: that Charles had allowed the clients of Robert the Strong to take over the abbacy of Saint-Calais and use its lands in support of Robert's appointment as head of the Breton march.[98] The sacrosanctity of ecclesiastical property also figures in the *Gesta pontificum Autissidorensium*, with its repeated criticism of bishops who dispersed church property or failed to prevent its dispersal by rulers and powerful laymen, and its equally frequent praise of those bishops who protected and increased the property of the church.[99] It is therefore probably not a coincidence that Saint-Germain of Auxerre was the recipient of an extraordinarily large number of Charles's diplomas guaranteeing the monks' control over a monastic *mensa*, while Saint-Étienne of Auxerre was one of the relatively few cathedral chapters to receive a diploma guaranteeing a capitular *mensa*.[100] As for episcopal statutes, although none are extant from either Auxerre or Le Mans, their *gesta* foreground many of the statutes' typical concerns. Both, for example, consistently call attention to the dependence of diocesan churches on episcopal control and the obligation of bishops to teach their clergy and preach to their laity.[101] Even more frequently, both works consistently cite episcopal statutes regulating the liturgical obligations of the clergy and laity in churches spread throughout the diocese.[102]

In other words, three to four decades before Regino wrote not just his chronicle but also his collection on episcopal synods and ecclesiastical discipline, the Carolingian church had already been reminded that it was a church founded in the blood of martyrs, that the history of political power was more often a story of tyranny than of righteousness, and that bishops, not kings, were the real leaders of a Christian society. So when the Carolingian empire failed, historians were not paralysed by cognitive dissonance. A new kind of history – a new kind of ecclesiastical history – had already been prepared. *That* is how writers of history were able to think about the unthinkable.

Notes

1 Mayke de Jong, *The Penitential State: Authority and Atonement in the Age of Louis the Pious, 814–840* (Cambridge: Cambridge University Press, 2009); Janet Nelson, 'History-writing at the courts of Louis the Pious and Charles the Bald', in *Historiographie im frühen Mittelalter*, ed. by Anton Scharer and Georg Scheibelreiter, Veröffentlichungen des Instituts für Österreichische Geschichtsforschung, 32 (Vienna: R. Oldenbourg Verlag, 1994), pp. 435–42.

2 Ado of Vienne, *Chronicon in aetates sex divisum*, *Patrologia Latina* 123: 23–138, especially cols. 135–7; see also G. H. Pertz's remarks in his partial edition of the *Chronicon*, in MGH SS 2: 315–25 (pp. 315–6), and Rosamond McKitterick, *Perceptions of the Past in the Early Middle Ages* (Notre Dame, IN: University of Notre Dame Press, 2006), pp. 29–30 and *passim*.

3 Regino of Prüm, *Chronicon*, ed. by Friedrich Kurze, MGH SRG, 50 (Hanover: Impensis Bibliopolii Hahniani, 1890), pp. 142–53 (aa. 894–906); trans. Simon MacLean, *History and Politics in Late Carolingian and Ottonian Europe: The 'Chronicle' of Regino of Prüm and Adalbert of Magdeburg* (Manchester: Manchester University Press, 2009), pp. 217–31.

4 Regino, *Chronicon*, p. 150 (a. 905); trans. MacLean, *History and Politics*, p. 228.

5 Regino, *Chronicon*, p. 145 (a. 897); trans. MacLean, *History and Politics*, pp. 221–2.

6 Stuart Airlie, '"Sad stories of the Death of Kings": Narrative Patterns and Structures of Authority in Regino of Prüm's *Chronicle*', in *Narrative and History in the Early Medieval West*, ed. by Elizabeth M. Tyler and Ross Balzaretti (Turnhout: Brepols, 2006), pp. 105–31 (p. 107).

7 Heinz Löwe, 'Regino von Prüm und das historische Weltbild der Karolingerzeit', *Von Cassiodor zu Dante: Ausgewählte Aufsätze zur Geschichtsschreibung und politischen Ideenwelt des Mittelalters* (Berlin: Walter de Gruyter, 1973), pp. 149–79 (pp. 165–8).

8 Hans-Henning Kortüm, 'Weltgeschichte am Ausgang der Karolingerzeit: Regino von Prüm', in *Historiographie im frühen Mittelalter*, ed. by Scharer and Scheibelreiter, pp. 499–513.

9 Löwe, 'Regino von Prüm', pp. 166–9.

10 Hayden White, *Metahistory: The Historical Imagination in Nineteenth-Century Europe* (Baltimore, MD: The Johns Hopkins University Press, 1973), pp. 7–9; Hayden White, 'Interpretation in History', *Tropics of Discourse: Essays in Cultural Criticism* (Baltimore, MD: The Johns Hopkins University Press, 1978), pp. 51–80.

32 Geoffrey Koziol

11 For the origin and early history of the model of the four empires, see Joseph Ward Swain, 'The Theory of the Four Monarchies: Opposition History under the Roman Empire', *Classical Philology* 35:1 (1940): 1–21.

12 Bede, *De temporum ratione liber*, ed. by Charles W. Jones, Corpus Christianorum Series Latina 123B (Turnhout: Brepols, 1977); trans. Faith Wallis, *The Reckoning of Time* (Liverpool: Liverpool University Press, 1999), pp. 156–237; Peter Darby, *Bede and the End of Time* (Farnham, UK: Ashgate, 2012), pp. 17–34.

13 Regino, *Chronicon*, p. 2; trans. MacLean, *History and Politics*, p. 62.

14 Bede, *Liber*, p. 495 (a.m. 3952); trans. Wallis, *Reckoning*, p. 195. The internal quotation is from Orosius.

15 Bede, *Liber*, p. 498 (a.m. 4031, 4033); trans. Wallis, *Reckoning*, p. 19.

16 Regino, *Chronicon*, p. 6; trans. MacLean, *History and Politics*, pp. 67–8.

17 Bede, *Liber*, p. 501 (a.m. 4132); trans. Wallis, *Reckoning*, p. 202.

18 Regino, *Chronicon*, pp. 7–8; trans. MacLean, *History and Politics*, pp. 70–1.

19 Bede, *Liber*, p. 509 (a.m. 4290); trans. Wallis, *Reckoning*, pp. 212–3.

20 Regino, *Chronicon*, pp. 14–5; trans. MacLean, *History and Politics*, p. 78.

21 Regino, *Chronicon*, pp. 15–6; trans. MacLean, *History and Politics*, pp. 79–80.

22 Regino, *Chronicon*, pp. 16–7; trans. MacLean, *History and Politics*, pp. 80–3.

23 Regino, *Chronicon*, pp. 41–2; trans. MacLean, *History and Politics*, pp. 122–4.

24 Cf. *Chronicon*, p. 40 (a. 742): 'Carlomannus eodem anno Alamanniam cum exercitu vastavit' (trans. MacLean, p. 121). For Cannstatt and its possible relationship to Carloman's abdication see Eric Goosmann, 'Politics and Penance: Transformations in the Carolingian Perception of the Conversion of Carloman (747)', in *The Resources of the Past in Early Medieval Europe*, ed. by Clemens Gantner, Rosamond McKitterick, and Sven Meeder (Cambridge: Cambridge University Press, 2015), pp. 51–67 (especially pp. 57–9).

25 Charles West, 'Knowledge of the Past and the Judgement of History in Tenth-Century Trier: Regino of Prüm and the Lost Manuscript of Bishop Adventius of Metz', *Early Medieval Europe* 24:2 (2016): 137–59.

26 On Regino's use of Justin's *Epitome* see Peter Emberger, 'Zum Fortwirken des Iustinus in der frühmittelalterlichen Chronik des Regino von Prüm', *Gymnasium* 118 (2011): 585–609; also Löwe, 'Regino von Prüm'.

27 McKitterick, *Perceptions of the Past*, pp. 35–61.

28 Frechulf of Lisieux, *Historiarum Libri XII*, in *Opera omnia*, ed. by Michal I. Allen, Corpus Christianorum Continuatio Mediaeualis, 169A (Turnhout: Brepols, 2002); also *ibid.*, 169 (Allen's introduction and commentary).

29 Nikolaus Staubach, 'Augustin und das Ende der alten Geschichte in der Weltchronik Frechulfs von Lisieux', *Frühmittelalterliche Studien* 29 (1995): 167–206.

30 See also Graeme Ward, 'All roads lead to Rome? Frechulf of Lisieux, Augustine and Orosius', *Early Medieval Europe* 22:4 (2014): 492–505; Graeme Ward, 'Lessons in leadership: Constantine and Theodosius in Frechulf of Lisieux's *Histories*', in *Resources of the Past*, ed. by Gantner et al., pp. 68–83.

31 Frechulf, *Historiarum Libri XII*, II.1.1–4, pp. 440–6.

32 *Ibid.*, II.1.10, pp. 454–5.

33 *Ibid.*, II.1.11–2, pp. 457–61.

34 *Ibid.*, II.1.15, pp. 467–8.

35 *Ibid.*, II.1.16, pp. 468–9.

36 *Ibid.*, II.2.13, pp. 496–8.

37 See Kortüm, 'Weltgeschichte', with the caveats of Hans-Werner Goetz, 'On the Universality of Universal History', in *L'Historiographie médiévale en Europe: Actes du colloque organisé par la Fondation Européenne de la Science au Centre de Recherches Historiques et Juridiques de l'Université Paris I du 29 mars au 1er avril 1989*, ed. by Jean-Philippe Genet (Paris: Éditions du Centre National de la Recherche Scientifique, 1991), pp. 247–61.

38 Ian Wood, 'Universal Chronicles in the Early Medieval West', *Medieval Worlds* 1 (2015): 47–60, www.medievalworlds.net/0xc1aa500e_0x00324b61.pdf (accessed February 2019); Helmut Reimitz, *History, Frankish Identity and the Framing of Western Ethnicity,*

The future of history after empire **33**

550–850 (Cambridge: Cambridge University Press, 2015); R. W. Burgess and Michael Kulikowski, *Mosaics of Time: The Latin Chronicle Traditions from the First Century BC to the Sixth Century AD*, vol. 1, *A Historical Introduction to the Chronicle Genre from its Origins to the High Middle Ages* (Turnhout: Brepols, 2013), chap. 1; Goetz, 'On the Universality of Universal History'; Ward, 'Lessons in Leadership'.

39 Frechulf, *Historiarum Libri XII*, ed. by Allen, CCCM 169A, pp. 58–9, 78★–78★.

40 Roman Deutinger, *Königsherrschaft im ostfränkischen Reich: Eine pragmatische Verfassungsgeschichte der späten Karolingerzeit* (Ostfildern: Jan Thorbecke Verlag, 2006), pp. 55–7, 61–3, 236–7; Geoffrey Koziol, *The Politics of Memory and Identity in Carolingian Royal Diplomas: The West Frankish Kingdom (840–987)* (Turnhout: Brepols, 2012), pp. 332, 337–40.

41 Frechulf of Lisieux*, Historiarum Libri XII*, pp. 17–20; Philippe Depreux, *Prosopographie de l'entourage de Louis le Pieux (781–840)* (Sigmaringen: Jan Thorbecke Verlag, 1997), pp. 235–40.

42 Frechulf, *Historiarum Libri XII*, pp. 435–7 (p. 436).

43 Regino, *Chronicon*, pp. 139, 147 (aa. 892, 899); trans. MacLean, *History and Politics*, pp. 213–4, 224–5.

44 Regino, *Chronicon*, p. 129 (a. 888); trans. MacLean, *History and Politics*, p. 199.

45 Philippe Depreux, 'L'actualité de Fréculf de Lisieux: à propos de l'édition critique de son oeuvre', *Tabularia* (2004), para. 2, www.unicaen.fr/mrsh/crahm/revue/tabularia/depreux.html (accessed February 2019). The position of Staubach, 'Augustin', is somewhat different but fundamentally compatible.

46 Étienne Delaruelle, 'En relisant le De institutione regia de Jonas d'Orléans: L'entrée en scène de l'épiscopat carolingien', in *Mélanges d'histoire du Moyen Âge dédiés à la mémoire de Louis Halphen*, ed. by Charles-Edmond Perrin (Paris: Presses Universitaires de France, 1951), pp. 185–92; Gerhard Ladner, 'Aspects of mediaeval thought on church and state', *Images and Ideas in the Middle Ages: Selected Studies in History and Art*, 2 vols. (Rome: Edizioni di storia e letteratura, 1983), II, pp. 435–56; Robert L. Benson, 'The Gelasian Doctrine: Uses and Transformations', in *La notion d'autorité au Moyen Âge: Islam, Byzance, Occident*, ed. by George Makdisi et al. (Paris: Presses Universitaires de France, 1982), pp. 13–44.

47 Frechulf of Lisieux, *Opera Omnia*, vol. 169A, pp. 727–9.

48 *Das Sendhandbuch des Regino von Prüm*, ed. by F. W. H. Wasserschleben and Wilfried Hartmann, Ausgewählte Quellen zur deutschen Geschichte des Mittelalters, 42 (Darmstadt: Wissenschaftliche Buchgesellschaften, 2004).

49 Paul the Deacon, *Liber de episcopis Mettensibus*, ed. and transl. by Damien Kempf, Dallas Medieval Texts and Translations, 19 (Leuven: Peeters, 2013), pp. 72–5; see also Damien Kempf, 'Paul the Deacon's *Liber de episcopis Mettensibus* and the role of Metz in the Carolingian realm', *Journal of Medieval History* 30 (2004): 279–99.

50 Paul the Deacon, *Liber*, pp. 86–7.

51 Thomas F. X. Noble, *The Republic of St. Peter: The Birth of the Papal State, 680–825* (Philadelphia: The University of Pennsylvania Press, 1984), pp. 262–3; Jörg Jarnut, 'Quierzy und Rom: Bemerkungen zu den "Promissiones Donationis" Pippins und Karls', *Historische Zeitschrift* 220 (1975): 265–97 (pp. 272–4); Josef Semmler, *Der Dynastiewechsel von 751 und die fränkische Königssalbung* (Düsseldorf: Drost, 2003), pp. 46–52.

52 *Gesta sanctorum patrum Fontanellensis coenobii*, ed. by Fernand Lohier and Jean Laporte (Paris: Société de l'Histoire de Normandie, 1936), I.2, p. 2. For such genealogies see Helmut Reimitz, 'Anleitung zur Interpretation: Schrift und Genealogie in der Karolingerzeit', in *Von Nuzten des Schreibens: Soziales Gedächtnis, Herrschaft und Besitz im Mittelalter*, ed. by Walter Pohl and Paul Herold (Vienna: Verlag der Österreichischen Akademie der Wissenschaften, 2002), pp. 167–81.

53 *Gesta sanctorum patrum Fontanellensis*, IV.1, p. 37 (Hugh); VIII.1, p. 59 (Raginfrid); XII.1, p. 84 (Gervold); XIII.2, p. 96 (Einhard); XIII, pp. 92–124 (Ansegis).

54 *Ibid.*, XI.1–2, pp. 85–6.

55 *Ibid.*, III.1, pp. 23–4.

34 Geoffrey Koziol

56 E.g., *ibid.*, IV.1, p. 39; V.3, pp. 45–6; VI.4, pp. 53–4; VIII.1–2, p. 59, 61–2; X.4, p. 77.
57 For example, the case of Raginfrid: *ibid.*, VIII, pp. 58–62.
58 *Geschichte des Bistums Le Mans von der Spätantike bis zur Karolingerzeit: Actus Pontificum Cenomannis in urbe degentium und Gesta Aldrici*, ed. by Margarete Weidemann, 3 vols. (Mainz: Verlag des Römisch-Germanischen Zentralmuseums in Kommission bei Habelt, 2002), especially vol. 1 for the *Actus*; Koziol, *The Politics of Memory*, pp. 365–81; Walter Goffart, *The Le Mans Forgeries: A Chapter from the History of Church Property in the ninth Century* (Cambridge, MA: Harvard University Press, 1966); Philippe Le Maître, 'L'oeuvre d'Aldric du Mans et sa signification (832–857)', *Francia* 8 (1980): 43–64; Steffen Patzold, *Episcopus: Wissen über Bischöfe im Frankenreich des späten 8. bis frühen 10. Jahrhunderts* (Ostfildern: Thorbecke, 2008), pp. 412–8.
59 *Actus*, ed. by Weidemann, vol. 1, XV, pp. 90–101.
60 *Actus*, ed. by Weidemann, vol. 1, XVI, pp. 102–3.
61 *Actus*, ed. by Weidemann, vol. 1, XVII, pp. 104–11.
62 *Actus*, ed. by Weidemann, vol. 1, XII, 71; Walter Goffart, 'Le Mans, St. Scholastica, and the Literary Tradition of the Translation of St. Benedict', *Revue Bénédictine* 77 (1987): 107–41.
63 *Actus*, ed. by Weidemann, vol. 1, I, pp. 33–8.
64 *Actus*, ed. by Weidemann, vol. 1, III, p. 40.
65 *Actus*, ed. by Weidemann, vol. 1, VI, p. 43.
66 *Actus*, ed. by Weidemann, vol. 1, IX, p. 56.
67 *Actus*, ed. by Weidemann, vol. 1, XV, p. 90.
68 *Actus*, ed. by Weidemann, vol. 1, I, p. 33; Patzold, *Episcopus*, pp. 414–5.
69 *Actus*, ed. by Weidemann, vol. 1, II, p. 39, III, p. 40.
70 *Actus*, ed. by Weidemann, vol. 1, IV, pp. 41–2.
71 *Actus*, ed. by Weidemann, vol. 1, V, pp. 42–3.
72 *Actus*, ed. by Weidemann, vol. 1, VI, p. 43.
73 *Actus*, ed. by Weidemann, vol. 1, VII, p. 47.
74 *Actus*, ed. by Weidemann, vol. 1, IX, p. 56, X, p. 61.
75 *Les Gestes des évêques d'Auxerre*, ed. by Michel Sot et al., 3 vols. (Paris: Les Belles Lettres, 2002–2009), vol. 1, pp. 1–157. For the dating see Pierre Janin, 'Heiric d'Auxerre et les Gesta pontificum Autissiodorensium', *Francia* 4 (1976): 89–105. Sot and his co-editors date it to 872–875.
76 Wolfert S. van Egmond, *Conversing with Saints: Communication in Pre-Carolingian Hagiography from Auxerre* (Turnhout: Brepols, 2006); René Louis, 'L'Église d'Auxerre et ses évêques avant saint Germain', in *Saint Germain d'Auxerre et son temps*, Société des sciences historiques et naturelles de l'Yonne (Auxerre: L'Universelle, 1950), pp. 39–88.
77 Van Egmond, *Conversing with Saints*, chap. 4.
78 *Les Gestes*, ed. by Sot et al., pp. 10–7.
79 *AASS* Maii III, cols. 561–4 (BHL 6623); Van Egmond, *Conversing with Saints*, pp. 81–5; Louis, 'L'Église d'Auxerre', pp. 42–7, 52, 58, 62–6.
80 Cf. Patzold, *Episcopus*, pp. 418–9.
81 *Les Gestes*, ed. by Sot et al., pp. 18–9.
82 *Les Gestes*, ed. by Sot et al., pp. 52–3.
83 *Les Gestes*, ed. by Sot et al., pp. 54–5.
84 *Les Gestes*, ed. by Sot et al., pp. 62–3.
85 *Les Gestes*, ed. by Sot et al., pp. 114–5.
86 *Les Gestes*, ed. by Sot et al., pp. 124–5.
87 *Les Gestes*, ed. by Sot et al., pp. 128–31.
88 *Les Gestes*, ed. by Sot et al., pp. 134–7.
89 *Les Gestes*, ed. by Sot et al., pp. 142–3.
90 *Les Gestes*, ed. by Sot et al., pp. 128–31, 134–7.
91 *Les Gestes*, ed. by Sot et al., pp. 126–7.
92 Jacques Dubois, *Les martyrologes du moyen âge latin*, Typologie des sources du moyen âge occidental, 26 (Turnhout: Brepols, 1978); Jacques Dubois, *Le martyrologe d'Usuard: Texte et commentaire*, Subsidia Hagiographica, 40 (Brussels: Société des Bollandistes, 1965).

93 Dubois, *Le martyrologe d'Usuard*, pp. 92–6, 128–37.
94 Patzold, *Episcopus*, especially pp. 279–87.
95 Carine van Rhijn, *Shepherds of the Lord: Priests and Episcopal Statutes in the Carolingian Period* (Turnhout: Brepols, 2007), pp. 139–40.
96 Koziol, *The Politics of Memory*, pp. 140–50, 154–87; Patzold, *Episcopus*, pp. 266–79; Geoffrey Koziol, *The Peace of God* (Leeds: ARC Humanities Press, 2018), pp. 19–24, 28–29.
97 *Les Gestes*, ed. by Sot et al., pp. 57–9; Dubois, *Les martyrologes*, p. 33; Dubois, *Le martyrologe d'Usuard*, p. 132; Henri Quentin, *Les martyrologes historiques du moyen âge: Étude sur la formation du martyrologe romain* (Paris: Librairie Victor Lecoffre, 1908), pp. 677–8, 685.
98 Koziol, *The Politics of Memory*, pp. 365–81.
99 *Les Gestes*, ed. by Sot et al., pp. 82–3, 122–3, 130–3, 134–7, 138–43, 148–57.
100 *Recueil des actes de Charles II le Chauve, roi de France*, ed. by A. Giry et al., 3 vols. (Paris, 1943–1955), no. 124 (850), for Saint-Étienne, and for Saint-Germain, nos. 156 (853), 200 (859), 214 (859), 215 (859), 233 (861), 235 (861), 262 (864), 269 (864), 427 (877); this list does not even include assignments of individual estates and reassignments of estates to and from the *mensa*.
101 A few examples of many: *Les Gestes*, ed. by Sot et al., pp. 14–5, 20–7, 66–7, 118–9, 150–1; *Actus*, ed. by Weidemann, vol. 1, pp. 33–4, 36–42, 47–8, 57, 61–2, 76, 80–1, 87, etc. Cf. also Patzold, *Episcopus*, pp. 416–7.
102 For example, *Les Gestes*, ed. by Sot et al., pp. 70–7, 116–23. For the *Actus*, note especially the suspiciously long and precise lists of episcopal ordinations of clergy and altars that consistently end the first fourteen lives.

3

REMEMBERING TROUBLED PASTS

Episcopal deposition and succession in Flodoard's *History of the Church of Rheims*

Edward Roberts

In the 1060s, Odalric, provost of the church of Rheims, appended a list of the city's bishops to a page in his personal psalter.[1] He omitted three prelates from his reckoning: Abel (743/4–747x762), Hugh (925–931, 940–946) and Gerbert (991–997). For different reasons, these men had not ended their lives in the see. Abel seems to have acted as bishop while the see was controlled by a layman named Milo. Some sources named Abel in the episcopal succession, but others asserted that he was only a chorbishop (an auxiliary or rural bishop). Hugh had been made bishop in 925 as a boy of just four years by his father, the count of Vermandois. Wider political conflicts twice led to Hugh's removal, in 931 and 946, and, eventually, to his excommunication in 948. Gerbert (of Aurillac, the later Pope Sylvester II) had been installed in 991 following the removal of his predecessor, Arnulf (989–991, 998–1021), deposed for treason against Hugh Capet. That deposition was contested, however, and when Gerbert's position eventually became untenable, he was forced to resign the see. While these were all reasonable grounds for Odalric to doubt the legitimacy of the bishops' tenures, his list nevertheless featured other bishops who had been unseated in similarly notorious circumstances. Egidius (573–590), for instance, was deposed after being found guilty of treason against Childebert II. Rigobert (*c.*692–717) was banished by Charles Martel for refusing his army entry into the city during the civil war of 715–717. And then there was Ebbo (816–835, 840–841), infamously compelled to resign the office following his starring role in the 833 rebellion against Louis the Pious. Ebbo was briefly restored following Louis' death but forced to abandon the bishopric once more within a year.

As this incidence of high-profile deposition shows, the office of archbishop of Rheims could be quite the poisoned chalice.[2] Indeed, not long after Odalric compiled his episcopal list, another Rheims archbishop, Manasses I (1069–1080), was condemned as a simoniac and deposed by Pope Gregory VII.[3] In terms of how a deposed bishop was remembered, however, it is unclear what made Egidius,

Rigobert and Ebbo apparently more legitimate than Abel, Hugh or Gerbert. This chapter therefore sets out to explore how the memories and reputations of Rémois bishops were received and, in some cases, reshaped in post-Carolingian Rheims. The critical text for such an enquiry is the *History of the Church of Rheims* (*Historia Remensis ecclesiae*), composed by the canon Flodoard in 948–952. This work, well known to Odalric and the community in the eleventh century, is a sprawling history of the bishops, saints and churches of the archdiocese, from the city's purported foundation in the eighth century BC down to 948, when a long-running schism between the aforementioned Hugh and a rival archbishop, Artold (931–940, 946–961), was resolved in the latter's favour. At a great synod in Ingelheim in 948, before Otto the Great, Louis IV, a papal legate and over thirty bishops, Hugh was declared an invader of the bishopric and excommunicated.[4] The settlement of this conflict was a driving factor in Flodoard's writing of the *History*, a work that has frequently been considered a landmark of early medieval institutional historiography (or *gesta*). The composite and varied nature of *gesta episcoporum* has led such texts to be interpreted in different ways. This is primarily a question of audience. On one level, *gesta* served as archives, bringing together charters, letters and other documents and situating property holdings and associated rights in a chronological framework for ease of reference. At the same time, taking their cue from the serialized biographies of the *Liber pontificalis*, authors of *gesta* often strove to enunciate a principle of apostolic succession in order to highlight a sequence of providential actions unfolding in a locality and thus to locate the bishops of a particular see within the sweep of Christian history. On this reading, *gesta* seek to harness an institution's glorious past and use it to reinforce social prestige and defend landed endowments. There is thus some debate about whether authors produced such works for the edification and benefit of their own communities or rather to advertise the power of their patron saints and the generosity of past benefactors. Clearly, these two views are not mutually exclusive, nor is there any one-size-fits-all approach to this highly flexible genre.[5]

Flodoard is well known for waxing lyrical about illustrious bishops of his church such as St Remigius and Hincmar.[6] But he also had to confront the controversial figures in Rheims' distant and recent past. These latter bishops' careers were stumbling blocks for an author intent on tracing an unbroken line of episcopal succession from his own day back to the first bishop of Rheims, Sixtus, who was thought to have been a disciple of St Peter.[7] How, then, did Flodoard deal with such difficult episodes? In what follows, I argue that specific contemporary concerns and recent turmoil at Rheims prompted Flodoard to reinterpret some of the church's more disreputable moments and to explain or justify these calamities by teasing out merit in the lives of controversial bishops. Far from being the reflexive, uncritical 'archivist' he is sometimes assumed to have been, Flodoard was uncommonly attentive to the rich sources he had at his disposal. He was particularly interested in episcopal trials and ecclesiastical property, both live issues in the Rheims of his day. Flodoard's treatment of deposed bishops, I suggest, allows us to observe how he juggled the competing demands of his task as an historian and of his mission to

38 Edward Roberts

memorialize Rheims' illustrious past within the confines of a delicate contemporary political situation. In a post-Carolingian playing field of political uncertainty and opportunity, authors drew on rights, privileges and powers from the past in order to negotiate the challenges of the present. At Rheims, with the benefit of rich archives and libraries and the intoxicating traditions of episcopal leadership in Merovingian and Carolingian high politics, Flodoard reimagined and revised the biographies of Rheims' bishops, especially those of questionable legitimacy.[8] His episcopal portraits thus emerge, more clearly than is usually thought, as products of his and his archbishop's agenda in the years around 950.

The treason of Egidius

The earliest Rheims bishop known to have been deposed was Egidius in 590.[9] Flodoard opened his chapter on the bishop by drawing on several charters to show how he had enriched the diocese by obtaining royal grants and purchasing property:

> [Egidius] is found to have enlarged the bishopric with arable lands and to have purchased slaves. Certain records of his acquisitions are found even today, such as that by which, it is read, he acquired for a fixed price two fields above the Retourne river from Bobolenus, one of which, it is written, supported a thousand *modii* of seed, the other four hundred.[10]

Flodoard summarized several other documents, including a privilege of immunity for Rheims issued by Childebert II, which is in fact the church of Rheims' earliest recorded immunity.[11] Such abridgments are typical of his archival methods. Flodoard occasionally retained the diplomatic language of charters, and frequently used verbs such as *invenitur* and *reperitur* to indicate that information had been learned from documents. He often specified charters with terms such as *testamentum*, *instrumentum*, *privilegium*, *carta*, *pagina*, *littera* and so forth.[12]

For the rest (and bulk) of this chapter, however, Flodoard relied on the witness of Egidius' contemporaries Venantius Fortunatus and Gregory of Tours, adding very little of his own summary, comment or interpretation. He first reproduced a poem by Fortunatus on Egidius' life and preaching.[13] Then, Flodoard turned to Gregory's works, primarily the *Histories*, but also his *Miracles of St Martin*. Flodoard quoted a number of passages from the *Histories* recounting Egidius' political activities, and in particular the intrigue that led to his deposition. Egidius, a key adviser to the king, had been involved in the negotiation of a new alliance between Childebert and his uncle, Chilperic, king of Neustria. In his promotion of Chilperic's interests at the Austrasian court, Egidius aroused the enmity of Childebert's other uncle, Guntram, king of Burgundy. Childebert soon struck a new alliance with Guntram, and, as Egidius' influence at court waned, the bishop was accused of having knowledge of a plot by Queen Fredegund (Chilperic's wife) to assassinate Childebert. At a council in Metz in 590, other charges of treason, corruption and forgery were brought against him. Egidius confessed his crimes and awaited his expected death sentence, but, following the intervention of his fellow bishops, 'after they had read the decrees of the canons' (*lectis canonum sanctionibus*), he was instead deposed and banished to Strasbourg.[14]

The absence of any comment from Flodoard on Egidius' downfall suggests that he felt Gregory's account spoke for itself, and he seems not to have had any further information on the matter with which to compare Gregory. Egidius had admitted his guilt and the trial had apparently, if vaguely, been canonically valid. Michel Sot has suggested that Flodoard quoted Gregory at length in this instance as 'less a literary source than a legal document' in order to demonstrate the procedural impeccability of Egidius' deposition.[15] The regularity of episcopal trials was certainly a concern in the tenth century, when archbishops of Rheims were deposed or expelled on five occasions, in 931 (Hugh), 940 (Artold), 946 (Hugh), 991 (Arnulf) and 996 (Gerbert). But Gregory's status as an historiographical authority surely also played a large part; Flodoard cited him by name, not something he usually did when drawing on earlier histories.[16] As a foil to Egidius' treason, however, Flodoard could stress his model diocesan work, which he backed up with reference to charters found in the archive and to the poetry of Fortunatus. In the following chapter, moreover, the historian emphasized that it was Egidius who had received the Aquitanian monk Basle (Basolus) and permitted him to pray in the area where an important monastery subsequently grew up in his honour (Saint-Basle at Verzy).[17] In sum, Flodoard could not contradict the weighty authority of Gregory's testimony, but he could soften Egidius' downfall by sandwiching it between his narrative of the bishop's commendable estate management and pious deeds.

The deposition of Rigobert

A little more than a century later, the bishopric was plunged into another crisis, one from which it did not easily recover. Rigobert became bishop around 692, and, like Egidius, served the church of Rheims well. This time, Flodoard had much more evidence available: he devoted four chapters to Rigobert's episcopate, and his account notably draws on a *vita*, for a local cult had grown up around the bishop.[18] Flodoard's admiration for Rigobert is clear, the historian beginning his biography by highlighting how he 'restored the religion of the canons to the clerics' of the cathedral (that is, Flodoard's own community) and assigned new properties for their livelihood. Rigobert augmented the episcopal patrimony with purchases and exchanges of land and obtained charters from Dagobert III and Theuderic IV. Flodoard once again summarized a number of these records and stated that the documents could still be found in the church archives. In fact, he cited more charters for Rigobert than for any other Rheims bishop.[19] Flodoard could also point to church-building activities such as his construction of an oratory in honour of the archangel Michael (Saint-Michel, Rheims).[20] Miracles drawn from the *vita* and its associated *translatio* accounts punctuate the narrative.[21]

Rigobert, as Flodoard mentioned, was the godfather of Charles Martel, which suggests good relations between the bishop and the Austrasian mayoralty in the

40 Edward Roberts

days of Pippin of Herstal's rule. In 717, during the war between Charles and the Neustro-Burgundian regime of Chilperic II and the mayor Ragamfred, Charles stopped off in Rheims in order to pray there. Rigobert, however, refused him entry, fearing that Charles' army would loot the city, as it was alleged to have done elsewhere. Charles, enraged, promised that he would take revenge should he prove victorious. This he did, promptly returning to Rheims following his defeat of Ragamfred at the Battle of Vinchy and expelling Rigobert. The ousted bishop went into exile in Aquitaine. Charles replaced him with his supporter Milo, 'a cleric only by tonsure' (*sola tonsura clerico* – i.e., not by lifestyle), and the two proceeded to divvy up Rheims' lands. Rheims, Flodoard wrote, was just one of many bishoprics that Charles gave away to laymen. The historian then recounted a story about Eucherius, bishop of Orléans, who had also been banished by Charles. Eucherius had a vision of Charles burning in hell, and an angel told him that the mayor had been condemned to eternal punishment for violating the property of the saints. When Charles' tomb was opened to test the truth of the vision, a dragon flew out, and the sarcophagus was found empty and scorched. Rigobert, Flodoard continued, eventually returned to Rheims, having been promised his see back by Milo. But when he arrived, Milo demanded that Rigobert give him all the property he had previously donated to the church. Rigobert refused, but nevertheless chose to live out his days locally, occasionally being allowed to celebrate mass in the cathedral.[22] It is also worth noting that the church of one of the villages Rigobert was said to have visited regularly, Cormicy, was a benefice held by Flodoard.[23]

Flodoard's source for the majority of this narrative was the aforementioned *Vita Rigoberti*, a text seemingly written under the aegis of Archbishop Fulk of Rheims (883–900) in the early 890s.[24] On the evidence of this text, Rigobert has been considered one of several late Merovingian bishops punished for resisting the expansion of Carolingian power. Memories of Charles Martel's treatment of such bishops as Rigobert, Eucherius, Ansbert of Rouen, Lambert of Maastricht and Bonitus of Clermont subsequently provided the basis for their veneration as saints.[25] They were also the foundation for Charles' later reputation as a systematic despoiler of church property, a charge now shown to have been a wholly ninth-century construction.[26] Thus, Eucherius' vision of Charles in hell, included in the *Vita Rigoberti* and reproduced by Flodoard, comes not from the eighth-century *Vita Eucherii*, but from a letter written in 858 by Archbishop Hincmar of Rheims on behalf of the synod of Quierzy to Louis the German in response to the king's invasion of West Francia. It is widely agreed that Hincmar invented this vision, which was a clear projection of his property ambitions onto an imagined eighth-century past. The archbishop's message to Louis was clear: royal misuse of ecclesiastical property risked eternal damnation.[27] Immediately after invoking Eucherius' vision, the author of the *Vita Rigoberti* turned to another dubious source, an undated letter purportedly sent by Pope Hadrian to Archbishop Tilpin of Rheims (762–794?). Hadrian lamented the injustices suffered by Rigobert, with particular attention to his deposition without apostolic consent or any judgement of his episcopal peers.[28] The letter has often been thought to contain an authentic kernel that was heavily augmented by Hincmar, who referred to a papal privilege for Tilpin on several occasions.[29] On this particular occasion, however, Hincmar's reputation as a forger has come before him, and there is little reason to suppose his involvement. For one, Hincmar is unlikely to have fabricated a document claiming that it was illegal to depose a bishop without synodal judgement or papal consent, because his own right to do so as a metropolitan was precisely the crux of his disputes with his suffragan bishops Rothad of Soissons and Hincmar of Laon.[30] Furthermore, although Hincmar did refer on several occasions to a privilege of Hadrian, he was extremely vague about it. He seems not to have known any of the details quoted by the author of the *Vita Rigoberti* or by Flodoard. Even more puzzlingly, Hincmar appears to have known virtually nothing about Rigobert. Only once, in a letter to Hincmar of Laon of 869, did Hincmar refer in passing to Rigobert's expulsion.[31]

If one recalls Hincmar's curious use of the example of Eucherius of Orléans rather than his own predecessor to highlight the suffering of the Frankish church under Charles Martel, these documentary problems strongly suggest that the account of Rigobert's deposition is a post-Hincmarian creation. This reworking is probably contemporary with the composition of the *Vita Rigoberti* around 890. That this cultural 'forgetting and remembering' coincided with the dislocation of the Carolingian political centre in 888 and a veritable caesura in contemporary historical writing is probably no coincidence.[32] It was also in these years that Archbishop Fulk sought further papal assurances of Rheims' apostolic and primatial status, as shown by his correspondence with successive popes. But we owe all these vignettes to Flodoard, who was the first to copy out and re-present these documents and stories in the overarching structure of his *History of the Church of Rheims* in the middle of the tenth century.[33] It is difficult to disentangle this past from the aims and priorities of his narrative. The story of Rigobert's expulsion would have had strong resonance around the time of the synod of Ingelheim.[34] The *History*, as mentioned, was composed in the wake of the difficult conflict between Archbishops Hugh and Artold. Flodoard dedicated his work to Archbishop Robert of Trier, who had taken a leading role in the settlement of the schism on Otto the Great's behalf.[35] Describing this recent turmoil, Flodoard contrasted the illegitimacy of Artold's forced abdication in 940 with the procedural regularity and canonical basis of Hugh's excommunication by a synod of over thirty bishops and a papal legate.[36] Artold's wholly unjust deposition at the hands of lay princes echoed Rigobert's, while Pope Hadrian's complaint about the absence of papal or synodal consent to Rigobert's deposition implied that Hugh's banishment had been lawful. Furthermore, Rigobert's expulsion, according to the Rémois authors, had ushered in a period of lay control of the see which resulted in the alienation of ecclesiastical property under Milo, about whom we shall hear more shortly. During the episcopate of the adolescent Hugh, the see was managed by his father, Count Heribert II of Vermandois, who also despoiled the church's lands. The detail Flodoard provided about the acquisition and defence of Rheims' property by bishops like Rigobert was grounded in the church's attempts to recover land lost during the struggles of the preceding decades.[37]

42 Edward Roberts

Flodoard thus inherited a recently-minted tradition concerning Rigobert's ill-treatment and deposition at the hands of Charles Martel, a narrative that probably developed alongside the bishop's local cult. But the historian was not merely a passive recipient of this tradition: he repurposed Rigobert's biography to address contemporary concerns. Flodoard did not simply recycle the contents of the *Vita Rigoberti*; he augmented the text with reference to charters and other documents not used by the author of the Life, such as Pope Zacharias' letter to Boniface in 751, which briefly discussed Milo.[38] Flodoard also excerpted longer quotations from the Hadrian–Tilpin letter for which he is the only source.[39] He may have felt the need to provide further justification because, as his sources showed, the nature of Rigobert's deposition was obscure. Drawing on the *Vita Rigoberti*, which in turn may have picked up on a brief remark in Hincmar of Rheims' letter to Hincmar of Laon in 869, Flodoard wrote that Rigobert had been allowed to return to Rheims and live out his years in quiet retirement at nearby Gernicourt.[40] Two charters mentioned by Flodoard muddy the waters, however. Both are confirmations obtained by Rigobert from Theuderic IV (r. 721–737), whose reign postdates the bishop's alleged deposition in 717 by several years.[41] These suggest that Rigobert continued to carry out episcopal functions at Rheims, and, as mentioned already, both the author of the Life and Flodoard state that he still occasionally held mass in the cathedral. Was Rigobert ever actually deposed? Another charter, not used by Flodoard but preserved by Folcuin of Lobbes in his *Gesta abbatum Sithiensium* (*Deeds of the Abbots of Saint-Bertin*, composed 962), may suggest that he was no longer bishop. According to this document, in 723 a certain Rigobert (no title is given) sold his property in Saint-Omer to Erkembold, abbot of Saint-Bertin and bishop of Thérouanne.[42] This could well be our Rigobert, who was from a well-born family in the Ardennes and had succeeded his kinsman Reolus as bishop of Rheims.[43] The absence of any episcopal title in Folcuin's version of the charter indicates that Rigobert no longer claimed the bishopric. In any case, the uncertainty produced by such documents was something that authors like Flodoard were happy to exploit in their attempts to recreate a morally instructive past. Rigobert's deposition, real or not, became a model illustrating the perils of the unlawful removal of a bishop and princely domination of a bishopric.

Milo and Abel

Rigobert is presumed to have lived until 743 or 744, at which point another Rheims bishop turns up in the historical record: Abel. However, we cannot grasp Flodoard's approach to Abel's episcopate without first reviewing the evidence for the infamous Milo. Until recently, there was a consensus that Milo had been installed as bishop of Trier and Rheims by Charles Martel, probably around 722, remaining in charge of both sees for about forty years. In 2010, Olaf Schneider challenged this understanding of Milo, arguing that the image of the tyrannical lay 'double-bishop' was entirely a creation of Hincmar of Rheims. As Schneider observed, there is no contemporary evidence that Milo was ever bishop of Rheims, or even any kind of

Remembering troubled pasts **43**

administrator of the *episcopium*.[44] The key text in the construction of this portrait would appear to be a memorandum composed by Hincmar in 863 for the trial of his suffragan bishop Rothad of Soissons. Discussing the constitution and rights of metropolitan bishops, Hincmar turned to explaining their history in the Frankish kingdom. He wrote that Boniface had sought to appoint apostolic representatives in *Gallia*, *Belgica* and *Germania* to oversee a stricter clerical adherence to the sacred canons. Boniface thus ordained Grimo in Rouen and Hartbert in Sens, but (unnamed) bishops designated for Rheims and Trier were not able to succeed because the cities were 'occupied' (*occupaverat*) by Milo, 'a cleric by tonsure, not by living' (*tonsura, non vita clericus*). After Milo's death, Hincmar continued, Weomad became bishop of Trier (*c*.762–791), but a vacancy ensued at Rheims because Milo had given away all the church's property to his sons and followers. Eventually, Tilpin became bishop of Rheims and was able to begin restoring the losses with the help of King Carloman.[45]

Hincmar's source for this was the correspondence between Pope Zacharias and Boniface, which in fact provides the only secure contemporary reference to a Milo who might possibly have been bishop of Rheims and Trier. Responding to a query from Boniface in a letter of 751, Zacharias urged him to strive to correct the behaviour of 'Milo and his like':

> As to Milo and his like, who are doing great injury to the Church of God, preach in season and out of season, according to the word of the Apostle, that they cease from their evil ways. If they listen to your admonitions they will save their souls, but if they die in their sins you who preach righteousness shall not lose your reward.[46]

The pope's allusive remark, it seems, was sufficient for Hincmar to cast Milo as Charles Martel's villainous right-hand man. But in his use of this correspondence, Hincmar was disingenuous, for he cannot have overlooked the fact that Zacharias' two letters of 744 named the bishop who was meant to succeed at Rheims as one Abel.[47] Why would he have omitted this information?

Flodoard's understanding of Milo was derived from the *Vita Rigoberti* and the writings of Hincmar. In Hincmar's view, Rigobert had been succeeded by Milo, a layman and pluralist and thus clearly illegitimate, and Milo had eventually been succeeded by Tilpin. But Flodoard did not accept this version of events. He also had access to the correspondence of Boniface and Zacharias. And here he learned that Boniface had sought to elevate a man named Abel to the rank of metropolitan bishop of Rheims through a grant of the pallium. As he wrote in a chapter entitled 'Abel, his successor':

> Abel is known to have followed the blessed Rigobert in the succession of the bishopric, although some relate that he was only a chorbishop. But I have found evidence of this bishop (*pontifex*) in an array of statements, and especially in the letters of Pope Zacharias to St Boniface.[48]

44 Edward Roberts

As Flodoard goes on to point out via a quotation from Zacharias' letter of 5 November 744, Boniface clearly stated that he had ordained Abel as well as Grimo and Hartbert. The historian also reproduced the portion of Zacharias' letter of 22 June 744 mentioning Abel. He then added, somewhat vaguely, that 'Some charters of this bishop are found with his name and title'.[49] Finally, Flodoard turned to the aforementioned Hadrian–Tilpin letter – a document forged or at least interpolated at an uncertain date – where he learned of Abel's expulsion:

> He was not permitted to remain in his see and, in defiance of God, he was ejected. For many seasons and many years the church of Rheims was without a bishop, and the properties of the church were stolen from this bishopric and divided among the laity, as happened in other dioceses, but to the greatest extent in the metropolitan city of Rheims.[50]

As Flodoard understood it, then, Milo had controlled the see, but was clearly never actually a bishop. Abel had been the legitimate successor of Rigobert but had been expelled at some point – presumably by Milo, though nowhere is this stated. A vacancy followed Abel's ousting, until eventually Tilpin was elected bishop, probably sometime after Milo's death in c.762.

The problem is that Abel, like Milo, does not seem ever to have been consecrated bishop, and, as Flodoard himself admits, was reported elsewhere to have been a chorbishop tasked with carrying out the episcopal ministry while Milo enjoyed the see's temporalities. Chorbishops, literally 'rural bishops', were assistants who helped urban bishops administer their dioceses. The institution had existed in the East since antiquity, and in the eighth century it became a feature of the Frankish kingdoms, particularly in the north, where dioceses tended to be large.[51] The early-ninth-century *Gesta* of the abbots of Fontenelle may also furnish evidence for a chorbishop at Rheims, for it asserts that Lando, abbot around 731–733, was also *episcopus de urbe Remensi*.[52] Boniface failed to implement his reform of the episcopal hierarchy: he apparently requested a pallium for Abel, but there is no evidence that he ever ordained Abel as a metropolitan.[53] There are two further contemporary references to Abel, neither mentioned by Flodoard. In the acts of the council of Soissons, held in March 744, he is named as one of the new archbishops Boniface wished to elevate, albeit without reference to Rheims.[54] And in a letter from Boniface to the Mercian king Æthelbald written in 746 or 747, Abel is named as a *coepiscopus*.[55] This is not definitely the same thing as a chorbishop (*corepiscopus*); it may simply mean 'fellow bishop'. But there are other instances in which *coepiscopus* clearly denotes a chorbishop.[56]

If Abel was indeed a chorbishop, this probably explains why Hincmar airbrushed him out during his recasting of the eighth century. In the early ninth century, the irregularity of the chorepiscopate had made it controversial. The 829 council of Paris moved to restrict the office's functions, and it became a target of the Pseudo-Isidorian forgers.[57] Hincmar himself was particularly concerned to extinguish chorbishops, in no small part because Gottschalk of Orbais, Hincmar's opponent in the predestination controversy, had been ordained priest by a Rheims chorbishop during the vacancy that followed the deposition of Ebbo in 835.[58] It is not hard to imagine that it suited Hincmar to overlook this evidence for an eighth-century Rheims chorbishop in order to emphasize the ambiguity of the office (and the illegitimacy of Gottschalk's ordination). Tilpin, as it happens, is another oddly elusive eighth-century bishop, for whose tenure there are no secure dates. This may be an indication that he served initially in a chorepiscopal capacity, before being consecrated bishop of Rheims only after Milo's death.[59] Since Hincmar wanted to make the point that Milo had been an illegitimate lay bishop, it suited him to leave Abel to oblivion.

Flodoard, on the other hand, was probably less worried by Abel's possible status as an auxiliary bishop. In fact, a remarkably similar situation had returned to Rheims in his day. When, in 925, Count Heribert placed his infant son Hugh on the see, he seconded a suffragan bishop of the province, Abbo of Soissons, to Rheims as an assistant to perform the liturgical and pastoral functions of the office, reserving for himself the right to administer the diocesan patrimony. In 928, Bishop Odalric of Aix-en-Provence (or perhaps of Dax in Aquitaine), having been driven from his see by Saracens, was appointed to perform the ministry.[60] Interestingly, Odalric was still in the area in 947, when Flodoard recorded his attendance at a synod in Verdun.[61] He may well have retained his auxiliary episcopal function in the province of Rheims throughout this time. Flodoard's acknowledgement and justification of Abel's episcopate, plain contrary to Hincmar's opinion, might best be understood as an effort to find historical precedent for what was essentially lay control of Rheims throughout Hugh's first pontificate. Carolingian canonists may have succeeded in substantially reducing the office of chorbishop, but the phenomenon of a prepubescent archbishop was clearly an irregularity that required a practical solution. In the Rheims of Milo and Abel, Flodoard found evidence for a similar *modus vivendi* which went some way in explaining a discreditable recent past.

Remembering Ebbo

Let us turn finally to Ebbo, arguably the most notorious figure in the episcopal history of Rheims. As has been explored recently in some detail, Ebbo's departure from Rheims produced complex controversies that reverberated throughout the ninth century.[62] In 833, Ebbo joined a rebellion against Louis the Pious and oversaw the emperor's deposition and public penance at Soissons in October. Soon, however, public opinion swung back in Louis' favour, and the emperor was released from confinement. Upon Louis' restoration, Ebbo became the fall guy for the entire affair. In February 835, at councils in Thionville and Metz, the archbishop admitted his role in Louis' deposition, confessed to unspecified crimes and resigned his episcopal office. However, the canonically ambiguous nature of this outcome, a compromise between defenders seeking Ebbo's restoration and opponents clamouring for his deposition, created a host of problems for his eventual successor,

46 Edward Roberts

Hincmar, who was appointed in 845 following a decade-long vacancy. After Louis' death in 840, Ebbo was restored to the bishopric by Lothar I, but when Rheims came under the control of Charles the Bald in 841, he was forced to abandon the see once again. During this brief stint, Ebbo ordained a number of priests, several of whom went on to careers of some prominence. Hincmar objected to these clerics' status, largely because the validity of Ebbo's ordinations controverted the legitimacy of his own succession to the archbishopric of Rheims. The question of whether Ebbo's removal in 835 had been procedurally regular therefore became a significant political issue, and it has been argued that this dispute was a driving factor in the production of the Pseudo-Isidorian False Decretals.[63] Hincmar was accordingly relentless in his efforts to blacken Ebbo's name. In a letter to Pope Nicholas I in 864, uniquely preserved by Flodoard in the *History*, Hincmar requested permission to scratch off Ebbo's name from the diptych in the cathedral church listing the bishops of Rheims since he had not ended his life in the see.[64]

Ebbo's career and downfall therefore posed several problems for Flodoard, who devoted two long chapters to the disgraced archbishop. In the first, Flodoard described Ebbo's rise to the archbishopric and his diocesan work, and the resulting portrait is the familiar ideal bishop: Ebbo was 'a diligent man, and learned in the liberal sciences'. Charters showed that he had ably concluded many exchanges and purchases of property. Ebbo restored and extended the decaying cathedral church and oversaw the construction of the church's archive, where Flodoard indicated he worked and prayed. He commissioned a new penitential from his suffragan bishop Halitgar of Cambrai, procured privileges from Carolingian rulers and embarked upon a successful mission on behalf of Pope Paschal to the Danes.[65] Flodoard backed up this account with characteristic citation and excerption of sources, drawing on charters, inscriptions, letters, Thegan's *Gesta Hludowici imperatoris*, and the *Annales regni Francorum*. Already at the end of this chapter, however, the historian signalled the coming storm, writing that Ebbo sided with Lothar against the emperor and participated in the 833 assembly that imposed Louis' penance. Flodoard also included the so-called 'Vision of Raduin', in which a Lombard monk was visited by the Virgin Mary, who complained to him about the amount of time Ebbo was spending at court.[66]

Flodoard devoted the next chapter to Ebbo's deposition and abortive restoration, asserting that the archbishop's expulsion in 835 was the result of 'his infidelity to the emperor' (*pro infidelitate imperatoris*). The historian narrated the affair almost entirely through documents and narrative sources, reproducing extracts from key texts such as the *Annales Bertiniani*, the *libelli* of the Frankish bishops' admissions of complicity at Metz, Ebbo's statement of abdication, the later account of the deposition by Bishop Theoderic of Cambrai, and the *edictum imperiale* of Lothar that restored Ebbo to Rheims in 840. Flodoard's access to these texts was most likely mediated by the acts of the synods of Soissons in 853 and Troyes in 867 (or perhaps dossiers of texts prepared by Hincmar for these councils), both of which met to address the fallout from Ebbo's deposition and reinstatement.[67] Nevertheless, the historian proved extremely diligent in his inspection and excerption of these materials. Flodoard concluded the chapter by briefly recounting how Ebbo was forced to abandon Rheims in 841 by Charles the Bald, and, after falling out with Lothar, eventually wound up in the East Frankish kingdom, where Louis the German appointed him to 'a certain bishopric in Saxony'.[68] Then, after beginning the third book with an account of Hincmar's monastic career and election to the archbishopric at the synod of Beauvais in 845, Flodoard described Ebbo's final bid to regain the see. Lothar complained to Pope Sergius II that Hincmar's election had been uncanonical because the archbishopric's legal occupant was still alive. Sergius attempted to intervene by arranging a council in Trier in April 846, but apparently his legates never arrived. The West Frankish bishops instead met in Paris in either autumn 846 or spring 847, where they confirmed Ebbo's deposition and Hincmar's appointment.[69] As a postscript, Flodoard reproduced one final Hincmarian text, the 'Vision of Bernold', in which Ebbo was seen burning in hell for spending too much time at the palace rather than in his own church.[70]

Recent assessments of Flodoard's treatment of Ebbo have tended to conclude that the historian embraced and embellished Hincmar's damning picture of a treacherous bishop, largely because Flodoard is widely considered – not wrongly – to have idealized Hincmar.[71] Indeed, Flodoard alone provided the incriminating details that Ebbo was Louis' *collactaneus et conscolasticus* ('milk-brother and classmate'), that he was given the monastery of Saint-Vaast in exchange for betraying the emperor, and that, following Louis' release from custody, Ebbo fled with the church's treasure to Denmark with a gang of Northmen. Flodoard is also the earliest witness to the vision of the monk Raduin. But the historian discerned two sides to this story: for all Ebbo's faults, his episcopate was clearly a high-water mark for the office's leading role in Frankish royal and imperial government. Flodoard did not reproduce the blatant hostility of sources like Thegan; he instead insisted that *all* the bishops had participated in Louis' deposition in 833 and did not assign any particular role to Ebbo. While Flodoard preserved the canonical arguments advanced in favour of Ebbo's deposition in 835, he also reproduced the full text of Lothar's edict restoring him in 840. And finally, Flodoard chose not to relate that Ebbo eventually became bishop of Hildesheim, stating only that Louis the German appointed him *in regione Saxonie quoddam episcopium*. The bishopric was clearly identified as Hildesheim in the documents Flodoard had before him.[72] This looks like an attempt to downplay a highly controversial – and, in the mid-tenth century, still canonically dubious – translation to another bishopric.[73] There is an interesting contrast here with his treatment of Egidius' treason and trial: whereas Flodoard, having no other evidence, submitted to Gregory of Tours' account without comment, in the case of Ebbo he was able to demonstrate precisely why the situation had been so complex. Flodoard's portrait is thus rather sympathetic, depicting Ebbo less as perfidious and unscrupulous than as naïve and tragic.

Steffen Patzold has observed that Flodoard's Ebbo looks like a prototypical Ottonian *Reichsbischof*.[74] Flodoard wrote the *History* in the same years that Otto, according to an older historiographical view, supposedly began to conceive of an 'imperial church system', the systematic appointment of loyal bishops as

48 Edward Roberts

counterweights to the Reich's mighty but unruly nobility. More recent research has tended to qualify or reject the notion of a coherent, long-term episcopal strategy on the part of the Ottonian–Salian rulers.[75] As Patzold notes, Ebbo's career was defined by his closeness with and service to the emperor. He used his position to promote Rheims' interests at court, obtaining valuable gifts and privileges for the church from the royal family. He lost his office *pro infidelitate imperatoris*. Patzold makes the point that Flodoard's portrayal of Ebbo was not inspired by any Ottonian political programme; it was shaped by his rich sources and by his own life in a city steeped in Carolingian tradition. Yet even if we discard outmoded conceptions of a *Reichskirchensystem*, it is clear that Flodoard composed the *History* in a distinctive Ottonian political milieu. As he wrote in his preface, he had been encouraged to produce such a history by its dedicatee, Archbishop Robert of Trier. Flodoard himself was in Otto I's presence on numerous occasions. The canon travelled to Aachen as part of a royal West Frankish delegation in 944.[76] He was present when Robert and Archbishop Frederick of Mainz restored Artold at Rheims before kings Louis IV and Otto in 946.[77] He attended the synod of Ingelheim in 948, where the dispute between Artold and Hugh was settled before Otto and virtually the entire Ottonian episcopate.[78] In 951, he was sent to Aachen to speak with Otto about the church of Rheims' disputed property in the Vosges.[79] Elsewhere in the *History* we find Flodoard explicitly linking Rheims with the Ottonian church, as when he recounted how, with Artold's consent, Otto oversaw the translation of the relics of St Timothy from Rheims to his new royal monastery of St Maurice in Magdeburg.[80] The archbishopric of Rheims owned considerable property in the East Frankish kingdom, and its suffragan diocese of Cambrai was actually in the Reich. In describing the activities of Ebbo and other Rheims bishops in the service of kings and emperors, Flodoard, acutely aware of an eastward transfer of imperial power in his own day, wanted to demonstrate that the office of the archbishop of Rheims still had a role to play in this new political order.[81] We might therefore read his sympathetic portrait of Ebbo as an attempt to show that, despite his catastrophic error of judgement in 833, he was not an inherently bad bishop.

Conclusion

Flodoard perceived the church of Rheims in his day as a storied institution at a low ebb. Yet calamity had befallen the see before, and the church had recovered its eminent position in the Frankish episcopate. Illegitimate bishops, lay appropriation of church property, arbitrary depositions and treasonous acts echoed the darkest moments of Rheims' past. But this past, Flodoard believed, offered some guidance for navigating the stormy waters of a fast-changing present. Because the *History of the Church of Rheims* gives an unparalleled look into an early medieval episcopal archive, there has long been a tendency to mine the text as the work of a humble 'archivist' who was simply taking cues from Archbishop Hincmar's project a century earlier. Flodoard certainly did celebrate Hincmar's life and deeds, but, as we have seen, he did not slavishly follow the great prelate when it came to history. Flodoard's Rheims was very different to Hincmar's, and he had his own duties and priorities. One of those priorities was reconciliation. The archiepiscopal schism of 925–948 was not resolved overnight by the synod of Ingelheim. Divisions within the church and province of Rheims and the West Frankish kingdom remained. When Artold died in 961, erstwhile supporters of the excommunicated Hugh clamoured for his restoration once more.[82] Recent turmoil could not simply be ignored, still less while Hugh lived. Thus, Flodoard did not disparage Hugh in the *History*, nor did he explicitly state that Hugh's tenure had been illegal, even though this was the verdict of the synod of Ingelheim. To help heal wounds, Flodoard fashioned an inclusive past that placed great emphasis on continuity and legitimacy yet remained faithful to his archival materials.[83] He engaged with the past in a decidedly thoughtful way, highlighting virtues in the church's less reputable prelates and drawing lessons from those who had been deposed in dubious or controversial circumstances. Flodoard did not just write to restore his community, however: in articulating the diocesan work, property rights, and royal privileges of the archbishops of Rheims, he was making a strong case for the role of the office in royal government at precisely the moment Otto I's rule was adopting a distinctly imperial tenor.

In 991, questions surrounding the deposition of a Rheims bishop surfaced once again at the synod of Saint-Basle, where Archbishop Arnulf was found guilty of treason, deposed, and replaced with Gerbert of Aurillac. According to Gerbert's own account of the synod, Arnulf was vilified through association with the seditious bishops Egidius and Ebbo.[84] Here, Flodoard's verdicts are nowhere to be seen, even though his *History* seems to have become authoritative: unusually for a work of *gesta*, his name became associated with it, and it was not continued in later generations. Other texts hint at changeable attitudes to episcopal legitimacy. As a list of benefactors of the monastery of Saint-Remi compiled during the second episcopate of Arnulf (who was restored in 998) reveals, there was no problem commemorating Hugh of Vermandois as 'Hugo archiepiscopus' for his gift of the *villa* of Crugny.[85] In his *Gesta abbatum Lobbiensium*, Folcuin of Lobbes, writing around 980, believed that Abel of Rheims was the same Abel who was attested as abbot of Lobbes in the mid-eighth century. He had consulted Flodoard's *History*, 'the *gesta pontificum* of Rheims'. But Folcuin had also learned in conversation with Archbishop Adalbero (969–989) that Abel was not commemorated in the episcopal succession. Folcuin was clearly puzzled by this and the fuzziness of Flodoard's account. He surmised that Abel had been appointed temporarily and had voluntarily withdrawn from the world, and so had not wished for his name to be included in the list.[86] Adalbero's remark suggests that Flodoard's case had not won support. About a century later, as we saw at the beginning of this chapter, the canon Odalric still did not subscribe to the historian's judgement of Abel, excluding him again from the episcopal series. As the circumstances surrounding Flodoard's reasons for writing the *History* faded from living memory, later generations of Rheims clerics turned again to the past and redeployed it with their own priorities firmly in mind.[87]

Notes

1 Rheims, Bibliothèque municipale MS 15, fol. 20v. See John S. Ott, *Bishops, Authority and Community in Northwestern Europe, c.1050–1150* (Cambridge: Cambridge University Press, 2015), p. 194.

2 For a sketch of early medieval Rheims, see Michel Sot, *Un historien et son Église au Xe siècle: Flodoard de Reims* (Paris: Fayard, 1993), pp. 17–42. Rosamond McKitterick, 'The Carolingian Kings and the See of Rheims, 882–987', in *Ideal and Reality in Frankish and Anglo-Saxon Society: Studies Presented to J. M. Wallace-Hadrill*, ed. by Patrick Wormald, Donald A. Bullough and Roger Collins (Oxford: Blackwell, 1983), pp. 228–49, remains a helpful overview of the archbishopric in the tenth century.

3 John S. Ott, '"Reims and Rome are Equals": Archbishop Manasses I (*c.* 1069–80), Pope Gregory VII, and the Fortunes of Historical Exceptionalism', in *Envisioning the Bishop: Images and the Episcopacy in the Middle Ages*, ed. by Sigrid Danielson and Evan A. Gatti (Turnhout: Brepols, 2014), pp. 275–302.

4 Flodoard of Rheims, *Historia Remensis ecclesiae*, ed. by Martina Stratmann, *MGH Scriptores* 36 (Hanover: Hahnsche Buchhandlung, 1998) [hereafter *HRE*]. The fundamental study of this work is Sot, *Un historien*. On Flodoard and the dispute of 925–48, see further Jason Glenn, *Politics and History in the Tenth Century: The Work and World of Richer of Reims* (Cambridge: Cambridge University Press, 2004), pp. 215–34; Edward Roberts, *Flodoard of Rheims and the Writing of History in the Tenth Century* (Cambridge: Cambridge University Press, 2019), pp. 29–74.

5 Within a substantial body of literature, see in particular Michel Sot, *Gesta episcoporum, gesta abbatum*, Typologie des sources du Moyen Âge occidental, 37 (Turnhout: Brepols, 1981); Constance B. Bouchard, 'Episcopal *Gesta* and the Creation of a Useful Past in Ninth-Century Auxerre', *Speculum*, 84 (2009), 1–35; Theo Riches, 'The Function of the *Gesta Episcoporum* as Archive: Some Reflections on the *Codex sancti Gisleni* (MS Den Haag KB75 F15)', *Jaarboek voor Middeleeuwse Geschiedenis*, 10 (2007), 7–46; Theo Riches, 'The Changing Political Horizons of *Gesta Episcoporum* from the Ninth to Eleventh Centuries', in *Patterns of Episcopal Power: Bishops in Tenth and Eleventh Century Western Europe*, ed. by Ludger Körntgen and Dominik Waßenhoven (Berlin: De Gruyter, 2011), pp. 51–62. See also Geoffrey Koziol, this volume. The classic work on 'creative memory' around the millennium is Patrick J. Geary, *Phantoms of Remembrance: Memory and Oblivion at the End of the First Millennium* (Princeton: Princeton University Press, 1994).

6 Remigius is the subject of the majority of the first book of the *History*, while the whole of the third is devoted to Hincmar: *HRE*, I.10–23, pp. 80–122; III.1–30, pp. 190–363.

7 *HRE*, I.3, pp. 66–7. Sixtus in fact lived in the third century: see Sot, *Un historien*, pp. 364–6; Marie-Céline Isaïa, *Remi de Reims: mémoire d'une saint, histoire d'une Église* (Paris: Cerf, 2010), pp. 599–602.

8 On the place of biography in broader historical analysis, see the comments of Stuart Airlie, this volume.

9 On Egidius, see Guntram Freiherr Schenk zu Schweinsberg, *Reims in merowingischer Zeit: Stadt, Civitas, Bistum. Anhang: Die Geschichte der Reimser Bischöfe in karolingischer Zeit bis zur Bischofserhebung Hinkmars 845* (Bonn: Rheinische Friedrich Wilhelms-Universität, 1971), pp. 99–109; Sot, *Un historien*, pp. 420–3.

10 *HRE*, II.2, pp. 132–3.

11 *HRE*, II.2, pp. 132–3; *Die Urkunden der Merowinger*, ed. by Theo Kölzer, *MGH DD. Mer.* 2 (Hanover: Hahnsche Buchhandlung, 2001), Dep. 79, p. 533; Martina Stratmann, 'Die Königs- und Privaturkunden für die Reimser Kirche bis gegen 900', *Deutsches Archiv*, 52 (1996), 1–55 (pp. 26–7, 48) (= nos. 5, 6, 7, 75).

12 On Flodoard's archival methods, see Harald Zimmermann, 'Zu Flodoards Historiographie und Regestentechnik', in *Festschrift für Helmut Beumann zum 65. Geburtstag*, ed. by Kurt-Ulrich Jäschke and Reinhard Wenskus (Sigmaringen: Thorbecke, 1977), pp. 200–14; Stratmann, 'Die Königs- und Privaturkunden'; Martina Stratmann, 'Die *Historia Remensis*

Ecclesiae: Flodoards Umgang mit seinen Quellen', *Filologia Mediolatina*, 1 (1994), 111–27; Roberts, *Flodoard*, pp. 114–22.

13 *HRE*, II.2, pp. 133–4; Venantius Fortunatus, *Opera poetica*, III.15, ed. by Friedrich Leo, *MGH Auct. ant.* 4.1 (Berlin: Weidmann, 1881), pp. 68–9.

14 *HRE*, II.2, pp. 134–6. The key passage of Gregory drawn on by Flodoard is *Libri historiarum decem*, X.18–19, ed. by Bruno Krusch and Wilhelm Levison, *MGH SRM* 1.1 (Hanover: Hahnsche Buchhandlung, 1951), pp. 509–13. On the political context of this episode, see Raymond Van Dam, 'Merovingian Gaul and the Frankish Conquests', in *The New Cambridge Medieval History, Volume 1: c.500–c.700*, ed. by Paul Fouracre (Cambridge: Cambridge University Press, 2005), pp. 193–231 (pp. 219–20); and on Gregory's account, Ian Wood, 'The Secret Histories of Gregory of Tours', *Revue Belge de Philologie et d'Histoire*, 71 (1993), 253–70 (pp. 267–9); Guy Halsall, 'Nero and Herod? The Death of Chilperic and Gregory's Writing of History', in *The World of Gregory of Tours*, ed. by Kathleen Mitchell and Ian Wood (Brill: Leiden, 2002), pp. 337–50 (pp. 345–7).

15 Sot, *Un historien*, p. 423 (quotation), 641, 745–6.

16 *HRE*, II.2, pp. 134: 'Qui tamen Gregorius in historia gentis Francorum de hoc presule narrat ... '. On the Carolingian reception of Gregory, see Helmut Reimitz, 'The Early Medieval Editions of Gregory of Tours' *Histories*', in *A Companion to Gregory of Tours*, ed. by Alexander Callander Murray (Brill: Leiden, 2016), pp. 519–65 (pp. 540–63).

17 *HRE*, II.3, pp. 137–40; Sot, *Un historien*, pp. 423–6.

18 *HRE*, II.11–15, pp. 156–66; Sot, *Un historien*, pp. 447–58.

19 *HRE*, II.11, pp. 156–9, quotation at p. 156; Stratmann, 'Die Königs- und Privaturkunden', pp. 12–3, 22–3, 30–1, 33, 52–3 (nos. 19, 20, 21, 26, 27, 87–91).

20 *HRE*, II.12, p. 160; Sot, *Un historien*, p. 454.

21 See especially *HRE*, II.13–15, pp. 162–6.

22 *HRE*, II.12, pp. 159–62, quotation at p. 160.

23 *HRE*, II.12, p. 162; cf. *HRE*, IV.28, p. 420. See further Roberts, *Flodoard*, pp. 135–6.

24 *Vita Rigoberti*, ed. by Wilhelm Levison, *MGH SRM* 7 (Hanover: Hahnsche Buchhandlung, 1920), pp. 54–80.

25 Paul Fouracre, 'The Origins of the Carolingian Attempt to Regulate the Cult of Saints', in *The Cult of Saints in Late Antiquity and the Middle Ages: Essays on the Contribution of Peter Brown*, ed. by James Howard-Johnston and Paul Antony Hayward (Oxford: Oxford University Press, 1999), pp. 143–65 (pp. 161–2).

26 Paul Fouracre, *The Age of Charles Martel* (London: Longman, 2000), pp. 122–6.

27 *Die Konzilien der karolingischen Teilreiche, 843–859*, ed. by Wilfried Hartmann, *MGH Conc.* 3 (Hanover: Hahnsche Buchhandlung, 1984), pp. 414–6; *Vita Rigoberti*, 13, p. 70. Paul Edward Dutton, *The Politics of Dreaming in the Carolingian Empire* (Lincoln: University of Nebraska Press, 1994), pp. 171–5; Fouracre, *Charles Martel*, pp. 123–5; Olaf Schneider, *Erzbischof Hinkmar und die Folgen: der vierhundertjährige Weg historischer Erinnerungsbilder von Reims nach Trier* (Berlin: De Gruyer, 2010), pp. 85–6. On various aspects of Hincmar's diocesan management, see Martina Stratmann, *Hinkmar von Reims als Verwalter von Bistum und Kirchenprovinz* (Sigmaringen: Thorbecke, 1991); and the essays of *Hincmar of Rheims: Life and Work*, ed. by Rachel Stone and Charles West (Manchester: Manchester University Press, 2015).

28 *Vita Rigoberti*, 14, pp. 70–1; *HRE*, II.13, pp. 162–3.

29 Émile Lesne, 'La lettre interpolée d'Hadrien I à Tilpin et l'église de Reims au IXe siècle', *Le Moyen Âge*, 26 (1913), 325–51, 389–413; Horst Fuhrmann, *Einfluß und Verbreitung der pseudoisidorischen Fälschungen. Von ihren Auftauchen bis in die neuere Zeit*, *MGH Schriften* 24, 3 vols (Stuttgart: Anton Hiersemann, 1972–4), I (1972), 116–7; Zimmermann, 'Flodoards Historiographie', p. 213; Stratmann, *Hinkmar*, p. 52; Schneider, *Hinkmar*, pp. 52–6. Hincmar refers to the letter in his 864 letter to Pope Nicholas I, transmitted only by Flodoard at *HRE*, III.13, p. 233 (= Hincmar of Rheims, *Epistolae*, no. 169, ed. by Ernst Perels, *MGH Epp.* 8.1 (Berlin: Weidmann, 1939), pp. 144–63); as well as in *Opusculum LV capitulorum*, 16, in *Die Streitschriften Hinkmars von Reims und Hinkmars von Laon, 869–871*, ed. by Rudolf Schieffer, *MGH Conc.* 4.2 (Hanover: Hahnsche Buchhandlung, 2003),

52 Edward Roberts

p. 196; *De iure metropolitanorum*, *PL* 126, c. 20, col. 200; and possibly *Vita Remigii*, preface, ed. by Bruno Krusch, *MGH SRM* 3 (Hanover: Hahnsche Buchhandlung, 1896), pp. 239–349 (p. 251).

30 For an overview and context, see Rachel Stone, 'Introduction: Hincmar's World', in *Hincmar*, ed. by Stone and West, pp. 1–43 (pp. 11–7); and further Fuhrmann, *Einfluß*, II, pp. 254–63 (on Rothad) and pp. 651–72 (on Hincmar of Laon).

31 *PL* 126, 515A-526A at 516C; see Schneider, *Hinkmar*, pp. 92–3. In his letter to Pope Nicholas of 864 (above, n. 29), Hincmar once again alludes to the expulsion of a bishop by Milo, but does not give his name: *HRE*, III.13, p. 233. See Schneider, *Hinkmar*, pp. 90–1. On the Hadrian–Tilpin letter, see further below.

32 Paul Fouracre, 'Forgetting and Remembering Dagobert II: The English Connection', in *Frankland: The Franks and the World of the Early Middle Ages. Essays in Honour of Dame Jinty Nelson*, ed. by Paul Fouracre and David Ganz (Manchester: Manchester University Press, 2008), pp. 70–89; Simon MacLean, 'The Carolingian Past in Post-Carolingian Europe', in *'The Making of Europe': Essays in Honour of Robert Bartlett*, ed. by John Hudson and Sally Crumplin (Brill: Leiden, 2016), pp. 11–28; and Koziol, this volume.

33 See further Edward Roberts, 'Construire une hiérarchie épiscopale: Flodoard de Reims et la correspondance de l'archevêque Foulques (vers 850 – vers 950)', *Cahiers de civilisation médiévale*, 61 (2018), 11–26.

34 Sot, *Un historien*, p. 452, makes a similar suggestion, but does not develop the point.

35 *HRE*, preface, p. 57.

36 Cf. *HRE*, IV.28, pp. 419–20, with IV.34, pp. 426–8 and IV.35, pp. 434–5. See further Ernst-Dieter Hehl, 'Erzbischof Ruotbert von Trier und der Reimser Streit', in *Deus qui mutat tempora: Menschen und Institutionen im Wandel des Mittelalters. Festschrift für Alfons Becker*, ed. by Ernst-Dieter Hehl, Hubertus Seibert and Franz Staab (Sigmaringen: Thorbecke, 1987), pp. 55–68.

37 See further Roberts, *Flodoard*, pp. 127–41.

38 *HRE*, II.12, p. 161.

39 *HRE*, II.16–17, pp. 167–9.

40 *PL* 126, 515A-526A at 516C; *Vita Rigoberti*, 16–19, pp. 72–4; *HRE*, II.12, pp. 161–2.

41 *HRE*, II.11, pp. 157–8; *MGH DD. Mer.* 2, Dep. 387 and 388, pp. 656–7; see discussion here and in Levison's introduction to *Vita Rigoberti*, pp. 54–5.

42 *Diplomata Belgica ante annum millesimum centesimum scripta*, no. 13, ed. by M. Gysseling and A. C. F. Koch, 2 vols (Brussels: Belgisch Inter-Universitair Centrum voor Neerlandistiek, 1950), I, 27–9. On Folcuin's use of charters, see Laurent Morelle, 'Incertitudes et faux-semblants: quelques remarques sur l'élaboration des actes privés carolingiens à la lumière de deux gisements de France septentrionale (Sithiu/Saint-Bertin, Saint-Denis)', in *Die Privaturkunden der Karolingerzeit*, ed. by Peter Erhart, Karl Heidecker and Bernhard Zeller (Zürich: Urs Graf, 2009), pp. 103–20 (pp. 103–11).

43 *Vita Rigoberti*, 1–2, pp. 61–2. Stratmann, 'Die Königs- und Privaturkunden', pp. 22, 54 (no. 92), identifies this Rigobert with the bishop of Rheims. The second abbot of Saint-Bertin was also named Rigobert, but he had clearly died before 723; Erkembold was the fourth abbot: Folcuin of Lobbes, *Gesta abbatum Sithiensium*, 12, ed. by O. Holder-Egger, *MGH SS* 13 (Hanover: Hahnsche Buchhandlung, 1881), pp. 607–35 (p. 610).

44 Schneider, *Hinkmar*, with findings summarized at pp. 388–9. The classic study of Milo is Eugen Ewig, 'Milo et eiusmodi similes', in his *Spätantikes und Fränkisches Gallien. Gesammelte Schriften (1952–1973)*, 2 vols, ed. by Hartmut Atsma (Munich: Artemis, 1976–9), II (1979), 189–219. Against Schneider's thesis that Milo was never bishop of Trier, see now Patrick Breternitz, 'Milo und die Münzen. Ein Beitrag zur Diskussion um Milos Trierer Episkopat', *Deutsches Archiv*, 72 (2016), 161–75.

45 *MGH Epp.* 8.1, no. 160, pp. 125–6; see Schneider, *Hinkmar*, pp. 88–90. For the wider reorganization of metropolitan bishoprics under the Carolingians, see Steffen Patzold, 'Eine Hierarchie im Wandel: die Ausbildung einer Metropolitanordnung im Frankenreich des 8. und 9. Jahrhunderts', in *Hiérarchie et stratification sociale dans l'Occident médiéval (400–1100)*, ed. by François Bougard, Dominique Iogna-Prat and Régine Le Jan

(Turnhout: Brepols, 2008), pp. 161–84; Daniel Carlo Pangerl, *Die Metropolitanverfassung des karolingischen Frankenreiches*, *MGH Schriften* 63 (Hanover: Hahnsche Buchhandlung, 2011).

46 *Die Briefe des heiligen Bonifatius und Lullus*, no. 87, ed. by Michael Tangl, *MGH Epp. sel.* 1 (Berlin: Weidmann, 1916), p. 198; trans. by Ephraim Emerton, *The Letters of St Boniface*, 2nd ed. (New York: Columbia University Press: 2000), p. 140. See also Fouracre, *Charles Martel*, p. 133.

47 *Die Briefe*, no. 57, p. 103; no. 58, pp. 106–7.

48 *HRE*, II.16, p. 166. For an overview of the evidence for Abel's career, including his probable Anglo-Saxon origin, see Marios Costambeys, 'Abel (*fl.* 744–747)', *Oxford Dictionary of National Biography* (Oxford: Oxford University Press, 2004).

49 *HRE*, II.16, p. 167.

50 *HRE*, II.16, p. 167.

51 The fundamental study is Theodor Gottlob, *Der abendländische Chorepiskopat* (Bonn: Ludwig Röhrscheid, 1928), pp. 77–8 for Abel. See also Jörg Müller, 'Gedanken zum Institut der Chorbischöfe', in *Medieval Church Law and the Origins of the Western Legal Tradition: A Tribute to Kenneth Pennington*, ed. by Wolfgang P. Müller and Mary E. Sommar (Washington: Catholic University of America Press, 2006), pp. 77–94. On chorbishops in the northern missions, see generally E. Knibbs, *Ansgar, Rimbert and the Forged Foundations of Hamburg-Bremen* (Farnham: Ashgate, 2011).

52 *Gesta sanctorum patrum Fontanellensis coenobii*, V.1, ed. by F. Lohier and J. Laporte (Paris: Picard, 1936), p. 43.

53 On the limits of Boniface's programme, see J. M. Wallace-Hadrill, *The Frankish Church* (Oxford: Clarendon Press, 1983), p. 157; Gregory I. Halfond, *The Archaeology of Frankish Church Councils, AD 511–768* (Brill: Leiden, 2010), pp. 203–4.

54 *MGH Conc.* 2.1, p. 34.

55 *Die Briefe*, no. 73, pp. 146–7.

56 Gottlob, *Chorepiskopat*, pp. 61–2.

57 Klaus Zechiel-Eckes, 'Der "unbeugsame" Exterminator? Isidorus Mercator und der Kampf gegen den Chorepiskopat', in *Scientia veritatis. Festschrift für Hubert Mordek zum 65. Geburtstag*, ed. by Oliver Münsch and Thomas Zotz (Ostfildern: Jan Thorbecke, 2004), pp. 173–90; Steffen Patzold, *Episcopus. Wissen über Bischöfe im Frankenreich des späten 8. bis frühen 10. Jahrhunderts* (Ostfildern: Jan Thorbecke, 2008), p. 234; Eric Knibbs, 'Ebo of Reims, Pseudo-Isidore, and the Date of the False Decretals', *Speculum*, 92 (2017), 144–83 (p. 152 n. 28).

58 Matthew Bryan Gillis, *Heresy and Dissent in the Carolingian Empire* (Oxford: Oxford University Press, 2017), p. 78.

59 On the problematic dates of Tilpin's tenure, see Schneider, *Hinkmar*, p. 83 n. 56.

60 Flodoard, *Annales*, ed. by Philippe Lauer (Paris: Picard, 1906), s.a. 925, pp. 32–3; 928, p. 42; *HRE*, IV.20, pp. 411–12; IV.22, p. 414.

61 *HRE*, IV.34, p. 426.

62 For an excellent summary of Ebbo's career, see Courtney M. Booker, 'The False Decretals and Ebbo's *fama ambigua*: A Verdict Revisited', in *Fälschung als Mittel der Politik? Pseudoisidor im Licht der neuen Forschung. Gedenkschrift für Klaus Zechiel-Eckes*, ed. by Karl Ubl and Daniel Ziemann, *MGH Studien und Texte* 57 (Wiesbaden: Harrassowitz Verlag, 2015), pp. 207–42 (pp. 216–23). On Ebbo's role in the deposition of Louis the Pious, see further Mayke de Jong, *The Penitential State: Authority and Atonement in the Age of Louis the Pious* (Cambridge: Cambridge University Press, 2009), pp. 252–9; Courtney M. Booker, *Past Convictions: The Penance of Louis the Pious and the Decline of the Carolingians* (Philadelphia: University of Pennsylvania Press, 2009), pp. 183–209; and on the ramifications of Ebbo's own deposition, see Patzold, *Episcopus*, pp. 315–57.

63 See most recently Knibbs, 'Ebo'.

64 *HRE*, III.13, p. 236.

65 *HRE*, II.19, pp. 175–83, quotation at p. 175. See Sot, *Un historien*, pp. 471–8; Patzold, *Episcopus*, pp. 353–7. On the two diplomas of Louis the Pious reproduced in this chapter,

see Philippe Depreux, 'Zur Echtheit einer Urkunde Kaiser Ludwigs des Frommen für die Reimser Kirche (BM² 801)', *Deutsches Archiv*, 48 (1992), 1–16.

66 *HRE*, II.19, pp. 182–3. This text does not seem to be contemporary with Ebbo's fall and is often attributed to Hincmar, but it may not be independent of Flodoard's *History*: outside this work, the vision survives in just one eleventh-century manuscript. See Stratmann, *HRE*, p. 182 n. 75; Dutton, *Politics*, pp. 230–3. On Flodoard's interest in visions, see Geoffrey Koziol, 'Flothilde's Visions and Flodoard's Histories: A Tenth-Century Mutation?', *Early Medieval Europe*, 24 (2016), 160–84.

67 *HRE*, II.20, pp. 183–9, quotation at p. 183. On Flodoard's use of his sources in this chapter, see Zimmermann, 'Flodoards Historiographie', pp. 208–11; Sot, *Un historien*, pp. 478–9; Patzold, *Episcopus*, pp. 355–6.

68 *HRE*, II.20, p. 189. On Ebbo's last years, see Hans Goetting, *Das Bistum Hildesheim. Die Hildesheimer Bischöfe von 815 bis 1221*, Germania Sacra, N. F. 2 (Berlin: De Gruyter, 1984), pp. 70–9; Booker, *Past Convictions*, p. 196 nn. 55–6.

69 *HRE*, III.2, pp. 191–3. See Elina Screen, 'An Unfortunate Necessity? Hincmar and Lothar I', in *Hincmar*, ed. by Stone and West, pp. 76–92 (pp. 77–80).

70 *HRE*, III.3, pp. 193–4. See Dutton, *Politics*, pp. 183–93.

71 See, for instance, Sot, *Un historien*, pp. 471–85, 647–9, 744; James T. Palmer, 'Rimbert's *Vita Anskarii* and Scandinavian Mission in the Ninth Century', *Journal of Ecclesiastical History*, 55 (2004), 235–56 (p. 253); de Jong, *Penitential State*, pp. 253–4; Booker, 'False Decretals', pp. 224–5.

72 *Die Konzilien der karolingischen Teilreiche, 860–874*, ed. by Wilfried Hartmann, *MGH Conc.* 4 (Hanover: Hahnsche Buchhandlung, 1998), p. 235 (a letter from Hincmar to Nicholas I on behalf of the 867 synod of Troyes). Sot, *Un historien*, p. 482, stresses Flodoard's concern to demonstrate the various canonical arguments made throughout the affair.

73 On this translation, see Knibbs, 'Ebo', pp. 168–73; and on tenth-century attitudes to the issue, see Conrad Leyser, 'Episcopal Office in the Italy of Liudprand of Cremona, *c*.890–*c*.970 , *English Historical Review*, 125 (2010), 795–817.

74 Patzold, *Episcopus*, pp. 356–7; and, similarly, Sot, *Un historien*, pp. 484–5.

75 A seminal criticism of the *Reichskirchensystem* was Timothy Reuter, 'The "Imperial Church System" of the Ottonian and Salian Rulers: A Reconsideration', *Journal of Ecclesiastical History*, 33 (1982), 347–74 (repr. in Timothy Reuter, *Medieval Polities and Modern Mentalities*, ed. by Janet L. Nelson (Cambridge: Cambridge University Press, 2006), pp. 325–54). For full bibliographic discussion, see Patzold, *Episcopus*, pp. 19–21.

76 Flodoard, *Annales*, s.a. 944, pp. 92–3.

77 Flodoard, *Annales*, s.a. 946, p. 103.

78 Flodoard, *Annales*, s.a. 948, pp. 109–16.

79 *HRE*, I.20, pp. 111–2.

80 *HRE*, I.4, p. 71.

81 See further Edward Roberts, 'Hegemony, History and Rebellion: Flodoard's *Historia Remensis ecclesiae* in Ottonian Perspective', *Journal of Medieval History*, 42 (2016), 155–76.

82 *Annales*, s.a. 961, p. 150; 962, pp. 150–4.

83 For a comparable assessment of Folcuin's *Gesta* of Lobbes, see Ingrid Rembold, 'History and (Selective) Memory: Articulating Community and Division in Folcuin's *Gesta abbatum Lobiensium*', in *Writing the Early Medieval West: Studies in Honour of Rosamond McKitterick*, ed. by Elina Screen and Charles West (Cambridge: Cambridge University Press, 2018), pp. 64–79. Similarly, Walter Pohl, 'History in Fragments: Montecassino's Politics of Memory', *Early Medieval Europe*, 10 (2001), 343–74 (p. 353).

84 Glenn, *Politics*, pp. 98–109; Charles West, *Reframing the Feudal Revolution: Political and Social Transformation Between Marne and Moselle, c.800–c.1100* (Cambridge: Cambridge University Press, 2013), pp. 163–7.

85 Rheims, Bibliothèque municipale MS 300, fol. 233v: *Hugo archieps Crusneium*. On this text, preserved in a twelfth-century copy, see J.-P. Devroey, 'Une liste des bienfaiteurs de Saint-Remi de Reims au début du XIᵉ siècle, témoin d'un obituaire rémois perdu', *Revue Bénédictine*, 114 (2004), 112–39.

Remembering troubled pasts **55**

86 Folcuin, *Gesta abbatum Lobbiensium*, 7, ed. by Georg Heinrich Pertz, *MGH SS* 4 (Hanover: Hahnsche Buchhandlung, 1841), pp. 52–74 (pp. 58–9). See Riches, 'Function', pp. 38–9; Rembold, 'History', pp. 74–5. It is unclear whether the bishop and abbot were one and the same: see Costambeys, 'Abel'.
87 See, for instance, the historiographical endeavours of Archbishop Gervais (1055–1067): Ott, *Bishops*, pp. 154–96.

4

IN THE SHADOW OF ROME

After Empire in the late-tenth-century chronicle of Benedict of Monte Soratte*

Maya Maskarinec

In the late tenth century an otherwise unknown monk, Benedict, penned a history of his monastery, S. Andrea at Monte Soratte. As it survives today, in a single manuscript (Vatican Chigi. F.IV.75), the chronicle extends from the mid- to late fourth century to Benedict's own day, sometime not long after 972.[1] Benedict's unusual – and very critical – perception of the past is the subject of this article. Writing from the vantage point of Monte Soratte, a site that has always been, and still remains, in the shadow of Rome, Benedict crafts a narrative that disparages but cannot ignore the city. Benedict portrays Rome's late antique and early medieval past as a spiral of chaos and oppression under a succession of 'foreign' empires that offers few feasible models of authority and legitimacy for the tenth-century present.[2] Nevertheless, so I argue, although Benedict is familiar enough with Rome to be able to turn the city's illustrious past against it, he is not distant enough to be able to find an alternative: Rome and the empires that have laid claim to the city still remain, after empire, the point of reference for the future.

Monte Soratte and Benedict of S. Andrea

Monte Soratte (691 m) is an isolated limestone outcropping, ca. 40 km north of Rome (in the present-day region of Lazio). On a clear day the ridge is easily visible from the city of Rome (Fig. 4.1). Monte Soratte rises above the surrounding countryside through which the Tiber snakes in tortuous bends (Map 4.1). In Roman times Monte Soratte formed the border of the agricultural territory

---

* The research for this essay was completed with the support of a Visiting Research Scholarship at the Institute for the Study of the Ancient World, NYU (2016–17) and a CAORC Mediterranean Regional Research Fellowship (2017–18).

FIGURE 4.1 Monte Soratte as viewed from Rome (Photo by author).

centred on the ancient town of Capena, the so-called 'Ager Capenas';[3] in medieval times it was part of the 'territorium Collinense'.[4] To the west of Monte Soratte ran the via Flaminia, to the east of the Tiber, the via Salaria: the routes most commonly frequented by travellers between Rome and the north. In the Middle Ages the via Salaria continued to be in use, although parts of the via Flaminia (especially to the north of Monte Soratte where the via Flaminia crosses the Treia valley) fell into disuse, with travellers preferring the ancient via Cassia further to the west, or the stretch along the Tiber.[5]

The ridge of Monte Soratte is an inhospitable outpost adjacent to fertile plains. Monte Soratte is covered in dense scrub, and wells cannot be dug into its limestone base. Until the 1820s (when much of the woods around Soratte were cleared), wolves roamed the environs, and their attacks on grazing sheep were a source of perennial concern to shepherds.[6] Yet, to the east of Monte Soratte, in close vicinity to the Tiber, Roman elites had established large agricultural estates (*villae rusticae*).[7] As analysed by Jones, the archaeological evidence from the Ager Capenas suggests extensive continuity in Roman-era settlement patterns through the eighth century (and often later),[8] and throughout the Middle Ages this continued to be an agricultural region in close contact with Rome. Oil, wine, grains, wood, and other heavy loads were carried to Rome down the Tiber, along which ran the via Tiberina.[9]

As viewed from atop the hills of Rome, Monte Soratte casts a striking visual profile: in the words of Lord Byron, it '[h]eaves like a long-swept wave about to break'.[10] The ridge was mentioned sporadically by Roman authors. 'You see how white with deep snow Soracte stands' is the first line of one of Horace's odes.[11] But neither the ancient ridge with its sanctuary dedicated to Apollo nor the medieval ridge with its monasteries ever achieved particular distinction. This

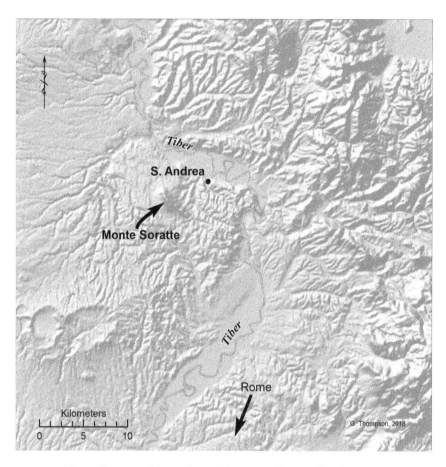

MAP 4.1 Monte Soratte and its environs (Map created by Gordie Thompson).

is a site that always has been – and still remains – in the shadow of Rome: far enough away to be outside the orbit of day-to-day urban politics, but not distant enough to be indifferent to the city. This explains the inability of our chronicler, Benedict, to ignore Rome and the vehemence of his attitude toward the city.

Benedict was a monk at the monastery of S. Andrea 'in Soracte' or 'in Flumine'.[12] As the two variants of S. Andrea's name indicate, this was a monastery that identified both with the ridge that loomed above it, and with the Tiber that connected it to Rome. As presented by Benedict's chronicle, the monastery of S. Andrea traced its lineage back to a church and monastery on the very peak of Monte Soratte, but the monastery of S. Andrea was itself located to the north-east, on a low hill below Monte Soratte, near the Tiber river (Map 4.1). Archaeological investigations conducted in the late 1990s confirmed that the monastery was located on the site of an earlier Roman villa; the remains thereof include fragments of a black and white mosaic pavement.[13] Like the Roman estate that preceded it, the monastery was well positioned to till the fertile fields around it and transport its goods to Rome via the Tiber. It had easy access to a Tiber port (at Badia), situated at a wide bend of the Tiber, which also served as a convenient spot for fording the river.

Our primary source for the monastery of S. Andrea is Benedict's chronicle, and the very little we securely know about its author, Benedict, derives from the text.[14] Indeed a passage of the chronicle that has substituted the name Benedict for Gerward (the librarian of Louis the Pious) in verses praising Charlemagne is the only evidence that our chronicler's name was Benedict, and that he was a monk (Fig. 4.2).[15] In 1013, as attested by a document in Farfa's cartulary, one Benedict, abbot of S. Andrea ('domnus benedictus uir uenerabilis abbas'), agreed to renounce a certain property; chronologically, so I suggest, it is not infeasible to identify this abbot with the author of our chronicle, though there is no firm evidence for such a conclusion.[16]

The evidence of Benedict's chronicle indicates that in the mid- to late tenth century S. Andrea was a well-endowed and active monastery with a library and a newly-completed circuit of walls. As presented by Benedict's chronicle, the monastery had entered into a new phase of prosperity with Alberic (II) (d. 954) after a long period of great instability.[17] The (heavily restored) church today *in situ* largely dates to a late-twelfth- to early-thirteenth-century reconstruction, but reused are Roman-era column capitals and early medieval architectural elements that must derive from the earlier church (Fig. 4.3).[18]

Benedict describes S. Andrea's land-holdings as extending throughout the *territorium Collinense*, as well as including property across the river in the Sabina and in Rome. Furthermore, as I have argued elsewhere, one of Benedict's primary motivations in composing his chronicle was to defend his monastery's rights to a piece of land outside of the distant town of Spoleto.[19] This property, so Benedict claims, had been donated to the monastery in the mid-eighth century by the Lombard king Ratchis and his wife Tassia. In his chronicle Benedict constructs a detailed narrative supported by legal arguments that explains and justifies the monastery's rightful ownership of the property in question. Moreover, I have suggested that Benedict may have composed his chronicle not long before or after 981, in the context of a dispute (or anticipated dispute) with the monastery of Farfa regarding this property. A diploma issued to Farfa by Otto II in 981 reasserts Farfa's claims to a piece of property in Spoleto in very close vicinity to that claimed by S. Andrea. Unlike Farfa, however, which benefited from the patronage of the Ottonian rulers, Benedict has, as we shall see, a distinctly negative attitude toward the arrival of the Ottonians in Italy; accordingly, we may read his chronicle as an attempt to assert his monastery's property claims in the absence of Ottonian support for the monastery.

As already mentioned, Benedict's chronicle survives in a single manuscript, now in the Vatican library: Chigi. F.IV.75 (Fig. 4.2).[20] The manuscript was long regarded as an autograph, but more recent scholarship has argued that this is an early-eleventh-century copy of the text, the product of an oral dictation of Benedict's

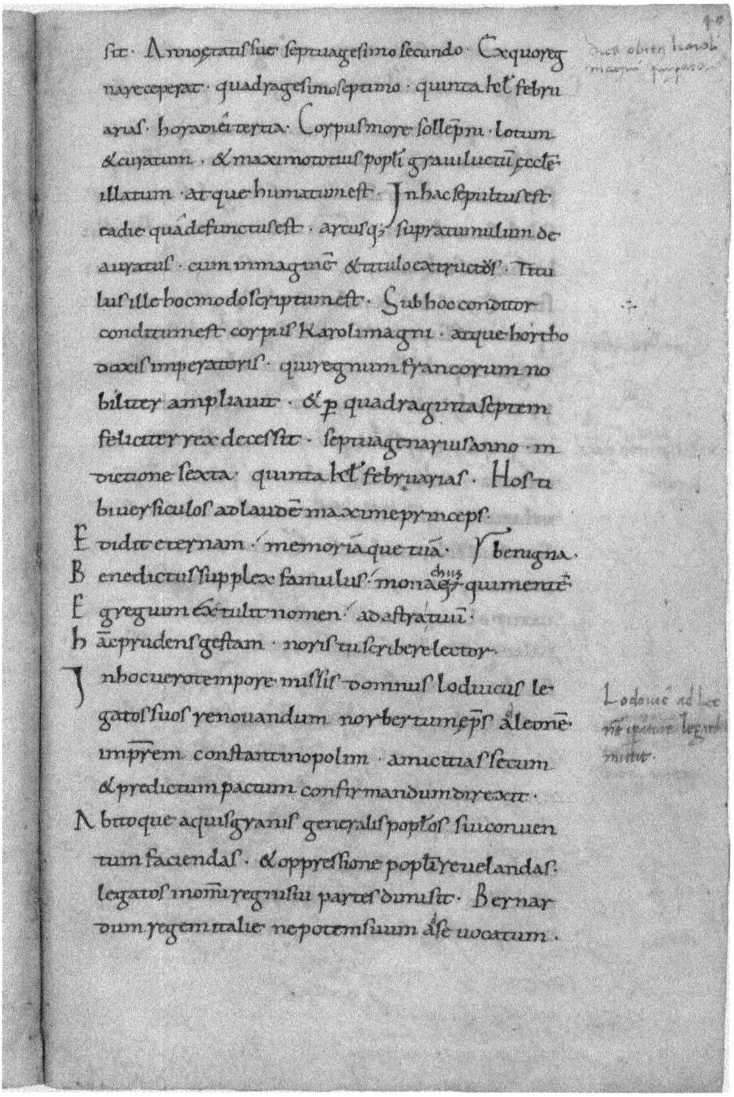

FIGURE 4.2 Vat. Chigi. F.IV.75, fol. 40r (courtesy of the Biblioteca Apostolica Vaticana, with all rights reserved).

text.[21] The surviving manuscript is incomplete; in it the chronicle both begins and ends mid-sentence. The amount of text missing from the beginning of the manuscript is impossible to reconstruct; however, as demonstrated by Paolo Chiesa, the codicology of the manuscript suggests that in its original form the chronicle probably only extended one folio longer than it does now.[22]

In the shadow of Rome 61

FIGURE 4.3 Reused architectural elements in the church of S. Andrea (Photos by author).

FIGURE 4.3 (*continued*)

Benedict's history of Rome: a downward spiral of oppression

Benedict's chronicle is written in praise and in defence of his monastery. Throughout the text, Benedict details the monastery's properties and privileges, and elaborates on the events, usually donations and the intervention of holy men, which strengthened the monastery over time. Rather than take a narrow view of his monastery's history, however, Benedict frames his text as a history of Rome and central-northern Italy more generally.[23] As Paolo Delogu has demonstrated, Benedict's preferred term for this is the 'kingdom of the Romans' (*regnum Romanorum*), a region whose borders Benedict never defines precisely; also referred to in the chronicle is the larger area of the 'kingdom of Italy/Italian kingdom' (*regnum Italiae/Italicum*).[24]

The history of the 'kingdom of Italy', and more specifically Rome, is the story of a people oppressed by 'foreign' rulers. When Pope Stephen decides to ask the Franks for assistance, Benedict has the pope exclaim: 'Woe is me, what should I do? The Italian kingdom has been suppressed by many peoples: first by the Medes and Alans, then by the Gauls, thirdly by the Goths, and fourthly by the Lombards'![25] Near the end of the chronicle, Benedict breaks out in lament: 'Alas, Rome! Oppressed and crushed by so many peoples, you have even been seized by a Saxon king'![26]

This would be a straightforward history of oppression, except that, as it turns out, the Romans are themselves to blame for their sad fate. Again and again, the decisive role in conflicts is played by the Romans themselves. They are under the yoke of their rulers because of their ineradicable bad customs: their grasping self-interest, their immoral practices and their propensity for strife and discord. This is a narrative of the history of Rome and Italy that is based on Benedict's sources but is inflected by biblical accounts of divine justice that, for Benedict, help make sense of it.

In Benedict's account of late antique history (primarily following Bede's chronicle), Italy, after it was ruled by Roman emperors (Julian, and then his Christian successors), was then ruled by Ostrogothic kings, beginning with Odovacer and ending with the worst, the *impiissimus* Totila.[27] Thereafter ruled one of the few individuals who Benedict suggests would have had the ability to establish a secure, stable government in Rome. This is Narses, that is, Justinian's general sent to conquer Italy but who is styled a ruler in his own right in Benedict's chronicle. According to Benedict, Narses was 'elected by all the Roman people'.[28] He is the first of the patricians who, Benedict tells us, ruled Rome.[29] Narses is presented in positive terms, yet the plots of 'wicked men from the territory of Rome (*viri scelerati de Romanis finibus*)' who conspire with the Goths cause his downfall.[30] Out of envy (*invidia*) they send an embassy to the Emperor Justin in Constantinople, accusing Narses of seeking to enslave them and possess Italy, not unlike the Goths.[31] On account of this, Narses writes to the Lombards, urging them to come and take possession of Italy. And when the Lombards arrive, multiplying like locusts (*sicut locuste*) throughout the whole kingdom of Italy, bringing pestilence and death, Narses makes a pact with them.[32]

The image of locusts descending upon Italy evokes the biblical image of the plague sent by God to punish the Egyptians.[33] That the Romans' depravity is linked to their destruction is made even more explicit later in the chronicle, again at a moment when foreign control over Rome is weak. After the reign of the Frankish kings Charlemagne and Louis the Pious, described by Benedict (following Einhard's *Life of Charlemagne* and the *Royal Frankish Annals*) as a period of comparative peace and prosperity,[34] Benedict is no longer following a known narrative source, and his succession of later Frankish rulers is confused. At one point Benedict reports that

> there arose dissension among the Romans, and evil men (*viri scelerati*) came forth and sent to the king of Babylon that he should come and possess the kingdom of Italy. And then the Hagarenes entered into Italy at the port of Centucellensis, and they covered the face of the earth, just as locusts cover crops in a field. And fear took possession of so many Romans that no one dared to leave the gates; and Rome was besieged, and the Leonine city was seized, and the church of St. Peter's was captured and plundered, and their horses were placed inside the monasteries of this very church. Thus the mother of all churches was turned to shame and all her dignity was torn away.[35]

The event in question appears to be the so-called 'Sack of Rome', the pillaging of St. Peter's by Arab maritime raiders in 846.[36] Benedict's description is also reminiscent of accusations levelled by Pope John VIII (r. 872–882) against his political opponents (the party of the bishop Formosus who, despite being excommunicated by Pope John VIII, went on to become pope), namely that they had invited in the

'Saracens'.[37] Accusing one's enemies of collaborating with Arab raiders may have been a conventional ninth- and tenth-century tactic of political defamation, but for Benedict it is an integral part of his historical narrative as to how Rome was sacked and plundered, confirming his worst suspicions about the wicked Romans, who bring the plague of the destructive 'Hagarenes' upon themselves – and the surrounding Roman countryside.

After this initial scene of devastation, again the pope calls upon foreign leaders for help, and the enemy is temporarily put to flight when the Romans team up with Guy, marquis of Spoleto. The Hagarenes, we are told, take to their ships again, bearing with them all their precious spoils from the Roman churches. Soon, however, the Romans proceed 'even more deceitfully' against the Franks and send to Palermo and Africa, again to the Hagarenes, that they might come and possess the Italian kingdom.[38] Again, the Hagarenes 'descend' like locusts, wreaking destruction by the sword and by fire throughout Italy, thereby ending the dominion of the Frankish kings in Italy. Thereupon, Benedict tells us, 'the Hagarenes ruled in the Roman kingdom for thirty years; the land was reduced to a wilderness (*redacta est terra in solitudine*), and the monasteries went without prayers'.[39]

Here Benedict is drawing on a verse from Jeremiah on the destruction of Babylon.[40] More immediately, the phrasing that the land was reduced to a wilderness is also found in a number of Roman sources commenting on Rome's misfortunes.[41] In particular, it is used in a homily of Gregory the Great, commenting on the book of Ezekiel, in which Gregory asks his listeners to look at the destruction around them that is the result, he explains, of divine justice for the sins of the people.[42] Gregory then elaborates on Rome's transformation from a city that was once mistress of the world to a city that has now become desolate and oppressed by her enemies, just as Ezekiel foretold regarding the city of Samaria. Likewise, Benedict implies that this destruction was deserved, for his chronicle continues, loosely quoting from the Book of Psalms, 'Truly, however, this was on account of the sins of the people, for as it is written, "From heaven the Lord looks upon all the sons who live on the earth, from his place of habitation"'.[43]

Benedict never spells out his charge fully, but by weaving biblical passages into his text at crucial moments, he repeatedly prompts his readers to conclude that Rome is a sinful city whose inhabitants are bringing upon themselves their own downfall, like Sodom and Gomorrah in the Book of Genesis, like Jerusalem or Babylon in Isaiah, or Samaria in Ezekiel. The Romans are not merely confused and misguided in some unremarkable way: this is a city morally corrupt to the core.

With the reign of the Hagarenes, Benedict's chronicle takes on an ever shriller tone of distress. Soon we have Rome under the sway of a powerful woman, the *domna senatrix*, as Benedict calls her.[44] This is Marozia, who controlled Roman politics in the late 920s. Benedict studiously omits her name, perhaps in an attempt to consign her to oblivion, but gives her a prominent role in the sequence of events. She gains power because Alberic takes her not as a legitimate wife but instead has

In the shadow of Rome **65**

an illicit affair (*consuetudinem malignam*) with her.[45] Again this leads to division and strife among the Roman people, and the Romans dispute amongst themselves. As a result, yet again, a foreign people descends upon Italy, this time the *gens Ungarorum*; again the scene is one of destruction by fire and the sword.

In telling of Marozia's influence, Benedict explains that Pope John XI (Marozia's son) 'was subjugated at Rome in the hands of a powerful woman, just as we read in the prophet, "Effeminate men will rule over Jerusalem".' Here Benedict is paraphrasing Isaiah 3 that describes how the Lord will pass judgement on the people of Jerusalem and Judah for their sins and will 'give children to be their princes, and effeminate men shall rule over them.'[46] Again the implication is that Rome is a degenerate city whose ills have been brought about by the sins of its inhabitants.

Marozia's rule is followed by another devastating attack by the 'Hungarians', which prompts a lament by Benedict and which, Benedict reports, was foretold by a series of omens and prodigies that took place in Rome in the seventh year of Pope John X's reign, that is 921. These warned, in vain, of the imminent destruction.

The first of these signs is stones falling from the sky in Rome and in the town of Narni (in Umbria), a form of heavenly wrath that appears in the Old Testament and in the Book of Revelation's description of Babylon's destruction.[47] Next are fiery torches that fall from the sky in parts of Rome, an image that, as Riccardo Santangeli Valenzani has pointed out, is reminiscent of the destruction of Sodom and Gomorrah in the Book of Genesis.[48] These flames of fire, so Santangeli Valenzani has suggested, target the properties of the Theophylact family, that is the family to which Marozia belonged. Thereupon there are three columns of flame on top of which are doves who attempt to extinguish the flames.

The next omen is a cooking pot (*olla*) in Rome that despite the best efforts of the local community cannot be moved until a priest recites prayers over it. Near the Salarian gate, we are told, a certain woman returning from St. Peter's, on the passion of our Lord, March 17, is cooking a stew.[49] After eating a plate of vegetables, she reaches for the pot, but it will not budge. Neighbours arrive, but they too are unable to move the pot. The pot adheres so firmly to the marble that it is as if the vessel were sculpted out of the marble itself. This omen recalls an analogy made in Ezekiel of the city as the pot and its people as the meat cooked within, an image prophesying the destruction of Jerusalem at the hands of foreigners.[50] Gregory the Great, in the same homily in which he chastises his congregation for the desolation of Rome caused by their sins, explicitly applies this prophecy to Rome, explaining that when the pot (*olla*) was put in place the city was first established; it boiled hot as the city grew in its glory and worldly powers, and now it is consumed.[51]

Another sign takes place at the church of S. Agata, on the vigil of the saint's feast day. The wooden image with the face of the saint leaps out from its usual spot and for a time remains suspended by its cord. Then it lies down before it again rights itself. And at the church of S. Angelo by the Tiber, the doors of the church are closed shut and cannot be opened, either by prayers or by force. Only the next day,

66 Maya Maskarinec

after a litany and a prayer, do they reopen of their own accord. Lastly, a bestial form, like an enormous dragon, is seen in the sky until it is covered up by a cloud.

By these signs the very fabric of the city of Rome rouses itself to warn the Romans. Benedict comments: 'Rome, afflicted by grief herself, began to vex the people'.[52] Here Benedict concludes his description of the signs, neither elaborating on their meaning, nor describing any immediate reaction in the city. The implication is that the Romans were numb to the portents and did not react, persisting in their usual habits. Benedict then proceeds with his narrative, describing how Marozia schemed to maintain her power over the city.

Something of a respite comes when the son of Marozia, Alberic (II), foils his mother's plots and, as 'princeps', reestablishes order to a certain extent. According to Benedict, he was 'exceedingly terrible, and the yoke over the Romans and the holy see was intensified'.[53] The Romans held in check, Alberic is able to turn his attention to monasteries outside of Rome. During Alberic's reign, Benedict tells us, no kings, neither Lombard nor from across the Alps, entered into Roman territory.[54] This, certainly from the perspective of Benedict's chronicle, is a noteworthy accomplishment.

Soon enough, however, the Romans 'according to their wicked custom', conspire how they may kill Alberic.[55] The plot is foiled, but the situation in Rome quickly disintegrates with the (natural) death of Alberic and the ascent to power of his fierce and debauched son Octavian as Pope John XII. As a result of Octavian's wickedness, certain Romans, a deacon and a high official, scheme against him – as usual turning to a foreign power. They invite in Otto, the king of the Saxons, to come and possess Italy and the Roman empire, just as Narses had once called upon the Lombards.[56]

Again, then, a foreign people descends upon Italy, and 'they cover the face of the earth, just like locusts'.[57] With Otto come other peoples and nations (*gentes nationes*) speaking languages unbeknownst to man. The image is again reminiscent of prophecies of destruction from the Old Testament.[58] Describing that Italy was devastated by the sword and by fire, again Benedict tells us that 'the land was reduced to a wilderness'.[59] As usual, strife breaks out in Rome. The pope (John XII) flees Rome, another is elected, and then the Romans 'according to their old customs (*secundum consuetudinem prisca*)' are divided amongst themselves.[60]

This leads Otto to lay siege to Rome, causing a terrible famine that prompts Benedict to draw on a line of Isaiah, 'it shall be a vexation only to understand the report'.[61] The context of this line is a prophecy regarding the destruction of corrupt rulers, priests and prophets; thus Benedict's chronicle implicitly suggests that the terror of the imperial assault was like that of the Lord's judgement. The implication is that the Romans must answer for their sins. Yet, as usual, the Romans misguidedly act out of self-interest, failing to see the consequences of their actions. They decide to betray the pope to the emperor, reasoning that: 'It is better that he alone should die for everyone so that we might free our souls from the torture of famine'.[62]

The chronicle concludes with yet another pope thrown out of the Lateran and legates sent to the Saxon emperor inviting him to come to Rome. Again Rome is oppressed by foreign peoples, and Benedict breaks forth into the lament with which, as it survives today, the chronicle ends.

Chris Wickham has convincingly argued that the tumultuous politics of ninth- and tenth-century Rome (as described by sources such as Benedict's chronicle) reflect the city's distinctive size and status.[63] What was different about Rome (in comparison to other contemporary cities) was its size (large for the tenth century), which allowed for a density and complexity of factions not found in other cities. Also unique were Rome's imperial connotations, on account of which foreign rulers were particularly prone to interfere in its politics. Wickham also argues that Rome followed a middle path between the northern model of urban government based on episcopal succession and the southern model of lay power. All of this was conducive to frequent shifts of alliance that created the appearance of seemingly perpetual strife.

As we have seen, however, this is not how Benedict explains the situation. At fault, according to him, are the age-old customs (*consuetudines*) of the Romans. This is a propensity for depravity that Benedict casts in a starkly sinister light. Rome is a city that is being destroyed by its sins, chastised by God. Roman history (at least since the time of Julian) is a litany of these sins and the failure of its inhabitants to react to the warnings and punishments of God. Despite centuries of misfortune, the Romans have persisted in their ways. The result is a Rome that is anything but a holy city. It is a grand city, circled by its walls and filled with churches; an imperial and papal city; but it is not, for Benedict, a sacred or blessed city.[64]

Leaving Rome to build Monte Soratte

Benedict's dismal 'Romescape' serves a purpose. Benedict was certainly familiar with the city of Rome, and he may even have identified as 'Roman' himself.[65] His attitude toward the city reflects a conscious attempt to denigrate it so as to magnify the merits of his monastery. Throughout the text, Benedict juxtaposes his negative portrait of Rome's urban politics with an idyllic view of monastic life at Monte Soratte. Here is to be found a bastion of coenobitic life maintained by individuals who took the initiative to leave Rome and frequently bolstered in subsequent centuries by non-Romans. Benedict thus construes Monte Soratte as a counter-image to Rome. To do so, he creatively draws on and at times twists his (often Roman) sources.

Repeatedly throughout the chronicle, Benedict alludes to the Emperor Constantine and Pope Sylvester as establishing the first church on Monte Soratte. It is likely that Benedict recounted this story in greater depth in the earlier part of his chronicle now missing; certainly it served as the monastery's foundation legend.

According to this well-developed late antique legend, at the beginning of his reign the Emperor Constantine persecuted Christians in the city of Rome.[66] To flee the persecutions the Roman bishop Sylvester and all his clerics withdrew from the city to Monte Soratte, where Sylvester bided his time reading scripture and praying, waiting for God's command, and indeed, Constantine, struck by leprosy, called Sylvester back to Rome and was baptized by him.[67] Thereafter, at least according to the version of events promoted at Monte Soratte, the Emperor Constantine had a church constructed at the very peak of the ridge, and it was here that Pope Sylvester was eventually buried.[68] (In contrast, according to the *Liber Pontificalis*, Pope Paul I [r. 757–767] had the body of the Sylvester removed from the catacombs and placed in the monastery of Sts. Sylvester and Stephen in Rome that he himself established.)[69] On Monte Soratte a late medieval church with crypt, rebuilt and restored extensively over the centuries – the site is prone to lightning strikes – hearkens back to this tradition.[70] Frescos of St. Sylvester attest to his continued commemoration in the church, and according to local folklore, an exposed limestone rock face incorporated into the crypt was identified as the bed of the bishop while in exile at the site.[71]

Sylvester's tomb, Benedict reports, attracted other Romans to the ridge. After the death of the Emperor Julian, we are told that Pope Damasus, a bishop who was remembered for his solicitude for Rome's saints, visited the tomb of Sylvester and there pronounced a lengthy prayer that was then inscribed in stone near to the saint's body. Thereupon many noble Romans began to abandon Rome and their worldly ways and flocked to the monastery, eager to embark on a holy life.[72] As presented by Benedict's chronicle, then, it is by leaving Rome that Romans can escape their pernicious past and present.

Not long thereafter the Gothic king Alaric sacks Rome, but the first monastery at Monte Soratte is on its way to becoming a site of miracles under its saintly abbot Nonnosus, whom Benedict (misconstruing his source, Gregory the Great's *Dialogues*) describes as being 'of Roman birth'.[73] The abbot Nonnosus, according to Benedict, was buried near the body of St. Sylvester, and a miracle performed by St. Nonnosus is one of the highpoints of Benedict's chronicle.[74]

Built on the foundation of individuals who left Rome, S. Andrea's status and independence from Rome is bolstered in subsequent centuries by donations and support from prominent individuals. The list of donors to the monastery through the centuries is impressive: in addition to certain popes, like Pope Damasus, its benefactors include a late-Roman noblewoman, Galla, the daughter of the consul Symmachus; the Lombard king Ratchis and his wife Tassia; Frankish kings including Charlemagne; and Alberic, son of the infamous Marozia. S. Andrea's property holdings, its churches and monasteries, and its spiritual treasures are the result of this patronage.

Especially significant is Carolingian support. Following the *Royal Frankish Annals*, Benedict relates how Carloman, the brother of the Frankish king Pippin, decided to renounce his claims to power and become a monk at Monte Soratte.[75] In contrast to the *Royal Frankish Annals*, however, which relates that Carloman went first to Rome and there was tonsured, before he constructed a monastery in honour of St. Sylvester at Monte Soratte, Benedict reports that Carloman went first to the threshold of the apostles, and then entered into the monastery at Monte Soratte, where he was tonsured and became a monk.[76] This subtle change indicates Benedict's characteristic desire to emphasize Monte Soratte, in contrast to Rome (or other monasteries), as the site most worthy of pious devotion and conducive to a spiritual vocation.[77]

While at Monte Soratte (as reported by Benedict), Carloman constructs the monastery of S. Andrea 'beside the river (*iuxta flumen*)' and donates extensively to the monastery. Most importantly, he receives the monasteries at Monte Soratte from the pope (Pope Zacharias), thereby placing them under imperial, not papal, protection.[78] This imperial status, from Benedict's perspective, is a cornerstone of S. Andrea's identity.[79] In turn, Pippin, and then Charlemagne, visit the monastery and confirm its privileges.[80] In addition, Charlemagne donates relics of St. Andrew to the monastery. Drawing on Einhard's account of Charlemagne's contacts with the eastern Mediterranean, Benedict constructs a fanciful narrative of Charlemagne's own voyage to the East; similar stories would enjoy a popular medieval afterlife.[81] Latowsky has suggested that Benedict's account is inflected by sibylline prophecies of the Last Emperor who would reunite the Empire before the coming of the Antichrist – even as Benedict, like Einhard, presents Charlemagne as a bringer of peace, rather than as a violent conqueror.[82]

Benedict narrates how Charlemagne travelled to the eastern Mediterranean, first to the Holy Land, where Aaron, 'king of the Persians', conceded to him the Holy Sepulchre, then, with Aaron, on to Alexandria, 'the Franks and the Hagarenes rejoicing together as if they were blood relatives'.[83] Thereafter Charlemagne travels to Constantinople where he receives relics of the Apostle Andrew from the Byzantine emperors.[84] When he returned to Italy, so Benedict reports, Charlemagne gave some of these relics (with the pope's permission – perhaps faintly evoking, as Latowsky has suggested, an image of a new Constantine and Sylvester)[85] to the monastery dedicated to Andrew at Monte Soratte.[86] This claim endows Monte Soratte with its own apostle, a bulwark of sanctity, a counterpart to Rome's Apostle Peter.

Louis the Pious, like his father Charlemagne, is presented in positive terms, above all as an upholder of the law, a trait that Benedict is keen to stress: 'Such was the ability of the Emperor Louis in Italy that not even a relative of the Roman pontiff would have been able to evade the law'.[87] More specifically, for the monastery, this entails the reaffirmation of the monastery's imperial status.

The end of the Carolingian order need not spell the end of the monastery's prosperity. Strong individuals – like Alberic – who break out of the cycle of Roman politics, have the good sense to patronize the monastery. This is a model, Benedict implies, that has potential – if only the Romans' propensity for strife were held in check, and foreign rulers, like Otto, would by their presence (or preferably absence), bring peace, rather than further devastation, to Italy.

S. Andrea was a monastery with a conflicted identity. This was a monastery that in the mid- to late tenth century still wished to imagine itself perched on the inhospitable ridge of Monte Soratte, as a bedrock of Christendom, worthy even of apostolic relics, a monastic idyll, disconnected from the urban strife of Rome. But the truth was that S. Andrea was down by the Tiber, in close contact with Rome, and embroiled in the same politics that engulfed the city. Romans had left Rome

70 Maya Maskarinec

to enter the monastery, but at S. Andrea they had not escaped the tentacles of the city's influence. The property and privileges of the monastery were dependent on the power struggles that were played out in the city. The same men who dominated Rome – rulers, popes, emperors, kings, patricians and others – cast their shadow over the monastery.

In composing his chronicle, Benedict was aware of this contradiction. He was conscious that Rome and his monastery were inextricably intertwined in their fortunes, and that Rome's past was also the past of his monastery. And yet rather than frame this link as one of joint responsibility, Benedict strives to twist Rome's past against the city, presenting the iniquities of Rome's inhabitants as the cause of the unending string of disasters that have come upon both Rome and its environs. As we have seen, in making sense of the past, Benedict frequently drew on biblical images of deserved destruction. In this respect we may situate his text not only in the late antique and medieval chronicle tradition, but also in that of prophetic texts, such as the Tiburtine Sibyl, a new version of which was redacted in Italy in opposition to Otto III (r. 996–1002).[88] The Tiburtine Sibyl foretells that 'Rome will be assaulted by persecution and the sword and seized by the hand of the king himself'.[89] Benedict would have agreed. Unlike the Sibyl, however, Benedict does not conclude that the end of times is near. Faced with the quickly shifting political order brought about by the Ottonians in Italy that did not favour his monastery, and faced with a past, which, from his perspective, offered little positive authority and legitimacy for his monastery, Benedict salvaged what he could. Above all, it was precisely the moral bankruptcy of Rome's past that Benedict found to his advantage, a justification for his monastery as a redemptive outpost that had weathered many a storm.

Notes

1 *Il Chronicon di Benedetto*, ed. by Giuseppe Zucchetti, Fonti per la storia d'Italia, 55 (Rome: Tip. del Senato, 1920) [henceforth Benedict, *Chronicle*]. The text was earlier edited by Georg Pertz, but omitting most passages where Benedict was following known sources: MGH SS 3 (Hannover: Hahn, 1839), pp. 695–719. There exists an Italian translation by Massimo Pautrier, *La Cronaca di Benedetto monaco del Soratte* (Rome: [n. pub.], 2010). The last securely datable event in the chronicle is Otto II's marriage to Theophanu in 972, but the chronicle ends with Otto's Italian expedition in 966.

2 See also Geoffrey Koziol, 'The Future of History After Empire', in the present volume. As in the historiographical texts discussed by Koziol, Benedict was confronted with the insufficiency of earlier triumphalist models of history to explain the 'failure' of the present; as in these texts, Benedict's chronicle emphasizes the depravity of the 'world', here contrasted with the sanctity of his monastery.

3 Regarding the area in Antiquity see G. D. B. Jones, 'Capena and the Ager Capenas: Part I', *Papers of the British School at Rome*, 30 (1962), pp. 116–207; G. D. B. Jones, 'Capena and the Ager Capenas: Part II', *Papers of the British School at Rome*, 31 (1963), pp. 100–58. Part I, p. 116: 'The ancient Ager Capenas occupied the elongated triangle of land north of Rome enclosed by the line of the Via Flaminia, M. Soracte and the lower Tiber valley'. Jones' survey also covers the area between Monte Soratte and the Tiber north of Ponzano Romano (in which the monastery of S. Andrea in Flumine is located), although this formed part of the Ager Faliscus, not the Ager Capenas.

In the shadow of Rome **71**

4 Regarding the area in the Middle Ages see Giuseppe Tomassetti, *La campagna romana antica, medioevale e moderna*, rev. by Luisa Chiumenti and Fernando Bilancia (Bologna: A. Forni, 1976), III, 280: 'il territorio *Collinense* ... formava un triangolo irregolare con la base sulla riva destra del Tevere, tra *S. Marta* e *Torrita*, e il vertice presso *Campagnano*, incluso anche il Soratte.' The term 'territorio Colinense' is found in Benedict's chronicle (Benedict, *Chronicle*, pp. 25, 26) and is well-attested in medieval property documents, especially from the monastery of S. Paolo. This region is not included in Pierre Toubert, *Les structures du Latium médiéval: le Latium méridional et la Sabine du IXe siècle à la fin du XIIe siècle* (Paris: De Boccard, 1973).
5 Martinori Edoardo, *Via Flaminia: studio storico-topografico* (Roma: Stab. Tip. Regionale, 1929), pp. 74–9 (According to Jones, pp. 117–8, to the north of Monte Soratte ran a track that connected S. Andrea with the via Flaminia); Jean-Marie Martin, 'Via Salaria: la documentazione medievale', in *La Salaria in età tardoantica e altomedievale: atti del convegno di studi, Rieti, Cascia, Norcia, Ascoli Piceno, 28–30 settembre 2001*, ed. by Enzo Catani and Gianfranco Paci (Rome: Erma di Bretschneider, 2007), pp. 265–74.
6 Mariano De Carolis, *Il Monte Soratte e i suoi santuari* (Rome: Tip. San Giuseppe, 1950), pp. 30–9; George Dennis, *The Cities and Cemeteries of Etruria* (London: J. Murray, 1848), pp. 186–7.
7 Jones, 'Capena and the Ager Capenas: Part II', pp. 101–2.
8 Ibid., p. 134.
9 Regarding transport on the Tiber see Toubert, *Les structures du Latium médiéval*, pp. 631–40.
10 *Childe Harold's Pilgrimage*, 4.75, cited in Jones, p. 125.
11 Horace, Odes, 1.9, trans. by Laurence Catlow, 'Fact, Imagination, and Memory in Horace: *Odes* 1.9', *Greece & Rome*, 23 (1976), pp. 74–81 (p. 75).
12 Regarding S. Andrea see *Il complesso monumentale di Sant'Andrea in flumine presso Ponzano Romano: restauri e studi interdisciplinari*, ed. by Stefania Cancellieri (Rome: Gangemi, 2007); Anna Maria Ramieri, *Ponzano attraverso i secoli: storia arte natura* (Ponzano Romano: Comune di Ponzano Romano, 2000), pp. 135–62; Irmgard Maria Voss, *Die Benediktinerabtei S. Andrea in Flumine bei Ponzano Romano* (Bonn: [n. pub.], 1985).
13 Stefania Cancellieri, 'Analisi storico critica del complesso monumentale di Sant'Andrea in flumine', in Cancellieri, *Il complesso monumentale* pp. 17–46; and Clementina Sforzini and Donatina Olivieri, 'L'area archeologica: evidenze e nuove acquisizioni', in ibid., pp. 105–38.
14 Zucchetti, VII-LXVI provides the most detailed introduction to the text and its author. For further bibliography on the chronicle see Maskarinec, 'Legal Expertise at a Late-Tenth-Century Monastery in Central Italy, or Disputing Property Donations and the History of Law in Benedict of Monte Soratte's Chronicle,' *Speculum* 94.4 (forthcoming, Oct. 2019).
15 Benedict, *Chronicle*, p. 124: 'Hos tibi versiculos ad laudem, maxime princeps,/ Edidit eternam memoriaque tua/ Benedictus supplex famulus monaque, qui mentem benigna/ Egregium extulit nomen ad astra tuum'. Einhard, *Vita Karoli Magni*, ed. by Oswald Holder-Egger, MGH SS rer. Germ. 25 (Hannover: Hahn 1911), p. XXIX, line 26: 'Gerwardus supplex famulus, qui mente benigna'.
16 *Il Regesto di Farfa di Gregorio di Catino*, ed. by Ignazio Giorgi and Ugo Balzani, 5 vols (Rome: Società romana di storia patria, 1879–1892), IV, no. 670 (1013); Voss, pp. 278–9 (translation), 48 (discussion).
17 Benedict, *Chronicle*, pp. 168–70; ibid., p. 39.
18 Cancellieri, 'Analisi storico critica', pp. 24, 26.
19 Maskarinec, 'Legal Expertise'.
20 Available online: http://digi.vatlib.it/view/MSS_Chig.F.IV.75. Benedict's chronicle is bound together with a collection of primarily legal texts; see further Maskarinec, 'Legal Expertise'.
21 First decades of the 11th century: Paola Supino Martini, *Roma e l'area grafica romanesca: secoli X–XII* (Alessandria: Ed. dell'Orso, 1987), pp. 290–1; and Matthias M. Tischler, *Einharts 'Vita Karoli': Studien zur Entstehung, Überlieferung und Rezeption* (Hannover:

72   Maya Maskarinec

Hahn, 2001), I, 469. Circa 1000: Hubert Mordek, *Bibliotheca capitularium regum Francorum manuscripta. Überlieferung und Traditionszusammenhang der fränkischen Herrschererlasse* (Munich: Monumenta Germaniae Historica, 1995), p. 756. Regarding the manuscript as the product of an oral dictation see Johannes Kunsemüller, *Die Chronik Benedikts von St. Andrea* (Erlangen-Nürnberg, 1963), pp. 22–57; Hartmut Hoffmann, *Deutsches Archiv für Erforschung des Mittelalters*, 20 (1964), pp. 596–97; and Paolo Chiesa, 'Benedictus sancti Andreae de Soracte mon.', in *La trasmissione dei testi latini del Medioevo. Medieval Latin Texts and their Transmission. Te. Tra I*, ed. by Paolo Chiesa and Lucia Castaldi (Florence: Edizioni del Galuzzo, 2004), pp. 32–7. Hoffmann and Chiesa agree with Kunsemüller's assessment but dispute, contra Kunsemüller, that Benedict himself was responsible for this dictation.

22 Chiesa, 'Benedictus sancti Andreae de Soracte', pp. 34–7.

23 Regarding Benedict's view of the past see Kunsemüller, *Die Chronik* pp. 80–95; Paolo Delogu, 'I Romani e l'Impero (VII–X secolo)', in *Three Empires, Three Cities: Identity, Material Culture and Legitimacy in Venice, Ravenna and Rome, 750–1000*, ed. by Veronica West-Harling (Turnhout: Brepols, 2015), pp. 191–226; Chris Wickham, *Medieval Rome: Stability and Crisis of a City, 900–1150* (Oxford: Oxford University Press, 2015), pp. 376–77. As discussed by Wickham, Benedict's view of the past has similarities with the *Libellus de imperatoria potestate*, edited by Zucchetti with Benedict's chronicle, pp. 191–210. Regarding the *Libellus* see most recently Lidia Capo, 'Iura regni et consuetudines illius: l'Impero carolingio a Roma', in *Honos alit artes. Studi per il settantesimo compleanno di Mario Ascheri, III, Il cammino delle idee dal medioevo all'età moderna*, ed. by Paola Maffei and Gian Maria Varanini (Florence: Florence University Press, 2014), pp. 183–90.

24 Cf. Delogu, 'I Romani e l'Impero', pp. 194–95.

25 Benedict, *Chronicle*, p. 69: 'Eum me, quid faciam? regno Italico a multis gentibus depressus: prius a Medis et Lanis, postmodum a Gallis, tertius a Gothi, quartus a Langobardis!' Cf. p. 37: 've regnum Italie, a multis depressus nationibus, que prius a Gallis, postea a Medis!'

26 Benedict, *Chronicle*, p. 186: 've Roma! qui a tantis gentis oppressa et conculcata; qui etiam a Saxone rege appreensa fuistis ... ' Cf. p. 39.

27 Benedict, *Chronicle*, p. 19: 'Odacer rex Gothorum Romam optinuit, quam ex eo tempore diutius eorum reges Gothorum regnum tenuerunt'. Based on Bede, but Benedict has added the phrase 'regnum tenuerunt'.

28 Benedict, *Chronicle*, p. 28: 'Narsus Rome patricius avocatus est, et ab omni populo Romano helectus'. For the title 'patricius romanorum' conferred upon Pippin by Pope Stephen II, see the discussion in Delogu, 'I Romani e l'Impero', p. 207. The title 'patricius' was also conferred upon Charlemagne by the pope. See also Laury Sarti, 'Frankish Romanness and Charlemagne's Empire', *Speculum*, 91 (2016), pp. 1040–58.

29 Benedict, *Chronicle*, p. 33: 'postea Roma per patricius principabantur'. Zucchetti, n. 2 notes that this same idea is found in the *Libellus de imperatoria potestate*.

30 Benedict, *Chronicle*, pp. 28–9: 'vox eius melliflua, rectoque ad investigandum Romanum imperium. tunc surrexerunt viri scelerati de Romanis finibus, cum Gothi laborantes et negotio tractantes de interitus Narsi patricii, qualiter expulsus et eiectus a Romano imperium'.

31 Benedict, *Chronicle*, p. 29: 'qui inde, per invidia Romanorum, pro quibus multa cum Gothos laboraverat, miserunt legationes a Constantinianam urbem a Iustinum principem et coniugem eius Sufficia accusationes, quod servitio premeret et possideret Italia et non esset ei dissimilis'.

32 Benedict, *Chronicle*, pp. 30–1: 'quo gens Langobardorum ingressi in Italia a traselpine montis usque ad traspidum, a mare Adriatica usque Terrina, impletum est regnum, et multiplicati sunt sicut locuste super regnum totum Italie'.

33 Exodus 10. 1–20.

34 As demonstrated by Delogu, however, Benedict slightly modifies his sources so as to minimize the suggestion that these Frankish kings/emperors ruled over the 'regnum Romanorum': Delogu, 'I Romani e l'Impero', pp. 193–4, 196–7.

35 Benedict, *Chronicle*, pp. 148–9: 'orta est persecutio Romani inter se; exierunt viri scelerati, et legatos miserunt a rex Babylonie, ut venirent et possidere regnum Italie. tanta denique

Aggareni in Italia ingressi a Centucellensis portus, sic impleverunt faciem terre, sicut locuste velut segetem in campo. tantos timor invasit Romanos, ut nullos extra portas egredi; obsedita est Roma, et civitas Leoniana appreensa, et ecclesia Sancti Petri capta et expoliata, et per monasteria ipius ęcclesie ęquos eorum stare precepit. versa est mater omnium ecclesiarum in opprobrium, et omnes decore suo abstractum'.

36 Regarding this 'Sack of Rome', see Tommi P. Lankila, 'The Saracen Raid of Rome in 846: An Example of Maritime *ghazw*', in *Travelling Through Time. Essays in Honour of Kaj Öhrnberg*, ed. by Sylvia Akar, Jaakko Hämeen-Anttila, and Inka Nokso-Koivisto (Helsinki: Finnish Oriental Society, 2013), pp. 93–120.

37 *Iohannis VIII. papae epistolae passim collectae*, no. 9, ed. by Erich Caspar and Gerhard Laehr, MGH Epp. 7 (Epistolae Karolini aevi V) (Berlin: Weidmann: 1928), pp. 326–9; F. E. Engreen, 'Pope John the Eighth and the Arabs', *Speculum*, 20 (1945), pp. 318–30.

38 Benedict, *Chronicle*, p. 152: 'Romani plus magis fraudulenter contra Francos miserunt legationes a Palarmo et Africe, ut venirent et possiderent Italico regno'.

39 Benedict, *Chronicle*, p. 153: 'regnaverunt Agarenis in Romano regno anni .xxx.; redacta est terra in solitudine, et monasteria sancte sine laudes'. Ugo of Farfa's late-10th-century *Destructio Farfensis* similarly reports on the Saracen presence in Italy for 48 years, but Ugo does not use the term 'regnare' or refer to the 'regnum Romanum'; cited by Zucchetti (ed.), *Il Chronicon di Benedetto*, p. 153 n. 4.

40 Jeremiah 50.13: 'ab ira Domini non habitabitur sed redigetur tota in solitudinem omnis qui transit per Babylonem stupebit et sibilabit super universis plagis eius'.

41 A letter of Pope John VII to the Emperor Charles in which he laments the devastation brought about by the Saracens likewise uses the phrase, although in that case the context is an appeal for help in this reversible situation: *Registrum Iohannis VIII*, no. 36, ed. by Erich Caspar, MGH Epp. 7 (Epistolae Karolini aevi V), pp. 35–6 (p. 35).

42 Gregory the Great, *Homiliae in Hiezechihelem prophetam*, 2.6.22, ed. by Marcus Adriaen, CCSL 142, pp. 295–313 (p. 310): 'Destructae urbes, euersa sunt castra, depopulati agri, in solitudine terra redacta est.' English translation by Theodosia Gray, *The Homilies of St. Gregory the Great. On the Book of the Prophet Ezekiel* (Etna, CA: Center for Traditionalist Orthodox Studies 1990), pp. 217–30.

43 Benedict, *Chronicle*, p. 154: 'verumtamen propter peccata populi, sicut scriptum est: "De celo prospexit Dominus super filios hominum omnes qui habitant horbem. de preparato habitaculo suo". qui superius diximus, per curricula triginta annorum usurpantem Agareni Romanum regnum'. Psalm 32 [33]. 13–4: 'De caelo respexit Dominus vidit omnes filios hominum; De praeparato habitaculo suo respexit super omnes qui habitant terram'.

44 Benedict, *Chronicle*, p. 161: 'donna senatrix, unde superius diximus, ordinavit Iohannes consanguineum eius in Sedem sanctissimus, pro quo undecimus est appellatus'. Nowhere in the chronicle does Benedict mention Marozia by name.

45 Benedict, *Chronicle*, pp. 158–9: 'accepit una de nobilibus Romani, cuius nomine superest, Theophilacti filia, non quasi uxor sed in consuetudinem malignam'.

46 Benedict, *Chronicle*, p. 161: 'subiugatus est Romam potestative in manu femine, sicut in propheta legimus: Feminini dominabunt Hierusalem'. Isaiah 3. 4: 'Et dabo pueros principes eorum, et effeminati dominabuntur eis'; trans. KJV (modified).

47 Benedict, *Chronicle*, p. 162: 'nam iuxta hurbe Roma lapides plurimi de celo cadere visi sunt'. Cf. for example, Joshua 10. 11.

48 Riccardo Santangeli Valenzani, 'Topografia del potere a Roma nel X secolo', in *Three Empires, Three Cities. Identity, Material Culture and Legitimacy in Venice, Ravenna and Rome, 750–1000*, ed. by Veronica West-Harling (Turnhout: Brepols, 2015), pp. 135–58 (pp. 137–8) draws a parallel to Genesis 19, the destruction of Sodom and Gomorrah, and more generally, cities destroyed by fire from the sky on account of their wickedness.

49 Benedict, *Chronicle*, pp. 163–4; the stew is described as a *pulmentum*, a generic term used to describe cooked dishes: Massimo Montanari, *Medieval Tastes: Food, Cooking, and the Table* (New York: Columbia University Press, 2015), p. 33.

50 Ezekiel 24; cf. Ezekiel 11.

51 Gregory the Great, *Homiliae in Hiezechihelem prophetam*, 2.6.22, ed. by Adriaen, pp. 311–2.

52 Benedict, *Chronicle*, p. 165: 'cępit Roma in se ipsa merore afflicta populi vexare'.
53 Benedict, *Chronicle*, pp. 166–7: 'Albericus princeps omnium Romanorum vultum nitentem sicut pater eius, grandevus virtus eius. erat enim terribilis nimis, et aggrabatum est iugum super Romanos et in sancte Sedis apostolice'.
54 Benedict, *Chronicle*, p. 170.
55 Benedict, *Chronicle*, p. 171: 'Romani secundum consuetudinem malignam consiliaverunt, ut principem occiderent'.
56 Benedict, *Chronicle*, p. 174: 'miserunt legatos ad Otto primus Saxones regem, ut veniret et possideret Italia et Romanum imperium'.
57 Benedict, *Chronicle*, p. 175: 'Otto rex veniente Italico regno, tanta pene multitudo gentis in Italia, que sic impleverunt faciem terre, sicut situle. habebat autem secum gentes nationes, quorum lingue non agnoscebant gentis'.
58 Deuteronomy 28. 49; Jeremiah 5. 15.
59 Benedict, *Chronicle*, p. 177: 'redacta est terra in solitudine, magis magisque famis valida pullularent'.
60 Benedict, *Chronicle*, pp. 179–80.
61 Benedict, *Chronicle*, p. 181: 'facta ingens famis in Romanos ignem et gladium, sicut scriptum est: "Sola vexatio daret intellectum etiam et auditu"'. Isaiah. 28. 19; trans. KJV.
62 Benedict, *Chronicle*, p. 181: 'cęperunt mollescere inter se, ut virtutes que prius habuerunt, ad nichilum redacti sunt. unoque consilio a minore usque ad maximum. et necessitate compulsi compreenderunt Benedictus papa, et in manus imperatoris illum dederunt; et dicebat ad alterutrum: "Melius est, ut iste solus moriatur pro omnibus, ut liberemur anime nostre a cruciatus famis"'.
63 Chris Wickham, '"The Romans According to Their Malign Custom": Rome in Italy in the Late Ninth and Tenth Centuries', in *Early Medieval Rome and the Christian West: Essays in Honour of Donald A. Bullough*, ed. by Julia M.H. Smith (Leiden; Boston: Brill, 2000), pp. 151–67.
64 Regarding Rome's walls see Benedict, *Chronicle*, p. 186. Benedict mentions Rome's gates and other city infrastructure (bridges and roads) fairly frequently, usually, but not exclusively, in the context of sieges. St. Peter's reoccurs throughout the chronicle (especially where Benedict is following the *Royal Frankish Annals*), for example as the site of synods and where emperors are crowned. Benedict rarely mentions relics in Rome, and when he does it is usually in the context of the city receiving relics from abroad (e.g., the Empress Eudoxia returns from Jerusalem with the relics of St. Stephen, and the relics of St. Anastasius the Persian are brought to the monastery *Ad Aquas Salvia*s).
65 For an overview of scholarship with further bibliography see Alfredo Cioni, 'Benedetto di S. Andrea', in *Dizionario biografico degli Italiani*, VIII (Rome: Istituto della Enciclopedia italiana, 1966), 446–51. Much has been made of the passage in which (in the context of relating the omens that took place in Rome) Benedict refers to the church of the Holy Apostles as 'que nos vocitamus Sancti Apostoli' (Benedict, *Chronicle*, p. 163). It is worth noting that Benedict's chronicle indicates a particular interest in sites in Rome or in the vicinity of Rome that are in the direction of Monte Soratte: for example, in a passage that has no known source, he reports how the Ostrogothic king, Totila, destroyed a bridge across the Tiber on the via Salaria (Benedict, *Chronicle*, pp. 27–8); also mentioned is the bridge's reconstruction by Narses (Benedict, *Chronicle*, pp. 32–3). The bridge that Benedict refers to, the Ponte Salario, is not over the main branch of the Tiber, but rather over the tributary, the Aniene, that flows into the Tiber from the west. This confirms the impression that Benedict is most interested in the city of Rome as it relates to his monastery.
66 The legend survives in various recensions; see Wilhelm Pohlkamp, 'Textfassungen, literarische Formen und geschichtliche Funktionen der römischen Silvester-Akten', *Francia*, 19 (1992), pp. 115–96; Wilhelm Pohlkamp, 'Kaiser Konstantin, der heidnische und der christliche Kult in den Actus Silvestri', *Frühmittelalterliche Studien*, 18 (1984), pp. 357–400. The most accessible version of the text remains that of Mombritius: *Sanctuarium seu Vitae Sanctorum*, ed. by Boninus Mombritius (Milan, 1475; reissued, Paris: Fontemoing, 1910; repr. Hildesheim: Olms, 1978), II, 508–31.

In the shadow of Rome **75**

67 Pohlkamp, p. 369 n. 46: Version A (1) (this is the longer recension that was more popular in the west): 'Silvester episcopus civitatis Romanae apud montem Soracten persecutiones tuas fugiens in cavernis petrarum cum suis clericis latebram fovet'; in Version B (1) Silvester's flight from Rome is already mentioned at the beginning of the narrative regarding Constantine's persecution: 'In illo tempore exiit edictum, ut christiani ad sacrificandum idolis cogerentur. Unde factum est, ut secedens sanctus Silvester ab urbe in monte Sirapti latibulum cum suis clericis collocaret'. The *Liber Pontificalis'* Life of Sylvester reports Sylvester's 'exile' on Monte Soratte: *Liber Pontificalis*, 34, ed. by Louis Duchesne, 2 vols (Paris: De Boccard, 1886–1892), I (1886), 170: 'Hic exilio fuit in monte Seracten et postmodum rediens cum gloria baptizavit Constantinum Augustum, quem curavit Dominus a lepra, cuius persecutionem primo fugiens exilio fuisse cognoscitur'.
68 Benedict, *Chronicle*, pp. 6, 9–10.
69 *Liber Pontificalis*, 95.5, ed. by Duchesne, I, 464. See also n. 79.
70 Elisabetta Scungio, '"In summo montis cacumine": il monastero di S. Silvestro al Soratte', *Arte medievale, 4th ser.*, 5 (2015), pp. 27–58; Ungarelli, 'L'edificio', in *Sant'Oreste e il suo territorio* (Soveria Mannelli: Rubbettino, 2003), pp. 239–50.
71 De Carolis, *Il Monte Soratte e i suoi santuari*, p. 102.
72 Benedict, *Chronicle*, p. 10: 'coeperunt multi nobiles Romani mundus relinquere ad eundem prefata aecclesia quasi cebium sanctę conversationis vitam ducere'.
73 Benedict, *Chronicle*, pp. 15–6: 'qui mirum Anastasius, virtutem venerabilis viro Nonnoso natione Romano preposito monasterii Sanctissimi Silvestri, quod in Syrapte montis sytum est …'. Gregory the Great, *Dialogues*, 1.7.1, ed. by Adalbert de Vogüé, *Grégoire le Grand. Dialogues*, 3 vols, Sources chrétiennes 251, 260, 265 (Paris: Les Editions du cerf, 1978–1980), II (1979), 66: 'Qui nimirum Anastasius uitae uenerabilis uiro Nonnoso, praeposito monasterii quod in Soractis monte situm est …'. Gregory the Great does specify (as Benedict quotes) that Anastasius was a notary in the Roman church but does not specify anything about Nonnosus' background.
74 Benedict, *Chronicle*, p. 22: 'hic [Nonnosus] sepultus est non longe a corpus beati Silvestri, mense december, die nono'. It is Nonnosus' miraculous expulsion of a demon from one of Ratchis' Lombard followers (p. 66) that prompts the Lombard king's generosity to the monastery (discussed above).
75 Benedict, *Chronicle*, p. 74: 'tunc Carlomagno Romam perrexit ad limina apostolorum, post hec ad montem Syrapti monasterium ingressus, ibique se totondit et monachus effectus est'.
76 *Royal Frankish Annals*, 746, ed. by Friedrich Kurze, MGH SS rer. Germ. 6 (Hannover: Hahn, 1895), p. 6: 'Tunc Carlomannus Romam perrexit ibique se totondit et in Serapte monte monasterium aedificavit in honore sancti Silvestri'. According to the *Royal Frankish Annals* only upon moving to the monastery of Montecassino did Carloman become a monk ('ibi monachus effectus est').
77 Similarly, Benedict modifies his sources in reporting Carloman's departure from Monte Soratte. Benedict reports (*Chronicle*, p. 77) that differences in customs/morals (*mores*) caused Carloman to leave the community at S. Andrea. Einhard's *Life of Charlemagne* (a source used extensively by Benedict) reports that Carloman was disturbed by the many Frankish nobles on their way to Rome who stopped by the monastery to pay their respects to him: Einhard, *Vita Karoli Magni*, 2, ed. by Holder-Egger, MGH SS rer. Germ. 25, p. 5. Other Frankish sources (such as the *Annales qui dicitur Einhardi*, 746) speak of Carloman receiving the advice to move.
78 Benedict, *Chronicle*, p. 70. This concession is attested in a letter from Pope Paul to Pippin (dating to 761–2), which annuls the earlier concession and grants the monasteries to Pippin: *Codex Carolinus*, no. 23, ed. by Wilhelm Gundlach, MGH Epp 3 (Epistolae Merowingici et Karolini aevi I) (Berlin: Weidmann, 1892), pp. 526–7.
79 However, according to a second letter from Pope Paul to Pippin (presumably postdating that in which Pope Paul had conceded the monasteries at Monte Soratte to Pippin, see n. 78), Pippin conceded the monastery of St. Sylvester on Monte Soratte to Pope Paul, who placed it under the monastery of Sts. Sylvester and Stephen in Rome that he

(the pope) had established (on the grounds that the monastery in Rome possessed the body of St. Sylvester): *Codex Carolinus*, no. 42, ed. by Gundlach, MGH Epp 3 (Epistolae Merowingici et Karolini aevi I), pp. 554–6. No mention is made in this letter of the monastery of S. Andrea. Benedict's chronicle reiterates both monasteries' imperial status under subsequent Carolingian rulers (for example, under Louis the Pious, see below).

80 Benedict, *Chronicle*, pp. 85–6, 96, 106, 108.

81 Benedict, *Chronicle*, pp. 113–4. For discussion see Matthew Gabriele, *An Empire of Memory: The Legend of Charlemagne, the Franks, and Jerusalem before the First Crusade* (New York: Oxford University Press, 2011), pp. 42–4; Anne Austin Latowsky, *Emperor of the World: Charlemagne and the Construction of Imperial Authority, 800–1229* (Ithaca: Cornell University Press, 2013), pp. 62–74.

82 Latowsky, *Emperor of the World*, pp. 69–74.

83 Benedict, *Chronicle*, p. 114: 'vertente igitur prudentissimus rex, cum Aaron rex usque in Alexandria pervenit; sicque letificantes Francis et Aggarenis, quasi consanguineis esset'.

84 Benedict, *Chronicle*, p. 114: 'rex piisimus atque fortis ad Constantinopolitano hurbem, Naciforus, Michahel it Leo, formidantes quasi imperium ei eripere vellet, valde subsceptu'; p. 115: 'qui mox imperator cum quanta donis et munera, et aliquantulum de corpore sancti Andreę apostoli, ad imperatoribus Constantinopolim accepto, in Italia est reversus!'.

85 Latowsky, *Emperor of the World*, p. 68.

86 Benedict, *Chronicle*, p. 116: 'deinde ad monasteria Sancti Andreę cum pontifice summo adest; qui rogatus imperator ad pontifice, ut aliquantulum reliquiarum de corpore sancti Andreę apostoli in hunc monasterium consecrationis constitueret; cuius loco positus est in hunc monasterium venerabile ecclesie, aput nos incognitum est'.

87 Benedict, *Chronicle*, p. 145: 'imperator Loduicus in tanta virtus in Italia estitit, ut sanguinium pontificis Romani a legibus non potuisset erueret'. Regarding the history of law-giving presented by Benedict's chronicle see Maskarinec, 'Legal Expertise'.

88 Levi Roach, 'The Legacy of a Late Antique Prophecy: the Tiburtine Sibyl and the Italian Opposition to Otto III', *The Mediaeval Journal*, 5 (2015), pp. 1–34; Anke Holdenried, 'Many Hands without Design: The Evolution of a Medieval Prophetic Text', *The Mediaeval Journal*, 4 (2014), pp. 23–42.

89 *Sibyllinische Texte und Forschungen: Pseudomethodius, Adso und die tiburtinische Sibylle*, ed. Ernst Sackur (Halle: Max Niemeyer, 1898), pp. 177–87 (p. 184): 'Roma in persecutione et gladio expugnabitur et erit deprehensa in manu ipsius regis'.

5

INFILTRATING THE LOCAL PAST

Supra-regional players in local hagiography from Trier in the ninth and tenth centuries

*Lenneke van Raaij**

Recent scholarship has embraced the role of locally-oriented powerbrokers and acknowledged the lack of cultural uniformity within the Ottonian Empire.[1] Archbishops and bishops exercised more direct power than in the Carolingian era and aristocrats increasingly served as lay abbots of major monasteries. As a result of this growing emphasis on the local in tenth-century society and culture, contemporary supra-regional 'grand narratives' appear to have lost their universal character. Whereas the *Annales Regni Francorum* were read in centres across the Frankish empire, chronicles describing the Ottoninan dynasty had a more regional or local character.[2] The *Annales Quedlinburgensis*, for example, contain a great deal of information about the Ottonian kings, but were mostly written with the interests of the monastery in Quedlinburg in mind.[3] Similarly, the *Chronicon* of Thietmar of Merseburg was not widely disseminated across the Ottonian realm, despite references to its kings.[4] These 'grand narratives' were not only sparsely distributed, they were also adapted to the needs of local or regional communities. Around the turn of the tenth century, Regino of Prüm wrote a universal *Chronicon* that covered the period from the Incarnation to 906 AD.[5] When Adalbert of Magdeburg continued this *Chronicon* to 962, he included many entries concerning regional and local politics.[6] These examples show that 'grand narratives' featuring the Ottonian dynasty were mostly communicated in a local or regional context.

Most local communities in the tenth century did not produce a 'grand narrative' of the Ottonian past; it was more common for supra-regional rulers to be embedded

---

* The research for this chapter was funded by the 'After Empire: Using and Not Using the Past in the Crisis of the Carolingian World, c.900–1050' HERA project, receiving funding from the European Union's Horizon 2020 research and innovation programme under grant agreement no. 649307.

in local narratives of particular communities through patronage. Gifts of land, or even the foundation of a monastery, could link the community to a king or ruler. Amy Remensnyder has studied the role of kings in foundation narratives of Aquitanian monasteries, focusing on charter evidence.[7] Similarly, in his study on saints' cults in Orléans, Thomas Head argues that local communities cherished royal patronage by preserving the specific charter in which the gift or exchange of property or land was issued.[8] This rather pragmatic interpretation of the relationship between kings and local communities, however, does not consider to what extent knowledge of this relationship was communicated to the members of the community beyond the highest echelons.

Perhaps the best way for supra-regional figures to find a way into the past of a local community was by encountering figures with a strictly local character, in particular local patron saints. These patrons were remembered by the community on a regular basis in a liturgical framework. Through prayers, sermons, the celebration of Mass and the Divine Office, and oral traditions that may have been fostered and then bolstered by the miraculous powers of local saints' physical remains, lay and religious members of local communities alike were reminded of their past, as well as their present, identity.[9] The backbone of this communicated local past is the hagiography produced for these local patron saints. Saints' *vitae* were used as a basis for other liturgical performances, such as sermons and *historiae* (accounts of the lives of saints alternated with prayers used during the celebration of the Matins Office).[10] Although the initial audience of these hagiographical works was limited to the literate clergy, the oral dissemination of the narratives in liturgical performances in various forms may have enlarged the audience significantly, including to lay people.[11]

The deeds of these saintly figures were based on a timeless vision of the past rather than actual events.[12] The acts of supra-regional figures within these narratives, however, often concerned worldly politics of little interest to future generations. In this respect, supra-regional figures had a hard time infiltrating local narratives. Nevertheless, we can think of several examples in which outsiders could find their way into the writings and performances of a local community. Supra-regional figures such as kings and archbishops could act as patrons for the foundation of a local church or monastery, or play a role in miracles or other interactions with the local patron saint described in *vitae*. This way, not only did worldly protagonists appear on the stage of a local community, but universally celebrated saints might make their appearance as well. A famous example in this respect is St Martin of Tours, who was considered a promoter of the Christian ideal, making him a popular exemplary figure for non-royal lay people and kings alike throughout the early Middle Ages.[13] Although recent scholarship has contested the active role of kings and rulers in the spread of St Martin's cult, St Martin remained, without a doubt, one of the most universally celebrated saints in the Middle Ages.[14] An example of St Martin's universality in the tenth century is given by Odo of Cluny, who wrote a sermon on the fire that ravaged the church of St Martin in Tours.[15] In this sermon, Odo showed awareness of many churches dedicated to St Martin, considering each of them to house the presence of the saint.[16] With so many shrines and churches, St Martin was embedded in many narratives of local communities.

Royal factors could more indirectly influence the local narrative. For example, Susan Boynton explains how royal influence could be translated into liturgy, as the 'language of royalty and empire' made its way into prayers performed in the royal abbey of Farfa.[17] The rewriting of hagiographical texts about local patrons by courtiers was another form of cultural connection between local and royal spheres. The Carolingian scholar and courtier Lupus of Ferrières, for example, wrote stylistically-amended versions of local saints *vitae* that were used in local communities. In the case of the *vita* of St Maximinus, patron of the royal abbey in Trier, the version written by Lupus became more popular and widespread than its locally-produced eighth-century predecessor.[18] These royal, mostly stylistic influences on local narratives only occur in local communities with connection to the court: both examples mentioned concerned royal abbeys.

Trier as case study

The city of Trier makes an interesting case study for researching the connection between central rulership and a local community. The city had been the setting for various supra-regional political events through the ages. Under Constantine the Great, it had been one of the fourth-century capitals of the Roman empire, and the city flourished while it counted Constantine and his mother Helena as residents. During the Merovingian period, Archbishops Nicetius and Magnericus resided in Trier as they maintained close relations with the Merovingian court.[19] Although it was not a centre of great importance in the Carolingian period, Trier became politically important again in the tenth century, as one of the most influential archiepiscopal centres in the Ottonian realm.[20] The archbishops of Trier were part of an extensive political network and were powerful figures in local society too, as they commissioned various churches and monasteries to be rebuilt in the second half of the tenth century.[21] Meanwhile, the royal abbey of St Maximinus had been renewed in 934 and was part of a great network of reformed monasteries. Monks from St Maximinus were sent to St Maurice, Magdeburg and Echternach to continue this movement.[22]

Alongside this important regional political function, Trier counted a large community of local patron saints: ten local patrons had been honoured with *vitae* by the early eleventh century.[23] Most of these saints were late antique archbishops, starting with Eucharius, who had converted the pagans living in Trier after being sent by St Peter himself.[24] These texts should be treated as an interrelated corpus, since the proximity of the cult centres represented is undeniable: even those furthest away from each other – St Eucharius in the south and St Paulinus in the north – are separated by no more than a forty minute walk.

The lives of the Trier patrons were not only intertwined geographically; they were connected through time. The saints Eucharius (ca. 250) and his two companions Valerius and Maternus, Agritius (ca. 314–329) Maximinus (ca. 329–346) and

80 Lenneke Van Raaij

Paulinus (ca. 347–358) together make up the first six entries of the earliest lists of archbishops of Trier, and all of them are honoured with a *vita* (see Table 5.1).[25] As direct successors, these protagonists were sometimes mentioned in each other's narrative. Archbishop Felix (386–399) also lived in the fourth century, ending the line of sanctified early bishops of Trier. Foundation narratives of the cathedral and various monasteries form the basis of this group of saints' lives. The episcopal saints Nicetius (526–566) and Magnericus (566–586) represent the sixth century, and their deeds are known from Gregory of Tour's work. Hildulphus (d. 707), Celsus (inv. 980) and Symeon (d. 1035) are the only saints who did not make it onto the list of famous early medieval archbishops of Trier. Hildulphus was bishop of Trier, but was better remembered for the foundation of a monastery outside Trier, in Moyenmoutier. Celsus' identity is unclear, as his ancient remains were discovered in the tenth century and he was declared a saint in 980. The true outsider in this group

TABLE 5.1 Hagiographical works of local patrons of Trier until the first half of the eleventh century (created by author)

Saint	Text	Edition	Date of composition
Nicetius	*Vita Nicetii*	B. Krusch, MGH SRM I (1885) 277–783.	591–594
Eucharius	*Vita Eucharii*	J. Bolland, AASS jan. II (1643) 918–922.	ca. 700–880
Maximinus	*Vita Maximini I*	G. Henschen, AASS mai VII (1866) 21–25.	751–ca. 800
Maximinus	*Vita Maximini II*	B. Krusch, MGH SRM III (1896) 74–82.	839
Felix	*Vita Felicis*	G. Henschen and D. Papebroch, AASS mar. III (1668) 622–625.	before 882
Paulinus	*Vita Paulini*	J. Pinius, AASS aug. VI (1743) 676–679.	882–ca. 1000
Hildulphus	*Vita Hildulphi*	H. Bolhommeus, AASS jul. III (1723) 221–227.	ca. 950–ca. 1000
Maximinus	*Historia Miraculorum Maximini*	G. Henschen AASS mai VII (1688) 25–33.	962–963
Maximinus	*Epigrammata Vita Maximini*	K. Strecker, MGH Poet. Lat. V 1 (1937) 147–152.	962– ca. 1000
Celsus	*Inventio et Miracula Celsi*	J. Bolland, AASS feb. III (1658) 396–404.	1007–1023
Magnericus	*Vita Magnerici*	J. Pinius, AASS jul. VI (1729) 183–192.	995–1035
Symeon	*Vita Symeonis*	G. Henschen, AASS jun. I (1695) 89–95.	ca. 1035
Agritius	*Vita Agritii*	J. Bolland, AASS jan. I (1643) 773–781.	ca. 1030–1072

of Trier cults is Symeon, a pilgrim who became a recluse in a city gate of Trier and was sanctified soon after his death in 1035. His life did not relate to the past as much as to early eleventh-century communities in Trier.

The temporal and geographic links between the different centres in Trier invite us to think about these centres as an amalgamated community. Nevertheless, we should not forget that every institution also had its own distinct profile.[26] Monastic institutions and canonical centres, regional centres and those with a more local character, all concentrated on different elements of the local pasts. Generally speaking, however, the narratives combined to make a coherent local 'grand narrative'. But this Trier 'grand narrative' lacked certain elements. Martyrs and saints from the Carolingian period are completely absent from the community of local saints.[27] Sanctified political or episcopal figures from the Carolingian or Ottonian periods did not appear on the tenth-century list of local saints. In the second half of the tenth century other German cities – notably Cologne and Augsburg – were privileged with new bishop-saints who enjoyed close connections with Ottonian court, but Trier did not.[28] Nor did Trier's monasteries have prominent founders who could be represented as the ancestors of Carolingian or Ottonian rulers.[29] Deprived of Carolingian and Ottonian saintly political figures, the question is whether – and to what extent – the local community in Trier was acquainted with royal or regional power through hagiography.

Carolingians in the local narratives

Despite their absence as protagonists from local Trier hagiography, Carolingian and Ottonian kings and rulers featured in some of the *vitae*. Their role, however, remained limited, as they competed with the power of local authorities and even with the active intervention of the local patron himself.

The narrative most closely related to the Carolingian court is that of the fourth-century archbishop of Trier St Maximinus, who was patron of the royal monastery just outside the city gates of Trier. Charles Martel and his son Pippin the Short occur in two Carolingian *vitae* of the saint: the *Vita Maximini I* (751–ca. 800) and its revision by Lupus of Ferrières (839). In these *vitae*, Carolingian rulers were beneficiaries of the miracles Saint Maximinus performed after his death.[30] In one miracle, Charles Martel had been ill with fever when he received a vision in which St Maximinus appeared to him.[31] Charles failed to recognize the saint and asked who he was. Maximinus explained that he was a bishop of Trier and that a visit to his grave would cure Charles. The king therefore visited the saint's sepulchre and was cured. As an act of gratitude, he donated several estates to St Maximinus' monastery. This narrative not only linked the monastery to Charles Martel, but also testified to the expansion of the monastery. Diplomata suggest that most estates of St Maximinus were acquired in the Merovingian and early Carolingian eras.[32] Although the monastery was not founded by Carolingian kings, the rulers did contribute to its wealth and expansion.[33] Looking closely at the role Charles Martel and Pippin the Short played in this local narrative, one notices that the Carolingians

82 Lenneke Van Raaij

were subordinate to the local patron.[34] St Maximinus appeared in a vision to Charles and asked him to come to his sepulchre, even though Charles had not been familiar with him before.[35] The power of St Maximinus, and the acceptance of his saintly authority by the Carolingian court, is also stressed in miracles featuring Pippin the Short, who actively sent his courtiers to St Maximinus to be cured.[36] As hagiographers drew attention to this matter, the Carolingian dynasty found its way into the local narrative of St Maximinus.

Along with the references to Carolingian rulers in *vitae* of St Maximinus, the people of Trier may have also been reminded of the Carolingian court during the feast of Hildulphus, a saint whose cult centre lay approximately 185 kilometres south of Trier. Hildulphus had been a bishop in Trier but abandoned his episcopal life to become a monk. He built a monastery in Moyenmoutier, in the Vosges and died in ca. 707. When the *vita* of Hildulphus was written in the second half of the tenth century, presumably in Moyenmoutier, the *Vita Maximini* was used as a source for knowledge on the deeds of Hildulphus as bishop of Trier: Hildulphus had been responsible for the translation of the bones of St Maximinus, after the crypt containing the sepulchre of the saint had flooded.[37] The *Vita Hildulphi* connects Hildulphus to the early court of the mayors of the palace by narrating that Hildulphus made an impression on King Pippin, father of Charlemagne, when he preached at court.[38] Moreover, Pippin is depicted here as a good king, who governed the *respublica Galliarum*.[39] The narrative, however, is anachronistic, as Hildulphus died before Pippin ascended the throne in 751 AD. The Pippin who was in charge during Hildulphus' life would have been Pippin of Herstal, the father of Charles Martel, who died in 714. The confusion of Pippins and Charleses might be understandable, but in this case it can hardly be called coincidental. As Goullet noted, other figures mentioned, such as Archbishop Milo of Trier (d. 762–763) and Jacob of Toul (r. 756–765), were contemporaries of Pippin the Short, not of Pippin of Herstal.[40] This anachronism was not corrected in the later eleventh-century *vitae* of Hildulphus, even though other discrepancies were amended.[41] This adaptation of the origins of Hildulphus to make him a Carolingian saint rather than a Merovingian one is understandable, given that the Benedictine monastery founded by Hildulphus became a royal monastery only under the former dynasty.

Aside from these two examples, no other local tenth-century narratives link Trier to the Carolingian dynasty. Instead, at the beginning of the century, hagiographers worried about the impact flawed lay abbots had on the local community. These lay abbots were mostly dukes or other regional aristocratic figures. The *Historia Miraculorum* (962–963), that dealt with the miracles performed by St Maximinus in the tenth century, criticized the lay abbots Megingaud (from the time of King Arnulf (894–899)) and Gisilbert (d. 939). In this narrative, Maximinus punished these men for treating the community poorly.[42] The period of lay abbacy at the beginning of the tenth century was not only a problem at the monastery of St Maximinus. In the *Vita Magnerici* the same sentiment is communicated.[43] It was a time of lack of respect, of rape, of fire and destruction, not only in the abbey of St Martin, but everywhere in Trier.[44] The relationships between lay abbots and

Infiltrating the local past **83**

monasteries were not fruitful in either account, but the length of the period of despair differed between the monasteries of Maximinus and Martin.[45] In 934 Abbot Ogo restored peace in St Maximinus through his reforms, whereas Archbishop Theodericus (965–977) did not revive St Martin until a few decades later.[46]

Archbishops and Ottonians in the local narratives

The authors of local hagiographies from the second half of the tenth century not only breathed a sigh of relief after the terrors of the lay abbacies, they also welcomed the new powerbrokers with open arms. Local *vitae* composed in the late tenth and early eleventh centuries began to display political perspectives absent from earlier *vitae*.[47] The archbishops of Trier, in particular, profited from these political messages.

In recent scholarship, several arguments have been made in favour of a direct link between archiepiscopal commissions of hagiography for Trier communities and the fight for primacy between Trier, Mainz, Cologne and Reims.[48] Notably, later *vitae*, especially those of Celsus (980), Magnericus (995–1035) and Agritius (1030–1072) show attempts to enhance the position of the tenth-century archbishops at the see of Trier. In the *Inventio Celsi* the archiepiscopal protagonist Egbert (977–993) was responsible for the renovation of the church of St Eucharius and the *inventio* (discovery) of the relics of Celsus.[49] In the *Vita Magnerici*, Archbishop Theodericus (965–977) is considered responsible for stopping the horrible rule of lay abbots and reviving the abbey of St Martin.[50] Meanwhile references to apostolic authority enhanced the leverage of the archbishops of Trier in regional politics, and the *Vita Agritii* stressed the primacy Trier held over *Gallia* and *Germania* and its position as *Roma secunda* on several occasions.[51] Thus, the local deeds of archbishops, especially Theodericus and Egbert, were promoted in the city's hagiography.

However, unlike other Lotharingian episcopal cities, the Trier centres did not produce any hagiographical works dedicated to the tenth or eleventh-century saintly bishops themselves.[52] It was through local saints from the distant past that authors conveyed the good deeds of contemporary archbishops to their audiences. It is noteworthy that the cults of both Celsus and Magnericus were only cultivated at the time of the composition of their *vitae* at the end of the tenth century.[53] The *Vita Agritii*, too, did not respond to an existing cult or discovery of relics: this *vita* is more about the cathedral and its relics and the other Trier patrons than Agritius himself.[54] The archbishops of Trier may thus have commissioned or used newly-written *vitae* of older saints to communicate their power and authority. The deeds of the archbishops that were communicated to this local audience had a strongly local flavour. Complex regional networks of knowledge and power that the archbishops were part of were rarely accounted for in the *vitae*.[55] The archbishops were given a strictly local function.

The Ottonian rulers, unlike Carolingian and episcopal actors, are not portrayed uniformly in the Trier hagiography. In one narrative, Henry I is depicted as subordinate to local rulers, whereas elsewhere, Otto II is considered a great source of authority. In the *Historia Miraculorum,* the monks of St Maximinus had

84   Lenneke Van Raaij

asked Henry I (d. 936) for help in a dispute with lay abbot Gisilbert. However, the king was unsuccessful. Only St Maximinus himself, who appeared to Gisilbert in a vision, was able to end the fight.[56] It indicates that Sigehard, the author of this text, did not consider the Ottonian ruler as powerful as a local saint, even though he introduced the king in a positive way.[57] Henry had not been strong enough to defend the monastery from other secular forces, and thus it was the saint himself who took responsibility for the earthly wellbeing of the monks. This is an interesting point of view, considering that St Maximinus was a royal abbey, supported by the Ottonian dynasty. Royal support, however, was not very strong in tenth-century Trier. Diplomas indicate that although the Ottonian rulers granted land and property to the monastery, it had been released from military duties and the duty to accommodate travelling kings.[58] To the people in St Maximinus abbey and in Trier, therefore, the king was not a particularly present figure in their lives, as he rarely visited the city.[59] The kings were thus not relevant to the local past. Even when the narrative mentioned the properties belonging to the monastery, kings were expunged from local narratives. Where Charles Martel had given property to St Maximinus, it was now the local saint who acted as the protagonist in the lands belonging to his abbey. In the *Historia Miraculorum*, St Maximinus exercised his power to protect his own estates outside the monastery in Trier.[60] Reading or listening to the *Historia Miraculorum*, a medieval audience would hear about how powerful an institution St Maximinus was, not about the patronage of the Ottonians. Clearly, the local power of the saintly patron was deemed to be more potent than that of a more distant king.

This presentation of the Ottonian rulers as less powerful was not shared by the authors of late tenth-century hagiography produced in St Eucharius on the other side of the city. On the contrary, in the *Inventio et Miracula Celsi*, Otto II is depicted as a powerful man to whom the archbishop and the newly discovered saint had to approach for approval. The text refers to Emperor Otto II as a Roman monarch and 'most catholic rector'.[61] In the *Inventio*, Archbishop Egbert of Trier asked the emperor for his blessing for the renovation of St Eucharius's church, using the apostolic authority he held as archbishop of Trier.[62] The emperor was enthused by the idea and told Egbert to quickly start restoration.[63] Having found the relics of Celsus during the renovation works, Egbert hurried to Ingelheim, where a large synod was held. At this synod, attended by bishops, abbots, and fathers from *Belgica* and *Germania*, Egbert showed off his discovery.[64] The emperor reacted joyfully and accepted Celsus as a new patron of the metropolitan see of Trier.[65]

Both the *Historia Miraculorum* (962) and the *Inventio et Miracula Celsus* (1007–1023) were composed a generation after the death of the two Ottonian rulers Henry I (d. 936) and Otto II (d. 983). However, unlike the depiction of Henry I in the *Historia Miraculorum*, Otto II is shown as an influential figure whose approval was indispensable for the sanctification of Celsus. He was also painted as a figure whose attention could only be obtained by powerful figures, such as by the archbishop of Trier with his apostolic authority. Indeed, by the time Otto II became emperor, the influence of archbishops on the emperor and vice versa was much greater than

Infiltrating the local past **85**

at the time of Henry I, who had been a mere king of a newly developing dynasty. By actively involving both Emperor Otto II and Archbishop Egbert of Trier in the narrative of St Celsus, the audience was made aware of the supra-regional power structures.

St Martin in Trier

Royal and regional rulers were not the only supra-regional authorities mentioned in the local Trier narratives; two well-known saintly figures made an appearance too. St Peter featured particularly prominently, as the apostle who sent St Eucharius to christianize the area.[66] The only other universally celebrated saint to feature in local hagiography is St Martin of Tours. He lived from ca. 336 to 397, making him contemporary with some of the local Trier patrons. The Roman soldier, who famously shared half of his cloak with a beggar, became bishop of Tours in 371 and performed many miracles. Through the works of Sulpicius Severus, Martin was depicted as a universal saint, promoting general Christian ideals.[67] Merovingian and Carolingian kings actively supported his cult and churches and chapels dedicated to Martin emerged all over the Frankish lands. Trier was no exception, with a monastery dedicated to St Martin just outside the city walls. An analysis of the perception of St Martin in the local narratives of Trier is helpful in further understanding the relationship between the powers of local saints and the role universal figures played in this.

The abbey of St Martin, for which Regino served as abbot during his exile from Prüm, was rather small, and did not play as prominent a role within the city as the monasteries of St Maximinus or St Eucharius. Klaus Krönert argues that the abbey of St Martin never played a role of importance in Trier at all, contrary to the abbeys dedicated to the saint in Mainz and Cologne.[68] He explains that its origins are obscure, that the earliest charters for the abbey suggest struggles for regaining property and the restoration of privileges, and that the narrative of the *Vita Magnerici,* written around the turn of the eleventh century, reveals that its past was not a prosperous one.[69]

More significantly, there are no clear signs of the active veneration of St Martin at this small abbey. In the charters, the abbey is not once referred to as St Martin's abbey. Instead the church is referred to as the place where 'the body of Magnericus rests', suggesting that the abbey was known by its local patron rather than its universal saint.[70] Magnericus, who held the archbishopric of Trier in the seventh century, actively supported the cult of St Martin in his lifetime, according to his *vita.* The *Vita Magnerici* was only written down at the end of the tenth or beginning of the eleventh century.[71] So, it was only in this period that St Martin was venerated, calling upon a seventh-century tradition.

The *Vita Magnerici* recounted the story of Wolfilaicus, one of Magnericus' pupils, who had heard about Martin' fame.[72] He went to pray at the sepulchre of St Martin in Tours and took some ashes from the sepulchre. Returning from the monastery, the ashes he kept in a little casket began to multiply and overflow.[73] In another miracle, Magnericus tore down an idolatrous statue to Diana, upon which he immediately got ulcers on every part of his body.[74] He went into the church alone and sprinkled oil that he took from the basilica of St Martin on the sores. He was then restored to health, and is said to have constructed three other churches dedicated to St Martin.[75] According to this *vita*, no doubt arises about the active cultivation of the cult of Martin in the region of Trier by Magnericus.

No traces of an active cult of St Martin can be found in other hagiographical works from Trier. In Carolingian hagiography for St Maximinus, Martin is only awarded a minor role, subordinate to the local saint himself. Nevertheless, St Martin's presence may have been vital for the dissemination of the narrative. The *Vita Maximini I* tells the story of Maximinus's journey to Rome, where he met Martin, and how the two visited the grave of the apostle Peter together.[76] After they left Rome, and St Martin went away to get provisions, St Maximinus succumbed to his tiredness and fell asleep. When St Martin returned and St Maximinus woke up, a bear had eaten their mule. Maximinus then ordered the bear to carry their belongings. The bear, miraculously, obeyed and was given back his freedom once the two had returned to Trier. In Trier, Martin asked Maximinus to teach his student Lubentius, after which Lubentius was ordained a priest.[77] This legendary narrative was also known beyond the city of Trier.[78] In the *Vita Mansueti,* written ca. 970 by Adso of Montier-en-Der (Châlons sur Marne), Maximinus and Martin visited the sepulchre of the founding bishop of Toul after the journey to Rome. This way, the community of Mansuy profited from the local narrative that had spread through the regions with time.[79] Also outside the diocese of Trier, the trope of a bear being commanded by a saint on a trip to Rome with a saintly contemporary was known: it also occurs in the first *vita* of Corbianus of Freising and that of Humbertus of Maroilles.[80] Both narratives are said to have been directly inspired by the *Vita Maximini I.*[81] Oral traditions, however, are hard to trace, and there is not enough evidence to firmly prove that the narrative originated from Trier. Nevertheless, this narrative of the encounter between Martin and Maximinus is one of the only local narratives that was known and used outside Trier. The other narrative that enjoyed wider dissemination, in which Eucharius received a staff from St Peter with which he could revive his companion, also concerned a universally-known figure.[82] Apparently, local narratives only became interesting for other communities once a universal saint got involved.

In the hagiography on St Paulinus and St Felix, who were contemporaries of St Martin, no connection between the local and universal figures is forged. In the *Vita Paulini* (882–ca. 1000) a relationship between the archbishop and St Martin is not cultivated. Although St Paulinus was a closer contemporary of St Martin than St Maximinus had been, he is not mentioned in any of the works of Sulpicius Severus on Martin, nor in other texts that might cultivate a relationship between the two. A connection between them would not be logical in the first place, since Paulinus died before Martin became bishop. The first *Vita Felicis* (before 882) briefly mentioned that Felix was consecrated bishop by Martin of Tours during a council held at Trier, citing the works of Sulpicius Severus.[83] The text's author, however, did not elaborate further on this matter, as there were no other sources to fall back on.

Neither the legendary version of St Martin as presented in the *vita* of St Maximinus, nor the historical version copied into the *Vita Felicis* can be considered a liturgical cry for veneration. This liturgical cry, and simultaneously the enhancement of the local cult of St Martin, can only be found in the *Vita Magnerici*, which mentions both the church of St Martin in Trier and the miracles Martin performed locally. For a true understanding of the veneration of St Martin in Trier, looking at local hagiographical sources does not suffice. St Martin was celebrated with his own feasts, hagiography and liturgy, separated from local protagonists.[84]

A timeless local identity

The past communicated in hagiographical texts composed in Trier in the ninth and tenth century was very local indeed. Despite its role in the region as the archiepiscopal centre and the presence of a royal abbey, the communities in and around the city did not identify to any great extent with supra-regional figures, at least not in their hagiographical traditions. Local traditions must also be associated with oral culture, which is usually hard to pin down. These local oral traditions were fluid and adapted to fit the needs of the local society: memories were added and others forgotten.[85] The memories of supra-regional rulers perhaps faded relatively quickly, because they did not share the timeless characters of saints. It is certainly worth noting in this respect, that the recording of the memory of Charles Martel and Pippin the Short in the *Vita Maximini I* is almost contemporaneous with their rule.[86] Similarly, the accounts featuring the Ottonian kings were written close to the periods of their rule.[87] Once remembered, the supra-regional rulers could retain their significance. The narrative of the miracles concerning Charles Martel and Pippin the Short remained relevant in the memory of the monks of St Maximin throughout the Ottonian period: in the chapter room of the monastery a series of epigrams accompanied by pictures of the life of St Maximinus reminded the community of this episode every day.[88]

Another problematic aspect of the memorializing of worldly rulers in the local past, is that their reputation was generally associated with a single monastery, cult or church. For example, Charles Martel had donated property to the monastery of St Maximinus, and Otto II acknowledged the veracity of the bones of Celsus, ensuring the authority of the newly found saint. The function of the kings was not relevant to other communities within Trier, which would not benefit from possible cross references or shared narratives. This was different to the narratives concerning archbishops, whose powers were associated with multiple centres. Already in the *Vita Nicetii*, written by Gregory of Tours in the sixth century, Archbishop Nicetius had the custom of secretly visiting the different churches in Trier at night.[89] In the local narratives produced in the second half of the tenth century, the active role of archbishops in different centres within Trier continued, indicating that their power was more relevant to the whole city than that of lay rulers. The archbishops of Trier

88 Lenneke Van Raaij

were a tangible force that people could identify with, not only because they walked around the city on a regular basis and performed liturgy for everyone to see, but also because the local narratives that shaped identity in Trier were filled with saintly archbishops, who had served and protected the different centres in Trier throughout the ages. They were more powerful than lay abbots and kings; they were acquainted with St Martin of Tours; and, above all, as successors of the saintly archbishops of Trier, they fitted into the liturgical frame of timelessness and transcendence.[90]

Notes

1 For an introduction to the tenth century and the Ottonian world, see: Charles West, *Reframing the Feudal Revolution* (Cambridge: Cambridge University Press, 2013); Timothy Reuter, 'Introduction: reading the tenth century', in *The New Cambridge Medieval History vol. 3: c. 900–1024,* ed. by Timothy Reuter (Cambridge: Cambridge University Press, 1999), pp. 1–24. An interesting study in this respect concerning litugy in the tenth century: Henry Parkes, *The Making of Liturgy in the Ottonian Church. Books, Music and Ritual in Mainz, 950–1050* (Cambridge: Cambridge University Press, 2015).

2 The Royal Frankish Annals communicated a wide sense of identity: Rosamund McKitterick, 'Constructing the Past in the Early Middle Ages: The Case of the Royal Frankish Annals', *Transactions of the Royal Historical Society* (1997), 101–29.

3 Martina Giese ed., *Die Annales Quedlinburgenses*, MGH SRG In Usum Scholarum Separatim Editi, 72 (Hannover, 2004); Sarah Greer, 'The Quedlinburg Annals: Writing the Ottonian Past in the 11th Century' on *After Empire: Using and Not Using the Past in the Crisis of the Carolingian World c. 900–1050* <https://arts.st-andrews.ac.uk/after-empire/2017/07/11/the-quedlinburg-annals-writing-the-ottonian-past-in-the-11th-century/> [accessed 7/10/2018].

4 Thietmar of Merseburg, *Thietmar von Merseburg: Chronik*, trans. by Werner Trillmich (Darmstatt, 2011), xxviii–xxx.

5 Simon MacLean, *History and Politics in Late Carolingian and Ottonian Europe. The Chronicle of Regino of Prüm and Andalbert of Magdeburg* (Manchester, 2009).

6 For example, Adalbert included entries of deaths and succession of bishops and abbots: MacLean, *History and Politics in Late Carolingian and Ottonian Europe,* pp. 259, 261, 269, 270.

7 Amy Remensnyder, *Remembering Kings Past. Monastic Foundation Legends in Medieval Southern France* (Ithaca and London: Cornell University Press, 1995).

8 Thomas Head, *Hagiography and the Cult of Saints: The Diocese of Orléans 800–1200* (Cambridge and New York: Cambridge University Press, 2000), p. 64.

9 Catherine Cubitt, 'Universal and local saints in Anglo-Saxon England', in *Local Saints and Local Churches in the Early Medieval West,* ed. by Alan Thacker and Richard Sharpe (Oxford: Oxford University Press, 2002), pp. 423–54 (pp. 437–8). For studies on the relation between liturgy and a local community: Susan Boynton, *Shaping a Monastic Identity: Liturgy and History at the Imperial Abbey of Farfa, 1000–1125* (Ithaca and London: Cornell University Press, 2006); Margot Fassler, *The Virgin of Chartres: Making History through Liturgy and the Arts* (New Haven and London: Cornell University Press, 2010). For the diversity and locality of liturgical practices in general, see Helen Gittos and Sarah Hamilton, *Understanding Medieval Liturgy. Essays in Interpretation* (Farnham: Routledge, 2016).

10 For an introduction to *historiae*, see: Jean-François Goudesenne, 'A typology of *historiae* in West Francia (8–10 c.)', *Plainsong and Medieval Music* 13:1 (2004), 1–31.

11 Wolfert S. van Egmond, 'The Audience of Early Medieval Hagiographical Texts: Some Questions Revisited', in *New Approaches to Medieval Communication* ed. by Marco Mostert (Turnhout: Brepols, 1999), pp. 41–67 (p. 43); Head, *Hagiography and the Cult of Saints: The Diocese of Orléans 800–1200*, p. 3.

Infiltrating the local past **89**

12 Fassler, *The Virgin of Chartres,* viii.
13 Yossi Maurey, *Medieval Music, Legend, and the Cult of St. Martin. The Local Foundations of a Universal Saint* (Cambridge: Cambridge University Press, 2014), p. 123.
14 According to Van Dam, Merovingian kings acknowledged the importance of the cult of St Martin, but were hesitant in actively promoting the cult of the saint. Raymond van Dam, *Saints and their Miracles in Late-Antique Gaul* (Princeton: Princeton University Press, 1993), pp. 21–8; Also compare: Eugen Ewig, 'Le culte de saint Martin de Tours à l'époque franque', *Revue d'Histoire de l'Eglise de France* 144 (1961), 1–18. Allan McKinley proposes other influences that improved the initial spread of the cult of St Martin: Allan S. McKinley, 'The first two centuries of Saint Martin of Tours', *Early Medieval Europe,* 14 (2006), 173–200. For the role of kings and the spread of St Martin central Europe, see Bruno Judic, 'Le culte de saint Martin dans le haut Moyen Age et l'Europe Centrale', *Sveti Martin Tourski kot simbol evropske kulture. Saint Martin de Tours, symbole de la culture européenne* ed. by Jasmina Arambaši (Ljubljana: Mohorjeva družba, 2008), pp. 32–44.
15 Bruno Judic, 'Le patronage martinien au xe siècle', *Annales de Bretagne et des Pays e l'Ouest* 119.3 (2012), 89–105.
16 Judic, 'Le patronage martinien au xe siècle', p. 98.
17 Boynton, *Shaping a Monastic Identity,* p. 97.
18 No tenth- or eleventh-centuriy copies of the *vita Maximini I* survive, whereas there are five copies extant from the life written by Lupus: Bern, Burgerbibliothek 24; Montpellier, Bibliothèque interuniversitaire, section médicine H 48; Paris, Bibliothèque Nationale de France, 5294; Vienna, Österreichische Nationalbibliothek 576; Metz, Bibliothèque municipale, 523 (lost in the second World War).
19 These relations are put to paper in their saints lives. *Vita Nicetii* in MGH SRM I (1885) ed. by Bruno Krusch, pp. 277–783, c. 1–2; *Vita Magnerici* in AASS jul. VI (1729) ed. by. Joannes Pinius, pp. 183–92, c. 2.16.
20 For an introduction to the tenth and eleventh-century rivalry between Trier and other major centres such as Mainz, Cologne, Liège and Rheims, see Klaus Krönert, 'Between Identity, History, and Rivalry: Hagiographic Legends in Trier, Cologne, and Liège,' in *Medieval Liège at the Crossroads of Europe: Monastic Society and Culture, 1000–1300* ed. by Steven Vanderputten, Tjamke Snijders and Jay Diehl, (Turnhout: Brepols, 2017), pp. 49–68.
21 Most famous archbishop is Egbert of Trier (975–993): Andreas Weiner, Rita Heyen, Franz J. Ronig eds., *Egbert Erzbischof von Trier 977–993. Gedenkschrift der Diozese Trier zum 1000. Todestag* (Trier: Selbstverlag des Rheinischen Landesmuseum, 1993).
22 John Nightingale, *Monasteries and Patrons in the Gorze Reform* (Oxford: Clarendon Press, 2001) p. 236.
23 Leading work in the field of hagiography in Trier is Klaus Krönert, *L'exaltation de Trèves: écriture hagiographique et passé historique de la métropole mosellane VIIIe – Xie siècle* (Ostfildern: Thorbecke, 2010). Krönert focusses on hagiography of Trier patrons until the end of the eleventh century, covering a wider timeframe than the present study.
24 *Vita Eucharii, Valerii et Materni* in AASS jan. II (1643) ed. by. Jean Bolland, pp. 918–22, c.1–2.
25 Several copies of lists of archbishops of Trier survive from the tenth century onwards. They are edited in: George H. Pertz, 'Series Archiepiscoporum Treverensium' *MGH SS* 13 (Stuttgart: 1881), 296–302. The oldest copies have a Trier origin: Brussels, Bibliothèque Royale II 976 (975–993) written in Trier; Wolfenbüttel, Herzog August Bibliothek cod. Guelf. 1109 Helmst. (994–1008) Trier; Paris, bibliothèque nationale de France, lat. 9433 (895–898) Echternach.
26 Boynton, *Shaping a Monastic Identity,* p. 4.
27 It is interesting to note that there are no local martyrs, as martyrs are considered to be at the top of the hierarchy of saints. For an introduction of the cult of saints, see: Peter Brown, *The Cult of the Saints. Its Rise and Function in Latin Christianity* (Chicago: University of Chicago Press, 1981).

90 Lenneke Van Raaij

28 For example, Bruno of Cologne was archbishop of Cologne and brother of Otto II: Henry Mayr-Harting, *Church and Cosmos in Early Ottonian Germany* (Oxford: Oxford University Press, 2007); Ualdoricus (Ulrich) was bishop of Augsburg, appointed by emperor Henry II and the first saint to be canonised by the pope: Manfred Weitlauff, 'Bischoff Ulrich von Augsburg (923–973) Leben und Wirken eines Reichsbischofs der ottonischen Zeit', *Jahrbuch des Vereins für Augsburger Bistumsgeschichte* 26–27 (1993), 69–142.

29 For example, the abbey of Prüm was founded by the grandmother of Pippin the Short, Bertrada, and St Denis in Paris was founded by King Dagobert. See also Remensnyder, *Remembering Kings Past.*

30 *Vita Maximini I* in AASS mai VII (1866) ed. by Godfrey Henschen, pp. 21–5, c. 12–3; *Vita Maximini II* in MGH SRM II (1896) ed. by Bruno Krusch, pp. 74–82, c. 12, 21–3.

31 The summary is based on *Vita Maximini I*, c. 12.

32 Nightingale, *Monasteries and Patrons in the Gorze Reform,* p. 185.

33 Charles Martel was a willing patron of the monstery of St Maximinus: Hans H. Anton and Alfred Haverkamp eds., *2000 Jahre Trier. Trier im Mittelalter* (Trier: Spee-Verlag, 1996), p. 50; Eric Wisplinghoff, *Untersuchungen zur Frühen Geschichte der Abtei S. Maximin die Trier von den Anfängen bis etwa 1150* (Mainz: Selbstverlag der Gesellschaft für mittlerheinische Kirchengeschichte, 1970), p. 17.

34 The *Vita Maximini I* speaks of a 'king Charles' and a 'king Pippin'. It is clear that Charles Martel and Pippin the Short are meant: 1) In the *Vita Maximini I,* the miracle of Charles is put before those of the court of Pippin, which suggests that Charles came before Pippin, as the rest of the work is chronological. 2) The miraculous healing of Charles is followed by gift giving of churches. The charters of Charles Martel to those churches still exist. Charles Martel was succeeded by Pippin the Short. 3) The Pippin in the *Vita Maximini I* is called 'rex', a term which would not have applied to Pippin of Herstal, who was mayor of the palace.

35 *Vita Maximini I*, c. 12. In the *vitae*, the vocative is used: 'perge mane ad sepulcrum meum'.

36 *Vita Maximini I*, c. 13. The beneficiaries are named and originate from all parts of society, like all miracles performed by St Maximinus in his first life: his cleric Brunicum, an Alemannic called Guerricus and a woman called Waltridus were cured from demons. It gives a rare insight into the type of people Pippin surrounded himself with, although it is unsure to what extent the tenth-century audience would relate to these figures.

37 *Vita Maximini I*, c. 9; *Vita Maximini II* c. 15.

38 *Vita Hildulphi* in AASS jul. III (1723) ed. by H. Bolhommeus, pp. 221–7, c. 3.

39 *Vita Hildulphi I,* c. 3: 'Pipinus itaque tunc temporis, uir magnae pietatis, genitor uidelicet magni Caroli, rempublicam Galliarum florentissime gubernabat, et Milone Archiepiscopo Treuirensium rebus humanis exuto, Treuirenses praesule indigebant'.

40 Monique Goullet, 'Les saints du diocèse de Toul (SHG VI)', in *Hagiographie du hâut moyen age en Gaule du Nord* ed. by Martin Heinzelmann, (Stuttgart : Jan Thorbecke Verlag, 2001), pp. 11–91 (p. 75).

41 Goullet, 'Les saints du diocèse de Toul', pp. 74–5.

42 *Historia Miraculorum* in AASS mai VII (1688) ed. by Godfrey Henschen, pp. 25–33, c. 10–12.

43 *Vita Magnerici*, c. 56–7.

44 *Vita Magnerici*, c. 56–7.

45 According to Nightingale, the period of lay abbots did not have seem to damage the religiosity of the abbey. Nightingale, *Monasteries and Patrons in the Gorze Reform,* p. 191.

46 *Historia Miraculorum*, c. 14; *Vita Magnerici*, c. 58.

47 Klaus Krönert argues in his work *L'exaltation de Trèves* that most hagiographical works from Trier have a political *causa scribendi*. He states that the texts written at the cathedral and St Eucharius wanted to show that the church of Trier had the right of primacy due to its ancient origin and its prominent position in Gaul and Germania. Krönert, *L'exaltation de Trèves,* p. 215. This argument is too generalising as it leaves out religious and cultural factors for composition of texts. Earlier hagiography like the *Vita Eucharii*,

Valerii et Materni is filled with references to St Peter and the apostolic heritage of Trier, but does not appear to be written with political motives. The text was composed in the Merovingian or Carolingian era, when primacy fights were not an issue, and there are no other political insinuations in the text.

48 Klaus Krönert, 'Production hagiographique et enjeux politiques à Trèves (xe-xie siècle)', in *Hagiographie, idéologie et politique au Moyen Âge en occident : Actes du colloque international du Centre d'Études supérieures de Civilisation médiévale de Poitiers, 11–14 septembre 2008* ed. by Edina Bozóky (Turnhout: Brepols, 2012), pp. 185–98 (p. 189); Head, 'Art and Artifice in Ottonian Trier', *Gesta* 36.1 (1997), 65–77 (pp. 68–70).

49 *Inventio et Miraculae Celsi* in AASS feb. III (1658) ed. by Jean Bolland, pp. 396–404, c. 10, 17.

50 *Vita Magnerici*, c. 58–60.

51 *Vita Agritii* in AASS jan. I (1643) ed. by Jean Bolland, pp. 773–81, c. 2, 8, 14, 28, 32.

52 On Lotharingian tenth and eleventh-century episcopal saints, see Anne Wagner, 'L'image du pouvoir épiscopal aux Xe -XIe siècle : l'exemple lorrain', in *Hagiographie, idéologie et politique au Moyen Âge en Occident: Actes du colloque international du Centre d'Études supérieures de Civilisation médiévale de Poitiers, 11–14 septembre 2008*, ed. by Edina Bozoky (Turnhout: Brepols, 2012), pp. 233–41.

53 The *Inventio Celsi* was written shortly after the actual *inventio* (discovery) in 980. There is no proof of a thriving cult of Magnericus in the ninth or tenth century. Only a vision of Archbishop Rotbert (930–955) in which he erects an altar on top of the grave of Magnericus. Ernst Winheller, *Die Lebensbeschreibungen der vorkarolingischen Bischöfe von Trier* (Bonn: Ludwig Röhrscheid Verlag, 1935), p. 109.

54 See also, Winheller, *Die Lebensbeschreibungen*, 143–5.

55 For the complex political and cultural activities of the archbishops of Trier, see: Weiner a.o. ed., *Egbert Erzbischof von Trier 977–993*. Anton and Haverkamp eds., *2000 Jahre Trier. Trier im Mittelalter*, pp. 94–104, 203–5.

56 *Historia Miraculorum*, c. 13.

57 *Historia Miraculorum*, c. 13: 'Ea autem tempestate, uir clarissimus Henricus, genitor Serenissimi Augusti Ottonis, cuius imperii anno uigesimo septimo haec scripsimus, monarchia regni potitus, subditos quidem iustitia, pace et clementia modestissime gubernauit, Imperii uero apicem uirtutibus et gloria omnique honestate singulariter decorauit'.

58 Bertram Resmini, e.o., *Das Erzbistum Trier 13. Die Benediktinerabtei St. Maximin vor Trier* (Berlin and Boston: De Gruyter, 2016), p. 239.

59 Bernhardt's study on the itineraries of Ottonian kings shows that royal monasteries that supported the Ottonian dynasty were mostly located in Saxony. John W. Bernhardt, *Itinerant Kingship and Royal Monasteries in Early Medieval Germany, c. 936–1075* (Cambridge: Cambridge University Press, 1993).

60 *Historia miraculorum*, c. 15.

61 *Inventio Celsi,* c. 5: 'Anno dominicae incarnationis 978, quando diuinae memoriae Otto secundus, Maximi Augusti, Ottonis relatiuus, Romanae monarchiae apicem strenue gubernando, Princeps agebat in sceptro'; *Inventio Celsi* c. 10: 'Imperator uero, uti Catholicissimus mundialis aulæ rector, tanto tanti Pontificis coniubilans voto, præ nimia mentis alacritate … '.

62 *Inventio Celsi*, c. 10.

63 *Inventio Celsi*, c. 11.

64 *Inventio Celsi*, c. 16–7.

65 *Inventio Celsi*, c. 17.

66 *Vita Eucharii, Valerii et Materni*, c. 1.

67 Maurey, *Medieval Music, Legend, and the Cult of St. Martin*, pp. 76–7; For the early development of the cult of St Martin, see: Van Dam, *Saints and their Miracles in Late-Antique Gaul*, pp. 13–28.

68 Klaus Krönert, 'Saint Martin, l'*abbatiola* de Trèves', *Annales de Bretagne et des Pays de l'Ouest* 119.3 (2012), 71–88 (p. 71).

69 Harald Zimmermann, *Papsturkunden 896–1046* (Vienna: Verlag der Österreichischen Akademie der Wissenschaften, 1984–1985) pp. 463–5; Heinrich Sauerland argues these charters are a forgery from the eleventh century. Heinrich Sauerland, *Trierer Geschichtsquellen des 11. Jahrhunderts* (Trier: Paulinus-druckerei, 1889) pp. 9–13; Krönert, 'Saint Martin, l'*abbatiola* de Trèves', pp. 75–6.

70 Zimmermann, *Papsturkunden 896–1046,* 465. no. 233: ' ... quoddam monasterium, ubi sanctus Magnericus corpore requiescit ... '.

71 In the last chapter of the *Vita Magnerici*, there is a reference to the composer of the *Vita Magnerici* being elected the successor of abbot Engilbert. Eberwinus was abbot between 995 and ca. 1047. Sauerland, *Trierer Geschichtsquellen,* p. 5; *Vita Magnerici,* c. 60.

72 *Vita Magnerici,* c. 35. The source of this miracle is Gregory of Tours, *Historiae* viii, 16.

73 *Vita Magnerici,* c. 36.

74 *Vita Magnerici,* c. 37–40; The source of this miracle is Gregory of Tours, *Historiae* viii, 16–17.

75 *Vita Magnerici,* c. 52.

76 The following summary is based on *Vita Maximini I*, c. 3. Lupus of Ferrières integrated the narrative of Maximinus' encounter with Martin in his *vita* as well. *Vita Maximini II*, c. 7. It is a summarised account, leaving out the discussion Maximinus and Martin have when they find their mule eaten by the bear.

77 *Vita Maximini I,* c. 4.

78 The plausibility of the veracity of the narrative is not relevant here. Martin was just a child when Maximinus was archbishop. Hans Hubert Anton stated that the narrative implied that Martin of Mainz, who was present at the synod in Cologne with Maximinus, was protagonist of this story instead of Martin of Tours. (Hans H. Anton, 'Neue Studien zu Trier um frühen und hohen Mittelalter: Zum Trierer hagiographischen Corpus und den Bischofsviten', *Rheinische Vierteljahrsblätter* 71 (2007), 43–83 (pp. 49–50). Krönert refuted this by stating that there was no other bishop called Martin in the fourth century (Krönert, *L'exaltation de Trèves,* p. 50). In any case, the text of the *vitae* continuously refers to Martin as 'confessor' and 'saint', which indicates that to the audience at least, there was no question about the identity of Maximinus' companion. For example *Vita Maximini I*, c. 3: 'Cumque reuersus fuisset beatus Martin et sanctum excitaset Maximinum, dixit ei: ... '. Ms London, BL addit. 19,967 shows that in the twelfth century, there was debate in Trier about the contemporaneousness of Martin and Maximinus. In this manuscript, a text is added (ca. 1140–1180 AD) on folio 39 in which this was debated. The author discussed both sides, but concluded that Maximinus and Martin were contemporaries. Lars Boje Mortensen, 'Twelfth-century studies in Trier's Roman past', *Cahiers de l'institut du Moyen Âge grec et latin,* 59 (1989), 297–322 (pp. 304–5).

79 *Vita Mansueti* in AASS sep. I (1746) ed. by Joannes Limpenus, pp. 637–651, c. 27; Monique Goullet, 'Les vies de saint Mansuy (*Mansuetus*) premier évêque de Toul. Aperçu du dossier et édition critique des textes inédits', *Analecta Bollandiana* 116 (1998), 57–105, (pp. 72–4).

80 Corbinianus (d. ca. 730) was the first bishop of Freising. He travelled with Ansericus to Rome, when a bear ate his mule. *Vita Corbiniani* in MGH SS rer. germ. 13, ed. by Bruno Krusch, pp. 100–234; Humbertus (fifth century) was founder of the abbey of Maroilles (North of France). He travelled with St Amand and Nicasius. *Vita Humberti Primi*: Anne-Marie Helvétius, 'Reécriture hagiographique et réforme monastique: les premières vitae de saint Humbert de Maroilles (xe -xie siècles)', in *La reécriture hagiographique dan l'occident médiéval. Transformations formelles et idéologiques* ed. by Monique Goullet and Martin Heinzelmann (Ostfildern: Thorbecke, 2003), pp. 195–230.

81 *Vita Corbiniani* ed. Krusch, p. 154; Helvétius, 'Reécriture hagiographique et réforme monastique', p. 210.

82 The trope of St Peter giving a staff to a disciple with which he could revive a companion from the dead is known in multiple local hagiographical works. Samantha K. Herrick, 'Apostolic founding bishops and their rivals. The examples of Limoges, Rouen and Pèrigueux', in *Espace sacré, mémoire sacrée: Le culte des évêques dans leurs villes (IVe–XXe*

siècle), ed. by Christine Bousquet-Labouéie and Yossi Maurey (Turnhout: 2015), pp. 15–35. Tenth- and eleventh-century manuscripts containing the *Vita Eucharii, Valerii et Materni* with no strong link to a Trier centre: Berlin, Staatsbibliothek Phill. Lat. 1874 (eleventh-century, Western Germany); Montpellier, Bibliothèque interuniversitaire, section médicine H 48 (eleventh-century, France); München, Bayerische Staatsbibliothek clm 4618 (eleventh-century, Southern Germany); München, Bayerische Staatsbibliothek clm 14031 (end of eleventh-century, St Emmeram); Paris, Bibliothèque Nationale de France, 5294 (eleventh-century, St Symphorien, Metz); St. Gallen, cod. Sang. 565 (tenth- or eleventh-century, St Gall); Trier, Dombibliothek 93 (eleventh- or twelfth-century, Paderborn).

83 *Vita Felicis*: Et ordinationis tempore seuerus sulpicius scriptor gestorum Martini turonorum pontificis quaedam significat qui tempore quo maximus imperator frequens episcoporum concilium treuiros conuocauerat, martinum quoque eodem uenisse commemorans, Postridie inquit felices episcopi ordinatio parabatur, sanctissimi sane uiri et plane digni qui meliori temper fieret sacerdos.

84 Head, *Hagiography and the Cult of Saints,* p. 1.

85 Julia Smith, 'Oral and Written: saints, miracles and relics in Brittany c. 850–1250', *Speculum* 65 (1990), 309–43 (p. 324).

86 The first Life of St Maximinus must have been written after 751, as Pippin, father of Charlemagne featured in one of the miracles as king, which he became in 751. The *terminus ante quem* is set at the end of the eighth century, as it is argued that the style of the text is not yet influenced by the Carolingian reforms. Krönert, *L'exaltation de Trèves,* pp. 52–3; Walter Berschin, *Biographie und Epochenstil im lateinischen Mittelalter, 3: Karolingische Biographie 750–920 n. Chr.* (Stuttgart: Hiersemann, 1991) p. 66.

87 The *Historia Miraculorum* was written in 962–963 by the monk Sigehard. *Historia Miraculorum* c. 25: 'Perinde etiam hoc celebre factum regi serenissimo, Ottoni uidelicet primo, ea luce Treueris existenti aperiens, puerum suae regali magnificentiae praesentiasti …'. See also Klaus Krönert, 'Les miracula sancti Maximini (BHL 5826): entre hagiographie et historiographie', *Revue Bénédictine* 115 (2005), 112–50 (pp. 149–50). The *Inventio Celsi* was written by Theoderic, a monk of St Eucharius. He became a monk in 1006. Abbot Richardus commissioned the works. He was abbot until 1023. Therefore, the works are written between 1006 and 1023. One of the miracles occur in 1007, which pushes the post quem date a little further. *Miracula Celsi*, c. 10.

88 The chapter room in which these epigrams were visible does not survive. In a manuscript from the third quarter of the tenth century, Gent, Universiteitsbibliotheek 9, the text survived. Helmutt Hoffmann, *Schreibschulen des 10. und des 11. Jahrhunderts im Südwesten des Deutschen Reichs,* MGH Schriften 53 (Hannover: Hahnsche Buchhandlung, 2004), pp. 470–1. The *terminus post quem* is 962, as the author of the epigrams mentioned Sigehard's *Historia Miraculorum* as a source. *Epigrammata Vita Maximini*, c. 23: Scripta retexentur studiosius et relegantur, / quae scripsere Lupus, Gregorius et Sigehardus'.

89 *Vita Nicetii*, c. 4.

90 Margot Fassler, 'The Liturgical Framework of Time and the Representation of History', in *Representing History 900–1300. Art Music History* ed. by Robert A. Maxwell (Philadelphia: Pennsylvania University Press, 2010), pp. 149–72.

6

AFTER THE FALL

Lives of texts and lives of modern scholars in the historiography of the post-Carolingian world

Stuart Airlie

We are fortunate, or seem to be so, in having such a historically conscious author to bring the curtain down on the Carolingian empire and raise it on its successors. Regino of Prüm's classic account of the evaporation of Carolingian dynastic exclusivity and the consequences of that drama stands at the head of any account of the post-Carolingian empire. Regino's dynastic concerns are echoed in subsequent texts such as Adalbert of Magdeburg's noting the end of the Carolingian line in the east, or Richer of Reims' explanation to his readers why there needed to be so many royal people called Charles and Louis in his narratives, an explanation that pointed to the importance of their disappearance in 987.[1]

And yet this dynastic crisis on its own need not in itself mean that a grand transformation of society took place as a result of kings called Louis and Charles being replaced by other highborn men who had seemingly more exotic names. This would not mean that the whole social order crashed out of Gramscian 'normal times' of 'submission and intellectual subordination' into 'abnormal times' where all that was solid dissolved into air.[2] The slow dissolution of the Carolingian dynasty and its empire was a crisis in political hegemony for various elites but did not in itself necessarily affect the basic social structures of that empire. Nor was dynastic change always as big a deal for contemporaries as it has been for historians keen to parcel up the past into periods. The 1002 succession of Henry II to Otto III in the German kingdom has been seen by modern historians as a break, since Henry was from a side-line of the Ottonian dynasty. But Henry's biographer Bishop Adalbold of Utrecht was not only undisturbed by this, he also glided over any unpleasantness associated with Carolingian disappearances in 888 and 911 by highlighting Henry's descent from Charlemagne himself.[3] Great institutions were inclined to stress their glorious continuity rather than to try and fit modern periodizations and caesuras; the twelfth-century *Deeds of the Archbishops of Magdeburg* proudly traced Magdeburg's origins and progress from the time of Julius Caesar to Charlemagne and Otto I. The eleventh-century chronicle of Hermann of Reichenau followed late ninth-century guides such as Regino and the *Annals of Fulda* and duly noted the upheavals of 888 and the fact that the death of Louis the Child in 911 marked the end of the royal line 'in our lands' (East Francia). But Hermann's vision and coverage of history were not a simple mirror of our categories, though we may glimpse reflections. And it should be remembered that not all history writing was on the grand scale of Hermann's; fragmentary knowledge, terse entries and a small community of under twenty monks are features of the historical work in the monastery of Rheinau on the upper Rhine in the early tenth century.[4]

Perhaps the various endings of the Carolingian empire south and north of the Alps were not a world-historical happening around which periods can still be organized. After all, the post-Carolingian world saw the creative formation of new kingdoms and territories in a Europe bigger than that ruled by Charlemagne's family. And tenth-century Europe itself can look rather small as global history catches imaginations and medieval Europe can be provincialized and diversified.[5] It is no accident that there has been a recent flurry of work on Islamic presences in post-Carolingian Europe.[6]

The disappearance of older master-narratives of this period such as, for example, the birth of France and/or Germany is surely liberating. The history of such master-narratives, however, remains important, not least because nationalisms are far from dead in contemporary Europe and elsewhere. It is thus certainly worth historians' while to detect and analyse the modern-era potency of myths of the Spanish 'Reconquista', or of Irish culture's fate at viking hands, to name just two enlightening examples.[7] Such analyses show that historians have not been innocent figures here. And the work of older generations of medieval historians tends to be best known and understood by later generations of medieval historians. But for medievalists to write about the modern era can be a daunting challenge, and how important is such older medieval scholarship in modern culture?

What follows is not so much an argument as a series of reflections on some aspects of the work of some medievalists whose research on some aspects of the post-Carolingian world can be profitably put under the interrogating spotlight of the previous paragraph. My coverage is partial and focuses on the work that I myself know through my own academic specialization. Other perspectives would present different pictures. But the existence of differing perspectives, and what can be revealed by exposing them, shifting between them, juxtaposing them, is precisely my point here. I focus, first, on the lives of some scholars and, secondly, on the lives of some medieval texts.

Scholarship in life and texts

For an era that did not produce a biographical best-seller to match Einhard's *Life of Charlemagne*, the post-Carolingian kingdoms have inspired a remarkable series of modern biographies.[8] Modern biographers of medieval figures face even more severe challenges of sources, concepts and methodology than their modernist counterparts. But all historical biographers are haunted by questions of validity and approach (how can a random life-span be a historical period? how to relate an individual to a wider field of forces? etc.). And while an earlier generation of medievalist biographers evoked writers such as Jacob Burckhardt or W.H. Auden as critical spirits for a biographer to placate or agree with, more recent scholarship has to face down the spectres of Anthony Giddens or Pierre Bourdieu and his sombre warnings on the biographical illusion.[9] Such biographers proceed by invoking such figures partly to exorcise them, partly to recruit them for ever more sophisticated approaches to biography which can critically consider agency, contemporaries' categories and expectations, etc., within a critical historical framework. Biographies necessarily tend to bring questions of agency into sharp focus and to highlight change over time, key aspects of historical analysis. And biographies of kings (and queens) can map onto medieval categories of authority and regnal structure, so we can read them with a clear intellectual conscience.[10]

Historiography here is not a zero-sum game; writing biographies does not prevent other kinds of historical analysis from being produced. And personal elements are not exclusive to biographies. A recent biography of Cnut argues for the king in England having a substantial entourage of Scandinavian warriors in attendance upon him; the evidence for this includes the startling image of the hero Sigurd and a savage wolf visible in a surviving fragment of a large stone frieze from the Old Minster complex in Winchester. The biographical spotlight on Cnut widens here to include his followers and indeed the culture of his Scandinavian homeland, and does so by pursuing a set of sources (skaldic verse, stone carvings) that feature material absent from the conventional narrative sources. The individual figure of Cnut is placed in a broad cultural context that in turn makes the distinctive nature of his court in England more sharply clear. Conversely, a more institutional perspective can draw on biographical, in the sense of personal, elements. For example, Cnut's Scandinavian-ness is also an active presence in Patrick Wormald's massive history of early medieval law where it stands in the way of attempts by sophisticated Anglo-Saxon prelates to limit feud: '[Archbishop Wulfstan of York] might have needed more than his formidable rhetorical powers to persuade his new royal master amid his Scandinavian entourage of the illegitimacy of kin-vengeance'.[11]

Cnut functions here as a piece of Danish/Scandinavian grit that affects the smooth running of Anglo-Saxon legal machinery. But if the legal history and the biography both stress the personal importance of Cnut, they both also rely on ideas and assumptions about identity: as a Scandinavian, Cnut was bound to be pro-feud and fully conversant with stories of Sigurd and the wolf. Varieties of cultural distinctiveness were indeed a prominent feature of the post-Carolingian world, as they had been in Carolingian Europe, and indeed in the Roman empire; Europe had to be Europeanized. But the identity of Cnut and his culture(s) was not necessarily as stable or as easily marked out as it can appear in studies such as these.[12] Of course identity and difference mattered, and could flare up into violence and conflict as in the St Brice's day massacre of 1002 when king Aethelred 'ordered to be slain all the Danish men who were in England'. Savage killings of targeted people followed, but this was not a massacre of all Danes simply because they were Danes; the victims may have been mercenaries, or new settlers; this horrific event was not about simply marking off Anglo-Saxons from Danes. And heroic figures such as Sigurd were internationally renowned; the eleventh-century author of the *Quedlinburg Annals* included in her Latin world-chronicle stories of Ermanric, Theoderic and Attila that were the stuff of sagas; Ermanric and Theoderic appear allusively in the late tenth-century Anglo-Saxon poem *Deor*; Wayland the smith is mentioned in the 'Germanic' *Deor* but he also appears in the (probably) Alfredian Old English prose Boethius in one of the 'riffs' on the original sixth-century Latin.[13] Such connections and contexts do not mean that the Winchester Sigurd loses its own distinctiveness when viewed against such a background. But when historical identity comes into our focus it can be harder to see.

Medieval rulers bulked large in the consciousness of (some) contemporaries. Their solemn gaze drills into our own eyes from the covers of their biographies piled up on bookshop tables. Perhaps rather more surprising is the presence of biographies of modern medieval historians, as even a writer of one such seems to think: 'the lives of scholars are seldom stuff for engrossing reading'.[14] And yet there are biographies, quite well-known ones, of, e.g., Marc Bloch, Eileen Power, Percy Ernst Schramm (over 600 pages), Ernst Kantorowicz, Steven Runciman (over 700 pages!). There is also a surprisingly large number of essay-length biographical-intellectual sketches, studies, obituaries of prominent medievalists of the nineteenth and twentieth centuries.[15] Some of the subjects of these biographies had themselves written about their own life and times. Marc Bloch did not write a biography of any medieval figure but did write a brief, cold-eyed memoir of his military service in 1939–40 that was also a wider anatomy of French defeat, though he did not publish this in his lifetime. Schramm's study of Otto III was not really a biography, but he did publish a massive history of his own family that was also a study of his native Hamburg.[16] Georges Duby wrote an account of his own intellectual and scholarly life, an example of the *égo-histoire* in vogue at the time.[17]

Such biographies raise some questions. Are medievalists the best people to write such accounts of figures who are themselves modern? And in this biographical field what exactly was the relation of life to work, and of life and work to the surrounding culture? In fact, the biographies of Bloch and Power were produced by modern historians, surely a good thing; professional medievalists might not always be convincing in sketching the context of the modern world. Medievalists, however, might hear some historiographical and cultural resonances more clearly. Of course, some medievalists can write about the modern era with the same sure touch and impressive erudition that characterizes their 'real' research.[18] Nonetheless, the modern period is not really our *Fach*. The two questions posed at the start of this paragraph are really one problem: why should we, as medievalists, read (or write) biographies of medievalists, what do we hope to get out of them that we can't from the works of the scholars themselves and our existing knowledge of the historiographical context, which is itself a cultural context?

98 Stuart Airlie

For medievalists, some aspects of these historians' lives are less fertile, not to say less appealing or interesting than others. Robert Lerner, for example, in his splendid biography of Kantorowicz labours mightily to explain the potency of the cult of the poet Stefan George under whose mystical thrall Kantorowicz, like many other distinguished figures, willingly fell. The cult, with its centre and members seemingly simultaneously self-denying and self-adoring, and the poetry are very hard to take now. George looks now like one of these figures whose status in a past culture makes some of its values and judgements almost impossible to comprehend, a sort of German Gracie Fields or George Formby. Lerner duly invokes awe-struck tributes to George from Weimar luminaries such as Walter Benjamin, though the biographical focus means that he does not have space to engage with Benjamin's (all too understandable) ambivalence about the poet. The fact that figures on the left, such as Benjamin and Rosa Luxemburg, could also fall under the spell of George and his poetry tells us something of its cultural importance for contemporaries. But a biographical approach cannot afford to move too far horizontally into the culture around its central figure.[19] The biographical approach tends to be linear. George had an important role as an impetus and an atmosphere for Kantorowicz's writing of his sensational biography of Frederick II. If we are interested in this part of Kantorowicz's life and work, we should be interested in George. We do not now tend to read Kantorowicz's study of Frederick to understand the thirteenth century; we read it, and write about it in order to understand Kantorowicz, and the twentieth century better.[20]

Frederick II himself and his incarnation in Kantorowicz's 1927 biography seem rather distant from the post-Carolingian world. But Kantorowicz wrote much more than this and he occupies an honoured place in sober bibliographies on, say, key images of sacred Christian kingship in the Ottonian and Anglo-Saxon kingdoms, where his 1957 analysis of the figure of Otto III in the Aachen Gospels remains 'a foundational if problematic text' in the study of this ruler image.[21] But this too can carry us to some of the stormier currents of twentieth-century thought. In his thoughtful study of ruler images of the Ottonian and Salian periods, Ludger Körntgen places Kantorowicz's study of this image as part of the critique of nineteenth-century concepts and terminology of the bourgeois liberal state which had held scholarly sway as timeless attributes of the state per se but which could, and should, be attacked as anachronistic. Körntgen does not say so explicitly, but this critique of bourgeois liberal assumptions about the state had been made, not just by historians, but also by a dark master of political and legal thinking in the 1920s and 1930s who countered liberal assumptions with the concept of political theology, Carl Schmitt. In the past few decades, Schmitt's work has passed from sinister obscurity to spotlit prominence and whereas Lerner snorts with a biographer's contempt at efforts to link Schmitt and Kantorowicz, scholars of political thought and philosophy have found it immensely fruitful to combine these two figures' ideas on 'political theology' and the legitimation of the state.[22]

All this takes us away from biography. Schmitt and Kantorowicz were both working in 1920s Germany (though *The King's Two Bodies* was written later, and in the USA), but that environment is not what much current medievalist scholarship focuses on. That focus is the thought, the work, rather than the life. The individual life of scholars can dissolve into broader themes; for example, Schramm's disturbing relationship with institutions of Nazi-era Germany can be illuminating for study of academic culture in that period and possibly for an assessment of Schramm's own *oeuvre* and significance.[23] Or the life and work of the historian can be sliced up, with particular themes and episodes selected for their ability to illuminate historiographical concerns. Rather than a full biography by a single author, collections of thematic essays can assess what still has value in the work of great scholars of the past or can take that work in new directions.[24]

And yet it is not always easy, or profitable, for historians to divorce the work from the life. Hans-Hennig Kortüm has recently examined an episode in the life of Otto Brunner who visited Berlin in January 1945 to give a lecture on Otto I's victory over the Hungarians at the Lech in 955. Kortüm deftly sketches the setting of bomb-shattered Berlin but does not seek to work at the level of biographical anecdote. Brunner died in 1982 but his work, for example on feud, remains of active value, and his historiographical influence remains strong. His eagerness to demonstrate his commitment to Nazi Germany in its death-throes is a stark example of the willingness of intellectual talent and expert scholarship to serve squalid regimes. This is what scholars' commitment to public engagement can look like and this is what Kortüm examines. He puts Brunner's lecture in the context of a series given in that winter at Berlin University on 'times of trial' (*Bewährungsstunden*) an expression that surely fits into that public discourse of the Nazi era catalogued by Viktor Klemperer as the *Lingua Tertii Imperii*. These lectures dealt with desperately catastrophic/triumphant battles against threateningly foreign hordes (Thermopylae/Marathon, Attila the Hun, Turks at Vienna). While Brunner railed against liberal-bourgeois tendencies to see the past in the light of the present, his lecture recruited Otto I for the long history of a German destiny culminating in the Third Reich.[25]

What matters to us, however, are the ideas. To place an episode of Brunner's career in its Nazi context may actually make such scholarship seem safely distant and remote. Biography may result in an antiquarian freezing of a scholar in the past; that is why Kortüm's approach was not primarily biographical. But the work of such scholars did not stop in 1945 and it is how that developed in the post-war world that needs scrutiny. Part of the power and interest of Brunner's work is his stress on the difference of the Middle Ages from the modern world, and his (vested) interest in long term developments. Here again, the connection with Schmitt is active, not least in its rejection of modern 'bourgeois liberal' assumptions about an essential identity of the state that can be back-projected onto the Middle Ages in unhelpfully anachronistic ways. Brunner also engaged with Schmitt's views on the friend-foe distinction as the hallmark of the (pre-modern) political community which led him to see no distinction between war and feud. This kind of thinking can have a problematic historiographical and conceptual legacy on the level of points of detail (blurring differences between private and public war in the Ottonian kingdom) as

100 Stuart Airlie

well as on the broader level of how we conceptualize the nature of royal rule in the Ottonian realm. Once we grasp the way that the shadow of the Schmitt-Brunner conceptualization of the 'state' (dissolved into a set of 'Germanic' communities of warriors bound by ties of lordship, not something separate from society,) falls over the historiography, we can better grasp what was at stake in the debates over *Staatlichkeit* in the 1990s and after.[26]

Such a perspective reveals what can look like very inward-looking historiographical debates (and could there be a more quintessentially German medieval historiographical debate than the work on *Staatlichkeit*?) as part of much broader and more resonant arguments about political cultures. This is not to deny the intrinsic interest of the biographical approach within current historiography; a biography of Kantorowicz turns out to be a page-turner. But what matters, what makes these figures of more than antiquarian interest, is if the problems exposed by biography, by the problematic nature of the life, mark the work and if that work itself is still alive. Schramm's connections with the Hitler era have attracted scholarly attention precisely from this angle. But Schramm's life was not confined to the Nazi era. Schramm's youthful encounter in Hamburg with the extraordinary art historian Aby Warburg mattered immensely to him and the impact of Warburg gives us a potentially important way of getting a sharper sense of Schramm's own work on images and objects; and of modern work on objects.[27] The imposing rows of older scholarship in institutional libraries should not all be destined to be reshelved in some basement annex. A motto above such shelves could be James Campbell's provocative verdict on the seemingly outmoded ideas of William Stubbs (d.1901): 'Stubbs's ideas belong not so much to the well-appointed zoo which students of intellectual history keep, but rather to the jungle of real debate, in which they are active and can bite'.[28]

Texts in the life of scholarship

Historiographies matter: 'There is medieval German history because there have been and are modern German historians'.[29] But amidst set agendas and categories, we as historians can pick and choose, and can shape and argue for changes in interest and focus. Examining shifts in gender roles and identities offers new perspectives on the transformation of the Roman world as well as on the transformation of the Carolingian world. Stilicho might interest us now less as a figure of mixed Roman and barbarian 'blood' than as an example of a general pattern of elite secular masculinity becoming more military, a form of identity becoming ever more marked in the transition to the early medieval west.[30] A focus on gender, particularly but not exclusively on social roles of women, is already revealing new pictures of changes around 1000 in the west.[31] If we are looking to shake up set historiographical patterns, new perspectives and concepts play a vital role here.

But in anatomizing historiographies, we should look at the source base on which they rest. It is admittedly a bit strained to follow a section on biographies of individuals by suggesting that sources have biographies. Scholars do know, however, that manuscripts have (after)lives and that this is part of their historical significance.[32] Some sources, particular types and genres as well as certain individual texts and objects, etc., can act as main characters in certain historiographies. This has all sorts of consequences. Paul Fouracre has argued that attempts to compare lord-serf relations across the Carolingian era into the eleventh century must confront the fact that 'we cannot compare like with like here. We have no cases from the Carolingian period that are as detailed or localized as our Marmoutier material'.[33] There may well therefore be some benefit in bringing separate historiographies together and juxtaposing them to shed light on each other, not to flatten them out, but precisely to expose their differences and the foundations (and assumptions) on which such differences depend.

One manageable way to do this is by looking at roles key sources play in their own historiographical theatre of debate. Here I offer a brief example. The first document is an 'official' report on an enquiry, an inquest held in Rižana in Istria in 802 to deal with misgovernment by patriarch Fortunatus of Grado-Aquileia and, more specifically, by duke John; Charlemagne's *missi* recorded the complaints of 172 local notables and brokered a resolution of the disputes. The second is a much less official looking account, from the 1020s, of the complaint of the castellan Hugh of Lusignan that he could not obtain justice from his lord, duke William V of Aquitaine; it gives vivid details of violence and harassment in Poitou.[34] They are very different kinds of document and comparing them is, of course, problematic. As we have seen, Fouracre has warned that the failure to compare like with like has not been helpful for efforts to define and understand the differences between Carolingian and post-Carolingian society. And Jennifer Davis, while discussing the 802 Istria report, has recently reminded us of the positive value of comparison within the same genre for detecting silence and weighing its significance.[35]

These documents are indeed different from each other, and while that may in fact be part of their appeal, in one area they are very similar indeed. Each of them has become historiographically significant, one might say emblematic in their worlds (Carolingian: well governed; post-Carolingian: violently chaotic). The Istria case plays an increasingly prominent role in surveys of Carolingian government; we can see something of its representative function in the fact that it is the only contemporary source deemed important enough to be fully translated in Philippe Depreux's admirable survey of early medieval social history. Hugh of Lusignan is also called on to speak for his era; his complaint is one of the four documents on the theme of lords and vassals translated in a source collection compiled by Patrick Geary; it features prominently in surveys of violence and anarchy in the era of feudal revolution.[36] This is significant in itself. And it means that they can be made to look quite different from how they normally appear if we bathe them in the light of a different historical perspective. From his vantage point in eleventh-century Marmoutier, Paul Fouracre is able to see that, while the Istria inquest does show 'public authority intervening to protect people against lords', we can 'also find that there are complaints about officials abusing their powers, so that the "state" appears in effect to be both protecting and abusing the people under its care. ...

The catalogue of oppressions would not have looked out of place in any account of eleventh-century "evil customs".' Conversely, Dominique Barthélemy, looking at Hugh's complaint through Carolingian spectacles, finds in it a continuity of terms, values and practices from the Carolingian era.[37]

I do not mean to suggest that everything stayed the same, and that we should abandon any quest for post-Carolingian transformations. Far from it. But these valuable correctives by Fouracre and Barthélemy may remind us how the self-reinforcing weight of historiography, i.e., our own expertise in a particular field can become *déformation professionelle*. Shaking up the historiographical framework can thus be a worthwhile exercise. Juxtaposing these two texts may not quite fulfil Lautréamont's dream ('as beautiful as the chance meeting of a sewing-machine and an umbrella on an operating table') but can help us escape the gravitational pull of historiographical master-narratives (Carolingian order; 'feudal' disorder) while still contemplating them.

My comparison of these documents will not be systematic. This is partly because of limits of my own abilities but also in homage to Susan Reynolds' warning against the seductions of a certain kind of systematic analysis: 'Of the trio, word, concept and phenomenon, the least significant for the historian of society is the word'. Looking at the term *convenientia*, for example, common to both documents, may not actually get us very far.[38]

What does an innocent eye see here? First, of course, documents. The inquest is a formal document, opening with an invocation of God and closing with subscriptions and details on the scribe. The *Conventum* is much less formally opened and closed, and in its content it seems overwhelmingly 'oral' (speeches, conversations) contrasting sharply with the *breves* referred to in the inquest. The inquest, however, also contains spoken statements (and they strike Stefan Esders as faithful to the speakers). And the *Conventum*, for all its orality, is itself a document, a fact that obviously mattered to contemporaries, even if we don't know precisely how it mattered.[39]

The records featured in the Inquest form part of a deeper past than that evoked in the *Conventum*. The Inquest refers back to 'the time of the Greeks', to the time of the '*magister militum* of the Greeks', to the time of 'Constantine and Basilius', etc. This stems from the particular historical developments of Istria, its Byzantine past. The *Conventum* very much inhabits the present with the past tending to appear only in immediate relation to the text's actors (a smaller group than in the Inquest) such as Hugh's father and uncles.[40] Here, however, the manuscript of the *Conventum* is interesting; it is preserved in an eleventh-century manuscript, probably written a couple of decades after the event, which also includes the Chronicle of Ademar of Chabannes and (part of) Einhard's *Vita Karoli*. Contemporaries could associate this seemingly journalistic text with a deeper past. In contrast, the 'imperial' document on Istria only comes down to us in an early modern copy.[41]

Both documents, in their concern to reach and record agreement in the present over wrongs of the past, look to a future. This is apparent in their concern with promises, with pledges (*Inquest*) and hostages (*Conventum*). But the future is also familial. In Istria, if bad duke John or his heirs or agents go on to commit more oppression, they are to pay the fines established by the *missi*.[42] In Poitou, duke William pledges that he and his son will keep faith. This is part of a familial concept and practice of office that is, if anything, more pronounced in the ninth-century Inquest than in the eleventh-century *Conventum*. In ninth-century Istria duke John is all too ably assisted in his wickedness by his sons, his daughters and his son-in-law.[43] This is hardly surprising but it is good for us to be reminded of a noble family's grip in the world of Carolingian public institutions. The explicit references to the duke's daughters are striking, not least because women are otherwise absent from the text. In the *Conventum*, women do appear: Hugh's wife is besieged in a fortress and this is important for Hugh. Women also appear as units (merely passive?) in a gift-exchange of favour, of networks and alliance, etc.[44]

The key actors are men and both documents let us hear the voice of the lords. The *Conventum*'s Count William speaks untrammelled wilful lordship in his response to Hugh's pleas: 'Don't expect me to do anything for you in this affair. If all the world were mine, I would not give you as much as I could hold on the tip of my finger'. But William also says more reasonable things; this response is not typical and it turns out to be a high (or low) point on the path towards a settlement. The lords in the ninth-century Inquest are much calmer. Patriarch Fortunatus disarms everyone with his reasonableness and even duke John admits that he has made a mistake in exploiting forests and meadows. The nature of that mistake is, however, intriguing. He had not exploited these resources out of lordly wilfulness but precisely because he had thought that they were 'public' ('*ego credidi quod a parte domini imperatoris in publico esse debeant*'). Lordly oppressiveness did not need the 'public' to collapse before it could get to work.[45] Both texts tell stories. The Carolingian inquest tells a story of, and results from, not only communal power (the anger against bad duke John) but also strong lordship (Charlemagne, all-seeing through his *missi*). The *Conventum* does not tell of a formless world; its stubborn repetition of key terms in the narrative of complaint points to the importance of oral confrontation, but the text overall narrates a vivid story of bad lordship.[46]

We could go further into these documents, observing more closely how they present and understand redress, how they present ceremony, and what they say about places, about palaces, fortresses, etc. But I hope that this solo workshop of an innocent eye has given some sense of what a simple comparison can yield. I have tried to avoid confining these documents to their fixed historiographical frames in the hope that we can get away from these frames but also hoping that we can get a more critical handle on them too. We cannot ignore them entirely, nor have I tried to do so; my eye is not completely innocent. But we have a range of frames of reference. If we step outside the contrast of Carolingian-public-realm-working-well vs-feudal-anarchy-trying-to-self-regulate we could choose other historiographical perspectives.

I have tried in this paper to indicate how historiographical perspectives can close off some views even as they open up others. That range of perspectives can be dizzying, but that actually makes the sheer amount to read and study less daunting, and the views more open.[47]

Notes

1 Regino, *Chronicon*, a.888, ed. F. Kurze, MGH SRG 50 (Hannover, 1890), pp. 129–30 and Adalbert, *Continuatio Reginonis*, a. 911, ed. F. Kurze, in same volume, p. 155; Richer of Saint-Rémi, *Histories*, Prologue, and Book 4, c.11, ed. and trans. Justin Lake (Cambridge, MA and London: Harvard University Press, 2011), 2 vols, 1, pp. 2–5, and 2, pp. 218–23. Simon MacLean, 'The Carolingian Past in post-Carolingian Europe', in *'The Making of Europe'. Essays in Honours of Rob Bartlett*, ed. J. Hudson and S. Crumplin (Leiden: Brill, 2016), pp. 11–31.

2 Steven Lukes, *Power: A Radical View*, (Houndsmills and New York: Palgrave Macmillan, 2nd edition, 2005), pp. 48–52. But cf. Chris Wickham, *Medieval Europe* (New Haven and London: Yale University Press, 2016), pp. 78–9. For a fresh perspective, with a view of Carolingian historical writing as much more than merely dynastic in its focus, see Geoffrey Koziol, 'The Future of History After Empire', in this volume.

3 Bernd Schneidmüller, 'Otto III – Henrich II. Wende der Königsherrschaft oder Wende der Mediaevistik?' in *Otto III.-Heinrich II. Eine Wende?* ed. B. Schneidmüller and S. Weinfurter (Stuttgart: Thorbecke, 2nd edition, 2000), pp. 9–46.

4 *Gesta Archiepiscoporum Magdeburgensium*, c.1, 2, 3 and 4, MGH SS 14, pp. 376–7. Hermann, *Chronicon*, a.888, a.911, MGH SS 4, pp. 109–110, p. 112; Hans-Werner Goetz, 'Das Geschichts- und Weltbild der Chronik Hermanns von Reichenau', in *Hermann der Lahme. Reichenauer Mönch und Universalgelehrter des 11. Jahrhunderts*, ed. F. Henzer, T. Zotz, H.-P. Schmidt (Stuttgart: W. Kohlhammer Verlag, 2016), 87–131 (89–92, 100–5, 121–30). Roland Zingg, 'Geschichtsbewusstsein im Kloster Rheinau im 10. Jahrhundert. Der Codex Modoetiensis f-9/176, die Annales Laubacenses und die Annales Alamannici', *Deutsches Archiv für Erforschung des Mittelalters* 69 (2013), pp. 479–502 (489–93, 499–502).

5 Björn Weiler, 'Tales of First Kings and the Culture of Kingship in the West, c. 1050-ca.1200', *Viator* 46.2 (2015), 101–27; Patrick J. Geary, *Writing History. Identity. Conflict and Memory in the Middle Ages*, ed. Florin Curta and Cristina Spinei (Bucharest: Editura Academiei Romane, Muzeul Brailei Editura Istros, 2012), pp. 279–89; Michael Borgolte, 'A Crisis of the Middle Ages? Deconstructing and Constructing European Identities in a Globalized World', in *The Making of Medieval History*, ed. G.A. Loud and M. Staub (Woodbridge and Rochester: York University Press and Boydell Press, 2017), 70–84.

6 Scott G. Bruce, *Cluny and the Muslims of La Garde-Freinet* (Ithaca: Cornell University Press, 2015); Mohammed Ballan, 'Fraxinetum: an Islamic frontier state in tenth-century Provence', *Comitatus: A Journal of Medieval and Renaissance Studies* 41 (2010), pp. 23–76; Klaus Herbers, *Europa: Christen und Muslime in Kontakt und Konfrontation. Italien und Spanien im langen 9. Jahrhundert* (Stuttgart: Franz Steiner Verlag, 2016); the new edition of the *Life of John of Gorze* devotes a substantial part of its Introduction to John's embassy to Cordoba, *Die Geschihcte des Lebens des Johannes, Abt des Klosters Gorze*, ed. and trans. Peter Christian Jacobsen, MGH SRG 81 (Wiesbaden: Harrassowitz Verlag, 2016), pp. 39–72. Also relevant here is William Blanc and Christophe Naudin, *Charles Martel et la bataille de Poitiers* (Paris: Libertalia, 2015).

7 Peter Linehan, *History and the Historians of Medieval Spain* (Oxford: Clarendon Press, 1993), at, e.g., pp. 206–7. Poul Holm, 'Between Apathy and Antipathy: The Vikings in Irish and Scandinavian History', *Peritia* 8 (1994), 151–69; Ruth Johnson, 'Mind the gap: the supposed hiatus in Irish art of the tenth century', in *The Vikings in Ireland and Beyond: Before and after the Battle of Clontarf* (Dublin: Four Courts Press, 2015), pp. 206–30.

8 A few examples: Gerd Althoff, *Otto III*, translated P.G. Jestice (University Park, PA: Pennsylvania State University Press, 2003), originally published in 1996 as part of the series *Gestalten des Mittelalters und der Renaissance*; Herwig Wolfram, *Conrad II 990-1039*, translated D. A. Kaiser (University Park, PA: Pennsylvania State University Press, 2006). Sarah Foot, *Aethelstan* (New Haven and London: Yale University Press, 2011); Levi Roach, *Aethelred the Unready* (New Haven and London: Yale University Press, 2016); Timothy Bolton, *Cnut the Great* (New Haven and London: Yale University Press, 2017). Pauline Stafford, *Queen Emma and Queen Edith* (Oxford: Blackwell, 1997).

9 Foot, *Aethelstan*, pp. 1–9; Roach, *Aethelred*, pp. 16–7 and cf. Knut Görich, 'Versuch zur Rettung von Kontingenz', *Frühmittelalterliche Studien* 43 (2009), 179–97 (179–84) and Knut Görich, *Friedrich Barbarossa. Eine Biographie* (Munich: C.H. Beck, 2014), p. 21; Bolton, *Cnut*, pp. 6–9 refers to Virginia Woolf and Orson Welles. Wolfram, *Conrad* II, pp. xii-xix. Michael Clanchy turns to W.H. Auden and Cole Porter to evoke Peter Abelard's reputation, *Abelard. A Medieval Life* (Oxford: Blackwell, 1997), p. 22, p. 329. For some of the standard academic objections to the genre, Ludmilla Jordanova, *The Practice of History* (London: Hodder Arnold, 2nd edition, 2006), 45–7.

10 Simon Dixon, *Catherine the Great* (Harlow: Longman, 2001), chapter 1. The importance of Eileen Power's 'biography' of Bodo the peasant is acknowledged in Chris Wickham, *Framing the Early Middle Ages* (Oxford: Oxford University Press, 2005), p. 405 (and Bodo makes it into the index).

11 Bolton, *Cnut*, pp. 176–82. Patrick Wormald, *The Making of English Law: King Alfred to the Twelfth Century* (Oxford: Blackwell, 1999), p. 364.

12 Classic here is Robert Bartlett, *The Making of Europe* (London: Allen Lane Penguin, 1993) and see also *'The Making of Europe'. Essays in Honours of Rob Bartlett*, ed. J. Hudson and S. Crumplin (Leiden: Brill, 2016); another classic is G. Woolf, *Becoming Roman. The Origins of Provincial Civilization in Gaul* (Cambridge: Cambridge University Press, 1998). See relevant reviews of Bolton's *Cnut* by J. Peltzer, *Francia* (2017) online and by A. Hicklin, *Journal of British Studies* 57.1 (2018), pp. 144–6.

13 Anglo-Saxon Chronicle, a.1002, in *English Historical Documents I, c.500–1042*, ed. Dorothy Whitelock (London: Eyre Methuen, 2nd edition, 1979), pp. 238–9; Roach, *Aethelred*, pp. 187–200. *Annales Quedlinburgenses*, ed. M. Giese MGH SRG 72 (Hannover, 2004), pp. 410–11, and see Giese's Introduction, pp. 101–21. Barbara Yorke, 'King Alfred and Weland: Tradition and Transformation at the Court of King Alfred', in *Transformations in Anglo-Saxon Culture. Toller Lectures on Art, Archaeology and Text*, ed. Charles Insley and Gale R. Owen-Crocker (Oxford and Philadelphia: Oxbow Books, 2017), 47–69 (p. 51).

14 Robert A. Lerner, *Ernst Kantorowicz. A Life* (Princeton: Princeton University Press, 2017), p. 3.

15 Carole Fink, *Marc Bloch. A Life in History* (Cambridge: Cambridge University Press, 1989) (Olivier Dumoulin, *Marc Bloch* (Paris: Presses de Sciences Po, 2000) is a rather different approach); Maxine Berg, *A Woman in History: Eileen Power, 1889–1940* (Cambridge: Cambridge University Press, 1996); David Thimme, *Percy Ernst Schramm und das Mittelalter* (Göttingen: Vandenhoeck und Rupprecht, 2006); Lerner, *Kantorowicz*; Minoo Dinshaw, *Outlandish Knight. The Byzantine Life of Steven Runciman* (London: Allen Lane Penguin, 2016). See also, for example, *Medieval Scholarship. Biographical Studies on the Formation of a Discipline, Volume 1, History*, ed. Helen Damico and Joseph B. Zavadi (New York and London: Garland Publishing, 1995), as well as *Interpreters of Early Medieval Britain*, ed. Michael Lapidge (Oxford: Oxford University Press for the British Academy, 2002), *Women Medievalists and the Academy*, ed. Jane Chance (Madison: University of Wisconsin Press, 2005), and the series *Rewriting the Middle Ages in the Twentieth Century*, published by Brill.

16 Marc Bloch, *Strange Defeat*, trans. G Hopkins (London: Oxford University Press, 1949); Marc Bloch, *Memoirs of War, 1914–15*, trans. C. Fink (Ithaca and London: Cornell University Press, 1969). Percy Ernst Schramm, *Neun Generationen: dreihundert Jahre deutscher Kulturgeschichte im Licht der Schicksale einer Hamburger Bürgerfamilie, 1648–1948* (Göttingen: Vandenhoeck and Ruprecht, 1963) 2 vols; Schramm's study of Hitler is also relevant here. I intend to explore Schramm's work more fully elsewhere.

17 Georges Duby, *L'Histoire Continue* (Paris: Éditions Odile Jacob, 1991).

18 Lerner's *Kantorowicz* is surely a convincing example. Hans-Werner Goetz's historiographical mastery remains impressive, see, for example, his 'Geschichtswissenschaft in Hamburg im Dritten Reich', in R. Nicolaysen and A. Schildt, eds, *100 Jahre Geschichtswissenschaft in Hamburg* (Berlin and Hamburg, 2011), pp. 103–60; and see also O. G. Oexle, *Die Gegenwart des Mittelalters* (Berlin: Akademie Verlag, 2013).

106   Stuart Airlie

19 Benjamin: Lerner, *Kantorowicz*, p. 82; and see H. Eiland and M. W. Jennings. *Walter Benjamin. A Critical Life* (Cambridge, MA. and London: Belknap Press, 2014), pp. 147–8, 407–8, but note that the Kantorowicz referred to on pp. 497–8 is misidentified as Ernst when it is surely Alfred Kantorowicz. Luxemburg: G. Adler, P. Hudis, A. Laschitza, eds, *The Letters of Rosa Luxemburg*, trans. G. Shriver (London and New York: Verso, 2011), p. 456. On George, M. S. Lane and M.A. Ruehl, eds, *A Poet's Reich. Politics and Culture in the George Circle* (Rochester: Camden House, 2011).

20 See, for example, Martin Ruehl, 'In this time without emperors: the politics of Ernst Kantorowicz's *Kaiser Friedrich der Zweite* reconsidered', *Journal of the Warburg and Courtauld Institutes* 63 (2000), pp. 187–242; Conrad Leyser, 'Introduction' to Ernst Kantorowicz, *The King's Two Bodies: A Study in Medieval Political Theology* (Princeton and Oxford: Princeton University Press, 2016), pp. ix–xxiii.

21 Eliza Garrison, 'Otto III at Aachen', *Peregrinations: Journal of Medieval Art and Architecture* 3.1 (2010), pp. 83–137 (p. 92, n.7); see also, for example Henry Mayr-Harting, *Ottonian Book Illumination* (London: Harvey Miller, 1991) 2 vols, vol. 1, pp. 60–64; Catherine Karkov, *The Art of Anglo-Saxon England* (Woodbridge: Boydell, 2011), pp. 111–12.

22 Ludger Körntgen, *Königsherrschaft und Gottes Gnade* (Berlin: Akademie Verlag, 2001), pp. 161–77, particularly pp. 161–3; Lerner, *Kantorowicz*, p. 347. G. Agamben is an egregious example of the trend; but see Victoria Kahn, *The Future of Illusion: political theology and early modern texts* (Chicago: University of Chicago Press, 2014), and Leyser, 'Introduction'.

23 E. Garrison, 'Ottonian Art and Its Afterlife: Revisiting Percy Ernst Schramm's Portraiture Idea', *Oxford Art Journal* 32 (2009), pp. 205–22; J. L. Nelson, 'Why Re-inventing Medieval History is a Good Idea', in G. A. Loud and M. Staub, eds, *The Making of Medieval History* (York: York Medieval Press, 2017), pp. 17–36. For a suggestion that Schramm's writing up of the wartime diary of the German army recalls medieval annals, see W. Ernst, 'Die Insistenz der Annalistik', in O.B. Rader, ed., *Turbata per aequora mundi. Dankesgabe an Eckhard Müller-Mertens*, MGH Studien und Texte, 29 (Hannover: Hahnsche Buchhandkung, 2001), pp. 223–31.

24 See, for example, D. Rollason, C. Leyser and H. Williams (eds), *England and the Continent in the Tenth Century: Studies in Honour of Wilhelm Levison (1876–1947)* (Turnhout: Brepols, 2010); M. Becher and Y. Hen, eds, *Wilhelm Levison (1876–1947). Ein jüdisches Forscherleben zwischen wissenschaftlicher Anerkennung und politischem Exil* (Siegburg: Franz Schmitt Verlag – Respublica Verlag, 2010); H. Fuhrmann, *Sind eben alles Menschen gewesen. Gelehrtenleben im 19. und 20. Jahrhundert* (Munich: C. H. Beck, 1996).

25 Hans-Hennig Kortüm, 'Otto Brunner über Otto den Großen: aus den letzten Tagen der reichsdeutschen Mediävistik', *Historische Zeitschrift* 299 (2014), pp. 297–333.

26 Peter N. Miller, 'Nazis and Neo-Stoics: Otto Brunner and Gerhard Oestreich before and after the Second World War', *Past & Present* 176 (August 2002), pp. 144–86, especially pp. 151–2 on the need to look at these people's postwar scholarship and pp. 152–8 on Schmitt and Brunner. See, for example, O. Brunner, *Land and Lordship* (1992, translated from the fourth edition of 1959), pp. 31–5, 95–102. H.-H. Kortüm, 'Wissenschaft im Doppelpaß? Carl Schmitt, Otto Brunner und die Konstruktion der Fehde', *Historische Zeitschrift* 282.3 (2006), esp. pp. 592, 607–8, 610. Note that A. Krah sees the term civil war as 'terminologically problematic' in her review of D. S. Bachrach, *Warfare in Tenth-Century Germany* (Woodbrdige: The Boydell Press, 2012) in *Historische Zeitschrift* 299.2 (2014), p. 463. On *Staatlichkeit*, see W. Pohl and V. Wieser, eds, *Der Frühmittelalterliche Staat – Europäische Perspektiven* (Vienna: Verlag der Österreichishen Akademie der Wissenschaften, 2009).

27 Garrison, 'Ottonian Art'; and see Thimme, *Schramm*. On objects, see J. M. H. Smith, 'Rulers and Relics c.750-c.950: Treasure on Earth, Treasure in Heaven', in A. Walsham, ed., *Relics and Remains*, Past and Present Supplements (Oxford: Oxford University Press, 2010), pp. 73–96.

28 James Campbell, 'Epilogue', in *The Anglo-Saxons*, ed. James Campbell (Oxford: Phaidon, 1982), p. 244.

29 Timothy Reuter, *Germany in the Early Middle Ages 800–1056* (Harlow: Longman, 1991), p. 1.

30 G. Nathan, 'The Ideal Male in Late Antiquity: Claudian's example of Flavius Stlicho', *Gender & History* 271. (2015), pp. 10–27; C. Wickham, *The Inheritance of Rome. A History of Europe from 400 to 1000* (London: Allen Lane, 2009), pp. 105–7.

31 Judith M. Bennet and Ruth Mazo Karras, 'Women, Gender and Medieval Historians', in *The Oxford Handbook of Women and Gender in Medieval Europe*, ed. J. Bennet and R. Karras (Oxford: Oxford University Press, 2013), p. 14. See also M. McLaughlin, *Sex, Gender and Episcopal Authority in an Age of Reform, 1000–1122* (Cambridge: Cambridge University Press, 2010), with S. Airlie 'A View from Afar', in L. Körntgen and D. Waßenhoven, eds, *Religion und Politik im Mittelalter/Religion and Politics in the Middle Ages* (Berlin and Boston: De Gruyter, 2013), pp. 71–88, at pp. 85–8.

32 One relevant example here is Christopher De Hamel, *Meetings with Remarkable Manuscripts* (London: Allen Lane, Penguin Random House UK, 2016), pp. 188–231 on a tenth-century manuscript. The book's title echoes that of Gurdjieff's autobiography, *Meetings with Remarkable Men*, thus evoking biography.

33 Paul Fouracre, 'Marmoutier and its Serfs in the Eleventh Century', *Transactions of the Royal Historical Society*, 6th series, 15 (2005), 29–49 (p. 44, with pp. 43–4, 47).

34 New edition and German translation in Stefan Esders, 'Regionale Selbstbehauptung zwischen Byzanz und dem Frankenreich. Die *inquisitio* der Rechtsgewohnheiten Istriens durch die Sendboten Karls des Grossen und Pippins von Italien', in *Eid und Wahrheitssuche*, ed. Stefan Esders and Thomas Scharff (Frankfurt: Peter Lang, 1999), pp. 49–112 (pp. 53–64). Jane Martindale, '*Conventum inter Guliielmum Aquitanorum Comitem et Hugonem Chiliarchum*', *English Historical Review*, 84 (1969), 528–53 (p. 541–530); reprinted with same pagination in Jane Martindale, *Status, Authority and Regional Power. Aquitaine and France, 9th to 12th centuries* (Ashgate: Aldershot and Brookfield, 1997) as chapter VIIb.

35 Fouracre, 'Marmoutier', pp. 43–4, 47; Jennifer Davis, *Charlemagne's Practice of Empire* (Cambridge: Cambridge University Press, 2015), p. 115.

36 A brief sample here. Istria: Philippe Depreux, *Les sociétés occidentales* (Rennes: Les presses universitaires de Rennes, 2006), pp. 293–9 and see pp. 221–4; Janet L. Nelson, 'Charlemagne and Empire', in *The Long Morning of Medieval Europe*, ed. Jennifer Davis and Michael McCormick (Aldershot and Burlington: Ashgate, 2008), pp. 223–34; Wickham, *The Inheritance of Rome*, pp. 389–90; Davis, *Charlemagne's Practice*, pp. 274–8. Hugh: Patrick J. Geary, *Readings in Medieval History*, vol.1 (1992), pp. 363–8; George T. Beech, 'The lord/dependant (vassal) relationship: a case study from Aquitaine c.1030', *Journal of Medieval History* 24.1 (1998), 1–30; Thomas N. Bisson, *The Crisis of the Twelfth Century* (Princeton and Oxford: Princeton University Press, 2009), pp. 52–3; Warren Brown, *Violence in Medieval Europe* (Harlow: Longman, 2011), ch.4; Wickham, *Medieval Europe*, pp. 99–100.

37 Fouracre, 'Marmoutier', p. 43, n.42, and cf. Wickham, *Inheritance of Rome*, pp. 389–92. Dominique Barthélemy, 'Autour d'un récit de pactes (Conventum Hugonis): la seigneurie chatelaine et le féodalisme, en France au xiè siècle', in *Il Feudalesimo nell'alto Medioevo*, Settimane di studio del Centro Italiano di Studi sull'alto Medioevo, 47 (Spoleto, Presso la Sede del Centro, 2000), 2 vols, 1, pp. 447–89.

38 Susan Reynolds, *Fiefs and Vassals* (Oxford: Oxford University Press, 1994), p. 13; on the *convenientia* as a genre that conceals the nature of dispute settlement as well as revealing it, see Adam Kosto, *Making Agreements in Medieval Catalonia: power, order and the written word 1000–1200* (Cambridge: Cambridge University Press, 2001), pp. 21–2, 101–7.

39 *Inquisitio*, ed. Esders, p. 53, pp. 63–4; *breves*, pp. 54 63; statements, see, e.g., pp. 54–5, p. 62; and Esders' comments, pp. 97, 99ff. Jane Martindale, 'Dispute, settlement and orality in the *Conventum inter Guillelmum Aquitanorum comitem et Hugonem Chilarchum*: A Postscript to the edition of 1969', in Martindale, *Status*, as ch.VIII, pp. 1–36, and see p. 11 on *brevis* in the *Conventum*.

40 *Inquisitio*, ed. Esders, pp. 54, 57, 61, with Esders' comments, pp. 77–8. *Conventum*, ed. Martindale, p. 543 and 543a.

41 Martindale, '*Conventum*', pp. 538–9 (Paris, Bibliothèque Nationale, manuscript latin 5927); Matthias Tischler, *Einharts Vita Karoli: Studien zur Entstehung, Überlieferung and*

Rezeption, Schriften der MGH 48 (Hannover, Hahnsche Buchhandlung, 2001), 2 vols, 2, pp. 1273–1301. Esders, pp. 50–1.

42 *Inquisitio*, ed. Esders, pp. 62–3, and Esders' comments, pp. 103–6.

43 *Conventum*, ed. Martindale, p. 548, 548a; *Inquisitio*, ed. Esders, p. 59.

44 *Conventum*, ed. Martindale, pp. 545, 543a.

45 Martindale, *Conventum*, pp. 547, p. 547a; *Inquisitio*, ed. Esders, p. 62, and see Esders' comments, p. 104. Barthélemy, 'Autour d'un récit'.

46 Davis, *Charlemagne's Practice*, pp. 274–8; Stephen D. White, 'Stratégie rhétorique dans la *Conventio* de Hugues de Lusignan', in *Histoire et société. Mélanges offerts à Georges Duby, vol. II Le tenancier, le fidèle et le citoyen* (Aix en Provence: Publications de l'Université de Provence, 1992), pp. 148–57.

47 My thanks to the Berlin After Empire audience (and to the original Transformation of the Carolingian World meeting in Vienna where I tried out some of these ideas.) And to Sarah Greer and Alice Hicklin for their patience.

PART II

Inscribing memories

7

HOW CAROLINGIAN WAS EARLY MEDIEVAL CATALONIA?*

Matthias M. Tischler (Barcelona)
*In memory of Bernhard Bischoff (1906–1991)***

Carolingian culture in early medieval Catalonia

Two of the unanswered questions within twentieth- and twenty-first-century Carolingian Studies are the role that the peripheries of Charlemagne's Empire played in its culture and religion, and what position these so-called *marcae* could establish in the Europe-wide network of knowledge transfer. These problems open up another unanswered question: what role did the Carolingian Spanish March (Catalonia) and its manuscripts play in the history of Europe-wide dissemination of the Carolingian minuscule and text culture since the ninth century onwards? To answer these questions, I will focus on central criteria of Carolingian culture such as the Carolingian script, religious texts of Benedictine and canonical life, the Bible and Homiliaries.

The Carolingian minuscule in early medieval Catalonia

Perhaps the most visible presence of Carolingian culture in early medieval Catalonia is seen in the diffusion of its cultural techniques and achievements, such as the dissemination of writing the new Carolingian minuscule in the Hispanic border region. Since the ninth century, this new script was a distinct feature separating the Northeast from the rest of the Iberian Peninsula. A closer look at Bernhard

---

* Prof. Dr. Matthias M. Tischler, Institució Catalana de Recerca i Estudis Avançats/ Universitat Autònoma de Barcelona, Edifici B, Campus de la UAB, E – 08193 Bellaterra.

** The research for this chapter was funded by the 'After Empire: Using and Not Using the Past in the Crisis of the Carolingian World, c.900–1050' HERA project, receiving funding from the European Union's Horizon 2020 research and innovation programme under grant agreement no. 649307.

112 Matthias M. Tischler

Bischoff's magisterial *Paläographie*[1] and his posthumously published four-volume repertory of the continental ninth-century manuscripts on the one hand,[2] and a review of his publications[3] and his also posthumously published *Handschriftenarchiv*[4] on the other hand provide some preliminary answers to our question about the introduction of Carolingian minuscule and texts in the Spanish March. Concerning the history of Carolingian minuscule in the Iberian Peninsula, Bischoff tells us that Catalonia was an exception in Spain in not continuing the use of the characteristic younger Visigothic minuscule until the early twelfth century (or even later); instead, Catalonia saw this change of script long before the rest of the Iberian Peninsula, where it was prompted by Cluniac influence and Pope Gregory's VII liturgical reform during the eleventh century.[5] Bischoff does not go into detail on the advance of the new Carolingian minuscule – he sees this phenomenon developing simultaneously with the use of the Visigothic script until the early ninth century – and mentions only the renowned monastery of Ripoll as a Catalan centre of its use. Yet recent research in modern Catalonia has shown that the story is more complicated: we now know that it took some time during the ninth century for the old Visigothic minuscule to be replaced by the new Carolingian script in the Spanish March.[6] In other words, we still find hybrid minuscule types in this century – either Visigothic minuscule under Carolingian influence or Carolingian minuscule with Visigothic substrate. We know today that the Carolingian minuscule increasingly infiltrated the Spanish March from the middle of the ninth century onwards through Carolingian manuscripts and charters imported from Septimania or even written in the Western Frankish realm.[7] This thus produced on the one hand a writing style in transition between the old Visigothic minuscule and the new Carolingian script; and on the other hand a specific form of Carolingian minuscule with Catalan earmarks written especially in the northern scriptoria of the Carolingian counties such as Vic and Ripoll. Girona and Barcelona, however, seem to have followed a more international Carolingian minuscule. That means that alongside Ripoll – and other monasteries under Carolingian influence whose early scriptoria are still difficult to reconstruct – the bishoprics and counties of Girona, Vic and Barcelona also played an important, but individualized role in the introduction of the Carolingian minuscule. Various types of this script were thus imported from early medieval Catalonia's political and cultural backyards in Septimania, Burgundy and Francia (Narbonne, Lyons, Tours …) and dominated in the development of a new general writing style in early medieval Catalonia from ca. 900 onwards.

Carolingian texts of religious life

Benedictine monasticism

It is an often-told story of early medieval monasticism that the diffusion of the Benedictine lifestyle across Europe was intrinsically connected to the Carolingians' reform of the Church. This older form of religious life came to dominate over other male (and female) monastic rules in the south-western periphery of the Carolingian Empire under Louis the Pious and his monastic counsellor Benedict of Aniane.[8] This second Benedict, originally baptized as Witiza, was the son of the Visigothic count of Maguelone in southern France (Septimania). When he became a Benedictine monk in Saint-Seine (near Dijon), he took his new name from his Italian forerunner and model of monastic life, Benedict of Nursia. We know a relatively large amount about Witiza-Benedict, including his involvement in the general introduction of a revised version of the *Regula S. Benedicti*, and his own and his disciples' works explaining the content and the superiority of this monastic rule in comparison to other contemporary monastic rules.[9] We even know that Benedict preached for a time against Adoptionism, a Hispanic form of Christology favoured by Bishop Felix of Urgell, which was disqualified, damned and eradicated as a heresy by the Frankish Church.[10] Due to the importance of his role, the transmission of his *Life*, which was written shortly after his death (821) by his own pupil Ardo of Aniane (ca. 822/823),[11] was not confined to his native region of Septimania. It is true that a twelfth-century copy from Aniane is the earliest preserved testimony of the full biographical text[12] – a statement we can read in recent scholarship –,[13] but it also left traces in medieval Catalonia: excerpts are seen in the lectionary of Santa Maria de Serrateix[14] and in the breviary of Saint-Michel de Cuxa.[15] As such, we can assume a certain level of circulation and knowledge of this Carolingian monastic biography in medieval Catalonia.

Another well-known story of early medieval monasticism is the equally Europe-wide enforcement of the Benedictine life accomplished by the tenth-century monastic movements which originated in various Frankish reform centres such as Cluny, Gorze, Fleury, Moissac and others. These movements aimed to continue, complete or transform the reform work of Benedict of Aniane. At least two of these monastic centres, Cluny and Fleury, which both had strong ties to Carolingian culture, had an early impact on the renewal of Catalonia's Benedictine life and the formation of the first congregations of exempt communities since the second half of the tenth century.[16]

Both of these stories of Catalan Benedictine monasticism are mostly told without an integral and integrative view of the manuscript tradition generated by these monastic reform movements. The full integration of Catalan evidence for the Europe-wide dissemination of new monastic literature into the history of oral and written communication, as well as its effects on religious identity-building in the various regions of the Iberian world, is an exciting task that remains to be achieved in full detail. What now follows can only be some preliminary observations on the Catalan landscape of text transmission and on its historical contextualization.

At the core of previous research interest in Catalan Benedictine life is the fundamental text, the *Rule of St. Benedict*.[17] The earliest known copy from ca. 850 is still written in Visigothic minuscule, but seemingly under the influence of Carolingian minuscule; as such, it was produced somewhere in the Spanish March, and is today preserved in the Escorial.[18] Other early copies are seen from the eleventh century: a book inventory of Sant Sadurní de Tavèrnoles from 1040

114 Matthias M. Tischler

mentions one – or possibly two – copies of St. Benedict's rule,[19] and the Ripoll catalogue of 1047 describes a 'Liber Sancti Benedicti', perhaps the (now-lost) personal exemplar of Abbot Oliba.[20] Manuscripts of the rule from the same century have been preserved from the Benedictine houses Sant Cugat del Vallès (given to its foundation, the monastery of Sant Llorenç del Munt)[21] and Santa Maria de Serrateix.[22] During his preparations of the critical edition of the Benedictine rule published in 1960,[23] the Viennese philologist Rudolf Hanslik could show that the text family of the rare Iberian testimonies depends on an archetype stemming from Narbonne or Septimania,[24] the home region of Benedict of Aniane.[25] But Hanslik did not compare the texts of all existing Catalan copies of the rule – the manuscript from Santa Maria de Serrateix in particular is missing in his edition – so we do not know the exact relationship between the Catalan copies and thus the forms of dissemination of Benedict's rule in early medieval Catalonia.[26]

Catalan Benedictine houses were also owners of a rich literature of commentaries and tracts on their father's Rule. All of these belonged to the school of Benedict of Aniane and his followers, especially Abbot Smaragdus of Saint-Mihiel. This manuscript panorama shows the great impact of the southern Carolingian-Septimanian network of monastic reformers which stood in open intra-Frankish conflict with older representatives of Benedictine life, especially the great Carolingian abbot, Adalhart of Corbie. In the early ninth century, Benedict wrote his *Concordia regularum*, a synopsis of regulations taken from different monastic rules.[27] In Catalonia, it is transmitted in an abbreviated text version (with lacunae) in a southern French copy of the late ninth century, which was later given to the Catalan Cistercian abbey of Santes Creus and thus could be the copy mentioned in Santes Creus' earliest book inventory dating from the last quarter of the twelfth century.[28]

In addition, though beyond our early medieval horizon, is a fourteenth-century copy perhaps from Saint-Victor de Marseille,[29] which transmits Benedict's tract *De diversarum poenitentiarum modo de regula Benedicti distincto*, a special short comparative text on various monastic penitential practices.[30]

Smaragdus, stemming from a noble Visigothic family who lived in the Iberian Peninsula or in Septimania, was abbot of Saint-Mihiel (near Verdun) since ca. 812 and wrote an explanation of the *Regula S. Benedicti* ca. 816/817, in the context of Benedict of Aniane's reform.[31] This *Expositio in Regulam S. Benedicti* must have played an important role in the Catalan monastic communities from the ninth century onwards. Whereas previous research perhaps wrongly identified the Smaragdus-codex mentioned in the testament of Bishop Idalguer of Vic from 908 as an early testimony of this exegetical work on Benedict's rule,[32] the oldest confirmed Catalan copy is preserved with a single folium from a tenth-century manuscript from the Benedictine house of Sant Benet de Bages[33] as well as the 'Espositum regule' in the previously-mentioned Ripoll catalogue from 1047. This was most probably a copy of this commentary on St. Benedict's rule.[34] Finally, one has also to mention Smaragdus's famous monastic speculum, the *Diadema monachorum*,[35] which, despite previous assumptions, is not mentioned in the testament of Bishop Riculf of Elne

(915),[36] but is later transmitted in a twelfth-century copy from the Benedictine abbey of Sant Cugat del Vallès.[37]

If we had more reliable early palaeographical data from Benedict's scriptorium in Aniane,[38] and if we knew much more about the earliest products of the ninth- and tenth-century Benedictine houses of Catalonia, then it would be much easier to identify further early manuscript material from the reform circle of Benedict and thus to better understand the relationship between our preserved manuscripts.

I would like to close my short overview on early medieval Benedictine life in Catalonia with a ninth-century folium, unknown to the specialists of Carolingian Benedictine reform: this fragment shows glosses on the Rule ch. 5–7, which is the spiritual core of the work.[39] They are different from the recently-edited anonymous compendium on the Rule, the so-called *Glosae de diversis doctoribus collectae in regula S. Benedicti abbatis*.[40] This latter work was composed by an anonymous author ca. 790/827, who put together a catena-glossary of ca. 1100 elementary terms of the *Regula Benedicti* and a florilegium of more than 500 extracts from a wide range of biblical, patristic and monastic texts. Our Barcelona fragment may have been part of a comparable schoolbook created for a new Benedictine community.[41] In any case, it is a further testimony of Carolingian study of the Benedictine rule chapter-by-chapter, commenting on central words or passages of the text. At the moment, we cannot say where exactly this manuscript was written. Its excellent ninth-century Carolingian minuscule is that of a Carolingian writing community,[42] and the glossed text of Benedict's rule belongs to the family of manuscripts disseminated by the church of Narbonne.[43] Together with other fragments, it came into the older Uncial manuscript of Gregory the Great's Homilies on the Gospels when it was rebound in the tenth century. The origins of this Uncial manuscript seem to be located in southern France near to the Mediterranean Sea,[44] so the fragments could also stem from this region. Yet, we cannot exclude the possibility that our Glossary on St. Benedict's rule was already in Catalonia, because another fragment, a folium of the *Breviarium apostolorum*, perhaps followed the same route from Septimania to Catalonia.[45] The namedropping of Bishop Vives of Barcelona (973–995) in this wonderful copy of Gregory's Homilies (fol. 159v) could be the decisive clue that it came (together with the fragments) to the Cathedral after the raiding of Barcelona by al-Manṣūr (985), as it was this bishop who had to restore the plundered book collection of his church.[46]

Canonical life

In stark contrast to the already intensely-studied introduction of reformed Carolingian Benedictine monasticism to early medieval Catalonia, our knowledge of the contemporaneous Carolingian reform of canonical life and its implantation in this border region through the famous *Institutio canonicorum Aquisgranensis* from 816[47] is still rather weak.[48] This rule seems to be introduced in the Spanish March during the ninth century. However, the first testimony for a community in Girona following the Aachen rule only dates from 887.[49] The foundation of the community

116 Matthias M. Tischler

of canons at Girona Cathedral followed the model of Barcelona (878). In 949, a first 'abba' of the collegiate church Sant Feliu is mentioned by name, a certain Teudesind.[50] In 1019, the Girona community of canons was reformed and granted privileges again.[51]

The establishment of canonical life at the Cathedral and collegiate church of Girona thus follows the general timeline of development of this form of religious life in early medieval Catalonia: the Cathedral chapters introduced the Aachen rule during the ninth century or in the first decade of the tenth century at the latest. The further reform of the 'vita canonica' at the Cathedral chapters continued from the middle of the tenth century onwards, starting with the renovation of common life at Vic Cathedral[52] – Urgell (835; reform 1010),[53] Barcelona (ca. 878; reform 1009)[54] and Vic (before 911; reform 957)[55] – whereas most collegiate churches followed the Aachen rule only from the late tenth or early eleventh century onwards – Solsona (928),[56] Besalú (977),[57] Sant Joan de les Abadesses (1017),[58] Sant Vicenç de Cardona (1019)[59] and Tremp (1079).[60]

This short story of the introduction of Carolingian canonical life in early medieval Catalonia can be confirmed, at least partially, by some preserved or recorded copies of the *Institutio canonicorum Aquisgranensis* from 816. Previous researchers knew of four Catalan manuscripts, but only the oldest one from Vic was mentioned in the MGH-edition provided by Albert Werminghoff in 1906.[61] This copy was written in a still-unidentified Catalan scriptorium, either in the second quarter of the tenth century or around the middle of this century.[62] It could be the original manuscript written for the community of canons of Vic Cathedral, which was mentioned in an inventory of Bishop Guadamir from June 14, 957;[63] it was Guadamir who introduced the use of the Aachen rule only a few days before his death.[64] The same manuscript also appears to be mentioned in another Vic inventory from August 971.[65]

The other Catalan copies of the Aachen rule have drawn less – if any – attention in medieval research.[66] These are the currently undiscoverable copy from Sant Joan de les Abadesses, probably dating from the eleventh century;[67] a second Vic copy from 1064,[68] which was arranged by the priest and canon Ermemirus Quintilianus, the most famous scribe of eleventh-century Vic;[69] and an obviously lost copy from Urgell Cathedral, which was perhaps copied on occasion of the reform in 1010 under Bishop Ermengol and then mentioned in an inventory from 1010/1040 and in another booklist from 1147.[70]

However, the oldest Catalan community of canons following the Aachen rule must have also possessed a copy of it. We have excerpts from this text preserved in an early modern copy from Sant Feliu de Girona dating from 1502, whose existence was mentioned in several specialist publications of the nineteenth and twentieth centuries, but has not been widely noted among the scholarly public.[71] This manuscript does not show the complete *Institutio canonicorum Aquisgranensis*, but rather is a selective collection of parts of the work, including the prologue, the collection of the patristic texts with the integrated epilogue, and the beginning of the rule itself. Its production in 1502 is no mere coincidence.[72] Exactly 500 years before, in December 1002, Pope Silvester II, who had strong ties to Catalonia since his juvenile studies there, confirmed the possessions of the Diocese of Girona and mentioned the church of Sant Feliu and Narcis in Girona and its position outside of the city gate.[73]

One cannot overrate the importance of the new Catalan copies of the Aachen rule for our view of the variegated Carolingian landscape of religious lifestyles in early medieval Catalonia. Up until now, we knew more-or-less since when each community followed the Aachen rule. Yet with the exception of the tenth-century copy from Vic, we had no deeper insight into the dissemination of the rule in Catalonia. In addition, the new copy from Girona impressively demonstrates how long and how deeply-rooted the introduction of this Carolingian rule for canons was in Catalonia. Alongside the Benedictine rule, this normative order for the canons was another basic text of the religious lifestyle. It came to prominence long before the introduction of the Augustinian rule in this periphery of Latin Christendom[74] and remained so in some traditional communities of canonical life even afterwards. Since Albert Werminghoff did not use the Catalan copies for his edition, we do not know which exact text version(s) they provide and which textual and historical interrelationship they have. As such, we cannot at present integrate these testimonies into the larger horizon of Carolingian canonical lifestyle.

Carolingian Bible tradition

Previous research on the Bible legacy of the medieval Iberian world has strongly focused on the production of Visigothic and Romanesque Bible pandects in northern Spain and has overlooked two further central phenomena of the north-eastern parts that became early medieval Catalonia, namely: 1) the strong role that the Carolingian Bible tradition already played in this middle ground between Italy, France and the rest of the Iberian Peninsula from the ninth century onwards; and 2) the import, production and edition of new Bibles in the long tenth century, which has not been told in the master narrative of the history of the Bible in Europe after the Carolingian reform. Our focus here lies on Carolingian Bible models, concentrating more on their outer forms than on their texts, since systematic investigation of the Latin texts they offer has not yet been accomplished.[75]

The production of the Bible in the late eighth- to early ninth-century Spanish March – that is, during the period of the Carolingian theologians' struggle against the Adoptionism of Bishop Felix of Urgell (781–799) and his followers – is only observable in some fragments. Like their northern Spanish counterparts and the unknown earliest products from the neighbouring Carolingian county of Ribagorça (see nevertheless the Deuteronomy fragments of a large ninth-century Visigothic Bible with three columns[76]), they are written in Visigothic minuscule – a script certainly used by Felix – and came from the territory of the 'ecclesia Narbonensis', where the new Carolingian minuscule had not been introduced at that time. From Felix's lifetime, we also have a bifolium of a late eighth-century liturgical Hispanic Psalter, already in the Gallican version, but full of Vetus Latina variants[77] and fragments from the Prophets[78] and the Psalter[79] from a large eighth- to ninth-century Visigothic Bible in several volumes. The place of production of this Bible is not yet clear. If it was produced in the still-Visigothic Narbonnais, it was an imported manuscript; but if it was a product of the Cathedral of Urgell or Girona, then it is the oldest known Bible produced under Carolingian dominion in the Spanish March. An argument in favour of the Cathedral scriptorium of Urgell could be strengthened by the exceptional position this episcopal see had in the Spanish March, which was undergoing a strong Carolingian reform influence due to the Felix affair. This scenario and the protected location of the bishopric allowed it to escape being immediately affected by Muslim raids in the ongoing ninth century – unlike Barcelona – and could explain why Urgell was the first important production centre of new Bibles in the Spanish March.

The further story of the Bible in early medieval Catalonia is marked by the introduction of the Carolingian Bible, thus by the import of book *and* text models of the revised Vulgata concerning formats, book orders and theological decisions behind these models. Analysis of understudied and new fragments in combination with the rich tradition of donations of biblical manuscripts on occasion of church dedications now allows us a view of a denser biblical panorama in early medieval Catalonia. At least three Bibles show the design of large Carolingian full Bibles with two columns and more than 40 lines per column. The most impressive copy is the oldest one: the still poorly-known late ninth-century Urgell Bible, a local product imitating the model of the Tours Bible.[80] But we have also a Genesis fragment from another giant Carolingian Bible (or Heptateuch) from later ninth-century Narbonnais, which was obviously imported to Vic Cathedral at the time of its restoration.[81] A high-quality product of the scriptorium of Urgell Cathedral from the first half of the tenth century was the giant Carolingian Bible from which a Jeremiah fragment is preserved.[82]

An unknown facet of the history of the biblical legacy of early medieval Catalonia are the first autochthonous products from the tenth century, all scattered in fragments. The earliest Bible of Barcelona Cathedral from ca. 900 is known from some pieces from Judges and the Psalter.[83] From the oldest Bible of the important Benedictine abbey of Sant Cugat del Vallès (near Barcelona), which was written by the deacon and judge Bonsom at the end of the tenth century, we have a fragment from the books of Kings[84] still showing the three column design of an old Spanish Bible that was also typical for the slightly later Ripoll Bibles. Finally, Girona also participated in the production of its own Catalan Bibles, as we can see from late tenth-century fragments from the Letters of St. Paul to Timothy[85] and the books of Kings,[86] as well as fragments of an early eleventh-century Bible from which pieces of the Old and New Testament are preserved.[87]

All this preparative work of copying and editing new Carolingian Bibles and further imports such as the extraordinary large, now fragmented, French Bible of late tenth century[88] were models for the magnificent Ripoll Bibles of the early eleventh century. These Ripoll Bibles, which have attracted so much research interest in the last decades, built the bridge to the ongoing Catalan and European Bible production.

When we contrast the biblical landscapes of early medieval northern Spain and Catalonia, the differences are obvious: in the latter region, the introduction of the Carolingian minuscule as the new and exclusive script of books and documents is remarkable. It was obviously promoted by the importation of Carolingian manuscripts, including Carolingian Bibles from Catalonia's metropolitan see of Narbonne and from other parts of the Western Frankish realm, which served as models for new orders of biblical books and texts. These imports nevertheless did not prevent the invention of hybrid forms in the outer and inner design of the new Catalan Bibles; those created up until the eleventh and twelfth centuries still evoke memories of the Visigothic Bibles of northern Spain, such as selected books of the Old Testament in the Vetus Latina version or texts belonging to Isidore of Seville's Bible edition. This interaction between imported manuscripts from the earliest period of Carolingian dominion and autochthonous products from the late ninth century is typical for early medieval Catalonia. Yet there remain questions in this panorama: what exact role did the Church of Narbonne play in the transmission of the biblical text to Catalonia? Did the Bible edition of the Visigoth Theodulf of Orléans play a role alongside the Bible revision accomplished by the Anglo-Saxon Alcuin? Only the systematic collation of the Catalan Bibles mentioned here and of hundreds of other biblical fragments will allow more insight into the routes of text transmission starting in the Frankish and Italian source grounds of the Carolingian Empire and beyond.

Carolingian exegesis and liturgy

The last point I want to make in my short assessment of Carolingian culture in early medieval Catalonia is to discuss the introduction of the exegesis and liturgy of the Church of Narbonne in the Spanish March since the beginning of the ninth century. A characteristic feature of the Gallo-Roman liturgy of this Church is that it remained enriched with Visigothic/Hispanic elements.[89] Yet during the ongoing ninth century, the growing Carolingian influence is undeniable and the import and use of new liturgical books and text traditions were a core issue in this process of liturgical transformation. Among them, the varying editions of Homiliaries – a booktype combining exegetical and liturgical functions – played a central role in the every day practice of liturgy and meditation. The so-called Homiliary of Luculentius in particular appears to mark the culmination of introducing Carolingian exegetical and liturgical traditions; I will now focus my final section on exploring this text.[90]

Luculentius is still a widely unknown author of Carolingian text culture. His work became part of the history of Latin medieval literature at a later stage, associated with an incorrect date and location. Earlier research favoured an Italian author from the late ninth century (ca. 900).[91] Angelo Mai, the discoverer of the first 18 homilies of this collection, already formulated this geographical hypothesis in the early nineteenth century.[92] He edited them from two manuscripts preserved at Roman libraries which mention Luculentius without further information about his position in the Latin Church.[93] Both manuscripts are supposed to have been written in central Italy in the late twelfth century, or even the first half of the thirteenth century.[94] Yet, the history of the text and its transmission in fact appears to be quite different. We know today that the oldest copies of Luculentius's much more voluminous collection stem from the Iberian Peninsula, especially two more-or-less complete manuscripts from the Catalan Benedictine monastery of Sant Cugat del Vallès. These two tenth-century copies are at present the two oldest known manuscripts from this abbey.[95] In these copies, the collection comprises 156 homilies with the majority on the Gospels and Epistles, starting the annual cycle with the Christmas vigil. Both copies, which were more-or-less contemporary, apparently had the same model. Despite the mutilated state of conservation of these copies, the Catalan palaeographer Anscari Manuel Mundó i Marcet was able to decipher the colophon of one of them (Ms. 17) on fol. 241va. From this, we know that the priest Truitari copied this manuscript in 956/957 under Abbot Landericus of Sant Cugat.[96] Following the Spanish Jesuit and Church historian Zacarías García Villada, who already postulated an author working in the so-called Spanish March because of the Carolingian script and content of these manuscripts, we now know that the two manuscripts represent the oldest text version, available in two further fragmentary manuscripts from tenth-century Catalonia and one fragment of twelfth-century Catalonia.[97] A second version with characteristic text features and variants,[98] datable to the middle of the tenth century, is also transmitted in many early Catalan manuscript fragments.[99] The complete text transmission of Luculentius's homiliary thus starts in the north-eastern part of the Iberian Peninsula with a strikingly early core area in the Diocese of Vic, whereas the peripheral and late Italian transmission shows common textual features with the second version[100] and offers only a small text selection of the whole homiliary.[101]

This scenario suggests an author working somewhere in the Spanish March. Yet there is another textual argument which should not be discounted. One of the main sources of Luculentius's work is the homiliary of the Visigothic Benedictine abbot, Smaragdus of Saint-Mihiel who came from the Septimanian-Carolingian boarder region.[102] With regard to this history of texts, García Villada had already supposed that 'Luculentius' is nothing else than the Latinized form of 'Smaragdus'.[103] 'Luculentius' thus would have been more a reference to the famous Visigothic-Carolingian author than a proper name.[104] On the other hand, this Latin name, combined with the use of the Carolingian homilies of the Benedictine monks Haimo and Heiric of Auxerre and of a source also used for the Franco-Catalan recension of the Carolingian Liverani homiliary,[105] suggests a younger author.[106] Can we thus locate him in the Spanish March (or in Septimania) and still place him in the ninth century?[107] A further persuasive argument for this region and date would be the liturgical and ecclesiastical influence that the Church of Narbonne exerted in this period on both sides of the Pyrenees.[108] In addition, we have also traces of the liturgical use of Luculentius from the ninth to the twelfth century in Narbonne,[109] Carcassone,[110] and Saint-Pons-de-Thomières.[111] Luculentius thus would have been one of the first Latin authors of this region writing after its integration into the Carolingian Empire and he seems to have been a Benedictine monk.[112] We can even further substantiate this geographical and chronological attribution by Luculentius's Vulgata version, as its features seem to be compatible with specific characteristics of some copies of the Catalan Bible tradition of the Benedictine abbey of Ripoll, the nearby episcopal see of Vic and the abbey of Saint-Michel de Cuxa in the Pyrenees that itself had strong connections with Ripoll and Vic.[113]

Another, still underrated argument for Luculentius's location in the Spanish March could be the specific interreligious content of his homiliary. García Villada was the first scholar to present this knowledge, though he did not indicate the exact place in this collection. He says that in one of his homilies, Luculentius focuses on the Muslims' excessive drinking of alcohol despite the Qur'ān's explicit prohibition.[114] In García Villada's eyes, only an author with exact knowledge of the new religious law could write comments like these.[115] What was unknown to García Villada when he was writing, is the fact that this homily forms part of the oldest text version.[116]

At present, without having a critical edition of the work, it is impossible to answer the question whether we deal with authentic knowledge of the Qur'ān in this passage or instead with oral Muslim traditions; or perhaps not even with specific Muslim behaviour but rather with a general objection against all drunkenness in different religious communities. If García Villada is however right, Luculentius would have been a new type of cultural broker of qur'ānic knowledge between two worlds if we locate him in the Spanish March around 900. Working in this frontier society, he would have been a representative of the mature monastic, exegetical and theological culture of the Carolingian reform church of the ninth century but would have now been confronted with the central problem of re-establishing and consolidating the new structures of the Latin Christian Church in immediate contact with the religious challenges facing this border-zone with al-Andalus. This religious and social context of his work could explain why Luculentius systematically confines his correct Catholic position against the erroneous opinions of the Jews, pagans and heretics in many of his homilies and why we thus must interpret the passage quoted above in the context of the polemics and apologetics of his liminal Mediterranean society.

Summary

What are the specific characteristics of our case study on early medieval Catalonia? This and other peripheries of the Carolingian Empire successfully carried out the Carolingian programme of reforms; as such we can say that this middle ground was Carolingian from a cultural and religious standpoint. In other words, we must break up the still-popular socio-political point of view on the Carolingian age which tells a history inflected by nineteenth-century priorities, focusing on a framework

122   Matthias M. Tischler

of dead dynasties and an old-fashioned concern about the loss and recovery of the Roman imperial title. In the case of Catalonia, using Carolingian cultural expressions such as scripture, manuscript models, religious texts and liturgy did not mean looking back to the fading Visigothic culture, but meant looking forward to ideas and models that would shape Europe in the centuries to come. The use of expressions of Carolingian culture was thus a project for the future, which shows that the very potential of the Carolingian reform efforts, the potential relevance of this engagement, was primarily constituted in cultural rather than political results (Latin language, scripture, exegesis, theology and forms of religious life). From this point of view, 'uses of the past' must be differentiated, insofar as we have to identify past cultural elements and those with the potential of creating the future. For our research in the coming decades, at a greater comparative level, this means that we must systematically contrast the cultural contribution of all these Carolingian peripheries – northern and central Italy, and the middle-eastern and south-eastern peripheries of the post-Carolingian Empire such as Bohemia, Poland, Hungary and the Balkans – to the development of the Carolingian minuscule, book models and religious and liturgical texts.

But what was the specific contribution of the Iberian-Catalan periphery to Carolingian culture with regard to the establishment of its forms of expression, when we compare it with the centres of this culture? Firstly, this and other peripheries of the Empire contributed to the homogenization of the Europe-wide culture despite a certain continuation of hybrid solutions of various degrees. Secondly, the Carolingian culture was established and confirmed as a result of the challenges facing the transcultural frontier societies of southern and south-eastern Europe, thus in the multicultural and multi-religious Mediterranean world.

It turns out to be a big scientific challenge for the future to sharpen exactly this double perspective on Carolingian (political) culture from the so-called centres *and* peripheries. Our work of deconstruction of what may have been 'Patristic', 'Visigothic', 'Carolingian', etc. in the eyes of medieval cultural brokers needs the full implementation of the rich manuscript material provided by Catalonia (and Septimania) as a middle ground *par excellence* of the Euromediterranean world. Uncovering these cultural layers deserve our full engagement – locally and internationally.

Notes

1 Bernhard Bischoff, *Paläographie des römischen Altertums und des abendländischen Mittelalters*, Grundlagen der Germanistik 24 (Berlin: E. Schmidt, 1986 (etc.)).
2 Idem, *Katalog der festländischen Handschriften des neunten Jahrhunderts* (mit Ausnahme der wisigotischen) 1: Aachen – Lambach (Wiesbaden: Harrassowitz, 1998); … 2: Laon – Paderborn (Wiesbaden: Harrassowitz, 2004); … 3: Padua – Zwickau (Wiesbaden: Harrassowitz, 2014); … 4: Gesamtregister (Wiesbaden: Harrassowitz, 2017).
3 The complete bibliography is published by Sigrid Krämer, *Bibliographie Bernhard Bischoff und Verzeichnis aller von ihm herangezogenen Handschriften*, Fuldaer Hochschulschriften 27 (Frankfurt am Main: Knecht, 1998).

4 *Handschriftenarchiv Bernhard Bischoff (Bibliothek der Monumenta Germaniae Historica, Hs. C 1, C 2)*, ed. by Arno Mentzel-Reuters, MGH Hilfsmittel 16 (München: Monumenta Germaniae Historica, 1997).

5 Bischoff, *Paläographie*, pp. 130, 136 and 160.

6 Anscari Manuel Mundó [i Marcet]/Jesús Alturo [i Perucho], 'La escritura de transición de la visigótica a la carolina en la Cataluña del siglo ix', in *Actas del VIII Coloquio del Comité Internacional de Paleografía Latina*, Estudios y ensayos 6 (Madrid: Joyas Bibliográficas, 1990), pp. 131–8; Jesús Alturo i Perucho, 'La cultura llatina medieval a Catalunya. Estat de la qüestió', in *Symposium internacional sobre els orígens de Catalunya (segles viii–xi)* 1, Memorias de la Real Academia de Buenas Letras de Barcelona 23 (Barcelona: Comissió del Millenari de Catalunya Generalitat de Catalunya, 1991), pp. 21–48; Idem, 'Manuscrits i documents llatins d'origen català del segle ix', in ibid., p. 273–80; Idem, 'Escritura visigótica y escritura carolina en el contexto cultural de la Cataluña del siglo ix', in *Las raíces visigóticas de la Iglesia en España*. En torno al Concilio III de Toledo. Santoral hispano-mozárabe en España, ed. by Agustin Hevia Ballina, Memoria Ecclesiae 2 (Oviedo: Asociación de Archiveros de la Iglesia en España, 1991), pp. 33–44 and 298; Idem, 'El fragment de còdex 2541, IV de la Biblioteca de Catalunya amb algunes notes sobre característiques paleogràfiques de la primitiva minúscula carolina catalana', in *Miscel·lània d'estudis dedicats a la memòria del Professor Josep Trench i Òdena* [= *Estudis castellonencs* 6, 1 (1994–1995)] (Castelló de la Plana: 1995), 95–103 [with 2 figures]; Idem, 'Els tipus d'escriptura a la Catalunya dels segles viii–x', in *Catalunya a l'època carolíngia*. Art i cultura abans del romànic (segles ix i x) (Exhibition catalogue) (Barcelona: Museu Nacional d'Art de Catalunya, 1999), pp. 131–4 [with 9 figures]; Anscari Manuel Mundó [i Marcet]/Jesús Alturo [i Perucho], 'Problemàtica de les escriptures dels períodes de transició i de les marginals', *Cultura neolatina* 58 (1998), 121–48 [with 17 figures] (pp. 127–31 and fig. 4–7); [Maria] Josepa Arnall [i Juan], 'La escritura carolina', in *Introducción a la paleografía y la diplomática general*, ed. by Ángel Riesco Terrero, Letras universitarias (Madrid: Síntesis, 1999) (etc.), pp. 89–110 [with 13 figures] (pp. 98–104).

7 On the influence of the Frankish diplomatic minuscule on the script of documents of the Spanish March: Ephrem [Ernest] Compte/Josep [Maria] Recasens [i Comes], 'Influències de l'escriptura de les cancelleries franques en els documents de la Marca Hispànica', in: *I Col·lqui d'història del monaquisme català, Santes Creus 1966: 2*, Publicacions de l'Arxiu bibliogràfic de Santes Creus 25 (Santes Creus: 1969), pp. 51–7 and figures 1–7.

8 Excellent overviews on the introduction of Benedictine life in the Spanish March and medieval Catalonia are: Antonio Linage Conde, *Los orígenes del monacato benedictino en la Península Ibérica* 2: La difusión de la 'Regula Benedicti', Fuentes y Estudios de Historia Leonesa 10 (León: Centro de Estudios e Investigacion 'San Isidoro', 1973), pp. 498–538; Idem, 'L'implantació de la regla benedictina als comtats catalans', in *Temps de monestirs*. Els monestirs catalans entorn l'any mil (Exhibition catalogue), ed. by Marina Miquel/ Margarida Sala, (Barcelona: 1999), pp. 44–61 [with 11 figures].

9 Walter Kettemann, *Subsidia Anianensia*. Überlieferungs- und textgeschichtliche Untersuchungen zur Geschichte Witiza-Benedikts, seines Klosters Aniane und der sog. 'anianischen Reform'. Mit kommentierten Editionen der 'Vita Benedicti Anianensis', 'Notitia de servitio monasteriorum', des 'Chronicon Moissiacense'/'Anianense' sowie zweier Lokaltraditionen aus Aniane 1–2, (PhD, Duisburg: 2000) [https://duepublico. uni-duisburg-essen.de/servlets/DocumentServlet?id=18245].

10 Manuel Ríu [i Ríu], 'Revisión del problema adopcionista en la diócesis de Urgel', *Anuario de estudios medievales* 1 (1964), 77–96 (p. 91 sq).

11 Ed. Georg Waitz, *MGH Scriptores* 15, 1 (Hannover: Monumenta Germaniae Historica, 1887), pp. 200–220; ed. Kettemann, *Subsidia Anianensia* 1, pp. 139–223.

12 Montpellier, Archives départementales de l'Hérault, 1H1, fol. 1r–13v, soon after 1131. For reasons of brevity, I give only selected bibliographical references to the mentioned manuscripts in the following footnotes. Full bibliographical data can be found on the homepage of my HERA-project "From Carolingian Periphery to European Central Region. The Written Genesis of Catalonia": http://pagines.uab.cat/unup/node/42.

124 Matthias M. Tischler

13 Paolo Chiesa, 'Ardo Anianensis mon.', in *La trasmissione dei testi latini del Medioevo*. Mediaeval Latin texts and their transmission 4, ed. by Idem/Lucia Castaldi, Millenio medievale 94. Strumenti e studi N. S. 32. TE.TRA 4 (Firenze: SISMEL Edizioni del Galluzzo, 2012), pp. 60–8.

14 Solsona, Arxiu Diocesà, Còdex 33 (olim Museu Diocesà, Ms. 3), fol. 23v–24r : Anscari Manuel Mundó [i Marcet], 'Regles i observances monàstiques a Catalunya', in *II Col·loqui d'història del monaquisme català*. Sant Joan de les Abadesses 1970 2, (Poblet: Abadía de Poblet, 1974), pp. 7–24 (p. 18); Francesc Xavier Altés i Aguiló, 'A propòsit del manuscrit llatí 3.806 de la Biblioteca Nacional de París. Un homiliari de Vilabertran', *Miscel·lània litúrgica catalana* 2 (1983), 13–47 (p. 28 with n. 69 and p. 45 with n. 169).

15 In the (lost) two-volume breviary of Saint-Michel de Cuxa, here first volume, fol. 63 sq., attested by the table of contents in Paris, Bibliothèque nationale de France, Fonds Baluze, Ms. 372, fol. 44r–48v, here fol. 44v: Pere Pujol i Tubau, 'El Breviari de Cuixà', *Butlletí de la Biblioteca de Catalunya* 6 (1920–1922), 329–41 (p. 333); Mundó i Marcet, 'Regles', p. 18; Altés i Aguiló, 'A propòsit', p. 28 with n. 69 and p. 45 with n. 169.

16 Ramon d'Abadal i de Vinyals, 'L'esperit de Cluny i les relacions de Catalunya amb Roma i la Itàlia en el segle x', *Studi medievali* III 2 (1961), 3–41; Anscari Manuel Mundó [i Marcet], 'Moissac, Cluny et les mouvements monastiques de l'Est des Pyrénées du xe au xiie siècle', *Annales du Midi* 75 (1963), 551–70 and 570–3 (Discussion) [repr. in *Moissac et l'Occident au xie siècle*. Actes du colloque international de Moissac, 3–5 mai 1963, Toulouse 1964, pp. 229–48 and 248–51 (Discussion)]; Karen Stöber, 'Cluny in Catalonia', *Journal of Medieval Iberian Studies* 9 (2017), 241–60 (pp. 241 and 244).

17 Linage Conde, *Los orígenes* 2, pp. 777–88 and 844–54.

18 El Escorial, Real Biblioteca del Monasterio de San Lorenzo, Ms. I. III. 13, fol. 7v–57v: Agustín Millares Carlo, *Corpus de códices visigóticos* 1: Estudio, ed. by Manuel Cecilio Díaz y Díaz e. a. (Las Palmas de Gran Canaria: Fundación de Enseñanza Superior a Distancia, 1999), p. 55 no 55; Idem: … 2: Álbum, ed. by Manuel Cecilio Díaz y Díaz e. a., (Las Palmas de Gran Canaria: Gobierno de Canarias, 1999), p. 54 no 55 (from fol. 203r); Linage Conde, 'L'implantació', p. 50. Some marginal notes show that the manuscript was already in the tenth century in a house under Benedictine influence in the more western regions of the Iberian Peninsula.

19 'regulas.ii.', ed. Cebrià Baraut [Obiols], 'Diplomatari del monestir de Sant Sadurní de Tavèrnoles (segles ix–xiii)', *Urgellia* 12 (1994–1995), 7–414 (pp. 128–33 no 59, p. 131 l. 37); Michel Zimmermann, *Écrire et lire en Catalogne (ixe–xiie siècle)* 1, Bibliothèque de la Casa de Velázquez 23, 1 (Madrid: Casa de Velázquez, 2003), p. 558; … 2 … 23, 2 (Madrid: Casa de Velázquez, 2003), pp. 761–3.

20 Ed. Rudolf Beer, *Die Handschriften des Klosters Santa María de Ripoll I*, Sitzungsberichte der Philosophisch-Historischen Klasse der Kaiserlichen Akademie der Wissenschaften 155, no 3 (Wien: 1908), pp. 101–9 (p. 103 no 78: ibid., p. 86 sq.).; Zimmermann, *Écrire et lire* 2, pp. 625 and 762.

21 Barcelona, Arxiu de la Corona d'Aragó, Ms. Sant Cugat 22, fol. 135v–155r: Linage Conde, *Los orígenes* 2, p. 782 n. 39, p. 831 with n. 194, 196 and 198–202, p. 839 n. 226 and p. 851 sq.; Mundó i Marcet, 'Regles', p. 15 with n. 27 and p. 18; Zimmermann, *Écrire et lire* 1, p. 605.

22 København, Det Kongelige Bibliotek, Ny Kgl. Samling, Ms. 1794, fol. 185r–201v: Linage Conde, *Los orígenes* 2, p. 810 (from fol. 201v; with the wrong shelfmark '1594') and 852 (with the wrong shelfmark 'S. 1.594'); Mundó i Marcet, 'Regles', p. 15.

23 Ed. Rudolf Hanslik, *Benedicti Regula*, CSEL 75 (Wien: 1960) (etc.), pp. 1–165.

24 Idem, 'Praefatio', in Idem (ed.): ibid., pp. xi–lxxiv (pp. lv–lviii); Manuel Cecilio Díaz y Díaz, 'La circulation des manuscrits dans la Péninsule Ibérique du viiie au xie siècle', *Cahiers de civilisation médiévale* 12 (1969), 219–41 and 383–92 [with 5 figures] (p. 238 n. 132); Zimmermann, *Écrire et lire* 2, p. 762.

25 Ríu i Ríu, 'Revisión' p. 96 indirectly assumed that it was Benedict of Aniane himself who brought this version of the rule to the Spanish March during his mission to Urgell.

26 Not collated are e. g. Tarragona, Biblioteca pública, Ms. 106, fol. 206r–287v, twelfth/thirteenth century, from the Cistercian abbey Santes Creus: Jesús Domínguez Bordona, 'Manuscritos de la Biblioteca Pública de Tarragona, Inventario general', *Boletín arqueológico* IV 53–54 (1953–1954), 50–75 [also separate: Idem, *Manuscritos de la Biblioteca Pública de Tarragona*, Instituto de Estudios Tarraconenses 'Ramon Berenguer IV'. Sección de arqueología e historia 6 (Tarragona: 1954)] (p. 57); and the fifteenth-century copy from the Girona Benedictine abbey Sant Pere de Gallicants, today Montserrat, Arxiu i Biblioteca del Monestir, Ms. 995, fol. 115r–136r: Linage Conde, *Los orígenes* 2, p. 853 n. 267; Mundó i Marcet, 'Regles', pp. 15 and 22; Alexandre Olivar [i Daydí], *Catàleg dels manuscrits de la Biblioteca del Monestir de Montserrat*, Scripta et documenta 25 (Montserrat: Abadía de Montserrat, 1977), p. 297.

27 Ed. Pierre Bonnerue, *Benedicti Anianensis Concordia regularum* [2]: Textus, CChr.CM 168 A (Turnhout: Brepols, 1999), pp. 3–669.

28 Tarragona, Biblioteca pública, Ms. 69, fol. 1r–176r (manuscript T): Jesús Domínguez Bordona, *El escritorio y la primitiva biblioteca de Santes Creus*. Noticia para su estudio y catálogo de los manuscritos que de dicha procedencia se conservan, Instituto de Estudios Tarraconenses 'Ramón Berenguer IV'. Publicación 1 (Tarragona, Sugrañes, 1952), p. 13; Idem, 'Manuscritos', p. 56; Mundó i Marcet, 'Regles', p. 18 (with the wrong date 'segle xiv'); Zimmermann, *Écrire et lire* 1, p. 582 sq.; Idem, *Écrire et lire* 2, pp. 763 and 824; Pius Engelbert, 'Ein karolingisches Fragment der "Concordia regularum" des Benedikt von Aniane in Reims', *Revue bénédictine* 126 (2016), 138–49 [with 2 figures] (p. 139).

29 Montserrat, Arxiu i Biblioteca del Monestir, Ms. 847, fol. 59r–62v: Josef Semmler, 'Legislatio Aquisgranensis', in Idem (ed.): *Initia consuetudinis Benedictinae*. Consuetudines saeculi octavi et noni, Corpus Consuetudinum Monasticarum 1 (Siegburg: Schmitt, 1963), pp. 423–582 (p. 566 sq. (with the wrong date 'saec. xii. ex.')); Mundó i Marcet, 'Regles', p. 18; Olivar i Daydí, *Catàleg*, p. 217.

30 Ed. Semmler, *Initia consuetudinis Benedictinae*, pp. 571–82 (manuscript L).

31 Ed. Alfred Spannagel/Pius Engelbert, *Smaragdi Abbatis Expositio in Regulam S. Benedicti*, Corpus Consuetudinum Monasticarum 8 (Siegburg: Schmitt, 1974), pp. 3–337.

32 'Smaragdum quodicem i', ed. Eduard Junyent i Subira, *Diplomatari de la Catedral de Vic*. Segles ix–x, Publicacions del Patronat d'Estudis Ausonencs. Documents 1 (Vic: Patronat d'Estudis Ausonencs, 1980–1996), p. 39 sq. no 41 (p. 39 l. 25): Linage Conde, *Los orígenes*, p. 796; Idem, 'L'implantació', p. 50; Zimmermann, *Écrire et lire* 1, p. 547. Yet Idem, *Écrire et lire* 2, p. 758 identified this manuscript also with the *Diadema monachorum* (*Écrire et lire* 1, p. 592 without identification). On the correct identification: as n. 90.

33 Montserrat, Arxiu i Biblioteca del Monestir, Ms. 793/I: Mundó i Marcet, 'Regles', p. 19 with n. 32 (with the wrong shelfmark '783-I'); Spannagel/Engelbert, *Smaragdi Abbatis Expositio*, p. xvii; Olivar i Daydí, *Catàleg*, p. 190 sq.

34 Ed. Beer, *Handschriften*, p. 105 no 162: Mundó i Marcet, 'Regles', p. 19; Zimmermann, *Écrire et lire* 1, p. 569 (unprecisely 'un manuscrit de la Règle bénédictine'); Idem, *Écrire et lire* 2, p. 762 sq. (wrongly thinking of a copy of Benedict of Aniane's *Concordia regularum*).

35 Ed. Migne, *PL* 102, 593–690.

36 'Smaragdum unum', ed. Migne, *PL* 132, col. 468 no X l. 48: Zimmermann, *Écrire et lire* 1, p. 549; Idem, *Écrire et lire* 2, p. 758; Éric Palazzo, 'Arts somptuaires et liturgie. Le testament de l'évêque d'Elne, Riculf (915)', in *Retour aux sources*. Textes, études et documents d'histoire médiévale offerts à Michel Parisse, ed. by Silvain Gouguenheim e. a., (Paris: Picard, 2004), pp. 711–7 (p. 714 (without identification)). For the correct identification of this work: as n. 90.

37 Barcelona, Arxiu de la Corona d'Aragó, Ms. Sant Cugat 90, fol. 1v–124v: Zimmermann, *Écrire et lire* 1, p. 605.

38 Bernhard Bischoff, 'Die ältesten Handschriften der Regula S. Benedicti in Bayern', *Studien und Mitteilungen zur Geschichte des Benediktinerordens* 92 (1981), 7–16 (p. 13 sq.); Pius Engelbert (ed.): *Der Codex Regularum des Benedikt von Aniane*. Faksimile der Handschrift Clm 28118 der Bayerischen Staatsbibliothek München (St. Ottilien: EOS Verlag, 2016), p. 49 sq.; Idem, 'Karolingisches Fragment', pp. 147–9.

126   Matthias M. Tischler

39 Barcelona, Arxiu Capitular, Còdex 120, fragment no 2: Anscari Manuel Mundó [i Marcet], 'Comment reconnaître la provenance de certains fragments de manuscrits détachés de reliures', *Codices manuscripti* 11 (1985), 116–23 [with 1 figure] (pp. 118 and 120–2); Jesús Alturo i Perucho, 'El glossari "in Regulam sancti Benedicti" de l'Arxiu de la Catedral de Barcelona', *Studia Monastica* 37 (1995), 271–7 (edition: pp. 275–7). The fragment is not mentioned by Bischoff, *Katalog* 1, p. 55.

40 Ed. Matthieu H. van der Meer, *Glosae in regula Sancti Benedicti abbatis ad usum Smaragdi abbatis Sancti Michaelis*, CChr.CM 282 (Turnhout: 2017), pp. 3–233: Idem, 'The "Glosae in regula S. Benedicti" – a text between the "Liber Glossarum" and Smaragdus' "Expositio in regulam S. Benedicti"', *Dossier d'HEL* 10 (2016), 305–19.

41 Thus, the fragment does not necessarily stem from a copy of the Rule with a glossary at its end, as assumed by Alturo i Perucho, 'El glossari', p. 273.

42 Following Anscari Manuel Mundó i Marcet probably Catalonia, tenth century, following Jesús Alturo i Perucho transpyrenaic, probably from the Narbonnais, ninth/tenth century. The first opinion is certainly wrong, the second perhaps concerning its date. We have here an excellent Carolingian Western Frankish minuscule of the ninth century always with a Carolingian 'a', rarely with a round 'd' and a 'g' in form of a '3'.

43 Alturo i Perucho, 'El glossari', p. 274.

44 Mundó i Marcet, 'Comment reconnaître', p. 121 sq.

45 Barcelona, Arxiu Capitular, Còdex 120, fragment no 3: Mundó i Marcet, 'Comment reconnaître', p. 121; Jesús Alturo i Perucho, 'Dos testimonis més del "Breuiarium apostolorum"', *Miscel·lània litúrgica catalana* 24 (2016), 19–32 [with 4 figures] (pp. 23–5 and 29 sq. fig. 1 sq. (from recto and verso)). The fragment is not mentioned by Bischoff, *Katalog* 1, p. 55.

46 This effort is not mentioned by Gaspar Feliu i Montfort, 'El bisbe Vives de Barcelona i el patrimoni de la Catedral (974–995)', in *Miquel Coll i Alentorn. Miscel·lània d'homentage en el seu vuitantè aniversari* (Barcelona,1984), pp. 167–91.

47 Josef Semmler, 'Reichsidee und kirchliche Gesetzgebung', *Zeitschrift für Kirchengeschichte* 71 (1960), 37–65 (pp. 43–5); Idem, 'Die Beschlüsse des Aachener Konzils im Jahre 816', in ibid 74 (1963), 15–82 (p. 16); Wilfried Hartmann, *Die Synoden der Karolingerzeit im Frankenreich und in Italien* (Konziliengeschichte. Reihe A: Darstellungen, Paderborn e. a.: Ferdinand Schöningh, 1989), pp. 157–60; Josef Semmler, 'Die Kanoniker und ihre Regel im 9. Jahrhundert', in *Studien zum weltlichen Kollegiatstift in Deutschland*, ed. by Irene Crusius, Veröffentlichungen des Max-Planck-Instituts für Geschichte 114. Studien zur Germania Sacra 18 (Göttingen:Vandenhoeck & Ruprecht, 1995), pp. 62–109; Egon Boshof, *Ludwig der Fromme*, Gestalten des Mittelalters und der Renaissance (Darmstadt:WBG, 1996), pp. 120–4.

48 Especially visible in Eduardo Carrero Santamaría, '"Ecce quam bonum et quam iocundum habitare fratres in unum". Vidas reglar y secular en las catedrales hispanas llegado el siglo xii', *Anuario de estudios medievales* 30 (2000), 757–805 (pp. 767–70), who did not understand the tremendous dimension of Louis the Pious's will to unify canonical life in his Empire.

49 Charter of Bishop Theothar of Girona from November 24, 887: ed. Ramon Martí [i Castelló], *Col·lecció diplomàtica de la seu de Girona (817–1100)*, Fundació Noguera. Col·lecció Diplomataris 13 (Barcelona: Fundació Noguera, 1997), p. 84 sq. no 17. The community is also mentioned in a charter of dedication and dotation by Bishop Sunifred from October 1, 858 which nevertheless is a falsification of the late eleventh century: ed. Ramon Ordeig i Mata, *Les dotalies de les esglésies de Catalunya (segles ix–xii)* 1: Preàmbul. Introducció. Documents 1–116 (segles ix–x) 1, Estudis històrics. Diplomatari 1 (Vic: 1993), pp. 24–6 no 6; Martí i Castelló, *Col·lecció diplomàtica*, p. 79 sq. no 11. Johannes Josef Bauer, 'Die vita canonica der katalanischen Kathedralkapitel vom 9. bis zum 11. Jahrhundert', in *Homenaje a Johannes Vincke para el 11 de mayo 1962* 1 (Madrid: CSIC, 1962–1963), pp. 81–112 (p. 88 sq.); Idem, 'Die vita canonica an den katalanischen Kollegiatkirchen im 10. und 11. Jahrhundert', in *Gesammelte Aufsätze zur Kulturgeschichte Spaniens* 21, Spanische Forschungen der Görresgesellschaft I (Münster in Westfalen: Aschendorff, 1963), pp. 54–82 (p. 56 with n. 7); Odilo Engels, 'Episkopat und Kanonie

im mittelalterlichen Katalonien', in ibid., pp. 83–135 [repr. in Idem, *Reconquista und Landesherrschaft*. Studien zur Rechts- und Verfassungsgeschichte Spaniens im Mittelalter, Rechts- und Staatswissenschaftliche Veröffentlichungen der Görres-Gesellschaft N. F. 53, (Paderborn e. a.: Ferdinand Schöning, 1989), pp. 149–201] (p. 84 with n. 5 and p. 114 sq.) do not really discuss these two charters. See also Gabriel Roura [i Güibas], *Girona carolíngia*. Comtes, vescomtes i bisbes (Del 785 a l'any 1000), Quaderns d'història de Girona (Girona, 1988), p. 68 sq.

50 Ed. Ramon Ordeig i Mata, 'Ató, bisbe i arquebisbe de Vic (957–971), antic arxiprest-ardiaca de Girona', *Studia Vicensia* 1 (1989), 61–97 (pp. 84 sq. no 4); ed. Martí i Castelló, *Col·lecció diplomàtica*, p. 125 no 85.

51 Ed. Martí i Castelló, *Col·lecció diplomàtica*, pp. 197–200 no 179: Bauer, 'Die Vita canonica an den katalanischen Kollegiatkirchen', p. 80.

52 Bauer, 'Die vita canonica an den katalanischen Kollegiatkirchen', p. 55 with n. 5.

53 Bauer, 'Die vita canonica der katalanischen Kathedralkapitel', pp. 86, 94 and 103 sq.; Idem, 'Die vita canonica an den katalanischen Kollegiatkirchen', p. 56 with n. 6, pp. 59 sq. and 80.

54 Bauer, 'Die vita canonica der katalanischen Kathedralkapitel', pp. 87, 94 and 101–3; Idem, 'Die vita canonica an den katalanischen Kollegiatkirchen', p. 80.

55 Bauer, 'Die vita canonica der katalanischen Kathedralkapitel', pp. 90 sq. and 96; Idem, 'Die vita canonica an den katalanischen Kollegiatkirchen', p. 80.

56 Manuel Ríu [i Ríu], 'La canònica de Santa Maria de Solsona. Precedents medievals d'un bisbat modern', *Urgellia* 2 (1979), 211–56 (pp. 221 sq. and 226).

57 Bauer, 'Die vita canonica an den katalanischen Kollegiatkirchen', p. 58 sq.

58 Ibid., pp. 57 sq. and 72.

59 Ibid., p. 61 sq. with n. 32–5.

60 Ibid., p. 65 with n. 53.

61 Ed. Albert Werminghoff, *MGH. Concilia aevi Carolini* 1, 1 (Hannover: Monumenta Germaniae Historica, 1906), pp. 312–421 [repr. in Jerome Bertram, *The Chrodegang Rules*. The rules for the common life of the secular clergy from the eighth and ninth centuries. Critical texts with translations and commentary, Church, Faith and Culture in the Medieval West (Aldershot: Taylor and Francis, 2005), pp. 96–131; ibid., pp. 132–74 follows an English version].

62 Vic, Arxiu i Biblioteca Episcopal, Ms. 128 C (XLVII C), fol. 1r–45v: Paul Ewald, 'Reise nach Spanien im Winter von 1878 auf 1879', *Neues Archiv der Gesellschaft für ältere deutsche Geschichtskunde* 6 (1881), 217–398 (p. 340); Werminghoff (ed.) *MGH. Concilia aevi Carolini*, p. 311 no 69; Josep Gudiol [i Cunill], *Catàleg dels llibres manuscrits anteriors al segle xviii del Museu Episcopal de Vich*. Amb un apéndix per Eduard Junyent [i Subirà] (Barcelona: Imprenta de la Casa de Caritat, 1934), pp. 133–5; Hubert Mordek, *Bibliotheca capitularium regum Francorum manuscripta*. Überlieferung und Traditionszusammenhang der fränkischen Herrschererlasse, MGH Hilfsmittel 15 (München: Monumenta Germaniae Historica, 1995), p. 1052.

63 'Vita Channonicha i', ed. Jaime Villanueva, *Viage literario a las iglesias de España* 6 (València: 1821), p. 273 sq. no XV (p. 274 l. 13); ed. Junyent i Subirà, *Diplomatari*, p. 256 no 303 l. 20: Bauer, 'Die vita canonica der katalanischen Kathedralkapitel', p. 91 sq.; Díaz y Díaz, 'La circulation', p. 238 n. 135; Miquel dels Sants Gros i Pujol, 'La vila de Vic i el monestir de Ripoll en els anys 967–970', in *Actes del Congrés internacional Gerbert d'Orlhac i el seu temps*. Catalunya i Europa a la fi del 1r mil·leni, Vic-Ripoll, 10–13 de novembre de 1999, ed. by Imma Ollich i Castanyer, Documents [Eumo] 31 (Vic: Eumo, 1999), pp. 747–61 (p. 753).

64 Ed. Junyent i Subirà, *Diplomatari*, pp. 254–6 no 302: Gros i Pujol, 'La vila de Vic', p. 750.

65 'Vita Chanonicha i', ed. Junyent i Subirà, *Diplomatari*, p. 346 sq. no 413 (p. 347 l. 8 sq.); Idem, 'La biblioteca de la canónica de Vich en los siglos x–xi', in *Gesammelte Aufsätze zur Kulturgeschichte Spaniens* 21, Spanische Forschungen der Görresgesellschaft I. 21 (Münster in Westfalen: Aschendorff, 1963), pp. 136–45 (p. 139); Miquel dels Sants Gros [i Pujol], 'Fragments de Bíblies llatines del Museu Episcopal de Vic', *Revista catalana de teologia* 3 (1978), 153–71 (p. 157 n. 10); Idem, 'La vila de Vic', p. 753; Jesús Alturo

128   Matthias M. Tischler

i Perucho, *Història del llibre manuscrit a Catalunya*, Generalitat de Catalunya. Textos i documents 23 (Barcelona: Generalitat de Catalunya, 2003), p. 97 sq.; Miquel dels Sants Gros i Pujol, *La Biblioteca Episcopal de Vic*. Un patrimoni bibliogràfic d'onze segles (Vic: Biblioteca Episcopal, Patronat d'Estudis Osonencs, 2006), p. 31 no 16 (with a figure of the inventory).

66 They are all missing in Albert Werminghoff, 'Die Beschlüsse des Aachener Concils im Jahre 816', *Neues Archiv der Gesellschaft für ältere deutsche Geschichtskunde* 27 (1902) 605–75 (pp. 637–45); Idem, (ed.): *MGH. Concilia aevi Carolini*, pp. 310–2; Rudolf Schieffer, *Die Entstehung von Domkapiteln in Deutschland*, Bonner Historische Forschungen 43 (Bonn: Röhrscheid, 1976), pp. 248–52; Marie-Hélène Jullien/Françoise Perelman, *Clavis scriptorum latinorum medii aevi*. Auctores Galliae 735–987 1, CChr.CM (Turnhout: Brepols, 1994), pp. 141 sq. and 231; Mordek, *Bibliotheca capitularium*, pp. 1045–56; Thomas Schilp, *Norm und Wirklichkeit religiöser Frauengemeinschaften im Frühmittelalter*. Die 'Institutio sanctimonialium Aquisgranensis' des Jahres 816 und die Problematik der Verfassung von Frauenkommunitäten, Veröffentlichungen des Max-Planck-Instituts für Geschichte 137. Studien zur Germania Sacra 21 (Göttingen: Vandenhoeck & Ruprecht, 1998), pp. 103–7; Gerhard Schmitz, 'Aachen 816. Zu Überlieferung und Edition der Kanonikergesetzgebung Ludwigs des Frommen', *Deutsches Archiv für Erforschung des Mittelalters* 63 (2007), 497–544.

67 Sant Joan de les Abadesses, Arxiu del Monestir, s. n.: José Janini [Cuesta], *Manuscritos litúrgicos de las bibliotecas de España* 2: Aragón, Cataluña y Valencia, Publicaciones de la Facultad de Teología del Norte de España. Sede de Burgos 38, 2 (Burgos: Aldecoa, 1980), p. 184 no 631. Although the manuscript also showed a copy of Ado of Vienne's *Martyrology*, it is not mentioned in Jésus Antoni Iglesias i Fonseca, 'El "Martirologio" de Adon in Cataluña. Consideraciones codicológicas y paleográficas sobre dos nuevos testimonios', in *Actas [del] III Congreso Hispánico de Latín Medieval (León, 26–29 de septiembre de 2002)* 1, ed. by Maurilio Pérez González (León: Universidad de León, Secretariado Publicaciones y Medios Audiovisuales, 2002), pp. 149–59.

68 Vic, Arxiu i Biblioteca Episcopal, Ms. 44 (XXXVI), fol. 84va–144vb: Gudiol i Cunill, *Catàleg*, pp. 61–3 and fig. 9 (from fol. 84r).

69 He died in 1080: Miquel dels Sants Gros i Pujol, 'Els antics necrologics de la Catedral de Vic (segles x–xiii)', *Studia Vicensia* 2 (2017), 7–174 (p. 57 no 302 with n. 112).

70 Mentioned as 'Vita canonica i.' or 'i. Vita canonica' respectively: Pere Pujol i Tubau, 'De la cultura catalana mig-eval. Una biblioteca dels temps romànics', *Estudis universitaris catalans* 7 (1913), 1–8 (p. 5 l. 32 and p. 6 l. 11); Díaz y Díaz, 'La circulation des manuscrits', p. 238 n. 135; Miquel dels Sants Gros [i Pujol], 'La biblioteca de la Catedral de la Seu d'Urgell als segles x–xii', *Acta Historica et Archaeologica Mediaevalia* 26 (2005), 101–24 (p. 107 no 8, p. 115 no 47 and p. 123).

71 Girona, Biblioteca Diocesana del Seminari, Fons de Manuscrits de Sant Feliu de Girona, Ms. 17 (olim Seminario, Ms. 150; olim Archivo de San Félix, Ms. 16), fol 104ra–160ra: José de la Canal, 'Noticia de los manuscritos y libros raros que hay en el archivo de la iglesia colegiata de Sant Félix', in *España sagrada* 45 (Madrid, 1832), pp. 259–65 Apéndice XI (p. 264); Jaime Villanueva, *Viaje literario a las iglesias de España* 14 (Madrid, 1850), p. 141 sq.; Rudolf Beer, *Handschriftenschätze Spaniens*. Bericht über eine in den Jahren 1886–1888 durchgefürte [!] Forschungsreise … , Abhandlungen über Handschriftenkunde 1 (Wien: 1894) [repr. Amsterdam: Gérard Th. Van Heusden, 1970], p. 239 no 40, p. 240 no 54 and p. 729; Alfred Cordoliani, 'Inventaire des manuscrits de comput ecclésiastique conservés dans les bibliothèques de Catalogne (avec notes sur les autres manuscrits de ces bibliothèques)', *Hispania sacra* 4 (1951), 359–84; ibid. 5 (1952), 121–64 (p. 375 sq.); José Janini [Cuesta]/ José María Marqués [Planagumà], 'Manuscritos de la Colegiata de San Félix de Gerona', *Hispania sacra* 15 (1962), 401–37 (p. 416 sq.); Janini Cuesta, *Manuscritos litúrgicos*, p. 112 sq. no 522; Roura i Güibas, *Girona carolíngia*, p. 68.

72 The Mercedarian friar Baltasar de Costa, a professional copyist, wrote his colophon at the end of the manuscript (fol. 176ra/rb): *Colophons de manuscrits occidentaux des origines*

au xvie siècle 1, Spicilegii Friburgensis Subsidia 2 (Fribourg, 1965), p. 199 no 1602 (without publishing the text).

73 ' …una cum ecclesia sancti Felicis martiris et sancti Narcissi, qui [!] est iuxta portam civitatis Gerundae, cum omnibus eorum pertinentiis', ed. Harald Zimmermann, *Papsturkunden 896–1046* 2: 996–1046, Österreichischen Akademie der Wissenschaften. Philosophisch-Historische Klasse. Denkschriften 177. Veröffentlichungen der Historischen Kommission 4 (Wien: Verlag der Österreichischen Akademie der Wissenschaften, 1989), p. 768 sq. no 404 (p. 768 l. 11 sq).

74 Karen Stöber, 'Religious and society on the borders of Christendom. The regular canons in medieval Catalonia', in *Monasteries on the borders of medieval Europe*. Conflict and cultural interaction, ed. by Emilia Jamroziak/Karen Stöber, Medieval Church Studies 28 (Turnhout: Brepols, 2013), pp. 173–92.

75 Armand Puig i Tàrrech, 'La Bíblia llatina en els països de llengua catalana fins al segle xiii', *Revista catalana de teologia* 28 (2003), 103–34; Jesús Alturo i Perucho, 'Corpus biblicum medii aevi Cataloniae. Códices, fragmentos, membra disiecta y referencias librarias. Una primera aproximación', in *Biblia y archivos de la Iglesia*. Santoral hispano-mozárabe en las diócesis de España. Actas del XXVI Congreso de la Asociacón celebrado en Bilbao (12 al 16 de septiembre de 2011), ed. by Agustín Hevia Ballina, Memoria Ecclesiae 38 (Oviedo: Asociación de Archiveros de la Iglesia en España, 2013), pp. 69–114 (without referring to the former).

76 Lleida, Arxiu Capitular, RC.0031 [olim Ms. 13] + Lleida, Museu Diocesà, s. n.: Millares Carlo, *Corpus* 1, p. 80 no 103 sq.; … 2: p. 98 no 103 (from fol. 2v).

77 Vic, Arxiu i Biblioteca Episcopal, Ms. 259: Miquel dels Sants Gros i Pujol, 'El fragment del "Liber psalmorum" hispànic, Vic, Mus. Epis., Ms. 259', *Revista catalana de teologia* 2 (1977), 437–52 [with 1 figure]; Puig i Tàrrech, 'La Bíblia llatina', p. 109 with n. 18 sq.; Gros i Pujol, *La Biblioteca Episcopal*, p. 14 sq. no 1 (with figure of fol. 1v/2r).

78 Barcelona, Biblioteca de Catalunya, Ms. 2541–1: Puig i Tàrrech, 'La Bíblia llatina', p. 109 with n. 17; Alturo i Perucho, 'Corpus biblicum', p. 96.

79 Barcelona, Arxiu de la Corona d'Aragó, Ms. Ripoll 395: Puig i Tàrrech, 'La Bíblia llatina', p. 109 with n. 17; Alturo i Perucho, 'Corpus biblicum', p. 96.

80 La Seu d'Urgell, Biblioteca Capitular, Ms. 1997: Pere Pujol i Tubau, 'El manuscrit de la Vulgata de la Catedral d'Urgell', *Butlletí de la Biblioteca de Catalunya* 6 (1920–1922), 98–145 and 2 plates [also separate: Barcelona 1923]; Puig i Tàrrech, 'La Bíblia llatina', pp. 108, 110–3, p. 116 n. 44, p. 118, p. 128 with n. 92 and p. 133; Alturo i Perucho, 'Corpus biblicum', p. 97; Bischoff, *Katalog* 3, p. 347 no 5981.

81 Vic, Arxiu i Biblioteca Episcopal, Ms. 255, I: Gros i Pujol, 'Fragments de Bíblies', pp. 153–71 (p. 154 sq. and p. 158 no 1); Puig i Tàrrech, 'La Bíblia llatina', p. 113 with n. 32 and 34; Gros i Pujol, *La Biblioteca Episcopal*, p. 16 no 2 (with figure of fol. 1v, upper part); Alturo i Perucho, 'Corpus biblicum', p. 98; Bischoff, *Katalog* 3, p. 470 no 7076.

82 La Seu d'Urgell, Biblioteca Capitular, Ms. 180. 1: Alturo i Perucho, 'Corpus biblicum', p. 98 sq.

83 Barcelona, Arxiu Diocesà, Fragm. 32 and Fragm. 33: ibid., p. 98.

84 Barcelona, Arxiu de la Corona d'Aragó, Fragm. 250: Puig i Tàrrech, 'La Bíblia llatina', p. 113; Alturo i Perucho, 'Corpus biblicum', p. 98.

85 Girona, Arxiu Capitular, Fragm. 7: Puig i Tàrrech, 'La Bíblia llatina', p. 114; Alturo i Perucho, 'Corpus biblicum', p. 99.

86 Montserrat, Arxiu i Biblioteca del Monestir, Ms. 821/V: Olivar i Daydí, *Catàleg*, p. 205; Alturo i Perucho, 'Corpus biblicum', p. 99.

87 Montserrat, Arxiu i Biblioteca del Monestir, Ms. 821/II: Olivar i Daydí, *Catàleg*, p. 205; Alturo i Perucho, 'Corpus biblicum', p. 102.

88 Vic, Arxiu i Biblioteca Episcopal, Ms. 255, II: Gros i Pujol, 'Fragments de Bíblies', pp. 154 sq., 158 and p. 159 no 2; Puig i Tàrrech, 'La Bíblia llatina', p. 113 with n. 32–4; Gros i Pujol, *La Biblioteca Episcopal*, p. 26 no 11 (with figure of fol. 1r); Alturo i Perucho, 'Corpus biblicum', p. 99.

130   Matthias M. Tischler

89 Miquel dels Sants Gros [i Pujol], 'La liturgie narbonnaise témoin d'un changement rapide de rites liturgiques', in *Liturgie de l'église particuliere et liturgie de l'église universelle*. Conférences Saint-Serge. XXIIe semaine d'études liturgiques, Paris, 30 juin – 3 juillet 1975, Bibliotheca Ephemerides liturgicae. Subsidia 7 (Rome: Edizioni liturgiche, 1976), pp. 127–54; Alexandre Olivar i Daydí, 'Survivances wisigothiques dans la liturgie catalano-languedocienne', in *Liturgie et musique (ixe–xive s.)*, Cahiers de Fanjeaux 17 (Toulouse: Privat, 1982), pp. 157–72; Miquel dels Sants Gros i Pujol, 'De l'església hispana a l'església carolíngia i el canvi de litúrga', in *Del romà al romànic. Història, art i cultura de la Tarraconense mediterrània entre els segles iv y x*, ed. by Père de Palol i Salellas/Antoni Pladevall i Font, (Barcelona: Enciclopèdia Catalana, 1999), pp. 397–407 [with 8 figures] (pp. 397 and 400–7).

90 The story of the Carolingian homiliaries in early medieval Catalonia has still to be written, so I will not give the first critical overview here. Beside later Catalan traces of the Homiliaries by Paul the Deacon and Haimo of Auxerre, we have at least five early testimonies: 1) a copy of Smaragdus of Saint-Mihiel's *Collectiones in Epistolas et Evangelia* mentioned in the testament of Bishop Idalguer of Vic of 908, who surely belonged to the Narbonnais clerics who restored the bishopric of Vic in late ninth century: as n. 32; 2) a copy of the same work in the testament of Bishop Riculf of Elne from 915: as n. 36; 3) the fragment of a Caroligian homiletic collection, Vic, Arxiu i Biblioteca Episcopal, Fragm. XXIII/27, Narbonnais, last quarter of the ninth century: Gros i Pujol, *La Biblioteca Episcopal*, p. 23 no 8 (with figure of fol. 1r); Francesc Xavier Altés [i] Aguiló, 'Un Homiliari i una col·lecció homilètica carolingis, copiats a l'entorn de l'any 900 (Vic, Arx. Cap., ms. 60, i Arx. Episc., frag. XXIII/27)', *Miscel·lània litúrgica catalana* 20 (2012), 15–45 [with 1 figure] (pp. 15, 18 and 32–6); Ludwig Vones, 'Bischofssitze als geistige Zentren eines katalanischen Kulturraumes im 10. Jahrhundert. Barcelona, Vic und Girona', in *Bischofsbild und Bischofssitz*. Geistige und geistliche Impulse aus regionalen Zentren des Hochmittelalters, ed. by Hanns Peter Neuheuser, Archa Verbi. Subsidia 9 (Münster in Westfalen: Aschendorff, 2013), pp. 173–203 (p. 176); 4) a copy of Hrabanus Maurus's *Homiliae in Evangelia et Epistolas* mentioned in the testament of Bishop Riculf of Elne of 915: 'librum Rabanum unum', ed. Migne, *PL* 132, col. 468 l. 49: Altés i Aguiló, 'A propòsit', p. 37 n. 123; Palazzo, 'Arts somptuaires', p. 214 (without identification); 5) the homiliary of an unknown Carolingian author for the morning office of the Sundays and the most important feast days of the liturgical year, Vic, Arxiu i Biblioteca Episcopal, Ms. 60 (LXXXVI): Gros i Pujol, *La Biblioteca Episcopal*, p. 17 (with figure of fol. 14v); Altés [i] Aguiló, 'Un Homiliari', pp. 15, 17–31 and 36–45. This last manuscript is the product of an unidentified scriptorium of the Narbonnais of the last quarter of the ninth century and thus seemingly also belongs to the first wave of manuscripts imported for the newly restored Vic Cathedral in late ninth century.

91 Zacarías García Villada, *Historia eclesiástica de España* 3: La Iglesia desde la invasión sarracena, en 711, hasta la toma de Toledo, en 1085, (Madrid: Compañia Ibero-Americana de Publicaciones, 1936), p. 386 suggested a date in Carolingian times ca. 850 because of the explicit reference to the reigning Emperor. This dating is seemingly taken from the colophon of Madrid, Biblioteca de la Real Academia de la Historia, Ms. 17, fol. 241va, which however does not mention Emperor Lothar I (817–855), but King Lothar III of West Francia (954–986): as n. 96.

92 Ed. Angelo Mai, *Scriptorum veterum nova collectio e Vaticanis codicibus edita* 9 (Roma: 1837), pp. 189–256 (= Migne, *PL* 72, col. 803–60).

93 Città del Vaticano, Biblioteca Apostolica Vaticana, Vat. lat. 6081 and Roma, Biblioteca Vallicelliana, Tomus XX. The Vallicelliana-manuscript was already known to Jean Mabillon/Michel Germain, *Museum Italicum seu Collectio Veterum Scriptorum ex Bibliothecis Italicis* … 1, (Paris: 1687), p. 69. Città del Vaticano, Biblioteca Apostolica Vaticana, Vat. lat. 6454, fol. 192–216 is a reorganized copy of the Luculentius-Homilies in Città del Vaticano, Biblioteca Apostolica Vaticana, Vat. lat. 6081 made by Giovanni Battista Bandini: Alfons Müller, 'Ein neues Fragment aus dem Schriftkommentar des Luculentius', *Theologische Quartalschrift* 93 (1911), 206–22 (p. 207). A fragment of the Homily on Eph

How Carolingian was early medieval Catalonia? **131**

3, 13–6, 10 is transmitted in Città del Vaticano, Biblioteca Apostolica Vaticana, Vat. lat. 6071, fol. 15: Werner Affeldt, 'Verzeichnis der Römerbriefkommentare der lateinischen Kirche bis zu Nikolaus von Lyra', *Traditio* 13 (1957), 369–406 (p. 388).

94 A further Homily on Gal 5, 25–6, 10 in Città del Vaticano, Biblioteca Apostolica Vaticana, Vat. lat. 6081, fol. 10–12 was published by Müller, 'Ein neues Fragment', pp. 211–8 (= Migne, *Suppl.* 4, Paris 1967–1971, coll. 1416–20).

95 Madrid, Biblioteca de la Real Academia de la Historia, Ms. 17 and Ms. 21: Joseph Lemarié, 'La collection carolingienne de Luculentius restituée par les deux codices Madrid, Real Academia de la Historia, Aemil. 17 et 21', *Sacris erudiri* 27 (1984), 221–371; Elisa Ruiz García, *Catálogo de la sección de codices de la Real Academia de la Historia*, (Madrid: Real Academia de la Historia, 1997), pp. 145–7 no 17 and pp. 169–73 no 21. Both manuscripts are now available in digitized form under the link: http://bibliotecadigital.rah.es. August Eduard Anspach discovered these copies and identifed their texts already in 1914: Ángel Custodio Vega [y Rodríguez], 'El Prof. Doctor August Eduard Anspach. Semblanza literaria', in José María Fernández Catón, *Catálogo de los materiales codicológicos y bibliográficos del legado científico del Prof. Dr. August Eduard Anspach.* Prólogo del P. Á. Custodio Vega, O.S.A., (León: 1966), pp. 9–28 (pp. 22 sq. and 28; ibid., p. 96 sq). The manuscripts' attribution to the productive scriptorium of Sant Cugat has been worked out by Anscari Manuel Mundó [i Marcet], 'Entorn de dos còdexs del segle xè de Sant Cugat del Vallès', *Faventia* 4, 2 (1982), 7–23 [with 3 figures]; Idem, 'Collectaneum seu Homiliae Luculentii in Epistolas et Evangelia (Madrid, R. Academia de la Historia, San Millán Ms. 17 i 21)', in *Catalunya romànica* 18: El Vallès Occidental, ed. by Antoni Pladevall i Font, (Barcelona: Enciclopèdia catalana, 1991), p. 190 sq. [with 2 figures].

96 'Explicit liber Deo gratias. Orate pro Truitario presbitero qui scripsit hunc librum collectaneum in honore sanctissimi Cucufati martiris sub Landerico abba anno iii regnante Leutario rege, et dedit illum ad Regiatus sacer propter remedium anime sue': Mundó i Marcet, 'Entorn', p. 20.

97 Vic, Arxiu i Biblioteca Episcopal, Fragm. XXIII/7, first quarter of the tenth century; Vilafranca del Penedès, Arxiu Comarcal de l'Alt Penedès, Comunitat de Preveres de Vilafranca, 17: G-8–79 and G-10–99 and Barcelona, Arxiu de la Corona d'Aragó, Col·lecions, Fragm. 249, Sant Cugat del Vallès (?), last quarter of the tenth century; Tarragona, Arxiu Històric Arxidiocesà, Ms. 21/3, twelfth century (not: end of the tenth century): Francesc Xavier Altés [i] Aguiló, 'La tradició codicològica i litúrgica de l'homiliari carolingi de Luculentius a Catalunya. La recensió catalana. Inventari i homilies recuperades', *Miscel·lània litúrgica catalana* 18 (2010), 71–241 [with 15 figures] (pp. 81, 87, 92–4, 99, 104 sq. and 118 sq., furthermore p. 195 no 87, p. 130 sq. no 3 and p. 135 (figure), p. 199 sq. no 95 and p. 185 (figure), and p. 166 sq. no 51 and p. 159 (figure)). Here as in n. 99 Altés i Aguiló's datings need a careful revision based on assured palaeographical data.

98 Lemarié, 'La collection', p. 238 n. 24 and p. 281. Altés i Aguiló, 'La tradició codicològica', p. 83 emphasises the posteriority of this redaction.

99 Altés i Aguiló, 'A propòsit', pp. 35–42; Idem, 'La tradició codicològica', pp. 81 sq., 87, 93, 104, 111 sq. and 118. Both cited articles also broach the issue of the rich further transmission of Luculentius's homilies in other liturgical manuscripts of Catalonia since the eleventh century, research already begun by Raymond Étaix, 'Quelques homéliaires de la région catalane', *Recherches augustiniennes* 16 (1981), 333–98 (pp. 337, 353 sq., 369 sq., p. 371 n. 27, pp. 375, 384 and p. 395 with n. 52).

100 In contrast to the first redaction, where from *Homilia* 57 onwards the biblical citations are abbreviated systematically, many biblical quotes are not abbreviated, but given in detail: Altés i Aguiló, 'La tradició codicològica', p. 82 sq.

101 Étaix, 'Quelques homéliaires', p. 395 n. 51.

102 With regard to the text and its order in the lectionary used by Smaragdus: Lemarié, 'La collection', pp. 229–35, 240 and 243–6. Nearly all other exploited homilies and other texts are older, coming from Jerome, Pelagius, Augustine, Gregory the Great and Bede

132 Matthias M. Tischler

the Venerable: García Villada, *Historia eclesiástica*, p. 386; Joseph Lemarié, 'Deux fragments d'homéliaires conservés aux archives capitulaires de Vich, témoins de sermons pseudo-augustiniens et du commentaire de Luculentius sur les Évangiles', *Revue des études augustiniennes* 25 (1979), 85–105 (p. 102); Idem, 'La collection', p. 243; Hildegund Müller, *Exemplarische Untersuchungen zu den Quellen des Luculentius-Homiliars*, Dipl. (Wien: 1988), pp. 26–9; Eadem, *Das 'Luculentius'-Homiliar*. Quellenkritische Untersuchungen mit Teiledition, Wiener Studien. Beiheft 23. Arbeiten zur Mittel- und Neulateinischen Philologie 3 (Wien: Verlag der Österreichischen Akademie der Wissenschaften, 1999), pp. 44–59.

103 García Villada, *Historia eclesiástica*, p. 385.

104 Altés i Aguiló, 'La tradició codicològica', p. 76 then collected a number of Catalan testimonies that show that 'luculentius' and 'luculenter' were favoured attributes of liturgical or exegetical texts. Already Johann Albert Fabricius, *Bibliotheca latina mediae et infimae aetatis* 4 (Hamburg: 1735), p. 844 assumed that we deal more with an epithet than a proper name.

105 Lemarié, 'Deux fragments', pp. 102–4; Altés i Aguiló, 'A propòsit', p. 41; Lemarié, 'La collection', pp. 240 and 243 sq. For this Carolingian homiliary see Henri Barre, *Les homéliaires carolingiens de l'école d'Auxerre*. Authenticité. Inventaire. Tableaux comparatifs. Initia, Studi e testi 225 (Città del Vaticano: Biblioteca Apostolica Vaticana, 1962), pp. 113–22; Francesc Xaxier Altes i Aguilo, 'La "pars aestiva" de l'Homiliari de l'ofici catalanonarbonès. Inventari i difusió. Reconstitució de la seva recensió de l'Homiliari carolingi de Liverani', *Miscel·lània litúrgica catalana* 8 (1997), 107–59 (pp. 118–59).

106 Hermann Josef Frede, *Kirchenschriftsteller*. Verzeichnis und Sigel, Vetus Latina. Die Reste der altlateinischen Bibel 1, 1 (Freiburg im Breisgau: Herder, 1995), p. 616 no 953; Eligius Dekkers, *Clavis patrum latinorum*, CChr.SL (Steenbrugge, 1995), p. 308 no 953 thus assumed an author from the ninth/tenth century and the latter omitted him in his *Clavis patrum latinorum*. Roger Gryson, *Répertoire général des auteurs ecclésiastiques latins de l'Antiquité et du Haut Moyen Âge* 2: Répertoire des auteurs: I–Z. Auteurs sans sigle propre. Tables, Vetus Latina. Die Reste der altlateinischen Bibel 1, 1[5] (Freiburg im Breisgau: Herder, 2007), p. 638 no 953 follows these repertories.

107 He is missing in Jesús Alturo i Perucho, 'La cultura llatina medieval a Catalunya. Estat de la qüestió', *Symposium internacional sobre els orígens de Catalunya*, 1, pp. 21–48; Zimmermann, *Écrire et lire* 1–2; Jose Carlos Martin [y Iglesias], *Sources latines de l'Espagne tardo-antique et médiévale (v[e]–xive siècles)*. Répertoire bibliographique. Avec la collaboration de Carmen Cardelle de Hartmann et Jacques Elfassi, Documents, études et repertoires publié par l'Institut de Recherche et d'Histoire des Textes 77 (Paris: CNRS éditions, 2010).

108 Altés i Aguiló, 'La tradició codicològica', p. 73 sq.

109 Gros i Pujol, 'Fragments de Bíblies', p. 155 n. 6 mentions the early extensive use of Luculentius's work in a Narbonne collection of patristic commentaries on the Epistle and Gospel lectures during the Holy Mass, although his dating to the first half of the ninth century is impossible.

110 Paris, Bibliothèque nationale de France, Ms. lat. 3829 is a copy of Luculentius's collection (in a revised version containing only 74 homilies on the Gospel lectures and some new homilies) from the last quarter of the twelfth century and was in use at Carcassonne Cathedral: Étaix, 'Quelques homéliaires', p. 394 sq.; Lemarié, 'La collection', p. 230 with n. 12, p. 238 sq., p. 245 n. 34, pp. 246–50 and 253–77; Idem, 'Les homélies pour la dédicace de la collection de Luculentius et du Parisinus 3829', *Miscel·lània litúrgica catalana* 3 (1984), 27–45 (pp. 27–30 and 35–44); Francesc Xaxier Altés i Aguiló, 'Una recensió del segle xi de les homilies sobre les epístoles estivals de l'Homiliari dit de "Luculenti(us)", testimoniada en els homiliaris de l'ofici del monestir de Serrateix i de la canòncia de Solsona', *Miscel·lània litúrgica catalana* 15 (2007), 273–304 [with 3 figures] (p. 274 with n. 6); Idem, 'La tradició codicològica', pp. 83, 99 sq. and 107 sq.

111 Paris, Bibliothèque nationale de France, Ms. lat. 5259 is a copy for the 'officium capituli', meaning a 'liber capituli' of this abbey made in the middle of the thirteenth century:

Francesc Xaxier Altés i Aguiló, 'Les "Homiliae capitulares" del monestir de Sant Ponç de Tomeres i l'homiliari de l'ofici catalanonarbonès', *Miscel·lània litúrgica catalana* 11 (2003), 131–57; Idem, 'La tradició codicològica', pp. 90 and 95.

112 Besides his preference for Benedictine sources, Bernard Capelle, 'Le Maître antérieur à S. Benoît?', *Revue d'histoire ecclésiastique* 41 (1946), 66–75 (p. 73); Altés i Aguiló, 'A propòsit', p. 39 sq. n. 132; Müller, *Das 'Luculentius'-Homiliar*, p. 59; Altés i Aguiló, 'La tradició codicològica', p. 75 could detect unquestionable traces of Benedictine monasticism in Luculentius's work.

113 Altés i Aguiló, 'A propòsit', p. 40 n. 133; Lemarié, 'Les homélies', p. 45; Müller, *Das 'Luculentius'-Homiliar*, pp. 30–4; Altés i Aguiló, 'La tradició codicològica', p. 74.

114 Sūrahs 2, 219, 4, 43 and 5, 90 sq.: They ask thee concerning wine and gambling. Say: "In them is great sin, and some profit, for men; but the sin is greater than the profit." They ask thee how much they are to spend; say: "What is beyond your needs." Thus doth God make clear to you his signs: in order that ye may consider ... O ye who believe! Approach not prayers with a mind befogged, until ye can understand all that ye say ... O ye who believe! Intoxicants and gambling, (dedication of) stones, and (divination by) arrows, are an abomination, of Satans handiwork: eschew such (abomination), that ye may prosper. Satan's plan is (but) to excite enmity and hatred between you, with intoxicants and gambling, and hinder you from the remembrance of God, and from prayer: will ye not then abstain?', trad. 'Abdullāh Yūsuf 'Alī, *The Holy Qur'an*. Text, translation and commentary 1, (Cambridge (Ma.): 1934 (etc.)), pp. 14a–726a (pp. 86a, 193a and 270a sq.).

115 García Villada, *Historia eclesiástica*, p. 386.

116 *Homilia* 128: 'ET NOLITE INEBRIARI VINO, IN QUO EST LUXURIA. Sicut enim homo non potest duobus dominis servire, Deo scilicet et mammonae, ita nullus potest inebriari vino pariter et SPIRITU SANCTO repleri. Qui Spiritu sancto repletus fuerit habebit prudentiam, castitatem, munditiam, pudicitiam, mansuetudinem, verecundiam. E regione qui vino inebriatur, habebit procacitatem, insipientiam, audaciam, furorem, libidinem. Et ideo praecipit Apostolus, non debere "inebriari vino, in quo est luxuria". Unde dicit Salomon: "Ne aspicias vinum cum flavescit in vitro; color enim blande [Cod., "blandis"] ingreditur, sed mordet ut coluber." Potest et aliter intelligi quod dicit: "Nolite inebriari vino", id est vino malitiae, de quo Moyses in cantico Deuteronomio: "De vinea Sodomorum, vinea eorum." Hoc vino inebriantur omnes amatores mundi. De quibus dicit Apostolus: "Quorum finis interitus, quorum Deus venter est, et gloria in confusione ipsorum qui terrena sapiunt"', ed. Migne, *PL* 72, col. 838 l. 10–29. The text has been checked against the two copies from Sant Cugat del Vallès, Madrid, Biblioteca de la Real Academia de la Historia, Ms. 17, fol. 202vb–203vb, here fol. 203rb–203va, and Madrid, Biblioteca de la Real Academia de la Historia, Ms. 21, fol. 222ra–223va, here fol. 222vb–223ra. Their common text shows some minor differences which nevertheless do not change the sense in general.

8

ORCHESTRATING HARMONY

Litanies, queens, and discord in the Carolingian and Ottonian empires

Megan Welton

Sometime during the second half of 791, the Carolingian Queen Fastrada received by letter a detailed account of a three-day litany organized by Charlemagne and his collected clergymen on the eve of battle with the Avars.[1] The letter details how all those present in the Frankish camp were asked to abstain from wine and meat throughout the three-day rite unless prevented by illness or age; those who still wished to partake in wine were required to pay.[2] As the gathered laity either fasted or gave alms, priests performed a special mass (*missam specialem*), while the clergy sang fifty of the psalms together and recited the litanies, all whilst barefoot.[3] At the beginning of his detailed description, Charlemagne, the sender of this letter, laid bare the rationale for the marathon liturgical venture: 'that He would vouchsafe to grant us peace and safety and victory and a successful expedition and that in His mercy and goodness He would be our helper and counsellor and defender in all our difficulties'.[4] Charlemagne concluded his letter by requesting that Fastrada, together with unnamed *fideles* in Regensburg, would organize litanies within the bounds of the Carolingian kingdom *qualiter ipsa letanias*, if she was in good health herself.[5]

Considered the only surviving personal letter from Charlemagne himself, this epistle is remarkable for a host of reasons.[6] It is, for instance, the only extant letter addressed to Queen Fastrada. Behind this single epistle lay an unknown series of exchanges, as indicated by Charlemagne's concluding complaint that Fastrada had not written more often since he last saw her, and his subsequent demand for more letters. More significant is the meat of the missive itself: namely, the litanies that Charlemagne and his itinerant court orchestrated and those that Fastrada and her court organized in the kingdom in Regensburg. Around the same time that this letter was composed and received, Fastrada's *nomen* appeared in another text, the so-called Montpellier Psalter, which ends with the earliest extant Carolingian *laudes regiae*.[7] Dated to the third quarter of the eighth century, the *laudes regiae* in the Montpellier Psalter comes as an addition at the end of the manuscript.[8]

Immediately preceding it, an extensive litany spanning almost three folios of two columns includes exhortations for prayers naming the Virgin Mary, cherubim and seraphim, the apostles, as well as a long series of martyrs, confessors, *virgines,* and other sainted figures. The litany ends with prayers for the stability of the king (*pro stabilitate rege*) and for the clergy. Near the bottom of the second column on f. 343v, a single blank line separates the final *Kyrie Eleison* and the opening *Christus uincit, Christus regnat, Christus imperat.* These *laudes regiae* prescribe specific prayers for Pope Hadrian, Charlemagne, and Charlemagne's sons. The last individual to be listed by name is Queen Fastrada, with prayers for her *salus et vita*, and petitions for the *virgines Christi* to pray directly to Christ for her continued health and life.[9] Immediately after Fastrada, the gathered congregation would then pray for all of the judges and the entire Frankish army.[10]

As demonstrated by Fastrada's letter and the Montpellier Psalter's *laudes regiae,* liturgy structured the world as harmony. For Carolingian and Ottonian rulers, litanies and the *laudes regiae* created what Ernst Kantorowicz termed 'the cosmic harmony of heaven, Church and State, an interweaving and twining of the one world with the other and an alliance between the powers on earth and the powers in heaven'.[11] This celestial concordance clearly informed the visual semiotics of many early medieval liturgical manuscripts. In the *laudes regiae* contained in a miscellany known as the Metz tonary, for instance, the entire rite is confined to a single folio, from the standard opening proclamations of *Christus uincit, Christus regnat, Christus imperat* to the final *Amen.*[12] Arranged in two neat columns, this *laudes* visually associates heavenly intercessors with individual secular leaders. In the first column, each unnamed ruler – whether pope, emperor, queen, or bishop – jumps off the page, as they command their own section of apostolic, angelic, and saintly intercessors who are subsequently invoked to come to the aid of the acclaimed ruler. The second column's supplications turn from acclamations for pontifical and temporal rulers to prayers for the entire community in Christ, their *Rex regum,* in whom they placed their hope as *our* impenetrable wall, *our* unconquerable army, *our* fortitude, *our* wisdom, *our* moderation, *our* virtue.[13]

This visual and textual representation of a cosmic harmony belies the real historical discord that litanies often sought to stave off. Such discord comes to the fore when we shift our gaze away from the figure most commonly studied in connection with these rites – namely the king or emperor – and fix onto the other leaders and the wider political community imbedded in liturgical manuscripts and in the epistolary exchanges and historical narratives that detail how these rites were performed. This present study focuses on one comparatively neglected category of rulers included in Carolingian and Ottonian litanies, namely, the queen or empress.[14] The goal of this analysis is not merely to *cherchez la reine,* but also to analyse the picture of political consensus that these rites presented and, as evidenced by historical narratives and letters, seemed to contemporaries to achieve in moments of potential discord and disaster.

This chapter will explore the role of Carolingian and Ottonian royal women in the royal liturgy, and particularly in the litanies and *laudes regiae* present in extant

136 Megan Welton

sacramentaries, graduals, tropers, and other liturgical manuscripts surviving from the late eighth, ninth, and tenth centuries. It explores a central tension between the manuscript evidence and the historical narratives, between the hope for a cosmic harmony and the reality of discord, disease, and war. This chapter examines this tension through queens and empresses who appear inconsistently in the liturgical manuscripts, but who consistently work within the wider political community at specific historical moments to oversee these important liturgical rites. It looks especially at those manuscripts that show the visible marks of this instability through the physical act of erasure. Precisely this element of instability and potential for discord, this chapter will argue, guaranteed that litanies attested not just to royal or imperial authority, but likewise to vulnerability.

Litanies, *laudes regiae*, and early medieval rulers

Although a distinctive religious rite with a formulaic structure, the early medieval litany served a multitude of purposes, and survives in a multitude of forms. Walahfrid Strabo defined litanies as public supplications (*rogationes publicas*), yet as Michael Lapidge has argued,

> the word *litaniae* (or *letaniae/laetaniae* as it came – wrongly – to be spelled) could embrace a wide range of meanings, from litanic or supplicatory prayers used in Mass and Office, to penitential processions accompanied by petitions or *rogationes* (which must have included litanic prayers of some sort), and to the annual feasts on which such processions took place, namely the Major Litanies (Great Rogations) of 25 April, and the Minor Litanies (Lesser Rogations) on the three days before the Ascension.[15]

Litanies could function as daily, habitual praxis and, at moments of unifying celebration and potential moments of discord, as extraordinary events. For Carolingian and Ottonian rulers, the extraordinary events included acclamations after one's coronation, a ruler's *adventus*, or the conclusion of an important synod, as in 876 at the Council of Ponthion. At the end of this council, Bishop Peter of Fossombrone and John of Toscanella brought Empress Richildis to stand beside Emperor Charles the Bald. As she stood next to the emperor,

> Everyone rose to his feet, each standing in position according to his rank. Then Bishop Leo and Bishop John of Toscanella began the *Laudes*, and when these had been duly performed for the lord pope and the lord emperor and the empress and all the rest, according to custom, Bishop Leo of Sabina said a prayer, and the synod was finally dissolved.[16]

This detailed description from the *Annals of St-Bertin* creates a visual scene of harmony, with each member of the gathered assembly positioned in their place, with Charles the Bald and Richildis standing next to each other, listening to the pope's and their own names acclaimed. The following analysis, however, is concerned with more tenuous moments in Carolingian and Ottonian politics, particularly in times of strife, when these same litanies and *laudes regiae* were enlisted to restore harmony to a discordant reality.

This plurality of purposes for the litany is reflected in their formal variability, for no two extant early medieval litanies are alike.[17] This mutability of form and function is likewise reflected in the inclusion or omission of the reigning queen or empress. Supplications for the reigning queen or empress take a variety of forms within litanies.[18] At times, the scribe inserted the reigning queen's *nomen* into the body of the litany, while in other manuscripts the placeholder of *illa* allowed the celebrant to insert the ruler's name at the appropriate moment.[19] Several Carolingian and Ottonian manuscripts containing litanies omit supplications or acclamations for the reigning queen or empress entirely, instead praying for the king or emperor and then for his children or some other parties.[20] However, these irregularities were not limited to queens alone, and extended to every party within the extant litanies. Indeed, in one late ninth- or early tenth-century manuscript now housed at Angers' Bibliothèque Municipale, a litany spanning several folios contains only prayers for the 'peace and unanimity of the Christian people', while another mid-ninth-century litany in Freiburg im Breisgau, Universitätsbibliothek, MS 363, contains various prayers only for the Frankish army.[21]

Both the litanies and the *laudes regiae* in their varied ways associate heavenly intercessors with temporal leaders.[22] The *laudes regiae*, in particular, provide interesting, if complex, insights into the protean nature of this association. Overall, the *laudes* tend to invoke early Christian female martyrs – often virgin martyrs – to intercede for the reigning queen or empress. In the Carolingian and Ottonian *laudes regiae* analyzed here, the saints Perpetua, Felicitas, Agatha, and Cecilia appear most frequently as intercessors for the queen.[23] However, some important caveats must be noted. First, there are a few *laudes* which associate the reigning queen or empress with male saints, as in Verona, Biblioteca MS XCII (87).[24] On f. 69r, the scribe composed acclamations for the Empresses Judith and Ermengard together, with the presiding celebrant invoking St. Martin and St. Benedict to intercede for their *salus et vita*.[25] Indeed, in a separate *laudes* contained within the same manuscript, the celebrant called upon St. Paul to intercede for these same empresses, while invoking *Sancta Maria* to pray for the Emperors Louis and Charles the Bald.[26] Likewise, various *laudes* called upon female saints to intercede for male rulers. On f. 76v of Metz, Bibliothèque-médiathèque, MS 351, the virgin martyrs Petronilla, Agnes, Cecilia, Anastasia, Genofeva, and Columba were all invoked to pray for the presiding bishop, while in an earlier version of the *laudes regiae* praying for Charles the Bald and Ermentrude, the rite calls for *Sancta Maria* to intercede for the king and the *Sancta virgo virginum* to intercede for the judges and the entire army of the Franks.[27] Indeed, the Virgin Mary – whether as *Sancta Maria, virgo virginum, genetrix Dei* or under some other designation – was called upon in numerous *laudes* to pray for the king or emperor, queen or empress, and other secular leaders.[28]

138   Megan Welton

Early medieval scribes only rarely produced royal votive masses, litanies, or *laudes regiae* in isolation.[29] These rites more commonly appear within psalters, sacramentaries, graduals, tropers and other liturgical manuscripts designed to perform a multitude of functions. Indeed, many of these manuscripts were not just produced by and for the clergy, but also served the quotidian needs of the wider community, from the temporal and sanctoral cycle of masses to the specific prayers for everything from difficulty conceiving children to the burial of the dead. Therefore, as scholars have demonstrated, modern readers must exercise caution in assessing a ruler's ideology or projection of power on the basis of these complex rites.[30]

Even with these caveats, Carolingian and Ottonian letters sent to and from rulers suggest the centrality of litanies performed on a regular and episodic basis, and particularly the incorporation of queens and empresses in their performance. Two letter collections from the early Carolingian period – namely, the *Codex epistolaris carolinus* and Abbess Theutild of Remiremont's *Indicularius* – preserve correspondence between religious leaders and the reigning ruler, with specific details of the performance of prayers and litanies for the king. Collected together in 791, the *Codex epistolaris carolinus* contains almost one hundred letters sent from the Lateran palace from 739 until the year the collection was produced.[31] Several letters in this collection either begin or end with the pope promising prayers for the reigning Carolingian king and queen, and for the longevity of their governance of the Frankish realm. In letter 18, dating to the beginning of 759, Pope Paul I ends his message to King Pippin by praying to God to preserve Pippin's life, to fulfil the *victoria regni gubernacula* and the promise of eternal life for him along with his 'sweetest wife, the most excellent queen, our spiritual *commatre*', Bertha, as well as for their children.[32] In a letter sent almost twenty years later in May of 778, Pope Hadrian related to Charlemagne that the church gave 'praise to God (*laudes Deo*) for the exaltation of your kingdom and of our daughter, the queen, your wife, your children and for all of the Franks, the *fidelis* of the blessed apostle Peter, and for you'.[33]

The pope was not the only religious leader to set down in letters his promise to pray for the reigning Carolingian king and queen. In her *Indicularius*, which survives solely in a tenth-century manuscript that gathered several letter collections, Abbess Theutild of Remiremont (d. 865) addressed a number of Carolingian dignitaries including Empress Judith and Emperor Louis the Pious. In her first letter to Louis, Abbess Theutild famously declared that her community at Remiremont prayed one thousand psalmodies and eight hundred masses with offerings and litanies each year, not only for the safety (*pro vestre incolomitate*) of Louis, but also for that of the most worthy queen (*dignissimeque regine*) and the royal children.[34] Such sentiments find corollaries in a template for entreating the king contained in a late ninth-century addition to a manuscript of a formulary contained in Vatican City, Biblioteca Apostolica Vaticana, Reg. lat. 612. On f. 33r, this particular formula advises its reader to state that the sender prays day and night (*die noctuque*) for the king *vel pro donna regina et pro filis et filiabus vestro vel pro stabilitate regni vestri*, doing so via masses and psalms.[35]

A few manuscripts suggest that rulers at least were prescribed to recite litanies for themselves in psalters created for their own use. Two such ornate psalters for

Charles the Bald contain litanies for the king and his queen Ermentrude. The king's sumptuous psalter, now Paris, Bibliothèque nationale de France, MS lat. 1152, concludes with three two-columned folios listing the Virgin Mary, angels, the apostles, martyrs, virgins, and others all embossed in gold, with the 'S' of their *Sancte* placed within a continuous red border. At the bottom of f. 171v, the scribe instructs the reader to pray for *Ut mihi karolo a te regi coronato uitam et prosperitatem atque uictoriam dones te rogo audi me*. At the top of the following folio, the reader would pray for *hirmindrudim coniugem nostram conseruare digneris . Te rogamus audi nos*.[36]

In another manuscript labelled on f.1r in gold lettering as the *Enchiridion Precationum Caroli Calvi Regis*, another litany tailored for the king begins on f. 22v in a format similar to the previous psalter.[37] Both begin with the title *Incipit Laetania* and contain two columns naming the collected saints, all picked out in gold lettering. However, the gilded 'S' of *sancte* is contained within a linear stripe of deep purple. Furthermore, the *ut* invocations start with prayers for the pope. The rite goes on to stipulate that the reader should pray *ut mihi tua misericordia uitam . et prosperitatem . uictoriam . atque post obitum requiem aeternam donare digneris te rogamus*.[38] Once again, there follows a prayer for Ermentrude, as well as for the conservation of peace for all of the Christian people, and for the eternal rest of Charles' ancestors.[39]

Even within these two manuscripts – created around the same time and for the same ruler – the litanies differ in important respects. In contrast to his psalter now in Paris, Charles' *Enchiridion* attached no title to Charles himself within the litany, although his title as king was sprinkled throughout the rest of the manuscript. Furthermore, prayers for the rulers could stand on their own, or they could be coupled with prayers for other important leaders (such as the pope) and, crucially, for their wider religious and secular communities.

Only one prayerbook for a tenth-century ruler survives, namely Otto III's *Gebetbuch* (Munich, Bayerische Staatsbibliothek, MS Clm 30111). Composed sometime between 983 and 996, this *libellus* also contains a litany for the young king to recite, with prayers for the pope and all those ordained within the church, the bishops and all their congregations, and the entire Christian people.[40] In between the pope and the bishops, the young king was instructed to pray for 'me, your servant and an unworthy king, and all our *principes*'.[41] Although there are no specific prayers for a queen or empress in this manuscript, scholars speculate that the youthful aspect of each of the three miniatures representing Otto III indicates that this text was composed during the regencies of Empress Theophanu and Empress Adelheid, perhaps even under their direction.[42] Furthermore, another manuscript possibly intended for Otto III's personal use and composed around the turn of the millennium – the Bamberg troper (Bamberg, Staatsbibliothek, MS Msc. Lit. 5) – contains a *laudes regiae* with prayers for an unnamed empress.[43]

Even as Otto III's *Gebetbuch* remains the only extant psalter for royal use, another now-lost psalter could have contained a litany, namely the psalter of Queen Emma of Francia (b.c. 948 – d. post-987). Presumably destroyed in a fire of 1774 along with many other manuscripts contained in the library of Saint-Remi, Mabillon in his *Annales ordinis Sancti Benedicti* described Emma's psalter as a *libellus precum*. Mabillon noted that there was a calendar at the beginning of the manuscript.[44] A catalogue of the Saint-Remi holdings compiled in 1640 provides a few more details, claiming that the first Psalm contained gold lettering written upon purpled parchment and 'that very many or even the greater part of the Psalms which followed were introduced by pictures inspired by the substance of the text'.[45] As Cahn has argued in his analysis of these descriptions of Emma's lost *libellus precum*, such a manuscript 'could also contain additional texts of particular concern to the owner: litanies and special devotions, penitential prayers and so forth'.[46] Cahn even goes on to draw comparisons to Charles the Bald's psalter in Munich's Schatzkammer and Ot to III's *Gebetbuch*.[47]

The mutability of liturgical manuscripts

Terrestrial threats could impel the performance of early medieval litanies. As medieval scribes copied, annotated, and corrected earlier liturgical rites, they were not only adapting formulae rooted in the Roman imperial and late antique past for use in present circumstances.[48] They were also inscribing and reinscribing words that would hopefully serve to steady an uncertain future by eliciting the intercession of saints for current rulers and by reminding these rulers of their personal and public responsibilities and ties to their *populum* and the wider Christian community.

These responsibilities merged in the discourse of political *virtus* which inflected both political thought and the liturgical language of the litanies.[49] Bishop Rather of Verona (b.c. 887 – d. 974), for instance, called upon kings to practice, train in, and be glorified by key features of kingship in his *Praeloquia*:

> Be prudent, just, brave, and temperate. Use these virtues as a four-horse chariot, as it were, in which to course the limits of your realm ... Protected by this four-fold breastplate, do not hesitate to meet the enemy unflinching; for you cannot be conquered by any adversaries if only you merit to be defended by such protection.[50]

Like Alcuin and the Carolingian *literati* before him, Rather admonished kings against basing their governance exclusively on martial strength. The king, in Rather's view, must grasp onto the 'four-horse chariot' of virtue in order to prove his ability to secure victories against his enemies and to govern his people correctly.

If a king could not, or would not, exhibit *virtus*, Rather did not consider him a king at all. Rather explicitly stated that any king who did not embody the four virtues of prudence, justice, courage, and moderation could not rightly be called king. 'We properly know these four virtues as "'royal"',' Rather averred,

> so that even some peasant who has them can fittingly be called king, whereas without them even he who holds almost total sovereignty of the world (though abusing it) cannot rightly be called king; for by bad government, as the thinker above says, the greatest empire is lost.[51]

Orchestrating harmony **141**

At a time when several rivals vied for the Carolingian crown, Rather's ideal king cloaked himself not in armour and physical strength but in the practice of political *virtus*.

Crucially, Rather expected the same display of *virtus* from queens that he did from kings. In his subsequent chapter, Rather asked 'Are you a queen? If so, much of the advice applies to you'.[52] Rather's expectation that a ruler's actions should embody justice, wisdom, moderation, and courage appears in other tenth-century political writings, including chronicles and annals, as well as letters, coronation *ordines*, and poetry. Carolingian and Ottonian authors alike crafted their narratives by using the discourse of *virtus* and *vitium* to assess the performance of secular rulers throughout western Christendom.[53]

To be of any consequence, the rulers' exhibition of these virtues required recognition from their political community.[54] As the litanies and, particularly, the *laudes regiae* associated leading religious and secular figures with the performance of these virtues as well as with saintly exemplars who had perfected such attributes, they also reminded all present of the requirements for a ruler to govern well. The ruler's performance of *virtus* required perpetual validation as their political community's response could and did constantly change. This mutability was reflected in the manuscripts preserving litanies and *laudes regiae* themselves as they often underwent additions, removals, and erasures depending on local context and broader political changes.

These alterations to liturgical manuscripts occur in the earliest Carolingian manuscript for the *laudes regiae*, the previously discussed Montpellier Psalter. Formerly known as the Psalter of Charlemagne, this small, yet deluxe manuscript contains two beautiful illuminations, one of David grasping a harp and the other of Christ holding a codex, along with over a hundred and fifty large initials embossed in gold and silver and more than 2000 smaller coloured initials scattered throughout the codex.[55] The culminating folios of the Montpellier Psalter contain the *laudes regiae*, which were added later to the original manuscript sometime before the death of Fastrada in 794.

Bernhard Bischoff first convincingly argued that this psalter did not originate at Charlemagne's court, but instead at Mondsee Abbey in Bavaria when it was still under the control of Duke Tassilo III of Bavaria.[56] Scholars have hypothesized that a dedication addressed to Tassilo or his family – or perhaps, as Johannes Fried has postulated, liturgical commemorations resembling the *laudes regiae* for the ruling Bavarian family – was ripped from the back of the manuscript and replaced with the Carolingian *laudes regiae*.[57] In either case, these *laudes regiae* have two further features of interest that scholars have highlighted. First, the scribe wrote the responses throughout the Montpellier Psalter's *laudes* not with the traditional *Tu illum/illa/illos adiuva*, but instead in the vulgar Latin form of *Tu lo iuua* and *Tu los iuua*. As Mary Garrison has aptly argued, 'this was what the participants had said themselves in their tongue, collectively imploring divine and supernatural help in a moment of prayer, ceremony and consensus'.[58] However, a final, concise litany inscribed with visibly darker ink on f. 345r immediately after this *laudes*

142 Megan Welton

regiae might suggest that resistance to this consensus could have continued. The litany culminates in a prayer for a *sororem nomine Rotrude*.[59] Two Rotrudes have been isolated as potential candidates: either the daughter of Charlemagne and Hildegard or, fascinatingly, the daughter of Duke Tassilo III himself.[60] If this Carolingian insertion at the end of the Montpellier Psalter was 'clearly a way of asserting authority', this assertion of authority and consensus was by no means immune from dissenting voices.[61]

These physical acts of removal and replacement find echoes in later Carolingian and Ottonian practice. Three individual rites of the *laudes regiae* conclude the liturgical manuscript Verona, Biblioteca capitolare Cod. XCII (87), composed in ninth-century Verona, but with significant emendations to two sets of the *laudes regiae* by contemporary hands.[62] The first *laudes* contains prayers for an unnamed bishop of Verona, an emperor, an empress, and the Christian army. In this manuscript, two additional *laudes* pray specifically for both Empress Judith and Empress Ermengarde, along with their respective husbands Louis the Pious and Lothar.[63] In the final set of *laudes* on fol. 70v-71v, which scholars have postulated could be the earliest, the original scribe acclaimed Empress Judith, with St. Paul as her intercessor. Subsequently, however, this entire clause was excised, visible only in a ghostly form on the folio, and replaced at a later date with the words *Ermingarde imperatrici victoria*, as well as with the reinscription of St. Paul as Ermengarde's saintly advocate.[64] A similar process occurs in the second set of *laudes*, beginning on fol. 68v. In this particular *laudes*, however, the original intended for a joint series of acclamations, beginning with Emperors Louis the Pious and Lothar and followed by *Judite et Ermengarde imperatricibus*.[65] Again, however, a later hand erased Judith's name, and corrected the plural ending of *imperatricibus* to *imperatrici*. As Westwell has recently argued, this unique triplicate series of *laudes* and the physical removal of Judith from the parchment 'suggest that the contents of the manuscript remained relevant and continued to be actively employed in the cathedral of Verona for decades'.[66]

The oldest Ottonian manuscript containing a *laudes regiae* likewise contains an excised queen's name. Munich, Bayerische Staatsbiliothek, MS Clm 27305 is largely composed of a martyrology, a computational text, a collectar, and a *laudes paschale* with royal acclamations amongst other texts, which scholars have dated to the late 950s or early 960s.[67] On page 241, the *laudes* began with the simple title: *Incipiunt laudes pascale*. As in many other *laudes*, the first acclamation was reserved for the preservation of an unnamed pope, written as *summo pontifici et universali papae*, with accompanying intercessions from the saints Peter, Paul, and Andrew.[68] Next, the celebrant would pray for King Otto I, who according to this *laudes*, was 'a great and peaceful king, crowned by God', and for whom the *Redemptor mundi*, as well as the archangels Michael, Gabriel, and Raphael, along with St. John and St. Stephan, should all intercede.[69] After prayers for the Ottonian queen, to which we will return shortly, appear acclamations for the royal couple's *nobilissime proli* followed by acclamations for Bishop Abraham of Freising and his *cunctae congregationi* at St. Mary's in Freising.[70] The final acclamations pray for the *vita et victoria* of all of the judges and the entire Christian army.

Initially, acclamations for Otto I were succeeded by prayers for the wellbeing and life of *Odae reginae*. As her intercessors, the rite called upon *Sancta Maria*, and the virgin martyrs Petronella, Agnes, Cecilia, Anastasia, Waltpurga, and Columba.[71] This Oda has been identified as the Anglo-Saxon Queen Edith, Otto I's first wife, who died prematurely in 946. Indeed, in 1858, Rockinger noted that Edith's name had been erased at some date, which prompts three further questions.[72] First, why did the scribe in the 950s or early 960s transcribe the name of a queen who had been dead for at least a decade? Second, did this scribe or their immediate contemporaries realize the incongruity of this ascription, and if so does this mean another queen – perhaps Adelheid, Theophanu, or even Mathilda – was substituted during a particular recitation of this rite? Finally, was there a lost exemplar that contained Edith's name, suggesting perhaps that this practice of liturgical acclamations extended earlier into the tenth century among the Ottonians?

Though it is not yet possible to answer these questions, the elision and erasure of these queens underscores the ephemeral nature of these rites. Tying an individual liturgical performance to a single historical moment is tenuous at best, particularly considering how modern scholars cannot access the on-the-spot decisions made by the presiding cleric or observe the response of the audience. The construction of community attempted through these litanies is equally ephemeral. Inscribing the queen into these sacred manuscripts and enlisting the prayers of individual saints not only elevated the queen and symbolically projected her royal authority; it also simultaneously forced the audience and the queen herself to question whether her actions and her life were, indeed, exemplary; if she was, indeed, virtuous enough to deserve these prayers and to lead her community to a safe and stable future.

As the Carolingian Queen Fastrada organized litanies within Saxony to ensure the success of Charlemagne's campaign against the Avars, Ottonian queens and empresses also utilized this liturgical form to avert disaster in troublesome times. There exists at least one specific parallel of a king on campaign requesting a queen who had remained at court to perform liturgical services in a time of war, albeit after the battle had been won. In 955 at the Battle of Lechfeld, Otto I famously defeated the Magyars. In the aftermath, Widukind of Corvey claimed that Otto I 'decreed that worthy honor and praise (*honoribus et dignis laudibus*) be given to God in every church'.[73] Widukind then states that Otto I quickly had sent word to his 'sainted mother', Queen Mathilda, of his victory.[74] Furthermore, Thietmar of Merseburg added to this messenger's letter and/or oral report that the victorious king sent a messenger to Mathilda

> with a complete report of what had happened, and also to arouse the souls of the faithful to the praise of Christ. All of Christendom, but especially that part committed to the king, received such a great gift of divine piety with ineffable joy, offering praise and thanks to God in the highest with one voice.[75]

144   Megan Welton

Charlemagne's implementation of litanies sought to shore up God's divine assistance in the midst of a military campaign; Otto I's similar practice offered praise and thanks in the glow of victory. Both instances, however, not only enlisted the queen or queen mother to implement these liturgies throughout Carolingian Francia and Ottonian Saxony respectively, but they also sought to bind their kingdoms together, under the king and queen, 'with one voice'.

A further example of the performance of litanies during a period of uncertainty appears in the late tenth- or early eleventh-century *Translatio et miracula sanctorum Senesii et Theopontii*.[76] The fifth and sixth chapters describe the translation of these two saints' bodies from Nonantola to Pavia. A severe outbreak of plague had struck the citizens of Pavia, and so the translation of the relics of the saints Sinesius and Theopontius to Pavia through several cities with three days of fasting was organized, with accompanying prayers, singing, and the recitation of psalms by multitudes.[77] As the relics approached Pavia, men and women greeted the bodies of the saints by praising God (*laudantes Deum*), as *regina gloriosissima* Adelheid sat in attendance.[78] At this precise moment, Adelheid enriched the relics with a multitude of gifts.[79] Thereafter, the city of Pavia 'was liberated from this deadly plague by these pious defences' and the citizens of Pavia praised and honoured Adelheid for ending their suffering.[80]

The tenuous nature of the performance of these liturgical rites for rulers is exemplified by a final example from a famously unstable period of Ottonian political history.[81] In 984 and 985, the canonesses of Quedlinburg sang out the divine *laudes* for two rival parties grasping for control over the Ottonian imperial throne. Otto II's death in Rome in December of 983 had struck the Ottonian court, as Thietmar of Merseberg claimed, like 'a harsh bolt'.[82] Central members of the Ottonian court – including Otto II's wife, Empress Theophanu, his mother, Empress Adelheid, and his sister, Abbess Mathilda of Quedlinburg – were all with Otto II in Italy before his sudden death. Yet, they had sent the three-year-old Otto III back to Saxony to be crowned king at Aachen a few months prior. This spatial distance caused an immense problem for the *dominae imperiales* and presented an irresistable opportunity for Otto III's uncle, Duke Henry II of Bavaria.

After news reached Saxony of Otto II's demise, Bishop Folcmar of Utrecht released Henry from his lengthy confinement in Utrecht. Henry acted quickly and asserted his claim to custody over the young, and newly anointed king, Otto III in Saxony. According to Thietmar's *Chronicon*, Duke Henry first gathered the leading nobles in Saxony to celebrate Palm Sunday in Magdeburg, and 'in the course of negotiations, demanded that they submit to his power and raise him to the kingship'.[83] Thereafter, Henry travelled the well-worn route to Quedlinburg to celebrate Easter, accompanied by 'the great men of the duchy ... and some who did not wish to come in person sent a representative who was to scrutinize everything carefully'.[84] Once in Quedlinburg, Henry's supporters 'openly greeted him as king and he was honoured with divine *laudes*'.[85]

Orchestrating harmony **145**

It is at this point in his narrative that Thietmar notes a rift in the Saxon nobility and Henry's wider base of support. Whereas the foreign dukes including Mieszko I of Poland and Boleslaus II of Bohemia swore an oath to confirm their support for Henry as king after these *laudes*, 'many others, not daring to violate their oath to the king, [and] for fear of God', thereafter began to switch their alliance.[86]

According to the *Annales Quedlinburgenses*, after Henry had 'tyrannically seized the throne', the empresses assembled a formidable force of Burgundians, Swabians, Italians, Franks, Thuringians, and Slavs and, together, they crossed into Saxony.[87] At a great assembly of both camps at Rohr, Henry 'was rightly deprived of the name and kingdom he had usurped'.[88] Henry was compelled to surrender his nephew, Otto III, to Adelheid, Theophanu, and Mathilda. The triumphant *dominae imperiales* travelled on to Saxony, where their first port of call was Quedlinburg. There, according to Quedlinburg's annalist, these two empresses and Quedlinburg's abbess 'were received most courteously with the sweet melody of praise by a great crowd of clergy and people, and also by the virgins serving Christ there who piously offered thanks' for their abbess's safe return and the empresses' triumph.[89] These several performances of the liturgy are remarkable not only for their divergent receptions, but perhaps even more so for their commonalities. Both Henry and the *dominae imperiales* utilized the sacred and historically significant space of Quedlinburg in order to solidify their imperial claim and control over Otto III. Even more crucially, Thietmar and the annalist of Quedlinburg noted the presence and response of the wider civic and political community.

Liturgy structured the world as harmony; yet the performance of liturgical rites could be triggered by discord. Evidence from Carolingian and Ottonian narrative sources shows how plagues, battles, and succession crises occasioned the performance of litanies and *laudes regiae*. At the same time, evidence internal to liturgical manuscripts shows how successive scribes and celebrants extracted, overwrote, or amended the very names and titles of rulers in order to accommodate immediate religio-political requirements. By attending to the presence and position of Carolingian and Ottonian queens and empresses in liturgy, this chapter has brought these background instabilities back into the foreground.

Royal and imperial women worked with clergy and their wider court to ensure the public, communal performance of liturgical rites, and they heard their own names recited amongst the heavenly saints along with their fellow temporal rulers. Such rites served to structure their performance as rulers, reminding them of their responsibilities and of the exemplars whose *virtus* they should emulate.

This internalization is finely displayed in Odilo of Cluny's description of Empress Adelheid's final day. In his *Epitaphium*, Odilo claimed that after Adelheid had received her last rites, she requested the recitation of the penitential psalms as well as the litany of saints to be sung by those attending her, both clergy and lay. As they began, the empress herself joined in 'psalming with those singing the psalms, and praying with those praying'.[90] In this moment of ultimate transition, she bound everyone in attendance to her and created a harmonious space through the use of liturgy.[91]

146 Megan Welton

Notes

1 *Nos autem, Domino adiuvante, tribus diebus letania fecimus.* Paris, Bibliothèque nationale de France, MS lat. 2777, f. 61r–61v (s.ix). *Epistolae variorum Carolo magno regnante scriptae*, no. 20, in *Monumenta Historica Germaniae (MGH) Epistolae (Epp.)* IV, ed. by Ernst Dümmler (Berlin: Weidmann, 1895), pp. 528–9, trans. P.D. King, *Charlemagne: Translated Sources* (Kendal: P.D. King, 1986), pp. 309–10. For more on the political and religious context of this letter see Michael McCormick, 'The Liturgy of War in the Early Middle Ages: Crisis, Litanies, and the Carolingian Monarchy', *Viator* 15 (1984), pp. 1–23. Janet L. Nelson, 'The Sitting of the Council at Frankfort: Some Reflections on Family and Politics', in *Das Frankfurter Konzil von 794: Kristallisationspunkt karolingischer Kultur. Akten zweier Symposien (vom 23. bis 27. Februar und vom 13. bis 15. Oktober 1994) anläßlich der 1200-Jahrfeier der Stadt Frankfurt am Main* I, ed. by Rainer Berndt SJ (Mainz: Der Gesellschaft für mittelrheinische Kirchengeschichte, 1997), pp. 149–65, at 159. Mayke de Jong, 'Charlemagne's Church', in *Charlemagne: Empire and Society*, ed. by Joanna Story (Manchester: Manchester University Press, 2005), pp. 103–35, at p. 128. For the manuscript context of this letter, see Mary Garrison, 'Letters to a King and Biblical Exempla: The Examples of Cathwulf and *Peregrinus*', *Early Medieval Europe* 7 (1998), pp. 305–28. Rosamond McKitterick, *Charlemagne: The Formation of a European Identity* (Cambridge: Cambridge University Press, 2008), pp. 43–8. Alice Rio, *Legal Practice and the Written Word in the Early Middle Ages* (Cambridge: Cambridge University Press, 2009), pp. 142–3. For more on Fastrada see, Janet L. Nelson, 'Women at the Court of Charlemagne: A Case of Monstrous Regiment?', in *Medieval Queenship*, ed. by John C. Parsons (New York: St. Martin's Press, 1993), pp. 43–61, reprinted in Janet L. Nelson, *The Frankish World 750–900* (London: The Hambledon Press, 1996), pp. 223–42. Matthew Innes, 'Queenship in Dispute: Fastrada, History and Law', in *Writing the Early Medieval West: Studies in Honour of Rosamond McKitterick*, ed. by Elina Screen and Charles West (Cambridge: Cambridge University Press, 2018), pp. 230–47.
2 *Epistolae variorum Carolo magno regnante scriptae*, no. 20, in *MGH Epp.* IV, ed. Dümmler, p. 528.
3 Ibid., pp. 528–9.
4 *… ut nobis pacem et sanitatem atque victoriam et prosperum iter tribuere dignetur, et ut in sua misericordia et pietate nobis adiutor et consiliator atque defensor in omnibus angustiis nostris exsistat. Epistolae variorum Carolo magno regnante scriptae*, no. 20, in *MGH Epp.* IV, ed. Dümmler, p. 528, trans. King, *Charlemagne: Translated Sources*, p. 310.
5 Ibid., p.529.
6 See note 1.
7 Montpellier, Bibliothèque Interuniversitaire, Faculté de Médecine, MS H 409, fol. 343v–344v (before 794). A digital facsimile of this Psalter can be found here: https://bvmm.irht.cnrs.fr/consult/consult.php?reproductionId=17271. See Elias A. Lowe, *Codices latini antiquiores: A Paleographical Guide to Latin Manuscripts Prior to the Ninth Century* VI (Oxford: Clarendon Press, 1962), no. 795. Ernst H. Kantorowicz, 'Ivories and Litanies', *Journal of the Warburg and Courtauld Institutes* 5 (1942), pp. 56–81. Bernhard Opfermann, *Die liturgischen Herrscherakklamationen im Sacrum Imperium des Mittelalters* (Weimar: Hermann Böhlaus, 1953), p. 101. Ernst H. Kantorowicz, *Laudes Regiae: A Study in Liturgical Acclamations and Mediaeval Ruler Worship* (Berkeley: University of California Press, 1958), pp. 21 and 33–7. Franz Unterkircher, *Die Glossen des Psalters von Mondsee (vor 788) (Montpellier Faculté de Médecine MS 409)*, Spicilegium Friburgense 20 (Freiburg: Universitätsverlag, 1974), pp. 30–45, with edition at p. 507ff. Bernhard Bischoff, *Die südostdeutschen Schreibschulen und Bibliotheken in der Karolingerzeit II: Die vorwiegend Österreichischen Diözesen* (Wiesbaden: Otto Harrassowitz, 1980), pp. 16–8. Mary Garrison, 'The Franks as the New Israel? Education for an Identity from Pippin to Charlemagne', in *The Uses of the Past in the Early Middle Ages*, ed. by Yitzhak Hen and Matthew Innes (Cambridge: Cambridge University Press, 2000), pp. 114–61, at pp. 140–6.
8 The circumstances of this addition will be discussed below.

9 *Exaudi Christe. Fastradane regina salus et vita. Alia virgines Christi, qualis volueris.* Montpellier, Bibliothèque Interuniversitaire, Faculté de Médecine, MS H 409, fol. 344r. Opfermann, *Die liturgischen Herrscherakklamationen*, p. 101.

10 *Exaudi Christe. Omnibus iudicibus vel cuncto exercitui Francorum vita et victoria.* Ibid. fol. 344r–344v.

11 Kantorowicz, *Laudes Regiae*, p. 62. The bibliography on early medieval litanies, with a particular focus on the *laudes regiae*, is extensive. In addition to note 3, see, Ludwig Biehl, *Das liturgische Gebet für Kaiser und Reich: ein Beitrag zur Geschichte des Verhältnisses von Kirche und Staat* (Paderborn: Schöningh, 1937). Maurice Coens, 'Anciennes litanies des saints', *Analecta Bollandiana* 54 (1936), pp. 1–37. Idem, 'Anciennes litanies des saints', *Analecta Bollandiana* 54 (1937), pp. 49–69. Idem, 'Anciennes litanies des saints', *Analecta Bollandiana* 54 (1941), pp. 272–93. Idem, 'Anciennes litanies des saints', *Analecta Bollandiana* 54 (1944), pp. 126–68. Reinhard Elze, 'Die Herrscherlaudes im Mittelalter', *Zeitschrift der Savigny-Stiftung für Rechtsgeschichte* 40 (1954), pp. 201–23. McCormick, 'Liturgy of War', pp. 1–23. Michael McCormick, *Eternal Victory: Triumphal Rulership in Late Antiquity, Byzantium and the Early Medieval West* (Cambridge: Cambridge University Press, 1990). Michael Lapidge, *Anglo-Saxon Litanies of the Saints*, Henry Bradshaw Society CVI (London: Henry Bradshaw Society, 1991). Yitzhak Hen, *The Royal Patronage of Liturgy in Frankish Gaul to the Death of Charles the Bald (887)*, Henry Bradshaw Society Subsidia 3 (Woodbridge: Boydell and Brewer, 2001). Astrid Krüger, *Litanei-Handschriften der Karolingerzeit*, MGH Hilfsmittel 24 (Hannover: Hahn, 2007). Ildar Garipzanov, *The Symbolic Language of Authority in the Carolingian World (c. 751–877)* (Leiden: Brill, 2008), pp. 46–53.

12 Metz, Bibliothèque-médiathèque, MS 351, f. 76r (s.ix/x). A digitized facsimile can be found here: www.flickr.com/photos/bnmetz/sets/72157640923158474/. Opfermann, *Die liturgischen Herrscherakklamation*, pp. 112–3. Walter Lipphardt, *Der karolingischer Tonar von Metz* (Münster: Aschendorffsche Verlagsbuchhandlung, 1965). For the manuscript's wider context, see Anna Maria Busse Berger, *Medieval Music and the Art of Memory* (Berkeley: University of California Press, 2005), pp. 60–7.

13 Metz, Bibliothèque-médiathèque, MS 351, f. 76r. Opfermann, *Die liturgischen Herrscherakklamationen*, p. 113. See Kantorowicz, *Laudes Regiae*, p. 19. Garrison, 'The Franks as the New Israel?', p. 142.

14 However, scholars have extensively analyzed one important liturgical rite for queens and empresses, namely coronation *ordines*. Amongst others, see Julie Ann Smith, 'Queen-Making and Queenship in Early Medieval England and Francia', (University of York, Ph.D. diss., 1993). Eadem, 'The Earliest Queen-Making Rites', *Church History* 66 (1997), pp. 18–35. Janet L. Nelson, 'Early Medieval Rites of Queen-Making and the Shaping of Medieval Queenship', in *Queens and Queenship in Medieval Europe*, ed. by Anne Duggan (Woodbridge: Boydell Press, 1997), pp. 301–16. Franz-Reiner Erkens, '*Sicut Esther regina*: Die westfrankische Königin als *consors regni*', *Francia* 20 (1993), pp. 15–37. Julie Ann Smith, 'The Earliest Queen-Making Rites', *Church History* 66 (1997), pp. 18–35. See also, Amalie Fössel, *Die Königin im mittelalterlichen Reich: Herrschaftsausübung, Herrschaftsrechte, Handlungsspielräume* (Stuttgart: Jan Thorbecke, 2000), pp. 15–20. Martina Hartmann, *Die Königin im frühen Mittelalter* (Stuttgart: Kohlhammer, 2009), pp. 146–8. Simon MacLean, *Ottonian Queenship* (Oxford: Oxford University Press, 2017), pp. 180–206.

15 Walahfrid Strabo, *Libellus de exordiis et incrementis quarundam in observationibus ecclesiasticis rerum*, c. 29, in *MGH Capitularia regum Francorum II*, ed. by Alfred Boretius and Victor Krause (Hannover: Hahn, 1897), p. 513. Alice L. Harting-Correa, ed. and trans., *Walahfrid Strabo's Libellus de exordiis et incrementis quarundam in observationibus ecclesiasticis rerum: A Translation and Liturgical Commentary* (Leiden: Brill, 1996), p. 186. Lapidge, *Anglo-Saxon Litanies*, p. 11. See also, Krüger, *Litanei-Handschriften der Karolingerzeit*, p. 20ff.

16 *…surrexerunt omnes, stantes quique in gradu suo. Tunc incoeperunt laudes Leo episcopus et Iohannes Tuscanensis episcopus, et post laudes peractas in domnum apostolicum et domnum imperatorem ac imperatricem et ceteros iuxta morem, data oratione a Leone Gavinense episcopo, soluta est synodus.* Annales Bertiniani, *MGH Scriptores rerum Germanicarum in usum scholarum separatim editi* 5,

148 Megan Welton

ed. by Georg Waitz (Hannover: Hahn, 1883), p. 131. Janet L. Nelson, trans. *The Annals of St. Bertin: Ninth-Century Histories* I (Manchester: Manchester University Press, 1991), p. 195. Kantorowicz, *Laudes Regiae*, p. 70.

17 Lapidge, *Anglo-Saxon Litanies*, p. 2.

18 The following manuscripts contain litanies and/or *laudes regiae* with prayers or acclamations for a queen or empress: Montpellier, Bibliothèque Interuniversitaire, Faculté de Médecine, MS H 409 (before 794); Verona, Biblioteca capitolare, Cod. XCII (87), fol. 67r–68r, fol. 68v–69v, fol. 70v–71v; Munich, Schatzkammer der Residenz, no MS number (842x869); Paris, Bibliothèque nationale de France, MS lat. 1152, fol. 170v–172r (842x869); Vatican City, Biblioteca Apostolica Vaticana, MS Reg. lat. 1997, fol. 160v (s.ix^med); St. Gall, Stiftsbibliothek, MS 397, pp. 2–3 (s.ix^med); Frankfurt am Main, Stadt- und Universitätsbibliothek, MS Barth. 179 (c.870); Cambridge, Corpus Christi College, MS 272, fol. 151r–154v (883/884); Paris, Bibliothèque Sainte-Geneviève, MS 111, fol. 23v–24r (887x882); Orléans, Bibliothèque Municipale, MS 196 (173), pp.136–40 (s.ix^{2/2}); Metz, Bibliothèque-médiathèque, MS 351, fol. 76r (s.ix/x); Monza, Biblioteca Capitolare, MS 7 B 15/98, fol. 48r (s.ix/x); Milan, Biblioteca Ambrosiana, MS A. 24 *bis* inf (s.x); Munich, Bayerische Staatsbibliothek, MS Clm 27305, pp. 241–5 (957x962); London, British Library, MS Add. 19768, fol.56v (967x972); Bamberg, Staatsbibliothek, MS Msc. Lit. 5, fol. 46r–47v (c.1000); Bamberg, Staatsbibliothek, MS Msc. Lit. 6, fol. 92r (c.1000).

19 For instance, the scribe of London, British Library, MS Add. 19768 named *Adelheide nobilissimae reginae* on f. 56v, while the scribe of Bamberg, Staatsbibliothek, MS Msc. Lit. 5 inscribed *Ill. Imperatrici salus et vita* on f. 46v. For a recent analysis of London, British Library, MS Add. 19768, see Henry Parkes, *The Making of the Liturgy in the Ottonian Church: Books, Music and Ritual in Mainz 950–1050* (Cambridge: Cambridge University Press, 2015), pp. 31–88. For a complete manuscript description of Bamberg, Staatsbibliothek, MS Msc. Lit. 5, see Friedrich Leitschuh, *Katalog der Handschriften der Königlichen Bibliothek zu Bamberg* I (Wiesbaden: Harrassowitz, 1966), pp. 143–45.

20 To take but one example, see another psalter composed around the same time as Montpellier, Bibliothèque Interuniversitaire, Faculté de Médecine, MS H 409: Paris, Bibliothèque nationale de France, MS lat.13159, fol. 163r (c.800), with acclamations for Pope Leo III, Charlemagne, his *nobilissime proli regali*, all of the kingdom's judges and the *cuncto exercitui Romanorum*.

21 Angers, Bibliothèque Municipale, MS 91 (83), fol. 130v–134r (s.ix/x). See Krüger, *Litanei-Handschriften*, no. 45. Freiburg im Breisgau, Universitätsbibliothek, MS 363, fol. 50r–52v (s.ix^med). See Krüger, *Litanei-Handschriften*, no. 67.

22 For a more in-depth analysis of the intricate connection between litanies and *laudes regiae*, see Opfermann, *Die liturgischen Herrscherakklamationen*, pp. 54–5. Krüger, *Litanei-Handschriften*, p. 31ff.

23 Perpetua: Vatican City, Biblioteca Apostolica Vaticana, MS Reg. lat. 1997, fol. 160v; St. Gall, Stiftsbibliothek, MS 397, pp. 2–3; Orléans, Bibliothèque Municipale, MS 196 (173), pp.136–40; Metz, Bibliothèque-médiathèque, MS 351, fol. 76r; Bamberg, Staatsbibliothek, MS Msc. Lit. 5, fol. 46r–47v; Bamberg, Staatsbibliothek, MS Msc. Lit. 6, fol. 92r. Felicitas: Vatican City, Biblioteca Apostolica Vaticana, MS Reg. lat. 1997, fol. 160v; St. Gall, Stiftsbibliothek, MS 397, pp. 2–3; Orléans, Bibliothèque Municipale, MS 196 (173), pp. 136–40. Agatha: Vatican City, Biblioteca Apostolica Vaticana, MS Reg. lat. 1997, fol. 160v; Metz, Bibliothèque-médiathèque, MS 351, fol. 76r; London, British Library, MS Add. 19768, fol. 56v; Bamberg, Staatsbibliothek, MS Msc. Lit. 5, fol. 46r–47v; Bamberg, Staatsbibliothek, MS Msc. Lit. 6, fol. 92r. Cecilia: Vatican City, Biblioteca Apostolica Vaticana, MS Reg. lat. 1997, fol. 160v; St. Gall, Stiftsbibliothek, MS 397, pp. 2–3; Munich, Bayerische Staatsbibliothek, MS Clm 27305, fol. 241–45; London, British Library, MS Add. 19768, fol. 56v.

24 Michel Andrieu, *Les 'Ordines Romani' du haut moyen age* I, Spicilegium Sacrum Lovaniense XI (Louvain: 'Spicilegium sacrum lovaniense' bureaux, 1931), pp. 473ff. Kantorowicz, *Laudes Regiae*, p. 33. Opfermann, *Die liturgischen Herrscherakklamationen*, pp. 24–6, with

edition at 103 and 115 (Nachtrag). Giles G. Meersseman, E. Adda, and Jean Deshusses, eds., *L'orazionale dell'arcidiacono Pacifico e il carpsum del cantore Stefano: Studie e testi sulla liturgica del duomo di Verona dal' IX all'XI sec.* (Freiburg: Edizioni universitarie, 1974), pp. 188–90. Susanna Polloni, 'Manoscritti liturgici della Biblioteca Capitolare di Verona (sec. IX)', in *Medioevo. Studi e documenti* II, ed. by Andrea Castagnetti et al. (Verona: Libreria Editrice, 2007), pp. 151–228, at 165–8.

25 *[Judit et] Ermingarde imperatrici(bus) vita. Sante Martine … Sancte Benedicte …* Opfermann, *Die liturgischen Herrscherakklamationen*, p. 115.

26 For the emperor: *… augusto (a Deo coronato magno et pacifico) imperatori vita (et victoria). Sancta Maria. Tu illum adiuva.* For Judith and Ermengarde: *Exaudi Christe. Judite imperatrici (nostre vita et victoria) ((Ermingarde imperatrici victoria)). Sancte Paule. Tu illam adiuva.* Opfermann, *Die liturgischen Herrscherakklamationen*, p. 115 and Nachtrag.

27 The earlier *laudes regiae* is Orléans, Bibliothèque Municipale, MS 196 (173), pp. 136–40. Opfermann, *Die liturgischen Herrscherakklamationen*, p. 108. See Marco Mostert, *The Library of Fleury: A Provisional Lists of Manuscripts*, Middeleeuwse Studies en Bronnen 3 (Hilversum: Verloren, 1989), no. 650.

28 For the king or emperor: Verona, Biblioteca capitolare, Cod. XCII (87), fol. 70v–71v; Orléans, Bibliothèque Municipale, MS 196 (173), pp. 136–40; Bamberg, Staatsbibliothek, MS Msc. Lit. 5, fol. 46r–47v; Bamberg, Staatsbibliothek, MS Msc. Lit. 6, fol. 92. For the queen or empress: Verona, Biblioteca capitolare, Cod. XCII (87), fol. 67v–68r; Vatican City, Biblioteca Apostolica Vaticana, MS Reg. lat. 1997, fol. 160v; Orléans, Bibliothèque Municipale, MS 196 (173), pp. 136–40; Metz, Bibliothèque-médiathèque, MS 351, fol. 76r; Munich, Bayerische Staatsbibliothek, MS Clm 27305, fol. 241–45; London, British Library, MS Add. 19768, fol. 56v. For the judges and army: Orléans, Bibliothèque Municipale, MS 196 (173), pp. 136–40.

29 An important exception would be the ornate and extensive litany known as the Lorsch Rotulus (Frankfurt am Main, Stadt- und Universitätsbibliothek, Ms. Barth. 179). See Astrid Krüger, '*Sancte Nazari ora pro nobis*: Ludwig der Deutsche und der Lorscher Rotulus', in *Ludwig der Deutsche und seine Zeit*, ed. by Wilfried Hartmann (Darmstadt: Wissenschaftliche Buchgesellschaft, 2004), pp. 184–202. Eric J. Goldberg, *Struggle for Empire: Kingship and Conflict under Louis the German, 817–876* (Ithaca: Cornell University Press, 2006), pp. 159–62.

30 As Garipzanov acutely states, one must be cautious when speaking 'of political messages disseminated by the Carolingians through royal liturgy if none of these liturgical texts were written by them, but by intermediaries such as monastics and prelates who were both royal servants and interested parties'. Garipzanov, *Symbolic Communication*, p. 51.

31 Vienna, Österreichische Nationalbibliothek, MS Cod. Vindob. 449 (s.ix^{ex}). For more on the *Codex epistolaris carolinus*, see Dorine van Espelo, 'A Testimony of Carolingian rule? The *Codex epistolaris carolinus*, its Historical Context, and the Meaning of *imperium*', *Early Medieval Europe* 21 (2013), pp. 254–82. Eadem, 'Rulers, Popes and Bishops: The Historical Context of the Ninth-Century Cologne *Codex Carolinus* Manuscript', in *Religious Franks: Religion and Power in the Frankish Kingdoms: Studies in Honour of Mayke de Jong*, ed. by Rob M. J. Meens, Dorine van Espelo, Bram van den Hoven van Genderen, Janneke Raaijmakers, Irene van Renswoude and Carine van Rhijn (Manchester: Manchester University Press, 2016), pp. 455–71.

32 *cum dulcissima coniuge, excellentissima regina, spiritale nostra commatre. Codex epistolaris carolinus*, no. 18, *MGH Epp.* I, ed. by Wilhelm Gundlach (Berlin: Weidmann, 1892), p. 518.

33 *… et cepimus Deo laudes referre et beato principi apostolorum Petro pro exaltatione regni vestri atque filiae nostrae, reginae, coniugis vestrae, prolis etiam et pro cunctis Francis, fidelis beati Petri apostoli atque vestris. Codex epistolaris carolinus*, ed. Gundlach, p. 586. As Dorine van Espelo has pointed out, even though Pope Hadrian made a rare reference to the Byzantine emperor Constantine in this letter, the late ninth-century scribe considered it more important to label this letter as *item exemplar epistolae adriani papae ad domnum carolum regem directa, in qua continentur gratiarum actiones pro vita et sanitatae domni regis et uxoris vel*

filiorum eius nec non et pro exaltatione snctae dei ecclesiae; et postulans, ut filium suum ex sacro baptismatis fonte suscipere mereretur. See Dorine van Espelo, 'A Testimony of Carolingian Rule: The *Codex epistolaris Carolinus* as a Product of its Time' (Utrecht University, Ph.D. diss., 2014), p. 141.

34 *... Scire igitur obtamus vestram inianter excellentiam, quod quasi reconpensantes ineffabilibus clementie vestre muneribus, huius volvente anni circulo praesentique hoc in tempore pro vestra incolomitate dignissimeque regine ac dulcissime diu servande regis prolis cecinimus psalteria mille, missas DCCC cum oblationibus ac letaniis creberrimis.* Zürich, Zentralbibliothek, MS Cod. 141, f.57 (s.x). Theutild of Remiremont, *Indicularius*, no. 1, ed. by Michel Parisse, *La correspondance d'un évéque Carolingien: Frothaire de Toul (ca. 813–847) avec les letters de Theuthilde, abbesse de Remiremont* (Paris, 1998), p. 154. For *Indicularius*'s wider context and relevant bibliography, see Hailey J. LaVoy, 'Why Have You Been Silent For So Long?': Women and Letter Writing in the Early Middle Ages, 700-900, (University of Notre Dame, Ph.D. diss., 2015), pp. 36–69 and passim. Steven Vanderputten, *Dark Age Nunneries: The Ambiguous Identity of Female Monasticism, 800–1050* (Ithaca: Cornell University Press, 2018), p. 40ff.

35 'or for the domina queen and for their sons and daughters or for the stability of their kingdom.' A digitized facsimile of this manuscript can be found here: https://digi.vatlib. it/view/MSS_Reg.lat.612. See Rio, *Legal Practice and the Written Word*, pp. 126–32.

36 It should be noted that no prayers for the rulers' children were included in this litany. A digitized facsimile of this manuscript can be found here: https://gallica.bnf.fr/ ark:/12148/btv1b55001423q/f349.item.r=lat.zoom

37 Munich, Schatzkammer der Residenz, no MS number (842x869), fol. 22v–27r. A digitized facsimile of this manuscript can be found here: http://daten.digitale-sammlungen. de/~db/0007/bsb00079994/images/index.html?id=00079994&nativeno=26v. See Robert Deshman, 'The Exalted Servant: The Ruler Theology of the Prayerbook of Charles the Bald', *Viator* 11 (1980), pp. 387–417, repr. in Robert Deshman, *Eye and Mind: Collected Essays in Anglo-Saxon and Early Medieval Art*, ed. by Adam S. Cohen (Kalamazoo: Western Michigan University Press, 2010), pp. 192–219. William Diebold, 'Verbal, Visual, and Cultural Literacy in Medieval Art: Word and Image in the Psalter of Charles the Bald', *Word & Image* 8 (1992), pp. 89–99.

38 Munich, Schatzkammer der Residenz, no MS number, fol. 26r–26v.

39 Munich, Schatzkammer der Residenz, no MS number, fol. 26v.

40 For an excellent analysis and description of this text, with relevant bibliography, see Sarah Hamilton, '"Most Illustrious King of Kings": Evidence for Ottonian Kingship in the Otto III Prayerbook (Munich, Bayerische Staatsbibliothek, Clm 30111)', *Journal of Medieval History* 27 (2001), pp. 257–88. A digitized facsimile of this manuscript can be found here: http://daten.digitale-sammlungen.de/~db/0007/bsb00075079/images/.

41 *Ut me famulum tuum et regem indignum et omnes principes nostros ...* Munich, Bayerische Staatsbibliothek, MS Clm 30111, fol. 18v.

42 Karl Leyser, 'The Tenth Century in Byzantine-Western Relationships', in *The Relations Between East and West in the Middle Ages*, ed. by Derek Baker (Edinburgh: Edinburgh University Press, 1973), pp. 29–63, reprinted in Karl Leyser, *Medieval Germany and its Neighbours 900–1250* (London: Hambledon Press, 1982), pp. 103–38. Henry Mayr-Harting, *Ottonian Book Illumination: An Historical Study* I (London: Harvey Miller, 1991), pp. 173–5. Hamilton, '"Most Illustrious King of Kings"', pp. 257–88.

43 Bamberg, Staatsbibliothek, MS Msc. Lit. 5 (c.1000), fol. 46r–47v. Leitschuh, *Katalog der Handschriften der Königlichen Bibliothek zu Bamberg* I, pp. 143–5. See Hartmut Hoffmann, *Bamberger Handschriften des 10. und des 11. Jahrhunderts*, *MGH* Schriften 39 (Hannover: Hahn, 1995), pp. 144ff. Rosamond McKitterick, 'Ottonian Intellectual Culture in the Tenth Century and the Role of Theophano', in *The Empress Theophano: Byzantium and the West at the Turn of the First Millennium*, ed. by Adelbert Davids (Cambridge: Cambridge University Press, 1995), pp. 53–74, at 59.

44 Jean Mabillon, *Annales ordinis Sancti Benedicti* IV (1707), pp. 32–3.

Orchestrating harmony **151**

45 *Psalterium ad usum Hemmae Reginae psalmus in membrana purpurea litteris aureis exaratur. Sequuntur alii psalmi quorum plerisque imagines psalmi argumentum exprimentes praehibentur.* Paris, Bibliothèque nationale de France, MS lat. 13070, fol. 5v. A digitized facsimile of the manuscript can be found here: https://gallica.bnf.fr/ark:/12148/btv1b10515927f/f18. image.r=latin%2013070. Transcription in Walter Cahn, 'The Psalter of Queen Emma', in *Studies in Medieval Art and Interpretation*, ed. by Walter Cahn (London: The Pindar Press, 2000), pp. 239–62, at p. 243. See also, MacLean, *Ottonian Queenship*, p. 165.
46 Cahn, 'The Psalter of Queen Emma', p. 243.
47 Ibid., pp. 243–44.
48 See note 1 and note 3.
49 For a recent analysis and relevant bibliography on the cardinal virtues in the Middle Ages, see István Bejczy, *The Cardinal Virtues in the Middle Ages: A Study in Moral Thought from the Fourth to the Fourteenth Century* (Leiden: Brill, 2011). For a more extensive discussion of this discourse of political *virtus*, see Megan Welton, '*Multiplex Virtus*: Queens, Ruling Women, and the Discourse of Political Virtue in Tenth-Century Europe' (University of Notre Dame, Ph.D. diss, 2017).
50 *His ergo utere, his exercere, his exornare. Esto prudens, iustus, fortis et temperatus. Hoc quasi quadriga euectus regni fines perlustra; hoc denique curru ista utere in uia … hoc quadruplici munitus thorace, hostibus ne cuncteris imperterritus occurrere, nec enim poteris aliquibus aduersis deuinci, si tamen tanta merueris tuitione uallari merueris.* Rather of Verona, *Praeloquia*, 3.i.2, in *Ratherii Veronensis Opera, Fragmenta, Glossae*, ed. by Petrus L.D. Reid et al., CCCM 46A (Turnhout: Brill, 1984), p. 78. Petrus L. Reid, *The Complete Works of Rather of Verona* (Binghampton: Medieval and Renaissance Texts and Studies, 1991), p. 95. For the historical and historiographical context of Rather's life and work, see Jelle Wassenaar's contribution in this volume. See also, Hans Martin Klinkenberg, *Versuche und Untersuchungen zur Autobiographie bei Rather von Verona. Archiv für Kulturgeschichte* 38 (Köln: Böhlau, 1956), pp. 265–314. Irene van Renswoude, 'The Sincerity of Fiction: Rather and the Quest for Self-Knowledge', in *Ego Trouble: Authors and their Identities in the Early Middle Ages*, ed. by Rosamond McKitterick, Richard Corradini, Matthew Gillis, and Irene van Renswoude (Vienna: Austrian Academy of Sciences, 2010), pp. 309–34.
51 *Hae quattuor ita regales proprie noscuntur esse uirtutes, ut eum his quilibet etiam rusticus rex non incongrue dici; sine his nec ipse uniuersam pene monarchiam obtinens mundi, quanquam abusiue, rex ualeat iuste uocari; male enim imperando, ut ait qui supra, summum imperium amittitur.* Rather, *Praeloquia*, 3.i.5, ed. Reid et al, p. 80. Reid, trans., *Complete Works of Rather*, p. 97.
52 *Regina es? Preter alias innumeras, multa etiam quae et tibi iam superius posita competunt documenta.* Rather, *Praeloquia*, IV.i.36, ed. Reid, et al, p. 141. Reid, trans., *Complete Works of Rather*, p. 155.
53 See note 49.
54 In particular, see Hen, *The Royal Patronage of Liturgy*, pp. 151–2 and Garipzanov, *Symbolic Language of Authority*, pp. 50–1 and passim.
55 See note 7.
56 Bischoff, *Südöstdeutschen Schreibschulen* II, pp. 16–8. For the wider context, see Stuart Airlie, 'Narratives of Triumph and Rituals of Submission: Charlemagne's Mastering of Bavaria', *Transactions of the Royal Historical Society* 9 (1999), pp. 93–119.
57 Johannes Fried, *Charlemagne*, trans. by Peter Lewis (Harvard: Harvard University Press, 2016), p. 155.
58 Garrison, 'The Franks as the New Israel?', pp. 142–3.
59 *Tu mihi Christe concede sororem nomine Rotrude esse beatam ut tibi semper seruiat illa.* Montpellier, Bibliothèque Interuniversitaire, Faculté de Médecine, MS H 409, fol. 344v.
60 Unterkircher, *Die Glossen des Psalters von Mondsee*, p. 41. Garrison, 'The Franks as the New Israel?', p. 140, ft. 110. McKitterick, *Charlemagne*, p. 338. Fried, *Charlemagne*, p. 115.
61 Fried, *Charlemagne*, p. 155.
62 Verona, Biblioteca capitolare, Cod. XCII (87), fol. 67r–68r, fol. 68v–69v, fol. 70v–71v (s.ix). Andrieu, *Les Ordines* I, pp. 367–73. Opfermann, *Die Liturgischen Herrscherakklamationen*,

152 Megan Welton

pp. 103, 115, Nachtrag. Meersseman, Adda, and Deshusses, eds., *L'orazionale dell'arcidiacono pacifico e il carpsum del cantore Stefano*, pp. 188–90. Polloni, 'Manoscritti liturgici della Biblioteca Capitolare di Verona', pp. 165–8. Arthur Robert Westwell, 'The Dissemination and Reception of the *Ordines Romani* in the Carolingian Church, c. 750-900' (University of Cambridge, Ph.D. diss, 2017), pp. 89–93.

63 Westwell, 'The Dissemination and Reception of the *Ordines Romani*,' pp. 90–1.

64 Opfermann, *Die Liturgischen Herrscherakklamationen*, pp. 103, 115, Nachtrag.

65 Ibid.

66 Westwell, 'The Dissemination and Reception of the *Ordines Romani*', p. 91.

67 Munich, Bayerische Staatsbibliothek, MS Clm 27305, pp. 241–5. L. Rockinger, *Drei Formelsammlungen aus der Zeit der Karolinger: aus Münchner Handschriften* (Munich: Georg Franz, 1858), pp. 473–4. Opfermann, *Die liturgischen Herrscherakklamation*, pp. 124–6. Hermann Hauke, ed., *Katalog der lateinischen Handschriften der Bayerischen Staatsbibliothek München: Clm 27270–27499* (Wiesbaden: Harrassowitz, 1975), pp. 23–8.

68 Opfermann, *Die liturgischen Herrscherakklamation*, p. 124.

69 Ibid., pp. 124.

70 Ibid., pp. 124–5.

71 Ibid., pp. 124.

72 Rockinger, *Drei Formelsammlungen aus der Zeit der Karolinger*, p. 473.

73 *… decretis proinde honoribus et dignis laudibus summae divinitati per singulas ecclesias.* Widukind, *Res gestae saxonicae*, III.49, in *MGH SS rer. Germ.* 60, ed. by H.-E. Lohmann and Paul Hirsch (Hannover: Hahn, 1935), pp. 128–9. Bernard S. Bachrach and David S. Bachrach, trans., *Widukind of Corvey: Deeds of the Saxons* (Washington, D.C.: The Catholic University of America Press, 2014), p. 129.

74 *et hoc idem sanctae matri eius per nuntios,* Widukind, *Res gestae saxonicae*, III.49, ed. Lohmann and Hirsch, p. 129. Bachrach and Bachrach, trans., *Widukind of Corvey*, p. 129.

75 *… qui, cuncta ordine pandentes, eam cura solverent mentesque fidelium in laudem Christi pariter accenderent. Tantum divinae pietatis donum omnis christianitas maximeque regi commissa ineffabili suscepit tripudio, gloriam et gratiam spallens unanimiter in altissimis Deo.* Thietmar of Merseburg, *Chronicon*, II.10, in *MGH SS rer. Germ. N.S.* 9, ed. by Robert Holtzmann (Berlin: Weidmann, 1935), pp. 50–1. David A. Warner, trans., *Ottonian Germany: The Chronicon of Thietmar of Merseburg* (Manchester: Manchester University Press, 2001), pp. 98–9.

76 *Translatio et miracula Sanctorum Senesii et Theopontii*, *MGH SS* 30.2, ed. by Percy E. Schramm (Leipzig: K.W. Hiersemann, 1926), pp. 984–92. See Aldo A. Settia, 'Pavia carolingia e postcarolingia', in *Storia di Pavia* 2 (1987), pp. 69–158, at 154–5.

77 *Translatio et miracula Sanctorum Senesii et Theopontii*, ed. Schramm, pp. 988–9.

78 *Translatio et miracula Sanctorum Senesii et Theopontii*, ed. Schramm, p. 989.

79 Ibid.

80 *Urbe vero Papia a predicta mortis clade eorum piis patrociniis liberata.* Ibid.

81 Amongst others, see Franz R. Erkens,' *… more grecorum conregnantem instituere vultis?* Zur Legitimation der Regentschaft Heinrichs des Zänkers im Thronstreit von 984 , *Frühmittelalterliche Studien* 27 (1993), pp. 273–89. MacLean, *Ottonian Queenship*, p. 166ff.

82 *Duro vecte.* Thietmar, *Chronicon*, III. 26, ed. Holtzmann, pp. 130–1. Warner, trans., *Ottonian Germany*, p. 148.

83 *Qui cum palmarum sollemnia in Magadaburg celebrare voluisset, omnes regionis illius principes huc convenire rogavit atque precepit, tractans, quomodo se suae potestati subderent regnique eum fastigio sublevarent.* Thietmar, *Chronicon*, IV. 1, ed. Holtzmann, pp. 132–3. Warner, trans., *Ottonian Germany*, p. 150.

84 *Inde egressus Heinricus proximum pascha Quidlingeburg festivis peregit gaudiis. Quo magnus regni primatus colligitur, a quibusdam autem venire illo nolentibus ad omnia diligenter inquirenda nuntius mittitur.* Thietmar, *Chronicon*, IV.2, ed. Holtzmann, p. 132–3. Warner, trans., *Ottonian Germany*, p.150.

85 *Hac in festivitate idem a suis publice rex appellatur laudibusque divinis attollitur.* Ibid.

Orchestrating harmony **153**

86 *Huc Miseco et Mistui et Bolizlovo duces cum caeteris ineffabilibus confluebant, auxilium sibi deinceps ut regi et domino cum iuramentis affirmantes. Multi ex his fidem violare ob timorem Dei non presumentes paululum evaserunt.* Ibid.

87 *quorundam etiam persuasione male illectus regnum tyrannice invasit. Annales Quedlinburgenses,* a. 984, in *Die Annales Quedlinburgenses, MGH SS rer. Germ.* 72, ed. by Martina Giese (Hannover: Hahn, 2004), p. 471. Warner, trans., *Ottonian Germany*, pp. 154–5, ft. 23.

88 *Qua visa perterrita moxque cedente parte iniusta Heinricus praefatus usurpato nomine et regno iure privatus regem. Annales Quedlinburgenses,* a. 984, ed. Giese, p. 473. Warner, trans., *Ottonian Germany*, pp. 154–5, ft. 23.

89 *Accepto itaque pignore unico praedictae imperiales dominae Saxoniam adierunt, ac primo saepe iam dictam Quedelignensis monticuli vertice eminentem usque civitatem una pervenientes dulcisona laudum melodia cleri scilicet ac populi Christoque inibi famulantium virginum occursu gemino gaudioque affecto et peroptato spiritualis matris adventu et pro triumpahli regis eventu pie gratulantium officiosissime susceptae, quod reliquum erat viae, summo cum honore transiere. Annales Quedlinburgenses,* a. 984, ed. Giese, p. 473. Warner, trans., *Ottonian Germany*, pp. 154–5, ft. 23.

90 *psallentibus psallebat, cum orantibus orabat.* Odilo of Cluny, *Epitaphium domine Adelheide auguste,* c. 20, in *Die Lebensbeschreibung der Kaiserin Adelheid von Abt Odilo von Cluny,* ed. by Herbert Paulhart (Graz-Cologne: Hermann Böhlaus, 1962), p. 44. For an alternate translation, see Sean Gilsdorf, *Queenship and Sanctity: The Lives of Mathilda and the Epitaph of Adelheid* (Washington, DC, 2004), p. 141.

91 The research for this chapter was conducted with the support of the Paul G. Tobin Dissertation Fellowship from the Nanovic Institute for European Studies at the University of Notre Dame (2016–2017) and the Arts and Letters Postdoctoral Fellowship at the London Undergraduate Program of the University of Notre Dame (2017–2018).

9

MODELS OF MARRIAGE CHARTERS IN A NOTEBOOK OF ADEMAR OF CHABANNES (NINTH- TO ELEVENTH-CENTURY)

Philippe Depreux

Charters are very valuable sources for historians interested in social and cultural history: they convey a great deal of varied information. Not only are the facts mentioned in them useful, their layout can reveal precious details about the aims and agency of the author;[1] their verbalization is itself the product of a historical phenomenon and as such provides valuable testimony about cultural exchange and the evolution of mentalities through time.[2] In addition to charters – whether kept as an original or copied in a cartulary – another kind of document is an important source of information: the so-called *formulae*, i.e. anonymized models for writing charters or letters. Most *formulae* were transmitted in collections,[3] some of which contain documents (like private everyday charters for laypeople) that are not preserved as an original or in copy elsewhere.[4] Sometimes such models were copied on free parchment leaves or in the margins of manuscripts dealing with other topics (for them Karl Zeumer, the editor of these *formulae* at the end of the nineteenth century, invented the subcategory '*formulae extravagantes*').[5] It was typical practice for medieval scribes not only to annotate manuscripts,[6] but also to write such little texts (songs, recipes or models) as marginal notes: such random testimonies of medieval culture are especially interesting because they reveal a lot about the networks and interests of medieval people.[7] This is also the case for two models of *libelli dotis* (dotal charters) copied into the personal notebook of Ademar of Chabannes, now kept at Leiden University Library under the shelfmark Vossianus Latinus 8° 15. This small manuscript (about 210 x 150 mm), written on poor quality parchment, contains not just texts but also drawings,[8] and is famous for its role as an important witness to the transmission of Antique knowledge and its reception during the Middle Ages.[9]

Ademar († 1034) was a monk of the abbeys of Saint-Cybard of Angoulême and – most importantly for us in the present article – of Saint-Martial in Limoges,[10] one of the most important cultural and liturgical centres in Aquitaine during the tenth to twelfth centuries.[11] The library of Saint-Martial kept Ademar's notebook at least until the beginning of the thirteenth century.[12] The codex was subsequently disassembled into fourteen separately bound booklets at the end of the nineteenth century. The last of these contains a series of heterogeneous texts:[13] the Fables of Avianus,[14] a collection of recreational mathematics problems attributed to Alcuin (*Propositiones ad acuendos iuuenes*, i.e. 'Problems to Sharpen the Young'),[15] instructions for making a crucifix.[16] Finally, it includes two models for writing *libelli dotis*,[17] most probably copied by Ademar himself:[18] these models are inserted into the *Propositiones ad acuendos iuuenes*, and are copied on fols 203⁵–205⁵ and 206⁵–210ʳ. The first *formula* (Zeumer, Form. extrav. n° 9) is copied on fol. 206ʳ; the second one (Zeumer, Form. extrav. n° 10) is copied on fol. 2105. On the lower half of that same folio are a number of drawings, including the calligraphy of an Arabic inscription in the form of a boustrophedon in Kufic writing – perhaps copied from an Islamic artefact brought to Aquitaine[19] – meaning 'In the name of God the Compassionate and the Merciful'.[20] This booklet forms a codicological unit, in which the appearance of the *libelli dotis* seems to be quite unremarkable.[21]

The preamble of Zeumer's Form. extrav. n° 9 focuses on theological considerations, while the preamble of Zeumer's Form. extrav. n° 10 explicitly refers both to Roman law on 'betrothal and prenuptial gifts' (*sicut in Theodosiano codice 'de sponsalibus et ante nuptias donationibus' auctoritas narrat*),[22] and to the necessity of the presence of a written record.[23] There is, however, also an allusion to the law in Zeumer's Form. extrav. n° 9 when the bridegroom in the document mentions the consent of his parents and friends (*mihi una per consensum parentum nostrorum et amicorum eam legibus sponsare decerno, et ad diem nuptiarum, Domino iubente, pervenire delibero*)[24] in quite a similar manner to the other charter model (Form. extrav. n° 10) copied in that notebook.[25] Both models make reference to the kiss (*osculum*) to be given for sealing the wedding: in this way, they implicitly allude to the Theodosian Code.[26] In the *dispositio* of Zeumer, Form. extrav. n° 9, the charter itself is denominated as a 'kiss': 'All this which is written above, I give, transfer and confer by this kiss to you, my aforementioned bride, so that from the present day on, you may do with it as you please without anyone opposing you'. (*Haec omnia superius conscripta, sponsa mea iam dicta, per hunc osculum a die presente tibi trado, transfero atque transfundo, ut facias exinde, quicquid volueris, nemine contradicente.*[27]) In both documents the charter is called '*osculum*' in the *sanctio*.[28] Many examples survive in contemporary Aquitaine in which a wedding charter is designated as an *osculum*.[29] These *libelli dotis* have already been investigated with regard to their formulaic and juridical structure,[30] as well as in respect of their theological meaning;[31] they have parallels with many other similar charters in Aquitaine,[32] so that there is no need to investigate their substance in this paper again, but it is necessary to compare them with other documents for situating them in a better way in their cultural context.

Another model of wedding charter is very close to Zeumer's Form. extrav. n° 10: this model was copied together with four other *formulae* in a manuscript now kept in the Vatican library (Reginensis Lat. 1050, fol. 164ʳ-5). This manuscript (unfortunately altered in its codicological structure) is a legal codex dating from

156   Philippe Depreux

the second half of the ninth century which contains (among other texts) the *Lex Romana Visigothorum* and the *Lex Romana Burgundionum*.[33] It once belonged to the abbey of Saint-Martial in Limoges. Evidence for this is provided by an additional note at the end of the codex: during the twelfth century someone noted that relics of saint Nicolas were 'present'[34] (we may complete: in a place which probably was the church St Mary and St Nicholas at Aubusson, a priory of Saint-Martial at that times)[35]. Four *formulae* have been copied at the end of the manuscript. Because of their similarities with the '*formulae* of Tours', K. Zeumer edited these texts as an appendix to that collection: these texts are a *cautio*, the *donatio in sponsa facta* which is interesting here, another *traditio* to the bride and a *mandatum, qualiter maritus uxoris negotium prosequitur*.[36] Their order corresponds to the order of the similar documents found in the Tours collection: the three first *formulae* in Reginensis Lat. 1050 correspond to numbers 13–15 of the *formulae* of Tours and the fourth model corresponds to number 20 of that collection. It is possible to consider these texts as a revised version of these original *formulae*. Alice Rio suggests that these models 'belonged to a reworking of the Tours collection made in the Carolingian period',[37] but one should not overestimate the similarities between these templates. While the scribe was inspired by the Tours collection, he wrote a new charter, as did the scribe who wrote the *donatio in sponsa facta* copied by Ademar.

The beginning of the Tours *formula* and the 'Touronian' *formula* in the Vatican manuscript (and the 'Ademarian' *formula* [Zeumer, Form. extrav. n° 10] as well) make clear that these *formulae* are not mere copies of the Tours model. They are all based on the Theodosian Code (III, V, 2), especially its *interpretatio*, the wording of which is quoted in the Tours *formula*. The *formula* in the Vatican manuscript and the 'Ademarian' *formula* explicitly refer to the Theodosian Code and deliver a free interpretation of that legal principle.

Hänel, Lex Romana, p. 78	*Interpretatio: Quoties* **inter sponsos et sponsas de futuris nuptiis** *specialiter* **fuerit definitum**, *et donationem sponsalitiae* **largitis vir** *in sponsam suam* **aut ex consensu parentum aut ipse, si sui iuris est,** *propria voluntate conscripserit et omni eam* **scripturarum solennitate firmaverit**, *ita ut et gesta legitime facta doceantur, et introductio locorum vel rerum traditio subsequatur* ... (Pharr, The Theodosian Code, p. 66: 'Whenever betrothed persons have made a specific arrangement concerning their future marriage, and the man, either with the consent of his parents or of his own free will if he is legally independent, has written a deed of gift of his betrothal bounty to his betrothed and has confirmed this deed of gift with all the formality of written documents, provided also that it shall be proved that public records were made in conformity with the law and that formal induction into the land and delivery of movables followed ...')
MGH, Formulae, p. 142 (Tours, n°14)	*Lex et consuetudo exposcit, ut, 'quicquid* **inter sponsum et sponsam de futuris nuptiis fuerit definitum** *vel* **largitum, aut ex consensu parentum aut ipsi, si sui iuris sunt, scripturarum sollemnitate firmetur'**. *Idcirco ego in Dei nomine ille* ... (Law and custom requires that 'whatever has been arranged and given between bridegroom and bride concerning their future marriage, either with the consent of the parents of of their own (will), if they are legally independent, must be confirmed through the formal means of written documents').

Models of marriage charters in a notebook of Ademar of Chabannes · 157

MGH, Formulae, p. 163 (Reginensis Lat. 1050)	*Latores legis aedicerunt, et antiqua consuetudo aedocet, ut prius arrarum coniugiae, postmodum osculum intercedentis personarum qualitate concedatur, sicut in Theodosiano codice 'de sponsalibus et ante nuptias donationibus' narrat auctoritas, ut, quicumque vir in sponsam suam ante die nuptiarum de rebus suis propriis donare vel conferre voluerit, per serie scripturae hoc alligare* <u>*percuret*</u>. *Igitur ergo ego in Dei nomine ille* ... (The law-givers have declared, and ancient custom teaches that, before the betrothal pledge and soon after the kiss is exchanged, according to the status of the persons involved, it should be allowed that if any man wants to give or confer something of his property to his betrothed before the day of their marriage, he should take care that this is registered by sentences in writing, as the authority of the Theodosian Code states in the title 'On betrothal and prenuptial gifts'. For this reasons, I, in the name of God, called N.N. ...)
MGH, Formulae, p. 539 (Vossianus Latinus 8° 15)	*Latores legis edicunt, et antiqua consuetudo edocet, ut prius arras coniugis, postmodo, osculo intercedente, personarum qualitate concedatur, sicut in Theodosiano codice 'de sponsalibus et ante nuptias donationibus' auctoritas narrat, videlicet ut, quicumque vir ad sponsam suam de rebus propriis ante dies nuptiarum aliquid concedere vel conferre voluerit, per seriem scripturae hoc alligare* <u>*per*</u>*mittat, vel* <u>*curet*</u>. *Idcirco etiam in Dei nomine ego* ... (The law-givers declare, and ancient custom teaches that before the betrothal pledge and soon after the kiss is exchanged, according to the status of the persons involved, it should be allowed that if any man wants to grant or confer something of his property to his betrothed before the day of their marriage, he should allow this to be registered by sentences in writing, or take care (that this should happen), as the authority of the Theodosian Code states in the title 'On betrothal and prenuptial gifts'. For this reason also, I, in the name of God ...)

The allusion to the legislators (*latores legis*) who stress the necessity of a written record is not specific to these *formulae*: we can find examples in other models for donations, like another *cessio* in the Tours collection or in a model of the Lindenbrog collection possibly originated in Elnone at the end of the eighth century.[38]

The affinity between the *formula* in the Vatican manuscript and the 'Ademarian' *formula* is obvious, although the second one is shorter than the first one (by about one third).[39] At the beginning of the *dispositio*, both *formulae* diverge in a markedly similar way from the Tours *formula*:

MGH, Formulae, p. 142 (Tours, n°14)	*Idcirco* **ego in Dei nomine** *ille. Dum* **multorum habetur percognitum**, *quod ego te illa, una cum* **consensu parentum** *vel* **amicorum** <u>**nostrorum**</u>, *tua spontanea voluntate sponsavi, mihi placuit, ut aliquid de rebus meis per hunc titulum libelli dotis ante dies nuptiarum tibi confirmare deberem; quod ita et feci.* (For this reason I, in the name of God, N.N. As is known by many, I have betrothed you, called N. N., according to your free will, with the consent of our parents or friends, it pleased me that before the day of our wedding I should confirm to you what I owe you from my property by this written dower title; and this is what I did.)

158 Philippe Depreux

MGH, Formulae, p. 163 (Reginensis Lat. 1050)	*Igitur ergo* **ego in Dei nomine** *ille,* filius *illius. Dum* **multorum habetur percognitum**, *qualiter ego aliqua femina aut* **puella nomine** *illa, filia illius, per* **consensu** *vel voluntate* **parentum** *vel* **amicorum** <u>***nostrorum*** *eam legibus</u> <u>sponsare*</u> *volo* **et, Christo propitio**, *sicut mos est et antiqua fuit consuetudo,* <u>**ad**</u> <u>**legittimum matrimonium vel coniugium sociare cupio.**</u> (For this reason I, in the name of God, N. N., the son of N. N. As is known by many, I want to marry a woman or girl named N. N., daughter of N. N., with the consent and will of our parents or friends, according to law and with God's help, as is practice and ancient custom, and I wish to join with her in a lawful marriage and union.)
MGH, Formulae, p. 539 (Vossianus Latinus 8° 15)	*Idcirco etiam* **in Dei nomine ego** *Barius, qui* filius *fui Arbini, et mater mea Ramigis, ut* **multorum** *noticiae* **habeatur percognitum**, *aliquam* **puellam nomine** *N., quae fuit filia Marini, et mater sua Urielia, una per* **consensum parentum** <u>***nostrorum***</u> *et* **amicorum** <u>***eam legibus sponsare*** *et Christo</u> <u>propitio ad legittimum matrimonium vel coniugium sociare cupio.*</u> (For this reason I, in the name of God, Barius, who was the son of Arbinus, and my mother Ramigis, as is known to the knowledge of many, wish to marry a girl named N.N., who was the daughter of Marinus. with the consent of our parents and friends, according to law and with God's help and wish to associate her in a lawful marriage and matrimony)

Further the differences are more obvious:

MGH, Formulae, p. 164 (Reginensis Lat. 1050)	**Propterea placuit mihi**, *atque bona decrevit voluntas pro amore vel dilectione ipsius feminae, ut* **ante die nuptiarum per hanc titulum osculum intercedentis** *ha diae praesente aliquid de rebus meis ei condonare vel conferre deberem*; **quod ita et mihi placuit fecisse**. *Dono tibi,* **dilecta sponsa mea** *illa, donatumque in perpetuum esse volo, hoc est locello, res proprietatis meae, nuncupante illo* ... (For this reason it pleased me, and my goodwill decided that for love and affection for this woman, I should give and confer her something from my property, before the day of the wedding, through this title with the exchange of the kiss today; this pleased me, so I did it. I give you this, my beloved betrothed N.N., and wish that whatever I have given you will be forever yours, that is the location, part of my property, called N. N.)
MGH, Formulae, p. 539 (Vossianus Latinus 8° 15)	**Propterea placuit mihi, ante diem nuptiarum** *a die presente aliquid de rebus meis propriis ei concedere debere, decernente bona voluntate, pro amore vel dilectione ipsius puellae* **per hunc titulum huius osculi intercedentis. Quod ita placuit mihi facere**, **dilecta sponsa mea** *nomine N. In pago Floriacensi, in vicaria Reinense, in villa quae dicitur Noriont, alodem meum, hoc sunt, terras, silvas adiacentes, quantumcumque in ipsa villa visus sum habere vel possidere, de mea parte, divisa cum fratribus meis, de integro medietatem tibi concedo, ut facias, quiquid volueris, nemine contradicente.* (For this reason it pleased me to give her something from my property today, before the day of the wedding, in goodwill for love and affection towards this girl, through this title with the exchange of this kiss. It pleased me to do exactly this, my beloved betrothed, named N. N. In the *pagus* of Fleury, in the *vicaria* of Reinense, in the village called Noriant, from my allod, that is, the lands and adjacent woods in as much as I seem to own and possess there from my part resulting from the division with my brothers, I give half of it to you so that you can do with it as you please, without anyone opposing you.)

The *sanctio* is definitely different:

MGH, Formulae, p. 164 (Reginensis Lat. 1050)	**Si quis vero, si ego ipse aut ullus de heredibus meis** *vel quislibet extranea aut obposita* **persona**, **qui contra** *hanc donatione, quod est* **osculus** *intercedentis a me factus, venire aut aliqua calumnia generare praesumpserit, cui litem intulerit solidos tantos* **conponat**, *et iniqua repetitio in nullisque modis obtineat firmitatem, sed praesens donatio ista a me facta, meis vel* **bonorum virorum** *manibus* **roborata** *cum stipulatione subnixa omnique tempore maneat inconvulsa.* (However, if anyone, whether myself, one of my heirs, or any stranger or hostile person, dares to contravene this donation made by me through the exchange of a kiss, or to give rise to any calumny, he who brings forward the contention should pay so many *solidi*, and unjust repetition should in no way gain validity, but the present donation, made by me and corroborated by my own hands as well as those of good men, with a fixed stipulation, should remain unviolated for all time.)
MGH, Formulae, p. 539 (Vossianus Latinus 8° 15)	**Si quis vero, si ego ipse aut ullus de heredibus meis** *vel proheredibus, aut aliqua* **persona** *fuerit,* **qui contra** *hunc* **osculum** *aliquid agere aut inquietare voluerit,* **componat** *solidos 100 argenti et 500 auri libras, coactus exsolvat, et vox sua nihil proficiat. Manu mea propria subter firmavi, et* **bonorum virorum** *testimonio cor***roborandam** *decrevi.* (However, if I myself, or anyone of my heirs or their representatives, or any person wants to do anything against this kiss or to disrupt it, he should be forced to pay 100 *solidi* of silver and 500 *librae* of gold, and his voice should be unsuccessful. I have confirmed this with my own hand below and have decreed it to be confirmed by the testimony of good men.)

At this point we can make some observations about the origin of these texts. A detail in the Leiden manuscript is very important, since it establishes a connection between both *formulae*. Instead of the wording *hoc alligare percuret* in the preamble of the Vatican manuscript we read in the Ademarian text: *hoc alligare permittat*, with a correction upon the line: *vel curet*, which gives *per-curet*. I conclude that Ademar was familiar with the Vatican manuscript (which was kept in Saint-Martial as discussed above) and that he made a collation of his own text with this manuscript. Unlike the text of the Vatican manuscript, the Ademarian *formula* is not completely anonymized: some names are copied (for instance, the bridegroom, his parents and the parents of the bride are all named within the text).[40] More interesting is the fact that we have geographical and chronological information within the *formula* text. The property given to the bride is situated in the region of Fleury (*in pago Floriacensi in vicaria Reinense in uilla quę dicitur Noriont* [I read *Noriona*]); and the charter upon which the *formula* is based was written under the reign of a king named Pippin (*in mense iulio regnante Pipino rege*). We can conclude that this text dates from between the years 814 and 848. It is not clear if the property given to the bride was located near Fleury Abbey as all historians interested in that text since Léopold Delisle have presumed; it could be located somewhere else – for example in northern Burgundy. With the exception of the toponym Fleury – or Fleuray (near Amboise in the

160   Philippe Depreux

Touraine, which is attested as a *villa* during the tenth century)[41] – no name can be identified. One detail could be used to argue in favour of an identification with Fleury-sur-Loire: in the other *formula* of the 'Ademarian' manuscript the properties are located in the region of Orléans (see below, this page). If we suppose that both *formulae* have the same origin, the *formula* mentioning Fleury should be connected with the famous abbey.

Let us sum up: The *formula* written by Ademar could be the copy of a real charter of the first half of the ninth century which was based on the *formula* kept in the Vatican manuscript, which is itself an adaption of a model from the Tours collection. It is possible that Ademar collated his text with the model in the Vatican manuscript, which belonged at that time to his own monastery (Saint-Martial). Unlike the *formula* of the Vatican manuscript, the 'Ademarian' *formula* ends with abbreviations for *signum* (i. e. the mention of the witnesses who should confirm the actual charter); after these *signa* Ademar wrote a Tironian note[42] meaning *omnimodis*[43] ('of various kinds') – this is also evidence for a copy directly based upon a real document.

The topic of the other *formula* copied by Ademar (Zeumer, Form. extrav. no. 9) is the same as Zeumer, Form. extrav. no. 10 and the juridical action is also similar (in this case, there is not only mention of a kiss but also of a ring).[44] The properties given are mentioned by name;[45] they are situated in the *pagus* of Orléans and one place can be identified with certainty: the *alodum de Sociaco* can only refer to Sougny.[46] The names of the witnesses are written according to the same layout as one would find in a real charter[47] which is a strong argument in favour of a copy having been made directly from the original charter, as in the case of the other *formula*. The *arenga* is very long.[48] In this text, marriage is legitimated by five quotation from the Bible (from both the Old and New Testament). This has been investigated by Philipp Reynolds and Ines Weber,[49] who were especially interested in other so-called *formulae extravagantes*, for instance n° 12 (in a manuscript from Senlis dating from the tenth century) and n° 13 (also dating from the tenth century; this manuscript belonged to Fleury Abbey). The 'Ademarian' *formula* fit into the ideology of the monastic reform of the era, but topics that they consider are much older, as one can see with the example of a *formula* of the Bourges collection (I am not convinced that we can actually speak of 'the' collection of Bourges, but it is not the place for discussing this here): *formula* n° 15 (copied in the manuscript Leiden University Library, PBL 114, a codex dating from the end of the eighth or the beginning of the ninth century that originated in Bourges) contains not only a theological legitimation of marriage,[50] but also mentions the kiss as a juridical instrument.[51]

Let us conclude. Both 'Ademarian' *formulae* are different, but both seem to have originated from the same region: the Loire valley. One of these *formulae* is related to the Tours collection with an intermediary: the model of the Vatican manuscript (or a charter connected to it). Both 'Ademarian' *formulae* mention the *osculum* as a juridical action, which excludes the possibility that the Tours collection was used as a model since there is no mention of the *osculum* in it. Ademar compared his text with the Vatican manuscript (as proven by the addition *vel curet*). Did Ademar merely copy these models from original charters without modifying them, or did he slightly change the text? It may be that the beginning of Zeumer's Form. extrav. no. 9 reveals some Ademarian influence: *Uniuersitatis cunctipotens creator ex cuius bonitate potestatiua ea quae sunt substantialiter esse ceperunt ...* [52] There is a degree of similarity with a liturgical text most probably sung at Saint-Martial, the Kyrie 'Cunctipotens': *Cunctipotens genitor, Deus omnicreator, eleison. / Fons et origo boni pie, luxque perennis, eleison. / Salvificet pietas tua nos, bone rector, eleison.* This trope was widely disseminated during the tenth century. For a long time, liturgists attributed it to the Sankt-Gall monk Tuotilo († 915), but this attribution is now controversial; some music historians think that this trope instead has an Aquitanian origin.[53] Since Saint-Martial was the most important musical centre in Aquitaine, I cannot overcome the temptation to imagine that the scribe of the *formula* was inspired by this topic.[54] Anyway if there is a connection between the *Kyrie* and the *formula*, it must be chronologically located sometime during the tenth century.

To finally conclude we must turn to an as-yet unaddressed important question: Why did Ademar copy these models for wedding charters? As a monk he evidently did not need them for himself. Should it be interpreted as an evidence that he was required by necessity to write such charters for members of his family or for some 'clients' of Saint-Martial of Limoges or of Saint-Cybard of Angoulême? Was he interested in Roman law, a kind of knowledge with an especially vivid tradition in the Loire valley and in Aquitaine?[55] Was it simply because he was interested in good examples of phrasing? Or did he have some contact with the family of the people involved in these documents? We do not know. It could also be possible that these documents obviously emanating from the Loire valley were brought to Limoges by Odo of Cluny, who was born in the Touraine, was active at Saint-Benoît and was closely connected to the bishop of Limoges, Turpio.[56] If my hypothesis is correct, Ademar's notebook is an interesting – and until now unknown – testimony to cultural exchange that occurred about two generations before the monk of Saint-Martial copied two quite insignificant models for inexperienced scribes in his personal notebook.[57]

Notes

1 Peter Rück, *Graphische Symbole in mittelalterlichen Urkunden. Beiträge zur diplomatischen Semiotik* (Sigmaringen: Thorbecke, 1996).

2 For some examples among a huge bibliography see *Charters and the Use of the Written Word in Medieval Society*, ed. by Karl Heidecker (Turnhout: Brepols, 2000); Benoît-Michel Tock, *Scribes, souscripteurs et témoins dans les actes privés en France (VIIe–début XIIe siècle)* (Turnhout: Brepols, 2005); *Die Privaturkunden der Karolingerzeit*, ed. by Peter Erhart, Karl Josef Heidecker and Bernhard Zeller (Dietikon-Zürich: Urs Graf-Verlag, 2009); Reinhard Härtel, *Notarielle und kirchliche Urkunden im frühen und hohen Mittelalter* (Vienna: Böhlau, 2011).

3 Alice Rio, *Legal Practice and the Written Word in the Early Middle Ages. Frankish Formulae, c. 500–1000* (Cambridge: Cambridge University Press, 2009).

4 Werner Bergmann, 'Verlorene Urkunden des Merowingerreiches nach den Formulae Andecavenses', *Francia* 9 (1981), 3–56; Warren C. Brown, 'When documents are destroyed or lost: lay people and archives in the early Middle Ages', *Early Medieval Europe* 11 (2002),

162 Philippe Depreux

pp. 337–66; Id., 'Laypeople and documents in the Frankish formula collections', in *Documentary Culture and the Laity in the Early Middle Ages*, ed. by Id., Marios J. Costambeys, Matthew Innes, and Adam J. Kosto (Cambridge: Cambridge University Press, 2013), pp. 125–51; Josiane Barbier, *Archives oubliées du haut Moyen Âge. Les* gesta municipalia *en Gaule franque (VIe–IXe siècle)* (Paris: Honoré Champion, 2014).

5 *Formulae Merowingici et Karolini aevi*, ed. by Karl Zeumer (Hannover: Hahnsche Buchhandlung, 1882–86) – thereafter MGH, Formulae; A. Rio, Legal Practice, *op. cit.*, pp. 162–64.

6 *The Annotated Book in the Early Middle Ages: Practices of Reading and Writing*, ed. by Mariken Teeuwen and Irene van Renswoude (Turnhout: Brepols, 2018).

7 This is for instance the case for the Lorsch Bee Charm or the Muspilli. See Cyril W. Edwards, 'German vernacular literature: a survey', in *Carolingian Culture: Emulation and Innovation*, ed. by Rosamond McKitterick (Cambridge: Cambridge University Press, 1994), pp. 141–70 (p. 143).

8 Danielle Gaborit-Chopin, 'Les dessins d'Adémar de Chabannes', *Bulletin archéologique du Comité des travaux historiques et scientifiques*, n.s., 3 (1967), pp. 163–225.

9 Léopold Delisle, 'Notice sur les manuscrits originaux d'Adémar de Chabannes', *Notices et extraits des manuscrits de la Bibliothèque Nationale et autres bibliothèques*, 35 (1896), pp. 241–358 (pp. 301–19); Georg Thiele, *Der illustrierte lateinische Aesop in der Handschrift des Ademar, Codex Vossianus Lat. Oct. 15, Fol. 195–205. Einleitung und Beschreibung* (Leiden: A.W. Sijthoff, 1905) – recently the attribution of that collection to Ademar was contested by Paolo Gatti, 'Ademaro, pseudo Ademaro? Anonimato nella favolistica latina fino all'XI secolo', *Filologia mediolatina* 23 (2016), pp. 155–66; Ad Van Els, 'A flexible Unity: Ademar of Chabannes and the Production and Usage of MS Leiden, Universiteitsbibliotheek, Vossianus Latinus Octavo 15', *Scriptorium* 65 (2011), pp. 21–66; Id., 'Een leeuw van een handschrift: Ademar van Chabannes en Ms. Leiden, Universiteitsbibliotheek, Vossianus Latinus Octavo 15' (unpublished thesis, Universiteit Utrecht, 2015); Id., 'Transmitting Knowledge by Text and Illustration: The Case of MS Leiden, UB, VLO 15', in *The Annotated Book in the Early Middle Ages, op. cit.*, pp. 465–99.

10 Richard A. Landes, *Relics, Apocalypse, and the Deceits of History. Ademar of Chabannes, 989–1034* (Cambridge, MA: Harvard University Press, 1995); Philippe Depreux, 'Adémar de Chabannes et le souvenir des abbés de Saint-Martial de Limoges', *Bulletin de la Société Archéologique et Historique du Limousin*, 137 (2009), pp. 5–23; Daniel F. Callahan, *Jerusalem and the Cross in the Life and Writings of Ademar of Chabannes* (Leiden: Brill, 2016).

11 *Saint-Martial de Limoges. Ambition politique et production culturelle (X^e–XIIIe siècles)*, ed. by Claude Andrault-Schmitt (Limoges: Presses Universitaires de Limoges, 2006).

12 Van Els, 'A flexible unity', *op. cit.*, p. 22.

13 Van Els, 'Een leeuw van een handschrift', *op. cit.*, p. 62.

14 Georg Thiele, *Der Lateinische Äsop des Romulus und die Prosafassungen des Phädrus. Kritischer Text mit Kommentar und einleitenden Untersuchungen* (Heidelberg: C. Winter, 1910).

15 Menso Folkerts, *Die älteste mathematische Aufgabensammlung in lateinischer Sprache: Die Alkuin zugeschriebenen* Propositiones ad acuendos iuvenes. *Überlieferung, Inhalt, kritische Edition* (Vienna: Österreichische Akademie der Wissenschaften, 1978); translation into English: John Hadley and David Singmaster, 'Problems to Sharpen the Young', *The Mathematical Gazette* 76, n° 475 (1992), pp. 102–26; Menso Folkerts and Helmuth Gericke, 'Die Alkuin zugeschriebenen *Propositiones ad acuendos iuvenes* (Aufgaben zur Schärfung des Geistes der Jugend)', in *Science in Western and Eastern Civilization in Carolingian Times*, ed. by Paul Leo Butzer and Dietrich Lohrmann (Basel: Birkhäuser, 1993), pp. 283–362.

16 Bernhard Bischoff, 'Anleitung zur Herstellung eines Crucifixus (vor 1034)', in Id., Anecdota novissima. *Texte des 4. bis 16. Jahrhunderts* (Stuttgart: Hiersemann 1984), pp. 226–32.

17 MGH, Formulae, pp. 538–9; short presentation in L. Delisle, Notice sur les manuscrits originaux, *op. cit.*, pp. 313–4; A. Van Els, Een leeuw van een handschrift, *op. cit.*, pp. 1263–4; transcription: *ibid*, pp. 1265–6. Zeumer's texts are reprinted and translated in German in: Ines Weber, *Ein Gesetz für Männer und Frauen: Die frühmittelalterliche Ehe zwischen*

Models of marriage charters in a notebook of Ademar of Chabannes **163**

Religion, Gesellschaft und Kultur, II (Ostfildern: Thorbecke, 2008), pp. 132–37. The first half of Zeumer, Form. extrav. n° 9 has been translated into English by Philip Lyndon Reynolds, 'Dotal Charters in the Frankish Tradition', in *To have and to hold. Marrying and its documentation in Western Christendom, 400–1600*, ed. by Philip Lyndon Reynolds & John Witte (Cambridge: Cambridge University Press, 2007), pp. 114–64 (p. 159). I will edit these texts again within the new edition of the *formulae* (see www.formulae.uni-hamburg.de). For the present article I quote from Zeumer's edition.

18 K. Zeumer meant that these *formulae* were written by two different hands during the tenth century (MGH, Formulae, p. 538), but there is no real argument for another attribution as to Ademar's hand (see Van Els, Een leeuw van een handschrift, *op. cit.*, p. 1263).

19 Gaborit-Chopin, 'Les dessins d'Adémar de Chabannes', *op. cit.*, pp. 213–4.

20 S. Denys T. Spittle, 'Cufic Lettering in Christian Art', *Archaeological Journal* 111 (1954), pp. 138–52 (p. 144).

21 Van Els, 'Een leeuw van een handschrift', p. 70.

22 MGH, Formulae, p. 539 l. 21–2.

23 MGH, Formulae, p. 539 l. 21–2: *ut, quicumque vir ad sponsam suam de rebus propriis ante dies nuptiarum aliquid concedere vel conferre voluerit, per seriem scripturae hoc alligare permittat* (addition upon the line: *vel curet*).

24 MGH, Formulae, pp. 538 l. 28–539 l. 2.

25 MGH, Formulae, p. 539 ll. 27–8: una per consensum parentum nostrorum et amicorum eam legibus sponsare *et Christo propitio ad legitimum matrimonium vel coniugium sociare cupio*.

26 *Lex Romana Visigothorum*, ed. Gustav Hänel (Leipzig: Teubner 1849) (hereafter Hänel, Lex Romana), p. 78 (= Codex Theodosianus III, V, 5): *... interveniente osculo*. English Translation: *The Theodosian Code and Novels and the Sirmondian Constitutions. A Translation with Commentary, Glossary, and Bibliography*, by Clyde Pharr (Princeton: Princeton University Press, 1952), pp. 66–7.

27 MGH, Formulae, p. 539 ll. 8–10; for comparison see the other document, ibid., p. 539 ll. 29–31: *propterea placuit mihi, ante diem nuptiarum a die presente aliquid de rebus meis propriis ei concedere debere, decernente bona voluntate, pro amore vel dilectione ipsius puellae per hunc titulum huius osculi intercedentis*.

28 MGH, Formulae, p. 539 ll. 10–12: *si autem fuerit, aut* ego ipse aut ullus de heredibus meis aut *ulla emissa* persona, qui contra hunc osculum aliquid agere aut inquietare voluerit ...; *ibid.*, p. 539 ll. 35–7: *si quis vero, si* ego ipse aut ullus de heredibus meis *vel proheredibus,* aut *aliqua* persona *fuerit,* qui contra hunc osculum aliquid agere aut inquietare voluerit ... On this part of a medieval charter see Joachim Studtmann, 'Die Pönformel der mittelalterlichen Urkunden', *Archiv für Urkundenforschung* 12 (1932), pp. 251–374.

29 Émile Chénon, 'Recherches historiques sur quelques rites nuptiaux', *Nouvelle revue historique de droit français et étranger* 36 (1912), pp. 573–660 (pp. 587–97).

30 Reynolds, *Dotal Charters, op. cit.*; Weber, *Ein Gesetz für Männer und Frauen, op. cit.*

31 Ines Weber, 'Die Bibel als Norm! Eheschließung und Geschlechterverhältnis im frühen Mittelalter zwischen biblischer Tradition und weltlichem Recht', in *Geschlechterverhältnisse und Macht. Lebensformen in der Zeit des frühen Christentums*, ed. by Irmtraud Fischer & Christoph Heil (Vienna: Lit Verlag, 2010), pp. 257–304.

32 Philippe Depreux, 'La dotation de l'épouse en Aquitaine septentrionale du IXe au XIIe siècle', in *Dots et douaires dans le haut Moyen Âge*, ed. by Régine Le Jan, Laurent Feller and François Bougard (Rome: École Française de Rome, 2002), pp. 219–44.

33 Hubert Mordek, *Bibliotheca capitularium regum Francorum manuscripta. Überlieferung und Traditionszusammenhang der fränkischen Herrschererlasse* (Munich: Monumenta Germaniae Historica, 1995), pp. 847–52; A. Rio, *Legal practice, op. cit.*, pp. 268–9.

34 Biblioteca Apostolica Vaticana, Reginensis Lat. 1050, fol. 163ʳ: *Per multa temporis et magna spacia sanctus Nihcolaus mansit in Grecia, nunc presens*.

35 *Acta pontificum Romanorum inedita. Urkunden der Päpste vom Jahre 748 bis zum Jahre 1198*, ed. Julius von Pflugk-Harttung, I (Tübingen: F. Fues, 1880), p. 74 (n° 81 = charter of

164   Philippe Depreux

Pope Paschalis II., 29th mai 1102): *in pago Lemovicensi, ecclesiam Sancte Marie et Sancti Nicolai in Castro Albuzonis.*

36 MGH, Formulae, pp. 163–5 (appendix to the Additamenta e codicibus formularum Turonensium). The wedding charter (*donatio in sponsa facta*) is document n° 2 (pp. 163–4).

37 Rio, *Legal Practice, op. cit.*, p. 114. See also Philippe Depreux, 'La tradition manuscrite des "Formules de Tours" et la diffusion des modèles d'actes aux VIIIe et IXe siècles', *Annales de Bretagne et des Pays de l'Ouest* 111 n°3 (2004), pp. 55–72 (pp. 60 and 68).

38 MGH, Formulae, p. 137 (Tours, n° 4); *ibid.*, p. 271 (Lindenbrog, Nr. 6)

39 MGH, Formulae, p. 163 (n° 2): 28 lines; *ibid.*, p. 539 (n° 10): 20 lines (without the *signa*).

40 MGH, Formulae, p. 539 (n° 10): *Idcirco etiam in Dei nomine ego Barius, qui filius fui Arbini, et mater mea Ramigis, ut multorum noticiae habeatur percognitum, aliquam puellam nomine N., quae fuit filia Marini, et mater sua Urielia, una per consensum parentum nostrorum et amicorum eam legibus sponsare et Christo propitio ad legitimum matrimonium vel coniugium sociare cupio.*

41 *Fragments de chartes du Xe siècle provenant de Saint-Julien de Tours*, ed. by Louis de Grandmaison (Paris: Picard, 1886), pp. 71–7 (n° 27).

42 There are many other Tironian notes in that manuscript, see Martin Hellmann, 'Tironische Tituli: Die Verwendung stenographischer Marginalien zur inhaltlichen Erschließung von Texten des frühen Mittelalters', in: *The Annotated Book in the Early Middle Ages, op. cit.*, pp. 263–83; Van Els, 'Transmitting Knowledge by Text and Illustration', *op. cit.*, p. 493.

43 Compare with Wolfenbüttel, Herzog August Bibliothek, Cod. Guelf. 9.8 Aug. 4°, fol. 2[v] (*Commentarii notarum tironianarum*, Saint-Bertin, 1. Half of the ninth century).

44 MGH, Formulae, p. 539 (n° 9): *Et coedo ei osculum intercedente anulo circumdata restringente in die nuptiarum aliquid de rebus meis propriis.*

45 *Ibid.*: *In pago Aurelianensi, in vicaria Pervei, dono tibi de terra, vineis, pratis, de silvis, de aquis, alodum de Sociaco, de integro medietatem. Et in loco alio, in villa quae dicitur Brono, coedo de terra, de vineis, de silva, de integro medietatem, et in alio loco de pratis Carbosanias de integro medietatem, et in alio loco qui dicitur Castello alodem meum de integro medietatem.* It is not possible to identify *Pervei*, see Jean-Pierre Brunterc'h, 'Le duché du Maine et la marche de Bretagne', in *La Neustrie. Les pays au nord de la Loire de 650 à 850*, ed. by Hartmut Atsma, I (Sigmaringen: Thorbecke, 1989), pp. 29–127 (pp. 105–6).

46 Département: Loiret, arrondissement: Orléans.

47 MGH, Formulae, p. 539 (n° 9): *Signum Borchardi, qui istum osculum fieri iussit et nobilium virorum astipulatione firmare rogavit. Signum Theodatus. Signum Bodo. Signum. Signum. Signum Iohannes. Signum Rainus. Signum. Signum. Signum Ioscelinus. Signum Tescelinus. Signum. Signum.*

48 MGH, Formulae, p. 538: *Universitatis cunctipotens Creator, ex cuius bonitate potestativa ea quae sunt substantialiter esse ceperunt, de limo terrae homini facto et in faciem eius spiraculo vitae inspirato, solitario, ne sine adiutorio sui similis appareret, de eius latere dormiendo costa assumpta, subsidium prebuit. Adiutorium enim factum est modo, scilicet ut intentio dilectionis a binario numero principium sumeret. De hac copulatione doctor gentium, apostolus Paulus, confirmanda atque inseparabiliter tenenda dixit: 'Viri, diligite uxores vestras, sicut et Christus ecclesiam dilexit' in confirmatione pacis. Patenter subostenditur: 'Vir non habet potestatem sui corporis, sed et mulier; similiter et mulier non habet potestatem sui corporis, sed vir'. Et de reddendo debito minime tacuit: 'Vir', inquiens, 'uxori debitum reddat, similiter et uxor viro'. His igitur ammonitionibus, et ut divino precepto oboedirem, quia Omnicreans dixit: 'Crescite et multiplicamini et replete terram'.*

49 See notes 30 and 31.

50 MGH, Formulae, pp. 174–5: *Dum Dominus omnipotens, creatur caeli et terrae, iuxta quod legitur, in principio masculum et femina cupolae consorcium sociavit, dum dicitur: 'Non est bonum homine esse solum, faciamus ei adiutorem similem sibi', infundetque benedictione: 'Crescitae', inquid tamquam, 'et multiplicatae et dominamini cuncta reptilia, que sub caelo sunt'; et Salvator intonuit: 'Quam ob rem relinquid homo patrem et matrem et adherebit uxore suae, et erunt dui in carne una'; et Spiritus sanctus per sagrorum imperatorem sensit auctoritas, et non inceste vel inlicitae ad procreandum humani generis coniunctio fiat. Hoc consultum est, ut, quicumque liberta persona de rebus propriis facultatis suae aliquid conferrae voluerit, hoc per seriem scripturarum laudabiliter debeat esse adlegatum adque subter firmatum, qui hac conditione et iurae postulat praeturium et gestis requirit municipalibus.*

51 MGH, Formulae, p. 175: *pro amorae dulcidinis vel osculum pacis cedo tibi a diae presentae cessumque in perpetuum esse volo et de a meo iurae in iurae et dominationis tuae.*
52 MGH, Formulae, p. 538.
53 Annie Dennery, 'Le *cantus firmus Kyrie Cunctipotens* des origines à la fin du XVIII siècle', in *Itinéraires du cantus firmus*, III: *De la théorie à la pratique*, ed. by Édith Weber (Paris: Presses de l'Université de Paris-Sorbonne, 1999), pp. 7–20 (edition of the text p. 19).
54 On the subject of such mental association see Alain Guerreau, 'Vinea', in *Les historiens et le latin médiéval*, ed. by Monique Goullet and Michel Parisse (Paris: Publications de la Sorbonne, 2001), pp. 67–73.
55 Jean-Pierre Brunterc'h, 'Un monde lié aux archives: les juristes et les praticiens aux IXe et Xe siècles', in *Plaisir d'archives. Recueil de travaux offerts à Danielle Neirinck* (Mayenne: Imprimerie de la Manutension, 1997), pp. 409–27.
56 Isabelle Rosé, *Construire une société seigneuriale: itinéraire et ecclésiologie de l'abbé Odon de Cluny, fin du IXe-milieu du Xe siècle* (Turnhout: Brepols, 2008).
57 I thank Stefan Esders, Sarah Greer and Alice Hicklin for their help in improving my English.

10

ALL IN THE FAMILY

Creating a Carolingian genealogy in the eleventh century

*Sarah Greer**

The genre of genealogical texts experienced a transformation across the tenth century. Genealogical writing had always been a part of the Judeo-Christian tradition, but the vast majority of extant genealogies from the Continent before the year 1000 are preserved in narrative form, a literary account of the progression from one generation to another. There were plenty of biblical models for this kind of genealogy; the book of Genesis is explicitly structured as a genealogy tracing the generations that descended from Adam and Eve down to Joseph.[1] Early medieval authors could directly imitate this biblical structure: the opening sections of Thegan's *Deeds of Louis the Pious*, for example, traced the begetting of Charlemagne from St Arnulf; in England, Asser provided a similarly shaped presentation of the *genealogia* of King Alfred.[2] In the late tenth/early eleventh century, however, secular genealogical texts witnessed an explosion of interest. Genealogies of kings began to make their way into narrative historiographical texts with much greater regularity, shaping the way that those histories themselves were structured.[3] The number of textual genealogies that were written down increased exponentially and began to move outside of the royal family to include genealogies of noble families in the West Frankish kingdoms and Lotharingia.[4] Perhaps most remarkable though, is that these narrative genealogies began – for the first time – to be supplemented by new diagrammatic forms. The first extant genealogical tables of royal and noble families that we possess date from exactly this period, the late tenth and eleventh centuries.[5]

---

*   The research for this article was funded by the 'After Empire: Using and Not Using the Past in the Crisis of the Carolingian World, c.900–1050' HERA project, receiving funding from the European Union's Horizon 2020 research and innovation programme under grant agreement no. 649307. I would like to thank Robert Bartlett, Stefan Esders, Alice Hicklin, Simon MacLean, Erik Niblaeus and the audience at the Edinburgh CMRS seminar series for their helpful feedback.

The earliest forms of these diagrams were relatively plain. Names of individuals in the table, often enclosed in roundels and occasionally embellished by sketches of the person in question, were connected vertically by lines indicating descent or inheritance of royal title. Chronological time was usually represented vertically, moving from the oldest ancestor at the top of the diagram to their most recent descendant at the bottom. Though the early examples are plainly decorated, the genre became more embellished through the late eleventh and twelfth centuries.[6] These later tables were heavily decorated with figurative medallions that depicted each individual, sometimes with the entire diagram situated in architectural settings of towers and windows. At the same time that these tables were becoming more elaborate, another genre of genealogical diagram emerged: the family tree, which placed the ancestor at the bottom of the diagram and the most recent descendant at the top, imitating the growth of a tree from its trunk to its branches. The most famous of these, the tree of Jesse, which depicted the genealogy of Christ, first emerged in its diagrammatic form in the eleventh century.[7]

Clearly, there was a considerable shift of interest in the tenth/eleventh century towards genealogical texts, which sparked the creation of new diagrammatic versions. It should not be underestimated how innovative this development was. In Ancient Rome, genealogical diagrams were described as *stemmata* by Pliny the Elder: these, he says, are *imagines pictae* of ancestors connected by *lineis* painted onto the atrium walls of patrician houses. However, even Pliny indicated that this practice had already fallen out of favour by the time he was writing in the reign of Vespasian, and no Roman *stemmata* survive.[8] Tenth century, extant examples of genealogical diagrams are vanishingly rare.[9] The decision to turn genealogies into diagram form in the tenth/eleventh century was a striking change after a thousand years of focus on the narrative form.

There have been several different explanations put forward for the growth of the genealogical genre in this period in general. One focuses on the concern shown by the Church in defining legitimate marriage, associating the boom in genealogical diagrams with a newly enforced prohibition against marriage to the seventh degree. Roman civil law had only prohibited marriage within four degrees (that is, four steps of descent) and the Roman method of counting these went both upwards to a common ancestor and then down to your potential spouse. For example, the relationship between parent and child was one degree; between siblings or grandparents and grandchildren was two degrees; between aunts/uncles and nieces/nephews was three degrees; and between first cousins was four degrees. A schematic form of these degrees of consanguinity was commonly shown in illustrations of Isidore of Seville's *Etymologies*, often in a crucifix form.[10] Until recently it was commonly thought that a new way of defining legitimate marriage emerged in the ninth century and became more strictly enforced in the tenth and eleventh centuries, which prohibited marriage within seven degrees and changed the method of counting, drawing on the so-called Germanic practice which only counted degrees back to the common ancestor.[11]

168   Sarah Greer

However, this view of the emergence of the new prohibition against marriage within seven degrees, counted in the Germanic method, has been comprehensively rewritten by Karl Ubl. He convincingly argues that before the eleventh century, the medieval Church had a fairly stable definition of consanguineous marriage as any union within three degrees of separation counted by the Germanic method back to the common ancestor. However, as papal decrees switched back and forward between the Roman and Germanic methods of counting, it appeared to modern (and some contemporary) observers that there were earlier attempts to introduce a much stricter definition of prohibition within seven degrees.[12] Instead, it was only in the eleventh century that incestuous marriage began to be defined in this much stricter sense at the court of Emperor Henry II, partially in an attempt to cast Henry as a devout enforcer of canonical law in opposition to his rival, King Robert the Pious of West Francia; Robert's decidedly incestuous marriage to his second wife, Bertha, had recently shocked contemporaries.[13] As such, while the increasing interest in genealogical texts in the earlier tenth century was very possibly a response to the growing desire for secular men and women to more easily identify their more distant ancestors, it is no coincidence that we see the boom of genealogical diagrams corresponding to exactly the same period that the definition of consanguineous marriage was rewritten.

Alternatively, we could see the growth of genealogical texts from the tenth century onwards linked to the development of noble familial identity and interest in succession rights as part of the feudal revolution. Georges Duby explicitly connected the rush of new textual genealogies for comital and ducal families in West Francia with the increased prestige and authority of local elite families, such as the counts of Flanders and Anjou.[14] By writing down their ancestors, tracing lines of descent back to legendary or heroic founding figures, noble families had a powerful tool to shape their identity as a group. The creation of a genealogy thus helped to legitimize the authority of that family's current representatives as rulers, which in turn led to a greater interest among contemporaries in the history of that family, and thus led to even more genealogical texts. Duby also situated the development of genealogies within his view of the changing nature of family structures around the year 1000, which proposed that there was a shift from cognatic, more expansive conceptions of family and kin groups to a more narrow, agnatic and patrilineal definition.[15] The increasing push towards primogeniture and stricter definition of inheritance rights within these families are thus seen as prompting more interest in accurate genealogical records within that family.[16] The identity of a family was shaped and reinforced as a consequence of defining who was considered to be one of its legitimate heirs.

Duby explicitly characterized this rise in ducal and comital genealogies as a response to the perceived breakdown of royal power in the tenth-century West Frankish kingdom. The Carolingian family continued to rule on-and-off across the tenth century over a much smaller area than their imperial predecessors, whilst facing serious competition for royal and imperial authority from the new Robertian/Capetian dynasty in West Francia and the Ottonian dynasty to the east. The idea of this erosion of contemporary Carolingian authority in the tenth century led Duby to argue that local noble families were able to lay claim to some of the former Carolingian glory, by creating their own genealogies in imitation of the royal versions of the past. Thus, the creation of genealogies from the tenth to twelfth centuries is characterized as a predominantly noble pre-occupation.[17]

However, this focus on the impetus for genealogical texts coming from noble families plays down the surge of royal genealogies being created in this same period. Noble genealogies themselves were often based on royal prototypes, with the recent generations of comital families often bolted on to a Carolingian genealogy to lend a regal lustre to their ancestry.[18] For example, one of the earliest sets of extant comital genealogical diagrams from France – those of the Counts of Anjou, created between 1066 and 1080 by the monks of Saint-Aubin in Angers – were joined by a manuscript from the monastery containing much more carefully drawn diagrams of the Merovingian, Carolingian and the Capetian dynasties.[19] In fact, the bulk of the new secular genealogies created in the tenth and eleventh centuries were focused on royal dynasties and, in particular, on the Carolingians. The genre of genealogy may well have appealed to noble concerns in this period, but it was clearly responding to concerns about royal authority and legitimacy in this period as well. There was an increasing focus on the legacy of the Carolingian dynasty after its last representative, Louis V, was replaced in 987 by Hugh Capet. Both the Capetians in the west and the Ottonians and Salians in the east attempted to latch onto the Carolingian aura as new royal dynasties, either by claiming that their line contained the real heirs of the Carolingian emperors and kings, or directly declaring their own Carolingian descent. There appears to have been an inverse relationship between the actual power of the Carolingian dynasty and its genealogy in the tenth century; as the political dominance of the Carolingian family contracted, the power and malleability of its genealogy increased as a source of authority for other dynasties.

Carolingian genealogical tables

In the spirit of this volume, then, Carolingian schematic genealogies serve as an interesting test-case for how and why the Carolingian past was used after the Carolingian Empire and dynasty had come to an end. We can now turn to look at these genealogies more closely. It appears that the first extant version we possess of a Carolingian genealogical diagram – and thus the earliest one known in the medieval west – is the sketch created at Saint-Gallen which has been dated to the late tenth century.[20] The diagram traces the rise of the Carolingian rulers in a single line, recording Pippin III; his sons, Carloman and Charlemagne; Charlemagne's wife, Hildegard; their son, Louis the Pious; Louis' son, Charles the Bald; and a King Pippin, wrongly described as a son of Charles the Bald. Two emperors, Charlemagne and Louis the Pious, receive small figurative sketches in roundels within the diagram as well. Each of the individuals depicted is surrounded by brief biographical notes, primarily focused on their relationship with the monastery of Saint-Gall and their

170 Sarah Greer

burial places; evidently creating the diagram was an attempt to keep track of the different Carolingian donors that had featured in the monastery's history.

Shortly after the monks of Saint-Gall, another diagram of the Carolingian dynasty was created in the German Empire; this version, however, provided a much greater amount of detail. The so-called Bamberg Table, on a sheet now in the Bayerische Staatsbibliothek, has been dated to the reign of Emperor Henry II (1002–1024).[21] It features a single line of male descendants in roundels stretching from Bishop Arnulf of Metz, who is represented by a small figurative sketch, down to Louis the Pious. From there, the diagram breaks into three branches with Louis's three sons, Lothar, Charles the Bald and Louis the German; the West Frankish line of Charles the Bald continues directly under his father down through Louis the Stammerer, Charles the Simple, Louis IV and Lothar, while Lothar and Louis's lines are pushed up and off to the sides of the page. Those men in the central vertical line who had been crowned as king from Pippin III down to Louis the Stammerer also received small figural representations of their faces within their roundels. While the diagram overwhelmingly focuses on male descent, with no wives mentioned, some lines of descent traced through Carolingian daughters are represented: including, famously, a line that led to Cunigund, the wife of Henry II. The page also includes another smaller family diagram representing the Ottonian descendants of King Henry I, though this is much less detailed than the Carolingian diagram that dominates the page.

This genealogy, with its inclusion of Cunigund and an Ottonian family diagram, has drawn considerable attention. Karl Schmid, in particular, has compared the Bamberg Table's Carolingian genealogy with a similar version contained in the later twelfth-century *Liber Aureus* of Prüm, to argue that both of these diagrams were based on an earlier, now-lost, Carolingian genealogical table which he describes as a *Stemma regum Franciae*. On the basis of the centrality of the West Frankish line of Charles the Bald in the diagram and the lack of imperial title given to Carolingian emperors from the Lotharingian/Italian or German lines, Schmid suggested it was likely that this stemma originated in West Francia. As the table includes Louis IV's son, Charles of Lower Lotharingia, and Charles's like-named son as the last two figures in the West Frankish line, Schmid dates the creation of the table to the 990s, just after the elder Charles had failed to claim the West Frankish throne and had rebelled against the new Capetian king, Hugh Capet.[22] This linear version of the Carolingian family tree, splitting into a tripartite division in the lower half to show the rulers of Lotharingia/Italy, East Francia and West Francia, continued to influence later versions of this genealogy, showing a remarkable stability of visual form; it was adopted for the eleventh-century Carolingian table in the original manuscript of Frutolf of Michelsberg's *Chronicle* as well as for the tables that were included in the various continuations of this text, including Ekkehard of Aura's *Chronicle*.[23]

We also have another different extant Carolingian stemma, which is found in the twelfth-century Steinfeld Codex as part of a compilation of different genealogical texts and diagrams.[24] On the basis of the diagram emphasizing a direct vertical line of descent from Pippin I down to Louis the Child, Nora Gädeke has persuasively argued that the Carolingian table in this manuscript is a copy of a now-lost, early tenth-century version, created at the court of Louis the Child. By some considerable rearranging of the Carolingian genealogical tree – including liberal mixing of lines of genealogical descent with lines of inheritance which results in Charles the Fat sitting directly below Charles the Bald – Louis the Child is cast as the direct, unquestioned heir in an unbroken line of Carolingian rulers.[25] This was clearly an argument rather than a reflection of reality; Louis was only six years old when he succeeded his father Arnulf of Carinthia in 900, and the young king faced serious opposition from his adult half-brother, the already-crowned Zwentibald of Lotharingia.[26] Gädeke suggests this document was created at the point that Louis's court was trying to secure his power as a Carolingian ruler and potentially claim the imperial title for him as well; there is little reason to have the short-lived Louis, who died in 911 when he was only seventeen, placed at the end point of this Carolingian genealogical table if it was not created at his court.[27]

The way that each of these diagrams represented the Carolingian family communicated different arguments about the nature of Carolingian legitimacy; as a result, historians have attempted to decipher what these arguments were. Those who have examined these tables have focused on the now-lost exemplars of these genealogies, trying to contextualize and thus decode the purpose of these diagrams. As such, there has been considerable attention paid to the careful structuring of these genealogies, including who is and who is not included, what connections between individuals and branches of the family are underlined, and what kinds of visual organization and emphasis are used. All of these elements are seen as tools used to construct the overall claim that the genealogy is making, and to give us insight into how the Carolingian family was seen in the tenth century and beyond.

A new Carolingian table: British Library Arundel MS 390, f.133r

Yet, for the attention that has been given to the Bamberg Table, the Carolingian table in the Steinfeld Codex and their other eleventh- and twelfth-century adaptations, there is one genealogical diagram from the eleventh century which has thus far not received the same level of attention. At the back of one of the earliest extant manuscripts of Regino of Prüm's *Chronicle*, British Library Arundel MS 390, we find a rather peculiar version of a Carolingian stemma (Fig. 10.1).[28] While the manuscript itself was most likely written in the early eleventh century, the family tree has been added in later on a flyleaf at the back, written in a hand that appears to date from the mid- to late-eleventh century. The same hand has also gone through the rest of the manuscript of Regino and annotated the text, namely giving very brief summaries of the lives of Carolingian rulers on the top of the manuscript pages where their death is recorded in the text. A few other texts are also written on the other leaves at the back of the manuscript, including: an *Epitaphium Heinrici* for the *dux* Henry who Regino reports died fighting against the vikings in the Siege of Paris in 887;[29] the *Iudicium de Regno et Sacerdotio*, which describes how an ordeal

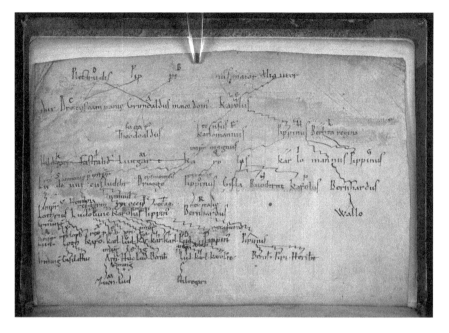

FIGURE 10.1   © The British Library Board, British Library, Arundel MS 390, f. 133r.

by water was used by a group of Italian churchmen to decide between the claims of Gregory VII and Henry IV, as well as the subsequent oath made to Henry IV;[30] and a list of popes.[31] However, these are in a different hand and ink and seem to be written after the genealogical diagram as they are placed on the folios immediately before and after it.

That this table has not received a great deal of attention is perhaps not surprising: the diagram is a mess. It is a far cry from the neat, linear diagrams that we see in the Bamberg Table or the table in the Steinfeld Codex. Instead, this one seems to begin with an attempt at a structure, placing the spaced-out name of Pippin centrally at the top of the manuscript, with Charlemagne's name almost (but not quite) directly underneath him further down the page. However, from Charlemagne onwards, it begins to break down; as some branches of the family begin to multiply and others sputter out, the diagram skews more and more to the left, forcing the author to begin to abbreviate names. The messiness of the table belies that this in fact might be a second attempt; there are remnants of erasures under the top half of the table. It also seems that once the names and links between individuals had been charted, the author added in further information, including titles of rulers, the names of their wives, and other pieces of information, such as the tonsuring of Charles Martel's son Carloman and the exile of Theodoald, the son of Grimoald II. The lack of space at the bottom of the table meant that some of these titles were heavily abbreviated as well. Some names also have single letters placed immediately above them.

The messiness and cramped presentation of the table does not, however, obscure the careful interest and attention paid by the author to certain elements of organization. It is immediately evident that the individuals in the diagram are methodically placed on horizontal levels indicating different generations of the Carolingian family, with connecting lines (both straight and wavy) showing either marriages or lines of descent. The cramped lower half of the table is a direct result of this; rather than shift certain branches up or down, or move siblings vertically to make it clearer, the author has relentlessly kept them on the same horizontal plane. The overall effect suggests less an attempt to shape the Carolingian family stemma into an argument, as we saw with the other diagrams we have encountered, and more an effort to make sense of all of the different parts of the complicated Carolingian family.

This sense of interest in the wider Carolingian family may also explain why we see so many Carolingian wives and daughters included in this diagram. The table includes seventeen named women and one unnamed woman, a striking increase compared to the four named women in the Bamberg Table and the two in the Steinfeld Codex.[32] These women are included all the way through the tree, beginning with the two wives of Pippin II at the top of the page and ending with Hildegard, the daughter attributed to Louis III at the bottom. The majority of the women are wives of Carolingian kings; at the top of the table, where space is plentiful, they are added alongside their husbands, while the cramped bottom half of the table sees these women sometimes tacked in over the top of the line of descent between their husband and son. Care is taken to distinguish which woman produced which son with separate lines: a clear example is the separation of Pippin II's sons Drogo and Grimoald by his wife Plectrude and his son Charles Martel by an *alia uxor*, but even at the bottom we can see cramped additions of 'Ansg.' and 'Addh.' on the lines leading to Louis the Stammerer's sons by his two wives, Ansgard and Adelheid. Almost all of these wives share something in common: all but one are mothers of Carolingian children.[33]

Sources

So, what then, are the sources for this new genealogical diagram of the Carolingians? The most notable source has already been identified by Gädeke: it is clear that this diagram has notable similarities with the version offered by the twelfth-century table in the Steinfeld Codex. The choice of Pippin II as the first individual rather than the more common decision to opt for St Arnulf of Metz, Pippin I, or Pippin III; the almost complete agreement on the male members of the family (including the unusual choice to include not just Charlemagne and Carloman, but also Pippin as the sons of Pippin III); the repetition of similar titles across the tables, and the conclusion with the generation including Zwentibald and Louis the Child all led Gädeke to suggest that both the Arundel and Steinfeld Carolingian tables may have drawn on a now-lost earlier diagram; perhaps the tenth-century version that had been drawn up at Louis the Child's court.[34] However, if this earlier diagram had

174 Sarah Greer

the same linear, extremely dynastically-minded structure that the Steinfeld Codex table did, then it is clear that the author of the Arundel 390 table chose to radically reimagine the visual layout of the genealogy.

The other main source for table in Arundel 390 is unsurprisingly the chronicle of Carolingian history written by Regino of Prüm which dominated this manuscript. Almost all of the new information included on the tree that is not seen in the Steinfeld Codex – that is, the vast majority of the Carolingian women included – is found in Regino's text. The wives of both Pippin III and Charlemagne, and Charlemagne's two daughters, Gisela and Rotrude, are named in the section of the *Royal Frankish Annals* which Regino quoted.[35] Ermengard, the wife of Lothar I features in the entry for 851; Emma, the wife of Louis the German is mentioned in 876; and Ermentrude, the wife of Charles the Bald appears in 870. The entry for 878 explains how Louis the Stammerer had two sons with his first wife, Ansgard, before being forced to repudiate her and marry Adelheid, with whom he had Charles the Simple. Gisela, the daughter of Lothar II, is discussed at length by Regino due to her marriage to the viking King Godafrid and her brother Hugh's rebellion in alliance with her husband.[36] This use of Regino fits with the author of this table annotating the rest of the manuscript in the way that we would expect if someone was using the Chronicle as a source to create a genealogy. The summaries noted at the tops of manuscript pages feature exactly the kind of short-form genealogical data that would help in creating a stemma.[37]

There are, however, a few additions which are not seen in either the Steinfeld Codex table or Regino's *Chronicle*. These are the two wives of Pippin II; the attribution of a son, Bernhard, and grandson, Wallo, to Carloman II; the inclusion of an Ermengard as the mother of Louis the Child; and the attribution of a daughter, Hildegard, to Louis III. We can deal with each of these in turn:

1) The inclusion of Pippin II's two wives as Plectrude and an *alia uxor*. This information matches up with the narrative Carolingian genealogy created at Compiègne in the tenth century which refers to both a 'Piletrudem' as the mother of Drogo and Grimoald and an unnamed other wife as the mother of Charles Martel.[38] It seems that the author did not have access to the chronicle of Fredegar where this *alia uxor* is named as Alpaida.[39]

2) The attribution of a son, Bernhard, and grandson, Wallo, to Carloman II. In his diagram of this table for the *Monumenta Germaniae Historica*, Georg Henrich Pertz suggested that this may be a misplacing of the Carolingian ancestry of Wala, Abbot of Corbie and Corvey.[40] Wala first appears in Regino's description of Charlemagne's delegation to King Hemming in 811.[41] The ancestry of Wala was then further explained in the following year's entry, where he is described as the son of Bernhard, making him the *patruelis* (paternal cousin) of Charlemagne.[42] Yet, in the table the author bumps Bernhard and Wala down two generations from their position as Charlemagne's uncle and cousin, instead making them Charlemagne's nephew and great-nephew respectively. Perhaps there was some confusion over exactly what the label of *patruelis* indicated, possibly being read more broadly as a description of a male relative descending from a fraternal line. If so, the author

may have tried to find a sensible place to put him, and opted to make him a son of Charlemagne's brother Carloman.

3) The inclusion of Irmingard as the mother of Louis the Child. Pertz described Irmingard, who is placed on a line between Arnulf and his son Louis the Child, as either the wife of Louis or possibly of his half-brother Zwentibald.[43] However, this overlooks the close positioning of Irmingard to Arnulf, as her name is written immediately underneath his name, with some distance between her and Louis. As such, it seems more likely that Irmingard is being positioned here as the wife of Arnulf and mother of Louis the Child. This contradicts the various sources that describe Uota as Arnulf's wife and Louis's mother. However, while Regino is at pains to emphasize the legitimacy of Louis the Child's parentage, compared to the illegitimacy of his half-brother Zwentibald, Louis's mother's name is not mentioned.[44] The sources which describe her at length and name her (the Regensburg Continuator of the *Annals of Fulda* and Hermann of Reichenau's *Chronicle*) evidently were not available to the author of this table.[45] However, where the name of 'Irmingard' as Louis's mother has come from is puzzling. If the author was not sure about the name of Arnulf's wife, or the mothers of his children, they could have omitted it; instead, Irmingard has been carefully added in over the line of descent leading to Louis alone. One outside possibility is that they have confused Louis the Child with Louis the Blind, whose mother was Irmingard, the daughter of Emperor Louis II. This seems unlikely for two reasons: firstly, Regino very clearly distinguishes between Louis the Child as the son of Arnulf and Louis the Blind as the son of Boso and Irmingard.[46] Anyone who was carefully reading the final sections of Regino's text would know to separate the two. Secondly, Irmingard is already present on the table in the correct place as Louis II's daughter. Either the author has made an unexplainable mistake, or was referring to some other source or tradition about Louis the Child's parents which has now been lost to us.[47]

4) The attribution of a daughter, Hildegard, to Louis III of West Francia. This seems to be an error, as it is clear from both Regino himself and other sources that Louis died in 883 without children.[48] There are several possibilities for where this error came from, as there are a number of Carolingian daughters named Hildegard at this point in the family tree, including the daughter of Louis II and the daughter of Charles the Simple.[49] However, I believe the most likely source for this error is the report in Regino's entry for 894, where he describes how a certain Hildegard, daughter of the King Louis who was the brother of Carloman and Charles, was deprived of her possessions and exiled to the monastery of Chiemsee.[50] This Hildegard was the daughter of Louis the Younger, and Louis's brothers were Emperor Carloman and Charles the Fat.[51] It would be an easy enough mistake to confuse that trio of brothers with the like-named trio of Louis III, Carloman II and Charles the Simple, especially as they are not far from each other on the bottom of the tree.

Alongside the additions to the table, we can also see which Carolingians have been removed or omitted from the author's two sources. There are a number

176 Sarah Greer

of omissions from the earlier generations of the family which are recorded in Regino's *Chronicle*, including some which also appear in the Steinfeld Codex table. These include Charles Martel's daughter Hiltrude and her son, Tassilo of Bavaria; Charles Martel's son, Grifo; Charlemagne's sons, Pippin the Hunchback, Hugh, and Theoderic; and Ermengard's son, Louis the Blind. Others who were not on the Steinfeld Codex table but were present in Regino's text include Lothar's two wives, Theutberga and Waldrada; Charles the Bald's wife, Richildis; Louis the Younger's wife, Liutgard; Hugh of Lotharingia's wife, Friderada; Charles the Fat's wife, Richgard; and Zwentibald's wife, Oda.[52] The underlying theme for these omissions seems to be related to a lack of descendants from these figures, or questions surrounding their legitimacy.[53] Tassilo, of course, was forced to give up his and his family's claim to Bavaria and entered a monastery and his uncle Grifo faced accusations of illegitimacy, was imprisoned in a monastery and then was killed in a rebellion against Pippin III.[54] The three sons of Charlemagne who were omitted included the famously illegitimate Pippin the Hunchback and two clerics who had no children.[55] Theutberga and Waldrada were the quintessential examples of problematic Carolingian marriages and questions around legitimacy. Richildis had no surviving male children.[56] Liutgard only produced one son for Louis the Younger, who died in childhood.[57] Hugh of Lotharingia's wife Friderada only had children from her previous marriage, and she remarried following the imprisonment and tonsuring of Hugh for his rebellion against Charles the Fat.[58] The scandal around Empress Richgard's sexual conduct and accusations of adultery were discussed at length by Regino, as well as her assertion of virginity and divorce from Charles the Fat.[59] Despite Zwentibald's marriage to Duke Otto of Saxony's daughter, Oda, the couple had no sons before Zwentibald's death in 900.[60] Although Regino and the exemplar of the Steinfeld Codex table serve as the sources for this table, it is evident that the information from them has not been copied over indiscriminately. Instead, members of the Carolingian family have been carefully weighed and decisions made about whether they are fit to include in this stemma on the basis of their production of legitimate heirs.

Consequently, this genealogical table is considerably different in purpose to the others that we have encountered of the Carolingian family. The Arundel 390 table is not, like the Bamberg Table, the Steinfeld Codex table and its lost exemplar, or the lost *Stemma regum Franciae*, focused on tracing the progression of dynastic power through the Carolingian family. Its intention is not to show which branch of Louis the Pious's sons dominated over the others, or to cast anyone as the main heir of Charlemagne or of Pippin III. Instead, the Arundel 390 table is intensely concerned with trying to map out the Carolingian family as opposed to the Carolingian dynasty. The genealogy is structured with horizontal layers corresponding to generations of the family contrasts with the vertical emphasis on the dynastic stemma, which instead prioritizes lines of inheritance. This allows a more comprehensive and more workable vision of the Carolingian family to appear. It is much easier to use the table in Arundel 390 to discover the relationships between siblings, cousins, nieces and nephews or more removed family relationships than to use the other convoluted dynastic diagrams that we have encountered. The information presented in Regino's *Chronicle* about the different members of the Carolingian family is here laid out for a reader to access easily, even if the format is cramped and messy. Much like modern editions and translations of Regino and other Carolingian chronicles include a genealogical diagram, the table in Arundel 390 offers a helpful visual guide for a reader who wants to make sense of who is who in this extensive, complicated family.

Provenance

Where did this rather different Carolingian stemma come from? Unfortunately, the provenance of Arundel 390 is somewhat opaque. Hartmut Hoffmann argued that the scribe of the main Regino text was from Reichenau, suggesting that the manuscript was written in the first third of the eleventh century.[61] However, the only certain information about its provenance after this comes from a stamp at the front of the manuscript which records that it was given to the Royal Society of London from the donation of Henry Howard, the sixth Duke of Norfolk (1628–1684). Howard donated the manuscripts collected by his grandfather, Thomas Arundel, the second Earl of Arundel, to the Royal Society in 1667, which were then later passed on to the British Library in 1831. No other definite information about the manuscript exists, though the donation from Arundel's collection suggests that it might have come into his ownership as part of his 1636 purchase of the library of Willibald Pirckheimer, the German humanist and intellectual.[62] Wolf-Rüdiger Schleidgen, who reassessed the various manuscripts of Regino's *Chronicle* in 1977, has suggested that this manuscript may have either originated in or was held in Soissons, mainly on the basis that the manuscript also contains a copy of the epitaph of Count Henry, who died fighting the vikings in the ninth century and was buried at Soissons. To support this, he notes that there is a later, fifteenth-century copy of this manuscript and of the table it contains as well, which is now held in the Universitätsbibliothek at Gießen.[63] This manuscript was either copied by or for a certain Eustachius, who was a canon of St Germanus at Speyer before later becoming a cantor at Worms. Eustachius studied canon law at Sens for two years, which Schleidgen notes is not far from Soissons, and so he could have made his copy of the manuscript while he was studying in the region.[64]

However, Schleidgen himself notes that there is another possibility: the manuscript may have come from the Middle Rhine area. Eustachius was, after all, based in this area for most of his career. Placing the manuscript in this region would then make more sense of its presence in the collection of Pirckheimer, who was based in Nuremburg.[65] This would also agree with one other element which Schleidgen did not note: the strong similarities between the tables in Arundel 390 and the Steinfeld Codex. Both the authors of the twelfth-century Steinfeld Codex table and the eleventh-century Arundel 390 table appear to be drawing on copy of a now-lost stemma. The monastery of Steinfeld lies just north of Würzburg, about

178 Sarah Greer

100 kilometres to the north-east of Worms. A Middle Rhine provenance for the Arundel manuscript would thus make sense of how the author was able to access the same exemplar. It would also explain why the twelfth-century *Codex Laureshamensis* from Lorsch appears to be based on the Arundel 390 version of Regino's *Chronicle*. It may also explain why a new Carolingian genealogical diagram appears in Lorsch at the same time that the Codex was being created which, like the Arundel 390 table, begins with Pippin II before tracing down to Louis the German and Louis the Younger, both of whom were buried in the monastery and are labelled as such on the table.[66] The majority of evidence that we have thus supports Arundel 390 being in the Middle Rhine region in the mid-to-late eleventh century, when this stemma was composed. It would have been relatively easy for someone to copy out the epitaph of Count Henry at Soissons, then travel back to the Rhine and later enter it into the manuscript.

This setting of Middle Rhine region helps to contextualize the very specific interest the author of the Arundel 390 table shows in the Carolingian family. The area stretching between Worms and Speyer was the heartland of the Salian imperial dynasty, which had risen to power after the death of the childless Henry II in 1024. From the middle of the eleventh century onwards – that is, at exactly the point that this diagram was created – the Salians began to steadily intensify their attention on the region, and on Speyer in particular, placing the cathedral at the centre of their imperial identity. The cathedral served as the imperial mausoleum for the Salian dynasty, containing the tombs of Conrad II and his wife Gisela; their son Henry III; their grandson Henry IV and his wife Bertha; and their great-grandson Henry V. This striking collection of Salian royal bodies was unusual for the time. The generations of the previous Ottonian dynasty had each been buried at different sites and there were few other mausolea that had such a wealth of emperors and empresses accumulate in such a short space of time. Under the reign of Henry IV, Speyer's identity as *the* Salian burial site intensified. In 1076, Henry arranged for his young daughter, Adelheid, to be buried in the cathedral; this marked a reorientation of the burial site from one which had been purely dynastic, housing the Salian ruling couples, to one which could include non-ruling members of their broader family as well.[67] Shortly afterwards, the cathedral began a period of intensive development, with the launch of a new building scheme on an unusually monumental scale. Over twenty years of construction, Speyer cathedral was transformed into one of the most spectacular buildings in the western Christian world, a very visible symbol of the power of the dynasty entombed there.[68]

The amplification of Speyer's identity as a Salian burial site was not just physical; Henry IV also made a concerted effort to promote the memorial function of the site and to craft a new image of his family. From the 1080s onwards, Henry gave a series of donations to Speyer in quick succession, transferring a number of properties to its bishop. These donations were made at significant points in Henry's reign; they tended to precede critical military and political events, such as on October 14, 1080, the day before Henry's battle against the anti-king, Rudolf of Rheinfelden.[69] Henry's success in quelling the threat Rudolf posed, followed by Henry's successful

Italian campaign and imperial coronation in 1084 and the death of his great rival, Pope Gregory VII, in 1086 were all accompanied by another swathe of memorial grants to Speyer; perhaps also intended as a reward for the bishop's loyal support during Henry's conflict with Gregory VII. From 1086 onwards, the emperor issued diplomas to Speyer which were granted for the souls of his grandparents, Conrad II and Gisela; his parents, Henry III and Agnes; his wife, Bertha; his brother, Conrad; his daughter, Adelheid; and his son, Henry.[70] He also arranged to have the bodies of some of his family members translated to Speyer: these included Bertha, who had been interred in Mainz cathedral; and Henry's brother, Conrad, and son, Henry, who were originally buried in the Harzburg.[71] This concerted effort by Henry IV to craft a Salian memorial identity at Speyer has led Stefan Weinfurter to argue that by the early twelfth century, Speyer would have been the most Salian place in the entire kingdom.[72]

As the central memorial site for the Salian family, Speyer would have been plugged into the increasing interest of the Salians and their supporters over the eleventh century in claiming that they were descended from the Carolingians. This attempt to latch onto the Carolingians as a source of identity had begun early; Conrad II was especially interested in Charlemagne, with the churches constructed at his royal palaces of Goslar and Nijmegen imitating the structure of his famous church at Aachen.[73] By the middle of the eleventh century, claims were being made about the direct Carolingian ancestry of the Salians. In addition to reporting that people said 'the stirrups of Charlemagne hung on Conrad's saddle', Conrad II's biographer, Wipo, stated that the emperor's wife, Gisela, was descended from Charlemagne 'when the fourth line is added after the tenth'.[74] This riddle appears to refer to Gisela's descent from Charlemagne through two different branches of her family, as well as making a neat biblical allusion to the book of Matthew proclaiming that there were fourteen generations from Abraham to David, from David to the exile to Babylon, and from the exile to Christ.[75] As both Gisela and her husband Conrad shared the line of ten generations of descent from Charlemagne through Otto I, their mutual great-great-grandfather, their marriage was clearly consanguineous by the new seven-degree definition, and the couple were dogged by criticism for this throughout their reign.[76] Their son, Henry III, also faced criticism for his second marriage to Agnes of Poitou in 1043 on the basis of their consanguinity: in two letters addressed to Abbot Poppo of Stavelot which must date to immediately before the marriage, Abbot Sigefried of Gorze pointed out that Agnes and Henry had common ancestors in both the fourth and fifth degree, lines he was able to trace with precision through successive female generations. Strikingly, he added that he had attached a *figura* of this genealogy, which he hoped Poppo would be able to show the king to help him make his case against the marriage; unfortunately, this *figura* has not survived.[77]

The Middle Rhine region, and the area around Speyer in particular, makes sense both as the location for Arundel 390 and as the context for the creation of the new Carolingian genealogical diagram in the late eleventh century. A wealth of evidence ties the manuscript to this location, from its use of the same exemplar as the Steinfeld

180 Sarah Greer

Codex, its similarities to the *Codex Laureshamensis*, the fifteenth-century copy made by a canon of Speyer (perhaps copied out so that he could take it with him after he moved to Worms) and its likely purchase as part of Pirckheimer's library. The setting of Speyer also perfectly fits with why the manuscript would be annotated and a new Carolingian genealogy created in the late eleventh century, just as Speyer saw an intensification of interest in the commemoration of the Salian family and attempts to link them explicitly to their Carolingian ancestors.

The purpose of the Arundel 390 table

With this in mind, we can begin to better understand why we see this particular version of a Carolingian genealogical diagram created in this manuscript. The table in Arundel 390 was created as part of an effort to map out the legitimate descendants of the Carolingian family; this must be linked to the context of Salian interests in Carolingian descent and in consanguineous marriage from the mid-eleventh century on. In Speyer, at a burial place that had been newly redefined as a familial burial place rather than simply a dynastic one, the Salians were intensely focused on concerns about consanguinity and Carolingian descent through female ancestors. In the face of serious challenges by other rival kings and by the pope, the Salian dynasty was in process of legitimizing its power and rulership through claiming that they were part of an unbroken line of emperors stretching back to Charlemagne. At the same time, we find a genealogical diagram of the Carolingians which paid careful attention to the division of the family into generations and to the inclusion of wives and mothers, being as comprehensive as possible in tracing the different legitimate lines of the family which had produced children. At the very point that the Carolingian family was a powerful source of authority that the Salians and their supporters sought to utilize, we see someone turn to the earliest extant copy of Regino of Prüm, precisely the text that helps to illuminate the Carolingian family tree.

As such, this tree may well have been created as the first part of an attempt to create a new version of a Carolingian stemma to help bolster Salian claims to Carolingian descent and legitimacy. The table looks strikingly like later examples from the Renaissance, where we have the summary diagrams of entire families sketched out in this very horizontal, generational form, before the creation of a more streamlined, argumentative form.[78] As Gädeke has pointed out, Arundel 390 is unique amongst the other eleventh-century Carolingian genealogical tables in the German Empire: it appears on its own, without a table of the contemporary ruling dynasty accompanying it.[79] Was the Arundel 390 diagram the preparatory work for a new table? This diagram could have been the first step of cataloguing the entire Carolingian family by someone who had been asked to create a new stemma. If that is the case, then we can compare this to the production of the Bamberg Table in the court of Henry II, a diagram that tacked the family of Empress Cunigund onto an earlier exemplar of a Carolingian genealogy. Doing so offered a way to skim over potentially consanguineous marriages in Cunigund's family and to promote a new

All in the family **181**

vision of the ancestry of Henry II and his wife.[80] Given the allegations of incest against Conrad and Gisela, and thus against all of their descendants, a new stemma that allowed a renegotiation of their family within a Carolingian framework may well have been appealing. Of course, this can only remain speculation, as no such diagram has survived today. We can only reconstruct hints of possible intention from the interests that we can see within the Arundel 390 table; whether this was acted upon cannot be proven.

Nevertheless, the practical purpose of this diagram finds a useful comparison with another genealogical text from the eleventh century. At the back of a tenth-century manuscript containing the historical texts of Liudprand of Cremona, Regino's *Chronicle*, and its continuation by Adalbert of Magdeburg, we find a table of royal genealogical information arranged in columns.[81] The primary column described the various rulers from the Carolingians down to the Ottonians and Salians, with the Carolingian information drawn almost entirely from Regino's text. Another column was then added to the left that discussed the Merovingians. Other bits of information, primarily to do with whether different individuals died with or without heirs, were added in around the table. To keep track of all the various people, the author used epithets and various scribal marks; so, for example, all references to Charles the Bald were marked by three horizontal dots.[82] Steffen Patzold has persuasively argued that this text was likely created for Bishop Abraham of Freising after Henry II died heirless in 1024, intended to help Abraham prepare for the upcoming assembly in Kamba to decide who would succeed as king. The genealogical table created was thus designed as a practical reference text, providing the bishop with information about the historical succession of kings that was easy to decipher quickly, added into the back of a manuscript containing the relevant texts. Later on, around the time of the coronation of Henry IV in 1084, the table was updated with information about the Salian rulers.[83] The similarities with Arundel 390 are striking: in these two manuscripts containing Regino's chronicle, we find a practical genealogical reference text designed to quickly summarize the information within the manuscript as a whole. It may also contextualize the apparently random letters included over the names of different figures in the table; they may have been a similar kind of device as the scribal marks in this table, or possibly refer to addenda which summarized pieces of biographical information in the way that we see on the Freising table.

It is clear that the Carolingian past lay at the heart of present concerns on the east of the Rhine in the late eleventh century. Genealogies of past dynasties were just as valuable a source as those of the present ruling dynasty. The inclusion of Carolingian genealogical diagrams in all of the copies of Ekkehard of Aura's *Chronicle* is testament to the continued interest in the Carolingians as a source of imperial legitimacy and authority when that topic was being fiercely debated.[84] Genealogies and genealogical diagrams were far from simply a noble concern; the table in Arundel 390 shows us how Carolingian sources were read, interpreted and used well after that dynasty had ended.

182 Sarah Greer

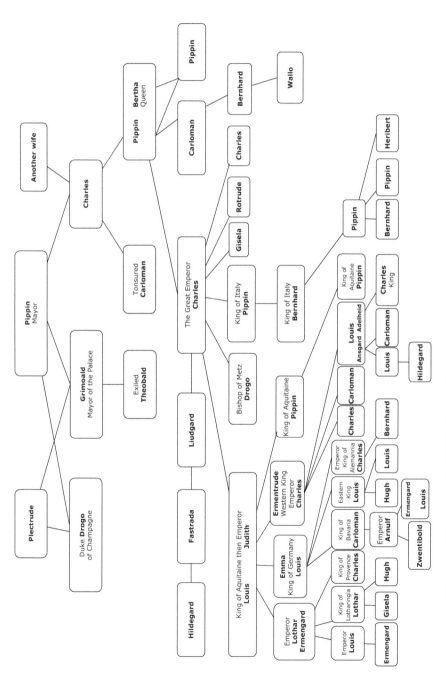

FIGURE 10.2 Diagram of the Arundel 390 Table (created by author).

Notes

1 T. Desmond Alexander, 'From Adam to Judah: The Significance of the Family Tree in Genesis', *The Evangelical Quarterly*, 61:1 (1989), 5–19.

2 Thegan, *Gesta Hludowici Imperatoris* 1 in *SS rer. Germ.* 64, ed. by Ernst Tremp (Hanover: Monumenta Germaniae Historica, 1995), pp. 174–6; Asser, *Vita Alfredi* in *Asser's Life of King Alfred, together with the Annals of St Neots, erroneously ascribed to Asser* ed. by William Henry Stevenson (2nd ed., Oxford: Clarendon Press, 1959), pp. 2–4. For a comprehensive discussion of early medieval textual genealogies, see Walter Pohl, 'Genealogy: A Comparative Perspective from the Early Medieval West', in *Meanings of Community across Medieval Eurasia* ed. by Eirik Hovden, Christina Lutter, Walter Pohl (Leiden: Brill, 2016), pp. 232–69.

3 Gabrielle Spiegel, 'Genealogy: Form and Function in Medieval Historical Narrative', *History and Theory* 22:1 (1983), 43–53.

4 For example, see the tenth-century genealogy created for the West Frankish Carolingians: *Genealogia regum Francorum* in *Scriptores* 13 (Hanover: Monumenta Germaniae Historica, 1881), p. 247; the *Genealogia Witgeri* created for the Flanders ducal house in 951–959: *Witgeri Genealogia Arnulfi Comitis* in *Scriptores* 9, ed. by Georg Henrich Pertz (Hanover: Monumenta Germaniae Historica, 1851), pp. 302–4; the *Genealogia de Arnulfo Comite* written in 961: in *Scriptores* 9, ed. by George Henry Pertz (Hanover: Monumenta Germaniae Historica, 1851), p. 304; and an eleventh-century short genealogical history of the Carolingian kings: P. Bernard, 'Une courte histoire des rois de France de Charles le Chauve à Louis V', *Bibliothèque de l'école des chartes* 84 (1923), 257–64. See also Karl Ferdinand Werner, 'Il y a Mille Ans, Les Carolingiens: Fin d'une Dynastie, Début d'un Mythe', *Annuaire-Bullentin de la Société de l'histoire de France* (1991–1992), 17–89 (pp. 50–7); Georges Duby, 'French genealogical literature: the eleventh and twelfth centuries', in *The Chivalrous Society* trans. by Cynthia Postan (Berkeley: University of California Press, 1977), pp. 149–57 (p. 150).

5 The genealogy of Christ also began to be depicted in graphic form in this period. The first extant examples come from illustrated manuscripts of Beatus of Liébana's commentary on the Apocalypse, which were produced in northern Spain from 940 onwards. However, the influence of these diagrams was apparently restricted to the Iberian peninsula in the tenth century. See Christiane Klapisch-Zuber, *L'Ombre des Ancêtres: Essai sur l'Imaginaire Médiéval de la Parenté* (Paris: Fayard, 2000), pp. 61–75; Gert Melville, 'Geschichte in graphischer Gestalt: Beobachtungen zu einer spätmittelalterlichen Darstellungsweise', in *Geschichtsschreibung und Geschichtsbewusstsein im Späten Mittelalter*, ed. by Hans Patze (Sigmaringen: Jan Thorbecke, 1987), pp. 57–4 (pp. 67–8).

6 Karl Schmid, 'Geschlechterbewusstsein am Beispiel ausgewählter karolingischer (Bild-) Stemmata aus dem hohen Mittelalter', in *Georges Duby: L'écriture de l'Histoire* ed. by Claudie Duhamel-Amado and Guy Lobrichon (Brussels: De Boeck-Wesmael, 1996), pp. 141–59 (p. 143).

7 Christiane Klapisch-Zuber, 'The Genesis of the Family Tree', *I Tatti Studies in the Italian Renaissance* 4 (1991), 105–29 (pp. 118–22); Marilyn Mitchell, 'Fitting issues: the visual representation of time in family tree diagrams', Σημειωτκη – *Sign Systems Studies* 2–3 (2014), 241–80 (pp. 253–6).

8 Pliny the Elder, *Natural History* 35, 2, ed. by H. Rackham (*Loeb Classical Library* 394, Cambridge MA: Harvard University Press, 1952), pp. 263–7; Mirelle Corbier, 'Painting and Familial and Genealogical Memory (Pliny, Natural History *35, 1–14*)' in *Vita Vigilia Est: Essays in Honour of Barbara Levick*, ed. by Edward Bispham and Greg Rowe with Elaine Matthews (London: Institute of Classical Studies SOAS, 2007), pp. 69–81 (pp. 70–6, 83). Corbier notes that Pliny appears to be describing paintings on walls, rather than the theory put forward by Theodor Mommsen that these *imagines* were masks connected by physical ribbons (pp. 81–3).

9 Anglo-Saxon royal pedigrees occupy the middle-ground between textual genealogies and visual stemmata: they relied on vertical organisation of text, but still lack the

184 Sarah Greer

visual elements (such as the roundels, lines, and different forms of arrangement) that mark out the genealogical stemmata dealt with here. David N. Dumville, 'The Anglian collection of royal genealogies and regnal lists', *Anglo-Saxon England* 5 (1976), 23–50; David N. Dumville, 'Kingship, Genealogies and Regnal Lists', in *Early Medieval Kingship* ed. by Peter Sawyer and Ian Wood, (Leeds: The School of History, 1977), pp. 72–104. Both of these essays are reprinted in David N. Dumville, *Histories and Pseudo-histories of the Insular Middle Ages* (Aldershot: Variorum, 1990). See also Pohl, 'Genealogies', pp. 249–55.

10 Mary Bouquet, 'Family Trees and their Affinities: The Visual Imperative of the Genealogical Diagram', *The Journal of the Royal Anthropological Institute* 2:1 (1996), 43–66 (p. 47); Klapisch-Zuber, 'The Genesis of the Family Tree', pp. 113–4.

11 See, for example, Jack Goody, *The Development of the Family and Marriage in Europe* (Cambridge: Cambridge University Press, 1983), pp. 136–7; Georges Duby, *Medieval Marriage: Two Models from Twelfth-Century France*, trans. by Barbara Bray (Baltimore: Johns Hopkins University Press, 1978); Constance B. Bouchard, 'Consanguinity and Noble Marriages in the Tenth and Eleventh Centuries', *Speculum* 56:2 (1981), 268–87.

12 There were some exceptions allowing closer marriages in more extreme circumstances, such as for missionaries in recently converted areas. Karl Ubl, *Inzestverbot und Gesetzgebung. Die Konstruktion eines Verbrechens (300–1100)* (Berlin: Walter de Gruyter, 2008), pp. 236–40, 374–83; David d'Avray, 'Review article: Kinship and religion in the early Middle Ages', *Early Medieval Europe* 20:2 (2012), 195–212 (pp. 199–205).

13 Ubl, *Inzestverbot*, pp. 384–440; d'Avray, 'Kinship and religion', pp. 206–9.

14 Duby, 'French genealogical literature', pp. 149–57.

15 This view has since fallen out of favour. See the commentary by Pohl, 'Genealogy', pp. 256–7.

16 Pierre Bourdieu explicitly linked the creation of genealogical texts and diagrams to interest in succession law and inheritance processes. Pierre Bourdieu, *Outline of a Theory of Practice*, trans. by Richard Nice (Cambridge: Cambridge University Press, 1977), p. 207 n. 71.

17 Duby, 'French Genealogical Literature', pp. 151–2.

18 Duby, 'French Genealogical Literature', pp. 152–3.

19 The comital genealogies are in Vatican, MS Reg.lat. 1283, fol. 65v; the royal genealogies are in Angers, Bibliothèque Municipale, 58(51), ff. 1v-3r. Klapisch-Zuber, *L'Ombre*, pp. 92–4. The royal genealogical diagrams appear to date to the reign of Philip I (r. 1060–1108), so were possibly written out at the same time as those of the Angevin counts.

20 BAV, MS Reg. lat. 339, fol. 7 (olim fol. 32); *Genealogiae Karolorum* VII in *Scriptores* 13 ed. by Georg Waitz (Hanover: Monumenta Germaniae Historica, 1881), p. 244, 248. See also Klapisch-Zuber, *L'Ombre*, p. 91. A high-resolution image of the manuscript is available online: http://digi.vatlib.it/view/MSS_Reg.lat.339.

21 Munich, Bayerische Staatsbibliothek, CLM 29880 (6). A high-resolution image of the manuscript is available online: http://daten.digitale-sammlungen.de/0005/bsb00059279/images/index.html?fip=193.174.98.30&seite=2&pdfseitex=.

22 Schmid, 'Ein verlorenes Stemma *Regum Franciae*. Zugleich ein Beitrag zur Entstehung und Funktion karolingischer (Bild-)Genealogien in salisch-staufischer Zeit', *Frühmittelalterliche Studien* 28 (1994), 196–225 (pp. 202–6). He argues that the inclusion of the younger Charles may suggest the table was created as an *ad hoc* response to the capture and imprisonment of the elder Charles and his older sons at Laon in 991, and was possibly written under the supervision of Archbishop Arnulf of Reims, himself the nephew of the elder Charles and cousin of the younger.

23 Schmid, 'Geschlechterbewusstsein', pp. 143–5. On the continuations and the various manuscript recensions of these texts, see T. J. H. McCarthy, *Chronicles of the Investiture Contest: Frutolf of Michelsberg and his Continuators* (Manchester: Manchester University Press, 2014), pp. 41–4.

24 London, British Library Additional MS 21109, f. 133v. This manuscript contains two stemmata, one of the Carolingians, one of the German emperors, and also includes a

All in the family **185**

textual genealogy running from Louis the Pious through to the twelfth-century German emperors which appears to have no apparent link to the schematic trees included. Nora Gädeke, 'Eine Karolingergenealogie des Frühen 10. Jahrhunderts?', *Francia* 15 (1988), 777–92 (pp. 778–80).

25 Gädeke, 'Eine Karolingergenealogie', pp. 785–6.

26 Timothy Reuter, *Germany in the Middle Ages c. 800–1056* (London: Longman, 1991), pp. 125–6; Simon MacLean, 'Shadow Kingdom: Lotharingia and the Frankish World, C. 850-C.1050', *History Compass* 11:6 (2013), 443–57 (p. 447).

27 Gädeke, 'Eine Karolingergenealogie', pp. 787–8.

28 London, British Library, Arundel MS 390, f. 133r. An edited version of this diagram as well as the various tables in the Steinfeld Codex can be found in 'Tabulae Karolorum et Ottonum', *Scriptores* 3 ed. by Georg Henrich Pertz (Hanover: Monumenta Germaniae Historica, 1839), pp. 213–5.

29 *Epitaphium Heinrici* in *Poetae Latini aevi Carolini* 4.1 ed. by Paul de Winterfeld (Berlin: Monumenta Germaniae Historica, 1899), p. 137. Arundel MS 390 includes an annotation on the page recording Henry's death in Regino's text directing the reader to the epitaph at the end of the manuscript.

30 This is edited in H. E. J. Cowdrey, *The Age of Abbot Desiderius: Montecassino, the Papacy, and the Normans in the Eleventh and Early Twelfth Century* (Oxford: Oxford University Press, 1983), pp. 245–9.

31 The papal list is edited with comments in Wilhelm Levison, 'Aus Englischen Bibliotheken', *Neues Archiv der Gesellschaft für Ältere Deutsche Geschichtskunde* 38 (1913) (643–664), pp. 662–4.

32 The women in the Arundel 390 table are Plectrude (wife of Pippin I) and his unnamed *alia uxor*; Bertha *regina*, wife of Pippin III; Charlemagne's wives Hildegard, Fastrada and Liudgard; Charlemagne's daughters Gisela and Rotrude; Judith, wife of Louis the Pious; Ermengard, the wife of Lothar I; Emma, the wife of Louis the German; Ermentrude, wife of Charles the Bald; Ermengard, daughter of Louis II; Gisela, daughter of Lothar II; Ansgard, first wife of Louis the Stammerer; Adelheid, second wife of Louis the Stammerer. There are two new inclusions: Ermengard as the mother of Louis the Child; and Hildegard as the daughter of Louis III of West Francia.

33 The exception is Charlemagne's wife, Liutgard. His other wife Fastrada is also included, though her two daughters with Charlemagne are not in the table.

34 Gädeke, 'Eine Karolingergenealogie', pp. 779–80, esp. n. 13, p. 780.

35 Regino of Prüm, *Chronicon* in *Scriptores rerum Germanicarum in usum scholarum separatim editi* 50 ed. by Friedrich Kurze, (Hanover: Monumenta Germaniae Historica, 1890), p. 53, 69.

36 Regino, *Chronicon*, p. 75, 101, 110–1, 114, 120, 123–5.

37 For more on the annotations, see Wolf-Rüdiger Schleidgen, *Die Überlieferungsgeschichte der Chronik des Regino von Prüm* (Mainz: Gesellschaft für Mittelrheinische Kirchengeschichte, 1977), p. 22.

38 'Hic [Pippin] cum haberet uxorem Piletrudem, de qua genuit Grimoaldum, aliam superduxit uxorem, de qua genuit Karolum seniorem et ducem, et obtinuit principatum annis 27.' *Genealogia regum Francorum*, p. 247.

39 *Chronicarum quae dicuntur Fredegarii* in Bruno Krusch (ed.), *Scriptores rerum Merovingicarum* 2, (Hanover: Monumenta Germaniae Historica, 1888), p. 172.

40 Pertz, 'Tabulae Karolorum et Ottonum', p. 214.

41 This section of Regino's *Chronicle* quoted extensively from the *Royal Frankish Annals*. *Annales Regni Francorum*, in Georg Heinrich Pertz (ed.), *Scriptores rerum Germanicarum in usum scholarum separatim editi* 6 (Hanover: Monumenta Germaniae Historica, 1895), p. 134; Regino, *Chronicon,* p. 70.

42 'Walonem filium Bernardi patruelis sui', Regino, *Chronicon*, p. 72.

43 Pertz, 'Tabulae Karolorum et Ottonum', p. 214, note b.

44 Regino, *Chronicon*, p. 134, 147–8.

45 *Annales Fuldenses*, in *Scriptores rerum Germanicarum in usum scholarum separatim editi* 7 ed. by Friedrich Kurze (Hanover: Monumenta Germaniae Historica, 1891), p. 132; Hermann of Reichenau, *Chronicon*, in *Scriptores* 5 ed. by Georg Heinrich Pertz (Berlin: Monumenta Germaniae Historica, 1844), p. 111. On Uota, see Timothy Reuter, 'Sex, lies and oath-helpers: the trial of Queen Uota', in *Medieval Polities and Modern Mentalities* ed. by Janet L. Nelson (Cambridge: Cambridge University Press, 2006), pp. 217–30.

46 Regino, *Chronicon*, p. 142.

47 This raises the tantalising opportunity to speculate about whether the source was the lost stemma of Louis the Child and the Carolingian family on which the Steinfeld Codex and Arundel 390 tables were based.

48 Regino records his death and that his kingdom passed to his brother Carloman (Regino, *Chronicon*, p. 120); the *Annals of St-Vaast* records the story of his death while chasing a girl into a house on a horse (*Annales Vedastini* in *Scriptores rerum Germanicarum separatim editi* 12 ed. by B. de Simson (Hanover: Monumenta Germaniae Historica, 1909), p. 52).

49 Witger, *Genealogia Arnulfi Comitis*, p. 303.

50 'Hildegardis filia Ludowici regis, fratris Carlomanni et Caroli, a quibusdam ad Arnulfum accusata regiis possessionibus privatur et privata in exilium destinatur in monasterio puellarum, quod Chemissem dicitur', Regino, *Chronicon*, p. 142. See D Arn 132, in *Die Urkunden der Deutschen Karolinger, Dritter Band, Die Urkunden Arnolfs* ed. by P. Kehr (Berlin: Monumenta Germaniae Historica, 1940), pp. 197–9; Karl Ferdinand Werner, 'Die Nachkommen Karls des Großen 1.-8.' in *Karl der Grosse. Das Nachleben* ed. by Wolfgang Braunfels and Percy Ernst Schramm (Dusseldorf: L. Schwann, 1967), pp. 403–84 and addition (b23, p. 456 and addition); Matthias Becher, 'Zwischen König und "Herzog"', in *Kaiser Arnolf: Das ostfränkische Reich am Ende des 9. Jahrhunderts* ed. by Franz Fuchs and Peter Schmid (Munich: C.H. Beck, 2002), pp. 89–121 (pp. 102–6).

51 Not to be confused with her eponymous aunt, Hildegard, the daughter of Louis the German.

52 Theutberga: Regino, *Chronicon*, pp. 77–8, 80–2, 84–9, 91; Waldrada: Regino, *Chronicon*, pp. 80, 82, 84–5, 87–9, 97; Richildis: Regino, *Chronicon*, p. 113; Liutgard: Regino, *Chronicon*, p. 118; Friderada: Regino, *Chronicon*, p. 121; Richgard: Regino, *Chronicon*, p. 127; Oda: Regino, *Chronicon*, pp. 145, 148.

53 An omission that does not fit this pattern though is Louis the Blind; he was a legitimate son of Irmingard and Boso, was proclaimed emperor and later married and produced children. This could perhaps be taken as further evidence for confusion around Louis the Blind and Louis the Child; or, alternatively, a rejection of this Louis on the basis of his descent from a Carolingian daughter rather than father. If so, that would also apply to the rejection of Hiltrude and her son Tassilo.

54 Regino, *Chronicon*, pp. 43–4.

55 Though this opens questions about why his other son, Drogo, was included. It is possible that the prestige of his position as bishop of Metz outweighed his lack of legitimate children.

56 She is also only briefly mentioned in Regino without reference to any children. Regino, *Chronicon*, p. 113. Werner, 'Die Nachkommen', b43-46, p. 454.

57 Regino, *Chronicon*, p. 119.

58 Ibid., p. 121.

59 Ibid., pp. 127–8.

60 Ibid., pp. 145, 148.

61 Hartmut Hoffmann, *Buchkunst und Königtum im ottonischen und frühsalischen Reich* (Stuttgart: Hiersemann, 1986), p. 331.

62 See Schleidgen, *Die Überlieferungsgeschichte*, p. 21; Bernhard Ebneth, 'Pir(c)kheimer, Willibald', in *Neue Deutsche Biographie*, Band 20 (2001), pp. 475–6.

63 This is Gießen, Universitätsbibliothek 650, which Schleidgen dates to c. 1486–1519. Schleidgen, *Die Überlieferungsgeschichte*, pp. 22–4, 139.

64 Ibid., p. 139.

65 Ibid.

66 'Genealogia Karolinorum' Straßburg, ehem. Sammlung Robert Forrer ohne Signatur. A digital reproduction of this stemma can be found online at: https://bibliotheca-laureshamensis-digital.de/view/slgrf_o-sig/0001/image. Schleidgen, *Die Überlieferungsgeschichte,* p. 139.

67 Caspar Ehlers, 'Die salischen Kaisergräber im Speyerer Dom', in *Die Salier. Macht im Wandel. Essays.* (Munich: Minerva, 2011), pp. 202–9 (p. 206); Stefan Weinfurter, 'Herrschaftslegitimation und Königsautorität im Wandel: Die Salier und ihr Dom zu Speyer', in *Die Salier und das Reich. Band 1: Salier, Adel und Reichsverfassung* ed. by Stefan Weinfurter (Sigmaringen: Jan Thorbecke, 1992), pp. 55–96 (p. 67).

68 Ehlers, 'Die salischen', p. 206; Weinfurter, 'Herrschaftslegitimation' pp. 91–2; Odilo Engels, 'Die Kaiserliche Grablege im Speyerer Dom und die Staufer', in *Papstgeschichte und Landesgeschichte. Festschrift für Hermann Jakobs zum 65. Geburtstag* ed. by Joachim Dahlhaus, Armin Kohnle (Cologne: Böhlau, 1995), pp. 227–54 (p. 227).

69 D HIV 325 in *Die Urkunden der Deutschen Könige und Kaiser, Sechster Band, Die Urkunden Heinrichs IV,* vol. 2 ed. by Dietrich von Gladiss and Alfred Gawlik (Weimar: Monumenta Germaniae Historica, 1952) p. 427. On the importance of this grant, see Weinfurter, 'Herrschaftslegitimation', p. 89; Karl Schmid, '"De Regia Stirpe Waiblingensium" Remarques sur la conscience de soi des Staufen', in *Famille et Parenté dans l'Occident Médiéval* (Rome: École française de Rome, 1977), pp. 49–56 (pp. 50–3).

70 DD HIV 379–385, pp. 505–11. Ingrid Heidrich, 'Beobachtungen zur Stellung der Bischöfe von Speyer im Konflikt zwischen Heinrich IV. Und der Reformpäpsten', *Frühmittelalterliche Studien* 22 (1988), 266–85 (pp. 269–72).

71 DD HIV 426, 474–5, pp. 571–2, 645–7; Heidrich, 'Beobachtungen zur Stellung', p. 272; Ehlers, p. 206; Weinfurter, 'Herrschaftslegitimation', p. 90.

72 Weinfurter, 'Herrschaftslegitimation', pp. 95–6.

73 Ibid., p. 71.

74 'Quando post decimam numeratur linea quarta, De Carolo Magno procedit Gisela prudens.'; 'Unde extat proverbium: Sella Chuonradi habet ascensoria Caroli.' Wipo, *Gesta Chuonradi II Imperatoris,* 4, 6, in *Scriptores rerum Germanicarum separatim editi* 61 ed. by Harry Bresslau (Hanover: Monumenta Germaniae Historica, 1915), pp. 28–9, 24–5.

75 Matt 1:17. My thanks to Chris Eddington for this observation. Donald C. Jackman has laid out the calculations of Gisela's Carolingian ancestry in detail, tracing the 'tenth' line ten generations back through her paternal ancestry to Otto I, and then through his mother Hadwig to Louis the Pious and Charlemagne and the 'fourth' line through her maternal grandfather King Conrad of Burgundy. Donald C. Jackman, Ius Hereditarium *Encountered III: Ezzo's Chess Match* (Pennsylvania: Archive for Medieval Prosopography, 2010), pp. 8–23, 67–74.

76 Herwig Wolfram, *Conrad II 990–1039: Emperor of Three Kingdoms* trans. by Denis A. Kaiser (University Park: Pennsylvania State University Press, 2006), pp. 46–7.

77 For a detailed discussion of Siegfried's case with an edition of his letter, see Michel Parisse, 'Sigefroid, Abbé de Gorze, et le mariage du roi Henri III avec Agnès de Poitou (1043). Un aspect de la réform Lotharingienne', *Revue du Nord* 356–7 (2003/4), 543–66.

78 See, for example, the diagrams of Scipione Ammirato in Klapisch-Zuber, 'The Genesis of the Family Tree', Figs. 6–8 between pp. 112–3, commentary pp. 110–1.

79 Nora Gädeke, *Zeugnisse Bildlicher Darstellung der Nachkommenschaft Heinrichs I.* (Berlin: Walter de Gruyter, 1992), p. 235.

80 Donald C. Jackman, *Studia Luxembourgensia* (Pennsylvania: Archive for Medieval Proposography, 2012), pp. 15–8.

81 Munich Codex Latinus 6388.

82 Steffen Patzold, 'Wie bereitet man sich auf einen Thronwechsel vor? Überlegungen zu einem wenig beachteten Text des 11. Jahrhunderts', in Matthias Becher (ed.), *Die*

Mittelalterliche Thronfolge im Europäischen Vergleich (Ostfildern: Jan Thorbecke Verlag, 2017), pp. 127–56 (pp. 141–2).

83 Patzold, 'Wie bereitet man sich auf einen Thronwechsel vor?' pp. 138–50.

84 For how the anonymous *Imperial Chronicle* which followed Ekkehard played with this concept of dynastic genealogy see Johanna Dale, 'Imperial Self-Representations and the Manipulation of History in Twelfth-Century Germany: Cambridge, Corpus Christi College MS 373', *German History* 29:4 (2011), 557–83 (p. 572).

11

'CHARLES'S STIRRUPS HANG DOWN FROM CONRAD'S SADDLE'

Reminiscences of Carolingian oath practice under Conrad II (1024–1039)

Stefan Esders[*]

'Without the oath being observed, the office of the royal dignity can in no way be administered'. This remarkable statement was made by the eleventh-century Saxon historian Bruno of Merseburg in a situation of fierce internal strife and indeed civil war.[1] It may remind the reader at the outset of this paper of the extraordinarily important role played by political oaths[2] in stabilizing and legitimizing monarchic rule in many, if not most societies of the past,[3] and even some of the present.[4] This feature can also be observed in cultures that encompassed different religious denominations, most prominently in the appointment of a new ruler, when oaths of loyalty become indispensable in legitimizing this ruler with regard to different groups of his 'subjects' by focusing on the essential religious values that united them. Thus, for instance, in the establishment of the Islamic caliphate, the general oath sworn to the caliph, the *bay'a*,[5] became an important topic in Sunni jurisprudence for which oath-based legitimacy could compensate for other factors such as the degree of close kinship to the prophet, whereas in Shia jurisprudence, which regarded the latter as indispensable, this was not the case.[6] Oaths were only one element among many in establishing monarchic legitimacy, but their importance could easily increase when other criteria of legitimacy were not at hand or not valued as relevant enough.

It thus may not be by chance that many historiographical sources focus in detail on practices of oath-taking when reporting the coming into power of a new dynasty which had no links with its predecessor. Wipo, a royal chaplain who composed an account of the deeds of Conrad II (1024–1039), the first ruler of the Salian dynasty, is no exception here. It seems that by the time he was writing it

---

[*] The research for this chapter was funded by the 'After Empire: Using and Not Using the Past in the Crisis of the Carolingian World, c.900–1050' HERA project, receiving funding from the European Union's Horizon 2020 research and innovation programme under grant agreement no. 649307.

190 Stefan Esders

was an established tradition in historiography to pay attention to oaths that were sworn. They often served to structure the narrative, to characterize political actors as reliable or, more often, as perjurers, and to explain how events ended as God, in the name of whom the oath had been sworn, finally intervened.[7] Models for this could already be found in the Old Testament,[8] while in Carolingian historiography oaths are frequently used to frame historical narratives and explain how things developed, if we think, for instance, of the *Royal Frankish Annals*[9] or of *Nithard's Histories*.[10] A tragic narrative line is drawn from the swearing to the breaking of an oath in order to explain – usually via the punishment of the perjurer – who was responsible for a conflict and why events turned out as they did.

Wipo, who is at the centre of the following contribution, had witnessed the election of Conrad II in Kamba in 1024, and as royal chaplain he was very close to the events he later reported in his work. The situation in 1024 was described by him as an extremely awkward one. The old dynasty of Saxon origin had died out in 1002 (or in 1024 by the latest), so it was clear that the new ruler would have to come from a different region. It is here that notions of the past come into play. To what extent would the new ruler and his dynasty simply claim to continue the old dynasty? Or would Conrad try to place himself at some distance from his immediate predecessors?[11] The Salians, who came to power with Conrad's election, originated in the Palatinate region in the Middle Rhine valley, a region of supposedly Frankish stock. As the Ottonian kingdom was composed of five duchies at this time – Saxony, Bavaria, Swabia, Lotharingia, and Franconia – this was an important point, for it entailed a special connection to the past only accessible for the new dynasty. The very name 'Salians', which came to be used to denote the dynasty only later, allowed for associating the family with the Franks, with the Salians as a Frankish subgroup, and also with Salic law.[12] The context of dynastic discontinuity could thus foster an increasing awareness of the relevance of the Carolingian past as part of the Frankish tradition for a kingdom that was not typically described as 'German' as early as the early eleventh century.[13]

For this reason, two topics came to be connected with the accession of Conrad II. Firstly, the relevance of oaths as a tool to legitimize a ruler from a new dynasty, and secondly, this dynasty's indebtedness to Carolingian traditions which could have an impact on the uses of the past. But, as we shall see when analysing Wipo's account of Conrad's election, it is not always clear to what extent the awareness of the Carolingian past exhibited in the work – that will become evident – illustrates a general state of indebtedness on the part of Conrad II and his advisers to Carolingian models, or whether we should attribute this clear Carolingian inheritance to Wipo as an original and learned political thinker. Since it is evident that the Carolingian past mattered to the Salian king as well as to his historian, it is almost impossible to separate the two interpretations.

Oaths by cognates

'Charles's stirrups hang down from Conrad's saddle'.[14] For the first ruler of the Salian dynasty, Conrad II, to whom this proverb refers, Carolingian traditions mattered a great deal: Conrad reportedly visited Aachen soon after his election to take possession of Charlemagne's throne and to emphasize his family's Frankish roots. But Wipo also wanted to make clear that Conrad managed to become a successful ruler through imitation of Carolingian models. As a political thinker, Wipo was influenced by classical historiographical writers such as Sallust. In his *Gesta Chuonradi II imperatoris*, written shortly after 1040 under Conrad's son and successor Henry III (r. 1028–1056), he often expressed his ideas in exemplary fashion, by inserting speeches into his narrative, elaborating on rituals, and even including poems and proverbs such as the one quoted above. Despite this, the *Gesta* is a surprisingly understudied text: its historical depth and allusiveness remain to be uncovered. As is revealed by his treatment of oaths, Wipo appears to have been familiar with oath-based models of 'narrative justice' to some extent, but on a number of occasions he also presents to his audience a much more complex and imaginative discourse on oaths and on their sophisticated uses.

This is aptly illustrated by an allusion to Carolingian oath practice in Wipo's account of the election of Conrad II at Kamba in 1024, which has to date been overlooked in modern scholarship. As Wipo wants to depict this election as an ideal and harmonious act during what in fact was an extremely dangerous situation with the potential for the outbreak of civil war, he reports that, right before the election to the kingship Conrad (the Elder) and his rival candidate and cousin, Conrad the Younger, negotiated the conditions under which the defeated party would accept defeat and agree to the winner being king. In the *Gesta*, Conrad the Elder delivers a speech in which he praises the two cousins' *familiaritas* and their *amicitia cognata*; indeed, his whole speech is actually centred upon the idea of the two candidates' *cognatio*. Conrad the Younger, in reaction to this speech, promises to comply completely with what was said, and that he, accordingly, if his cousin be elected king, would undoubtedly swear to him full royal fidelity (*et omnem regiam fidelitatem facturum certissime promisit*). Interestingly, Conrad the Younger qualified his promise by adding that he would be faithful to Conrad the Elder 'as towards a most beloved cognate' (*sicuti cognato carissimo*).[15] Wipo goes on to say that in the course of his speech Conrad the Elder, as many could see, drew closer for a short while and kissed his cousin, an act through which it was understood that both candidates had finally arrived at an agreement.[16]

What strikes the reader here from a Carolingian perspective – apart from the ritual and the kiss – is the recurrent emphasis placed on the two candidates' *cognatio* and the oath formula to which Wipo was apparently alluding. Conrad the Younger promised *fidelitas regia ... sicut cognato carissimo*, which seems to echo the oath-formulas of the treaties concluded between the ninth-century Carolingian kings.[17] In fact, starting from the time of Charlemagne, quite a number of oath-formulas were constructed with such a *sicut*-clause, as I once called it, to specify the oath's contents.[18] As the Carolingian rulers promised each other mutual charity and loyalty 'as a brother should show towards his brother' (*si cum om per dreit son fradra saluar dist, soso man mit rehtu sinan bruodher scal*) so famously in the oaths of Strasbourg in 842),[19] or, in 845, 'as a nephew towards his uncle' (*fidelis sicut nepos patruo*),[20] the intention was to make fidelity and kinship converge. In 921, when there was no

192 Stefan Esders

longer a Carolingian ruling over the East Frankish kingdom, the Saxon Henry I and the West Frankish king Charles III concluded a treaty near Bonn, where they promised each other under oath 'to be a friend, as a friend should be towards a friend': if you were not related to each other anymore, you could only be friends.[21] But it seems clear that Wipo, when writing about the two cousins called Conrad in 1024, must have thought of models from the Carolingian period when rulers were still descended from or belonging to the same family.

Reference to the Carolingian dynasty and its members' mutual affection conveyed the idea that there still was some overarching idea of 'brotherhood' or close kinship that allowed writers to conceive of the divided Frankish kingdom as a coherent whole.[22] Although concluded by two rulers, these treaties were often in fact multilateral agreements, as the interest of numerous lay and ecclesiastical nobles were at stake here, many of which transcended the contemporary political borders.[23] But what was Wipo's intention when referring to these ideas? It has recently been shown that in the wake of the forthcoming election of 1024, clerical and lay nobles were gathering information and arguments they thought could be put forward in favour of one of the candidates (or against an opponent) in the course of the negotiations. Detailed knowledge of Carolingian dynastic succession and, moreover, of the Carolingian divisions of the realm, was regarded as highly relevant in this situation.[24] From such a perspective, one should indeed refrain from adopting the perspective of German constitutional historiography that the Ottonians simply gave up the Carolingian practice of dividing the kingdom, which, it used to be believed, had simply become too small for such a strategy and consisted of five duchies alone.[25] On the contrary, although the primogeniture principle of succession succeeded in the long term, it continued to be challenged early on during Ottonian rule. Wipo thus seems to have modelled the compromise made between the two Conrads on the Carolingian idea of the realm being a community of closely related kings that came from the same family or dynasty – a familiarity strengthened by the bond of oaths. Focusing on the two cousins' *cognatio*, he sought to understand the East Frankish kingdom as a peaceful, harmonious entity governed in concord by rulers that came from the same family. In so doing, he set the scene for the tragic history that would follow when King Conrad would have to fight against his rebellious younger cousin and others soon after. We know from the Annals of St Gall that as early as Easter 1025 there was a first clash between the cousins at Augsburg, as the newly appointed king was not willing to fulfil his younger cousin's expectations or even promises he seemed to have given right before the election.[26] Apparently the younger Conrad had expected to somehow participate in his cousin's rule.[27] Wipo, however, does not mention that Conrad the Younger made a common cause with the rebellious Duke Ernst of Swabia, whom he blames for being treacherous alone, as we shall see below. It was not until 1036 that Conrad the Younger was invested with the duchy of Carinthia, which he, according to Wipo, administered 'being faithful to Conrad and his son Henry and serving well' (*fidus et bene militans imperatori et filio suo Heinrico*), but he died in 1039, as did his cousin Conrad II.[28] By referring to the Carolingian idea of joint rulership of two or more rulers from the same dynasty, Wipo thus seems to advocate the solution that the king and duke both came from the same family, a situation that would not cause the break-up of the kingdom. The history of the Ottonians offered ample evidence for the dangers inherent in the competition between the royal family and the important positions held by aristocratic families.[29]

It therefore seems clear that Wipo did not simply invent the parts of his narrative that dealt with oaths, but shaped these narratives in exemplary style to convey his own vision of what politics should be like. In retrospect, from the eleventh century, the Carolingian kings and emperors could appear as 'masters of the oath', who forged bonds of fidelity between rulers and their subjects, lords and their vassals and even between each other as rulers. Though it remains a challenge to trace the precise channels through which knowledge of Carolingian political thought and oath practice was transmitted to the first Salian ruler and to his chaplain, their reflection and sophisticated use of Carolingian models points to a consciousness of a new beginning which is often condensed into a renewed interest in the past.

A revitalization of the Carolingian general oath of loyalty under Salian rule?

In the Carolingian period, general oaths of fidelity like those sworn to Charlemagne, Louis the Pious or Charles the Bald created a direct personal bond between the adult male free population and the Carolingian ruler and his family.[30] This has always been taken to indicate a comparatively high degree of statehood, as the oaths had many political and legal implications, including performing military service in the great host, obeying the royal ban by which the capitularies were enacted, and acting as witness when interests of the fisc were dealt with in an inquest.[31] However, operating under the same assumption, it has been questioned whether these oaths continued to be sworn in the tenth century to the rulers of the Ottonian dynasty in the East Frankish kingdom.[32] Most historiographic references seem indeed to point to oaths sworn by the royal vassals and the higher clerics alone, while the Ottonians apparently issued only a few new capitularies.[33] For this reason, constitutional historians such as Walter Kienast have assumed that the Carolingian practice of having the whole adult male population swear an oath of fidelity was abandoned in the later Carolingian or Ottonian period.[34] It seems clear that behind such assumptions lie master narratives of a supposed 'feudalization' of the political order in the tenth century. However, while it can hardly be denied that the intermediate powers gained a stronger position during the dissolution of Carolingian power, it is a different question whether this issue has to be directly linked to the practice of general oaths. It has been shown recently that, even under Ottonian rule, fiscal inquest was practised on certain occasions,[35] while Ottonian warfare surely did not include vassals alone.[36]

Looking at this issue from a later perspective, it becomes clear that under the third Salian ruler, Henry IV (1053/56–1105), general oaths of loyalty must have mattered a great deal – otherwise Pope Gregory VII's powerful political manoeuvre to absolve Henry's subjects from the oaths they had sworn to him would not have made any

194 Stefan Esders

sense.[37] This topic is so prominent in the 'Streitschriften' of that time that it must have had a considerable impact that extended far beyond the relationship between the ruler and his ecclesiastical and lay magnates.[38] When Bruno of Merseburg wrote on the Saxon War shortly after 1080, he described the indispensability of the oath for royal governance, as quoted at the beginning of this article.[39]

One may thus ask how far we can trace this practice back, and when the Carolingian practice of general oaths was taken up again (if it was ever abandoned). A suitable candidate for this would indeed be Conrad II (1024–1039), the first Salian: there are considerable and significant reminiscences of Carolingian oath practice found once again in Wipo's *Gesta Chuonradi*. Wipo deals with this issue for the first time when narrating the establishment of Conrad II's rule as new king right after his election:

> As regards the establishment of fidelity (*De fidelitate facta*) I think it is less necessary to mention this, as it is attested by frequent use that all bishops, dukes and the remaining princes, the soldiers of the first category, the gathered soldiers, even all free men, if they were of any importance, make fidelity towards their kings. But to him (Conrad) all submitted by their oath even more sincerely and voluntarily.[40]

Although Wipo seeks to suggest some sort of universal consensus to Conrad's rule and interprets the obligation to swear loyalty to extend to most freemen, there is some understatement in this passage, as he explicitly admits that he is only mentioning in passing the usual steps following the election of a new king. He thus refers to the established routine of a general oath of fidelity in monarchies, while only the second sentence refers specifically to Conrad. Following this, Wipo goes on to report Conrad's first deeds and the circuit he made around the kingdom to have his rule accepted in all provinces of the kingdom.[41]

One major difference between the Carolingian and the Salian oaths that becomes clear from this, is that Conrad apparently did not send out his *missi* throughout his kingdom to accept the oath on his behalf, as had been the case in Carolingian oath practice.[42] Instead, he received a personal oath from the important secular and ecclesiastical magnates and their troops at his election, while in the course of his circuit further oaths were sworn to him by local groups and also by delegates from Italy.[43] However, that Wipo refers to the *fidelitas facta* only in passing does not mean that he did not regard the oath as a vital instrument, since he places emphasis on the fact that most free men of a certain standing swore this oath. That Conrad may have indeed followed the Carolingian practice of oath-taking becomes clear from a charter that reports the proceedings of a meeting held in Regensburg in 1027, where the king, among other things, carried out an inquisition procedure to pinpoint fiscal properties in Bavaria. For this purpose all Bavarian counts and selected judges were compelled by the oath sworn to the king (*per sacramentum regale*) to testify publicly when asked – based on this very oath (*eodem sacramento publice interrogati*) – what they knew about which possessions in their province belonged to the throne (*ad solium sui imperii iure pertinere*).[44] This is a clear nod to Carolingian oath practice, as we already find reference to the use of the imperial oath in inquest procedures under Charlemagne as early as 802, as is frequently attested in general capitularies and local charters from Bavaria.[45] It seems clear that Conrad II followed Carolingian models here, both in his order to register fiscal property and in reminding his functionaries of the oath of fidelity sworn to him on the occasion of his accession to the throne.

A second issue connected to this is the habit of swearing fidelity under reservation.[46] Wipo showcases this feature in his account of a general meeting Conrad assembled in Ulm in 1027. Here Duke Ernst of Swabia, the stepson of the king whom Wipo portrays as an arrogant and disloyal rebel against the king, addressed his *milites*, reminding them of the oath-based fidelity they had promised to him and admonishing them not to leave him, but to preserve their honour instead; they should never forget that according to old tradition, the Swabians were famous for their good faith (*bona fide*) and their adherence to their lords; by staying loyal to him, they would earn benefits, and glory and honour for their descendents. A reply to this made by two Swabian counts on behalf of the whole group is presented by Wipo in direct speech:

> We cannot deny that we firmly promised you fidelity (*fides*) against all except the one who has given us to you (*contra omnes praeter eum, qui nos vobis dedit*). If we were slaves (*servi*) of our king and emperor and subjected by him to your right (*iuri vestro mancipati*), we would not be allowed to separate from you. However, since we are free (*liberi sumus*) and have our king and emperor as the highest protector (*defensor*) of our liberty (*libertas*) on earth, we would, as soon as we forsook him, lose our liberty (*libertas*), which no good man, as someone says, loses except together with his life. This being so, we will obey to you in everything honest and just that you will require from us. However, if you want something against this, we will frankly return to the place from where we have come to you conditionally (*conditionaliter*).[47]

The discourse on the interconnection of fidelity and liberty, which would eventually cause the duke to surrender unconditionally to the king, has of course many historical roots.[48] Again, the Carolingians' insistence on liberty being the prerequisite of fidelity, which is so evident in the capitularies that concern the *liberi homines*' obligation to swear the oath, may have served as a model here;[49] provisions on the superiority of fidelity owed to the king may have also been included as a model.[50] At the same time, the speech of the two counts apparently alludes to contemporary discussions on the inalienability of liberty which stressed the king's ultimate responsibility for protecting all people of free status.[51] Moreover, Conrad II took care of the *censuales*, manumitted church dependents who were living under ecclesiastical patronage in the episcopal cities, being eager to have their status fixed by written law.[52] To this one may add that we find such a notion of conditional fidelity ('*Treuevorbehalt*') also occasionally expressed in contemporary documents.[53]

Conclusion

The picture that emerges from this brief discussion warns against approaching issues such as oaths of loyalty by proceeding from general assumptions about the degree of statehood and feudalization in the tenth and eleventh centuries that historians have been drawing for a long time. The aim of this contribution, as of the whole volume, is to question such master narratives and to ask instead to what extent a certain awareness of the Carolingian past may be found in contemporary sources from the tenth and early eleventh centuries. Interdependences between the more distant past and the immediate present thus call for a much more complex and nuanced approach to such ostensibly clear issues.

It has become clear from this discussion that the Carolingian past mattered a great deal in the situation of the early eleventh century when a new dynasty established itself that sought to emphasize its Frankish origin. For the issue of oath-taking the Carolingian period offered various important models, which could be found in manuscripts and texts that were available. Yet there remains the difficulty of tracing precisely the sources that made Conrad II and his advisers aware of models and traditions that they believed to be Carolingian, and of course also the methodological problem of distinguishing accurately between Wipo and Conrad. Nonetheless, one should not succumb the temptation to deny early eleventh-century contemporaries at least some historical awareness of the more distant past, and of the particular character of Carolingian statehood. The Carolingian past was of course instrumentalized here for the purpose of legitimating the new ruling dynasty, but one should not rule out the possibility that it was also regarded as a model to which Conrad II and his advisers sought to return at least to some extent. After all, there must have been a certain capacity to historicize the past even before the age of historicism.

Notes

1 Bruno, Bellum Saxonicum, c. 108: *Sine sacramentorum autem observatione regiae dignitatis officium nequaquam administrari potest. Brunos Buch vom Sachsenkrieg*, ed. Hans-Eberhard Lohmann, MGH Deutsches Mittelalter 2, (Leipzig: Hiersemann, 1937), pp. 356–7.
2 Paolo Prodi, *Das Sakrament der Herrschaft: Der politische Eid in der Verfassungsgeschichte des Okzidents*, (Berlin: Duncker & Humblot, 1997; Italian version: *Il sacramento del potere. Il giuramento politico nella storia costituzionale dell'Occidente*, (Bologna: Il mulino, 1992).
3 Andre Holenstein, *Die Huldigung der Untertanen. Rechtskultur und Herrschaftsordnung (800–1800)*, (Stuttgart: Gustav Fischer, 1991); Stefan Esders, '"Faithful believers". Oaths of Allegiance in Post-Roman Societies as Evidence for Eastern and Western "Visions of Community"', in Walter Pohl, Clemens Gantner and Richard Payne (eds.), *Visions of Community in the Post-Roman World. The West, Byzantium and the Islamic World, 300–1100*, (Aldershot: Ashgate, 2012), pp. 357–74.
4 Bettina Dennerlein, 'Legitimate Bounds and Bound Legitimacy. The Act of Allegiance to the Ruler (*Bai'a*) in 19th Century Morocco', *Die Welt des Islams*, N.S., 41 (2001) pp. 287–310.
5 Andrew Marsham, *Rituals of Islamic Monarchy. Accession and Succession in the First Muslim Empire* (Edinburgh: Edinburgh University Press, 2009).

'Charles's stirrups hang down from Conrad's saddle' **197**

6 Émile Tyan, *Institutions du droit public musulman, vol. 2, Sultanat et califat* (Paris: Siray, 1957), pp. 344–51 and 474–5.

7 Karl Ferdinand Werner, '*Gott*, Herrscher und Historiograph: Der Geschichtsschreiber als Interpret des Wirkens *Gottes* in der Welt und Ratgeber der Könige Gott (4. bis 12. Jahrhundert)', in Ernst-Dieter Hehl, Hubertus Seibt, and Franz Staab (eds.), *Deus qui mutat tempora. Menschen und Institutionen im Wandel des Mittelalters. Festschrift für Alfons Becker zu seinem 65. Geburtstag* (Sigmaringen: Thorbecke, 1987), pp. 1–32, repr. in id., *Einheit der Geschichte. Studien zur Historiographie* (Sigmaringen: Thorbecke, 1999), pp. 89–119.

8 Yael Ziegler, *Promises to Keep: The Oath in Biblical Narrative* (Leiden: Brill, 2008).

9 Matthias Becher, *Eid und Herrschaft. Untersuchungen zum Herrschaftsethos Karls des Großen* (Sigmaringen: Thorbecke, 1993), pp. 21–77.

10 Thomas Scharff, *Die Kämpfe der Herrscher und der Heiligen. Krieg und historische Erinnerung in der Karolingerzeit* (Darmstadt: Wissenschaftliche Buchgesellschaft, 2002), pp. 158–65.

11 This seems to become clear from the Salians' avoidance of Ottonian name-giving practicse, see Karl Schmid, 'Die Salier als Kaiserdynastie', in Hagen Keller, and Nikolaus Staubach (eds.), *Iconologia sacra. Mythos, Bildkunst und Dichtung in der Religions- und Sozialgeschichte Alteuropas. Festschrift für Karl Hauck zum 75. Geburtstag* (Berlin – New York: De Gruyter, 1994), p. 461–95, at pp. 463–5.

12 Matthias Springer, 'Gab es ein Volk der Salier?', in Dieter Geuenich, Wolfgang Haubrichs and Jörg Jarnut (eds.), *Nomen et gens. Zur historischen Aussagekraft frühmittelalterlicher Personennamen* (Berlin – New York: De Gruyter, 1997), pp. 58–73.

13 On this issue, naturally the subject of great debate in German historiography, see Joachim Ehlers, *Die Entstehung des deutschen Reiches* (4th edition, Munich: Oldenbourg, 2012).

14 Wipo, *Gesta Chuonradi II. imperatoris, c. 6: Unde extant proverbium: 'Sella Chuonradi habet ascensoria Caroli'. Die Werke Wipos*, ed. Harry Bresslau, MGH SS rer. Germ. in us. schol. 60 (Hannover: Hahn, 1915), pp. 28–9

15 Wipo, *Gesta Chuonradi II. imperatoris, c. 2: Ad haec iunior Chuno respondit, totam hanc sententiam sibi acceptam fore, seque illi sicuti cognato carissimo, si eum res summa vocaret, omnem regiam fidelitatem facturum certissime promisit. Die Werke Wipos* (above, n. 14), p. 18.

16 Ibid.

17 Reinhard Schneider, *Brüdergemeine und Schwurfreundschaft. Der Auflösungsprozeß des Karlingerreiches im Spiegel der caritas-Terminologie in den Verträgen der karlingischen Teilkönige des 9. Jahrhunderts* (Lübeck: Mathisen, 1964).

18 Stefan Esders, 'Fidelität und Rechtsvielfalt. Die *sicut*-Klausel der früh- und hochmittelalterlichen Eidformulare', in François Bougard, Dominique Iogna-Prat and Régine Le Jan (eds.), *Hiérarchie et stratification sociale dans l'Occident médiéval (400–1100)* (Turnhout: Brepols, 2008), pp. 239–55.

19 Nithard, *Historiarum liber III*, 5. Most recent edition: Kurt Gärtner and Günter Holtus, 'Die erste deutsch-französische 'Parallelurkunde'. Zur Überlieferung und Sprache der Straßburger Eide', in Id. (eds.), *Beiträge zum Sprachkontakt und zu den Urkundensprachen zwischen Maas und Rhein* (Trier: Kliomedia, 1995), pp. 97–128, at p. 105.

20 Annales Bertiniani ad. ann. 845: *Annales Bertiniani*, ed. Georg Waitz, MGH SS rer. Ger. in us. schol. 5 (Hannover: Hahn, 1883), p. 32.

21 Treaty of Bonn: *Constitutiones et acta publica imperatorum et regum inde ab a. DCCCCXI usque ad a. MCXCVII (911–1197)*, ed. Ludwig Weiland, MGH Constitutiones et acta publica imperatorum et regum I, (Hannover: Hahn, 1893), no. 1, pp. 1–2. See Karl Ferdinand Werner, 'Bonn, Vertrag v.', in *Lexikon des Mittelalters* 2 (1983), col. 428–9.

22 Schneider, *Brüdergemeine und Schwurfreundschaft* (above, n. 17).

23 Patrick Geary, 'Oathtaking and Conflict Management in the Ninth Century', in Stefan Esders (ed.), *Rechtsverständnis und Konfliktbewältigung im Mittelalter* (Cologne: Boehlau, 2007), pp. 239–54.

24 Steffen Patzold, 'Wie bereitet man sich auf einen Thronwechsel vor? Überlegungen zu einem wenig beachteten Text des 11. Jahrhunderts', in Matthias Becher (ed.), *Die*

198   Stefan Esders

mittelalterliche Thronfolge im europäischen Vergleich (Ostfildern: Thorbecke, 2017), pp. 127–56.

25   Karl Schmid, 'Das Problem der "Unteilbarkeit des Reiches"', in id. (ed.), *Reich und Kirche vor dem Investiturstreit. Vorträge beim wissenschaftlichen Kolloquium aus Anlass des 80. Geburtstages von Gerd Tellenbach* (Sigmaringen: Thorbecke, 1985), pp. 1–16.

26   Annales Sangallenses maiores a. 1025: *Saeve contentionis fomes exarsit in sacrosancto die paschali apud Vindelicam Augustam inter Chuonradum regem et patruelem eius Chuonradum. Cui etiam Ernest consobrinus eius, dux Alamanniae, et Welfhardus comes postea confoederati simul regi rebellare sunt ausi. Sed hoc temere incaeptum Deo prohibente non habuit effectum. Die Werke Wipos* (above, n. 14), p. 91.

27   Herwig Wolfram, *Conrad II, 990–1039: Emperor of Three Kingdoms* (University Park, PA.: The State University of Pennsylvania Press, 2006), pp. 42–5.

28   Wipo, *Gesta Chuonradi II. imperatoris*, c. 21: *Die Werke Wipos* (above, n. 14), p. 41.

29   See, e.g., Gerd Althoff, *Die Ottonen. Königsherrschaft ohne Staat* (Stuttgart: Kohlhammer, 2000), pp. 138–41 and pp. 154–61.

30   Stefan Esders, 'Rechtliche Grundlagen frühmittelalterlicher Staatlichkeit: Der allgemeine Treueid', in Walter Pohl/Veronika Wieser (eds.), *Der frühmittelalterliche Staat – Europäische Perspektiven* (Vienna: Verlag der Österreichischen Akademie der Wissenschaften, 2009), pp. 423–32.

31   Stefan Esders, 'Treueidleistung und Rechtsveränderung im frühen Mittelalter', in id./ Christine Reinle (eds.), *Rechtsveränderung im politischen und sozialen Kontext mittelalterlicher Rechtsvielfalt* (Münster: Lit, 2005), pp. 25–62.

32   Walther Kienast, *Untertaneneid und Treuvorbehalt in Frankreich und England. Studien zur vergleichenden Verfassungsgeschichte des Mittelalters* (Weimar: Hermann Böhlaus Nachf., 1952).

33   Steffen Patzold, 'Capitularies in the Ottonian realm', *Early Medieval Europe* 27 (2019), pp. 112–32.

34   Kienast, *Untertaneneid und Treuevorbehalt* (above, n. 32), pp. 1–4.

35   For the use of inquisition procedure under the Ottonian rulers see David Bachrach, 'Inquisitio as a Tool of Royal Governance under the Carolingian and Ottonian Kings', *Zeitschrift der Savigny-Stiftung für Rechtsgeschichte, Germanistische Abteilung* 133 (2016), pp. 1–80

36   Karl Ferdinand Werner, 'Heeresorganisation und Kriegführung im deutschen Königreich des 10. und 11. Jahrhunderts', in *Ordinamenti militari in occidente nell'alto medioevo* (Spoleto: Centro italiano di studi sull'alto medioevo, 1968), Vol. 2, pp. 791–843; David S. Bachrach, *Warfare in 10th-century Germany* (Woodbridge: The Boydell Press, 2012), pp. 70–101.

37   See, most famously, Gregory's Dictatus papae, c. 27: *Quod a fidelitate iniquorum subiectos potest absolvere. Das Register Gregors VII.*, ed. Erich Caspar, MGH Epp. 4, Epistolae selectae 2,1 (Berlin: Weidmann, 1955), p. 208.

38   Tilman Struve, 'Das Problem der Eideslösung in den Streitschriften des Investiturstreites', *Zeitschrift der Savigny-Stiftung für Rechtsgeschichte, Kanonistische Abteilung* 106 (1989), pp. 107–132.

39   See above n. 1.

40   Wipo, *Gesta Chuonradi II. imperatoris*, c. 4: *De fidelitate facta regi minus necessarium dicere puto, frequenti usu teste, quod omnes episcopi, duces et reliqui principes, milites primi, milites gregarii, quin ingenui omnes, si alicuius momenti sint, regibus fidem faciant; huic tamen sincerius et libentius iurando omnes subiciebantur. Die Werke Wipos* (above, n. 14), p. 24.

41   Wipo, *Gesta Chuonradi II. imperatoris*, c. 5–6: *Die Werke Wipos* (above, n. 14), pp. 26–9.

42   Stefan Esders, Massimiliano Bassetti, and Wolfgang Haubrichs, *Verwaltete Treue. Ein oberitalienisches Originalverzeichnis mit den Namen von 174 vereidigten Personen aus der Zeit Lothars I. und Ludwigs II.* (in press).

43   Wipo, *Gesta Chuonradi II. imperatoris*, c. 6: *Die Werke Wipos* (above, n. 14), pp. 27–9.

44   Inquisitio bonorum regalium in Bawaria (1027. Iun.-Aug.): *Constitutiones et acta publica imperatorum et regum* (above, n. 21), No. 439, pp. 645–6.

45   Heinrich Brunner, 'Zeugen- und Inquisitionsbeweis der karolingischen Zeit' (1865), in Id., *Forschungen zur Geschichte des deutschen und französischen Rechts. Gesammelte Aufsätze*

(Stuttgart: J. G. Cotta, 1894), pp. 88–247, at pp. 155–7; Holenstein, *Die Huldigung der Untertanen* (above, n. 3), pp. 127–38; Stefan Esders, 'Die römischen Wurzeln der karolingischen *inquisitio* in Fiskalsachen', in Claude Gauvard (ed.), *L'enquête au moyen âge* (Rome: École française de Rome, 2008), pp. 13–28, at pp. 26–7; for Ottonian inquests see Bachrach, '*Inquisitio* as a Tool …' (above, n. 35).

46 This topic is dealt with in the monograph by Kienast, *Untertaneneid und Treuvorbehalt* (above, n. 32).

47 Wipo, *Gesta Chuonradi II. imperatoris*, c. 20: '*Nolumus inficiari, quin vobis fidem firmiter promitteremus contra omnes praeter eum, qui nos vobis dedit. Si servi essemus regis et imperatoris nostri et ab eo iuri vestro mancipati, non nobis liceret a vobis separari. Nunc vero, cum liberi simus et libertatis nostrae summum defensorem in terra regem et imperatorem nostrum habeamus, ubi illum deserimus, libertatem amittimus, quam nemo bonus, ut ait quidam, nisi cum vita simul amittit. Quod cum ita sit, quicquid honesti et iusti a nobis exquiritis, in hoc parere volumus vobis. Si autem contra hoc vultis, illuc revertemur liberaliter, unde ad vos venimus conditionaliter.' Die Werke Wipos* (above, n. 14), p. 40.

48 For some of them, see Karl Hans Ganahl, 'Bäuerliche Freiheit als Herrschaftsanspruch des Grafen', in *Abhandlungen zur Rechts- und Wirtschaftsgeschichte. Festschrift Adolf Zycha zum 70. Geburtstag überreicht von Freunden, Schülern und Fachgenossen* (Weimar: Hermann Böhlaus Nachf., 1941), pp. 103–22; see also the references quoted below, n. 50.

49 Eckhard Müller-Mertens, *Karl der Große, Ludwig der Fromme und die Freien. Wer waren die Liberi homines der karolingischen Kapitularien (742/743–832)? Ein Beitrag zur Sozialgeschichte und Sozialpolitik des Frankenreiches* (Berlin (Ost): Akademie-Verlag, 1963); Johannes Schmitt, *Untersuchungen zu den Liberi homines der Karolingerzeit* (Frankfurt/M.: Peter Lang, 1977).

50 Capitulare missorum in Theodonis villa datum secundum generale a. 805, c. 9: *De iuramento, ut nulli alteri per sacramentum fidelitas promittatur nisi nobis et unicuique proprio seniori ad nostram utilitatem et sui senioris; excepto his sacramentis quae iuste secundum legem alteri ab altero debetur. Et infantis, qui antea non potuerunt propter iuvenalem aetatem iurare, modo fidelitatem nobis repromittant. Capitularia regum Francorum* 1, ed. Alfred Boretius (Hannover: Hahn, 1883), No. 44, p. 124.

51 See the contributions in Johannes Fried (ed.), *Die abendländische Freiheit vom 10. zum 14. Jahrhundert: Der Wirkungszusammenhang von Idee und Wirklichkeit im europäischen Vergleich* (Sigmaringen: Thorbecke, 1991); for contemporary discussions on this issue, see also Stefan Esders, *Die Formierung der Zensualität. Zur kirchlichen Transformation des spätrömischen Patronatswesens im früheren Mittelalter* (Ostfildern: Thorbecke, 2010), pp. 102–9.

52 Esders, *Die Formierung der Zensualität* (above, n. 51), pp. 102–6.

53 See Wolfram, Conrad II (above, n. 27), p. 70. By contrast, Walther Kienast had believed that Wipo's account on the two Swabian counts was completely fictitious and has been invented by Wipo; see his 'Untertaneneid und Treuvorbehalt. Ein Kapitel aus der vergleichenden Verfassungsgeschichte des Mittelalters', *Zeitschrift der Savigny-Stiftung für Rechtsgeschichte, Germanistische Abteilung* 66 (1948), pp. 111–47, at p. 129; Id., Untertaneneid und Treuvorbehalt (above, n. 32), pp. 12 and 277–8. On the *salva fidelitate talis*-clause see also Jean-Pierre Poly and Eric Bournazel, *The Feudal Transformation, 900–1200*, trans. Caroline Higgitt (New York and London: Homes & Meier, 1991), p. 73.

PART III

Recalling Communities

12

NOTIONS OF BELONGING

Some observations on solidarity in the late- and post-Carolingian world

Maximilian Diesenberger[*]

Introduction

The late- and post-Carolingian world saw the emergence of new modes of identification and group-formation in the Latin West.[1] Firstly, the Carolingian empire gave way to a pluralistic political landscape; and secondly, there was a shift in patterns of social organization, often termed the 'rise of feudalism.'[2] Each phenomenon created new forms of social cohesion, but also conflict. Traditional forms of social cohesion and intergroup relationships were frequently challenged. In this respect, local communities and larger political blocs intertwined. However, studies on group-formation at both the larger and smaller scales to date have given little attention to solidarity and the vocabularies of belonging applied to these processes.

Solidarity is an essential component of human collectivity, a specific type of connection through which a group is held together.[3] Solidarity builds on expectations and bases itself on an emotionally laden trust; a promise for the future that draws upon a common past. According to current research it represents often (but not necessarily) an equality of its members, reinforced through common belief and ritual. To maintain a framework of solidarity, social norms are required, which are sometimes confirmed through legal agreements. These normative practices were monitored according to moral standards, making it difficult to disregard them. Solidarity represents a mutual bond. It is an integrating element, which simultaneously excludes outsiders. Small face-to-face groups, such as families, village communities, etc. have boundaries with out-groups which are defined more-or-less clearly, while larger collectives possess more open boundaries and

---

[*] The research for this chapter was funded by the 'After Empire: Using and Not Using the Past in the Crisis of the Carolingian World, c.900–1050' HERA project, receiving funding from the European Union's Horizon 2020 research and innovation programme under grant agreement no. 649307.

204   Maximilian Diesenberger

were consequently more integrative. Solidarity was an impetus for group action, or arose from such activity. It became actualized when group members had to contribute to it, such as when the group was threatened. In this sense, solidarity was always situational. It therefore has to be analysed according to its contexts.

The late- and post-Carolingian period provides us with a particularly interesting context for a study of the formation and transformation of solidarity. In the fragmentation of the Carolingian empire we observe various changes in regard to the organization and conceptionalization of social bonds and political boundaries. The period provided and confronted contemporaries with multiple possibilities of social entities to align themselves with, or be assigned to. New designations had to be made, or existing nomenclature adapted, to describe these formations. The fragmented post-Carolingian world is therefore characterized by the continuous differentiation and categorization of groups. In fact, it seems that the empire, which produced a hierarchically-organized frame of belongings on different scales, had established a scope for alternative organizational approaches, which remained open even when the empire failed as a political framework. One question is: to which socio-political frameworks did the authors of the late- and post-Carolingian world apply solidarity to motivate or affect group behaviour? They positioned solidarity within variable frames of reference, which can be explicitly understood only through an investigation of the specific contexts in which they were used.

A remarkable source for an early definition of what solidarity means is given in the early 840s. In the *Liber Manualis* Dhuoda instructs her son, William, about the proper conduct at the court of Charles the Bald. For this purpose the author draws on an edifying example based on Pliny's *Naturalis historia* and commenting on Psalm 41, 'Like the stag':

> Stags habitually behave in following way: When a herd sets out to swim across bodies of water, or wide rivers with turbulent currents, one stag after the other lays its head and horns on the back of the one before it. By resting a little, they may quickly and more easily cross the water. They are so intelligent and have such subtle instinct that, when they sense the leader is beginning to flag, they let him drop back to second place and choose the rearmost stag to swim at the head, so as to support and refresh the others. This way, as each changes place with the others in turn, a fraternal creaturely kindness surges through all of them. They always take care to hold head and antlers above the water and to breathe, lest they be swallowed up in the depths of the river.[4]

For Dhuoda this example of 'mutual support' (*subportatio*), 'reciprocity' (*mutatio vicisstudinis*), and 'brotherly compassion' (*compassio dilectionis fraterna*) towards the weaker and the stronger applies to humans as well. In order to make this point clear she quotes Acts 4: 34: 'There was no needy among them but they shared everything in common.' With these words she addresses an idealized Christian community of solidarity, which was characterized by equality and unity: 'they had one heart and one mind' (*cor unum et anima una*). Applying this to her own time she advises her son: 'Be eager to render service and honour – in word and deed, and with mildness of speech – to great and small, toward your peers and those of lesser degree.'[5] The differences in rank within a community of solidarity are levelled through the *compassio fraterna dilectionis*[6] and the *conglutinatio dilectionis*.[7]

Solidarity means first and foremost to undertake tasks for others that do not lead to any immediate compensation, or could even lead to disadvantages for the individual. The early Saxons exemplified this principle according to Widukind, when the Britons asked them for help against the Scots and the Picts: 'Know that the Saxons will be reliable friends to the Britons and will stand by them as much in good times as in bad.'[8] The leader of the Saxons later emphasized to the Franks: 'that we can show no greater favour to our friends than to despise death for them ...'[9] For both a young nobleman at the court of a foreign king, and for a *gens* allying themselves with another, solidarity behaviour served as the basis for survival and prosperity in an increasingly differentiated social environment.

Whether in the early 840s or the mid-tenth century, whether a *Liber Manualis* or a historiographical text, whether in Uzès within Septimania, or in Corvey within Saxony, whatever the gender or the social rank of the author (the aristocrat Dhuoda or the monk Widukind), the cohesion of a group of any size (the court of Charles the Bald, the Saxons) is expressed in the solidarity behaviour of its members. Acts of solidarity are mostly taken for granted to such an extent, as Dhuoda implies in her example of the stags, that they do not even need to be mentioned in the texts.

Lack of solidarity

Solidarity often appears in the sources when its existence is threatened: the need for solidarity is stressed, or its loss bemoaned.[10] It is addressed when breaches and transformations are observed, that is when contemporaries reported violations of the ideas of due return and of social exchange, the denial of support, the disruption of social bonds and associations built on oaths, and the maltreatment of the *pauperes*. Dhuoda's 'Manual' for her son, William of Septimania, is a good example for a wide-reaching breach of solidarity at the highest level (and in a lower one). When she wrote the text, her son William was at the court of Charles the Bald, where he had been since 25 June 841. On that date, Charles and Louis had fought against their brother Lothar at Fontenoy. Bernhard of Septimania, William's father, failed to bring aid to Charles as promised and had to pay for this error dearly. When Dhuoda, writing shortly afterwards, speaks of the necessity of brotherly love she is referring to both the situation of her sons at the court of Charles the Bald and the bloodshed between the royal brothers which shocked public opinion in Francia and led to a loss of confidence in Carolingian rulership.[11] Fears of further conflicts proved to be well founded. Continuing disputes between the brothers fostered the divergence of powers, as we can see with the ultimately unsuccessful attack of Louis the German on Western Francia in 858.

Dhuoda's example of the stags shows one way in which solidarity was conceptualized in the wake of conflict. How does this compare to the language

206 Maximilian Diesenberger

of solidarity employed by other authors in reference to the conflicts among the Franks from the 840s onwards? In 859 the bishops who had gathered in Metz complained of the *discordia* and *pernicia* between the brothers, going on in detail to characterize the loss of solidarity as a 'sin against god,' as 'stamping upon the *ecclesia*,' as depopulation of Christendom, as a 'disturbance of peace' and as a 'betrayal of the fatherland.'[12] These were important points of reference, but there were others as well: in the 870s Adrevald of Fleury saw the reason for the quarrels among the *gens Francorum* in light of Matthew 24:12 as an 'increasing cooling of charity (*caritas*) among many people.'[13] As an effect of the atmosphere of mistrust between the elites and the kings, he said the *boni homines* even felt that they themselves were against the people (*genti contraria sentire*). This had an effect not only on the stability of the empire, but also on social life at a regional level. In Adrevald's view the secular oppression of the religious communities in his region intensified in this time. Equity was not always guaranteed by law and some of the responsible officeholders even tried to seize possessions of Fleury.[14]

The onset of viking attacks in these years further tested the solidarity between harried periphery and the centres of the empire. At Rouen and Paris in the 840s, the common people complained bitterly when local monasteries started removing relics, protesting that their lands were being laid open to devastation.[15] In the case of Rouen, Charles the Bald had commanded monks of Saint Medard to bring Gildard's relics from there to his favoured monastery in Soissons. The citizens of Rouen,

> struggling to oppose the will of those seeking the relics (since they were unable to sustain so great a loss to their whole province without either great injury or even civil sedition), all came out into the open and almost reached the point of war.[16]

In the end they had to give in, because 'the leaders of the region were terrified lest the royal force be turned upon them with grave fury and the whole region be thus devastated.'[17] Obviously, in the eyes of the author the ties between the court and the province were put to the test. There are different aspects of solidarity in this episode. On the one hand, there is a breach of solidarity: the protection of a province was arbitrarily cancelled and with that the expectation of mutual aid. Instead there was the risk that the province would be destroyed by royal forces. On the other hand, we can see that the citizens of Rouen were concerned about the wellbeing of the whole province. The king's demand provoked collective action to fight against this breach of trust. The people of the province were ready to fight. Eventually they 'acquiesced, but not without the greatest melancholy,' as the author reports. This is what sociologists and philosophers call 'fighting solidarities' or 'political solidarities': a shared social justice aim, which 'unites the group and maintains the movement.' It is a 'response to oppression, injustice and social vulnerabilities.'[18]

External threats and the lack of internal support necessarily shaped the self-defence activities of the population. In some cases the inhabitants of an area threatened by enemies made vows of mutual assistance. One such oath-community, which was formed for self-defence in response to the gathering of a large number of *Dani* in 859 in the Schelde-area, was completely destroyed: not by Danes, as one might expect, but by *nostri potentiores*, as Prudentius of Troyes emphasizes. This unauthorized association of the *vulgus promiscuum* clearly seemed too dangerous.[19]

Fault lines in solidarity groups could occur not only between royal brothers, between monasteries and secular officeholders in local contexts, or between the centre and periphery, but also between social hierarchies. Such a conflict is documented in a sermon written in the early 920s by Abbo of Saint-Germain. In this text he rebukes the *milites* who kill or take captive peasants, servants of their own realm, although these people are needed to tend to the farms, pay tribute, and supply the soldiers with such essential military goods as food, clothes and horses:

> Brothers, every day you see how this realm is going to ruin. Our peasants and servants and all of those who used to keep our farms and plough our lands, whence we should have had both our food and our clothing and with which we used to buy our horses and armour, now are dead or captives. What need we have without these people! We ourselves know neither how to plough nor sow the lands, nor prune nor cultivate the vines. What shall we do now?

This misbehaviour also had an impact on success in war: 'How can you please God and get a victory, you who have your hands forever full of perjuries and plunderings?'[20]

It was this lack of internal solidarity that (for some authors) made it possible for external enemies to destroy Christian communities. Regino of Prüm sees this reflected in the division amongst the Bretons, which the Normans were able to exploit;[21] Liutprand of Cremona sees it in the jealousy among the inhabitants of Provence, which strengthened the small group of Saracens of Freinet.[22] According to Liutprand, the crushing defeat at the hands of the Hungarians at the Brenta in 899 came about when, after the battle practically had been won, some groups failed to support each other when the steppe riders made a desperate counter attack in order to profit from one another's demise.[23] And, finally, Ermentarius blamed the civil war for the success of the Northmen.[24]

Maintenance of solidarity

In all these examples it is clear that group solidarity could not simply exist but had to be constantly affirmed through rules and common experience. Group solidarity must be maintained through control mechanisms.[25] This is done for instance with the *capitula* of synods, where the *populus* as a whole or specific groups are exhorted to just behaviour. Assemblies and the decrees that they produced served to support already existing structures of solidarity. This is made clear by numerous calls in council acts to provide mutual assistance under various circumstances. This applies to the unity of the church throughout the various Frankish kingdoms,[26] as well as to the relationship of the kings both to one another and to their subjects[27], and also official co-operation between bishops and counts.[28] Some stipulations attempt to fundamentally correct disturbances of internal cohesion. The capitulary of a *missus* from Burgundy, which was supposed to implement the decisions of the synod of Quierzy of 14 February 857 in the area of the office bearers' authority, is a much discussed testimony of such efforts. According to this text, those who cause destruction or enrich themselves at the expense of and to the disadvantage of those who live in the *patria* are threatened with heavy penalties.[29] The bishops who assembled at Pîtres in 862 promised to administer *medicamenta* against sins that had been committed in the recent past. These *medicamenta* were expressly conceived for all, including those *raptores et praedatores*, who attempted to expand their power in the Western kingdom during and after the chaos caused by Louis the German's attack.[30] The *medicamenta* were not free: the culprits had to provide compensation by a fixed date.

The convocation of a synod in itself contributed to the strengthening of internal cohesion and the assurance of mutual solidarity. The common prayers and discussions strengthened the feeling of community.[31] As Janet Nelson put it: 'Repeated meetings over time, collective action, and the articulation of common concerns fostered a conscious solidarity on the part of bishops ...'.[32] In June 909 the participants at the synod of Trosly discussed the *status regni*, which had been worsened by the *infestatio paganorum*, through *perturbationes gravissimi regni* and by *insectationes* of pseudo-Christians. First of all, however, the participants affirmed their unity, mutual love, unanimity, and concord between the various ranks of the church.[33] Such expressions made it all the more painful when a church removed itself from this kind of solidarity union, as had happened ca. 50 years earlier with the Breton church.[34]

While these decisions were taken at synods or assemblies and therefore ideally affected the whole kingdom or church province, naturally there were also assemblies at regional and local levels and in alternative contexts. For example, Archbishop Hincmar of Reims tried to strengthen the social cohesion among his regional priests, by ordering them to have lunch together once a month.[35] Feast days presented another possibility to maintain cohesion within a group. These provided an opportunity for groups to demonstrate their solidarity to one another, in that the poor were fed, guests welcomed, and signs of social distinctions diminished. So-called *coniurationes* or *gildae* were important horizontal solidarity groups that confirmed their unity though oaths, meetings, and communal drinking. We do not know anything more about their organization or ideals, as their existences are only attested by bans.[36]

Another occasion where group cohesion and solidarity were extremely important was war, and not only for reasons of camaraderie.[37] When Charlemagne went on campaign against the Avars in 791 he waited together with his army at the river Enns, where they fasted and did penance for three days, and only afterwards crossed the symbolic boundary.[38] The collective confrontation of everyone's individual sin in this episode strengthens their common ties as Christians and as a solidarity group. In the tenth century, Widukind reports that the Saxons took additional steps when they fought against a coalition of Northern Slavs in 929,[39] or against the Hungarians in 955.[40] Before both battles the Saxons made oaths, both to the commander as well as to one another, in which they swore to offer one another mutual assistance. In this case the social cohesion between those who were assembled was not seen as sufficient on its own.[41] Solidarity during battle had to be confirmed beforehand by oath! Perhaps this was the fruit of experiences of several Carolingian kings in the second half of the ninth century. The warriors followed the lead of their magnates rather than that of the king.[42] At the first glance these are conflicts of loyalty. In a wider context however, there are also changes in emphasis across the different solidarity frames that members of these groups belonged to: the *regnum*, the *gens*, and the Christian *populus*.

Equality within groups

Equality is often an issue when it comes to solidarity. In research it is regarded as the main difference between solidarity and patronage or loyalty, which are both constructed vertically rather than horizontally. In a functioning solidarity frame, an individual or a group could rely on equality before the law. During the synod of Pîtres in 862 Hincmar of Rheims developed an idealized picture of a society of equals.[43] He illustrated this with a powerful biblical picture: 'The archangel who is now the Devil fell from Heaven with his minions because he refused to be the subject to his maker and scorned to be an associate with his fellow angels in the equality of charity.'[44] But reality was different, as Hincmar conceded in his text. Many hagiographical narratives from the second half of the ninth century complain about the inequality before the law, which monasteries had to endure from local officeholders. Therefore saints fought for justice for their communities in situations of inequality. Alternative frames of solidarity arose.

There were several levels of equality within the hierarchy of a Carolingian and post-Carolingian society. In 891, a Frankish and a viking army met at the Dyle. As the battle took place on marshy ground, the Franks were not able to fight on horseback, as they were accustomed to. For this reason, Arnulf of Carinthia addressed his warriors, reminding them of past defeats, the cruelty of the enemy, the violent deaths of their parents and the murders of priests and exhorting them to take revenge for these crimes (*sceleris factores*). He said he would dismount and go into battle on foot with the banner in his hand. With this, the Regensburg continuator of the *Annales Fuldenses* reports that the battle (which the Franks ultimately won) began: 'Fired up by these words, all both old and young were inspired by the same zeal and courage to march into battle on foot.'[45] One could add to this that the readiness of the king to go into battle on foot just like the rest of the warriors was probably decisive in allowing the army to take the field with motivation. It was precisely the overcoming of inequality in these situations that influenced collective action in a positive way.

Common values and common pasts

A solidarity group often marks out common values and a common past. Referring to the past or to shared experience strengthens cohesion, especially in extreme situations like the one Arnulf faced on the banks of the river Dyle in 891. Widukind of Corvey approaches this theme from various perspectives. In the early days of the Saxons, the Franks called upon them for help against the Thuringians. When the ruler of the Thuringians saw that he had no chance against this alliance, he sent a negotiator to the Frankish king to ask for peace. The negotiator pointed to the familial relations between the Frankish king and the wife and sons of the Thuringian king, appealed to his sympathy, and reminded him of an undefined *natura communium rerum*.[46] Whatever this *natura communium rerum* might have been, it caused the Frankish king to change his mind and turn against the Saxons instead. When the Saxons realize the Franks have betrayed them, the warrior Hathagat, known as the 'Father of Fathers' due to his advanced age and renowned deeds, encourages the Saxons to take heart against Frankish faithlessness, and exhorts his follow combatants to fight the enemy together, calling upon the *exempla* of their ancestors and of those already fallen in battle.[47] In his previously mentioned sermon, Abbo of Saint-Germain refers to the *milites* who assaulted their own population as well as to the deeds of the forefathers (*boni patres*), but then looks further into the past to the Romans and Jews. He uses the Romans as a positive example, even though they were pagan before the birth of Christ: 'These Romans, indeed, because they lived righteously (*iuste*), chastely (*caste*) and soberly (*sobrie*), conquered and defeated all *gentes*.' But because the Jews constantly sinned against God, 'foreign nations always came upon them, and slew and captured them, and burned their strongholds.'[48]

The past of a group is often used to impose moral obligations of solidarity in the present, with an eye on the future. These binding moral values can be built on past successes, but also on defeats, and are central to the study of group solidarity. Both lay mirrors like Dhuoda's *Liber Manualis* or synodal acts offer a variety of moral standards and obligations. In tenth-century France, Gerald of Aurillac served as an example of moral conduct in many different ways, even in courts of law. 'He went fasting to the law court, lest failing in temperance he should be unable to give a reasonable judgement. For he sought what was of Christ, what was of peace, what might further the common good.'[49] Gerald has noticed this effect in his immediate environment as well as outside of it. Yet, as a lay saint, he was an exception in his time, as was his *Vita*. Most of his peers did not voluntarily rise to the moral obligations of solidarity promoted in Gerald's *Vita*. This does not mean that other laypeople lacked solidarity: they followed alternative moral obligations, which operated on a smaller scale. Help and support for the all-encompassing common good was not a given, and often had to be demanded.

Demand of solidarity

Solidarity has an appellative character. In 859 the Synod of Savonnières called upon the kings to restore *caritas fraterna* and *concordia pacis*. The bishops were admonished to preserve their *unitas* and to hold synods.[50] In 864 Charles the Bald proclaimed in the context of the synod of Pîtres that all, without any excuse, were to come to the defence of their homeland.[51] Such clear demands were deemed necessary by contemporaries, but Ermentarius reports around 862 that no one was left who was prepared to resist the vikings, and only a few who were even prepared to call for it: '... *rarus est qui dicat: "State, state, resistite, pugnate pro patria, liberis et gente.'''*[52] In the previously mentioned sermon of Abbo of Saint-Germain, the preacher exhorts his audience to collective action: '*Francia*, defend yourself! Do not multiply and increase your enemies, but as scripture commands, fight for your fatherland. Do not fear to die in God's battle. Surely, if you are killed in it, you will be holy martyrs ...'[53] Abbo of Saint-Germain thought to evoke a sense of belonging and emotionally-charged solidarity in the *milites*, who were plundering the farmlands of their own people, by using the label *Francia*.

Solidarity and group labels

Using group labels in the late- and post-Carolingian world was thus associated with the search for sustainable and resilient groups, where cohesion and solidarity were still present or were being renegotiated.[54] With regards to this, the authors of that troubled time were reflecting on the scope of social cohesion and solidarity. Abbo's identity, as revealed in his *De bello Parisiaco*, was 'layered, rippling out in concentric circles from his home: he was a man of Saint Germanus, a Parisian, a Neustrian, and a man from *Francia*,' as Simon MacLean put it.[55] Just as his identities were multiple and fluid, so were the meanings of the group labels he used. In his sermons it is *Francia*, the *regnum* and the *patria*, but it could also be the *patria*, the *imperium*, the *res publica* at a larger scale,[56] which is also the case for instance in Paschasius Radbertus. He uses these three labels almost synonymically when he discusses Wala's ideas of the common good. According to the *Epitaphium Arsenii*, Wala followed the example of Scipio and other citizens, who set aside their personal interests in order to give priority to the common good. To Wala, a divided empire has negative consequences for the care of the *patria* and its citizens, for *fides* and *pax*, for the *prosperitas ullarum rerum*. And what is more, there is in his mind *nullus qui sociis et amiciis debitam caritatem impendat*.[57] In the middle of the ninth century, debates about the unity of the empire were combined with reflections on solidarity. It was a time when 'efforts were being made to find appropriate terms to express the group-consciousness of the faithful men' as Janet Nelson put it.[58] These are terms like *nostra omnium societas* or *bar(o)natus*.[59]

But the term *christianitas* was also used in different ways that had different meanings. While Charlemagne practised politics for the *populus christianus* and in its name,[60] and the concept of *christianitas* mainly referred to the proper Christian moral behaviour of the individual, that is, their personal Christianity, in the wake of the viking attacks over the ninth century the term becomes more territorialized.[61] A remarkable new use of *christianitas* occurs in a sermon of Abbo of Saint-Germain around 920, in which the term is spatialized to refer to church estates and is directed

212 Maximilian Diesenberger

against internal opponents.[62] But as the concept of *christianitas* expresses a universal claim, a shift seems to have occurred here in the labelling and perception of the social big picture. *Christianitas* took the place of *imperium*. This had consequences for the localization of solidarity. In his sermon, Abbo equates *christianitas* with (*nostra*) *fraternitas* and thus refers to both the clergy and the secular population.[63] Here we can also see how the transformation of political concepts of order was also a matter of solidarity, or rather that this transformation was perceived as a reformation and modification of solidarity frames.

Different levels of solidarity

The fact that solidarity is a driving force in small groups as well as in larger collectives raises the question of what the relation between these collectives was in terms of solidarity issues. In the first years of the tenth century, Bishop Radbod of Utrecht wrote the *Libellus de miraculo sancti Martini* on the viking attacks on Tours in June 903.[64] Radbod had studied in Tours himself and was therefore interested in the events of 903, when vikings attacked the city in late June. The attack was beaten back, but caused severe losses and damage to the inhabitants of Tours and the vicinity. In his portrayal, the author uses the image of social unity in the city. It is Saint Martin who was the broker between different groups within Tours and beyond. Any conflicts and social differences are suppressed in the text.[65] In order to avoid differentiation within the city, the text used terms such as '*Turonici*' and '*oppidani*.' In doing so the bishop of Utrecht projects an image of social cohesion, mutual aid, and solidarity.[66]

Radbod wrote his text for his flock in the diocese of Utrecht, where he was consecrated as bishop in 899. However, because of viking attacks, Radbod was not able to take up his residence in Utrecht itself but instead took his seat further east at Deventer, where his predecessor Odilbold had moved in 895. Radbod lamented the fact that he could only visit Utrecht 'in times of peace' and that 'circumstances would not allow him to live there uninterruptedly.' In writing about the miracles of Saint-Martin in Tours and the successful defence of the city due to the joint effort of the *oppidani*, he created a model of cohesion and solidarity behaviour which he wanted to implement in Utrecht, where Saint Martin was also venerated. But there were some obstacles to the translation of this model to the north. Radbod admits that Tours is far away from Utrecht. He insists that he did not add anything to the story, but he concedes that the number of Northmen killed by the *Turonici* might be exaggerated.[67] But, as always, the attribution of the victory to Martin cannot be denied. In a comparison between Martin in his lifetime and now as a saint, Radbod refers to 'the free power of the most powerful man,' which Martin once possessed and which is also subject to the saint now.[68]

The question arises whether it was possible to transfer a model of social cohesion and solidarity to another community at all. The prestige of Martin was limited in this time and had to be enforced. Radbod needed a bigger frame to connect the *Turonici* with the inhabitants of Utrecht. Firstly it is the *civitas* of Tours which Radbod describes as the most precious place, even better than Alexandria or Carthage. Secondly Radbod compares Martin's miraculous deliverance of Tours to the divine assistance that had supported the military successes of the Christian Roman emperors Constantine and Theodosius, two emperors used in Carolingian times as models for Charlemagne or Louis the Pious. Moreover, Martin's corpse was more powerful than Alexander the Great, Xerxes, and Augustus had once been.[69] Already in the prologue Radbod argues that Christianity rules the whole world, because the *christiana religio* had subdued many kingdoms and defeated the most powerful kings. Therefore the *religio christiana* should be called *domina* and *imperatrix*![70] This is quite an interesting shift of imperial vocabulary from the Carolingians to Christianity in general and to Saint Martin in particular. This imperial frame was needed to explain that Martin's power still existed and was not only limited to Tours but could be activated at each site where he was venerated. There is more. At the end of his text Radbod invites his audience to pray to Martin unanimously for help, including the request 'to save the *statum regni Francorum*, while the lineage of the former Charles the Great never dies out, so that the *regnum* will never be conquered by an invisible or visible enemy.'[71] Obviously for Radbod the Carolingian family itself was still a reference point to address the larger social whole, bridging the physical and mental borders of different social and political units at the beginning of the tenth century, in order to transfer a successful model of civic unity and solidarity to another region. But he demonstrates that the bond between the Carolingian family, Saint Martin, and the *regnum Francorum* was not as strong as it was in earlier times. When the Carolingians are first mentioned in the text they testify to the disintegration of the realm, exemplified by the battle of Fontenoy. Concerning the appearance of the Normans, Radbod argues:

> For this was the result of the depredation by the aforementioned people, which, in the same year, they say, when four kings, progeny of the same father, delivering battles among themselves with their armies, polluted the plains of Fontenoy with much Christian blood, had entered the basin of the river Seine with their piratical fleet.[72]

Carolingian failure immediately led to punishment. Different solidarity frames are in play in this text: the city, Christianity, the empire, and even the royal family. They demonstrate the difficulties of establishing a solidarity group in a complex social world. Of course the authors of these texts were themselves always components of the groups and solidarity-communities, presenting concurrent perspectives on the existence and significance of the solidarity norms of these groups.

Solidarity in the late- and post-Carolingian world

The social changes in the late- and post-Carolingian world also had wide-reaching consequences from the perspective of solidarity. The range of solidarity had, from an empire that formulated binding solidarity norms for all social ranks in very different regions, become much smaller. This process is not extraordinary; the difficulty is transferring the experiences and quality of micro-level solidarity to large-scale abstract entities. From an empire that had been created through expansion and was now challenged by incursions from different regions, the quality and composition of solidarity had changed drastically. If (political) solidarity is characterized above all by being created through resistance, then, paradoxically, it is precisely the conflict-heavy late- and post-Carolingian era that was formed by solidarity. There were many different groups who organized themselves into fighting solidarities. That was caused not only by incursions from outside, especially those of the vikings and Hungarians, but also by divisions in kingdoms. There were also many political centres of equal rank to which one could associate or disassociate oneself or others. This also created the conditions for a multiplication of possible groups to which one could belong. At the same time, this diversity also meant a greater limitation due to the numerous competing groups. The irritation in this game of belongings chiefly consisted in the fact that the relationship inside and outside [groups?] also ran along social lines: one did not just belong to a certain regional or politically defined group; fault lines could also run between different social classes. Abbo of Saint-Germain attempted to close this gap in his sermons. Others attempted to turn a group to fight against itself as happened at the Schelde in 859, when the *potentiores* were sent against the *vulgus promiscuum*. Fragmentation also meant a growth in collective action, in the course of which some of these groups became solidarity groups.

At the same time, complaints about the lack of solidarity became louder. When a moved Odo of Cluny stood at the grave of Gerald of Aurillac around 925, he marvelled

> that in this age of ours, when charity has almost entirely grown cold, …, the miracle of the saints should not cease, but He is mindful of the promise, that He makes by Jeremiah 'I will not turn away from doing good [to my people].'[73]

In the past there were examples of unity and solidarity that could be held up against the lack of solidarity. In these texts, priority is conceded to the role of social solidarity: that is that language which emphasizes cultural, linguistic, or ethnic commonalities. In the *Annals of St Bertin* it is Louis the Pious who was 'deeply worried about spilling the blood of a people who felt themselves one,' when it comes to sending his army into battle against that of his son, Louis the German.[74] Only two years later, that was exactly what his sons would do. But Prudentius seems to think that Lothar is to blame for this, as both his brothers are described in the rhetoric of unity and fraternity immediately before the battle of Fontenoy: 'Charles, full of joy and affection, came to meet Louis as he approached. There was a complete union between them: they were bound by brotherly love, and they even pitched camp together, sharing each other's company and counsels.' And furthermore: 'They made every effort, by sending very frequent missions, to come to an agreement with Lothar for peace and harmony and the government of the whole people and realm.'[75] Their deeds went beyond their own interest, according to the author; they only had the big picture uppermost in their minds. In the *Annals of Saint Bertin*, it is the *populus* that Louis the Pious and his good sons care for. The text does not mention the *gens Francorum* as a solidarity frame, as Adrevald does somewhat later (c. 870) in the context of the dispute between the Carolingian brothers. Instead, it is the *populus* in a more Christian sense.[76] One might ask whether the transformation of the Carolingian world, in addition to changing collective action and group solidarity, did not also change the language of solidarity itself.

Dramatic events like the battle of Fontenoy had effects on how one talked about this big picture and how one spoke (or did not speak) about group solidarity. Dhuoda, whom I mentioned at the beginning, transferred the image of the apostolic solidarity community, which had been used as a monastic ideal for centuries, onto court society. At the same time, she advanced the impression of the naturalness of solidarity behaviour through her use of the examples of the stags and of other natural imagery.[77] Later, Odo of Cluny transferred the qualities of a saint to a secular *comes* through the consistent transformation of solidarity action when he composed the *vita* of St Gerald of Aurillac. A rhetoric of solidarity was now increasingly applied even to smaller groups and administrative districts. In the *Life of John of Gorze*, the district of the feared Count Boso is described as a space deeply lacking in solidarity, in that more-or-less all of its inhabitants steal one another's property.[78] In this manner, the author indirectly makes it clear that the good and just ruler should be the guarantor of a solidarity society, or that a society shaped by solidarity should reflect the positive attributes of a ruler. The late- and post-Carolingian world is thus also a time of alternative solidarity models and moral obligations, which sometimes competed.

Simon MacLean has pointed to the fact that historiographic texts of the tenth century scarcely, or only very rudimentarily look to a Carolingian past.[79] Perhaps this is also the reason why Abbo does not merely invoke the memory of the *boni patres* in his sermon, but digs deep into antiquity, just as Radbod of Utrecht compares the power of Martin with that of Alexander the Great, Xerxes, and Augustus.[80] It may have been the lack of suitable examples in later Carolingian history that was responsible for this, as well as the increasing fragmentation of the empire and of the church.[81] This fragmentation also led to old group-terms and administrative names coming into use again and new terms being formed. The accounts of miracles from Saint-Vaast around the end of the ninth century are an eloquent testimony to the use of old names. Ulman, a cleric from St Vaast, sees all *Gallia comata*, due to its own sin, as a victim of the vikings. According to his account, when the remains of Vedastus were again laid in the basilica of St Vaast in 853, innumerable people gathered from all directions to be at the grave of the saint: 'One could see the entire province (*provincia*) bloom and at the same time Francia rejoice after the invasion of Getae (*diluvium Getarum*)', he reports.[82]

Such sources attempt to delimit the geographical frame of common experiences, or to determine the area of validity of collective action with the aid of old as well

216 Maximilian Diesenberger

as new names. Unaccustomed collective action or new solidarity groups led to blurring in terms for outsiders, such as the aforementioned *vulgus promiscuum* in the *Annales Bertiniani*.[83] Mostly, a (negative) evaluation is attached. In all cases, the sources make clear that there was a heightened number of active groups. The social and political processes of late- and post-Carolingian societies can be investigated to determine how strongly collective action was implied by solidarity, which solidarity frames had validity and how much the range of solidarity changed. Social changes can be analysed in terms of the carrying capacity of horizontal social ties and in terms of the 'discourse of common life'. In order to understand the processes that forged, maintained, or destroyed group solidarity in the late- and post-Carolingian world, we need to investigate two areas: the actual dynamics of solidarity within groups and the discourse of solidarity, as well as how these two intertwine.

Notes

1 I would like to thank Andreas Fischer, Paul Gazzoli, Christina-Maria Lutter, Simon MacLean, Janet L. Nelson, Walter Pohl and Jelle Wassenaar for comments on this text.

2 For a useful problematization of the concept see still Timothy Reuter and Chris Wickham, 'The "Feudal Revolution"', *Past & Present*, 155 (1997), 177–208.

3 Emile Durkheim, *On Morality and Society* (Chicago: University of Chicago Press, 1973); Michael Hechter, *Principles of Group Solidarity* (Berkeley: University of California Press, 1987); *Solidarity*, ed. by Kurt Bayertz (Dordrecht: Kluwer Academic Publishers, 1999); Graham Crow, *Social Solidarities: Theories, Identities and Social Change* (Philadelphia: Open University Press, 2002); Sally J. Scholz, *Political Solidarity* (University Park: Pennsylvania State University Press, 2008); *Solidarity: Theory and Practice*, ed. Art Laitinen and Anne Birgitta Pessi, (Lanham: Lexington Books, 2015); Siniša Maleš[e]vi , 'Where does group solidarity come from? Gellner and Ibn Khaldun revisited', *Thesis Eleven*, 128, 1 (2015), 85–99. See historical research on solidarity: Marina Rustow, 'Patronage in the context of solidarity and reciprocity: two paradigms of social cohesion in the Premodern Mediterranean', in *Patronage, Production, and Transmission of Texts in Medieval and Early Modern Jewish Cultures*, ed. by E. Alfonso and J. Decter (Turnhout: Brepols, 2014), pp. 13–44. Gervase Rosser, *The Art of Solidarity in the Middle Ages. Guilds in England, 1250–1550* (Oxford: Oxford University Press, 2015).

4 Dhuoda, *Liber Manualis*, III, c. 10, ed. and trans. by Marcelle Thiébaux, Cambridge Medieval Classics 8 (Cambridge: Cambridge University Press, 2006), pp. 112–3: *Cervi hanc habent consuetudinis morem, ut, cum pluraliter maria vel spatiosa maritimis undarum gurgitis flumina transverhi coeperint, unus post unum caput cum cornibus super dorsa compare suo colla submittant, ut paululum quiescentes facilius amnem possint transcurrere veloces. Est in illis talis intellectus et talis aequa discretio, ut, cum priorem senserint adgravari, mutant primum posteriorem, et extremum, ad ceteros sublevandum vel refocilandum, eligunt primum: sicque in singulis versa vice mutantes, talis per singular in illis transcurrit compassio dilectionis fraterna: hoc semper caventes ut caput cum cornibus, ne in amnis mergantur profundis, superos tendi et anelari satagunt.* About Dhuoda see Janet L. Nelson, 'Dhuoda', in *Lay Intellectuals in the Carolingian World*, ed. by Patrick Wormald and Janet L. Nelson (Cambridge: Cambridge University Press, 2007), pp. 106–20.

5 Dhuoda, *Liber Manualis* III, c. 10, pp. 110–1: *Hanc in subportationem vel vicissitudinis mutationem, delectionem tam in majoribu quam in minoribus per compassionem fraternitatem omnimodis per cuncta in genere humano ostendit esse tenendam.*

6 Dhuoda, *Liber Manualis* III, c. 10, pp. 112–3.

7 Dhuoda, *Liber Manualis* III, c. 10, pp. 114–5.

8 Widukind of Corvey, *Res gestae Saxonicae* I, c. 8, ed. by Paul Hirsch and Hans-Eberhard Lohmann, MGH Scriptores rerum Germanicarum in usum scholarum separatim editi

60 (Hannover: Hahnsche Buchhandlung, 1935), p. 9: '*Certos amicos Brettis Saxones sciatis et eorum necessitatibus atque commodis aeque semper affuturos.*'

9 Widukind, *Res gestae Saxonicae* I, c. 9, p. 15.

10 The best example for this is Salomon of Constance, *Carmen* 1, ed. by Paul von Winterfeld, MGH Poetae latini aevi Carolini 4, 1 (Berlin, Weidmann, 1899), pp. 297–306; an extended discussion of this text is in preparation.

11 Janet L. Nelson, 'Carolingian violence and the ritualization of ninth-century warfare', in *Violence and Society in the Early Medieval West*, ed. Guy Halsall (Woodbridge: Boydell Press, 1998), pp. 90–106 at 101 and 103–4: 'the trauma of Fontenoy'.

12 *Synodus Mettensis*, c. 1, ed. Wilfried Hartmann, *MGH, Concilia 3, Die Konzilien der karolingischen Teilreiche 843–859* (Hannover: Hahnsche Buchhandlung, 1984), pp. 435–44, at p. 438: *Nota et – pro dolor! – nimis est nota discordia atque calamitatis pernicies, quae factione quorumdam seditiosorum hominum nuper inter fratres, reges nostros Hludowicum et Karolum accidit;* c. 8, p. 441: *Nam sicut quisque in se peccantibus debet propter deum dimittere, ita in deum peccantes et ecclesiam conculcantes et regni pervasores et in christianitatis depopulatores et in pacis perturbatores et in patriae proditores debet minister domini rex debitam vindictam propter deum exercere.* See John Van Engen, 'Christening, the Kingdom of the Carolingians, and European Humanity', in *Rome and Religion in the Medieval World: Studies in Honor of Thomas F.X. Noble*, ed. by Valerie L. Garver and Owen M. Phelan (London: Routledge, 2014), pp. 101–28, at 124.

13 Adrevald of Fleury, *Miracula Sancti Benedicti*, c. 27, ed. Oswald Holder-Egger, *MGH Scriptores*, xv, 1 (Hannover: Hahnsche Buchhandlung, 1887), pp. 474–97, at 491.

14 Thomas Head, *Hagiography and the Cult of Saints. The Diocese of Orléans, 800–1200* (Cambridge: Cambridge University Press, 1990), pp. 138–52.

15 *Vita Sancti Gildardi episcopi Rotomagensis et ejusdem translatio Suessiones anno 838–840 facta*, ed. Albert Poncelet, *Analecta Bollandiana*, 8 (1889), pp. 389–405, at 404–5. See *Translatio S. Germani Parisiensis anno 846 secundum primævam narrationem. E codice Namurcensi*, c. 8, ed. by Charles de Smedt, *Analecta Bollandiana*, 2 (1883), pp. 69–98, at 75.

16 *Vita Sancti Gildardi episcopi*, p. 404.

17 *Vita Sancti Gildardi episcopi*, p. 405.

18 Arto Laitinen and Anne Birgitta Pessi, 'Solidarity. Theory and Practice. An Introduction', in *Solidarity: Theory and Practice*, ed. by Art Laitinen and Anne Birgitta Pessi, (Lanham: Lexington Books, 2015), p. 10; see Scholz, *Political Solidarity*, pp. 190–1.

19 *Annales Bertiniani auctore Prudentio*, a. 859, ed. Georg Waitz, *MGH, Scriptores in rerum germanicarum in usum scholarum seperatim editi*, 5 (Hannover: Hahnsche Buchhandlung, 1883), p. 51; trans. by Janet L. Nelson, *The Annals of St-Bertin* (Manchester: Manchester University Press, 1991), p. 89. See Janet L. Nelson, 'Peers in the early middle ages', in *Law, Laity and Solidarities: Essays in Honour of Susan Reynolds*, ed. by Pauline A. Stafford, Janet L. Nelson, and Jane Martindale (Manchester: Manchester University Press, 2001), pp. 27–46, at 39.

20 Abbo of Saint-Germain, *Sermo adversus raptores bonorum alienorum*, ed. Ute Önnerfors, *Abbo von Saint-Germain-des-Pres, 22 Predigten*. Lateinische Sprache und Literatur des Mittelalters, 16 (Frankfurt am Main: Verlag Peter Lang, 1985), pp. 94–99. Translation: James E. Cross and Alan Brown, 'Literary Impetus for Wulfstan's Sermo Lupi', *Leeds Studies in English*, n.s. 20 (1989), 271–91, at 285–7.

21 Regino of Prüm, *Chronicon*, a. 890, ed. by Friedrich Kurze, *MGH, Scriptores in rerum germanicarum in usum scholarum seperatim editi*, 50 (Hannover: Hahnsche Buchhandlung, 1890), p. 135; Translation: Simon MacLean, *History and Politics in Late Carolingian and Ottonian Europe. The* Chronicle *of Regino of Prüm and Adalbert of Magdeburg* (Manchester: Manchester University Press, 2009), p. 208.

22 Liutprand of Cremona, *Antapodosis* I, 4, ed. by Joseph Becker, *MGH, Scriptores in rerum germanicarum in usum scholarum seperatim editi*, 41 (Hannover: Hahnsche Buchhandlung, 3. reprint, 1915), pp. 1–158, at 6.

23 Liutprand of Cremona, *Antapodosis* II, 15, pp. 44–5.

24 Ermentarius, *De translationibus et de miraculis sancti Filiberti, prologus*, ed. by Renè Poupardin, Monuments de l'histoire des abbayes de Saint-Philibert (Noirmoutier, Grandlieu,

218   Maximilian Diesenberger

Tournus) publiés d'après les notes d'Arthur Giry (Collection de textes pour servir à l'étude et à l'enseignement de l'histoire 38, Paris, 1905), pp. 19–70, at 60.

25 See Hechter, *Principles of Group Solidarity*, pp. 176–7.

26 E.g. '*Invitation letter for a synod in Troyes*' (860 or 861), ed. by Wilfried Hartmann, *MGH, Concilia 4, Die Konzilien der karolingischen Teilreiche 860–874* (Hannover: Hahnsche Buchhandlung, 1998), pp. 43–5, at 44. See *Hlotarii et Karoli Conventus Leodii Habitus* (854. Febr.), Hoc est sacramentum, quod sibi mutuo iuraverunt', ed. by Alfred Boretius and Victor Krause, *MGH, Leges 2, Capitularia regum Francorum 2* (Hannover: Hahnsche Buchhandlung, 1897), pp. 76–8, at p. 78.

27 E.g. '*Synod of Yülz*' (844), c. 1, ed. by Wilfried Hartmann, *MGH, Concilia 3, Die Konzilien der karolingischen Teilreiche 843–859* (Hannover: Hahnsche Buchhandlung, 1984), pp. 27–35, at 30.

28 '*Synod of Pavia*' (845–50) c. 12, ed. by Wilfried Hartmann, *MGH, Concilia 3, Die Konzilien der karolingischen Teilreiche 843–859* (Hannover: Hahnsche Buchhandlung, 1984), pp. 207–15, at 214.

29 '*Capitulary of a missus from Burgundy*' c. 3 ed. by Wilfried Hartmann, *MGH, Concilia 3, Die Konzilien der karolingischen Teilreiche 843–859* (Hannover: Hahnsche Buchhandlung, 1984), p. 398: *III. De his vero, qui intra patriam residentes rapinas exercent, domos infringunt, homines sine causa occidunt, trustes commovent aut alios dampnant et opprimant, prata defensoria depascunt, fruges aliorum devastant, ex his mandat senior noster: ut primum episcopali auctoritate iudicentur et sic postea a comitibus legaliter constringantur et insuper bannum nostrum, id est solidos LX, componant. Et si eos constringere non potuerint, ad regalem praesentiam deducantur, ut dignam suscipiant vindictam.*

30 '*Synod of Pîtres and Soissons 862*', c. 2, ed. by Wilfried Hartmann, *MGH, Concilia 4, Die Konzilien der karolingischen Teilreiche 860–874* (Hannover: Hahnsche Buchhandlung, 1998), pp. 90–122, at pp. 100–1.

31 Timothy Reuter, 'Debating the "feudal revolution"', in Idem, *Medieval Polities and Modern Mentalities* (Cambridge: Cambridge University Press, 2006), p. 79.

32 Janet L. Nelson, 'National synods, kingship as office and royal anointing: an early medieval syndrome', *Studies in Church History*, 7 (1971), 41–60, at 43–4. For episcopal solidarities in the late- and post Carolingian era see the contribution of Jelle Wassenaar in this volume.

33 '*Synod of Trosly*' (26. June 909), praefatio, ed. by Wilfried Hartmann, Isolde Schröder und Gerhard Schmitz, *MGH, Concilia 5, Die Konzilien der karolingischen Teilreiche 875–911* (Hannover: Hahnsche Buchhandlung, 2012), pp. 497–562, at 503–4.

34 See for instance *Synod of Soissons 866*, '*Zweites Synodalschreiben an Nikolaus I.*', ed. by Wilfried Hartmann, *MGH, Concilia 4, Die Konzilien der karolingischen Teilreiche 860–874* (Hannover: Hahnsche Buchandlung, 1998), pp. 218–20.

35 Janet L. Nelson, 'Making ends meet. Wealth and poverty in the Carolingian church', in *The Frankish World, 750–900*, ed. by Janet L. Nelson (London: The Hambledon Press, 1996), pp. 145–4, at 153.

36 Otto-Gerhard Oexle, 'Gilden als soziale Gruppen in der Karolingerzeit', *Das Handwerk in vor- und frühgeschichtlicher Zeit, 1. Historische und rechtshistorische Beiträge und Untersuchungen zur Frühgeschichte der Gilde*, ed. by Herbert Jahnkuhn, Walter Janssen, Ruth Schmidt-Wiegand, and Heinrich Tiefenbach (Göttingen: Vandenhoeck & Ruprecht, 1981), pp. 284–354. Otto-Gerhard Oexle, 'Gilde und Kommune. Über die Entstehung von "Einung" und "Gemeinde" als Grundformen des Zusammenlebens in Europa', in *Theorien kommunaler Ordnung in Europa*, ed. by Peter Blickle (Schriften des Historischen Kollegs. Kolloquien, 36, München: Oldenbourg Verlag, 1996) pp. 75–98.

37 See Scholz, *Political Solidarity*, p. 117, to the difference between camaraderie and solidarity.

38 Walter Pohl, *The Avars. A Steppe Empire in Central Europe, 567–822* (Cornell: Cornell University Press, 2018), pp. 232–3.

39 Widukind of Corvey, *Res gestae Saxonicae* I, c. 36, ed. by Hans-Eberhard Lohmann and Paul Hirsch, *MGH SS rerum Germanicarum in usum scholarum*, 60 (Hannover: Hahnsche Buchhandlung, 1935), p. 52.

40 Widukind, *Res gestae* III, c. 44, p. 124.
41 Karl Leyser, *Rule & Conflict in an Early Medieval Society* (Oxford: Blackwell, reprint 1989), p. 13.
42 For examples see Simon Coupland, 'The Carolingian army and the struggle against the Vikings', *Viator*, 35 (2004), 49–70, at 60.
43 *Synod of Pîtres and Soissons 863*, c. 1, p. 100.
44 See Nelson, 'Peers', p. 43.
45 *Annales Fuldenses, Continuatio Ratisbonensis*, a. 891, ed. by Friedrich Kurze MGH Scriptores rerum Germanicarum in usum scholarum separatim editi 7 (Hannover: Hahnsche Buchhandlung, 1891), pp. 119–21.
46 Widukind, *Res gestae Saxonicae* I, 10, p. 17.
47 Widukind, *Res gestae Saxonicae* I, 11, pp. 18–9.
48 Abbo of Saint-Germain, *Sermo adversus raptores bonorum alienorum*, p. 96.
49 Odo of Fleury, *The life of saint Gerald of Aurillac*, c. 11, trans. by Gérard Sitwell, *Saints and Saints' Lives from Late Antiquity and the Early Middle Ages*, ed. by Thomas F. X. Noble and Thomas Head (University Park: Pennsylvania State University Press, 1995), pp. 293–362, at 306. See Stuart Airlie, 'The Anxiety of Sanctity: St Gerald of Aurillac and his Maker', *The Journal of Ecclesiastical History*, 43, 3 (1992), 372–95.
50 *Synod of Savonnières* (14. June 859) c. 1 and 2, ed. by Wilfried Hartmann, MGH, Concilia 3, Die Konzilien der karolingischen Teilreiche 843–859 (Hannover: Hahnsche Buchhandlung, 1984), pp. 447–89, at pp. 458–9.
51 *Edictum Pistense* (864, Iun. 25), c. 27, ed. by Alfred Boretius and Victor Krause, *MGH Leges* 2, *Capitularia regum Francorum* 2 (Hannover: Hahnsche Buchhandlung, 1897), pp. 310–28, at 322: *Et qui ad defensionem patriae non occurrerint, secundum antiquam consuetudinem et capitulorum constitutionem iudicentur.*
52 Ermentarius, *De translationibus et miraculis sancti Filiberti II, prologus*, p. 62.
53 Abbo of Saint-Germain, *Sermo adversus raptores bonorum alienorum*, p. 98.
54 For studies on the context of geographical and political terms see Margret Lugge, '*Gallia' und 'Francia' im Mittelalter. Untersuchungen über den Zusammenhang zwischen geographisch-historischer Terminologie und politischem Denken vom 6.-15. Jahrhundert* (Bonner Historische Forschungen, 15, Bonn: Ludwig Röhrscheid Verlag, 1960); Bernd Schneidmüller, *Nomen patriae. Die Entstehung Frankreichs in der politisch-geographischen Terminologie, 10.–13.* Jahrhundert (Nationes 7, Sigmaringen: Thorbecke, 1987); Thomas Eichenberger, *Patria. Studien zur Bedeutung des Wortes im Mittelalter, 6.-12. Jahrhundert* (Nationes 9, Sigmaringen: Thorbecke, 1991).
55 Simon MacLean, *Kingship and Politics in the Late Ninth Century. Charles the Fat and the End of the Carolingian Empire* (Cambridge: Cambridge University Press, 2003), pp. 61–2.
56 See Abbo of Saint-Germain, *Sermo de fundamento et incremento christianitatis*, pp. 133–46.
57 *Radbert's Epitaphium Arsenii* II, 6–7, ed. by Ernst Dümmler, Preussische Akademie der Wissenschaften Berlin, Abhandlungen der historisch-philologischen Klasse (Berlin, 1900), pp. 18–98, at 70. For Paschasius Radbertus see Mayke de Jong, 'The Empire that was always decaying: the Carolingians (800–880)', *Medieval Worlds: Comparative & Interdisciplinary Studies*, 1, 2 (2015), 6–25.
58 Janet L. Nelson, 'Kingship and empire in the Carolingian world', in *Carolingian Culture: Emulation Culture*, ed. by Rosamond McKitterick (Cambridge: Cambridge University Press, 1995), pp. 52–87, at 67.
59 *Capitula ad Francos et Aquitanos missa de Carisiaco* (856. Iul. 7) c. 10, ed. by Alfred Boretius/ Victor Krause, MGH, Capitularia regum Francorum 2 (Hanover, 1897), pp. 279–82, at 281; *Karoli II. et Hlotharii II. Conventus apud sanctum Quintinum* (857.Mart. 1), *Tertia adnuntiatio Karoli* ed. by Alfred Boretius/Victor Krause, MGH, Capitularia regum Francorum 2 (Hanover: Hahnsche Buchhandlung, 1897), pp. 293–5, at 295.
60 Mayke de Jong, 'The state of the church: ecclesia and early medieval state formation', in *Der frühmittelalterliche Staat: Europäische Perspektiven*, ed. by Walter Pohl and Veronika Wieser (Forschungen zur Geschichte des Mittelalters 16, Wien: Verlag der Österreichischen Akademie der Wissenschaften, 2009), pp. 241–55, at 248.

220   Maximilian Diesenberger

61 John Tolan, 'Constructing Christendom', in '*The Making of Europe*'. *Essays in Honour of Robert Bartlett*, ed. by John Hudson and Sally Crumplin (Leiden: Brill, 2016), pp. 277–98, at 279–82.

62 Piroska Nagy, 'La notion de Christianitas et la spatialisation du sacré au Xe siècle: un sermon d'Abbon de Saint-Germain', *Médiévales*, 49 (2005), 121–40.

63 Abbo of Saint-Germain, *Sermo de fundamento et incremento christianitatis*, pp. 133–46, at 143: *nostra fraternitas, que est Dei civitas et Christianitas Christum habens fundamentum*. Eine Studie zu den Sermones Abbos von Saint-Germain ist in Vorbereitung.

64 Radbod of Utrecht, *Libellus de miraculo sancti Martini*, ed. by Oswald Holder-Egger, MGH Scriptores 15, 2 (Hannover: Hahnsche Buchhandlung, 1888), pp. 1239–44. Bernhard Vogel, 'Der heilige Martin von Tours und der *Libellus de miraculo sancti Martini* Bischof Radberts von Utrecht (Anfang des 10. Jahrhunderts)', in *Mirakelberichte des frühen und hohen Mittelalters*, ed. by Klaus Herbers, Lenka Jiroušková and Bernhard Vogel (Ausgewählte Quellen zur deutschen Geschichte des Mittelalters, 43, Darmstadt: Wissenschaftliche Buchgesellschaft, 2005), pp. 125–47.

65 Sharon Farmer, *Communities of Saint Martin. Legend and Ritual in Medieval Tours* (Ithaca: Cornell University Press, 1991), pp. 31–34.

66 Radbod, *Libellus de miraculo sancti Martini*, cc. 5 and 6, p. 1243.

67 Radbod, *Libellus de miraculo sancti Martini*, c. 7, pp. 1243–4.

68 Radbod, *Libellus de miraculo sancti Martini*, c. 8, p. 1244.

69 Radbod, *Libellus de miraculo sancti Martini*, c. 3, p. 1242.

70 Radbod, *Libellus de miraculo sancti Martini*, prologus, p. 1240.

71 Radbod, *Libellus de miraculo sancti Martini*, c. 8, p. 1244.

72 Radbod, *Libellus de miraculo sancti Martini*, c. 4, p. 1242.

73 Glenn W. Olsen, '"One heart, one soul" (Acts 4:32 and 34) in Dhuoda's "Manual"', *Church History*, 61 (1992), 23–33.

74 *Annales Bertiniani*, a. 839, pp. 16–7: '*Imperator autem, sanguinem communis populi fundi admodum metuens …*'; trans. Nelson, p. 41.

75 *Annales Bertiniani*, a. 841, p. 25: *Hlodowico denique propinquanti Karolus frater summo desiderio atque amore obvius venit, pariterque coniuncti, sicut fraterna caritate, ita etiam castrorum metatione, convivii etiam consilioruraque unitate, apud fratrem Hlotharium super pacis et unanimitatis, totius quoque populi et regni gubernatione, creberrimis legationibus satisagunt*; trans. Nelson, p. 50. See also Nithard, *Historiae* III, 6, ed. by Ernst Müller, MGH Scriptores rerum Germanicarum in usum scholarum seperatim editi, 44 (Hannover: Hahnsche Buchhandlung, 1907), pp. 37–8.

76 Adrevald of Fleury, *Miracula Sancti Benedicti*, c. 27, p. 91. See above p. 3.

77 Dhuoda, *Liber manualis* 3, 10, pp. 114–5.

78 *Hystoria de vita domni Iohannis Gorzie coenobii abbatis*, c. 105, 1 and 107–8, ed. Peter Christian Jacobsen, MGH Scriptores rerum Germanicarum in usum scholarum seperatim editi, 81 (Wiesbaden: Harrassowitz Verlag, 2016), pp. 394–5 and 400–3.

79 Simon MacLean, 'The Carolingian past in post-Carolingian Europe', in '*The Making of Europe*'. *Essays in Honour of Robert Bartlett*, ed. by John Hudson/Sally Crumplin (Leiden: Brill, 2016), pp. 11–31.

80 Abbo of Saint-Germain, *Sermo adversus raptores bonorum alienorum*, p. 96; Radbod of Utrecht, *Libellus de miraculo sancti Martini*, 3, p. 1242.

81 See for instance 'Zweites Synodalschreiben an Nikolaus I.', ed. by Wilfried Hartmann, *MGH, Concilia* 4, *Die Konzilien der karolingischen Teilreiche 860–874* (Hannover: Hahnsche Buchhandlung, 1998), pp. 218–21. For the events in Brittany see Julia M. H. Smith, *Province and empire: Brittany and the Carolingians* (Cambridge: Cambridge University Press, 1992), p. 161.

82 Ulmarus, *Libellus de virtutibus sancti Vedasti episcopi*, cc. 1 and 2, ed. Oswald Holder-Egger, *MGH Scriptores*, xv, 1 (Hannover: Hahnsche Buchhandlung, 1887), pp. 399–402, at 399.

83 *Annales Bertiniani*, a. 859, p. 51.

13

BISHOPS, CANON LAW, AND THE POLITICS OF BELONGING IN POST-CAROLINGIAN ITALY, C. 930–C. 960

Jelle Wassenaar[*]

Introduction

In 934, Rather, Bishop of Verona (887/890–974), rebelled against his king, Hugh of Italy (r. 924–947). Together with the local count, Milo (r. 931–955), Rather invited Duke Arnulf of Bavaria and Carinthia (r. 907–937) to invade the kingdom. The rebellion failed: Arnulf's forces lost an initial skirmish with the Italian king, upon which the Bavarians promptly retreated to their homeland, leaving Rather behind. After a short investigation, Hugh imprisoned Rather as a traitor in Pavia. That is where the now deposed bishop began to write the *Praeloquia*, a fascinating treatise that Rather is likely to have finished only after his imprisonment ended, while still living in Italy under house arrest with Azzo, the bishop of Como.[1]

The *Praeloquia* provides tantalizing glimpses of a tenth-century author self-consciously portraying himself as an individual, and above all as an outsider.[2] This 'individualist' dimension of his work has acquired most attention in modern studies of this text.[3] But in spite of the individualism apparent in Rather's justification of his rebellion against the king, the *Praeloquia* can also be seen – in places – as a markedly anti-individualistic work. Rather explicitly connected his own ordeal to the interests of the episcopacy at large: King Hugh had not only persecuted Rather, but also others 'of our *fraternitas*, of our ministry, of our rank and office'.[4] The king had thrown some bishops into prison, had sent others into exile, and had thus 'driven them from their rightful seats'.[5]

---

[*] The research for this chapter was funded by the 'After Empire: Using and Not Using the Past in the Crisis of the Carolingian World, c.900–1050' HERA project, receiving funding from the European Union's Horizon 2020 research and innovation programme under grant agreement no. 649307.

Rather suggested that the bishops had brought this oppression upon themselves by having failed to uphold age-old ideals of episcopal solidarity.[6] As fellow clergymen, bishops were supposed to help each other, 'encourage each other with mutual support', while 'having genuine love [...] of our brothers', and 'reciprocating our brother's love in turn'.[7] But in the Italian kingdom, bishops were 'divided and forsaken, each for each'.[8] Rather compared his fellow bishops to the priest and Levite in the parable of the Good Samaritan (Lk. 10.30–36): much like they had passed by the wounded victim of robbers before the arrival of the Good Samaritan, the Italian bishops had not brought any aid to their 'wounded brother'.[9] Rather presented the absence of church councils in the Italian kingdom as an important symptom of this breakdown in episcopal solidarity. He lamented that '[...] there are no councils of the Church, nowhere synods and conventions [...]'.[10] Instead '[...] everything is commanded, executed and allowed by secular might, power, and decision'.[11]

Rather's words suggest that Italian bishops had broken with tradition, and there was some truth in this. The tenth-century Italian kingdom was an anomaly in that its kings and bishops attended very few synods until the 950s, and none of these were held in the Italian *regnum* proper.[12] In West and East Francia, church councils continued to be organized regularly throughout the tenth century, albeit less frequently than before. In these two kingdoms, a strong, originally Carolingian, episcopal *esprit de corps* centred on the regnal church seems to have endured.[13] Nor can the importance of church councils in fostering a sense of solidarity among bishops be denied.[14]

Rather might well have had specific past church councils in mind when he lamented the lack of church councils and episcopal cooperation in the Italian kingdom. While still a young monk at Lobbes, Rather likely read or heard about the Council of Tribur (895), held close to his native Lotharingia.[15] Regino of Prüm described this council as a defence of episcopal authority in his *Chronicon*; the gathered bishops decreed 'against the very many laypeople who were trying to diminish episcopal authority'.[16] Rather's experience with church councils would, however, not have been unequivocally positive. In 920, a provincial synod took place in Cologne under circumstances that intimately involved Rather.[17] His then patron, Hilduin, had just been installed in the see of Liège, and had promptly switched his allegiance from the West Frankish king, Charles III, to the East Frankish ruler, Henry I. The affair ended with Hilduin's deposition in 921, forcing Rather and his patron to seek their fortunes at the court of Hugh of Italy in 926.[18] Shortly before his rebellion, while still bishop of Verona, Rather would have heard of several other church councils: Henry I and his bishops organized a major synod at Erfurt in 932, and that same year Arnulf of Bavaria, whom Rather would later invite to invade the kingdom of Italy, also organized two synods.[19]

Despite few similar displays of episcopal solidarity and cooperation in the post-Carolingian Italian kingdom, Rather's disparaging words on the collegiality of his fellow bishops should not be taken at face value. Irene van Renswoude has shown how Rather consciously presented himself as an outcast in his works, and his narrative of being abandoned by a divided Italian episcopacy might well have been designed as part of the same rhetorical strategy.[20]

Moreover, several texts written and used by other northern Italian prelates suggest that ideals of episcopal solidarity were not as absent in the Italian kingdom as implied by Rather. This chapter will discuss some of these texts in an attempt to provide a context for Rather's episcopal call to arms. It will first consider how Rather's own notions of episcopal solidarity were similar to, and partly influenced by, a then widespread and popular collection of canon law, the *Collectio Anselmo dedicata*. It will suggest that Rather's invective on the mentality of his fellow bishops in the *Praeloquia* was in part built on this collection. The next part of the essay will discuss how Rather and other tenth-century Italian bishops described the episcopacy as a unified *ordo* (social rank) with a discrete set of interests. It will argue that the reproduction, transmission, and use of canon law allowed originally Carolingian ideals of episcopal solidarity and unity to thrive in post-Carolingian northern Italy, even when church councils were absent. Finally, it will ascertain the functions and limits of episcopal solidarity, concluding that while Rather's ideas on what it meant to belong to the episcopacy competed with other ideologies of episcopal group belonging, the notion that bishops constituted an ideally united *ordo* with a shared a set of interests was eminently meaningful and politically salient in tenth-century Italy.

The *Collectio Anselmo dedicata*

The *Collectio Anselmo dedicata* is a large canon law collection comprising some 2000 canons. It was compiled in northern Italy between 882 and 896, and was one of the most widespread canon law collections to circulate in the post-Carolingian Italian kingdom in the first half of the tenth century.[21] A considerable number of the collection's canons were taken from the so-called abbreviated A2 recension of the Pseudo-Isidorian forgeries.[22] This famous ninth-century forged collection of canon law is itself well known for its defence of episcopal rights: 'Pseudo-Isidorians wanted the Frankish episcopacy to have *de facto* immunity, always and everywhere'.[23] One rubric in the A2 recension of the Pseudo-Isidorian forgeries, which was also copied in the *Collectio Anselmo dedicata,* captures this spirit best in that it states quite plainly that bishops are not to be harmed, but revered.[24]

In addition to this articulation of shared episcopal rights, the Pseudo-Isidorian forgeries also show a marked concern for the unity and solidarity of the episcopacy as a distinct *ordo*. One rubric, taken over *verbatim* in the *Collectio Anselmo dedicata*, simply but effectively stipulates 'That the *ordo episcoporum* should be one'.[25] Other canons copied in the *Collectio Anselmo dedicata* evoke obligations of solidarity among bishops: one rubric in this collection thus states that bishops should aid their oppressed brothers.[26] And much like Rather does in his *Praeloquia*, the canon itself connects episcopal solidarity to the deposition of bishops: the source of the canon is a forged letter by the first-century Pope Zephyr, in which the unjust expulsion of bishops is condemned.[27]

Besides such rubrics and canons borrowed from the Pseudo-Isidorian forgery complex, the *Collectio Anselmo dedicata* features a notably large number of excerpts from Gregory the Great's register.[28] Gregory's letters are replete with the rhetoric of episcopal *fraternitas*, which would in itself have impressed ideals of mutual support on the minds of their readers. Moreover, the compiler of the *Collectio Anselmo dedicata* appears to have inferred that some of these letters ultimately dealt with the brotherly obligations that bishops owed towards each other. One rubric, unique to this collection, states 'that one bishop should step forth as assistant to another for the defence of truth in all things'.[29] Gregory's original point was that in defending one party or the other one should always insist on justice.[30] The rubric in the *Collectio Anselmo dedicata* instead focuses on the principle that bishops should aid each other, something that Gregory might have implied, but did not articulate explicitly in his letter. Episcopal solidarity thus seems to have been something that was very much on the compiler's mind.

Rather of Verona was likely one of the many northern Italian prelates who had read the *Collectio Anselmo dedicata*. As Edward Roberts notes in an insightful study, every Pseudo-Isidorian decretal that Rather cited in his writings can also be found in the *Collectio Anselmo dedicata*.[31] Although his indebtedness to these decretals is much clearer in his later writings, Rather also slightly obliquely paraphrases parts of several such decretals in his *Praeloquia*.[32] Addressing the *ordo episcoporum* at the beginning of the fifth book, Rather paraphrased part of a forged letter attributed to Pope Alexander the First, which is also transmitted in the *Collectio Anselmo dedicata*. The letter condemns those bishops who refused to help their *fratres*, and evokes the brotherly unity of the episcopacy as an ideal: bishops who refused to help their fellows are shown to be schismatics instead of priests.[33] The rubric in the *Collectio Anselmo dedicata* evokes the same sentiment of episcopal solidarity.[34]

In his later writings Rather used this letter by Pseudo-Alexander to invoke the duty of bishops to help their peers more explicitly. In 951, Rather, now deposed from the bishopric of Verona for a second time after a short-lived return to his see in 946, wrote to Pope Agapet II (r. 946–955), seeking to give his account of his two expulsions from the bishopric of Verona. Rather complained of the lack of support he received from his 'brother bishops', and, citing the letter by Pseudo-Alexander transmitted through the *Collectio Anselmo dedicita*, argued that if any of his fellow prelates had borne him any goodwill, 'they did so out of fear of the great Pope Alexander's decretals, who said: "Any of your college who refuses help to them" – the bishops, that is, and the deprived – "will be judged a schismatic, not a priest"'.[35] Rather clearly thought this was an important point: in later writings to his fellow bishops, Rather would cite the same canon three more times, and he always did so to drive home the message that prelates ought to mutually support one another.[36]

Articulating shared interests among bishops

Equally significant as his evocation of ideals of mutual support among bishops is that Rather described the episcopacy as a discrete, ideally unified, *ordo*, whose members

Bishops, canon law, and the politics of belonging in post-Carolingian Italy **225**

shared a set of interests, a representation also found in many of the canons in the *Collectio Anselmo dedicata*. In his third book Rather asked the king if he did not

> hear it said every day that it is customary in the world for a king to speak up for a king, though they may be the worst enemies, since each looks to his own interest, and a bishop for a bishop, a cleric for a cleric […].[37]

According to Rather, bishops spoke up for bishops (just like kings do for kings) 'out of fellowship in the same rank (*ordo*)'.[38]

Rather framed his rebellion against King Hugh as standing up to royal infringements on episcopal rights, especially in regards to church property. As noted above, Rather claimed that he was not the only bishop who had suffered under Hugh. To Rather, Hugh had despised the symbols of episcopal authority ('the stole, chasuble, belt, hose, and sandals'), and would prefer 'have bishops robbed and killed than protected by them'.[39] In the fourth book of his *Praeloquia*, Rather admonished the king for being an 'open robber of the church […] who wanted to hold all the Church's property and to have the bishop as your hired hand', and a 'wolf' who would 'like to find the shepherd timid and the dog barkless'.[40] In a later chapter, Rather again picked up this theme of church robbery: the king should 'not slip from his *ministerium*', and, following the example of his predecessors, should restore God's churches. Moreover, the king should 'take care that there can never be anyone who can urge you to take something from these institutions for your own use or that of your friends'.[41] Rather claimed that it was because of exactly such unjust treatment of bishops and church property on the part of the king and his *milites* that he rebelled.[42]

In a later letter to his fellow bishops, sent in 951, Rather used a Pseudo-Isidorian decretal likely taken from the *Collectio Anselmo dedicata* to lend further authority to these sentiments. He addressed the letter to the 'most reverend fellow-bishops throughout all Italy, Gaul, and Germany', and in it demanded a council to be held to resolve whether Rather was truly the rightful bishop of Verona. Most probably citing the *Collectio Anselmo dedicata*, Rather framed his deposition as an affront to the entire *ordo episcoporum*:

> It will be your choice, not my silence, which decides whether, with Pope Callixtus and a vast crowd of bishops, his predecessors, to use his very words, "it seems best to strike with the spiritual sword the crimes of conspiracies and the dissension of a congregation against its bishop or allow it in sufferance to grow and multiply to the prejudice of our whole order".[43]

A similar conception of the episcopacy as an *ordo* with a discrete set of interests is found in the works of another tenth-century bishop who was Rather's contemporary in northern Italy: Atto of Vercelli (885–961).[44] The works of Atto not only suggest that bishops other than Rather conceived of the episcopacy as a unified *ordo* with common interests, but also that this depiction could be evoked to mobilize bishops against a perceived threat to their authority and interests.

Around 951, Atto wrote a letter to his 'beloved *confratres*', here likely referring to all the bishops of the Italian kingdom.[45] The letter referred to a request made by the king to his bishops: as the king feared a hostile invasion, he asked that 'we, meaning the bishops' provide him with hostages, to ensure their loyalty.[46] Atto pleaded with his bishops to deny the king's request – based on the fact that there are no precedents for such an action in the works of the Holy Fathers – while still asserting his enduring loyalty to those he calls 'our most glorious kings'.[47] At the end of his letter, Atto described the *ordo episcoporum* as a group whose interests could, as he implies was the case in his day and age, be at odds with the king.[48] But he left open the question of whether the king or the prelates were to blame for this sorry state of affairs:

> if that bond of faith, which was once strong among our princes and predecessors [i.e. earlier bishops], is believed to be very little preserved by us, the princes are shown to be inferior or we are shown to be more base.[49]

Although Atto did not use the Pseudo-Isidorian decretals in his letter to his fellow bishops, he did use these heavily in two other works: in his episcopal capitulary and in a treatise titled *De pressuris ecclesiasticis*. In both works he invoked Pseudo-Isidorian canons, culled largely from the *Collectio Anselmo dedicata*, in defence of the age-old rights of the episcopacy.[50] In the first book of his *De pressuris ecclesiasticis*, dedicated to the judgement of bishops (*De iudiciis episcoporum*), Atto reproduced Pseudo-Isidorian decretals (likely culled from the *Collectio Anselmo dedicata*) to stipulate that bishops are not to be lightly accused, and that priests and deacons are not to raise incitement against their bishops.[51] In his episcopal capitulary, Atto used Pseudo-Isidorian decretals in a similar fashion: one of the canons he copied from the *Collectio Anselmo dedicata* forbade priests from visiting the diocese without the permission of the prelate, and another stipulates that local clerics were barred from seeking the defence of secular power in attempts to subvert ecclesiastical discipline.[52]

Conrad Leyser has shown how canon law collections like the *Collectio Anselmo dedicata* could be read by ambitious clerics to 'imagine the Church as a career', and were used in defence of increasing episcopal mobility.[53] Rather moved sees no fewer than four times, and he used Pseudo-Isidorian decretals, most likely taken from the *Collectio Anselmo dedicata*, to defend these relocations.[54] But these canon law collections were also deployed by bishops in more local, quotidian contexts. Bishops could use the authorities transmitted in canon law collections to rebut dissenting clerics within their dioceses, who would have presented quite a common challenge to episcopal authority.[55] It has been suggested that Atto himself experienced some local opposition in his diocese.[56] Rather certainly did: his episcopal authority was undermined by rebellious clerics during his second (946) and final (962–968) tenures as bishop of Verona. In a letter to a fellow bishop explaining the conflict during his final reign as bishop, Rather listed a number of Pseudo-Isidorian canons defending episcopal authority. As the conflict between

Bishops, canon law, and the politics of belonging in post-Carolingian Italy **227**

the Veronese bishop and his clergy was sparked by Rather's attempt to reform how church property was distributed among the ranks of the clergy, most of these canons explicitly defended the bishop's exclusive control over church property. Yet Rather also wielded canons to defend the rights of bishops on a more fundamental level, noting that the canons stipulated that 'nothing should be done without the permission of the bishop'.[57]

Canon law did not only evoke the shared interests of the episcopacy, but it was also in the interest of individual prelates to reproduce and transmit canon law collections: it provided them with a set of authoritative texts that could be used in defence of challenges to their authority. This depicted shared interest would in itself have facilitated the transmission of collections like the *Collectio Anselmo dedicata*. The way these texts were transmitted may have functioned as what social scientists call a 'control economy': a set of norms that allows selfish behaviour to serve a common cause.[58] Roberts has suggested that Rather likely played an important role in the transmission of the *Collectio Anselmo dedicata* north of the Alps, and he clearly did so to defend his own transfers between bishoprics.[59] Atto also promoted the diffusion of the *Collectio Anselmo dedicata*: he donated a full copy of the collection to the chapter library of Vercelli, and some of the clergymen who read the collection in the years afterwards likely became bishops themselves.[60] Although individual bishops like Rather might ultimately have used the *Collectio Anselmo dedicata* to support their own ends, the dissemination of this text – and the ideologies contained therein – were of value to the episcopacy as a whole. Being able to draw on such collections benefitted all prelates, by providing them with authoritative decrees that could be (and, in Rather's case, demonstrably were) wielded in defence of local challenges to their authority. At the same time, the diffusion of manuscripts containing canon law collections and the enthusiastic use bishops like Rather and Atto made of these texts in their writings to other bishops furthered a collective self-awareness among their fellow prelates: they belonged to an ideally cohesive, mutually supportive, group with a discrete set of interests.

The functions and limits of episcopal solidarity

The authority and popularity enjoyed by the *Collectio Anselmo dedicata* and similar texts in tenth-century northern Italy suggests that an ideology of episcopal solidarity was thriving, even when overt displays of episcopal cooperation, such as those of the near-contemporary East Frankish and Bavarian church councils, were absent. Some of this episcopal *esprit de corps* is in fact visible in the letter collections of Rather and Atto, which show a lively inter-diocesan scholarly exchange facilitated by the language of episcopal *fraternitas*.[61] But episcopal solidarity among northern Italian prelates went further than mere scholarly cooperation, as Atto's letter to his fellow bishops regarding the king's demand for hostages has already shown.

Rather's fate in the wake of his revolt suggests this too. Although the deposed bishop himself implied otherwise, it is quite likely that he benefitted from this *esprit de corps* among the northern Italian episcopacy. In his *Praeloquia* Rather made

228 Jelle Wassenaar

several, albeit veiled, references to enjoying some support after his rebellion. First of all, he claimed that his fellow bishops 'permitted one of their own number [i.e. Rather] [...] to be strangled by anyone in their presence with their mouths damnably hardened by one of the same rank [i.e. another bishop]'.[62] This cryptic sentence suggests that some bishops wanted to come out in defence of Rather, but were restrained from doing so by another bishop.[63] Secondly, whilst in exile with Bishop Azzo in Como, Rather wrote a letter to a group of Provençal bishops who had invited him to a synod to discuss his deposition from the see in Verona.[64] In it, Rather explained that he was unable to come due to his exile, but also implied that some bishops had vouched for their brother-bishop with the Provençal prelates: he stated that 'is a thousand times less in every respect than what I am reported to be in the words of my friends'.[65]

One of these friends might well have been Azzo, with whom Rather stayed – nominally under house arrest – after having been released from King Hugh's 'persecution' and imprisonment in Pavia between 937 and 939.[66] Azzo does not seem to have been close to King Hugh, although he did briefly join Hugh's patronage network. Azzo first appeared in Hugh's charters in 937, just around the time that he became the warder of Rather as his exile under house arrest. In that year Hugh gave the church of Como as well as the local canons a very generous donation; Azzo personally acted as the intercessor.[67] The charter stresses Azzo's loyalty to the king: he is named a 'beloved *fidelis*'.[68] Azzo gained the prestigious title of *archicancellarius* in the same year.[69] Notably, Italian kings tended to give this title to potentially rebellious prelates – sometimes to bishops who had revolted in the past.[70] Azzo would hold onto the title of archchancellor for just a few years; by 940, he had lost the title again, and it is at this time Azzo also disappears completely from Hugh's charters, even though he remained in office until 947.[71]

Although the events surrounding Rather's exile and escape are murky at best, they do suggest a plausible narrative: Azzo received Rather in 937, possibly as the result of an agreement or compromise between Rather's allies and the king. Hugh then sought to ensure that the bishop of Como – at that point not yet part of his patronage network – would remain loyal to him by granting Azzo a generous donation and promoting him to the prestigious office of archchancellor. Rather fled the kingdom in 939, and, as he noted himself, was able to do so because he 'had been released even against his [the king's] wishes'.[72] He could hardly have done so without Azzo's assent, or at least acquiescence, and consequently the bishop of Como seems to have been punished for having allowed Rather to leave by promptly being banished from Hugh's patronage network again.

Rather certainly looked back fondly on his stay with Azzo, whom he called the 'venerable bishop of Como' in a later letter recounting his exile to the monks of Lobbes.[73] He also enjoyed the freedom to write his *Praeloquia*, and was allowed to use the cathedral library.[74] Ideals of episcopal solidarity transmitted through canon law would have informed Azzo's attitude to Rather's stay in Como: in hosting his brother-bishop, Azzo was, consciously or not, following a precept transmitted in the *Collectio Anselmo dedicata* and a substantial number of other canon law collections,

Bishops, canon law, and the politics of belonging in post-Carolingian Italy **229**

according to which persecuted bishops who were expelled from their sees should be hosted by their fellow bishops.[75]

Rather thus likely benefitted from a kind of episcopal *esprit de corps* among northern Italian prelates in the wake of his revolt, yet his narrative, pieced together from the *Praeloquia* and his letters, suggests that he thought his fellow bishops had not gone far enough. One reason for what Rather portrayed as a lack of support for a fellow prelate could be that some Italian bishops had very different ideas about what it meant to belong to the episcopacy. Such a different ideology of group belonging is visible in Atto of Vercelli's reaction to the case of another rebellious bishop: Waldo of Como, who was installed in the late 940s by Berengar II.[76] Berengar was Hugh's rival to the Italian throne, who would later expel Hugh from the Italian kingdom and hold the Italian throne for himself between 950 and 961, after which the East Frankish King Otto I took over the kingdom.[77] Although Waldo was installed by Berengar II, he rebelled against his king, likely during Liudulf of Swabia's incursion into Italy in 956. Right after Waldo had rebelled, Atto wrote a letter to his fellow prelate urging him to cease his rebellion and reaffirm his loyalty to the king.[78]

Atto connected the episcopacy closely to royal power, and stated that it is the duty of the *ecclesia* to serve the kings – a sentiment he repeated consistently in many of his other writings.[79] By rebelling, Waldo had not only abandoned his king but also his 'benevolent brothers (*confratribus*)'.[80] Waldo should 'be mindful of royal dignity, and be mindful of your rank (*ordo*)'.[81] Citing a long excerpt from the acts of the Third Council of Toledo, Atto asserted that those belonging to the ecclesiastical orders (*ecclesiastici ordinis*) ought to support the 'strength of kings and the stability of kingdoms'.[82] One Toledan decree tying episcopacy to the *regnum* cited by Atto can also be found in the *Collectio Anselmo dedicata*, and seems to have been explicitly aimed at potentially rebellious bishops on the borders of a kingdom: it forbids priests on the boundaries with the enemy from exchanging messages with a foreign *gens* without the permission of the king.[83] Finally, Atto used the example of the Old Testament People of God to warn Waldo of the dangers of rebellion: whenever they had opposed their kings 'they were completely oppressed by the pagans, and therefore trampled upon by the neighboring *gentes*'.[84]

To Atto, the unity of the *regnum* had to be defended at all costs, and this superseded concepts of episcopal solidarity. This sentiment is also apparent in his other writings. Atto wrote an obscure political treatise which he entitled *Polipticum*, addressed to an anonymous fellow bishop. As Giacomo Vignodelli argues in an insightful article, this unidentified bishop might well have been Rather, as Atto seems to allude to Rather's imprisonment.[85] He would certainly have known of Rather's difficulties, as Atto of Vercelli was demonstrably in contact with Azzo of Como, Rather's host during his exile.[86] In his treatise, Atto developed a conception of the *regnum* that can rightly be called 'transpersonal': the *regnum* is the *patria*, and its division must be avoided. Inviting a foreigner to take over the throne would always threaten to divide the *regnum*, and only those kings who avoided factionalism among the *populus* would acquire the blessing of the *patria*.[87]

Rather was more ambivalent about the relationship between royal power and the *ordo episcoporum* in his *Praeloquia*, and seems to have been much more concerned about the unity of the episcopacy than about that of the kingdom. Asking his fellow prelates to stand up in defence of their fellow prelate, Rather bluntly admonished them not 'to pander to the enemy', and urged them not to be afraid of offending their 'lord'.[88] Where Atto had warned his fellow bishops of the dangers posed by foreign *gentes* to the unity of the kingdom, Rather instead modelled the Italian episcopacy after the persecuted people of God: '[…] we bishops have been touched, scorned, driven, routed; the structure which seemed to stand on our foundation has fallen. "Other lords have possessed us without you" (Is. 26.13); "we have become a taunt to our neighbours, mocked and derided by those around us" (Ps. 78.4)'.[89] In his later writings, Rather's conception of the episcopacy also seems much less tied to a *regnum* than it appears to be in Atto's works. When asking his fellow prelates to convene a synod, he did not write to the prelates of the Italian kingdom, but instead addressed his letter to 'to the lord fathers and most reverend fellow-bishops throughout all Italy, Gaul, and Germany established in the Lord', borrowing from an earlier transregnal Carolingian vocabulary.[90] Rather's idea of the episcopacy was thus altogether much more free-standing than Atto's.

As Atto's letter to Waldo shows, authoritative texts like the *Collectio Anselmo dedicata* and the rhetoric of episcopal fraternity could be used to promote an ideology of episcopal group belonging that was strongly at odds with Rather's more idiosyncratic vision of the episcopacy. But one wonders whether Rather's contemporaries thought his rebellion had much to do with defending the *ecclesia* and the shared interests of the episcopacy in the first place. Rather rebelled alongside the local count and clergy, which suggests that the dissent that sparked the rebellion was of a more local nature than Rather wanted his readers to believe. Nor do the rebels seem to have acquired any support from other magnates within the kingdom. And although Liudprand of Cremona was sympathetic to Rather's cause, his later version of Rather's rebellion in his *Antapodosis* makes no mention of episcopal interests at all, simply stating matter-of-factly that the bishop had invited Arnulf together with the count to revolt against Hugh.[91] Yet Liudprand did, as we will see[92], depict other instances of the oppression of bishops by Italian kings, and connected rebellions by prelates other than Rather to episcopal interests.

Episcopal interests and polemics

Whatever the actual context of his revolt, Rather might have wanted to frame his rebellion as a near-heroic defence of episcopal rights because this would appeal to the sensibilities of his northern Italian brother-bishops, fellow readers of texts like the *Collectio Anselmo dedicata*. It is unclear how well known the *Praeloquia* was among the prelates of the Italian kingdom, but Rather's deposition was clearly a hotly-debated issue in his own day, as suggested by the Provençal bishops who invited Rather to a synod: they had heard of his deposition and thought it was also of interest to them.

Rather likely sent them that part of his *Praeloquia* which deals with the lack of church councils and episcopal solidarity.[93] Rather finished his *Praeloquia* inside the kingdom of Italy, while being hosted by the bishop of Como. Moreover, Vignodelli has persuasively argued that Atto of Vercelli entered into a kind of 'dialogue' with Rather.[94] In his *Polipticum*, Atto seems to reply to Rather's *Praeloquia*, and in his *De pressuris ecclesiasticis* Atto appears to allude to Rather's deposition.[95] This suggests that the message of Rather's *Praeloquia* was known to some northern Italian prelates in the years following Rather's exile, and that these bishops formed part of the initial intended audience of Rather's invective against King Hugh.

What would they have made of Rather's notion that all Italian prelates were subject to a bishop-oppressing king? After all, Rather claims that not only he, but the entire Italian episcopacy, was oppressed by King Hugh. When taken at face value these words could today be read as circumstantial evidence to support an older, but still at times repeated, scholarly tradition, according to which King Hugh's eventual demise was ultimately due to him pursuing 'anti-episcopal' policies that antagonized his bishops. According to this scholarly narrative, Berengar I, King Hugh's predecessor, was an ardent promoter of episcopal interests and actively increased their powers. The two kings who held the Italian throne after Berengar I, Hugh and Berengar II, were supposedly much less supportive of bishops, which ultimately led to their demise at the hands of rebellious prelates who shifted their support to other lords. According to one more recent reading in this vein, these kings' lack of enthusiasm in promoting episcopal interests ultimately convinced the Italian bishops to support Otto I, the East Frankish ruler who would defeat Berengar II in 962 and take over the Italian throne.[96]

As several studies have shown, such reductive dichotomies – placing pro-episcopal kings against anti-episcopal ones – are much too simplistic.[97] Yet the notion of Hugh as an 'anti-episcopal king' is not necessarily anachronistic, in that Rather himself contrasted Hugh's 'anti-episcopal' policies with the purportedly more 'pro-episcopal' ones of rival rulers. In his *Praeloquia* Rather wrote that his denunciation of King Hugh as an oppressor of bishops was not applicable to 'those who now energetically govern the north in four divisions', which most likely refers to the dukes of Bavaria, Swabia, Franconia, and Saxony. Unlike Hugh, so claimed Rather, these were 'Christian rulers', not tyrants. And even if they threatened to rule in the same way that Hugh did, their bishops would restrain them.[98] In his 951 letter to Pope Agapet II, Rather portrayed Otto I's first invasion of the Italian kingdom as intimately connected to the abuses of canon law by Italian kings:

> I believe that you, Father, neither wished nor dared to give anyone the license of doing anything against canon law, and that he [Otto I] wanted the kingdom of Italy for no other pressing purpose than by imperial power to force the kingdom that had been wracked by many instances of wrongdoing of this kind and other injustices into the justice of Christian law.[99]

232 Jelle Wassenaar

Such partisan statements tell us little about the nature of these kings' policies towards their bishops, but they do show that tenth-century prelates could convince themselves, and likely at least some of their fellows as well, that the behaviour of a given king was detrimental to the interests of their *ordo* as a whole. This suggests that while ideals of episcopal solidarity among northern Italian bishops did not allow for the shows of episcopal cooperation visible at church councils in nearby East Francia and Bavaria, appealing to the episcopacy as an *ordo* could play an important role in polemics aimed at rulers.

Conclusion

In the five years following his escape from the kingdom of Italy, Rather travelled to the Provençe, Reims, and Lobbes, and sent his *Praeloquia* to Bruno (the younger brother of Otto I, Rather's patron, and soon-to-be archbishop of Cologne), Rotbert of Trier, and Flodoard of Reims.[100] His movements and letters at this time reveal what Timothy Reuter has called 'a network of dioceses across Europe which was more homogenous than the kingdoms or counties that at least in name were also to be found across Europe'.[101] By the middle of the 940s, bishops and clerics in Vienne, Reims, Trier, and Lobbes had heard of Hugh's vile deeds against their 'brother-bishop'. Moreover, they liked what they had read: according to Folcuin, around the year 950 Rather 'was considered the first among the philosophers of the [i.e. Bruno's] palace'.[102]

One of the *Praeloquia*'s readers was Liudprand of Cremona, who would go on to write his own invective against another Italian king, Berengar II, in the 950s. Liudprand praised it as a work 'written with great elegance and refinement'.[103] Liudprand had his own reasons for targeting an Italian king with a polemic. Like Rather, he had been exiled from the kingdom, albeit not by Hugh but because of a conflict between his family and Berengar II.[104] Like Rather, Liudprand found refuge at Otto I's court, and his *Antapodosis* was at least in part written in support of his patron's claim to the Italian throne.[105]

Much recent research has shown how Liudprand effectively attempted to undermine the legitimacy of Berengar II and other Italian kings by shaming them 'with accusations of sexual promiscuity and deviance'.[106] Liudprand similarly attacked the legitimacy of Italian kings by portraying them as veritable oppressors of episcopal rights and violators of canon law in his *Antapodosis*. He claimed that the rebellion against Berengar I, which eventually allowed Rather's nemesis Hugh to take the throne, was ultimately sparked by the king's oppression of a single prelate's episcopal rights (although the revolt itself also involved a group of secular magnates): 'The reason for their rebellion was this. While Lambert, once his predecessor had died, was supposed to be ordained archbishop of the Milanese, King Berengar demanded no small sum from him, against the rules of the holy fathers'.[107] After Rather's revolt, King Hugh, 'against justice and law', commended 'the Veronese, Tridentine, and Mantuan churches' to Archbishop Manasses of Arles.[108] Berengar II, finally, had deprived Bishop Joseph of Brescia from his see 'with no council being held, no decision by the bishops'.[109]

Bishops, canon law, and the politics of belonging in post-Carolingian Italy **233**

It has recently been argued that Liudprand's and Rather's narratives of Hugh's family as sexually suspect 'intervened in contemporary politics not simply as records of Hugh's inadequacies but as real political actors that helped to make that failure happen'.[110] The great currency enjoyed by canon law collections defending the rights of the episcopacy suggests that their texts were also aimed specifically at a shared awareness among northern Italian prelates of their common rights as bishops. Liudprand's and Rather's portrayals of Italian kings as anti-episcopal tyrants might in this way have played a more significant role in Hugh's and Berengar II's expulsions from Italy than the anti-episcopal policies that modern historians have tried to read into their diplomas.

Notes

1 Liudprand, *Antapodosis*, III, cc. 49–52, ed. Paolo Squatriti, *Corpus Christianorum Continuatio Mediaevalis* CLVI (Turnhout: Brepols, 1998), p. 94, trans. Paolo Squatriti, *The Complete Works of Liudprand of Cremona* (Washington, DC: The Catholic University of America Press), pp. 137–38. For an introduction to Rather's life and works, see *The Complete Works of Rather of Verona*, trans. Peter L. D. Reid (Medieval and Renaissance texts and studies, 76, Binghamton, NY: Center for Medieval and early Renaissance studies, 1991), pp. 4–16. I would like to thank Max Diesenberger, Alice Hicklin, Simon MacLean, Edward Roberts, Giacomo Vignodelli, and the participants at the 2018 Leeds IMC After Empire session for their helpful comments on an earlier version of this paper. The views expressed remain, of course, my own.

2 Irene van Renswoude, 'The Sincerity of Fiction. Rather and the Quest for Self-Knowledge', in *Ego Trouble: Authors and Their Identities in the Early Middle Ages*, in *Forschungen zur Geschichte des Mittelalters*, 15, ed. R. Corradini *et al.* (Vienna: Verlag der Österreichischen Akademie der Wissenschaften, 2010), pp. 227–42.

3 Georg Misch, *Geschichte der Autobiographie*, vol. 2.1: *Das Mittelalter – Die Frühzeit* (Bern/ Frankfurt am Main: Francke/Schulte-Bulmke, 1955), p. 520; Aaron Y. Gurevich, *Das Individuum im europäischen Mittelalter* (Munich: C. H. Beck, 1994), p. 146.

4 Rather of Verona, *Praeloquia*, III, c. 20, ed. Peter L. D. Reid, *Corpus Christianorum Continuatio Medievalis* XLVI A (Turnhout: Brepols, 1984), p. 93, trans. Reid, *Complete Works*, p. 109.

5 Rather, *Praeloquia*, III, c. 20, ed. Reid, *CCCM* XLVI A, p. 93, trans. Reid, *Complete Works*, p. 109.

6 See the contribution by Maximilian Diesenberger in this volume for a more wide-ranging and theoretical application of the concept of 'solidarity' to tenth-century ideologies and groups.

7 '[…] *exhortando mutuo nos exhortantes, commoda pro necessitate alterutrum in simplicitate tribuentes, prelaturam in sollicitudine amministrantes, in hilaritate nobis invicem miserantes, dilectionem Dei et fraternam sine simulatione habentes, odientes malum, adherentes bono, karitatem fraternitatis invicem custodientes* […]': Rather, *Praeloquia*, V, c. 17, ed. Reid, *CCCM* XLVI A, p. 155, trans. Reid, *Complete Works*, p. 169.

8 '*Nunc vero, ut (proh nefas!) in nobis illud compleatur propheticum dicentis: Unusquisque carnem brachii sui vorabit, Manasses Ephraim et Ephraim Manassen, simul ipse contra Iudam, hoc est confessione Dei insignem Ecclesiam, ab invicem mordentes, ab invicem consummimur divisique ab alterutro desolamur*': Rather, *Praeloquia*, V, c. 17, ed. Reid, *CCCM* XLVI A, p. 156, trans. Reid, *Complete Works*, p. 169.

9 '*Verum ut iam ad inceptum redeam: preterit sacerdos et levita, non se intellegentes eadem descendere via, nec ulla fratri vulnerato conferunt remedia*': Rather, *Praeloquia*, III, c. 30, ed. Reid, *CCCM* XLVI A, p. 103, trans. Reid, *Complete Works*, pp. 118–9.

234   Jelle Wassenaar

10 '*Concilia dehinc Ecclesiae nusquam, conventus synodici non alicubi* [...]': Rather, Praeloquia, V, c. 13, ed. Reid, *CCCM* XLVI A, p. 152, trans. Reid, *Complete Works*, p. 166.

11 '[...] *nil ecclesiastica lege aut approbatur aut inprobatur, accusatur vel excusatur, defenditur aut opponitur, sed omnia vi, potestate et iudicio seculari imperantur, perficiuntur et tolerantur* [...]'; Rather, *Praeloquia*,V, c. 13, ed. Reid, *CCCM* XLVI A, p. 152, trans. Reid, *Complete Works*, p. 166.

12 Pope Benedict IV (r. 900–903) called a synod in 900, inviting the archbishops, kings, dukes, counts and Christians from Gaul to discuss the deposition of Bishop Argrim of Langres in Rome: Wilfried Hartmann, *Die Synoden der Karolingerzeit im Frankenreich und in Italien* (Paderborn: Schöningh, 1989), p. 395; in early 901 Pope Benedict IV organized a synod at which both northern Italian and Tuscan bishops discussed a conflict between the Bishop of Lucca and an inhabitant of the same city (ruling in the bishop's favour): Hartmann, *Die Synoden* p. 395; Pope Sergius III (r. 904–911) organized a synod discussing the infamous trial of Formosus in 904, although no acts have survived: Hartmann, *Die Synoden*, p. 396; In 921 Pope John X (r. 914–928) convened a synod to discuss the conflict between Hilduin and Richer over the see of Liège; no northern Italian bishops seem to have taken part: on this see Harald Zimmermann, 'Der Streit um das Lütticher Bistum vom Jahre 920/921', *Mitteilungen des Instituts für Österreichische Geschichtsforschung*, 65.1–2 (1957), 30–5; in 949 the Pope confirmed the decrees of the 948 Ingelheim synod, and here some northern Italian bishops do seem to have taken part, but no acts survive: Ernst-Dieter Hehl, *Die Konzilien Deutschlands und Reichsitaliens 916–1001*, vol. 1: *916–960* (Hannover: Hahn, 1987), pp. 171–2.

13 Janet L. Nelson, 'Rulers and Government', in *The New Cambridge Medieval History*, vol. 3: *c. 900–c.1024*, ed. by Timothy Reuter (Cambridge: Cambridge University Press, 1999), pp. 95–129 (p. 122); on the West-Frankish synods see Isolder Schröder, *Die westfränkischen Synoden von 888 bis 987 und ihre Überlieferung. MGH Hilfsmittel* 3 (Munich: Monumenta Germaniae Historica, 1980); on the East Frankish and Italian synods see Heinz Wolter, *Die Synoden im Reichsgebiet und in Reichsitalien von 916 bis 1056* (Paderborn: Schöningh, 1988) and Ernst-Dieter Hehl, 'Die Synoden des ostfränkisch-deutschen und des westfränkischen Reichs im 10. Jahrhundert: Karolingische Traditionen und Neuansätze', in *Recht und Gericht in Kirche und Welt um 900*, ed. Wilfried Hartmann (Berlin/Boston/Oldenbourg: De Gruyter, 2007), pp. 125–50.

14 On church councils and episcopal solidarity see Janet L. Nelson, 'National Synods, Kingship as Office, and Royal Anointing: an Early Medieval Syndrome', *Studies in Church History*, 7 (1971), 41–59; *ead.*, 'Charlemagne and the Bishops', in *Religious Franks: Religion and Power in the Frankish Kingdoms – Studies in Honour of Mayke de Jong*, ed. Rob M. J. Meens *et al.* (Manchester: Manchester University Press, 2017), pp. 350–69; Timothy Reuter, 'Debating the "Feudal Revolution"', in *Medieval Polities and Modern Mentalities*, ed. Janet L. Nelson (Cambridge: Cambridge University Press, 2010), pp. 72–88 (pp. 79–80).

15 On which see Christopher J. Carroll, 'The Last Great Carolingian Church Council: The Tribur Synod of 895', *Annuarium Historiae Conciliorum*, 33 (2001), 9–25.

16 '[...] *contra plerosque seculares, qui auctoritatem episcopalem inminuere temptabant*': Regino of Prüm, *Chronicon, s.a.* 895, ed. Friedrich Kurze, *MGH Scriptores rerum Germanicarum* 50 (Hannover: Hahn, 1890), p. 143, trans. Simon MacLean, *History and Politics in Late Carolingian and Ottonian Europe. The Chronicle of Regino of Prüm and Adalbert of Magdeburg* (Manchester/New York: Manchester University Press, 2009), p. 218.

17 On this synod see Wolter, *Die Synoden*, pp. 21–2.

18 Zimmermann, 'Der Streit um das Lütticher Bistum', esp. pp. 35–6.

19 On the synod of Erfurt see Wolter, *Die Synoden*, pp. 30–4; for the two synods organized by Arnulf in 932, held in Dingolfing and Regensburg, *ibid.*, pp. 35–8.

20 Renswoude, 'Sincerity of Fiction', esp. pp. 230–1.

21 Klaus Zechiel-Eckes, 'Quellenkritische Anmerkungen zur "Collectio Anselmo dedicata"', in *Recht und Gericht in Kirche und Welt um 900. Schriften des Historischen Kollegs* 69, ed. Wilfried Hartmann and Annette Grabowsky (Munich: Oldenbourg, 2007), pp. 49–65

Bishops, canon law, and the politics of belonging in post-Carolingian Italy **235**

(p. 64); on the diffusion of the *Collectio Anselmo dedicata* see Irene Scaravelli, 'La collezione canonica Anselmo dedicata: lo status quaestionis nella prospettiva di un'edizione critica', in *Le storie e la memorie. In onore di Arnold Esch*, ed. Roberto Delle Donne and Andrea Zorzi (Florence: Firenze University Press), pp. 33–52.

22 Zechiel-Eckes, 'Quellenkritische Anmerkungen', p. 59. See also Horst Fuhrmann, *Einfluss und Verbreitung der pseudoisidorischen Fälschungen: von ihrem Auftauchen bis in die neuere Zeit. MGH Schriften* 24, vol. 2 (Stuttgart: Anton Hiersemann, 1973), p. 430.

23 Eric Knibbs, 'Ebo of Reims, Pseudo-Isidore, and the Date of the False Decretals', *Speculum,* 92 (2017), 144–83 (p. 155).

24 The *Collectio Anselmo dedicata* has not yet been edited in full, but its rubrics can be found in the *Clavis Canonum* database [www.mgh.de/ext/clavis/(consulted 12/10/2018)]; *Collectio Anselmo Dedicata* (henceforth *CAD*) 2.124; Ps.-Alexander I, JK †25, ed. Paul Hinschius, *Decretales pseudo-Isidorianae* (Leipzig: Scientia Verlag, 1863), pp. 102–3.

25 *CAD* 2.131: '*Quod unus sit ordo episcoporum*'; the compiler of the *Collectio Anselmo dedicata* seems to have reduced a rubric to a letter by Ps.-Anacletus in the A2 recension of the Pseudo-Isidorian decretals to that core message: '*De ordinatione eipscoporum. Quod unus sit ordo episcoporum. Item de primatibus et patriarchis, de archiepiscopis et metropolitanis*', Ps.-Anacletus, JK †4, ed. Hinschius, *Decretales*, p. 82.

26 *CAD* 2.127: '*Ut episcopi oppressis fratribus vicissim succurrant in recta fide et bona voluntate*', Ps.-Zephyrinus, JK †81, ed. Hinschius, *Decretales*, p. 134.

27 *Ibid.*

28 On the use of Gregory's letters in tenth-century collections see the stimulating article by Conrad Leyser, 'The Memory of Gregory the Great and the Making of Latin Europe, 600-1000', in *Making Early Medieval Societies: Conflict and Belonging in the Latin West, 300–1200*, ed. Kate Cooper and Conrad Leyser (Cambridge: Cambridge University Press, 2016), pp. 181–201, esp. p. 199.

29 '*Ut unus episcopus alteri pro veritate defendenda in omnibus adiutor existat*': *CAD* 2.245.

30 Gregory the Great, *Registrum, Lib.* VIII, *Ep.* 15, ed. Dag Norberg, *Corpus Christianorum Series Latina* CXL A (Turnhout: Brepols, 1982), p. 534: '*Nulla ergo vos res ab aequitatis studio, nulla suspendat potentia personarum, sed innitens praeceptis dominicis onia quae sunt rectitudinis adversa contemne. In defendendas partes iustitiae constanter insiste*'.

31 Edward Roberts, 'Bishops on the Move: Rather of Verona, Pseudo-Isidore, and Episcopal Translation', in *Bishops in the Long Tenth Century. Episcopal Authorities in France and Lotharingia, c. 900–c. 1050. Special Issue of The Medieval Low Countries*, ed. Brigitte Meijns and Steven Vanderputten (In print; Turnhout: Brepols, 2019), who also provides a comprehensive overview of Rather's use of Pseudo-Isidorian decretals. I am grateful to the author for having allowed me to consult this article before publication.

32 Roberts, 'Bishops on the Move'.

33 Rather, *Praeloquia,* V, c. 7, ed. Reid, *CCCM* XLVI A, p. 148; Ps.-Alexander I, JK †25, ed. Hinschius, *Decretales*, pp. 102–3: '*Qui autem ex vestro collegio fuerit et ab auxilio vestro se subtraxerit, magis scismaticus quam sacerdos esse probabitur. Ecce, inquit propheta, quam bonum et quam iocundum habitare fratres in unum*'.

34 *CAD* 2.120: '*De episcopis qui sunt inter se discordes et canino dente se derodere conantur et de his qui se a collegio episcoporum et ab auxilio subtrahunt*'.

35 Rather of Verona, *Letter to Pope Agapet II*, c. 2, ed. Fritz Weigle, *Die Briefe des Bischofs Rather von Verona. MGH Briefe* 1 (Weimar: Hermann Böhlaus Nachfolger, 1949), pp. 33–43 (p. 34), trans. Reid, *Complete Works*, p. 224.

36 Rather of Verona, *Letter to Bishops of Italy, Gaul, and Germany*, c. 1, ed. Weigle, *Die Briefe*, p. 45, trans. Reid, *Complete Works*, p. 230; Rather of Verona, *Phrenesis*, c. 12, ed. Reid, *CCCM* XLVI A, pp. 207–8, trans. Reid, *Complete Works*, pp. 253–4; Rather, *Letter to Milo*, trans. Reid, *Complete Works*, p. 426, ed. Weigle, *Die Briefe*, p. 124.

37 Rather, *Praeloquia,* III, c. 21, ed. Reid, *CCCM* XLVI A, p. 94, trans. Reid, *Complete Works*, p. 110: '*Nonne audis cotidie istud et hoc usitari in seculo, regem pro rege, licet sint inimicissimi, dum unusquisque videlicet prospicit sibi, sepissime loqui, episcopum pro episcopo […]*'.

236   Jelle Wassenaar

38 *Ibid.*: '*Si ergo nos invicem sic pro participio iuvamus ordinis, in quibus est maxima imperfectio caritatis* […]'.

39 Rather, *Praeloquia*, IV, c. 12, ed. Reid, *CCCM* XLVI A, p. 116, trans. Reid, *Complete Works*, p. 131: '*Quae etiam tibi ne tuo iudicio obvenerint, non nihil timeo, dum tam vilipendi a te considero, ut magis predari et occidi quam his optes defendi*'; on Rather's notions of good kingship see Megan Welton's contribution in this volume.

40 Rather, *Praeloquia, IV*, c. 20, ed. Reid, *CCCM* XLVI A, p. 124, trans. Reid, *Complete Works*, p. 139: '*Lupus enim cum sis ipse, pastorem timidum canemque mutum velles invenire. Et cum Ecclesiae sis publicus predo, contradictorem inveniri velles nullum*'.

41 Rather, *Praeloquia IV*, c. 34, ed. Reid, *CCCM* XLVI A, p. 140, trans. Reid, *Complete Works*, p. 154: '*Cave ne unquam aliquis existat, qui possit suadere, ut aliquid ex his aut ad tuos aut ad tuorum auferas usus*'.

42 Rather, *Praeloquia IV*, c. 20, ed. p. 124, trans. p. 139.

43 Rather, *Letter to Bishops of Italy, Gaul, and Germany*, c. 1, ed. Weigle, *Die Briefe*, p. 44, trans. Reid, *Complete Works*, p. 230; Ps.-Calixtus I, JK †86, ed. Hinschius, *Decretales*, p. 138.

44 For an introduction to Atto of Vercelli's life and works see Suzanne F. Wemple, *Atto of Vercelli. Church, State, and Christian Society in Tenth-Century Italy* (Rome: Edizioni di Storia e Letteratura, 1979).

45 Atto of Vercelli, *Letter to His Beloved Brethren*, ed. and trans. George A. Willhauck, 'The Letters of Atto, Bishop of Vercelli: Text, Translation, and Commentary' (unpublished doctoral thesis, Tufts University, 1984), pp. 132–49 (p. 132). On the date of the letter see now Germana Gandino, *Contemplare l'ordine. Intellettuali e potenti dell'alto Medioevo. Biblioteca Nuovo Medioevo* 73 (Naples: Liguori, 2004), pp. 88–9.

46 Atto, *Letter to His Beloved Brethren*, ed. Willhauck, 'The Letters', p. 132, trans. *ibid.*, 142: '*Novit Karitas vestra, quia nostri principes et domini, gloriosissimi scilicet reges, dum hostilem se dicunt suspicari impetum, nostra, scilicet episcoporum contra haec quaerunt suffragia*'.

47 'Kings' is here in the plural because Berengar II ruled together with his son Adalbert: Gandino, *Contemplare l'ordine*, p. 88

48 Atto, *Letter to His Beloved Brethren*, ed. Willhauck, 'The Letters', p. 140, trans. *ibid.,* p. 149: '*Etsi fragilitatis causa aut ipsi in nobis aut nos contra illos aliquid iniquum commisimus, sic eius clementia deleatur ut nulla iam in posterum ultio exinde preparetur*'.

49 Atto, *Letter to His Beloved Brethren*, ed. Willhauck, 'The Letters', p. 139, trans. *ibid.,* p. 149: '*Unum tamen scio procul dubio, quod ubique dicetur quia, si illud fidei vinculum, quod olim inter principes nostrosque valuit predecessores, minime apud nos servari creditur, aut principes deteriores aut nos nequiores esse probamur*'.

50 On Atto's use of the *Collectio Anselmo dedicata* see Suzanne F. Wemple, 'The Canonical Resources of Atto of Vercelli', *Traditio*, 26 (1970), 335–50.

51 Atto of Vercelli, *De pressuris ecclesiasticis libellus*, ed. Joachim Bauer, 'Die Schrift "*De pressuris ecclesiasticis*" des Bischofs Atto von Vercelli' (unpublished doctoral thesis, Eberhard Karls Universität Tübingen, 1975), pp. 56–7: '*Episcopos non leviter accusandos sanctorum statuta patrum pleniter interdicunt. Nec aliquem ad eorum accusationem sancti canones admittunt, nisi qui vita et moribus fideli examinatione dignis sacerdotibus quoequandus inveniatur*' (Ps.-Lucius, JK †246, ed. Hinschius, *Decretales*, p. 175, *CAD* 2.82); '*Beatissimus etiam Silvester summus pontifex et universalis apostolus collecta synodo in sancta et venerabili Romana ecclesia per omnia interdixit, et ut presbiter non adversus episcopum, non diaconus adversus presbiterum* […] *det accusationem aliquam, et non dampnetur praesul*' (Ps.-Silvester, JK †*Synodus (secunda) episcoporum* 284, ed. Hinschius, *Decretales*, p. 449, *CAD* 3.96 and 3.141).

52 Atto of Vercelli, *Capitulare*, c. 35, ed. Rudolf Pokorny, *MGH Capitula episcoporum* 3 (Hannover: Hahnsche Buchandlung, 1995), pp. 277–78: '*Ut nullus presbiter absque permissu episcopi aliquid in eius parroechia agat*' (*CAD* 4.41); c. 51, ed. Pokorny, *Capitula episcoporum* 3: '*Ut clerici secularem defensionem adversus ecclesiasticam disciplinam non requirant*' (*CAD* 5.109).

53 Leyser, 'Memory of Gregory the Great', p. 193; *id.*, 'Episcopal Office in the Italy of Liudprand of Cremona, c. 890–c. 970', *The English Historical Review*, 125.515 (2010), 795–817.

Bishops, canon law, and the politics of belonging in post-Carolingian Italy **237**

54 Roberts, 'Bishops on the Move'.
55 On episcopal justice in tenth-century Italy see Sarah Hamilton, 'Inquiring into Adultery and Other Wicked Deeds: Episcopal Justice in Tenth- and Early Eleventh-Century Italy', *Viator*, 41.2 (2010), 21–43, and pp. 31–3 in the same article for a discussion of Rather's conflicts with the local clergy.
56 Rob M. J. Meens, 'In the Mirror of Eusebius. The Episcopal Identity of Atto of Vercelli', in *Ego Trouble: Authors and Their Identities in the Early Middle Ages. Forschungen zur Geschichte des Mittelalters*, 15, ed. R. Corradini *et al.* (Vienna: Verlag der Österreichischen Akademie der Wissenschaften, 2010), pp. 243–48 (p. 248).
57 Rather, *Letter to Bishop Hubert of Parma*, ed. Weigle, *Briefe*, p. 73, trans. Reid, *Complete Works*, p. 354; Ps.-Clemens, *JK* †12, ed. Hinschius, *Decretales*, p. 57.
58 Helmut Thome, 'Solidarity: Theoretical Perspectives for Empirical Research', in *Solidarity. Philosophical studies in contemporary culture*, 5, ed. Kurt Bayertz (Dordrecht: Springer, 1999), pp. 101–31 (p. 113); Walter Pohl, 'Staat und Herrschaft im Frühmittelalter: Überlegungen zum Forschungsstand', in *Staat im frühen Mittelalter. Forschungen zur Geschichte des Mittelalters* 11, ed. Stuart Airlie, Walter Pohl, and Helmut Reimitz (Vienna: Verlag der Österreichischen Akademie der Wissenschaften, 2006), pp. 9–38 (p. 25).
59 Roberts, 'Bishops on the Move'.
60 I am indebted to Giacomo Vignodelli for suggesting this and making me aware of Atto's donation; Pokorny, *Capitulare*, p. 253; the manuscript is Vercelli, Biblioteca Capitolare, MS XV.
61 Rather: *Letter to Priest Patricus*, ed. Weigle, *Die Briefe*, pp. 66–9; *Letter to Hubert of Parma*, ed. Weigle, *Die Briefe*, pp. 71–106; *Letter to Bishop Odalrich of Bergamo*, ed. Weigle, *Die Briefe*, pp. 109–11; *Letter to Bishop Martin III of Ferrara*, ed. Weigle, *Die Briefe*, pp. 155–6. Atto: *Letter to Bishop Azzo of Como*, ed. Willhauck, 'The Letters', pp. 38–51; letters sent to Atto from other dioceses: Gunzo of Novara, *Letter to Atto*, ed. Willhauck, 'The Letters', pp. 69–71. For a discussion of scholarly exchange and learned culture in tenth-century Italy see the contribution by Giorgia Vocino in this volume.
62 Rather, *Praeloquia* IV, c. 22, ed. Reid, *CCCM* XLVI A, pp. 127–8, trans. Reid, *Complete Works*, pp. 141–2.
63 The bishop who had silenced Rather was likely his former patron, Hilduin of Milan: Reid, *Complete Works*, p. 5.
64 For a discussion of Rather's representation of his experience of exile see Barbara Schlieben, 'In Exilio. Innen-, Außen- und Zwischenansichten frühmittelalterlicher Exilanten', *Saeculum*, 63 (2013), 189–203. For a wide-ranging collection of studies on the medieval phenomenon of exile, see *Exile in the Middle Ages: Selected Proceedings from the International Medieval Congress. University of Leeds, 8–11 July 2002*, ed. Laura M. Napran and Elisabeth M.C. van Houts (Turnhout: Brepols, 2004).
65 Rather of Verona, *Letter to Archbishops Wido and Sobo*, ed. Weigle, *Die Briefe*, pp. 20–1, trans. Reid, *Complete Works*, pp. 209–10.
66 Rather, 'Letter to Pope Agapet II', c. 5, trans. 225, ed. Weigle 34.
67 On tenth-century bishops acting as intercessors see Sean Gilsdorf, *The Favor of Friends: Intercession and Aristocratic Politics in Carolingian and Ottonian Europe* (Leiden: Brill, 2014), pp. 125–52.
68 Luigi Schiaparelli, *I diplomi di Ugo e di Lotario, di Berengario II e di Adalberto* (Rome: Tipografia del Senato, 1925), No. 44, pp. 134–6 (p. 134).
69 On this see Luigi Schiaparelli, *Ricerche storico-diplomatiche*, vol. V: *I diplomi di Ugo e Lotario* (Rome: Forzani, 1914), p. 154.
70 Hagen Keller, *Zur Struktur der Königsherrschaft im karolingischen und nachkarolingischen Italien: der 'consiliarius regis' in den italienischen Königsdiplomen des 9. und 10. Jahrhunderts* (Tübingen: Niemeyer, 1967), p. 167.
71 Schiaparelli, *Richerche*, p. 154.
72 Rather, *Letter to Pope Agapet II*, c. 5, ed. Weigle, *Die Briefe*, p. 34, trans. Reid, *Complete Works*, 225.
73 Rather of Verona, *Letter to the monks of Lobbes*, ed. Weigle, *Die Briefe*, pp. 27–9 (p. 27).

238 Jelle Wassenaar

74 *Ibid.*
75 Based on a query for the *incipit* to the synodal decree in question ('*Suggerente fratre et coepiscopo nostro olimpio*') in the *Clavis Canonum* database [www.mgh.de/ext/clavis/search.php (consulted 12/10/2018)], among which are *CAD* 5.58; *Benedictus Levita* 7.14; *Dionysiana* Pal. Lat. 577; *Collectio Hispana* 1.5.21; ed. Hinschius, *Decretales*, p. 269.
76 Liudprand, *Antapodosis*, V, c. 29, ed. Squatriti, *CCCM* CLVI, p. 139 trans. *id.*, *Complete Works*, p. 191.
77 For an overview of the political events leading up to Otto I's takeover of the throne see Giuseppe Sergi, 'The Kingdom of Italy', in *The New Cambridge Medieval History*, vol. 3: *c. 900-c.1024*, ed. Timothy Reuter (Cambridge: Cambridge University Press, 1999), pp. 346–70.
78 The dating of this letter has been subject to some debate, on which see Gandino, *Contemplare*, pp. 88–90. I am grateful to Giacomo Vignodelli for having shared his recent assessment of the letter with me before publication. In his upcoming edition of Atto's *Polipticum* Vignodelli has now convincingly argued for 956/7 as the time of Waldo's rebellion and thus also of the years in which Atto's letter was most likely written.
79 Atto, *Letter to Bishop Waldo of Como*, ed. Jacques-Paul Migne, *Patrologia Latinia*, 134 (Paris: Migne, 1854), col. 97A: '*Unde et ipse tanta Magistri eruditus doctrina, admonet Ecclesiam omnimode regibus servare obedientiam*'; on Atto's conception of obedience to kings see Wemple, *Atto of Vercelli*, pp. 70–9.
80 Atto, *Letter to Waldo*, ed. Migne, *PL* 134, col. 95C: '*unde vestra mens tam cito potuit concitari, ut sacerdotalis immemores reverentiae, ex improviso a vestro discederetis seniore, vestrisque benevolis confratribus, et gratis in ipsos insurgere non vereremini?*'.
81 *Ibid*, col. 101B: '*Memores estote regiae dignitatis, memores estote et vestri ordinis*'.
82 *Ibid.*, cols 99B–99D: '*Sancti quoque Patres sacra celebrantes concilia, pro robore regum et stabilitate regni sagacissima protulerunt decreta* […] *Ex concilio Toletano cap. 75, post instituta quaedam ecclesiastici ordinis, vel decreta quae ad quorumdam pertinent disciplinam*'.
83 *Ibid.*, col. 101A: '*Confinitimi hostium sacerdotes, praeter eos qui regia potestate licentiam accepere, quodlibet mandatum ad gentem extraneam occulte accipere vel dirigere non praesumant*'.
84 *Ibid.*, col. 98B: '*Quia donec regibus repugnare quaerunt, et a paganis undique opprimuntur, et a finitimis gentibus ideo conculcantur*'.
85 Giacomo Vignodelli, 'Attone e Raterio: un dialogo tra storiografia e filologia', *Filologia mediolatina*, 24 (2017), 221–88 (esp. pp. 274–5). On Atto's *Polipticum* see now Giacomo Vignodelli, *Il filo a piombo: il Perpendiculum di Attone di Vercelli e la storia politica del regno italico*. Istituzioni e società, 16 (Spoleto: Fondazione Centro italiano di studi sull'alto Medioevo, 2011) and his 'Politics, Prophecy and Satire: Atto of Vercelli's *Polipticum quod appellatur Perpendiculum*', *Early Medieval Europe*, 24.2 (2016), 209–35.
86 Atto sent Azzo of Como a letter in reply to an apparently earlier request for advice on a religious matter (marriage between spiritual kin): Atto: *Letter to Bishop Azzo of Como*, ed. Willhauck, 'The Letters', pp. 38–51.
87 Atto of Vercelli, *Polipticum quod appellatur Perpendiculum*, c. 14, ed. Georg Goetz, *Abhandlungen der philologisch-historischen Klasse der sachsischen Akademie der Wissenschaften*, 37.2. (Leipzig: Teubner, 1922) p. 23.
88 Rather, *Praeloquia*, V, cc. 14–5, ed. Reid, *CCCM* XLVI A, pp. 153–4, trans. Reid, *Complete Works*, p. 167: '*Ne ergo lenocineris hosti* […] "*Metuo*", *ais*, "*offensam senioris.*" *Econtra Apostolus: Ego, inquit, si adhuc hominibus placerem, Christi servus non essem*'.
89 *Ibid.*, III, c. 14, ed. p. 87, trans. p. 103: '*Sed tacti sumus, elisi sumus, spreti sumus, impulsi sumus, versati sumus, cecidit quae super nos videbatur stare structura. Possiderunt nos domini absque te; facti sumus opprobrium vicinis nostris, subsannatio et illusio his qui sunt in circuitu nostro*'.
90 Rather, *Letter to the Bishops of Italy, Gaul, and Germany*, ed. Weigle, *Die Briefe*, pp. 43–5, trans. Reid, *Complete Works* pp. 230–1: '*Dominis patribus et reverentissimis compraesulibus per universam Italiam, Galliam atque Germaniam in Domino constitutis Ratherius peccator et exul*'; this 'imperial' perspective first seems to have been introduced by the *Annales of Lorsch*, on which see now Helmut Reimitz, *History, Frankish Identity and the Framing of Western Ethnicity, 550–850* (Cambridge: Cambridge University Press, 2017), p. 353.

Bishops, canon law, and the politics of belonging in post-Carolingian Italy **239**

91 Liudprand, *Antapodosis*, III, c. 49, ed. Squatriti, *CCCM* CLVI, p. 94: '*Arnaldus Bagoariorum et Carentanorum dux, cuius superius fecimus mentionem, cum non multum ab Italia longe distaret, collectis copiis quatinus Hugoni regnum auferret advenit. Qui Tridentinam ea ex parte primam Italiae marcam pertransiens, Veronam usque pervenit in qua a Milone comite atque Raterio episcopo libenter, ut qui eum invitarant, suscipitur*'.

92 See p. 232.

93 Reid, *Complete Works*, p. 6.

94 Vignodelli, 'Attone e Raterio', esp. pp. 276–8.

95 *Ibid.*, p. 279.

96 Sergi, 'Kingdom of Italy', p. 357: 'The increase in the episcopate's temporal powers, energetically initiated by Berengar I, had become an unstoppable process, even though it had received only intermittent support from Hugh and Berengar II. It was probably these men's lack of enthusiasm in promoting their interests that led the bishops to give such enormous support to Otto I. What Hugh and Berengar II had both done, on the other hand, was to upgrade the status of the counts'.

97 Barbara H. Rosenwein, 'The Family Politics of Berengar I, King of Italy (888–924)', *Speculum*, 71.2 (1996), 247–89 (pp. 279–80); Igor S. Salazar, 'Crisis? What Crisis? Political Articulation and Government in the March of Tuscany through Placita and Diplomas from Guy of Spoleto to Berengar II', *Reti medievali rivista*, 17.2 (2016), 251–79 (p. 267ff.)

98 Rather, *Praeloquia*, IV, c. 22, ed. Reid, *CCCM* XLVI A, p. 127: '*Sed ut ad aliquem horum, quos nunc Boreae divisionis tethrarchiam satis strenue novi gubernare, haec cuncta referam: ociose me ista prelibasse puto, in quantum te Christianissimum fore conspicio, nec tyrannide imperium nec potestatem insania commutavisse*'.

99 Rather, 'Letter to Pope Agapet II', c. 8, ed. Weigle, *Die Briefe*, p. 42, trans. Reid, *Complete Works*, p. 228: '*Vestram credo paternitatem neque voluisse neque ausam fuisse contra legem canonicam alicui quidlibet agendi dare licentiam, illum non alia necessitate regnum ambiisse Italicum, nisi ut distortum per multimoda iniustitiarum huiusmodi scilicet et aliarum inrectitudinum volumina ad rectudinem Christianae legis potestate imperiali cogeret regnum*'.

100 Folcuin of Lobbes, *Gesta abbatum Lobbiensium*, ed. Georg H. Pertz, *MGH SS* 4 (Hannover: Hahn, 1841), c. 20, pp. 63–4; the letter to Flodoard does not survive (Folcuin notes that there is a copy in the Lobbes library), although those to Rotbert and Bruno do.

101 Timothy Reuter, 'A Europe of Bishops. The Age of Wulfstan of York and Burchard of Worms', in *Patterns of Episcopal Power: Bishops in Tenth and Eleventh Century Western Europe*, ed. Ludger Körntgen and Dominik Waßenhoven (Berlin/Boston: De Gruyter, 2011), pp. 17–38 (pp. 28–9).

102 Folcuin, *Gesta Abbatum Laubiensium*, ed. Pertz, *MGH SS* 4, c. 22. p. 64.

103 Liudprand, *Antapodosis*, III, c. 52, ed. Squatriti, *CCCM* CLVI, p. 94; as Nikolaus Staubach has shown, Liudprand's work was also influenced by a reading of Rather's *Praeloquia*: 'Historia oder Satira? Zur literarischen Stellung der *Antapodosis* Liudprands von Cremona', *Mittellateinisches Jahrbuch*, 24/25 (1989/90), 461–87.

104 On Liudprand's life and works see Squatriti, *Complete Works*, pp. 3–40, and Jon N. Sutherland, *Liudprand of Cremona, Bishop, Diplomat, Historian: Studies of the Man and his Age*. Biblioteca degli studi medievali 14. (Spoleto: Centro italiano di studi sull'Alto Medioevo, 1988).

105 Philippe Buc, 'Italian Hussies and German Matrons. Liutprand of Cremona on Dynastic Legitimacy', *Frühmittelalterliche Studien*, 29 (1995), 207–25.

106 Ross Balzaretti, 'Men and Sex in Tenth-Century Italy', in *Masculinity in Medieval Europe*, ed. Dawn Hadley (London: Routledge, 1998), pp. 143–59 (p. 154).

107 Liudprand of Cremona, *Antapodosis*, II, c. 57, ed. Squatriti, *CCCM* CLVI, p. 58, trans. Squatriti, *Complete Works*, pp. 100–1. '*Causa autem rebellionis horum haec fuit. Dum Lampertus, defuncto decessore suo, Mediolanensis archiepiscopus ordinari debuisset, non parvam ab eo rex Berengarius contra sanctorum instituta patrum pecuniam exigebat*'.

108 *Ibid.*, IV, c. 6, ed. trans. pp. 142–3: '*Hugo autem rex, regnum securius obtinere sperans si affinitate sibi coniunctis regni officia largiretur, contra ius fasque Veronensem, Tridentinam atque Mantuanam commendavit, sed quod verius est in escam dedit, ecclesiam*'.

109 *Ibid.*, V, c. 29, ed. trans. p. 191: '*Hoc in tempore Ioseph quidam, moribus senex, diebus iuvenis, Brixianae civitatis clarebat episcopus. Quem Berengarius, ut erat Dei timens, ob morum probitatem episcopio privavit, eius loco Antonium, qui nunc usque superest, nullo concilio habito, nulla episcoporum deliberatione constituit*'.

110 Ross Balzaretti, 'Narratives of Success and Narratives of Failure: Representations of the Career of King Hugh of Italy (c.885–948)', *Early Medieval Europe*, 24.2 (2016), 185–208 (p. 185).

14

MIGRANT MASTERS AND THEIR BOOKS

Italian scholars and knowledge transfer in post-Carolingian Europe

Giorgia Vocino

In the intellectual history of the medieval Latin West, the tenth century is reputed to have brought to the fore a new kind of scholar, arguably the forerunner of the modern intellectual: an individual deliberately using his knowledge, training, and skills as means of social mobility which, if handled cleverly, could grant access to *Konigsnähe* and lead to high office in the Church.[1] A politically successful career had its springboard in the classroom: Liudprand of Cremona, trained in Italy and active on both sides of the Alps at the service of Otto I, has long been considered the prototype of such an intellectual who cynically played his cards to climb the social ladder.[2] Knowledge and learning, affiliation to a well-established prestigious school (or renowned master), and participation in scholarly networks across political borders appear to have been used by tenth-century intellectuals with a higher degree of awareness. In truth, learning had always been a highly valued resource placing renowned *magistri* within the recruiting radar of the ruling elites: career opportunities would open up for them while, at a more informal level, intellectual standing allowed them to exert influence by exploiting the occasions offered by early medieval elite sociability (court life, assembly meetings, letter exchanges, etc.). The court of Charlemagne provides an outstanding early medieval example of headhunting: intellectuals were recruited and deployed to help shape the expanding polity under Frankish rule.[3] Italians played an important role in the early years of Charlemagne's reign (770s and 780s); however, the recruitment of Italian *magistri* north of the Alps was limited to the immediate aftermath of the Lombard defeat in 774.[4] Surviving sources do not disclose the names of other intellectuals educated in Italian schools who would become leading scholars at the courts of Charlemagne's successors. Furthermore, as Donald Bullough already noticed, we find no mention of *grammatici* across the Italian *regnum* for almost one and a half centuries after Peter of Pisa, Paulinus of Aquileia and Paul the Deacon.[5]

242 Giorgia Vocino

A radically different scenario can be observed for the following one hundred and fifty post-Carolingian years that are the focus of this volume: Italian scholars joined the court and travelled north of the Alps, taught there and significantly contributed to cultural and intellectual life under the Ottonian and Salian rulers. Why were they recruited? Why did they decide to move north? What knowledge did they have to offer that could not be found elsewhere but in Italy? How did they earn public acknowledgement in scholarly circles north of the Alps? And finally, what was their legacy? Looking for answers to these questions enables us to better understand the reasons why Italian *magistri* were held in high esteem by post-Carolingian political and intellectual elites. Moreover, the analysis of their scholarly profiles brings out the distinctive features of tenth- and early eleventh-century court culture, in which the crucial role played by specialized and technical knowledge – such as mastery of Greek, rhetorical competence, and legal training – was widely acknowledged and with them the qualities Italians could bring along.

The disciples of the Auxerre school

Between 900 and 1050, we can identify four waves of Italian scholars who travelled north and earned a reputation for themselves: the disciples of the Auxerre school (890s–930s), the early Ottonian recruits (950s–960s), the ideologues of the empire (970s–1000), and the imperial careerists (1010s–1050s).

The earliest migration during the decades around the year 900 was directed towards Francia. Ademar of Chabannes (d. 1034) is a late witness of this movement. In his personal handbook (Leiden, Universiteitsbibliotheek, MS Vossianus Latinus Octavo 15), the learned monk and *grammaticus* from Saint-Martial in Limoges copied down, in a somewhat disorderly way, an intellectual genealogy.[6] This family tree of *scholastici*, better known as *Grammaticorum διαδοχή*, harks back to the seventh century, to Theodore and Hadrian of Canterbury.[7] Their intellectual heirs drank from the source of knowledge and doctrine which poured forth from them: an uninterrupted line is thus traced from Theodore and Hadrian to Hucbald of Saint-Amand (d. 930) via some of the most renowned early medieval scholars. The reconstructed intellectual family tree is clearly an imagined and at times disconcerting one (Hrabanus Maurus would have been Alcuin's teacher!), but the ensuing description of the school of Auxerre and its disciples is a precious testimony of the crucial role played by this intellectual centre in the hectic decades around 900.

The reputation of Remigius of Auxerre among his contemporaries had earned him many students, some of them coming from distant regions. Ademar mentions a master named Ambrose, who would in turn have been the teacher (*preceptor*) of two disciples, Israel and *Gontio*. Later, these disciples illuminated Britain and Italy respectively with their knowledge of the liberal arts.[8] Israel is well known to specialists of Anglo-Saxon England and is none other than the grammarian active at Æthelstan's court. Later, in Trier, he was chosen to be the tutor of Otto I's youngest brother Bruno, future archbishop of Cologne.[9] We shall shortly come back to the identity of the second pupil, *Gontio*, but let us first focus on his master, Ambrose. Only the name of this disciple of Remigius is known, which betrays an Italian origin and points to the metropolitan province of Milan as his place of birth. Ambrose had crossed the Alps, attended Remigius's school in Francia (in Auxerre, Rheims or Paris) and came back to Italy where he became a teacher himself. In the 910s or early 920s, Israel, a Brittonic speaker transiting the Italian peninsula, perhaps on his way to or back from Rome, entered his classroom.[10] Israel must have learned Greek with him and this circumstance has led historians to assume that Ambrose was teaching in Rome, where the ancient language had not yet been completely obliterated. However, this is not necessarily accurate, as acquiring knowledge of Greek was possible in ninth- and tenth-century northern Italy as well, and a particularly strong case can be made for Milan. The *Psalterium Graeco-Latinum*, also known as the Psalter of Symeon (Berlin, Staatsbibliothek – Preußischer Kulturbesitz, MS Hamilton 552) was copied in the monastery of Sant'Ambrogio during the second half of the ninth century and testifies to the presence of scribes capable of reading and writing Greek.[11] The local availability of Greek-Latin glossaries has also been recently demonstrated,[12] while the probable existence of an Irish colony in the Ambrosian city and its plausible involvement in the production of a famous group of Greek-Latin biblical books further corroborates the hypothesis that it was indeed possible to learn Greek in late and post-Carolingian Milan.[13]

Ambrose could therefore have been a Milanese master who also taught the rudiments of the Greek language. His presence in Remigius's classroom makes sense with what we know from recent scholarship highlighting the intense circulation of scholars and books between Italy and the Auxerre region in the last decades of the ninth century.[14] The anonymous author of one of the most remarkable post-Carolingian celebrative poems, the *Gesta Berengarii* written for the newly crowned Emperor Berengar I, also attended Remigius's school before coming back to Italy where he wrote his panegyric in 915–916. Frédéric Duplessis has even entertained the idea that he might be the Italian disciple of Remigius mentioned in Ademar's *Διαδοχή*.[15] The use of Greek titles (with accentuation and minuscule letters) in the *Gesta Berengarii* suggests that its author had a remarkable knowledge of the language, which would indeed be compatible with the intellectual profile of Ambrose.[16] The identity of the author of the *Gesta Berengarii* cannot be known for certain, but what we know about Ambrose and Berengar's panegyrist shows that, even in a time of undeniable political instability and military confrontations, cultural networks continued to function across post-Carolingian polities: Italian advanced students of the liberal arts crossed the Alps to attend the school of the most famed teacher of their time, after which they came back with a cultural capital allowing them to establish themselves as masters in their own right.

The early Ottonian recruits

Ademar mentioned a second pupil educated by Ambrose, *Gontio*, traditionally identified with *Gunzo italicus*, the boastful grammarian recruited by Otto I and

244 Giorgia Vocino

the author of the vitriolic *Epistola ad Augienses*.[17] A cleric with the same name was a deacon at Novara, whence he addressed a letter to Atto of Vercelli (924–958) asking for advice on canonical matters.[18] It would be tempting to conclude that the brilliant disciple of Ambrose mentioned by Ademar, the grammarian travelling north with Otto's retinue, and the deacon from Novara are one and the same person, but this seems unlikely. The author of the *Epistola ad Augienses* must have been an already established master when he met the German ruler, and maybe even an independent professional scholar if we are to believe his claim to possess a personal fortune that freed him from the obligation to accept the emperor's offer.[19] His vindication of social and economic independence (*non alicui ita subiciebar neque tam humilis fortunae habebar, ut cogi possem*) would rule out a monastic background, but his classical and biblical knowledge fits with a clerical status and an education received in a cathedral school of the Italian kingdom.

The name Gunzo is indeed well attested in the Milanese region in the ninth and tenth centuries, when we find several homonyms mentioned in documentary sources. Among them a priest redacting a charter for Archbishop Walpert of Milan in July 963 is a particularly interesting figure.[20] The elegant style in which the charter was written suggests that this Gunzo was not only a priest trained to work for the cathedral chancery, but that he had also received an advanced education in the arts of speech. He does not appear to have drafted other documents for the Milanese church, which would make sense if he left Italy to follow Otto I.[21] If the Gunzo recruited by the German emperor is the Milanese priest who drafted a charter in 963 – as Donald Bullough was also inclined to think[22] – he could indeed have met and impressed the Saxon ruler on at least three occasions (late 961, January 965 or July 972).[23] Otto I's second stay in Milan, and his itinerary, fit perfectly with the information Gunzo provides in his *Epistola*: he crossed the Alps in winter and we know the emperor was in St. Gallen on January 18th, 965 and in Reichenau soon thereafter on the 23rd.[24] It was at St. Gallen that the unfortunate accident took place which hurt Gunzo's pride and prompted the writing of a complaint (*querela*) addressed to the monks of Reichenau. This letter was written as a judicial oration and denounced the unfair treatment Gunzo had been subjected to at St. Gallen, where he was derided for a trivial grammatical mistake (using the accusative at the place of the ablative). As both a defence against this insult and a testimony to his learning, Gunzo made a display of his classical and biblical learning: he filled the letter with quotations from ancient authors providing examples of *casuum mutationes* and claimed to have brought with him a hundred books, including rare works such as Plato's *Timaeus*, Aristotle's *De interpretatione*, and Cicero's translation of Aristotle's *Topica*.[25] Gunzo's boastful claim is probably an exaggeration to impress his readers and might have been targeting an area of knowledge, namely dialectic, on which the reputation of the school at St. Gallen relied heavily.[26] However, the Italian master was undoubtedly an experienced grammarian and a scholar well acquainted with classical rhetorical theory and devices, a knowledge only a very limited number of early medieval scholars could display.[27] The informed implementation of Ciceronian principles is remarkable for a tenth-century author: Gunzo used texts (Cicero's *De inventione* and the *Rhetorica ad Herennium*) that are traditionally thought to have been reintegrated into the school curriculum only from the eleventh century onwards.[28] His familiarity with the ancient poets (including rare authors such as Statius) shows that the *enarratio poetarum* constituted an essential part of his education and probably also teaching practice. Horace, Juvenal, and Persius occupy a place of honour among the quoted authors, which not only confirms the post-Carolingian heightened interest in the ancient satirists, but is also an indicator of the genre and literary tradition within which the *Epistola* should be situated.[29] The satirical quality of much tenth-century literature has been thoroughly explored and Italian scholars educated in Lombardy (the anonymous author of the *Gesta Berengarii*, Atto of Vercelli, Liudprand of Cremona) figure prominently among the most skilled authors using classical satire as a benchmark for their own work.[30] Although probably inspired by an actual event, the *Epistola ad Augienses* was constructed as a classical *controversia*, that is a fictional judicial oration and a display piece at the same time. The letter was both a defence and an accusation in which a satirical register was adopted to ridicule adversaries and give a morally debased portrait of them.[31] The eloquence of Gunzo's speech thus testified to his excellent rhetorical skills, while his literary references illustrated the extent of his learning and a knowledge he deemed superior than the one expressed by his opponents, the monks of St. Gallen.

Gunzo therefore did indeed have something to offer Otto I: a familiarity with Roman judicial rhetoric and Boethian dialectic and, if he is the Ambrosian priest who drafted a charter in 963, also useful training in documentary practice. The circulation of the *Epistola ad Augienses* in north-eastern Francia (Saint-Amand, Marchiennes) and Lotharingia (Gorze, Toul, Stavelot) draws a map within which Gunzo's final destination could have been located.[32] Manuscript transmission also testifies to the scholarly reputation earned by the Italian master, whose name was always given in the title introducing his letter. It is no longer surprising that Gunzo was not forgotten and that he earned a mention in the *Grammaticorum* διαδοχή. Considering what we know from the analysis of the *Epistola ad Augienses*, its author and the Italian pupil of Ambrose mentioned by Ademar could very well be the same person. This conclusion is also corroborated by Gunzo's familiarity with the teaching of the Auxerre school, which might have facilitated his knowledge of Plato's ideas through the study of Calcidius's translation, Boethius and Martianus Capella.[33] Before the momentous encounter between Gerbert of Aurillac and Otto I, it thus was an Italian scholar who contributed to the *translatio studii* from late Carolingian Francia to Ottonian Germany via Italy.

Gunzo was not the first scholar to accept an invitation to cross the Alps and teach in a German school: during the first Italian campaign of Otto I, Stephen, a *grammaticus* from Novara (d. *post* 985), impressed one of the closest counsellors of the king, the chancellor and Bishop Poppo I, who introduced him to court and recruited him to teach at his cathedral school at Würzburg.[34] We are better informed about Stephen's life thanks to his epitaph of which two versions are known: one transmitted in a book containing Gregory the Great's *Homilies on*

246 Giorgia Vocino

Ezechiel (Würzburg, Universitätsbibliothek, MS M. p. th. f. 6, f. 115v), the other in the collection of canons and councils known as *Collectio Novariensis* (Novara, Biblioteca Capitolare, MS Cod. XXX, f. 117r).[35] Stephen was born in Novara, but later moved to Pavia where he probably completed his education before himself becoming a master teaching in both cities (*Urbe, velut potui, doctor utraque fui*, from the Novara manuscript). He then followed Poppo I to Würzburg where he taught in the local cathedral for eighteen years (952–970), after which Stephen returned to Novara, where he resumed his teaching and lived at least until 985 when he appended his signature (*Stephanus gramaticus*) to a local charter.[36] Before moving back to Italy, Stephen bequeathed to the Würzburg cathedral the few books (*paucos libros*) in his possession, at least one of which can be identified as a sermon collection copied in late eighth-century Italy (Vienna, Österreichische Nationalbibliothek, MS Cod. lat. 1616).[37] Professional scholars such as Stephen and Gunzo certainly owned books and could therefore bring them along when taking on a new appointment.[38] The nature of Stephen's teaching is difficult to assess: only a vague remark to his contribution to the study of wisdom (*sophiae studiis dogmata crebra dedi*) is mentioned in the Würzburg version of his epitaph.[39] The manuscripts connected to him (two sermon collections and the *Collectio Novariensis*) do not appear to be traditional didactic material for a grammarian, but might have been used to train soon-to-be or newly ordained priests.[40] Evidence for this Italian master's teaching of the arts of speech and proof of his reputation north of the Alps can however be found in the eleventh-century *Vita sancti Wolfkangi* written by Otloh of St Emmeram: Stephen's lectures on Martianus Capella and his school attracted many students, amongst whom were some of the scions of the German elite.[41] The existence of latent competition between scholars from the two sides of the Alps – which is also suggested by Gunzo's *Epistola* – can be read in the episode narrated in Otloh's *Life* that sees a young Wolfgang succeeding where Stephen had failed: he provided his fellow students with a more accurate explanation of the metrical complexities of Martianus Capella's verses, thus infuriating the Italian master who banned him from his lectures. Taking hagiographic stories at face value is often risky, but the episode reveals that the acknowledgement of their northern peers was not easily earned by those masters who left Italy at the request of the German rulers. It was not only Stephen and Gunzo who experienced scepticism towards their knowledge and skills as well as competition within the scholarly elites. Other promising scholars faced the same challenges with, as we shall see, variable fortunes.

Liudprand is a well-known example of a successful, if somewhat shrewd intellectual, whose life and work hardly need rehearsing.[42] It is however interesting here briefly to recall his career and the transmission of his works. Liudprand was born into a wealthy Lombard family well-connected at court in Pavia: he was educated in the capital of the kingdom and became a deacon at the local cathedral.[43] One might have expected him to have easy access to the royal palace, but obtaining a position in the chancery was not a given: Liudprand lamented the substantial financial investment (*inmensis oblatis muneribus*) required from his family to secure him a place at court and the office of *signator epistolarum* for the *de facto* new ruler of Italy since 945, Berengar II.[44] His service for the Italian king did not last long: Liudprand soon sought out Otto I in the 950s and joined his court, where he was initially singled out probably more for his diplomatic experience and linguistic skills (knowledge of Greek) than for his learning or training in the chancery.[45] His introduction into *Königsnähe* thus appears to have been granted on different grounds to the majority of the Italian scholars who served the Ottonian and Salian rulers – with the exception of Johannes Philagatos, as we shall see. The definitive ousting of Berengar II and his son in 962 paved the way for Liudprand's promotion: on January 14th, 962 he had already been appointed bishop of Cremona, but he continued to serve Otto I, for whom he carried out numerous travels and missions until his death in 972–973.[46] Liudprand's remarkable learning and mastery of the arts of speech are witnessed by his literary production, but there is no evidence that he ever worked as a teacher, promoted the local school at Cremona, or even increased the holdings of his cathedral library, which did not even own a copy of his writings a decade after his death.[47] However, a didactic vocation and a familiarity with grammatico-exegetical school practices can be observed in the idiograph copy of the *Antapodosis* owned by Abraham of Freising (Munich, Bayerische Staatsbibliothek, MS Clm 6388): the text is here accompanied by a set of glosses (transliterations, translations, and grammatical considerations) designed to help the reader unacquainted with the Greek language.[48] Moreover, Liudprand's awareness of the importance of scholarly acknowledgement for career advancement needs to be further stressed. His earliest work, an Easter homily composed before his appointment as bishop (957–961), is an outstanding demonstration of the author's mastery of rhetorical and dialectical techniques applied to a dialogic and polemical text, the length of which was hardly appropriate for a reading in the church.[49] François Bougard rightly wonders whether 'Liudprand did not turn a test for his accession to the episcopate into a school exercise'.[50] If Liudprand's impressive career relied heavily on his diplomatic experience, his scholarly education helped him secure the public acknowledgement of the learned attendees of Otto I's court:[51] the king's brother Bruno might have been impressed by his Greek fluency and facilitated his ascent, but Abraham of Freising acknowledged his literary talents and decided to copy his eloquent homily into his pastoral vade mecum, that is a reference book for personal use (Munich, Bayerische Staatsbibliothek, MS Clm 6426).[52] The manuscript transmission of Liudprand's works owes much to the Bavarian bishop: if the Ottonian court did not actively promote their circulation, the impression Liudprand made on the scholarly elites and the bonds he created with high-ranking German prelates ensured the swift and widespread dissemination of his masterpiece, the *Antapodosis*, north of the Alps.[53]

The ideologues of the empire

The fascination of the Ottonian court with Byzantine culture and the value attached to the knowledge of Greek, already apparent in Liudprand's writings, increased notably as a consequence of the marriage between Otto II and the Byzantine princess

248 Giorgia Vocino

Theophanu in 972.[54] Intellectuals and diplomats gathered around the new empress, and among them was an Italo-Greek monk from Rossano whose star rose quickly. Johannes Philagathos was chancellor for the Italian kingdom in 980–982, appointed abbot of Nonantola by Otto II in 982, chosen by Theophanu as the tutor of her son in 987 and promoted to the bishopric of Piacenza in 988.[55] If the ambitions of the Calabrian monk eventually led him to his own downfall, his role in the education of Otto III should not be underestimated: the famous ninth-century *Lorscher Arzneibuch* (Bamberg, Staatsbibliothek, MS Msc. Med. 1, f. 42v) preserves a brief note in a blank space listing a selection of twelve books gathered in Piacenza for Otto III. It is an interesting collection: Orosius (two books), the satirist Persius, Livy (two books), a medical miscellany, two law books (*capitulares*), a grammatical miscellany (containing Fulgentius and Isidore), a dialectical miscellany (Porphyry accompanied by Boethius's commentary) and two glossaries.[56] This is a fitting selection for the education of an emperor still in his teens who was being groomed for rulership in the late 980s and early 990s: books for the study of grammar and dialectic, for a knowledge of Roman history and an acquaintance with the laws of his kingdoms were necessary tools in the hands of the tutor in charge of Otto III's education. One is left wondering whether the two glossaries might have included Greek-Latin word lists to familiarize the future emperor with the Greek language, also in view of the Byzantine marriage that was being negotiated by Johannes Philagathos himself. The Saxon emperor's fascination with Rome and Byzantium is well known, and his Italo-Greek tutor certainly contributed to feeding it in his adolescence. The booklist thus gives us glimpses of the disciplines and the typology of texts selected for the education of the future *imperator Romanorum* and his training in the exercise of power.

If Johannes Philagathos nurtured Otto III's Roman dream, Leo of Vercelli helped him give it shape. The charismatic Italian bishop was dubbed the 'spokesman of the Empire' by the late Ronald Witt.[57] Doubts about his Italian origin have long been entertained, but palaeographical and diplomatic studies published in the last two decades have convincingly demonstrated that his graphomaniac hand had been trained in Italy.[58] Leo of Vercelli is certainly one of the most prolific and easily identifiable manuscript annotators: his highly distinctive script and the use of signed *notae* (often abbreviated N. L. for *Nota Leo*) can be found in many early medieval manuscripts preserved in Vercelli and other European libraries. Nothing is known about Leo's education and early career until 996, when we find him in Mainz at the court of Otto III, where he most likely served as chaplain and was counted among the ruler's closest counsellors.[59] Appointed bishop of Vercelli in 998 or 999, he continued to work for Otto III: together with Gerbert of Aurillac and other politically influential churchmen, Leo is considered one of the masterminds behind the ideological project of the *Renovatio imperii Romanorum*.[60] His loyalty to the empire never wavered and the bishop of Vercelli was among the staunchest supporters of both Henry II (1002–1024) and Conrad II (1024–1039). Leo of Vercelli is an outstanding example of an intellectual engaged and excelling in both documentary culture and book culture. According to Wolfgang Huschner, the Italian bishop could be identified with the notary 'Heribert E' drafting diplomas for Otto III and Henry II.[61] He had also been involved in Otto III's imperial chancery where he acted as *logotheta* and *protoscrinarius*. Moreover, he attended and probably presided the court hearings at the palace,[62] he was a legal expert and it has also been suggested that he played an active role in Ottonian law-making.[63] If Leo did not write much and was not much read, judging by the manuscript transmission of his works, his literary products (two panegyrics for Ottonian rulers, a verse animal fable, two letters and a short poem lamenting the death of his predecessor) and the analysis of their sources reveal the breadth of his learning. References to and borrowings from barely known authors such as the southern Italian poet Eugenius Vulgarius and even rarer works such as Seneca's *Apocolocynthosis* and Cicero's *Epistolae ad familiares* delineate a remarkable intellectual profile.[64] The examination of the manuscripts annotated by Leo confirms the impressive range of his interests and readings: the Fathers of the Church, exegesis, and canon law represent a hardly surprising share of the *codices* containing his *marginalia*, but his distinctive hand can also be found next to Cicero's letters, Church and Ancient history,[65] on the book reuniting the works written by his predecessor Atto of Vercelli (Vatican City, Biblioteca Apostolica Vaticana, MS lat. 4322), and next to the polemic writings of Eugenius Vulgarius gathered in a manuscript shortly afterwards incorporated in the library of Otto III donated to Bamberg Cathedral by Henry II.[66] The remarkable career of Leo of Vercelli and his political engagement at the side of the German emperors have long been the focus of scholarly attention. However, the Italian bishop was also a scholar and teacher: while reading the *Scriptores historiae Augustae*, Leo flagged several passages for a young pupil (*puer*), who in one case is explicitly named Odelricus.[67] His didactic interest appears to have been limited to the selection of moralistic examples to show his student, which might imply Leo was not working as a traditional *grammaticus*, but more as a mentor or a personal tutor, in which case the court, where the scions of the elites where educated, could be suggested as the place where Leo read the book and annotated it for his teaching.[68] The Italian bishop read classical authors to learn from their eloquence and showed interest in their philosophical reflection: the *marginalia* accompanying Cicero's letters in the beautiful copy produced at the court of Louis the Pious (Florence, Biblioteca Medicea Laurenziana, MS Plut. 49.09) highlighted remarkable stylistic passages and the Roman orator's consolatory thoughts on the civil wars, which might have resonated with Leo's personal experience in the tumultuous years following Otto III's death.[69]

The charismatic and eclectic personality of Leo of Vercelli emerges from his reading, which might conceal traces of his teaching activities at the German court. As with many other Italian scholars, Leo was recruited not only for his technical legal training and the experience he acquired in the chancery, but also as a brilliant scholar whose services at court might have included assistance in the education of the future elites of the empire.

Imperial careerists

Access to the court meant access to political opportunities. By the early eleventh century, the Italian scholastic system had been restructured to offer a tailored education for students hoping for a future position in the administration of the empire. Peter Damian, the most influential scholar of the Gregorian reform and himself living proof of the excellent education achievable in early eleventh-century Italy, recalls in one of his letters the unfortunate demise of Hugh, a brilliant cleric from Parma who had set his sights on high office in the *Reichskirche*:

> Since he aspired to the episcopal dignity, he took the position of chaplain to the emperor Conrad. On his return from the court, loaded with the king's promises and with never a doubt in his mind that he would win the high office, he was attacked by brigands. […] Then, indeed, he clearly understood that what he had learned was of no value, for together he lost both the sweetness of life […] and the high dignity to which he aspired.[70]

The by-then customary path to success and power for the clerical elites is clearly laid out and openly criticized by Peter Damian: Hugh was betting on his learning and on his knowledge of the liberal arts to climb the social ladder and he considered service in the emperor's chancery to be his best shot at the ultimate prize, a bishopric. A *cancellarius* named Hugh did indeed work for the Italian chancery of Henry II and Conrad II between 1023 to 1027 and had been promoted to be chaplain of the latter in 1027.[71] He was appointed bishop of Parma in 1027 and held the *cathedra* until his death (ca. 1044–1046), which appears to contradict Peter Damian's account of his violent death before he could get the coveted *culminis dignitatem*. The distance in time between the writing of the letter (after 1064) and the events remembered might explain the confusion, assuming that the learned reformer and ascetic did not intentionally fabricate the story for the sake of his argument, which was to demonstrate that liberal arts are an obstacle on the path to spiritual perfection.[72] Either way, Hugh's career and Peter Damian's anecdote testify to the existence of well-oiled social mechanisms as well as to the new importance of the city of Parma both as a centre of learning and as a key political hub in the Italian kingdom. This was hardly a novelty: since the episcopate of Wibod (*ante* 860–895), the church of Parma had been closely tied to the *regnum*, and under the Ottonians the connection grew even stronger.[73] It is no surprise that the local cathedral school acquired importance and prestige: the education offered in its classrooms prepared young clerics to serve in the administration of the empire and, to the most skilled and ambitious of them, it threw open the doors to the hallways of power.

The cathedral school of Parma not only educated Hugh and Peter Damian, but also a slightly younger Milanese scholar whose life and work both illustrate a changed cultural world and shed light on the social practices that regulated access to the court, secured scholarly acknowledgement and led to high office. Anselm de Besate belonged to one of the most influential families in the Italian kingdom, a *Bischofsfamilie* as Wolfgang Huschner describes it.[74] His political and social connections undoubtedly facilitated his access to the most reputable schools in the kingdom as well as his integration into the Milanese cathedral clergy.[75] The eleventh century has long been described as a time of flourishing for cathedral schools and Anselm's educational itinerary corroborates this reconstruction: he attended the Milan cathedral school during the incumbency of the charismatic Archbishop Aribert da Intimiano (1018–1045), then decided to further polish his skills in the arts of speech with three respected masters (the philosopher Drogo, his pupil Sichelm, and the otherwise unknown Aldeprand) teaching in Parma and Reggio Emilia. While he learned dialectic with Drogo, he studied Ciceronian rhetoric and Roman law with Sichelm, whom he described as 'a Cicero above all others in his rhetorical skills and a Justinian above all others in his imperial edicts and legal judgements'.[76] The economic backing of his aristocratic family allowed him to travel, first as a student and later as a scholar in Italy, Francia, and Germany, as Anselm boastfully recalls in his *Rhetorimachia*.[77] His education and precocious career stand out for their itinerant nature, but this undoubtedly was the path followed by many more wealthy students and professionals whose lives are not documented.[78] Like other tenth- and eleventh-century Italian intellectuals (Liudprand of Cremona, Leo of Vercelli, Hugh of Parma, and possibly Gunzo), Anselm had been trained to serve in the chancery, an experience that laid the foundations for a brilliant career. In 1045 the Milanese cleric, most likely still in his twenties, drafted a charter for Suidger of Bamberg (1040–1046), who was promoted to the throne of St Peter as Pope Clement II (1046–1047) only a year later.[79] In March 1047 Anselm was back in Italy and already working for the Italian chancery of Henry III, while in the summer of 1048 we again find him in Germany, where he drafted an imperial diploma of immunity for the bishopric of Minden.[80] The writing of his masterpiece, the *Rhetorimachia*, dates to the winter of 1047–1048, before Anselm moved back to Germany to serve in the emperor's chancery.

Anselm's biography shows that he pursued his study of the liberal arts when he had already acquired a solid foundation of professional experience in documentary culture. In all likelihood, he also taught rhetoric (or planned to do it) after attending Sichelm's classes in Reggio Emilia: his *Rhetorimachia* is a fictional *controversia*, an illustration of the principles of the discipline he had expounded elsewhere, in a handbook entitled *De materia artis*, which unfortunately does not survive.[81] Like Gunzo's *Epistola ad Augienses*, the *Rhetorimachia* was a showpiece: Anselm decided to address it to Emperor Henry III, asking him to commend it and further circulate it within the court, which he describes as a rather unwelcoming environment:

> Accept this little work of mine at this time for your commendation, Caesar […]. And, to your many crowds of learned men (*choris doctorum*) […] hand it over ascribed as literature, so that your court may be deemed worthy of praise and that no problem with rantings may be there again (*sit nullis denuo molestia latracionum*).[82]

Anselm was with Henry III and Leo IX at the synod of Mainz in October 1049 and on that occasion most likely engaged in a public debate with local scholars, whom he failed to impress.[83] Anselm's account of this disputation is included in a letter to his master Drogo: his young age did not help him and his dialectic argumentation did not convince the audience. The dedicatory letter to Henry III probably contains echoes of this failed opportunity. Anselm decided to offer his work directly to the emperor, hoping to gain a better chance at success by exploiting a centuries-old effective social practice: book dedications to rulers provided a parallel channel for validation and public acknowledgement.[84] The letter to the emperor was also a display of Anselm's familiarity with Roman law, and more particularly his acquaintance with the Justinianic *Corpus Iuris Civilis*: the opening line, stressing that legislation is an imperial prerogative, was thus directly borrowed from the *Institutiones*.[85] The marginal notes to Book III of the *Rhetorimachia* further testify to Anselm's knowledge of Justinianic law, with two quotations from the *Novellae* possibly drawn from the *Epitome Iuliani*.[86] Epideictic and judicial rhetorical skills, knowledge of Roman (imperial) law, and an excellent education in the arts of speech were thus offered by the Milanese scholar to Henry III with the hope to receive the yearned-for public acknowledgement. But Anselm's ambitions were not fulfilled and his professional career did not bring him much further: his last diploma for the imperial chancery was drafted on September 16th, 1050 and the only surviving evidence for the following years is a charter for Hezilo of Hildesheim produced between 1054 and 1067.[87] Anselm's scholarly success also appears to have been rather limited: his literary output only survives in two manuscripts (antigraph and apograph), one of which was copied in eleventh-century Italy, the other in twelfth-century Trier.[88] The earlier copy (Paris, Bibliothèque nationale de France, MS fonds latin 7761) was undoubtedly produced for didactic purposes, as suggested by the set of annotations accompanying the *Rhetorimachia* that illustrate the rhetorical precepts applied in this judicial speech. The manuscript has a pocket-size format (184 x 140 mm) and might have been copied, and later travelled, in the entourage of the author.[89] The later copy (Cusanusstift, Bernkastel-Kues, MS 52), produced in the *scriptorium* of St. Matthias at Trier, used the Italian manuscript as exemplar, but added the introductory poem and the dedicatory letter to Henry III, which strengthens the hypothesis that Paris, BnF lat. 7761 was indeed hastily prepared in Italy before travelling to Germany in Anselm's luggage.[90] The limited manuscript transmission of the *Rhetorimachia* echoes Anselm's failure in obtaining career advancement, while the fact that he never got around to writing the announced fourth book dedicated to deliberative rhetoric suggests that he also gave up the idea of teaching rhetoric.

Conclusions

Post-Carolingian Europe might have been shaken by numerous political crises and endured violent military confrontations, but these did not affect the circulation of scholars and books before and after the so-called 'Ottonian Renaissance'.[91] Cultural and intellectual exchange continued to create links among people, schools and institutions, and Italian students and *magistri* relied heavily on those connections to

Migrant masters and their books **253**

boost their careers. The articulated Milanese scholastic system described in the late eleventh century by Landulf Senior in his *Historia Mediolanensis* no longer appears an exaggeration: clerics educated in the local cathedral were used to travelling and studying abroad.[92] The origins of such an educational curriculum can be traced back, as we have seen, to the late Carolingian period.

Retracing the lives of those Italian scholars who left their cities and institutions to pursue their studies and create the conditions for their recruitment at court helps us unveil the functioning of an evolving social and cultural framework. First, the analysis confirms the growing professionalization of self-aware independent intellectuals, which has been highlighted by Claudio Leonardi as one of the distinctive features of the period 900–1050.[93] The story of Hugh of Parma and the writings of Anselm de Besate are straightforward testimony to the definition of an Italian tailored path to high office in the imperial administration. The profiles of the post-Carolingian intellectuals accepted into *Königsnähe* also show a high degree of homogeneity. Educated in city cathedrals (not in monasteries as it often was the case north of the Alps), well versed in both book culture and documentary culture, relying on their mastery of technical knowledge (Greek language, judicial rhetoric, Roman law), Italian scholars were increasingly aware of their talents and willing to use them as means of social mobility. The distinctive twelfth-century culture emanating from cathedral schools that has been compellingly described by C. Stephen Jaeger had roots in Italy going further back than the eleventh century:[94] Italian masters efficiently combined centuries-long literary traditions (epideictic literature) and school practices (fictional controversies) cultivated in the centres of learning of the *regnum italicum* with the grammatico-exegetical approach to the written word that had been the quality brand of the Auxerre school.[95] The sophisticated (archaic, often obscure, and rich in loanwords) language favoured by Italian intellectuals is the result of such a cultural merge: it is no surprise that stylistic similarities have been recently highlighted in the works produced by post-Carolingian Italian authors (Berengar's panegyrist, Liudprand, Atto of Vercelli) and northern scholars whose connections to the Auxerre school are well known (Heiric of Auxerre, Abbo of St Germain, Odo of Cluny).[96]

Secondly, this study sheds light on the evolution of social practices of disputation, patronage, *Publizistik* and public opinion in an age of transition from typically Carolingian cultures of debate mostly, but not exclusively, centred on doctrinal controversies to the quarrelsome times of the Investiture Contest with its abundant polemical literature, over half of which was produced in Italy.[97] A ruler was no longer needed to act as the arbiter of debates; scholarly communities could now regulate and settle them by themselves. Gunzo and Anselm de Besate confronted the northern scholarly elites (the monks of St. Gallen and Reichenau, and the scholars gathered at Mainz in 1049) with opposite results. Their polemical writings reveal the degree of maturation achieved by such social phenomena, the roots of which also go back to the Carolingian period.[98]

Lastly, the intellectual profile of the Italian masters recruited at court shows the fields in which they excelled and the knowledge they could offer to beat the competition. On the one hand, the promotion of Ciceronian oratory and Roman

254 Giorgia Vocino

law in Italian cathedral schools foreshadows the emergence of the new rhetorical and legal culture traditionally associated with the rise of the Communes.[99] On the other hand, advanced rhetorical education and technical training in episcopal chanceries paved the way to the formalization of a new genre, the *artes dictaminis* composed in Italy from the late eleventh century onwards.[100] Despite the post-Carolingian 'brain drain' – or rather encouraged by the opportunities it offered –, Italian scholarly elites accelerated the shaping of their 'cultural uniqueness'.[101] They thus got a decisive head start which made them the forerunners in the social and intellectual transformations that eventually led to the birth of the European lay intellectual and to Humanism.

Notes

1 Claudio Leonardi, 'Intellectual Life', in *New Cambridge Medieval History*, III, ed. by Timothy Reuter (Cambridge: Cambridge University Press, 2000), pp. 186–211 (pp. 189–90).

2 Conrad Leyser, 'Episcopal Office in the Italy of Liudprand of Cremona, c.890-c.970', *English Historical Review*, CXXV n. 515 (2010), pp. 795–817.

3 Donald Bullough, '*Aula renovata*: the Carolingian Court before the Aachen Palace', *Proceedings of the British Academy*, 71 (1985), pp. 267–301.

4 On the Lombard intellectuals who stood out at Charlemagne's court see Claudia Villa, '*Itinera italica* nel secolo VIII: i libri e i viaggi', in *Paolino d'Aquileia e il contributo italiano all'Europa carolingia*, ed. by Paolo Chiesa (Udine: Forum, 2003), pp. 453–70; also Ronald G. Witt, *The Two Latin Cultures and the Foundation of Renaissance Humanism in Medieval Italy* (Cambridge: Cambridge University Press, 2012), esp. pp. 17–23 as well as Giorgia Vocino, 'Between the Palace, the School and the Forum. Rhetoric and Court Culture in Late Lombard and Carolingian Italy', in *After Charlemagne. Carolingian Italy and its Rulers*, ed. by Clemens Gantner and Walter Pohl (Cambridge: Cambridge University Press, forthcoming).

5 Donald Bullough, 'Le scuole cattedrali e la cultura dell'Italia settentrionale prima dei Comuni', in *Il pragmatismo degli intellettuali. Origini e primi sviluppi dell'istruzione universitaria. Antologia di Storia medievale*, ed. by Roberto Greci (Torino: Scriptorium, 1996), pp. 23–46 (p. 31).

6 Ad van Els, 'Transmitting Knowledge by Text and Illustration: The Case of MS Leiden, UB, VLO 15', in *The Annotated Book in the Early Middle Ages. Practices of Reading and Writing*, ed. by Mariken Teeuwen and Irene van Renswoude (Turnhout: Brepols, 2017), pp. 465–99. A thorough study of this manuscript has been carried in Ad van Els, 'Een Leeuw van een Handschrift: Ademar van Chabannes en MS Leiden, Universiteitsbibliotheek, Vossianus Latinus Octavo 15' (unpublished doctoral thesis, University of Utrecht, 2015), available online: https://dspace.library.uu.nl/handle/1874/306223.

7 Walter Berschin, *Griechisch-lateinisches Mittelalter: Von Hieronymus zu Nikolaus von Kues* (Bern: Francke, 1980), pp. 149–57. Cf. Ad van Els, 'Een Leeuw', pp. 979–82.

8 VLO 15, f. 147v: *Ambrosius quoque hisraelis preceptor auditoris. egroalis. Gontio nihilominus. quorum alter britanniam. alter italiam septemplici minerua celebrem reddidit.*

9 For a reassessment of Israel's biography, see now Franck Cinato, 'Israel, Bishop, Monk, Grammarian', in *Knowledge and Culture in Times of Threat. Europe around 900*, ed. by Pierre Chambert-Protat and Warren Pezé (Stuttgart, forthcoming).

10 Michael Lapidge argued for a Breton, rather than an Irish identity, 'Israel the Grammarian in Anglo-Saxon England', in *From Athens to Chartres: Neoplatonism and Medieval Thought*, ed. by Haijo J. Westra (Leiden: Brill, 1992), pp. 97–114. On the problems related to the date of Israel's pilgrimage to Rome, see Cinato, 'Israel'. However, his education in Italy must be located in the years preceding the development of his career in England and Germany, therefore before the 930s.

11 The first page of the manuscript bears Symeon's beautifully decorated Greek colophon, which can be admired online: https://digital.staatsbibliothek-berlin.de/ansicht?PPN=PPN736607951&PHYSID=PHYS_0018&DMDID=DMDLOG_0006 (last accessed on September 11th, 2019).For the Greek-Latin biblical books copied by a group of Irish scribes (Basel, Universitätsbibliothek, MS A VII 3; St. Gallen, Stiftsbibliothek, MS 48; Dresden, Sachsichesbibliothek, MS A 145 b) see Simona Gavinelli, 'Irlandesi, libri biblici greco-latini e il monastero di S. Ambrogio in età carolingia', in *Il monastero di S. Ambrogio nel Medioevo. Convegno di studi nel XII centenario: 784–1984* (Milan: Vita e Pensiero, 1988), pp. 350–60 (pp. 357–8).

12 Frédéric Duplessis, 'De Laon à Brescia: le *Glossarium Monacense* (München, BSB, lat. 14420, fol. 144v)', *Archivum Latinitatis Medii Aevi*, 73 (2015), pp. 79–147.

13 Simona Gavinelli, 'Per un'enciclopedia carolingia (Codice Bernese 363)', *Italia medioevale e umanistica*, 26 (1983), pp. 1–25, esp. pp. 6–9. The Milanese Archbishop Arnulf II (998–1018) also probably knew Greek and this might explain why he was chosen by Otto III as his emissary for the diplomatic mission in Constantinople that would have acquired for him a Byzantine bride had the young emperor not died prematurely, see Michele Baitieri, 'Episcopal Diplomacy at the Turn of the First Millennium. Archbishop Arnulf II (998–1018) between the Reigns of Otto III and Henry II', in *Bishops as Diplomats, 1000–1400*, ed. by Peter Coss, Chris Dennis, Melissa Julian-Jones and Angelo Silvestri (Turnhout: Brepols, forthcoming).

14 Frédéric Duplessis, 'Les sources des gloses des *Gesta Berengarii* et la culture du poète anonyme', *Aevum*, 89/2 (2015), pp. 205–63.

15 Frédéric Duplessis, 'Réseaux intellectuels entre France et Italie (IXe-Xe s.): autour des *Gesta Berengarii imperatoris* et de leurs gloses' (unpublished doctoral thesis, École Pratique des Hautes Études, 2015), I, pp. 409–10.

16 Duplessis, 'Réseaux intellectuels', pp. 8–10.

17 On Gunzo, the 'vindicator of Italian scholarship', see Witt, *The Two Latin Cultures*, pp. 93–6.

18 On the thorny question of Gunzo's identity see Paolo Chiesa, 'Gunzone', *Dizionario Biografico degli Italiani*, 61 (2004), pp. 564–5.

19 Gunzo, *Epistola ad Augienses*, MGH *Die deutschen Geschichtsquellen des Mittelalters 500–1500*, II, ed. by Karl Manitius (Weimar: Monumenta Germaniae Historica, 1958), p. 21.

20 The original charter is today in Parma, Archivio di Stato, Fondo diplomatico, sec. X, mazzo II – Monastero di S. Sisto di Piacenza, cf. Giovanni Drei, *Le carte degli Archivi Parmensi dei sec. X-XI*, I (Parma, 1924), n. LXV.

21 We find however another *humilis presbiter* named Gunzo subscribing a provincial synod convened by Archbishop Walpert in 969: the original document is not preserved, but the text was quoted in full in the proceedings of a later *placitum* (Pavia, 985), see *Die Konzilien Deutschlands und Reichsitaliens 916–1001*, ed. by Ernst-Dieter Hehl (Hanover: Hahnsche Buchhandlung, 1987–2007), II, no. 33.

22 Bullough, 'Le scuole cattedrali', p. 38 as well as Bullough's review of the MGH edition of Gunzo's *Epistola ad Augienses* published in the *English Historical Review*, 75, n. 296 (1960), pp. 487–91. The British scholar mentions the existence of 'noticeable similarities' between the literary style of the charter and the *Epistola*. The rhetorical training of the Milanese priest is indeed apparent in his use of alliterations (e.g. *clementiam lamentando et miserabiliter lacrimando*) and highly figurative expressions such as *homines decocte aetatis* and *post longi taciturnitatem silentii*.

23 Otto I probably stayed in Milan in late 961, but the mention of his coronation in Sant'Ambrogio related by Landulf Senior is not entirely reliable; on January 3rd, 965 the ruler, on his way north, stopped in Milan where he issued a diploma; on July 30th, 972 the emperor was again in Milan where he held his last Italian *placitum*. On Otto I's Milanese coronation in 961, see Landulf Senior, *Historia Mediolanensis*, II, ed. by Ludwig Conrad Bethmann and Wilhelm Wattenbach, MGH SS 8 (Hanover: Monumenta Germaniae Historica, 1848), pp. 53–4. For the diploma and the *placitum*, see MGH DD O I nos. 274 and 416.

24 Gunzo, *Epistola ad Augienses*, p. 21. *Regesta Imperii*, II, ed. by J. F. Böhmer (Innsbruch, 1893), pp. 176–7: the mention of Otto I's stay in St Gallen recorded in the *Annales Sangallenses maiores* was read by Philipp Jaffé under erasure on St. Gallen, Stiftsbibliothek, Cod. Sang. 915. For the diplomas issued at Reichenau on January 23rd, see MGH DD O I nos. 275 and 276, on these see Hagen Keller, 'Otto der Große urkundet im Bodenseegebiet. Inszenierungen der "Gegenwart des Herrschers" in einer vom König selte besuchten Landschaft', in *Mediaevalia Augiensia. Forschungen zur Geschichte des Mittelalters*, ed. by Jürgen Petersohn (Stuttgart: Thorbecke, 2001), pp. 205–45 (pp. 222–3).

25 Gunzo, *Epistola ad Augienses*, p. 37.

26 On dialectical knowledge at St. Gallen in the tenth century, see Anna A. Grotans, *Reading in Medieval St. Gall* (Cambridge: Cambridge University Press, 2006), pp. 79–91.

27 John O. Ward, 'What the Middle Ages Missed of Cicero, and Why', in *Brill's Companion to the Reception of Cicero*, ed. by William H. F. Altman (Leiden: Brill, 2015), pp. 307–26. Focusing on the early medieval period, John Moorhead, 'Aspects of the Carolingian Response to Cicero', *Philologus*, 129 (1985), pp. 109–20.

28 The increasing use of Ciceronian treatises in the classroom since the early eleventh century is confirmed by the writing of commentaries, see John O. Ward, 'Ciceronian Rhetoric and Oratory from St. Augustine to Guarino da Verona', in *Cicero Refused to Die: Ciceronian Influence through the Centuries*, ed. by Nancy van Deusen (Leiden: Brill, 2013), pp. 163–96 (pp. 179–80 also for further bibliography). However, at least two other slightly younger tenth-century scholars, Gerbert of Aurillac and Abbo of Fleury, studied and taught Ciceronian rhetoric, see Justin Lake, 'Gerbert of Aurillac and the Study of Rhetoric in Tenth-Century Rheims', *The Journal of Medieval Latin*, 23 (2013), pp. 49–85, esp. pp. 63–5. Interestingly, Gerbert might have acquired Victorinus's commentary on the *De inventione* from the monk Rainard of Bobbio.

29 Frédéric Duplessis speaks of an *aetas iuvenaliana* for the late ninth and the tenth century which underlines the late integration of Juvenal and Persius into the canon of authors studied in the classroom, see Frédéric Duplessis, 'L'Europe post-carolingienne et les débuts de l'*aetas iuuenaliana*', in *Knowledge and Culture*.

30 Again Duplessis, 'Les sources', pp. 216–7 and 249–52; On Atto of Vercelli see Giacomo Vignodelli, 'La tradizione scoliastica a Persio e Giovenale nel Polittico di Attone di Vercelli e nelle sue glosse (953–958)', in *Il ruolo della scuola nella tradizione dei classici latini. Tra Fortleben ed esegesi*, ed. by Grazia Maria Masselli and Francesca Sivo (Campobasso: Il Castello, 2017), II, pp. 377–428 as well as idem, 'Politics, prophecy and satire: Atto of Vercelli's *Polipticum quod appellatur Perpendiculum*', *Early Medieval Europe*, 24 (2016), pp. 209–35. Still invaluable is Nikolaus Staubach, '*Historia* oder *Satira*? Zur literarischen Stellung der *Antapodosis* Liudprands von Cremona', *Mittellateinisches Jahrbuch*, 24/25 (1989–1990), pp. 461–87.

31 For the connection between satire and rhetorical declamations in classical literature, Susanna Morton Braund, 'Declamation and Contestation in Satire', in *Roman Eloquence. Rhetoric in Society and Literature*, ed. by William J. Dominik (London: Routledge, 1997), pp. 147–65.

32 Cologny, Fondation Martin Bodmer, MS Bodmer 80 was copied in late tenth-century Alamannia possibly from the original addressed to the monks of Reichenau. The *Epistola* was also available in eleventh-century Saint-Amand where it was included in a schoolbook containing Boethius and an anthology of verse and prose exemples of hermeneutic writing (Valenciennes, Bibliothèque Municipale, MS 298). From the Saint-Amand manuscript were chosen the excerpts gathered under the title *Exempla Gunzonis* that can be read in a twelfth-century didactic *florilegium* from Marchiennes (Douai, Bibliothèque Municipale, MS 749). On the indirect witnesses of the circulation of the text in Lotharingia, see Gunzo, *Epistola ad Augienses*, p. 16.

33 Interestingly Gerbert and Gunzo are the only tenth-century scholars to make explicit references to Plato's *Timaeus* and more particularly to his idea of the World Soul, which had been commented upon by John Scottus Eriugena and Remigius of Auxerre, see John Marenbon, 'Platonism – A Doxographic Approach: The Early Middle Ages', in *The*

Platonic Tradition in the Middle Ages. A Doxographic Approach, ed. by Stephen Gersh and Maarten J. F. M. Hoenen (Berlin: De Gruyter, 2002), pp. 67–90 (pp. 84–5 on Gunzo). On the renewed interest in Boethius in late Carolingian Francia, see Mariken Teeuwen, 'Reading Boethius around 900: Manuscripts of Boethius' texts and their annotations', in *Knowledge and Culture*. It is worth mentioning that Remigius's commentary on Martianus Capella was available in Milan already around 900 when it was copied in the beautiful didactic miscellany that is today Paris, Bibliothèque nationale de France, MS Fonds latin 7900A, see again Duplessis, 'Les sources'.

34 Witt, *The Two Latin Cultures*, p. 77 for a synthetic overview of what we know about Stephen. For more information, see Simona Gavinelli, 'Lo studio della grammatica a Novara tra l'VIII e il XV secolo', *Aevum*, 65/2 (1991), pp. 259–78 (pp. 264–5); Ettore Cau, 'Scrittura e cultura a Novara (secoli VIII-X)', *Ricerche medievali*, 6–9 (1971–1974), pp. 1–87.

35 Both epitaphs are published in MGH *Poetae* 5, *Die Ottonenzeit*, I, ed. by Karl Strecker (Leipzig: Monumenta Germaniae Historica, 1937), pp. 554–6.

36 Othloh, *Vita sancti Wolfkangi*, ed. by Georg Waitz, MGH SS IV, pp. 521–42 (p. 528). For Stephen's signature see Cau, 'Scrittura e cultura', p. 70 and plate XXIV.

37 For a thorough study of this *codex* see Ettore Cau, 'Osservazioni sul cod. lat. 1616 (sec. VIII ex.) della Biblioteca Nazionale di Vienna', in *Palaeographica Diplomatica et Archivistica. Studi in onore di Giulio Battelli*, ed. by Scuola speciale per archivisti e bibliotecari dell'Università di Roma (Rome, 1979), I, pp. 85–97.

38 This had already happened in the ninth century with the Irish scholar Dungal who had been appointed master at Pavia, see Mirella Ferrari, '« In Papia conveniant ad Dungalum »', *Italia medioevale e umanistica*, 15 (1972), pp. 1–5 (pp. 32–40).

39 MGH *Poetae* 5, I, p. 555.

40 In the Novara version of his epitaph, Stephen declared that he taught both children and adults (*erudiens pueros instituensque viros*), MGH *Poetae* 5, I, p. 556.

41 Othloh, *Vita sancti Wolfkangi*, p. 528.

42 Paolo Chiesa, 'Liutprando di Cremona', *Dizionario Biografico degli Italiani*, 65 (2005), pp. 298–303. For updated bibliography see the introductions to the new French and Italian translations of Liudprand's works: Liutprando *Antapodosis*, edited by Paolo Chiesa (Rome: Fondazione Lorenzo Valla, 2015) and Liudprand de Crémone, *Oeuvres*, edited by François Bougard (Paris, CNRS éditions, 2015) as well as the new study by Anastasia Brakhman, *Außenseiter und 'Insider'. Kommunikation und Historiographie im Umfeld des ottonischen Herrscherhofes* (Husum: Matthiesen Verlag, 2016).

43 His father and stepfather had both been trusted with a diplomatic mission to Constantinople for King Hugh of Italy (926–947).

44 Liudprand, *Antapodosis*, V, 30, ed. by Paolo Chiesa, CCCM 156 (Turnhout: Brepols, 1998), p. 141.

45 Liudprand de Crémone, *Oeuvres*, p. 12, cf. Johannes Koder, 'Liutprand von Cremona und die griechische Sprache', in *Liutprand von Cremona in Konstantinopel. Untersuchungen zum griechischen Sprachschatz und zu realienkundlichen Aussagen in seinem Werken*, ed. by Johannes Koder and Thomas Weber (Vienna: Verlag der Österreichischen Akademie der Wissenschaften, 1980), pp. 9–70.

46 Liudprand de Crémone, *Oeuvres*, p. 17.

47 Witt, *The Two Latin Cultures*, p. 90. Bullough stresses the impressive range of authors known to Liudprand: 'Liutprando conosceva un numero maggiore di scrittori classici degli altri studiosi del X secolo, e fra essi alcuni poco conosciuti anche più tardi' (Bullough, 'Le scuole cattedrali', pp. 39–40). On the medieval reception of Liudprand's works see also Paolo Chiesa, 'Per una storia del testo delle opere di Liutprando di Cremona nel medioevo', *Filologia mediolatina* 2 (1995), pp. 165–91, on the lack of an Italian manuscript transmission p. 171.

48 Paolo Chiesa, 'Testi provvisori, varianti d'autore, copie individuali. Il caso dell'*Antapodosis* di Liutprando', in *La critica del testo mediolatino*, ed. by Claudio Leonardi (Spoleto: Centro italiano di studi sull'alto Medioevo, 1994), pp. 323–38.

49 Bernhard Bischoff, 'Eine Osterpredigt Liudprands von Cremona (um 960)', in idem, *Anecdota novissima* (Stuttgart: Hiersemann, 1984), pp. 20–34.

50 Liudprand de Crémone, *Oeuvres*, pp. 17–22 (p. 21): 'Liudprand n'a pas sacrifié à l'exercice d'école, celui du clerc devant faire ses preuves pour accéder à l'épiscopat.'

51 While I do think Liudprand's *Homelia Paschalis* was the early work of a cleric and scholar trying to impress a court audience, I do not agree with Anastasia Brakhman's understanding of his much longer and elaborate historical work, the *Antapodosis*, as a 'Bewerbungsschrift', see Brakhman, *Außenseiter und 'Insider'*, pp. 43–59 (p. 59).

52 See Benedetta Valtorta, 'Uno *speculum episcopi* nel manoscritto Clm 6426', *Studi medievali*, 54 (2013), pp. 305–28; cf. Chiesa, 'Per una storia', pp. 173–74, n. 33. The manuscript can be consulted online: http://daten.digitale-sammlungen.de/~db/0000/bsb00003258/wimages/ (last accessed on September 11th, 2019).

53 On the role of Abraham and Theoderic of Metz in the early transmission of Liudprand's works see again Chiesa, 'Per una storia', pp. 172–8.

54 Rosamond McKitterick, 'Ottonian intellectual culture in the tenth century and the role of Theophanu', *Early Medieval Europe*, 2 (1993), pp. 53–74. Also Berschin, *Griechisch-lateinisches Mittelalter*, pp. 222–5.

55 Luigi Canetti, 'Giovanni XVI, antipapa', *Dizionario Biografico degli Italiani*, 55 (2001), pp. 590–5.

56 On this list, see Hartmut Hoffmann, *Bamberger Handschriften des 10. und des 11. Jahrhunderts* (Hanover, Hahnsche Buchhandlung, 1995), pp. 6–12.

57 Witt, *The Two Latin Cultures*, pp. 96–100.

58 On the diplomas he drafted as 'Heribert E', Huschner, *Transalpine Kommunikation im Mittelalter: diplomatische, kulturelle und politische Wechselwirkungen zwischen Italien und dem nordalpinen Reich (9. – 11. Jahrhundert)* (Hanover: Hahnsche Buchhandlung, 2003), pp. 267–70 and plate no. 39 for his autograph subscription; for a more cautious assessment cf. Hoffmann, 'Notare, Kanzler und Bischöfe am ottonischen Hof', *Deutsches Archiv für Erforschung des Mittelalters*, 61 (2005), pp. 435–80 (pp. 467–8). For an analysis of his marginal annotations, see Simona Gavinelli, 'Leone di Vercelli postillatore di codici', *Aevum*, 75/2 (2001), pp. 233–62, (p. 242, n. 34: 'il tratteggio della scrittura confermerebbe la sua origine italiana').

59 Leo of Vercelli is mentioned with the title *episcopus palatii* in the *Passio Adalberti* written by Bruno of Querfurt, who also praised him for his intelligence and eloquence, see Bruno of Querfurt, *Vita secunda sancti Adalberti episcopi*, ed. by Georg H. Pertz, MGH SS 4 (Hanover: Monumenta Germaniae Historica, 1841), p. 605. For an overview of Leo's biography, and his literary output Andrea Bedina, 'Leone', *Dizionario Biografico degli Italiani*, 64 (2005), pp. 478–82; focusing on Leo's books, his works and their dissemination Roberto Gamberini, *Metrum Leonis. Poesia e potere all'inizio del secolo XI* (Tavarnuzze: Sismel-Edizioni del Galluzzo, 2002), pp. VII–XIX as well as Idem, 'Leo Vercellensis ep.', in *La trasmissione dei testi latini del Medioevo. Medieval Latin Texts and their Transmission*, ed. by Paolo Chiesa and Lucia Castaldi, I (Florence: Sismel-Edizioni del Galluzzo, 2004), pp. 248–61; analysing his career and political ideology Heinrich Dormeier, 'Un vescovo in Italia alle soglie del Mille: Leone di Vercelli « Episcopus imperii, servus sancti Eusebii »', *Bollettino Storico Vercellese*, 2 (1999), pp. 37–74.

60 The bibliography on the subject is too vast to be presented here, but can be found in the recent article by Hagen Keller, 'Identità romana e l'idea dell'*Imperium Romanorum* nel X e nel primo XI secolo', in *Three empires, three cities: identity, material culture and legitimacy in Venice, Ravenna and Rome, 750–1000*, ed. by Veronica West-Harling (Turnhout: Brepols, 2015), pp. 255–82.

61 Huschner, *Transalpine Kommunikation*, pp. 263–70, on the weak points of this identification Hoffmann, 'Notare', pp. 467–68.

62 Dormeier, 'Un vescovo', p. 46.

63 Nicolangelo D'Acunto, 'Ottone III e il *regnum Italiae*', in *San Romualdo di Ravenna. Atti del XXIV Convegno del Centro Studi Avellaniti. Fonte Avellana 2001* (Negarine di S. Pietro in Cariano, 2003), pp. 45–84, for a maximal, although not entirely reliable, assessment of

Leo's output, see Hermann Bloch, 'Beiträge zur Geschichte des Bischofs Leo von Vercelli und seiner Zeit', *Neues Archiv der Gesellschaft für ältere deutsche Geschichtskunde*, 22 (1897), pp. 11–136.

64 On the sources of the *Metrum Leonis* see Gamberini, *Metrum Leonis*, pp. XXII-XXVI.

65 His marginal annotations can be found in the exceptional ninth-century copy of the *Scriptores historiae Augustae* written at Fulda (Bamberg, Staatsbibliothek, MS Msc. Class. 54) and in Justin's *Epitome* of the *Historiae Philippicae* produced in late Carolingian northern Francia (Vercelli, Biblioteca Capitolare, MS CLXXVII).

66 For further details on these manuscripts and Leo's annotations see Gavinelli, 'Leone di Vercelli'.

67 Cf. Gavinelli, 'Leone di Vercelli', pp. 255–6. The Italian palaeographer does not ascribe the annotation on f. 86r to Leo, but the reference to a *puer* can also be found in other *marginalia* whose attribution is not disputed, as for instance on f. 114r.

68 Gavinelli, 'Leone di Vercelli', p. 255 and Heinrich Dormeier, 'Die *Renovatio Imperii Romanorum* und die "Außenpolitik" Ottos III. und seiner Berater', in *Polen und Deutschland vor 1000 Jahren*, ed. by Michael Borgolte (Berlin, 2002), pp. 163–91 (pp. 179–80).

69 Gavinelli, 'Leone di Vercelli', pp. 251–2. On Leo's fierce resistance against Arduin of Ivrea, see Francesco Panero, *Una signoria vescovile nel cuore dell'impero. Funzioni pubbliche, diritti signorili e proprietà della Chiesa di Vercelli dall'età tardocarolingia all'età sveva* (Vercelli: Società storica vercellese, 2004), esp. pp. 77–97 as well as Alfredo Lucioni, 'Re Arduino e il contesto religioso: monachesimo e vescovi fra inimicizie e protezioni', in *Arduino fra storia e mito*, ed. by Giuseppe Sergi (Bologna: Il Mulino, 2018), pp. 25–84.

70 Peter Damian, *Letter 117*, in *The Letters of Peter Damian 91–120*, translated by Owen J. Blum (Washington, DC: Catholic University of America Press, 1998), pp. 318–31, quoted passage at pp. 325–6, cf. *Die Briefe des Petrus Damiani*, ed. by Kurt Reindel, MGH *Briefe*, 4 (Munich: Monumenta Germaniae Historica, 1983–1993), III, pp. 323–4.

71 Harry Bresslau, *Handbuch der Urkundenlehre für Deutschland und Italien* (Berlin: De Gruyter, 1969), I, pp. 452 and 471–2. On Hugh of Parma also Huschner, *Transalpine Kommunikation*. pp. 818–9, 824–30 and 929–31 who does not mention Peter Damian's letter.

72 The story of the learned wandering scholar Walter, assistant of Peter Damian's master Ivo, has an equally violent ending: after thirty years of travelling across Europe to pursue his studies, he settled in Italy to teach boys and was later mortally wounded by the supporters of another teacher. Instead of asking for a priest to make his last confession, he only kept uttering the same words 'Oh what a loss! What a loss', see Peter Damian, *Letter 117*, p. 325.

73 On the political relevance of the church of Parma in the Ottonian and Salian empire, see Huschner, *Transalpine Kommunikation*, pp. 913–28.

74 Huschner, *Transalpine Kommunikation*, p. 247. See also Cinzio Violante, 'L'immaginario e il reale. I "da Besate" una stirpe feudale e "vescovile" nella genealogia di Anselmo il Peripatetico e nei documenti', in *Nobiltà e chiese nel Medioevo e altri saggi. Scritti in onore di Gerd Tellenbach*, ed. by Cinzio Violante (Rome: Jouvence, 1993), pp. 97–157. Anselm's maternal and paternal family trees are reconstructed in the appendix published by Karl Manitius in MGH *Die deutschen Geschichtsquellen des Mittelalters 500–1500*, II.

75 Witt, *The Two Latin Cultures*, pp. 120–39; Herbert E. J. Cowdrey, 'Anselm of Besate and Some Other Italian Scholars of the Eleventh Century', *Journal of Ecclesiastical History*, 23 (1972) pp. 115–24; Cinzio Violante, 'Anselmo da Besate', *Dizionario Biografico degli Italiani*, 3 (1961), pp. 407–9. Anselm's student years can be reconstructed by gleaning information from his writings edited by Karl Manitius and published in the same volume as Gunzo's *Epistola ad Augienses*, MGH *Die deutschen Geschichtsquellen des Mittelalters 500–1500*, II, pp. 95–183. An English translation is available in Beth Susan Bennett, 'The *Rhetorimachia* of Anselm de Besate. Critical Analysis and Translation' (unpublished doctoral thesis, University of Iowa, 1981), pp. 78–160.

76 At Parma he studied dialectic (Porphyry and Boethius) with Drogo (*philosophus, flos et Italiae decus*) with whom he established a lasting bond of mentorship and friendship. On Sichelm, see Anselm de Besate, *Rhetorimachia*, p. 99.

77 *Ibidem*, p. 154. English translation by Bennett, *The Rhetorimachia*, p. 135 (slightly modified): *the glory of my name would not flourish thus, nor in this manner, with ANSELM, would resound all of Italy and the rest of the provinces which we have perambulated from childhood, from sunrise to sunset, in the teaching of logic. Not at my arrival would* Francia *ring, nor, to be sure, would* Alamannia*, nor indeed the royal palace itself which has been for a long time now awaiting me as its chaplain.*

78 Landulf Senior, *Historia Mediolanensis*, p. 71.

79 Anselm's hand has been identified in Henry III's diplomas as the notary 'Heinrich C', see Carl Erdmann, *Forschungen zur politischen Ideenwelt der Frühmittelalters* (Berlin: Akademie-Verlag, 1951), pp. 119–24. Erdmann's findings are summarized by Karl Manitius in MGH *Die deutschen Geschichtsquellen des Mittelalters 500–1500*, II, pp. 66–74.

80 Manitius, MGH *Die deutschen Geschichtsquellen*, p. 67, cf. MGH *Die Urkunden der Deutschen Könige und Kaiser*, V, ed. by Harry Bresslau and Paul F. Kehr (Berlin: Monumenta Germaniae Historica, 1931) no. 221.

81 Anselm de Besate, *Rhetorimachia*, pp. 102–3.

82 *Ibidem*, p. 100 (translated by Bennett, *The Rhetorimachia*, p. 83).

83 The episode narrated in the second letter to Drogo could be fictional, but the mention of the Byzantine legation presenting gifts to the emperor confirms Anselm's attendance. For an analysis of the letter, Beth S. Bennett, 'The Significance of the *Rhetorimachia* of Anselm de Besate to the History of Rhetoric', *Rhetorica: A Journal of the History of Rhetoric*, 5/3 (1987), pp. 231–50 (pp. 235–41). On the blossoming high medieval culture of debate see Leidulf Melve, *Inventing the Public Sphere. The Public Debate during the Investiture Contest (c. 1030–1122)* (Leiden: Brill, 2007).

84 Sita Steckel, *Kulturen des Lehrens im Früh- und Hochmittelalter. Autorität, Wissenskonzepte und Netzwerke von Gelehrten* (Cologne-Weimar-Vienna: Böhlau, 2011), on the Ottonian and early Salian period pp. 689–862.

85 Anselm de Besate, *Rhetorimachia*, p. 97.

86 *Ibidem*, pp. 163 and 167.

87 Manitius, MGH *Die deutschen Geschichtsquellen*, pp. 73–4.

88 *Ibidem*, pp. 86–90.

89 *Ibidem*, p. 88: Dümmler thought the manuscript could have been copied from Anselm's autograph, but Manitius was skeptical about the assumption.

90 The manuscript was probably originally unbound, as suggested by the blackened look of the first page of each quire (e.g. f. 10r or 34r). Decoration (missing two ornate initials, on f. 16v and 34v) and a parchment slip integrating a lacuna (f. 4bis) further corroborates the impression of a *codex* certainly prepared with care, but in a hurry.

91 I am reluctant to use the label 'Ottonian Renaissance' which implies a cultural and intellectual decadence during the late ninth and first half of the tenth century which is not supported by manuscript evidence, school activities and literary production, see the forthcoming volume *Culture and Knowledge*; also Mirella Ferrari, 'Manoscritti e testi fra Lombardia e Germania nel secolo X', *Mittellateinisches Jahrbuch*, 24/25 (1989/1990), pp. 105–15.

92 Landulf Senior, *Historia Mediolanensis*, p. 71.

93 Claudio Leonardi, 'Intellectual Life', pp. 189–90.

94 C. Stephen Jaeger, *The Envy of Angels: Cathedral Schools and Social Ideals in Medieval Europe* (Philadelphia: University of Pennsylvania Press, 1994), in the conclusion at p. 329 the author wonders 'to what extent the eleventh century was the *auctor absconditus* or *architectus absconditus* of the twelfth'.

95 *L'école carolingienne d'Auxerre, de Murethach à Remi, 830–908*, ed. by Dominique Iogna-Prat, Colette Jeudy and Guy Lobrichon (Paris: Beauchesne, 1991).

96 On the influence of the Auxerre school on glossematic (or hermeneutic) writings from both sides of the Alps see the introduction to Attone di Vercelli, *Polipticum quod appellatur Perpendiculum*, ed. by Giacomo Vignodelli (Florence, forthcoming). Also for a wider overview see Michael Lapidge, 'The hermeneutic style in tenth-century Anglo-Latin literature', *Anglo-Saxon England*, 4 (1975), pp. 67–111.

97 See the special issue dedicated to Carolingian cultures of debates edited by Mayke de Jong and Irene van Renswoude for *Early Medieval Europe*, 25/1 (2017). On the Gregorian period again Melve, *Inventing the Public Sphere*.

98 A clear antecedent has been studied by Warren Pezé, *Le virus de l'erreur. La controverse carolingienne sur la double prédestination* (Turnhout: Brepols, 2017).

99 Cum verbis ut Italici solent ornatissimis. *Funktionen der Beredsamkeit im kommunalen Italien*, ed. by Florian Hartmann (Göttingen:Vandenhoeck & Ruprecht, 2011).

100 See Renato de Filippis, 'Die Freude (an) der Rhetorik in Anselm von Besates Rhetorimachia', *Quaestio*, 15 (2015), pp. 333–41; and again Bennett, 'The Significance of the *Rhetorimachia*'. On the emergence of the *Ars dictaminis* see now *Le* dictamen *dans tous ses états. Perspectives de recherches sur la théorie et la pratique de l'ars dictaminis (XIe-XVe siècle)*, ed. by Benoît Grévin and Anne-Marie Turcan-Verkerk (Turnhout: Brepols, 2015), particularly the articles by Grévin, Bognini and Hartmann.

101 Witt, *The Two Latin Cultures*, p. 1.

15

THE DIGNITY OF OUR BODIES AND THE SALVATION OF OUR SOULS

Scandal, purity, and the pursuit of unity in late tenth-century monasticism

Steven Vanderputten

Contemporary accounts of the introduction or reintroduction of Benedictine monasticism in England provide a (by tenth-century standards) detailed insight into the ideology and objectives of its principal agents. Considered together, Aethelwold of Winchester's 966 refoundation charter for New Minster, the Winchester council's *Regularis Concordia*, and a small but significant collection of saint's *Lives*, letters, and legal documents form a solid basis against which local manifestations of change can be tested.[1] In particular, analysis of these texts allows us to reconcile the *Regularis Concordia*'s call for unity in monks' and nuns' observance with the numerous indications that absolute uniformity was never actually achieved, let alone pursued.[2] In comparison, the evidence for two similar campaigns on the Continent, one in 950s–early 960s Cologne and another in early 970s Reims, is decidedly underwhelming. Very few theoretical, programmatic, or apologetic treatments of monastic change – a more apt term than 'reform' – from these regions are known to us,[3] and explicit testimony of the two attempts at monastic unification is limited to a single instance each. For Cologne, we have a mere handful of lines in Ruotger's 967/69 *Life* of Archbishop Bruno (953–965), where he states that Bruno admonished 'the multitudes from different congregations that belonged to his honourable see' to be 'one heart and mind' and live 'according to the fixed rule', so that they would avoid disrepute and dress appropriately.[4] And for Reims, there is the longer account by the chronicler Richer of Saint-Remi of a synod, held in 972/974 by Archbishop Adalbero (969–988), where the archbishop and a number of abbots from the region debated the lack of unity in monastic observance, and denounced the scandal caused by monks' illicit relationships with both men and women, their loose attitude to enclosure and obedience, and their penchant for luxurious and frivolous clothes.[5] Besides the fact that there are few sources to inform us of the impact of these campaigns, Ruotger's ultra-brief testimony has discouraged detailed investigation of Bruno's objectives and arguments,[6] while that of Richer, although far longer, is considered suspect.[7]

Initially, there were some historians who accepted the Reims synod's scathing criticisms. Nineteenth-century French historian Ferdinand Lot called the commentary of the two prelates typical of the medieval 'puerile and formalistic mind',[8] while the German monastic specialist Kassius Halinger argued that it must be read as an attack not on indigenous groups of monks, but on the Cluniacs, whom Gorze-inspired Adalbero and his associates presumably saw as a threat to their vision of monastic observance and governance.[9] But as scholars became more acquainted with Richer's methods as a historian, they also became more vocal in acknowledging that neither his account of various speeches held at the synod nor the truth-value of their criticism of the monks' behaviour can be verified using independent sources.[10] Throughout his chronicle, Richer reworked authentic speeches and invented new ones to instruct his readership on the practical benefits of using eloquence in government and debate.[11] The speeches allegedly delivered at the synod not only bear the formal traces of Richer's intervention, but presumably were also tailored to deliver a highly charged oratory in support of his didactic agenda.[12] Additionally, some authors have suggested that Richer, whilst writing in the turbulent setting of 990s Reims, was looking to create vivid memories of a glorious, bygone era in the history of the archdiocese and his own abbey of Saint-Remi, and grossly exaggerated Adalbero's achievement and that of former Abbot Rodulph in restoring monastic observance. Building on these suspicions, Mechtild Müller concluded that the criticisms in the text strictly reflect Richer's personal objections against the conduct of his contemporaries.[13] The combined result of these observations and interpretations is that specialists of tenth-century monastic ideology and reform have all but forgotten his testimony, despite its length and its fascinating contents.

So, is Richer's account of the synod a mere literary folly by a lone monk who was eager to show off his rhetorical skills and recall the golden years of Adalbero's tenure? In the following pages I hope to show that this is not the case. For one, the basic element of his account – Adalbero's calling of a synod to discuss unity in monastic observance – reminds us of the stated goals of the aforementioned campaigns in Cologne and England, regions with which Adalbero's circle maintained strong links. Secondly, the remainder of Richer's text provides us with a rare late tenth-century commentary on monastic identity that merits serious investigation in its own right, regardless of how accurately it describes the 972/974 synod. More specifically, it echoes broadly attested discourses of monastic purity and normative rectitude, including those in Cluny- and Gorze-influenced circles, in the aforementioned campaigns in England and Cologne, and finally also in mid-to-late tenth-century Reims itself. And finally, the distinct traces of literary invention and intervention in the speeches particularly should not distract us from the fact that the chronicler built his discourse on locally and more widely attested traditions of constructing scandal over the conduct of religious – in other words, of giving generalized feelings of unease over the behaviour of religious a local

264 Steven Vanderputten

specificity. While we shall never be able to verify if these things were truly discussed at the 972/974 synod, in a more general sense they shed light on contemporary 'reformist' methodology and discourse in a region that remains under-represented in the study of monastic thought and identity. As such, Richer's report also shows that discourses from other parts of Europe may be less unique, or less original, than some specialists have suspected.

Richer's account of the 972/974 synod and its interpretation(s)

Richer's account of the synod is preceded by a passage describing how in May 972, Adalbero held an archdiocesan synod to consolidate the previous year's transformation of Mouzon, a former house of canons, into a Benedictine monastery.[14] Towards the end of the meeting, 'a very grave enquiry was held over the religious conduct of monks, concerning the fact that the observance (*ritus*) established by the elders appeared to have been corrupted and changed by certain individuals'. The archbishop decreed that abbots from diverse places would convene, 'so that they would consult over this matter in a useful manner'.[15] A follow-up meeting was duly held sometime between the summer of 972 and 974.[16] Adalbero opened the proceedings by admonishing the attending abbots: 'the old religion of your order has excessively deviated from its old honour and reputation'. To repair this, he exhorted them to 'have the same desires, and the same opinions, and to work together towards the same goals'. The reason for his intervention, so he stated, was a lack of consensus over the 'custom of monastic life, with different people wanting and thinking different things', resulting in a state of 'neglected virtue and ... the disgrace of immoral conduct'.[17]

Abbot Rodulph of Saint-Remi (970–983), who acted as the abbots' primate (*praecipuus et primas*) and spokesman, responded by stating that it was 'obvious that we have incurred some dishonour', and that the inappropriate behaviour of monks was bearing 'upon the dignity of our bodies and the salvation of our souls'.[18] He then delivered three speeches – the structure of which reveals Richer's interventions – each of which was followed by a formal rejection of the stigmatized practices on the part of the archbishop and the assembled abbots. First, Rodulph discussed monks who had a male or female companion (*compater* and *commater*), arguing that this type of personal relationship harmed their reputation and moral status. Then, he denounced those monks who left the monastery on their own, without having consulted their fellow brothers: this, Rodulph argued, brought them into disrepute and gave rise to suspicions that the monks owned private property. And in a final, longer address, he criticized the monks for their clothing, denouncing hats that covered the ears, the use of exotic fur pelts, and fringed garments made out of expensive fabrics. He also expressed his disapproval of monks who were fastidious about the even colouring of their black tunics; the use of linen bedding; and their preference for narrow, luxuriously cut shoes and for tunics cinched up on both sides, with long sleeves and heavy folds. The monks' drawers, Rodulph complained, were made with extravagant amounts of the finest fabric. Following this final speech, he stated that the abbots would in future seek to correct such issues of monastic misconduct in 'private councils' (*in privatis conciliis*), a proposal that Adalbero accepted. According to Richer, the archbishop's enthusiastic supervision of the reform guaranteed that, in subsequent years, monastic life in the Reims region once again flourished.[19]

A number of commentators have hailed the 972/974 synod as symptomatic of a paradigm shift in approaches to monastic reform.[20] Until then, interventions in religious communities had been managed strictly on a case-by-case basis, with new modes of conduct and governance being communicated *verbo et exemplo* by individuals recruited from prominent institutions. Presumably, a lack of coordination and structural oversight meant that, post reform, each community retained its individual identity and that differences between local practices grew as long-term processes of institutional and disciplinary change unfolded. In Michel Bur's interpretation, the recently appointed Adalbero, who was looking to remediate this situation for the Reims area and was basking in the glory of the successful eviction of the canons at Mouzon, drew inspiration from England's recent Winchester council and pushed for a unified regional observance in Benedictine houses.[21] As an abundant source record shows, the institutional, intellectual, and personal networks in which major agents of monastic change from England and the Continent (particularly the Reims area, Cologne, and Lotharingia) operated were closely interlinked.[22] Monks from Fleury and Saint-Peter's in Ghent had also attended the Winchester council, guaranteeing that on the Continent (including at the archiepiscopal court in Reims) there was a swift awareness of its decisions and of the objectives of its main participants.[23] But if we accept that Adalbero did call for monastic unity in the early 970s – and there truly is no good reason to discredit that part of Richer's testimony – he probably gained inspiration from other sources too. One was his education at the abbey of Gorze and his subsequent career as a cathedral cleric at Metz, where his uncle Adalbero of Metz (929–962) had led several male and female institutions through a Benedictine reform.[24] Another influence on Adalbero was his relative Bruno of Cologne, whom we saw had launched a reform initiative with strikingly similar aims some ten to fifteen years earlier, and who throughout his adult life maintained close connections with both Adalbero's own region of Lotharingia and the Reims area.[25]

We have no indication of serious attempts to align the outcomes of all of these regional campaigns,[26] and Richer's text suggests that there was also resistance on the part of the leaders of the Reims monasteries to abdicating their abbatial prerogatives and accepting the creation of an institution that would impose unified customs on all the region's monastic communities.[27] Regardless, there were other ways in which the attempts to bring unity to the monastic observance in Cologne, England, and Reims were indeed linked. To begin with, in all three cases agents of monastic change took inspiration from the reform synods of the early ninth century, particularly the Aachen ones of 816/817, and the way the Carolingian reformers had linked uniformity in religious' observance to ritual purity and effective intercession

266 Steven Vanderputten

with the divine.[28] A theme that runs throughout Ruotger's biography of Bruno is the opposition between *dissensio in ecclesia* ('dissent in the Church') and *sinceritas religionis* ('sincerity of religion'),[29] and as we saw at the beginning of this paper, the main protagonists of the campaigns in England and presumably also Reims held very similar views.

Secondly, the 'reform' of Benedictine observance and governance in all three regions took place against the background of interventions in all sorts of religious communities, including those of clerics. The decrees of the Aachen synods, besides targeting both cloistered religious and communities of clerics, show many overlaps as regards the conduct expected of members of the two cohorts.[30] And as we saw earlier, Bruno's biographer indicates that the archbishop called upon 'the various communities (*congregationes*) belonging to his honourable see', with *congregationes* presumably meaning groups of monks (or nuns) and those of clerics.[31] For England, evidence relating to the reorganization of cathedral communities in the later decades of the tenth century allows us to argue that there too, 'reforms' of monastic and clerical communities (particularly of cathedral chapters) often went hand in hand.[32] The same is true for Adalbero's own 972/974 synod, which appears to have coincided with a major intervention at Reims cathedral. Besides commissioning an extensive building campaign for the cathedral itself (an intervention that, besides impacting on the clerics' experience of sacred space, no doubt transformed their liturgical practices too),[33] he apparently told the canons to take residence inside the cloister, sleep and eat in communal rooms, undertake daily readings of the *Rule* of St Augustine and the 'decrees of the Fathers', and observe silence at specific times of the day.[34] While this intervention most fell short of Aethelwold of Winchester's full 'benedictinization' of English cathedral clerics – inspiration for Adalbero's action most likely came from his uncle Adalbero's reform of the canons at Metz cathedral[35] –it nonetheless must have brought profound changes to the lives of the Reims clerics. And as we shall see further, the criticism that was apparently directed at the region's clergy in the 940s–970s is echoed in that which Richer reports was voiced at the 972/974 synod.

Finally, all three campaigns (or at least the (near-)contemporary accounts of these) also reference narratives of scandal. Regarding Cologne, Ruotger tells us how Bruno had admonished all of his ecclesiastical subjects to 'cut out … the superfluity of clothing, divergent virtues, and whatever of this kind seemed effeminate or inappropriate in his Church'.[36] In comparison, England's *Regularis Concordia* issued a more discreet – tactful even – warning that 'differing ways of observing the customs of one rule and one country bring (monks' and nuns') holy conversation into disrepute'.[37] But if we broaden our perspective to include commentaries on the conduct of clerics, we find that in this region too, agents of change were able and willing to adopt a fierce rhetoric of scandal.[38] Richer's testimony about Rodulph haranguing the Reims monks for their disregard of the rules, their aberrant sexuality, and the way they presented themselves to the world may be the most suspect of all three regional case studies. However, we also find that Adalbero from his background in the Metz area must have been familiar with the use of an accusatory discourse in the context of attempts to turn religious houses into Benedictine monasteries. In the *Life of John of Gorze*, the author dismisses the clerics who had served at Gorze prior to the arrival of Benedictine monks in 934, referencing their impurity by referring to the 'filth' that surrounded the altar.[39] And if we pay attention to the documentation regarding criticism of the (mis)conduct of clerics and women religious in mid-tenth-century Reims, it additionally becomes obvious that witnesses of the 972/974 synod would hardly have batted an eye at hearing violent rhetoric of the type Rodulph allegedly delivered.

Reformist rhetoric in tenth-century Reims

By the time Adalbero held his 'synod of abbots', the Reims region had witnessed scandal being constructed around the conduct of religious personnel for at least two-and-a-half decades. A notable presence at the archiepiscopal court in the years 944/946 was the polemicist Ratherius, formerly bishop of Verona, who wrote that transgressions of sexual boundaries catastrophically impacted upon the virile morality of clergymen, and as such also jeopardized their claims to legitimacy, power, and property.[40] That he found a receptive audience for his ideas locally becomes evident if we consider the 940s *Visions of Flothildis*, an anonymous narrative that accuses clerics of disregarding celibacy, and being negligent in carrying out divine office.[41] More generally speaking, the criticisms voiced by both Ratherius and the *Visions* must be linked to a broadly attested discourse – including in Odo of Cluny's 917/927 *Conferences*, Bishop Aethelwold of Winchester's 966 refoundation charter for New Minster, and the 980s *Life of John of Gorze* – that accused impure religious of polluting holy places, and that argued that observance of a specific rule, preferably a monastic one, was the best guarantee for the purity and efficient intercession of those serving these places.[42]

By the look of things, application of these ideas at Reims soon exceeded (as it did in other places) the limits of the written page, including attempts to justify drastic interventions (all of which were politically motivated) in the organization and observance of religious groups. The evidence for Homblières, a female house that was first turned into a Benedictine nunnery (946), and then into a house of Benedictine monks (949), illustrates the application of narratives of scandal in concrete settings.[43] A charter issued by King Louis IV of Western Francia following the institution's second transition states that the nuns had been living a life that was 'insufficiently honest', and had been unwilling to accept a regular observance.[44] The 950s *Miracles of St Hunegondis* added to this that an earlier, 946 'restoration' of the sisters' Benedictine observance had failed because of 'the obscene enticements of carnal desire', and because the sisters had stubbornly refused to acknowledge their errors and amend their ways.[45] Around the same time the *Miracles* were written, in 952, Archbishop Artald (946–961) forced the canons at Saint-Basle to accept that their community be turned into a Benedictine house. A 955 charter by King Lothar of Western Francia presumably attests to the use by the reformers of a discourse of scandal, when it states that the canons had behaved 'in a worldly manner'.[46]

268   Steven Vanderputten

Following the reform of Saint-Basle, the political situation at Reims presumably became too unstable politically to make further interventions in religious communities possible. Archbishop Odelric (962–969), a former lay abbot of the nunneries of Remiremont and Bouxières in the diocese of Toul and Bruno of Cologne's appointee as archbishop, was locally remembered for his efforts to restitute usurped properties to religious houses.[47] But as far as historiographical memory is concerned, it was only Adalbero who, upon his accession to the archiepiscopal throne in 969, revived former narratives of scandal to address the misconduct of clerical communities. Almost immediately, he set out to turn the rural communities of canons at Mouzon and Saint-Thierry into Benedictine houses. Thanks to recent work by Ortwin Huysmans, we have a detailed understanding of the political background to these interventions, the ruthless reshuffling of property rights (affecting multiple religious communities, including Rodulph's institution of Saint-Remi), and the psychological and physical warfare through which Adalbero pressured the canons and their leadership.[48] We can confidently assume that Adalbero used scandalous rhetoric to push his agenda. According to the *Chronicle of Mouzon*, a narrative that is usually dated to the 1030s/1040s but surely derives partly from much earlier accounts, the archbishop stated that the Mouzon inmates merely pretended to be canons, as '(their) life is in nothing different from that of laymen. Slaves to the world, they enjoy marriage and via this business bring forth boys and girls'.[49] And speaking of Saint-Thierry, it declares that the canons there had held a prebend 'not to serve God and his saints, but themselves and the count'.[50] As with such contemporary accounts from England, it is possible that the Mouzon chronicler was first and foremost trying to justify the then-current Benedictine identity of his monastery, and bolster the self-confidence of his fellow monks.[51] But then we must also consider that his judgement of the pre-intervention group of canons at Reims cathedral, whom he calls 'ignorant and poor', is strikingly benign.[52] This might be taken to suggest that he is not simply looking to argue the superiority of a Benedictine observance, but is in fact reproducing memories of selective criticism (correlated to the nature of Adalbero's intervention) as it had been expressed in the early 970s.

By the time Richer drafted his account of the 972/974 synod, circumstances in the archdiocese had again changed drastically. Following Adalbero's death, a power struggle over the archiepiscopal throne erupted that ended in 995 with the definitive installation of Arnulf, son of the penultimate Carolingian sovereign of West Francia. Arnulf's appointment triggered an exodus of Adalbero's former associates,[53] while Richer stayed behind, wallowing in nostalgia for the glorious 970s and 980s and compiling his chronicle. The two main passages in which he looks back on Adalbero's achievements with the region's religious communities are markedly different. In the first, covered by Chapters 24 and 25 of the chronicle, he portrays the archbishop as a benign *corrector* of canons and monks, striving to establish them as unified cohorts that were clearly distinct from secular society.[54] In describing Adalbero's treatment of canons, he suppresses any memories of the contested abolition of the two communities at Mouzon and Saint-Thierry and of

The dignity of our bodies and the salvation of our souls **269**

possible resistance to his intervention at Reims cathedral.[55] And in Chapter 25, in his version of the archbishop's 'reform' of monastic observance, he does not make any reference to the misconduct that was allegedly decried at the 972/974 synod. Instead, he states,

> one cannot say enough about the love and diligence with which he corrected monks' customs, and distinguished their dress from a worldly one. Not only did he strive to make them look distinguished in accordance with the dignity of their religious status, but he also wisely saw to it that the (monks') material possessions that had grown were in no way diminished. Although his love for (all of them) was profound, it was exceptionally so for the monks of the blessed Remigius, patron of the Franks.[56]

The second time Richer addresses the archbishop's achievement, in Chapters 32 to 42, the contents and tone of his testimony are very different. Gone are all the references to interventions in communities of canons; and the argument about a benign *correctio* of the monks' customs is now significantly expanded, and recast to focus on Adalbero's plea for unity at the 972/974 synod, his pointing out of monastic disrepute at this point in time, and finally on Rodulph's stringent *correptio*. Reversing the *Chronicle of Mouzon*'s argument about the canons at Reims cathedral c. 970, Richer has Rodulph state that the monks had acted inappropriately *not* because of poverty or ignorance – in other words, that they knew full well what they had been doing so far was wrong, and that they did not lack the resources to pursue an honourable life.[57] The abbot concludes that they had failed to '(steel the) mind to pursue those things that (one) ought to desire and to reject the things which ought to be shunned'.[58] What monks were lacking was a masculine resolve to look for 'the dignity of (their) bodies and the salvation of (their) souls' – that is to say, to act as they were supposed to act, and represent the ideals they were supposed to represent.

How can we explain this discrepancy? Perhaps it is true, as some scholars have suspected, that Chapters 32–42 were simply a vehicle for Richer that enabled him to simultaneously do several things: to demonstrate the effectiveness of rhetorical speech to his readership; turn memories of Adalbero and especially Rodulph into that of heroic saviours of monastic life; transform memories of a failed attempt at unifying observance and creating a semi-formal body for monastic governance across institutional boundaries into a tale of resounding success; and perhaps also to lament the fragmented observance and misconduct of his 990s peers. But we must also consider the possibility that Richer's statement in Chapter 25 is likewise deceptive, and that *correctio* and *correptio* had been integral parts of Adalbero's reform discourse all along. As we saw, criticism of the general type Rodulph is said to have aimed at the monks was far from unheard of in the early 970s Reims, as was a general methodology of weakening one's opponent by referring to the scandal of their conduct and an already-damaged reputation. And if we compare his statements with what Ruotger has to say about Bruno of Cologne's objections to the outward

270 Steven Vanderputten

appearance of religious, the risk of scandal, and compromised masculinity, it does seem reasonable to assume that Richer's account, even though it inaccurately reports on what was literally said at the synod, in terms of its overall argument comes closer to the early 970s views and arguments than specialists have suspected.[59]

The problem of distinction

Even if we admit that Rodulph's speeches are completely invented, as a commentary on the foundations of monastic identity and the relationship between inner and outer moralities, Richer's report of the 972/974 synod remains a highly valuable, almost criminally disregarded text. Its approach is reflective of a broader quest, initiated in the context of late eighth- and early ninth-century reforms and re-emerging time and again over the next century and a half, to realize what Mayke de Jong has called 'a singularly powerful ideal of differentiation which defined the separateness of those who mediated between God and mankind'.[60] That quest was just as relevant and current in the early 970s as it was some twenty to twenty-five years later, when Richer was writing his chronicle. Ninth-century commentators like Smaragdus of Saint-Mihiel and Hildemar of Corbie had portrayed the world of the cloister as a tightly choreographed stage play, where the conduct, interactions, and outward appearance of its members functioned as indicators of their success in achieving a distinct masculinity, meaning steadfastness in pursuing one's purpose in life.[61] These and other arguments were well known to Adalbero and his circle, and to his contemporaries in the Empire and England.

Yet, while these and other tenth-century agents found the inner stage play in the cloister of great importance, they also explicitly envisaged a second, outer play, encompassing society as a whole. So Ruotger's comments on Bruno's call for unity also references a need for religious to represent a masculine resolve in pursuing and representing their distinct purpose in life, so that they would not be thought of as 'effeminate' or 'indecent'. And as Christopher Reidel recently argued, Aethelwold of Winchester's warnings against worldly conduct by monks were not intended to argue the enforcement of strict enclosure, but to create a *habitus*, a mode of conduct, that would protect monks while they were playing an active role in society.[62] Finally, Rodulph's comments focus on scandal that emerges not in the inner world of the cloister, but in the physical and virtual spaces where encounters with the outside world take place, and where outsiders can observe the monks' conduct and outward appearance. Revealing in this respect is his stressing of the notion that the practices he denounces are not morally reprehensible as such. When discussing male or female companionship for monks, he clarifies that 'I do not see this (companionship) as an objection for those living in the world, but denounce it as illicit for our order', as if he is looking to avoid disturbing the minds of his lay listeners. And when he talks about monks leaving the monastery without consultation, he asks his audience to 'consider how much this is in disagreement with our order'.[63]

Because of the porosity of the metaphorical walls between the cloister and the world, impurity was a central concern for all of these commentators. In their understanding, even the slightest suspicion that a 'return into the world' had happened or might happen had catastrophic consequences.[64] The first of Rodulph's three speeches, that on male and female companions, references canon 14 of the decrees of the Aachen synod of 817, which also prohibits the kissing of women, thereby referencing the same sexual implication that is present in Richer's text.[65] But Richer gives added impact to the abbot's statement by using the dialectic trope of *notatio*, which explains a word by dissecting its different parts – to argue that companions are in fact 'fathers' (*com-pater: pater cum*, 'father with' or 'of') and therefore sexually active beings ('fornicators').[66] Likewise, the second speech and its comments on stability and poverty derive from canon 13 of the decrees of the aforementioned Aachen synod,[67] and Chapter 67,1 of the *Rule of St Benedict*. But in Richer's text, Rodulph adds that these inappropriate practices are not just forbidden, but actually give rise to suspicions that these monks might own property, be depraved in their customs, and generally lead a life of debauchery.[68]

Finally, the speech on monastic dress contains various references to the *Rule* and Benedict of Aniane's interpretation of that text.[69] It is here also that Richer most fully develops the argument that inner and outer moralities must be perfectly aligned: in doing so, he echoes Odo of Cluny's *Conferences*, where the latter associates worldly dress with 'living according to the flesh', and adds that 'a pretty piece of clothing is a sign of a lascivious mind'.[70] Yet here too, references to public scandal and the indignation of the laity are more prominent than in ninth-century commentaries. So Rodulph says that underneath (the costly tunics) one could see their haunches 'pressed close together and buttocks clenched tight', giving them the appearance of *meretriculae*, literally 'little harlots'; and talking about the monks' drawers, he refers to the fact that the fabric is so fine, that observers 'can see their privates'.[71] Besides sexualizing inappropriate dress, the abbot also questions the offending monks' masculinity, not just in a physical sense, but also metaphorically in regard to their steadfastness in pursuing their purpose in life. Earlier we saw how, speaking of Bruno's campaign in 950s or early 960s Cologne, Ruotger had already written that 'superfluity of clothing' was one of the things that made servants of the Church look 'effeminate'.[72] These statements also remind us of Odo's *Conferences*, where he notes that 'laypeople themselves (are) indignant about the quality and modification of (monks') dress', and cites Jeremiah 3:3, *Frons mulieris meretricis facta est tibi*, 'Thy forehead became that of a whoring woman'.[73] If we consider these antecedents and implications, the accusation that the Reims monks looked like 'little harlots' (*meretriculae)* does not seem so random after all.[74]

Rodulph's/Richer's thinking about the relationship between the inner morality and outward appearance of clerics and monks, particularly their clothing, reminds us of increased concerns regarding rich dress as documented for the later eighth and early ninth centuries. Presumably responding to a trend initially seen in Anglo-Saxon England and then also in Francia, Boniface insisted that monks who wore clothes with embroidered bands were likely to fall victim to lust and fornication. And in his letters, Alcuin of York repeatedly stated that inappropriate, rich clothing constituted a danger to the soul. Writing to Bishop Higbald and the monks at Lindisfarne, he stated

272 Steven Vanderputten

'When [God] has taken care to forbid ostentation and costly clothing to women, how much more unseemly vanity in clothing is in men. It is especially harmful to those who serve God as monks, who should in all things show self-control and live religiously, so that their conduct should be beyond reproach.' In a letter to Abbot Frithwine of Wearmouth and Jarrow, he urged him 'adorn your chest with the stole of holiness not with the cultivation of empty clothes'.[75] Perhaps in response to these concerns, Carolingian royal and conciliar legislators, particularly those who authored the decrees of the Aachen synod of 816, prescribed a unified dress code for all monks, the most distinctive aspect of which was the knee-length cowl.[76] Throughout the later ninth and the tenth centuries, observance of this principle continued to be regarded as emblematic of monasticism's distinct status within the Christian community. But as far as we can tell, in the first century after these mandates were issued the point was pushed less aggressively than in the writings of Odo, Ruotger, and indeed also Richer.[77]

This suggests a 'rediscovery' of sorts, in the middle decades of the tenth century, of late-eighth- and early ninth-century commentaries on monastic and clerical dress. That there was considerable interest in material from that period can be easily argued. In an eleventh-century list of books kept at Gorze – the abbey where Adalbero had been educated – we find references to Theodemar of Monte Cassino's letter to Charlemagne; Benedict of Aniane's *Concordia regularium*; the decrees of the 817 synod; and Smaragdus's admired *Diadema monachorum*, all of which explicitly address the issue of proper monastic dress.[78] Evidence of their reception is legion. We already saw how, in his *Conferences*, Odo makes a number of comments on luxurious dress, denouncing it as a sign of compromised monastic masculinity. And in another part of that text, he objects to aristocratic individuals who, once they had entered the cloister, continue to represent their 'physical nobility' in the colour and cut of their clothing, and who decline to wear the *cuculla*, the 'emblem of monastic life' (*monasticum schema*).[79] 'Is it not apostasy', he writes, 'to have contempt for the instructions of the Fathers as regards clothing and food?'[80] And in the 980s *Life of John of Gorze*, a text that is thought to represent 'Gorzian' attitudes in the mid-tenth-century, John refuses to wear anything other than what 'a monk has the right to wear, neither capes or textiles of any colour other than black'.[81] Rodulph in Richer's text also speaks of the need to uphold 'the observance (*ritus*) established by the elders'.[82]

The question, though, is why is the scandal of inappropriate monastic dress argued so aggressively and so prominently in these tenth-century commentaries? While it is beyond the scope of this paper to attempt to formulate a comprehensive answer, these authors probably sought to do two things. One, as we saw earlier, was to construct narratives of scandal to influence the public perception of monks' (and also clerics and women religious') compromised ritual purity and effectiveness as intercessors with God, as part of efforts to pressure them into accepting an agenda of spiritual and/or institutional reform. And a second was to establish non-ambiguous, visual dividing lines between the ecclesiastical cohorts and the laity in the context where changing clerical and monastic fashions clashed with hardening views on the relation between inner and outer moralities. Recently, Maureen Miller has

The dignity of our bodies and the salvation of our souls **273**

shown how the higher clergy in several regions of Europe were in the process of adopting a more luxurious style to represent the distinct moral and functional identity of clerics within the ecclesiastical system and society in general.[83] It is possible that a similar movement to adapt the appearance of monks to reflect their distinct, elevated status and morality was taking place around the same time.

More than half a century ago, Kassius Hallinger suspected that Richer's text implicitly criticizes the Cluniacs' adoption of a *duplex vestis* or double habit as an overly luxurious, frivolous, and counter normative tradition.[84] But differences of opinion about the matter do not seem to have run exclusively along a fracture line that separated Cluniac from 'Lotharingian' or 'Gorzian' monasticism. In 'Gorzian' ciricles too, groups of monks were experimenting with new dress codes. Following a 979 intervention by newly appointed Abbot Ramwold, a former monk from Trier, the community at Sankt Emmeran in Regensburg adopted a dress code that included a very wide habit worn possibly over a brightly blue tunic.[85] Meanwhile, at Reichenau, the monks had also taken to wearing a wide habit; whereas at Fulda, the monks wore a very narrow, pale one.[86] By the second quarter of the eleventh century, the Echternach community had also adopted a wide, ankle-length variant of the *cuculla*, while the dress code at Sankt Emmeran continued to be in a state of flux.[87] If some of these communities faced criticism for their non-traditional appearance, their response may not have been very different from the one recorded in the chronicle of Thietmar of Merseburg. Writing about an 1005 archiepiscopal intervention at the abbey of Bergen, Thietmar calls the new strictness in dress and food habits laudable, but states that 'the God-pleasing fruit of virtue lies in a good heart and is sometimes hidden with the pious under a pretty and golden dress'.[88]

The general impression we get from these scattered testimonies is that of widespread experimentation happening in the decades around the turn of the millennium. Judging by Abbot Ramwold's tolerance of a non-traditional dress code at Sankt Emmeran, at least in some cases the monks' reasons for wearing a 'pretty and golden dress' presumably went further than a mere desire to show off their wealth or their (former) position in life, but actually included a proper, logical argument on the need to represent their distinct moral status as members of the monastic cohort. Pending systematic analysis of iconographic and other evidence, we can only guess if such experiments were taking place in the Reims area too. When Notker of Sankt Gallen (d. 1022) denounced as counter to the Lord's example the recent custom among certain French monks of wearing the *duplex vestis* or double *cuculla*, his criticism was aimed at Lotharingian reformers Richard of Saint-Vanne and Poppo of Stavelot.[89] These institutional settings and the men who operated in them bring us close to the context of the 972/974 synod, as Richard in the 980s and 990s had been a cleric at Reims cathedral, and Poppo had entered the monastic life at Saint-Thierry.[90] But then we must also be attentive to the possibility that Notker was playing into the prejudices of his audience against foreigners and their customs,[91] and relied on satire to reference more fundamental resentments over what these individuals had done to his community.

274 Steven Vanderputten

For their part, members of the Reims cathedral circle in the decades around the year 1000 were no strangers to satire either. Richard himself was known for the terrifying visions he summoned when describing the fate of his adversaries in hell, and famously wrote a scorching letter accusing the monks of Saint-Vaast and Saint-Bertin (both in Flanders) of gross misconduct.[92] Another, much-cited example from the 1020s is Bishop Adalbero of Laon's depiction of a monk who upon returning from a journey to the south of France had taken up wearing lay clothes, and carrying weapons.[93] Conceivably, Richer's account of the Reims synod should be read at least in part as a deliberate attempt to ridicule groups and individuals with dissenting views on monastic observance by creating scandal over their general worldliness, calling them 'little whores', and attacking their aberrant outward appearance. Whether the satire actually originated with Adalbero and Rodulph in the 970s, or with Richer in the 990s, is perhaps less important than the observation that the text brings together all kinds of arguments and rhetorical strategies that were designed to make a statement on the inextricable link between the monks' inner and outer morality, the need for distinction and purity, and the rooting of these principles in ninth-century tradition.

Conclusions

Historical truth, selective reporting, and literary invention are so entangled in Richer's chronicle that we should not want to choose between accepting and rejecting his account of what was said at the 972/974 synod. Instead of trying to find out whether Adalbero and Rodulph's criticisms were truly theirs and whether they truly referred to real-life situations in the Reims monasteries c. 970, we probably must read Richer's account as reflective of a particular approach to monastic identity as it was propagated by Adalbero's circle, and of the rhetorical means the archbishop and the abbot relied upon to push those views upon his monastic subjects, and justify an aggressive campaign of monastic unification. Whether these views truly made much impact, at the time or when Richer reported on them, is a different matter altogether.

Notes

1 Discussion in Julia S. Barrow, 'The Ideology of the Tenth-Century English Benedictine "Reform"', in *Challenging the Boundaries of Medieval History: The Legacy of Timothy Reuter*, ed. by Patricia Skinner (Turnhout: Brepols, 2009), pp. 141–54. On the debate since 2009, Tracey-Anne Cooper, *Monk-Bishops and the English Benedictine Reform Movement* (Toronto: Pontifical Institute of Mediaeval Studies, 2015); Christopher T. Reidel, *Monastic Reform and Lay Religion in Aethelwold's Winchester* (unpublished doctoral dissertation, Boston College, 2015); and Rebecca Stephenson, *The Politics of Language. Byrhtferth, Aelfric, and the Multilingual Identity of the Benedictine Reform* (Toronto: University of Toronto Press, 2015). I should like to thank Melissa Provijn for her comments on the draft version of this paper.
2 *The Monastic Agreement of the Monks and Nuns of the English Nation*, ed. by Thomas Symons (London: Nelson, 1953). Real-life application of changes to the liturgy inevitably led to local variations; see the discussion in *Aelfric's Letter to the Monks of Eynsham*, ed. by Christopher A. Jones (Cambridge: Cambridge University Press, 1998), pp. 49–51.

The dignity of our bodies and the salvation of our souls **275**

3 Julia Barrow, 'Ideals and Applications of Reform', in *The Cambridge History of Christianity 3. Early Medieval Christianities, c. 600 – c. 1100*, ed. by Thomas Noble and Julia Smith (Cambridge: Cambridge University Press, 2008), pp. 359–60.

4 Ruotger, *Vita Brunonis archiepiscopi Coloniensis*, ed. by Irene Ott (*Monumenta Germaniae Historica* (henceforth MGH) *Scriptores Rerum Germanicarum ns 10*) (Weimar: Böhlau, 1951), p. 22: 'De religione primo et cultu Dei ... instituit, ut multitudinis, quae in diversis congregationibus ad eius honorabilem sedem pertinentibus erat, unum cor esset et anima una'; all translations for this text are from Henry Mayr-Harting, *Church and Cosmos in Early Ottonian Germany: The View from Cologne* (Oxford: Oxford University Press, 2007), p. 41. Bruno also instructed all the hermits in the region to become recluses, adopt a specific lifestyle, and forge a permanent connection to an established religious house; Ruotger, p. 34.

5 Richer, *Historiae*, ed. by Hartmut Hoffmann, *MGH Scriptores* 38 (Hannover: Hahnsche Buchhandlung, 2000), chs. 32–42, pp. 187–91. On the dating of this archdiocesan or diocesan synod, Isolde Schröder, *Die westfränkischen Synoden von 888 bis 987 und ihre Überlieferung* (Munich: Monumenta Germaniae Historica, 1980), pp. 290–2 and 297.

6 Some attempts to reconstruct and contextualize Bruno's ecclesiastical (in particular monastic) policies may be found in Friedrich Lotter, *Die Vita Brunonis des Ruotger. Ihre historiographische und Ideengeschichtliche Stellung* (Bonn: Röhrscheid, 1958), pp. 84–90; Hugo Stehkämper, 'Erzbishof Brun I. und das Mönchtum', *Jahrbuch des Kölnischen Geschichtsvereins*, 40 (1966), pp. 1–18; and Gunther Wolf, 'Erzbischof Brun I. Von Köln, Kaiserin Theophanu und die Blütezeit des Klosters St. Pantaleon zu Köln', in *Satura mediaevalis: Gesammelte Schriften. 2: Ottonenzeit* (Heidelberg: Hermes, 1995), pp. 229–43. Also the references further, in n. 25, 29, and 41.

7 Michel Bur suspects that the Reims synod led to an overall 'unity of behaviour ... a monolithism typical of the Reims abbeys within the Benedictine world'; 'Saint-Thierry et le renouveau monastique dans le diocèse de Reims au Xe siècle', in *Saint-Thierry, une abbaye du VIe au XXe siècle*, ed. by Michel Bur (Saint-Thierry: Association des Amis de l'Abbaye de Saint-Thierry, 1979), pp. 39–49 (p. 48). Manuscript evidence suggests a focus on aligning liturgical practices, as was the case in contemporary England; Jason Glenn, *Politics and History in the Tenth Century. The Work and World of Richer of Reims* (Cambridge and New York: Cambridge University Press, 2004), pp. 75–7.

8 Ferdinand Lot, *Les derniers Carolingens. Lothaire – Louis V – Charles de Lorraine (954–991)* (Paris: Bouillon, 1891), p. 71: 'Rien ne montre mieux l'esprit puéril et formaliste du moyen âge que les plaintes de l'abbé Raoul'.

9 Kassius Hallinger, *Gorze-Kluny. Studien zu den monastischen Lebensformen und Gegensätzen im hochmittelalter*, 2 vols. (Rome: Studia Anselmiana, 1950–1951), ii, p. 699.

10 Bur, p. 41 and Hoffmann's comments in Richer, *Historiae*, pp. 1–8 and p. 187, n. 33.

11 On Richer's reputation and methodology as a historiographer, Glenn, *Politics* and Justin Lake, *Richer of Saint-Rémi. The Methods and Mentality of a Tenth-Century Historian* (Washington D.C.: Catholic University of America Press, 2013), esp. pp. 22–9.

12 Many of the speeches in Richer's chronicle begin with a *conquestio*, an opening speech intended to arouse the pity of his readers, followed by a *comparatio*, where a problem is pointed out but a solution is immediately offered; Lake, p. 200 onwards. To aid his readers, Richer inserted marginal notes in his autograph manuscript, pointing out exactly how these parts gave structure to the speeches, and how they made them particularly effective: these are included in Hoffmann's edition. In his account of the 972/974 synod, a double *conquestio* (chs. 31 and 33) is followed by three *indignationes* (chs. 35–41), while a reconciliatory speech (ch. 42), confirming the synod's decisions and pointing out their intended effect, closes the passage.

13 Mechtild Müller, *Die Kleidung nach Quellen des frühen Mittelalters. Textilien und Mode von Karls dem Grossen bis Heinrich III.* (Berlin and New York: De Gruyter, 2003), p. 115. Glenn (pp. 77–84) suspects that Richer and his peers at Saint-Remi followed an observance influenced by monastic practice at Gorze and Fleury.

276 Steven Vanderputten

14 On this intervention, Ortwin Huysmans, 'Pious Foundation or Strategic Masterstroke? The Chronicon Mosomense and the Reform of Mouzon by Archbishop Adalbero of Reims (969–989)', *Revue d'Histoire Ecclésiastique*, 110 (2015), pp. 103–34.

15 Richer, *Historiae*, ch. 31, p. 186: 'de monachorum religione ... motu gravissimo conquestio habita est, eo quod ritus a maioribus constituti, a quibusdam depravati et inmutati viderentur. Unde ... decretum est ut diversorum locorum abbates convenirent, et inde utiliter consulerent'. All translations of Richer's text are from Richer of Saint-Remi, *Histories*, ed. and trans. Justin Lake (Cambridge, MA.: Harvard University Press, 2011).

16 Bur (p. 44) speculates that the monastic participants of the synod were mainly abbots from institutions in the diocese of Reims, joined by the leaders of Saint-Médard in Soissons, Corbie, and perhaps also (through links with Insular abbots there) Saint-Vincent in Laon and even Saint-Felix in Metz. The abbots whom we know participated in the May 972 meeting are Rodulph of Saint-Remi, Odoleus of Saint-Médard, Ratoldus of Corbie, and Adzo of Saint-Basle; Schröder, p. 290.

17 Richer, *Historiae*, ch. 33, p. 187: 'Vestri ordinis antiqua religio, ab antiquitatis honestate ut fama est supra modum aberravit. Dissidetis enim inter vos in ipsa regularis ordinis consuetudine, cum aliter alter, alter aliter velit ac sentiat ... Unde et utile duxi, ut vobis hic gratia dei in unum collectis, suadem idem velle, idem sentire, idem cooperari, ut eadem voluntate, eodem sensu, eadem cooperatione et virtus neglecta repetatur et pravitatis dedecus vehementissime propulsetur'.

18 Ibid., ch. 34, p. 188: 'Quod hic, inquit, a te promulgatum est pater sanctissime, alta memori a condendum est eo quod et corporum dignitatem, et animarum salutem affectes ... Unde et patet nos aliquid dedecoris contraxisse, quod ab appetendis aliquanto aberravimus'.

19 Ibid., chs. 35–42, pp. 188–91.

20 'Nowhere,' wrote the German historian Ernst Sackur, 'was ... reform taken in hand so systematically and so earnestly'; *Die Cluniacenser in ihrer kirchlichen und allgemeingeschichtlichen Wirksamkeit bis zur Mitte des elften Jahrhunderts*, 2 vols. (Halle a.d. Saale: Niemeyer, 1892–1894), ii, p. 194. Presumably it was this remark that led the Benedictine scholar Ursmer Berlière to view the synod as a distant precursor to the earliest, twelfth-century 'general chapters' of Benedictine abbots, the first of which was held in Reims in late 1131; 'Les chapitres généraux de l'ordre de St. Benoit', *Revue Bénédictine*, 18 (1901), pp. 364–98 (pp. 366–7) and 'Les chapitres généraux de l'ordre de S. Benoit', *Revue Bénédictine*, 19 (1902), pp. 38–75, 268–78, 374–411 (p. 385).

21 Bur, p. 43.

22 A fairly recent state of the art is in *England and the Continent in the Tenth Century, Studies in honour of Wilhelm Levison (1876–1947)*, ed. by David Rollason, Conrad Leyser, and Hannah Williams (Turnhout: Brepols, 2010).

23 *The Monastic Agreement*, pp. 71–2. On interactions between Fleury and English centres, John B. Nightingale, 'Oswald, Fleury and Continental Reform', in *St Oswald of Worcester*, ed. by Nicholas B. Brooks and Catherine R.E. Cubitt (London: Bloomsbury Publishing, 1996), pp. 23–45 and several of the papers in *England*, ed. by Rollason, Leyser, and Williams. On interactions between Adalbero and the two abbeys of Fleury and Ghent, Bur, pp. 44–5.

24 John Nightingale, *Monasteries and Patrons in the Gorze Reform: Lotharingia, c. 850–1000* (Oxford: Oxford University Press, 2001), pp. 71–86.

25 Ludwig Vones, 'Erzbischof Brun von Köln und der Reimser Erzstuhl', in *Von sacerdotium und regnum. Geistliche und weltliche Gewalt im frühen und hohen Mittelalter. Festschrift für Egon Boshof zum 65. Geburtstag*, ed. by Franz-Reiner Erkens and Hartmut Wolff (Cologne: Böhlau, 2002), pp. 325–45.

26 Donald A. Bullough, 'The Continental Background of the Reform', in *Tenth-Century Studies. Essays in Commemoration of the Millennium of the Council of Winchester and Regularis Concordia*, ed. by David Parsons (London: Phillimore, 1975), pp. 2–36, 210–4 (p. 33).

27 Bur, p. 45 and Patrick Demouy, *Genèse d'une cathédrale. Les archevêques de Reims et leur Eglise aux XIe et XIIe siècles* (Paris: D. Guéniot, 2005), pp. 299–300.

The dignity of our bodies and the salvation of our souls **277**

28 Glenn, pp. 25–35. Also the discussions in Patrick Wormald, 'Aethelwold and His Continental Counterparts: Contacts, Comparison, Contrast', in *Bishop Aethelwold: His Career and Influence*, ed. by Barbara A.E. Yorke (Woodbridge: Boydell Press, 1988), pp. 13–42 (pp. 15–9); Mechtild Gretsch, 'Cambridge, Corpus Christi College, 57: A Witness to the Early Stages of the Benedictine Reform in England?', *Anglo-Saxon England*, 32 (2003), pp. 111–46; and Barrow, *Ideology*.

29 Hartmut Hoffmann, 'Politik im ottonische Reichskirchensystem: zur Interpretation der *Vita Brunonis* von Ruotger', *Rheinische Vierteljahrblätter*, 22 (1957), pp. 31–55, with additional commentary in Henry Mayr-Harting, 'Ruotger, the *Life of Bruno* and Cologne Cathedral Library', in *Intellectual Life in the Middle Ages. Essays Presented to Margaret Gibson*, ed. by Lesley Smith and Benedicta Ward (London: Continuum, 1992), pp. 33–60 (pp. 34–5).

30 Mayke De Jong, 'Imitatio Morum. The Cloister and Clerical Purity in the Carolingian World', in *Medieval Purity and Piety. Essays on Medieval Clerical Celibacy and Religious Reform*, ed. by Michael Frassetto (New York, NY: Garland, 1998), pp. 49–80. Several authors have observed how, in post-reform England, moral and even functional distinctions between monks and clerics remained vague; Francesca Tinti, 'Benedictine Reform and Pastoral Care in Late Anglo-Saxon England', *Early Medieval Europe*, 23 (2015), pp. 229–51 and Reidel.

31 Ruotger, p. 22; also Rebecca Browett, *The Cult of St Aethelwold and Its Context, c. 984–c. 1400* (unpublished doctoral dissertation, University of London, 2016), pp. 54–5 and 67 (with thanks to the author for sharing her unpublished work).

32 Julia S. Barrow, 'English Cathedral Communities and Reform in the Late Tenth and the Eleventh Centuries', in *Anglo-Norman Durham 1093–1193*, ed. by David Rollason, Margaret M. Harvey, and Michael C. Prestwich (Woodbridge: Boydell Press, 1994), pp. 25–39 (pp. 34–7).

33 Michel Bur, 'A propos de la Chronique de Mouzon. II: Architecture et liturgie à Reims au temps d'Adalbéron (vers 976)', *Cahiers de civilisation médiévale*, 27 (1984), pp. 297–303 and Glenn, pp. 30–5.

34 Richer, *Histories*, p. 138; also the later testimony in the *Chronique ou livre de fondation du monastère de Mouzon. Chronicon Mosomense seu Liber fundationis monasterii sanctae Mariae O.S.B. apud Mosomum in dioecesi Remensi*, ed. by Michel Bur (Paris: Centre national de la recherche scientifique, 1989), p. 170 and the commentary in Glenn, pp. 35–52.

35 It is unclear what observance the cathedral canons at Metz had been following while the younger Adalbero was a cleric there. The most likely inspirations are Chrodegang of Metz's *Rule* for canons, his legacy as transmitted through the 816 Aachen synod's *Institutio canonicorum*, or some adaptation of that latter text; Glenn, p. 36.

36 Ruotger, p. 22: 'ut vestium superfluitas, morum inequalitas et quicquid hoc modo effeminatum et indecens in eius ecclesia videretur, vera et spirituali circumcisione, quod est inicium sapientie, diligentissime abscideretur, ut divinis ministeriis omnes, quorum id intererat, intentissime secundum prefixam sibi regulam viverent nec aliam sibi sue salutis causam ullatenus estimarent'.

37 *The Monastic Agreement*, p. 3: 'ne impar ac varius unius regulae ac unius patriae usus probrose vituperium sanctae conversationi irrogaret'.

38 Stephenson, pp. 68–101.

39 John of Saint-Arnoul, *Vita Johannis Gorziensis*, ed. by Paul C. Jacobsen (*Die Geschichte vom Leben des Johannes von Gorze*) (Wiesbaden: Harrassowitz Verlag, 2016), pp. 242 and 244.

40 Ortwin Huysmans, 'Peace and Purges: Episcopal Administration of Religious Communities and the Contested See of Reims (c. 931–953)', *Revue Bénédictine*, 126 (2016), pp. 287–323 (p. 296); on Rather's views and those of other polemicists in northern Italy, Ross Balzaretti, 'Men and Sex in Tenth-Century Italy', in *Masculinity in Medieval Europe*, ed. by D.M. Hadley (London: Taylor & Francis, 1999), pp. 143–59.

41 *Visiones Flothildis*, ed. by Philippe Lauer (*Les annales de Flodoard*) (Paris: A. Picard et fils, 1905), pp. 173–74. Some of Rather's influence might also be discernible in the policies as archbishop of Bruno, a noted supporter of Rather's; Gunther G. Wolf, 'Erzbischof

Brun I. von Köln' und die Förderung gelehrter Studien in Köln, in *Satura mediaevalis: Gesammelte Schriften. 2: Ottonenzeit* (Heidelberg: Hermes, 1995), pp. 219–28 (pp. 221–2).

42 Isabelle Rosé, *Construire une société seigneuriale. Itinéraire et ecclésiologie de l'abbé Odon de Cluny (fin IXe-milieu du Xe siècle)* (Turnhout: Brepols, 2008), pp. 603–20; Barrow, *Ideology*, p. 150; and above, n. 38.

43 Two different reconstructions of the Homblières reform are in Fraser McNair, 'A Saint, An Abbot, His Documents and Her Property: Power, Reform and Landholding in the Monastery of Homblières under Abbot Berner (949–82)', *Journal of Medieval History*, 41 (2015), pp. 55–68 and Huysmans, *Peace*, pp. 311–2.

44 *Recueil des actes de Louis IV, roi de France (936–54)*, ed. by Maurice Prou and Pierre Lauer (Paris: Imprimerie nationale, 1914), nr. 32, p. 77: 'non satis honeste viventibus et regulari districtioni subiici'.

45 Berner, *Translatio corporis sanctae Hunegundis*, ed. in *AASS Augusti* V (Antwerp, 1741), p. 233: 'inibi per misera carnalis desiderii lenocinia turpissime volutabantur' and 'crebris exhortationibus ad sui imitationem juxta monita Apostoli, arguendo, obsecrando, necnon etiam increpando, continuo invitabat'.

46 *Recueil des actes de Lothaire et de Louis V, rois de France (954–987)*, ed. by Louis Halphen and Ferdinand Lot (Paris: Imprimerie nationale, 1908), nr. 6, pp. 13–5. C. 948, Artald put the canons of St Timothy, a small community outside the Reims city walls, on a path to extinction by removing the relics of their patron saints. Nothing is known of how he justified this intervention; Huysmans, *Peace*, pp. 313–5.

47 Eduard Hlawitschka additionally suspects that he is the same Odelric, a deacon of the cathedral of Metz, who was involved in the 933 restoration of Gorze and the 941/942 removal of canons (and subsequent their replacement by Benedictine monks) at the abbey of Saint-Arnoul in Metz; 'Zur Lebensgeschichte Erzbischof Odelrichs von Reims', *Zeitschrift für die Geschichte des Oberrheins*, 109 (1961), pp. 1–20 (p. 16).

48 Huysmans, *Pious Foundation*. Additionally, Adalbero may have tried to intervene at another house of canons at Saint-Vivent in Braux-sur-Meuse; Id., *Tutor ac nutritor. Episcopal Agency, Lordship and the Administration of Religious Communities. Ecclesiastical Province of Rheims c. 888–1073* (unpublished doctoral dissertation, Leuven, 2016), p. 138.

49 *Chronique*, p. 161: '... eorum vita nihil a laicorum differat cohabitatione: nuptiis quippe fruuntur, filiorum et filiarum quaestuosis mercimoniis inservientes, usibus saeculi coutuntur ...'.

50 Ibid., p. 157: 'praebendariis, non Deo et sanctis eius, sed sibi ipsis et comiti servientes'.

51 The *Chronicle* notes that at the time of writing – which can be at any point between the late tenth century and the 1030s – the 'reformed' canons of the cathedral have long abandoned the strict observance Adalbero taught them in the early 970s; *Chronique*, p. 170. On the low opinion Aethelwold had of the clergy, Barrow, *The Ideology*, p. 146 and Stephenson, pp. 68–101.

52 *Chronique*, p. 170: 'rusticos et pauperes'.

53 Two notable departures were Richard, a deacon and Lotharingian native who later became prominent as abbot of Saint-Vanne in Verdun, and his friend and patron Count Frederic of Verdun; Steven Vanderputten, *Imagining Religious Leadership in the Middle Ages. Richard of Saint-Vanne and the Politics of Reform* (Ithaca, NY: Cornell University Press, 2015), p. 7.

54 The Reims nunneries of Saint-Pierre d'Avenay and Saint-Pierre-les-Dames may have attracted Adalbero's attention at some point, but are absent from the source record for his tenure; Françoise Poirier-Coutansais, *Gallia monastica. Tableaux et cartes de dépendances monastiques 1. Les abbayes bénédictines du diocèse de Reims* (Paris: Picard, 1974), p. 454 and 483.

55 Richer, *Historiae*, p. 138. The continuation of Flodoard's *Annals* refers to Adalbero's construction works at the cathedral as 'destructions'; *Les Annales*, pp. 160–1.

56 Richer, *Historiae*, ch. 25 p. 183: 'Monachorum quoque mores, quanta dilectione et industria correxit, atque a seculi habitu distinxit, sat dicere non est. Non solum enim

The dignity of our bodies and the salvation of our souls **279**

religionis dignitate eos insignes apparere studuit, verum etiam bonis exterioribus augmentatos nullomodo minui prudens adegit. Quos cum multo coleret amore, precipua a tamen beati R(emigii) Francorum patroni monachos caritate extollebat'.

57 Ibid., ch. 34, p. 188: 'Quod etiam multa obiurgatione reprehendendum est cum nec ignavia nos precipitaverit, nec inopia ad id impulerit'.

58 Ibid.: 'Constat enim ad habitum virtutis neminem pervenisse, nisi quem talis animus munivit, quo et appetenda appetenda peteret, et vitanda refelleret'.

59 Typically for the scepticism some historians have had vis-à-vis the second part of Richer's account, Auguste Dumas makes no mention of the synod; 'L'Église de Reims au temps des luttes entre Carolingiens et Robertiens (888–1027)', *Revue d'histoire de l'église de France*, 30 (1944), pp. 5–38 (p. 22).

60 Mayke De Jong, 'Charlemagne's Church', in *Charlemagne: Empire and Society*, ed. by J. Story (Manchester: Manchester University Press, 2005), pp. 103–35 (p. 124).

61 Lynda L. Coon, *Dark Age Bodies. Gender and Monastic Practice in the Early Medieval West* (Philadelphia, PA: University of Pennsylvania Press, 2011), pp. 98–113 and Christopher A. Jones, 'Monastic Identity and Sodomitic Danger in the Occupatio by Odo of Cluny', *Speculum*, 82 (2007), pp. 1–53 (pp. 45–53).

62 Reidel, pp. 14–6 and Id., 'Debating the Role of the Laity in the Hagiography of the Tenth-Century Anglo-Saxon Benedictine Reform', *Revue Bénédictine*, 127 (2017), pp. 314–46.

63 Richer, *Historiae*, ch. 35, p. 188: 'Hoc licet verisimile dicens, secularibus non preiudico, sed nostro ordine illicita reprehendo' and 'O quantum nostro ordini dissentiat considerate'.

64 Albrecht Diem, *Das monastische Experiment. Die Rolle der Keuschheit bei der Entstehung des westlichen Klosterwesens* (Münster: LIT Verlag, 2005), pp. 93–4; also Jones, pp. 39–45.

65 Edited by Josef Semmler in *Corpus consuetudinum monasticarum* 1, ed. by Kassius Hallinger (Siegburg: Schmitt, 1963), c. 14, p. 460: 'Ut sibi conpatres conmatresue non facient et nullam quamlibet mulierem osculentur'. On how ninth-century commentators viewed male friendships, Coon, pp. 124–7 and Jones, p. 42.

66 Refer to Lake's commentary in *Richer, Histories*, ii, p. 458.

67 *Corpus consuetudinum monasticarum*, i, c. 13, p. 460.

68 Richer, *Historiae*, ch. 36, p. 189: 'Inde est quo turpitudo vitae, morum pravitas, proprietatis peculium, nobis a calumniantibus intenduntur'.

69 For instance, Rodulph's attributed comments on the 'regular cap' (*pilleo regulari*) allude to ch. 55,7 of the *Rule of St Benedict*.

70 Odo of Cluny, *Collationes*, ed. in *Patrologia Latina* 133, c. 554: 'secundum carnem viventes et corporea nobilitate gloriantur' and c. 555: 'pulchra vestis animae lascivientis indicium est'; similar statements may be found at c. 562 and 603. We can only speculate whether Richer had access to a copy of Odo's text, which may or may not have arrived at Reims through Abbot Archembald of Fleury, who in the mid-940s was involved in the 'restoration' of Benedictine observance at Saint-Remi. On the transmission history of the *Collationes* and Fleury's ownership of a copy in the eleventh century, see Rosé, p. 132, n. 365 and Id., 'Les Collationes d'Odon de Cluny (+ 942). Un premier recueil exempla rédigé en milieu "clunisien"?', in *Le tonnerre des exemples: 'Exempla' et médiation culturelle dans l'Occident médiéval*, ed. by Marie-Anne Polo de Beaulieu, Pascal Colomb, and Jacques Berlioz (Rennes: Presses Universitaires de Rennes, 2010), pp. 145–60 (p. 153).

71 Richer, *Historiae*, ch. 37, p. 189: 'Nam tunicas magni emptas, plurimum cupiunt, quas sic ab utroque latere stringunt, manicisque et giris diffluentibus diffundunt, ut artatis clunibus et protensis natibus potius meretriculis quam monachis a tergo assimilentur', and ch. 41, p. 190: 'Horum etenim tibiales quater sesquipede patent, atque ex staminis subtilitate etiam pudenda intuentibus non protegunt'.

72 Ruotger, p. 22.

73 Odo of Cluny, *Collationes*, c. 607: 'De vestitus autem qualitate vel immutatione ipsi saeculares contra monachos indignantur'. Also c. 562: 'Qui perverso ordine colunt carnem, quae non prodest, quicunque et negligunt spiritum, qui vivificatur, revera vani

et mendaces filii hominum, populus Gomorrhae, ut ait Isaias, cultores vestium; cum Deus per Ezechielem queratur, quod in superbia ornamentis ipsius utantur. Qui etiam, sicut Josephus Judaeos ante excidium fecisse commemorat, vestimentis exoticis induuntur. Nam de his Hegesippus refert, quia tunc femineis utebantur, et mutilabant sibi barbas, atque suas facies more meretricum dealbabant'.

74 Reaching back even further in time, Rodulph's attributed comments also turn into a narrative of scandal – and catastrophic loss of monastic masculinity – a seemingly innocent remark by Smaragdus of Saint-Mihiel in his commentary on the *Rule of St Benedict*, where he states that monks' drawers – *femoralia* – are also called *feminalia;* Leah Shopkow, 'A Tale of Disorder, Vulgarity, Ethnicity, and Underwear in the Monastery', in *Prowess, Piety, and Public Order in Medieval Society: Studies in Honor of Richard W. Kaeuper*, ed. by Craig Nakashian and Daniel P. Franke (Leiden and Boston: Brill, 2017), pp. 179–98 (p. 186).

75 On this, Valerie Garver, '"Go humbly dressed as befits servants of God": Alcuin, Clerical Identity, and Sartorial Anxieties', *Early Medieval Europe* 26 (2018), pp. 203–30. I am grateful to Dr. Garver for sharing her work prior to publication.

76 Discussions in Hallinger, ii, pp. 675–9; Pius Engelbert, 'Grundlinien einer Geschichte des Benediktinischen Habits', *Studia Monastica*, 41 (1999), pp. 277–302 (pp. 283–5); and Müller, pp. 109–34.

77 Josef Semmler, 'Das Erbe der karolingischen Klosterreform im 10. Jahrhundert', in *Monastische Reformen im 9. und 10. Jahrhundert*, ed. by Raymund Kottje and Helmut Maurer (Sigmaringen: Jan Thorbeke Verlag, 1989), pp. 29–77 (pp. 51–2). On scandal over monastic clothing in later centuries, Henri Platelle, 'Le problème du scandale: les nouvelles modes masculines aux XIe et XIIe siècles', *Revue belge de philologie et d'histoire*, 53 (1975), pp. 1071–96.

78 Anne Wagner, *Gorze au XIe siècle. Contribution à l'histoire du monachisme bénédictin dans l'Empire* (Turnhout: Brepols, 1997), pp. 123–4.

79 Odo of Cluny, *Collationes*, c. 554.

80 Ibid., c. 603: 'An non est apostasia, de habitu vel victu traditiones patrum contemnere?'. For a similar statement, see the passage at c. 574. Odo tells the tale of a monk from the abbey of Dôle who was not recognized by his abbot because of his blue cowl (Ibid., 606); in his *Life of Odo*, John of Salerno turned this into a vision where the abbot is St Benedict himself (*Vita Odonis*, ed. by M. Marrier and A. Quercetanus (*Bibliotheca Cluniacensis*) (Paris: Protat, 1614), c. 43).

81 John of Saint-Arnoul, p. 454 and 456; also the discussion in Giulia Barone, 'Jean de Gorze, moine Bénédictin', in *L'abbaye de Gorze au Xe siècle*, ed. by Michel Parisse and Otto G. Oexle (Nancy: Presses Universitaires de Nancy, 1993), pp. 141–58 (p. 156).

82 Richer, *Historiae*, ch. 33, p. 186: 'ritus a maioribus constituti'.

83 Maureen C. Miller, *Clothing the Clergy. Virtue and Power in Medieval Europe, c. 800–1200* (Ithaca, NY: Cornell University Press, 2015), pp. 121–33.

84 Hallinger, ii, pp. 699–704. Writing in 1093, a monk from Hersfeld famously referred to the debate over Cluny's *duplex vestis* as a 'long and embittered battle'; *Liber de unitate ecclesiae conservanda*, ed. by W. Schwenkenbecher, *MGH Libelli de lite imperatorum et pontificum* 2 (Hannover: Hahnsche Buchhandlung, 1892), p. 275.

85 Prior to the reform, the older monks had taken to wearing a second, linen tunic, while the younger ones wore a single, woollen one; Arnold of Sankt Emmeran, *Liber de Sancto Emmeranno*, ed. by Georg Waitz (*MHG Scriptores* 4) (Hannover: Hahnsche Buchhandlung, 1841), p. 559.

86 Müller, pp. 129–30.

87 Ibid., pp. 121–3. In eleventh-century Monte Cassino, short and long *cucullae* were simultaneously in use, meaning that different groups in the monastery were following a different dress code; Ibid., p. 124.

88 Thietmar of Merseburg, *Chronicon*, ed. by R. Holtzmann (*MGH Scriptores rerum Germanicarum ns* 9) (Berlin: Weidmannsche Buchhandlung, 1935), pp. 288–90: 'hii,

The dignity of our bodies and the salvation of our souls **281**

quorum nova conversatio ei in habitu et in victu laudabilis extat, vero non sunt sepe quod simulant ... Omnis hominum Deo acceptabilis fructus in corde bono consistens, a bonis veste pulchra et aurea cibi potusque mediocritate nonnumquam dissimulatur'.

89 Notker, *Commentarii in Psalmos*, ed. by P. Piper (*Die Schriften Notkers und seiner Schule 2. Psalmen und Katechetische Denkmäler nach der St. Galler Handschriftengruppe*) (Freiburg i.B. and Tübingen: Mohr, 1883), Psalm 21, 19 (p. 70) and 65,15 (p. 249).

90 Vanderputten, pp. 47–8 and Bur, *Saint-Thierry*, pp. 46–7.

91 In a 1043 letter, Abbot Sigefrid of Gorze criticized newfangled fashions and beard-wearing customs among the laity in France; Michel Parisse, 'Sigefroid, abbé de Gorze, et le mariage du roi Henri III avec Agnès de Poitou (1043). Un aspect de la réforme lotharingienne', *Revue du Nord*, 86 (2004), pp. 543–66 (p. 563).

92 Vanderputten, pp. 149–51.

93 Adalbero of Laon, *Poème au roi Robert*, ed. by Claude Carozzi (Paris: Les Belles Lettres, 1979), p. 8.

16

LAW AND LITURGY

Excommunication records, 900–1050

*Sarah Hamilton**

I

The bishops of tenth- and eleventh-century Europe have attracted a good deal of scholarly attention in the past thirty years.[1] Researchers investigating the political and religious landscapes of Latin Europe have emphasized the importance of bishops to local and regional politics and at the same time traced the ways in which their authority manifested itself in their roles as pastors, reformers and local rulers. Tim Reuter, in particular, drew attention to how bishops anticipated later developments by central medieval rulers.[2] Stressing the importance of symbolism and episcopal charisma to the development of ideas of community, he also recognized the significance of dioceses, with the bishop as sovereign. To date, the emphasis in the work of those that have followed him has been on identifying what might be termed the 'secular dimensions' of episcopal power, including bishops' revenue raising and judicial powers, their roles in collective assemblies, as architectural patrons, and as instigators of the reform of clerical and monastic communities, and political ritual behaviour such as *adventus* ceremonies. Most scholars are, of course, aware of the apostolic responsibilities of episcopal office – in Reuter's words 'in the last resort they held an office for which they would have to render an account' for those in their charge to the Lord – but in practice they pay little attention to them.[3]

This neglect contrasts sharply with more recent work on the significance of the ninth-century Frankish Empire for the development of episcopal identity. Steffen Patzold underlined the need to recognize the full range of episcopal activity, and the

---

* The research for this chapter was funded by the 'After Empire: Using and Not Using the Past in the Crisis of the Carolingian World, c.900–1050' HERA project, receiving funding from the European Union's Horizon 2020 research and innovation programme under grant agreement no. 649307.

importance of avoiding artificial distinctions between secular and spiritual power when drawing attention to the significance of the ninth century for the expectations which medieval churchmen came to have of what bishops should be and do.[4] Both he and Mayke de Jong showed the importance of the councils of Louis the Pious's reign for the development of these shared norms, and the centrality of the manifestations of apostolic authority, that is the rituals of confession, penance and excommunication, for episcopal identity.[5] At the same time, Patzold demonstrated that the rolling out of the 'model' articulated most clearly at the Council of Paris in 829 was by no means universal across the Frankish Empire, reaching East Francia only in the 880s. His conclusions thus complement those of Wilfried Hartmann, whose study of canon law highlighted how the rites and laws of penance and excommunication developed in the ninth century became the focus of increased attention and reflection for churchmen in the years around 900.[6]

The texts of the rites for penance are well documented from the late eighth century onwards, but it is only from the years immediately after 900AD that the earliest records of actual rites for excommunication survive. They do so as a record of the sentence imposed by the bishops of the province of Rheims on the murderers of Archbishop Fulk on July 6th 900, and as seven chapters in the collection of canon law which Regino of Prüm compiled for the archbishops of Trier and Mainz, c. 906 x 913.[7] As Patzold and Hartmann observed, it is clear from both conciliar and epistolary evidence that ninth-century Frankish bishops – like their predecessors – not only practised excommunication but invested time and thought in developing the church law surrounding it. However, they felt no need to record its rites. Quite how, when and why in the years *after* the end of the Carolingian Empire bishops and their clergy chose to set down the rites for excommunication are questions to which the answers are only imperfectly understood.

The prevailing interpretation melds canon law and liturgy into an account whereby in East Francia formal excommunication rites of the type in Regino were initially recorded in canon law, and only later in liturgical books. In contrast, in West Francia, the earliest records are of the more informal, *ad hoc* formulae, like the Rheims example, which went on to have a vibrant history. This account therefore ignores differences in genre and geography. It traces the evolution of formal rites from the Lotharingian Regino of Prüm in the early tenth century to the Rhineland Burchard of Worms in the early eleventh century only turning to the West Frankish Ivo of Chartres in the later eleventh century.[8] Meanwhile, there has been a good deal of research into the West Frankish evidence, which, in the absence of legal collections, has relied instead upon charters and letters and linked the increasing evidence for the practice of excommunication to changes in lordship.[9] Even recent work on the West Frankish evidence relies on outdated interpretations of the normative evidence and ignores the relatively plentiful evidence for informal excommunication *formulae*.[10] The result is historians of both East and West Francia seem happy to accept the picture given by Regino and Burchard as normative for the post-Carolingian period, despite the disparities in the source base from different regions. Two further issues also need to be taken into account. Anglo-Saxon evidence is neglected by scholars

284   Sarah Hamilton

working on continental material. This is because, as Michael Elliot has observed, scholars of continental canon law have largely ignored Anglo-Saxon canon law, whilst those working on Anglo-Saxon church law have tended to look backwards to earlier Insular sources rather than at developments across the Channel; excommunication is no exception to this rule.[11] Secondly, recent studies of liturgical formulae for excommunication in this period have identified a considerable variety in the texts of excommunication rites from the tenth and eleventh centuries, pointing to the role of local agency in the making of these records in West and East Francia and also in England.[12] The end result of such specialization has been to emphasize geographical difference. What has therefore not properly been considered is the extent to which the pictures emerging from different areas and different types of evidence can in fact be compared, and whether doing so provides a clearer answer to the question of not only how but why excommunication rites came to be recorded for the first time only in the post-Carolingian period.

Any comparative study risks contrasting apples with oranges, but there are good reasons for assessing the development of the tenth- and eleventh-century recording of excommunication rites in the kingdoms of England, Germany and West Francia. Late Anglo-Saxon England and Ottonian and early Salian Germany both had relatively unified episcopates and strong kings. Contrastingly, as is well known, West Frankish politics were much more fragmented.[13] The second section of this paper will therefore investigate the specific contexts in which excommunication rites were recorded in these three realms in the years c.900–c.1050, and consider why these records were made, before in the final part turning to consider some of the implications of this cross-realm comparison for our current understandings of episcopacy in this period.

II

The Reich

The earliest record of the excommunication liturgy to survive from the Reich is that in the collection of canon law Regino of Prüm composed for the archbishops of Trier and Mainz, c. 906 x 913. As both its contents and his preface make clear, Regino intended it to serve as a practical handbook to support the bishop during the visitation of his diocese; it thus has a tight focus on pastoral care and ecclesiastical discipline. Regino's record is widely recognized by historians of excommunication as fundamental to later medieval canon law and pontifical liturgies.[14] Over seven chapters Regino prescribed how excommunication should be conducted as follows:

- it should take place within the Mass after the reading of the Gospel, that is before the consecration of the Eucharist;[15]
- the bishop should first address those people and clergy present, naming the offender, explaining the offence which had incurred the sentence, and that due process had been followed;[16]

- then the bishop should declare the sentence of excommunication, using one of the four formulae provided;[17]
- those present should acclaim the sentence;[18]
- using the vernacular, the bishop should then explain the consequences of the sentence for both the offender and those in the community i.e. that those having any contact with the excommunicant would themselves incur an excommunication sentence;[19]
- finally, the bishop should notify the priests in his own diocese and the bishops of neighbouring sees of the case via letters so as to ensure that no one has contact with the excommunicant.[20]

These prescriptions were followed by instructions for the rite to be followed for the reconciliation of excommunicants: the bishop should meet the penitent excommunicant(s) outside the church, and after establishing that they have performed penance, lead them by the hand into the Church, before notifying the clergy of their restoration to the Christian community.[21] Unlike most of the canons in his collection, Regino did not provide any authorities for these two excommunication rites. It is, however, probable that they are based on customs followed in early tenth-century Trier because, as Wilfried Hartmann has demonstrated, Regino's other unattributed canons generally reflect Carolingian law.[22] Moreover, Regino's text echoes later ninth-century evidence from Rheims. A letter of Archbishop Hincmar to the priests of his diocese granted them permission to read the sentence before the Gospel rather than after as offenders had taken to leaving church so as to avoid being notified of their excommunication.[23] Further evidence for Regino's record being grounded in earlier traditions is suggested by the linguistic echoes between one of Regino's excommunication formula (*Libri duo*, II.416, rubricated 'Terribilior') and two tenth-century formulae from Rheims: that recorded as being imposed on the murderers of Archbishop Fulk of Rheims, and an anonymized formula added in a north-eastern French hand to a late ninth-century canon law manuscript sometime in the second third of the tenth century.[24] The most probable explanation for these parallels between practices and texts in Rheims and Trier is that they draw on common, if undocumented, earlier practices.

Historians of canon law have traced how Regino's texts were taken up by Burchard in his twenty-book *Decretum* and thence widely circulated across the cathedral libraries of eleventh-century Europe.[25] But what is less well recognized by scholars of excommunication is that in the tenth century Regino's canons circulated mainly within the Reich, especially in Lotharingia and the Rhineland, and therefore cannot be accepted straightforwardly as representative of wider practices.[26] Regino's collection survives in two recensions and is now preserved in eleven manuscripts and in four fragments from the tenth and eleventh centuries, of which only two come from outside the Reich, from the close-by sees of Rheims and Arras.[27] Its later influence is similarly geographically restricted: Regino's canons on excommunication are found in only three later tenth- and early eleventh-century collections, all compiled in the Reich:

286 Sarah Hamilton

- *Collectio IV Librorum* (Lotharingia, s. x[1]);[28]
- Burchard of Worms's *Decretum* (Worms, *c.* 1020);[29]
- *Collectio XII Partium* (Freising, s. xi[in], with an augmented version from 1039).[30]

The texts surrounding Regino's canons suggest the compilers of these collections regarded excommunication as fundamental to claims to episcopal authority rather than merely a form of punishment. All of Regino's canons on excommunication were copied as a block into Book I of the *Collectio IV Librorum*, which deals with the bishop's financial and judicial authority rather than into Book III which deals with those offences which incur a sentence of excommunication.[31] Like the compiler of the *Collectio IV Librorum*, Burchard consciously linked excommunication to episcopal authority. He devoted all of Book XI to excommunication, beginning with a canon drawn from the Pseudo-Isidorean tradition, via Pseudo-Remedius of Chur's *Collectio Canonum*, which outlines the grounds on which the bishop has authority to judge, namely the apostolic power of the keys.[32] Regino's block of canons on the rites for imposing and reconciling excommunicants follows immediately.[33] Whereas both Regino and the compiler of the *Collectio IV Librorum* had left the canons prescribing how excommunication should be conducted unattributed, Burchard included spurious authorities, as was his practice elsewhere in the *Decretum*. In this case he attributed them to a Council of Rouen, perhaps because this was the authority Regino had given for the preceding canon in his collection.[34] Where Burchard differed most substantively from his source is in his prescription of the reconciliation rite for excommunication. Whereas Regino had opined that crimes should be corrected in accordance with divine and human law, Burchard omitted the reference to human law.[35] This accords with Burchard's more general views which, as Greta Austin has suggested, privileged canon law as 'the law of God', grounded in biblical authority, above that of secular law.[36] Further, Burchard also interpolated details of the psalms, verses and prayers into the text of Regino's outline, turning a legal prescription into a liturgical *ordo*.[37]

Burchard composed his *Decretum* to educate the clergy in his diocese, although how it was used by later communities remains a matter of debate.[38] The exact nature of the relationship between the two early eleventh-century collections, the *Decretum* compiled in Worms and the *Collectio XII Partium* compiled in Freising, continues to preoccupy scholars.[39] But it is widely acknowledged that close parallels indicate that there was co-operation between Worms and Freising, where the *Collectio XII Partium* was originally compiled in the early eleventh century, with a second, longer version, being finished there c. 1039.[40] Like Burchard, the *Collectio XII Partium* devotes a whole book to excommunication: book X 'de diversis conditionibus hominum et de excommunicatione reproborum'.[41] Both versions of the *Collectio* include the same block of canons on excommunication rites from Regino, but with Burchard's spurious attributions to earlier councils.[42] The compiler(s) also followed those for Burchard and *Collectio IV Librorum* in connecting excommunication to the defence of episcopal authority: this block of canons in both versions of the *Collectio XII Partium* was preceded by a canon from the Council of Tribur (895)

Law and liturgy **287**

defending the ban imposed by the bishop on pain of excommunication.[43] Here, as in Burchard, spiritual law is regarded as superior to secular law and connected to the defence of the bishop's authority in all spheres.

The citation of Regino's canons in the *Collectio XII Partium* differ from both the original, and from the version in Burchard, in two significant regards. First, the rite for the imposition of excommunication in the augmented *Collectio* includes an expanded rubric headed 'Incipit *ordo* ad excommunicandum incorrigibilis'.[44] This rubric expands on that in Regino and Burchard to set out how the rite should be conducted in a public mass. The bishop should enter the church in full procession from the sanctuary and deliver the sentence standing on the top step of the lectern, with twelve priests standing around, holding lights in their hands which they throw to the ground at the conclusion of the anathema. Before declaring excommunication, the bishop should make clear the rebel has already been summoned three times that he should return to the bosom of Holy Church. This rubric is followed by Regino's full text of the address which the bishop should deliver. The effect is to enhance the solemnity of the occasion, by spelling out details of the rite which are otherwise hidden in Regino's description. Another copy of this *ordo*, with an identical title and rubric, can be found in a pontifical from Freising compiled sometime in the first half of the eleventh century (now Munich, Bayerische Staatsbibliothek, Clm 21587).[45] In adapting Regino's canons into an *ordo*, Freising's churchmen demonstrate the significance they attached to legal process – the rebel must be summoned three times – and to enhancing episcopal authority, surrounded by twelve priests, standing at the top of the lectern. Moreover, just as Burchard had done, the churchmen of Freising revised the reconciliation rite in the original *Collectio XII Partium*, although their amendments were rather less extensive than those undertaken at Worms.[46] This analysis suggests East Frankish churchmen made conscious choices when copying Regino's canons. The enhancements they made to Regino's original texts and the canons copied alongside them reflect local traditions but also imply that for these compilers the delivery of excommunication was intimately linked to the articulation of episcopal authority.

The Freising pontifical highlights the value of liturgical evidence. It is one of several from eleventh-century Germany to include examples which are more independent of the Regino-Burchard tradition.[47] Whilst the degree of local agency at work in such collections makes it much harder to approach them collectively, at least one group of manuscripts offers a means of doing so; these are the manuscripts now known as Romano-German Pontificals. Henry Parkes has demonstrated in his research that this set of *ordines* and legal texts was a much more varied and looser collection than was implied by its editors, and that it was not compiled in Mainz in the 960s, but rather only circulated widely across the Reich from the early eleventh century onwards.[48] Its influence outside the Reich was also much more restricted than presumed by earlier generations of scholars.[49] Cyrille Vogel and Reinhard Elze's edition of the Romano-German Pontifical includes all Regino's texts, together with an excommunication formula attributed to a Pope Leo.[50] The reconciliation rite represents an expansion of Regino's text along similar lines to

288 Sarah Hamilton

that in Burchard, but it draws on wider traditions for its prayers.[51] Examination of the contents of these manuscripts suggests the texts of excommunication rites in these manuscripts are not nearly as uniform as the modern edition suggests. Only six out of sixteen eleventh- and twelfth-century codices labelled by Michel Andrieu as Romano-German Pontificals contain all the excommunication rites in Vogel and Elze's edition, and these tend to be later copies, made from the second half of the eleventh century.[52] Conversely, perhaps the earliest example of a Romano-German Pontifical manuscript, that constructed for Henry II's new see at Bamberg in the early eleventh century, includes as an afterthought, as part of a supplement added in a slightly later hand, just the formula attributed to Pope Leo and the reconciliation rite.[53] The Leonine formula contains a clear statement of apostolic authority:

> And just as the Lord gave to Blessed Peter the Apostle and his successors, whose succession we hold, however unworthy, the power that whatever they bind on earth shall be bound on earth and in heaven, and whatever they loose on earth shall be loosed on earth and in heaven, thus to those [people], if they do not wish to be corrected, we close heaven and we deny the earth for burial and may they be plunged into the lower fire, and may they be consumed for what they did without end.[54]

A further seven manuscripts in the sample include an *ordo* for imposing excommunication based on that in Regino, but omit Regino's alternative address and other formulae in favour of that attributed to Leo, followed by the Romano-German reconciliation *ordo*.[55] Collectively, they point to communities which envisaged the bishop relying on the language of pseudo-papal authority to pronounce excommunication and which sought to articulate apostolic authority in the episcopal reconciliation rite.

The limited circulation of the East Frankish rites means they should not be treated as normative for practice elsewhere in Europe. At the same time the preoccupation with linking the recording of excommunication rites with statements of the bishop's apostolic authority is common to compilers of both canon law and liturgical records. Can a similar pattern be found in areas with rather different patterns in the evidence for records of excommunication rites?

Anglo-Saxon England

The earliest Anglo-Saxon records of excommunication rites are recorded in manuscripts of texts associated with Archbishop Wulfstan of Worcester and York (996–1023).[56] They first survive in a miscellaneous manuscript of the type often categorized as an episcopal handbook: Cambridge, Corpus Christi College, MS 265.[57] Written in the third quarter of the eleventh century, probably at Worcester, it contains, amongst other texts, the collection of Anglo-Saxon canon law associated with Wulfstan, now known as the *Collectio Wigorniensis*.[58] Copied together at the end of the *Collectio* are a rite for imposing 'excommunication against those in contempt of the laws of the Lord and the enemies of holy church', a short text outlining the excommunication of those who had attacked one of the community's estates at *Ontelawe*, and a rite for the reconciliation of excommunicants. They were all written in a different, slightly later hand to that which copied the main part of the *Collectio*, and seemingly serve as a supplement to it.[59] It is therefore unclear whether these rites represent a core element of the *Collectio* as it existed in Wulfstan's time, or a mid-eleventh-century addition. I follow here Michael Elliot, the *Collectio*'s most recent editor, who has suggested that it is likely that they are part of the core because there is evidence that they were also copied with two other recensions of the *Collectio* – there are five in all – including one written in the first half of the eleventh century.[60] Other texts in these other recensions of the *Collectio* reveal an interest in asserting the superiority of divine law, and in defining how and when excommunication should be imposed.[61] These texts, as with many of Wulfstan's other writings, are indebted to ninth-century Carolingian traditions.[62]

It is therefore unsurprising that the *Collectio*'s rites for excommunication have some basic similarities with those in Regino. However, as I have demonstrated elsewhere, they are clearly independent of the East Frankish traditions.[63] In basic structure they are comparable: for the imposition of excommunication, the excommunication sentence should be read out from the pulpit after the Gospel, and the terms of the excommunication sentence be made clear. The sentence itself should be delivered accompanied by maledictions, and those present should acclaim it with an Amen. Then the candles being held by the clergy (number unspecified) should be thrown down on the floor followed by a sacerdotal prayer. The cantor then begins the offertory. But the differences are equally revealing: the address should be delivered by the deacon, not the bishop, and its text, despite the inclusion of various phrases also found in the East Frankish material, is seemingly independent of them. These differences highlight the significance of local agency in the making of liturgical records. At the same time, the emphasis on the apostolic origins of episcopal authority, and upon their pastoral responsibility for disciplining sinners, also echo concerns found in Regino a century earlier, and in the almost contemporary compilations made at Worms and Freising. For example, the declaration of excommunication includes the statement:

> Therefore in separating we excommunicate and in anathematizing we bind those rebels, N., from the company of all Christians, through all the power of those of whom it is spoken in the Gospel, saying 'Whatsoever you bind upon earth, shall be bound in heaven'. For the Lord gave to the apostles, and to their successors, that is the bishops, the aforesaid power of binding and loosing and instructed them to build and to plant good in the house of the Lord, to uproot and tear down sinners from the house of the Lord, which is from the church of Christ.[64]

The reconciliation rite is even more intriguing. Both the Anglo-Saxon and East Frankish rites frame the reconciliation around the bishop taking the penitent excommunicants by the hand and introducing them to the physical church as a token of their spiritual reconciliation. But the Anglo-Saxon rite departs from the East Frankish traditions in mentioning and attributing a significant role to those acting as intercessors (*intercessores*) on behalf of the penitent excommunicants with the bishop in its opening rubric.[65] The intercessors should promote the excommunicants' cause to the bishop, before the excommunicants meet the bishop. The Anglo-Saxon rite further underlines the bishop's apostolic authority in its choice of absolution prayers. Whilst in the East Frankish rites the ministers requested God to absolve the penitent excommunicant, in the Anglo-Saxon rite they declaimed absolution in the first person plural, citing the source of their power: 'Let us, as successors to blessed Peter to whom the Lord granted the power to bind and loose, absolve you'.[66] This prayer articulating the Petrine grounds for episcopal authority circulated in Anglo-Saxon England from at least the mid-tenth century.[67] Although this particular manuscript is associated with Worcester, this reconciliation rite later circulated more widely within southern England because it is also found in a mid-twelfth-century pontifical manuscript from Canterbury.[68]

Archbishop Wulfstan was a prolific author of laws, tracts, and homilies in both Latin and Old English. Like Regino and Burchard, he had a strong interest in disciplining and educating the clergy in order to raise the standards of pastoral care, and his *Collectio* was integral to his efforts.[69] But the Anglo-Saxon tradition for recording excommunication rites is a century later than that in the Reich. Formal excommunication rites are recorded first in an early eleventh-century canon law context; more *ad hoc*, informal records of excommunication formulae of a type which did not circulate independently in East Francia begin to be added to liturgical and legal manuscripts only from the second half of the eleventh century, and may be a product of the post-Conquest period.[70] The Anglo-Saxon trajectory for initially recording excommunication rites is therefore remarkably similar to that in East Francia. In both realms churchmen constructed canon law collections to educate the secular clergy in the law and authority of the Church, and in doing so, found it useful to record excommunication rites. In both places these rites record local traditions. In both kingdoms they only moved later to copying them in a liturgical context. The picture for West Francia is, however, rather different.

West Francia

The earliest records of excommunication rites to survive in the Latin west come from West Francia, or more precisely from north-eastern France. The nature of these records differs from those for the Reich and Anglo-Saxon England but the manuscript context is similar. The earliest dateable rite, as mentioned earlier, is that imposed on the assassins of Archbishop Fulk of Rheims on July 6th 900.[71] It survives now as an addendum, written around 1000, to a tenth-century Rheims manuscript containing two Carolingian canon law collections.[72] It is a record of the 'excommunication ... read out in the church of Saint Mary's in Rheims', and lists the names of all the bishops in attendance.[73] It therefore lacks the prescriptive details

Law and liturgy **291**

about how the rite should be administered recorded in the East Frankish texts, except for the incidental reference in the final curse to the accompanying action: 'And just as these lights, thrown down from our hands today, are extinguished, so may their lights be extinguished in eternity'.[74] Rather it is presented as a record of a particular event in the see's history, when the bishops assembled for the consecration of Fulk's successor, Heriveus, and excommunicated those named as his murderers. This sentence is one of several records of key occasions in the ninth- and tenth-century history of Rheims's bishops added to this manuscript: others include the penitential ordinance Archbishop Seulf issued after the Battle of Soissons in 923, and the oath sworn by Gottschalk.[75] It seems to be included as a historical record of a key moment in the bishopric's history rather than as a prescriptive record of how to conduct excommunication.

There are two contenders for the actual earliest manuscript of a West Frankish excommunication formula; again both lack the prescriptive rubrics and detail of the East Frankish tradition. The first was also recorded in Rheims in a later hand as an *addendum* to a canon law collection: the *Collectio Dionysio-Hadriana*, copied in north-eastern France in the third quarter of the ninth century.[76] The *Dionysio-Hadriana* was one of the fundamental Carolingian canon law collections, having originally been presented by Pope Hadrian to Charlemagne in 774, and circulated widely across the Frankish kingdoms. It set out the responsibilities and duties of different members of the church, providing 'a comprehensive plan for the building of … Christian society'.[77] The excommunication formula was added in a mid-tenth-century hand into a blank space at the end of the *Collectio*. This text is an anonymized version of that used at Rheims, shorn of the contextual detail.[78] Its appearance in this context is suggestive of the same processes which half a century or so earlier led Regino to record excommunication rites in his collection: excommunication is a disciplinary process in which the bishop asserts his authority to maintain ecclesiastical order.

The second contender is the record added post 977 to a pontifical written around 900 for the use of the archbishop of Sens.[79] It begins by deploring those who, having been purified by baptism, now 'voluntarily subject themselves to the old enemy'. It excommunicates and anathematizes 'Ragenard and his son Rodmund and their fellow soldiers and invaders of ecclesiastical things' as being the leaders amongst 'all those who, after I had received the blessing of the archbishop, did not let me enter the place of the church of Sens in the way of my predecessors, rejecting truth and embracing falsehood'.[80] Ragenard was Count of Sens from 948 to 996, and his son, Fromund II, Count of Sens from 996 to 1012. The twelfth-century *Chronicle of Saint-Pierre-le-Vif* puts flesh on the cryptic reference to those who obstructed the bishop from entering the church of Sens. In 976/77 the count and his son, with some of the leading clergy of the diocese of Sens, had sought to prevent the installation of the new archbishop, Seguin, who responded by putting the whole see under interdict. Seguin was only able to enter his see some eight months after his election.[81] The excommunication formula seems, therefore, to have been recorded because it referred to a historical event, just as that for Rheims had been. But it was

292 Sarah Hamilton

later amended in a second (undated) hand, seemingly to excommunicate several named individuals suggesting it was also later reused for a different occasion.[82] This particular manuscript was also used to record other texts of historical significance to the archbishop of Sens's authority in this period, including the texts of the oaths of suffragan bishops added in its margins.[83]

As in England, only one canon law collection was compiled in West Francia in this period, that of Abbo of Fleury.[84] Abbo did not include any excommunication rites, although he cited a canon from the Council of Meaux-Paris (845/6) which enjoined that anathema should usually be prescribed only with the support of the archbishop and fellow bishops because it had such grave consequences; this canon had wider currency on the Continent in this period as it is found in Regino and Burchard.[85] Although Regino's collection was known in eleventh-century north-eastern France, it seems that West Frankish churchmen preferred to read and copy Carolingian canon law and episcopal *capitula* rather than compile new collections.[86] Their conservatism explains, at least in part, why there is no evidence for the sorts of formal rites recorded by bishops in East Francia and Anglo-Saxon England.

Rather, the sorts of pedagogic concerns which seem to have inspired Regino, Burchard and Wulfstan to prescribe excommunication rites, emerge instead in the letter collections of two secular clerics, bishops and teachers: Gerbert of Aurillac (d.1003), sometime Archbishop of Rheims and Pope Sylvester II, and Fulbert, bishop of Chartres (1006–28). Both letter collections owe much to their authority as teachers, and to the efforts of their pupils; they serve as both memorials and exemplars.[87]

One of the leading scholars of the late tenth-century Latin west, Gerbert wrote the letters under consideration here during his time at Rheims cathedral. As well as teaching in the school, he wrote letters on behalf of Archbishop Adalbero (969–89), before later becoming archbishop of Rheims himself for a short period in difficult and contentious circumstances, and then leaving for the court of Otto III. Gerbert's letters suggest he had a clear understanding of the canonical process to be followed for the imposition of anathema. In 995 he wrote a warning letter against 'those encroachers, scoundrels and tyrants whose names are written below' for theft from, and murder of, the clergy:

> We, all the bishops of Rheims, summon your consciences and invite you to make satisfactions. We are allowing time for penitence until the first of next month. Then we shall either recognize you as the fruitful branches of the church or with the sword of the Holy Spirit cut you off from the field of God as useless wood.[88]

If they remained contumacious in the face of this warning, they would be cut off. Whilst both the canon law and formal liturgical rites referred to the need to warn excommunicants, they were often vague about the precise timetable; here Gerbert seems to demonstrate a firm grasp of process.

Law and liturgy **293**

In April 994 he replied to a complaint he had received from a bishop, saying that he had 'dispatched reproving letters to those who scorn you' but that if they continued their evil ways:

> then we order that the documents of our summons be placed for reading in the well-known place of the church; and then, that a sentence of excommunication, written out accurately and pronounced solemnly, be affixed in [the] well-known place and that a copy of it be directed to us in order that the same may be carried out in our churches.[89]

Gerbert's proposed actions for publicizing the sentence essentially conformed to those in ninth-century canon law, as Regino's rites made clear. A warning should be issued to the people concerned, and then placed publicly in the church, and then, if they remained contumacious, a sentence of excommunication should be read out, and then stuck up, and copies of the sentence notified to other churches. Gerbert's reference to the 'well-known place' echoes a canon found in Burchard's *Decretum*.[90] Burchard falsely attributed it to the decretals of Pope Honorius II, but in fact it is taken from the 875 Council of Rome, c. 11.[91] In other words, Gerbert is demonstrating a knowledge of ninth-century practice, and even, in his echoes of the text, of ninth-century conciliar legislation, similar to that articulated in the East Frankish rites. Others of Gerbert's letters show him acting out the canonical requirement that the bishop should notify neighbouring bishops of the sentence of excommunication.[92]

Like Gerbert, Fulbert of Chartres was a renowned teacher and his correspondence was preserved by his pupils as a testament to his teachings.[93] Like Gerbert, his letters display the same implicit awareness of the procedures associated with excommunication.[94] He wrote a joint letter with Avesgaudus, bishop of Le Mans, to Archbishop Ebalus of Rheims requesting that he join them in excommunicating Count Herbert of Le Mans for his attacks on the bishop of Le Mans.[95] He received similar requests from other bishops but did not always act on them, writing to Bishop T.:

> In my warm sympathy for you I have made the wrong done to you my own, and I am burning with zeal against those who have committed a shameful crime against the episcopate. But since I do not see that it would be useful to you or safe for me if we let our zeal break forth and take vengeance by excommunicating them, I think we should rest content with sending them letters of warning until they are corrected by doing penance or punished by order of the Supreme Judge.[96]

He was also aware of the need to warn the malefactor before issuing a sentence of anathema. In 1008 he wrote to Count Fulk of Anjou that he had been asked to excommunicate him for sending men to murder Count Hugh of Beauvais, and subsequently protecting them from royal justice.[97] The case was a *cause célèbre* in the early eleventh century, for the count's murder took place in 1008 in front of the king, Robert the Pious, whilst both were out hunting. Although Fulbert had been asked to excommunicate Fulk, he wrote 'since we were concerned for your salvation, we asked for this to be postponed for three weeks so we could write and admonish you'.[98] He warned the count that he 'will not remain in Christian communion with us after date' unless he ensured that the men guilty of the actual murder were brought to trial or repudiated them.[99] In the end, Fulk opted to avoid a potentially difficult situation by going on pilgrimage to Jerusalem. The threat of excommunication in this case seems to have been effective as a form of 'coercion', or 'bend punishment', as Lotte Kéry termed it.[100]

Excommunication was, however, not always easily delivered. Fulbert wrote to the bishop of Paris asking that the issuing of a sentence be put off until a council of bishops had been held:

> With regard to the woman from Laon who is committing sacrilege by ravaging your church's possessions, we have put off excommunicating her for the following reasons: first, because there was no one who would dare to notify her that we had excommunicated her; second, since it would be of little, or perhaps no profit to you, if she were excommunicated in our church without knowing it; third, because we believe that this could be done to better advantage in a provincial council of our fellow bishops. I think that we should wait until then …[101]

In doing so he looked back to the teachings of the 845/6 Council of Paris which enjoined that excommunication should be delivered in synod by more than one bishop. Fulbert's letters, like those of Gerbert before him, exemplify similar themes to those found in canon law collections from England and the Reich: a twin concern to ensure that excommunication was practised in accordance with church law, and to link it to the defence and articulation of episcopal authority.

III

Bishops in all three realms maintained the concern to articulate and promote the correct practice of excommunication throughout the tenth and into the eleventh century. Although Hartmann identified the years of crisis for the former Frankish kingdoms immediately after the end of the Carolingian Empire as crucial to this preoccupation, it remained an episcopal concern throughout this period. Indeed, records of the *formulae* to be used for the imposition of excommunication, and the rites to be followed for the reconciliation of excommunicants, only began to be recorded in the years after Empire. These records, as with other liturgical records, were never straightforward prescriptions, but the differences between them point to the liveliness of excommunication practices, and the rite's importance to local bishops, across East and West Francia and Anglo-Saxon England.

Law and liturgy **295**

Whilst current accounts of the emergence of medieval excommunication rites bring evidence together from different genres and geographical regions to construct a universal practice, it is worth recognizing the different evolution in recording practices between these three realms. In East Francia excommunication rites were initially recorded in an early tenth-century canon law collection compiled to support Lotharingian bishops in the government of their diocese, and taken up by Rhineland and Bavarian bishops anxious to provide the clerics teaching in their cathedral school with a comprehensive guide to pastoral care and discipline. Excommunication rites only began to be added into liturgical compilations from the early eleventh century. In Anglo-Saxon England, the practice of excommunication was promoted and regulated in tenth-century royal law codes, but its rites only became a matter of record in the early eleventh century.[102] This is when Wulfstan, a bishop whose other writings testify to this commitment to the education of the clergy, set them down in his canon law collection. Moreover, it was not until the post-Conquest period that excommunication formulae came to be widely recorded in liturgical books.[103] The nature of evidence from West Francia is even more different. Here, churchmen chose to record the texts of specific sentences, not formal, rubricated rites. In the tenth century these seem to have been recorded as much as a matter of historical record, as for prescription. But they appear in liturgical as well as legal compilations. Far from being normative, as some of the work on the spiritual consequences of post-Carolingian dispute settlement implies, the West Frankish experience appears unusual.

But the similarities across these three case studies are also striking. In all three regions, one of the main contexts in which excommunication rites were recorded is a pedagogic one. Both Regino's and Burchard's collections were intended to support bishops in the education and discipline of their clergy in Lotharingia and the Rhineland, as was Wulfstan's in Anglo-Saxon England. In West Francia, the letters of Gerbert and Fulbert capture the pronouncements and practice of two renowned teachers. All these texts show the debt tenth- and early eleventh-century churchmen owed to ninth-century legislation. And all link the practice of excommunication to the articulation of the bishop's apostolic authority. This study therefore shows how an investigation of the context in which rites were recorded has the potential to move beyond the local to investigate how bishops across the post-Carolingian world of northern Europe sort to express and record their authority in a challenging world. At the same time, it highlights the dangers of treating any one record of how excommunication should be carried out as representative of a normative, universal practice for the whole of Christendom.

Notes

1 In addition to the works cited below see Olivier Guyotjeannin, *Episcopus et comes: Affirmation et déclin de la seigneurie épiscopale au nord du Royaume de France (Beauvais-Noyon, Xe-début XIIIe siècle* (Geneva: Droz, 1987); Geneviève Bührer-Thierry, *Éveques et pouvoir dans le royaume de Germanie. Les Églises de Baviere et de Souabe, 876–973* (Paris: Picard, 1997); *Bischof Burchard von Worms 1000–1025*, ed. by Wilfried Hartmann

(Mainz:Verlag der Gesellschaft für mittelrheinische Kirchengeschichte, 2000);Wilfried Hartmann, 'L'évêque comme juge: la pratique du tribunal épiscopal en France du Xe au XIIe siècle', in *Hiérarchies et services au Moyen Âge*, ed. by Claude Carozzi and Huguette Taviani-Carozzi (Aix-en-Provence: Publications de l'Université de Provence, 2001), pp. 71–92; *The Bishop: Power and Piety at the First Millenium*, ed. by Sean Gilsdorf (Münster: LitVerlag, 2004); Steffen Patzold, 'L'épiscopat du haut Moyen Âge du point de vue de la médiévistique allemande', *Cahiers de civilisation médiévale*, 48 (2005), 341–58; *The Bishop Reformed: Studies of Episcopal Power and Culture in the Central Middle Ages*, ed. by John S. Ott and Anna Trumbore Jones (Aldershot: Ashgate, 2007); Anna Trumbore Jones, *Noble Lord, Good Shepherd. Episcopal Power and Piety in Aquitaine, 877–1050* (Leiden: Brill, 2009); *Patterns of Episcopal Power: Bishops in Tenth and Eleventh Century Western Europe*, ed. by Ludger Körntgen and Dominik Wassenhoven (Berlin: Walter de Gruyter, 2011); John Eldevik, 'Bishops in the Medieval Empire: New Perspectives on the Church, State and Episcopal Office', *History Compass*, 9 (2011), 776–90; John Eldevik, *Episcopal Power and Ecclesiastical Reform in the German Empire. Tithes, Lordship, and Community, 950–1150* (Cambridge: Cambridge University Press, 2012); *Religion und Politik im Mittelalter: Deutschland and England im Vergleich*, ed. by Ludger Körntgen and Dominik Wassenhoven (Berlin: Walter de Gruyter, 2013); John S. Ott, *Bishops, Authority and Community in Northwestern Europe c. 1050–1150* (Cambridge: Cambridge University Press, 2015); Julia Barrow, *The Clergy in the Medieval World. Secular Clerics,Their Families and Careers in North-Western Europe, c. 800-c.1200* (Cambridge: Cambridge University Press, 2015); Florian Mazel, *L'évêque et le territoire. L'invention médiévale de l'espace (Ve-XIIIe siècle)* (Paris: Éditions du Seuil, 2016); Special Issue: *Bishops in the Age of Iron*, ed. by Brigitte Meijns and StevenVanderputten, 'Medieval Low Countries' 6 (2019), 137–56

2 Timothy Reuter, 'Ein Europa der Bischöfe. Daz Zeitalter Burchards von Worms', in *Bischof Burchard*, ed. by Hartmann, pp. 1–49; translated as 'A Europe of Bishops. The Age of Wulfstan of York and Burchard of Worms', in *Patterns of Episcopal Power*, ed. by Körntgen and Wassenhoven, pp. 17–38.

3 Reuter, 'A Europe of Bishops', p. 37.

4 Steffen Patzold, *Episcopus. Wissen über Bischöfe im Frankenreich des späten 8. bis frühen 10. Jahrhunderts* (Ostfildern: Jan Thorbeke Verlag, 2008).

5 Mayke de Jong, *The Penitential State. Authority and Atonement in the Age of Louis the Pious, 814–840* (Cambridge: Cambridge University Press, 2009); Mayke de Jong, 'Ecclesia and the Early Medieval Polity', in *Staat im frühen Mittelalter*, ed. by Stuart Airlie,Walter Pohl, Helmut Reimitz (Vienna: Österreichische Akademie der Wissenschaften, 2006), pp. 113–32.

6 Wilfried Hartmann, *Kirche und Kirchenrecht um 900. Die Bedeutung der spätkarolingischen Zeit für Tradition und Innovation im kirchlichen Recht*, MGH Schriften, 58 (Hannover: Hahnsche Buchhandlung, 2008), pp. 267–316.

7 Berlin, Staatsbibliothek Preussischer Kulturbesitz, MS Phillips 1765, fols 95r-v; *Die Konzilien der karolingischen Teilreiche 875–911*, ed. by Wilfried Hartmann, Isolde Schröder and Gerhard Schmitz, MGH Concilia 5 (Wiesbaden: Harrassowitz, 2014), pp. 455–8; Regino of Prüm, *Libri Duo de Synodalibus Causis et Disciplinis Ecclesiasticis*, ed. by F.G.A. Wasserschleben and rev. by Wilfried Hartmann as *Das Sendhandbuch des Regino von Prüm* (Darmstadt:Wissenchaftliche Buchgesellschaft, 2004), II. 412–8, pp. 438–46.

8 Elisabeth Vodola, *Excommunication in the Middle Ages* (Berkeley: University of California Press, 1986); Roger E. Reynolds, 'Rites of Separation and Reconciliation in the Early Middle Ages', *Segni e Riti nella Chiesa Altomedievale Occidentale, Spoleto, 11–17 aprile 1985*, Settimane di studio del Centro italiano di studi sull'alto medioevo, 33 (Spoleto, 1987), pp. 405–33, repr. in his *Law and Liturgy in the Latin Church, 5th–12th Centuries* (Aldershot: Ashgate, 2004), no. X; Christian Jaser, *Ecclesia maledicens. Rituelle und zeremonielle Exkommunikationsformen im Mittelalter* (Tübingen: Morhr Siebeck, 2013). The exception is a 2015 collection which focuses mainly on the Carolingian period and West Francia: *Exclure de la communauté chrétienne. Sens et pratique sociales de l'anathème*

et de l'excommunication (IVe–XIIe siècle), ed. by Geneviève Bührer-Thierry and Stéphane Gioanni (Turnhout: Brepols, 2015).

9 Lester K. Little, *Benedictine Maledictions. Liturgical Cursing in Romanesque France* (Ithaca, NY: Cornell University Press, 1993) suggested it was a phenomenon mainly of West Francia north of the Loire and linked to political fragmentation; more recently scholars working on charter sanction clauses and the Peace of God movement in southern France have challenged the assumption that recourse to cursing is a north French phenomenon: Jeffrey Bowman, 'Do Neo-Romans Curse? Law, Land and Ritual in the Midi (900-1100)', *Viator*, 28 (1997), 1–32; François Bougard, 'Jugement divin, excommunication, anathème et malédiction: la sanction spirituelle dans les sources diplomatiques', in *Exclure*, ed. by Bührer-Thierry and Gioanni, pp. 215–38; Isabelle Rosé, 'Judas, Dathan, Abiron, Simon et les autres. Les figures bibliques-repoussoirs dans les clauses comminatoires des actes originaux français', *Archiv für Diplomatik*, 62 (2016), 59–106.

10 Laurent Jégou, *L'évêque, juge de paix. L'autorité épiscopale et le règlement des conflits (VIIIe–XIe siècle)* (Turnhout: Brepols, 2011), pp. 462–75; Michel Lauwers, 'L'exclusion comme construction de l'ecclesia. Genèse, fonction et usages du rite de l'excommunication en Occident entre le IXe et le XIe siècle', in *Exclure*, ed. by Bührer-Thierry and Gioanni, pp. 263–84.

11 Michael Elliot, 'New Evidence for the Influence of Gallic Canon Law in Anglo-Saxon England', *Journal of Ecclesiastical History*, 64 (2013), pp. 700–30, at pp. 700–1.

12 Genevieve Steele Edwards, 'Ritual Excommunication in Medieval France and England, 900-1200' (unpublished doctoral dissertation, Stanford University, 1997); Sarah Hamilton, '*Absoluimus uos uice beati petri apostolorum principis*: Episcopal Authority and the Reconciliation of Excommunicants in England and Francia c. 900 – c. 1150', in *Frankland. The Franks and the World of the Early Middle Ages. Essays in Honour of Dame Jinty Nelson*, ed. by Paul Fouracre and David Ganz (Manchester: Manchester University Press, 2008), pp. 209–41; Sarah Hamilton, 'Interpreting Diversity: Excommunication Rites in the Tenth and Eleventh Centuries', in *Understanding Medieval Liturgy. Essays in Interpretation*, ed. by Helen Gittos and Sarah Hamilton (Farnham: Ashgate, 2016), pp. 125–58; Sarah Hamilton, 'Medieval Curses and Their Records', *Haskins Society Journal* (forthcoming).

13 For example, Gerd Tellenbach, *The Church in Western Europe from the Tenth to the Early Twelfth Century*, trans. by Timothy Reuter (Cambridge: Cambridge University Press, 1993), p. 41; Jean Dunbabin, *France in the Making, 843–1180* (Oxford: Oxford University Press, 1985).

14 For example, Reynolds, 'Rites of Separation', pp. 411–4; Little, *Benedictine Maledictions*, pp. 36–8, 143–4.

15 Regino, *Libri duo*, II.412, ed. by Hartmann, p. 438.

16 Regino, *Libri duo*, II.412, ed. by Hartmann, pp. 438–40.

17 Regino, *Libri duo*, II.413–417, ed. by Hartmann, pp. 442–4. Hartmann's edition omits two *formulae*; these are edited in Regino of Prüm, *Libri duo de synodalibus causis et disciplinis ecclesiasticis*, ed. F.G.A. Wasserschleben (Leipzig: Engelmann, 1840), II.414–15, pp. 373–4.

18 'Et repondeant omnes tertio: *Amen*, aut: *Fiat*, aut: *Anathema sit*.' Regino, *Libri duo*, II.413, ed. by Hartmann, p. 442.

19 Regino, *Libri duo*, ed. by Hartmann, II. 413, p. 442.

20 Regino, *Libri duo*, ed. by Hartmann, II.413, pp. 442–4.

21 Regino, *Libri duo*, ed. by Hartmann, II. 418, p. 446.

22 Wilfried Hartmann, 'Die *Capita incerta* im Sendhandbuch Reginos von Prüm', in *Scientia veritatis. Festschrift für Hubert Mordek zum 65. Geburtstag*, ed. by Oliver Münsch and Thomas Zotz (Ostfildern: Thorbecke, 2004), pp. 207–26.

23 Epistle XVII, *Patrologia Latina* 126, col. 101.

24 *MGH Concilia* 5, pp. 455–8; Brussels, Bibliothèque royal de Belgique, MS 495–505, fols 204r-v; there is broadly accurate transcription by Steele Edwards, 'Ritual Excommunication', pp. 139–40 (albeit erroneously attributed to MS 295–505), who noted the similarities of both Rheims formulae with one of Regino's texts.

25 See now Hartmut Hoffmann and Rudolf Pokorny, *Das Dekret des Bischofs Burchard von Worms. Textstufen – Frühe Verbreitung – Vorlagen*, MGH Hilfsmittel 12 (Munich: Monumenta Germaniae Historica, 1991); also Lotte Kéry, *Canonical Collections of the Early Middle Ages (ca. 400–1140). A Bibliographical Guide to the Manuscripts and Literature* (Washington, DC: Catholic University of America Press, 1999), pp. 133–55.

26 For example, the excommunication rite in Regino is accepted by Jégou as representative of wider West Frankish practice: *L'évêque*, p. 470.

27 Kéry, *Canonical Collections*, p. 129: Arras, Bibliothèque municipale, MS 723 (s. xi, Saint-Vaast); Paris, Bibliothèque nationale de France, MS lat. 17527 (s. xi¹, Rheims).

28 Linda Fowler-Magerl, *Clavis Canonum. Selected Canon Law Collections Before 1140*, MGH Hilfsmittel 21 (Hannover: Hahnsche Buchhandlung, 2005), pp. 68–70; for further bibliography see Kéry, *Canonical Collections*, p. 189. The contents suggest it was compiled in Lotharingia in first half of the tenth century but it now survives in only one late eleventh-century manuscript in a central Italian hand (Cologne, Erbischöfliche Diözesan-und Dombibliothek, MS 124) and citations in other collections suggest it circulated in eleventh-century Italy.

29 Burchard of Worms, *Decretum*, PL 140, cols 537–1065; Greta Austin, *Shaping Church Law Around the Year 1000. The Decretum of Burchard of Worms* (Ashgate: Farnham, 2009).

30 Jorg Müller, *Untersuchungen zur Collectio Duodecim Partium* (Ebelsbach: R. Gremer, 1989); Kéry, *Canonical Collections*, pp. 155–7.

31 *Collectio IV Librorum*, I. 67–74 = Regino, I.412–418: Linda Fowler Magerl, *Clavis Canonum. Selected Canon Law Collections Before 1140. Online Database* (www.mgh.de/ext/clavis/) (last accessed 19th October, 2018).

32 Burchard of Worms, *Decretum*, XI.1, PL 140, cols 855–6; for source as Pseudo-Remedius c. 49, see Hoffmann and Pokorny, *Das Dekret*, p. 218. On Burchard of Worm's intentions, with a consideration of his working methods in Book XI, see Greta Austin, *Shaping Church Law Around the Year 1000. The Decretum of Burchard of Worms* (Ashgate: Farnham, 2009).

33 Burchard, *Decretum*, XI.2–8, PL 140, cols 856–61.

34 Regino, *Libri duo*, ed. by Hartmann, II. 411, pp. 436–8: 'De presbytero accusato: Ex Concilio Rotomagensi'.

35 Burchard, *Decretum*, XI.8, PL 140, col. 860: 'Et ibi secundum leges diuinas opportet damnum commissum emendari, aut si iam emendatum est, eorum testimonio comprobari'; cf. Regino, *Libri duo*, ed. by Hartmann, II.418, p. 446: 'et ibi secundum legis diuinas et humanas oportet damnum commissum emendari, aut si iam emendatum est, eorum testimonio comprobari.'

36 Greta Austin, 'Jurisprudence in the Service of Pastoral Care: The *Decretum* of Burchard of Worms', *Speculum*, 79 (2004), 929–59, (pp. 933, 946).

37 Burchard, *Decretum*, XI.8, PL 140, cols 860–1; Regino, *Libri duo*, ed. by Hartmann, II.418, p. 446. On these changes see Sarah Hamilton, 'The Anglo-Saxon and Frankish Evidence for the Rites for the Reconciliation of Excommunicants', in *Recht und Gericht in Kirche und Welt um 900*, ed. by Wilfried Hartmann with Annette Grabowsky, Schriften des Historischen Kollegs Kolloquien 69 (Munich: R. Oldenbourg Verlag, 2007), pp. 169–96 at pp. 171–6, 190–4.

38 Sarah Hamilton, *The Practice of Penance, 900–1050* (Woodbridge: Boydell Press, 2001), pp. 31–2.

39 Greta Austin, 'Freising and Worms in the Early Eleventh Century: Revisiting the Relationship Between the *Collectio Duodecim Partium* and Burchard's *Decretum*', *Zeitschrift der Savigny-Stiftung für Rechtsgeschichte, kanonistiche Abteilung*, 124 (2007), pp. 45–108.

40 Fowler-Magerl, *Clavis Canonum*, pp. 91–3.

41 Book XI: 'De penitentia et reconciliatione'.

42 Regino, *Libri duo*, ed. by Hartmann, II. 412–418; *Collectio XII Partium*, X.115–121; the augmented *Collectio XII Partium*, X.264–270; see Fowler-Magerl, *Clavis Canonum* at www.mgh.de/ext/clavis/ (last accessed 11th October, 2018).

Law and liturgy **299**

43 Council of Tribur (895), Versio Vulgata, c. 8, *Die Konzilien der karolingischen Teilreiche 875–911*, ed. by Wilfried Hartmann, Isolde Schröder and Gerhard Schmitz, MGH Concilia 5 (Wiesbaden: Harrassowitz Verlag, 2014), p. 348 = Original *Collectio XII Partium*, X.108, augmented *Collectio XII Partium*, X.262.

44 Augmented *Collectio XII Partium*, X.264.

45 fols 152r-152v. A digitized version is available at Münchener DigitalisierungsZentrum Digitale Bibliothek: available at https://app.digitale-sammlungen.de/bookshelf/bsb00060092/images (last accessed 11th October 2018), on which see Hamilton, 'Interpreting Diversity', pp. 139–43.

46 *Collectio XII Partium*, X.121.

47 Hamilton, 'Interpreting Diversity'.

48 Henry Parkes, 'Questioning the Authority of Vogel and Elze's *Pontifical romano-germanique*', in *Understanding Medieval Liturgy*, ed. by Gittos and Hamilton, pp. 75–102; Henry Parkes, *The Making of Liturgy in the Ottonian Church. Books, Music and Ritual in Mainz, 950–1050* (Cambridge: Cambridge University Press, 2015).

49 Hamilton, *The Practice of Penance*, pp. 211–23.

50 *Le Pontifical Romano-Germanique du dixième siècle*, ed. by Cyrille Vogel and Reinhard Elze, 3 vols, Studi e testi 226–27, 263 (Vatican City: Biblioteca Apostolica Vaticana, 1963–1972), I, pp. 308–21.

51 Hamilton, 'The Anglo-Saxon and Frankish Evidence', pp. 173–76.

52 Montecassino, Ms 451 (s. xi^2); Rome, Biblioteca Vallicelliana, MS D.5 (s. xi2); Vendôme, Bibliothèque municipale, MS 14 (s.xi) (s.xi^1, Lorsch?); Paris, Bibliothèque nationale de France, MS lat. 820 (s. xi^2, Angers); Vitry, Bibliothèque municipale, MS 36 (s. xi^{ex}, Châlons); Eichstätt, Diözesanarchiv, Cod. B.4 (s. xi^2). In addition two codices include all the PRG excommunication rite except for the Leonine formula: Munich, Bayerische Staatsbibliothek, Clm 21585 (s. xi^{med}) and Metz, Bibliothèque municipale, Cod. 334 (s. xi). This analysis is only possible thanks to Henry Parkes's comparative analysis of the contents of various Romano-German Pontifical manuscripts, as version of which is available here: *PRG Database: A tool for navigating Le Pontifical Romano-Germanique, ed. Cyrille Vogel & Reinhard Elze* available at http://database.prg.mus.cam.ac.uk/ (last accessed 19th October 2018).

53 Hamilton, 'Interpreting Diversity', pp. 134–9; Henry Parkes, 'Henry II, Liturgical Patronage and the Birth of the "Romano-German Pontifical"', *Early Medieval Europe* (forthcoming).

54 'Et sicut dominus beato Petro apostolo eiusque successoribus, cuius uicem tenemus, quamuis indigni, potestatem dedit, ut quodcumque ligarent super terram ligatum esset et in caelis et quodcumque soluerent super terram solutum esset et in caelis, ita illis, si emendare noluerint, caelum claudimus et terram ad sepeliendum negamus et dimergantur in ferno inferiori, soluantque quod gesserunt sine fine.' *Le Pontifical Romano-Germanique*, ed. by Vogel and Elze, I, pp. 316–7; Bamberg, Staatsbibliothek, MS Lit. 53, fol. 191v.

55 Paris, Bibliothèque nationale de France, MS Lat. 1231 (s. xi); Vienna, Österreichische Nationalbibliothek, Cod. 1817 (s. xii); Milan, Biblioteca Ambrosiana, Cod. Z.52 sup (s.xi); Münster, Westfälische Wilhelms Universität Münster Universitäts-und Landesbibliothek, MS 1133 (s. xi); Merseburg, Domstiftsbibliothek, Cod. I.57 (s.xi); Augsburg, Bistumsarchiv, MS 21 (s. xi^2); Munich, Bayerische Staatsbibliothek, Clm 3909 (s. xii).

56 On Wulfstan see Patrick Wormald, 'Archbishop Wulfstan: Eleventh-century Statebuilder', in *Wulfstan, Archbishop of York. The Proceedings of the Second Alcuin Conference*, ed. by Matthew Townend (Turnhout: Brepols, 2004), pp. 9–27.

57 Edited in Hans Sauer, 'Die Exkommunikationsriten aus Wulfstans Handbuch und Liebermanns Gesetze', in *Bright is the Ring of Words. Festschrift für Horst Weinstock zum 65. Geburtstag* (Bonn: Romanistischer Verlag, 1996), pp. 283–307. A digitised facsimile and manuscript description is available at Parker Online: available at https://parker.stanford.edu/parker/catalog/nh277tk2537 (last accessed 12th October 2018). See also that in Mildred Budny, *Insular, Anglo-Saxon and Early Anglo-Norman Manuscript Art at Corpus*

300 Sarah Hamilton

Christi College, Cambridge: An Illustrated Catalogue, 2 vols (Kalamazoo, MI: Medieval Institute Publications, Western Michigan University), I, pp. 605–7.

58 This is the title given by Michael D. Elliot, 'Canon Law Collections in Anglo-Saxon England c. 600–c.1066' (unpublished doctoral dissertation, University of Toronto, 2013), 170–171, and Michael D. Elliot, 'New Evidence for the Influence of Gallic Canon Law in Anglo-Saxon England', *Journal of Ecclesiastical History*, 64 (2013), 700–30 (p. 702, n. 4); it was previously known as *Excerptiones Egberti* and the *Canon Law Collection of Archbishop Wulfstan*. Michael Elliot has generously published an edition of all 5 recensions on-line: *Anglo-Saxon Canon Law*, available at http://individual.utoronto.ca/michaelelliot/ (last accessed 12th October 2018); this supersedes the partial edition: *Wulfstan's Canon Law Collection*, ed. by J.E. Cross and Andrew Hamer (Cambridge: D.S. Brewer, 1999). Crucial to understanding the make-up of this collection is Hans Sauer, 'Zur Überlieferung und Anlage von Erzbischof Wulfstans "Handbuch"', *Deutsches Archiv für Erforschung des Mittelalters*, 36 (1980), pp. 341–84 (translated as 'The Transmission and Structure of Archbishop Wulfstan's "Commonplace Book"', in *Old English Prose: Basic Readings*, ed. by Paul E. Szarmach (New York: Garlanda Publishing, 2000), pp. 339–93; and Patrick Wormald, *The Making of English Law. King Alfred to the Twelfth Century. Volume I: Legislation and its Limits* (Oxford: Blackwell, 1999), pp. 210–24.

59 Cambridge, Corpus Christi College, MS 265, pp. 209, 211–5.

60 *Collectio Wigorniensis* C, ed. by Michael D. Elliot, p. 121, available at http://individual.utoronto.ca/michaelelliot/ (last accessed 12th October 2018). The other recension in which these rites appear towards the end is found in the later manuscript, Oxford, Bodleian Library, MS Barlow 37, fols 41r–41v (England, s.xii^ex–/s.xiii^in); the contents list for a mid-eleventh-century manuscript with an Exeter provenance, now Cambridge, Corpus Christi College, MS 190, suggests that a quire which is now missing between pp. 110–1 included similar texts.

61 E.g. *Collectio Wigorniensis* C, c. 221; *Collectio Wigorniensis* I, cc. 169–171; *Collectio Wigorniensis* O, cc. 158, 164, 166. Elliot, 'Wulfstan's Commonplace Book Revised', p. 17, n. 52.

62 Michael D. Elliot, 'New Evidence for the Influence of Gallic Canon Law in Anglo-Saxon England', *Journal of Ecclesiastical History*, 64 (2013), 700–730; *The Political Writings of Archbishop Wulfstan of York*, ed. and trans. by Andrew Rabin (Manchester: Manchester University Press, 2015), pp. 29–30.

63 Hamilton, 'The Anglo-Saxon and Frankish Evidence'.

64 'Nos autem segregando excommunicamus et anathematizando ligamus illos rebelles N. a consortio christianorum omnium per omnipotentiam illius, qui in euuangelio locutus est dicens: "Quodcumque ligaueritis super terram, erit ligatum et in celis" et reliqua. Dedit enim dominus apostolis et successoribus eorum, id est episcopis, potestatem uidelicet ligandi atques soluendi, et precepit eis edificare et p(l)antare bonos in domo domini, euellere et dissipare peccatores de domo domini, hoc est de ecclesia Christi.' Cambridge, Corpus Christi College, MS 265, p. 211.

65 Cambridge, Corpus Christi College, MS 265, p. 213: 'De his qui post excomunicationem cum lucu penitentie ad reconciliationem ueniunt. Placuit uniuerso senatui ut hi qui excommunicati ad emendationem ueniunt et indulgentie ueniam petunt, ac cordec conpuncto penitentie subdantur, et cum intercessoribus ad cimiterii portam perueniunt maneant illic discalciati laneisque induti, quousque eorum interuentores promoueant episcopum quecumque modo potuerint.' On this text see Hamilton, 'Rites for the Reconciliation of Excommunicants', pp. 176–86.

66 'Absoluimus uos uice beati petri cui dominus potestatem ligandi atque soluendi dedit': Cambridge, Corpus Christi College, MS 265, p. 215. This prayer is unique to Anglo-Saxon tradition: Hamilton, 'Rites for the Reconciliation of Excommunicants', p. 182.

67 Hamilton, 'Remedies for "Great Transgressions": Penance and Excommunication in Late Anglo-Saxon England', in *Pastoral Care in Late Anglo-Saxon England*, ed. by Francesca Tinti (Woodbridge: Boydell Press, 2005), pp. 83–105 at p. 100.

68 London, British Library, MS Cotton Vespasian D. xv; on its medieval provenance see Hamilton, 'Absoluimus', p. 211.

69 In addition to the works cited in notes 55, 57 and 61 see Michael Elliot, 'Wulfstan's Commonplace Book Revised. The Structure and Development of Block 7 on Pastoral Privilege and Responsibility', *Journal of Medieval Latin*, 22 (2012), 1–48.

70 Hamilton, 'Remedies', pp. 93–105.

71 *MGH Concilia* V, pp. 456–8.

72 Kéry, *Canonical Collections*, p. 88 (*Collectio Dacheriana*, s.ix^{in}), 174 (the *'Additiones' to the Capitula of Isaac of Langres*, s.ix$^{4/4}$).

73 'Lecta est excommunicatio haec quae sequitur in aecclesia Sanctae Mariae Remis praesentibus episcopis infrascriptis': *MGH Concilia* V, p. 456.

74 'Et sicut hae lucernae de nostris projectae manibus hodie extinguuntur, sic eorum lucerna in aeternum extinguatur.': *MGH Concilia* V, p. 458.

75 *MGH Concilia* V, p. 455.

76 Brussels, Bibliothèque royale de Belgique, MS 495–505; Kéry, *Canonical Collections*, pp. 13–20.

77 Rosamond McKitterick, *The Frankish Church and the Carolingian Reforms, 789–895* (London: Royal Historical Society, 1977), p. 4.

78 For a transcription see Steele Edwards, 'Ritual Excommunication', pp. 139–40.

79 Saint Petersburg, National Library of Russia, MS Q.v.I.no. 35, fols 105v-107r. See Niels Krogh Rasmussen, *Les Pontificaux de haut Moyen Âge. Genèse du livre de l'évêque* (Leuven: Spicileigum Sacrum Lovaniense, 1998), pp. 89–135 for a description. The text has been edited most recently by Steele Edwards, 'Ritual Excommunication', pp. 150–4.

80 'Igitur cognoscat universalis ecclesia hostes seuissimos et tirannos improbos, aduersarios et persecutores pessimos sanctae dei aecclesiae, Ragendardum et Rodmundum eius filium eorumque commilitones ecclesiasticarum rerum peruasores ... ... Hos et omnes qui postquam archiepiscopalem suscepi benedictionem, sanctum Sennensis ecclesiae locum ingredi non permiserunt more antecessorum meorum, desistentes a veritate adherentes mendatio, insuper anathematizamus per Patrem et filium et spiritum sanctum et per auctoritatem nobis a deo concessa.': Saint Petersburg, National Library of Russia, MS lat. Q.v.I.35, fols 105v- 106r.

81 *Chronique de Saint-Pierre-le-Vif-de Sens, Dite de Clarius: Chronicon Sancti Petri Vivi Senonensis*, ed. by Robert-Henri Bautier and Monique Gilles (Paris: Centre national de la recherche scientifique, 1979), p. 90.

82 Guy Lobrichon, 'Nouvelles recherches sur le rituel pontifical de Sens au IXe siècle', *Bulletin de la Société Nationale des Antiquaires de France* (13, May, 1992), pp. 191–200.

83 Georg Waitz, 'Obedienzklärungen burgundischer und französischer Bischöfe', *Neues Archiv*, 3 (1878), pp. 195–202.

84 Composed 988x996, it survives in only one eleventh-century manuscript: Kéry, *Canonical Collections*, pp. 199–201; ed. *PL* 139, cols 473–508.

85 Abbo, *Collectio Canonum*, c. 36: 'De inuste excommunicatum', *PL* 139, col. 494, cites 3 canons under this heading, including the Council of Meaux-Paris (845/6), c. 56, *MGH Concilia III*, pp. 110–1. Cf. Regino, *Libri Duo*, II.310, and Burchard, *Decretum*, XI.10, *PL* 140, cols 861–2.

86 Confirmed by a review of the evidence for local collections in Kéry, *Canonical Collections*, pp. 161–202. There are two West Frankish manuscripts of Regino: Arras, Bibliothèque municipale, MS 723 (s. xi, Saint-Vaast, Arras) and Paris, Bibliothèque nationale de France, MS lat. 17525 (s. xi^1, Rheims). Note also the copy of *Collectio XII Partium*, now Troyes, Bibliothèque municipale, MS 246 (s. xi^1, East Francia, prov. cathedral of Troyes).

87 *Die Briefsammlung Gerberts von Reims*, ed. Fritz Weigle, MGH Die Briefe der deutschen Kaiserzeit 2 (Weimar: Hermann Böhlaus, 1966); Pierre Riché, 'Nouvelles recherches sur les lettres de Gerbert d'Aurillac', *Comptes rendus des séances de l'Académie des Inscriptions et Belles-Lettres*, 131 (1987), pp. 575–85; *The Letters and Poems of Fulbert of Chartres*, ed. and trans. Frederick Behrends (Oxford: Oxford University Press, 1976).

302 Sarah Hamilton

88 'Conuenimus ergo conscientiam uestram omnes episcopae Remorum diocesos ad satisfactionem inuitamus. Spaciumque paenitentiae usque in proximis kalendis attribuimus, tunc uos aut in fertiles ecclesiae palmites recognituri aut tanquam inutile lignum ab agro Dei gladio sancti spiritus excisuri', *Die Briefsammlung Gerberts*, ed. Weigle, no. 199, pp. 241–2; translation: *The Letters of Gerbert with his Papal Privileges as Sylvester II*, ed. and trans. Harriet Pratt Lattin (New York: Columbia University Press, 1960), no. 195, pp. 229–30.

89 'Quod si, quod absit, in malitia perseueraverint, tunc in celebri ecclesiae loco nostrae vocationis scripta ad legendum proponi iubemus, deinde excommunicationem rationabiliter conscriptam et a vobis sollempniter celebratam celebri affigi loco eiusque exemplar nobis dirigi, ut idem in nostris fiat aecclesiis': *Die Briefsammlung Gerberts*, ed. Weigle, no. 202, p. 244; translation, based on an earlier edition with a different dating and suggested addressee, *Letters of Gerbert*, no. 206, p. 267.

90 *Decretum*, XI.49, *PL* 140, col. 868.

91 Hoffmann and Pokorny, *Das Dekret*, p. 221; *MGH Concilia* V, p. 12.

92 *Die Briefsammlung Gerberts*, ed. Weigle, nos 100, 113, pp. 129–30, 141.

93 On Fulbert and his circle see Pierre Riché, 'Autour du millénaire de Fulbert, le maître et ses disciples', *Bulletin de la Société archéologique d'Eure-et-Loir*, 92(2007), 1–10, repr. in Pierre Riché, *Les Lumières de l'an mille* (Paris: Centre national de la recherche scientifique, 2013), pp. 199–212; Bernard Gowers, 'Fulbert of Chartres and His Circle: Scholarship and Society in Eleventh-century France' (unpublished doctoral dissertations, University of Oxford, 2007).

94 Jean Leclercq, 'L'interdit et l'excommunication d'après les lettres de Fulbert de Chartres', *Revue historique de droit français et étranger*, 4th ser. 22 (1944), 67–77; Wilfried Hartmann, 'Die Briefe Fulberts von Chartres als Quelle für die Praxis des bischöflichen Gerichts in Frankreich am Beginn des 11. Jahrhunderts', in *Grundlagen des Rechts. Festschrift für Peter Landau zum 65. Geburtstag*, ed. by Richard H. Helmholz, Paul Mikat, Jörg Müller, and Michael Stolleis (Paderborn: F. F. Schöningh, 2000), pp. 93–103.

95 *Fulbert*, ed. Behrends, no. 87, pp. 154–6.

96 *Fulbert*, ed. Behrends, no. 54, p. 94: 'Illatam uobis iniuriam uere meam facio conpassionis affectu, in eos qui sacro ordini fecere contumeliam zelo feruens. Sed quia nec uobis utile esse uideo nec mihi tutum ut zelus noster ad uindictam excommunicacionis erumpat, expectandum et commonitoriis utendum esse reor, donec illos aut penitentia corrigat, aut summi iudicis sentencia multet.'

97 *Fulbert*, ed. Behrends, no. 13, p. 26.

98 'Sed nos tuae prouidentes saluti, trium ebdomadarum ab ipso die petiuimus inducias, ut litteris te conuenire possemus.', *Fulbert*, ed. Behrends, no. 13, p. 26.

99 'Christianam communionem nobiscum ulterius non habebis', *Fulbert*, ed. Behrends, no. 13, p. 26.

100 Lotte Kéry, *Gottesfurcht und irdische Strafe. Der Beitrag des mittelalterlichen Kirchenrechts zur Entstehung des öffentlichen Strafrechts* (Cologne: Böhlau, 2006), p. 108.

101 'Laudonensem illam sacrilegam res ecclesiae uestrae diripientem propter has causas excommunicare distulimus: primo, quia defuit qui ipsi ferre auderet nostram excommunicacionem; deinde, quia parum uobis aut nihil fortasse prodesset, si illa nesciens excommunicaretur in ecclesia nostra; tercio, quia expectauimus ut in conuentu nostrorum conprouincialium episcoporum utilius hoc fieret. Quod etiam adhuc expectandum nobis uidetur, si animi uestri serenitas adquiescat.': *Fulbert*, ed. Behrends, no. 79, pp. 138–41. Leclercq, 'L'interdit', p. 76.

102 Hamilton, 'Remedies', pp. 98–9.

103 Hamilton, 'Remedies', pp. 94–7; Elaine Treharne, 'A Unique Old English Formula for Excommunication from Corpus Christi College 303', *Anglo-Saxon England*, 24 (1995), 185–211.

INDEX

Abbo of Saint-Germain-des-Près 207, 210–212, 214–215, 253
Abel, bishop of Reims 36–37, 42–45, 49
Abraham, bishop of Freising 142, 181, 247
Actus pontificum Cenomanensis in urbe degentium 24–30
Æthelred II, king of England 3, 44, 96
Adalbero, bishop of Metz 265–266
Adalbero, archbishop of Reims 49, 262–270, 272, 274, 292
Adalbert of Magdeburg, *Chronicon* of 77, 94, 181
Adam 16, 19, 166
Adelheid, empress and wife of Otto I 139, 143–145, 173–174
Adelheid, daughter of Henry IV 178–179
Ademar of Chabannes 9; *Chronicle* of 102; notebook of 154–155, 159–161, 242–245
adventus 136, 282
Aethelwold, bishop of Winchester 262, 270
Agnes, empress and wife of Henry III 179
agriculture and farming 56–57, 207, 211
Agritius of Trier 79–80, 83
Alberic II, *princeps* and son of Marozia 59, 66, 68–69
Alcuin 119, 140, 155, 242, 271
Alexander the Great 213, 215
Annales Bertiniani / *Annals of St-Bertin* 46, 136, 215–216
Annales Quedlinburgensis / *Annals of Quedlinburg* 77, 97, 145

Annales regni Francorum / *Royal Frankish Annals* 18–19, 46, 63, 68, 74, 88, 190; audience of 77
Annales Fuldenses / *Annals of Fulda* 95, 175, 209
Anselm de Besate 252–253
Aquitaine 40, 45, 154–155, 161
Arnulf of Carinthia, king of East Francia 175; death of 15, 171; in battle 209–210
Arnulf of Metz, bishop-saint 23, 166, 170, 173
Arnulf, archbishop of Reims 36, 39, 49
Artold, archbishop of Reims 37, 39, 41, 48–49
Atto, bishop of Vercelli 225–227, 249, 253
Augustus, emperor 16–17, 19–21, 213, 215
Avars 134, 143, 208
Azzo, bishop of Como 221, 228–229

baptism 25, 68, 113, 291
Bede 17–19, 21–22, 29, 63
Benedict of Aniane 113–115, 271–272
Benedict of Nursia 25, 113
Benedict of St Andrea 56, 58–59, 62–70
Benedictine monasticism 82, 111–121, 262–268
Berengar I, king and emperor 15, 231–232, 243
Berengar II, king of Italy 229, 231–233, 247, 253
Bertha, empress and wife of Henry IV 178–179
betrothal 155–158

304   Index

Bible, the 111, 117–122, 160, 166; Book of Ezekiel 64–65; Book of Genesis 64–65, 166; Book of Isaiah 64–65; Jeremiah 64, 118, 214, 271; Book of Psalms 64; Book of Revelation 65; Old Testament 65–66, 119, 190, 229

Boethius 97, 245, 248

Bohemia 122, 145

Boniface, archbishop of Mainz and martyr 42–44, 271

Bretons 30, 205–207

Britain 2, 17, 242; its people 205

Bruno, archbishop of Cologne 232, 242, 247, 262–266, 268–271

Bruno of Merseburg 189, 194

Burgundy 2–3, 27, 38, 40 112, 145, 156, 159, 208

Cambrai 46, 48

canon law 47, 223–229, 233, 285–287, 292; collections 44, 223–230, 286–291

canonical life, canons 115–117, 128, 269; *see also* Benedictine monasticism

Capetians 3, 36, 168–170

capitularies 7, 193, 208, 226, 248; Ansegis 23; *see also* judicial inquest

Caroline minuscule 9, 111–113

Carolingian dynasty 6–7, 25–26, 29, 81, 195, 213; 'Renaissance' 6–7; and the *Annales Mettenses priores* 231; church reform of 112; genealogies *see entry*

Carloman, mayor of the palace and brother of Pippin II 19, 68–69, 172–173

Carloman I, king of the Franks and brother of Charlemagne 43, 169–170, 175

Carloman II, king of West Francia 174–175

Celsus of Trier 80, 83–87

Charlemagne 1–2, 15, 18, 23–25, 59, 63, 68–69, 111, 142–144, 211, 213; campaigns of 208; coronation of 28; court culture 241; death of 18; genealogies of *see entry*; letters of/to 134–135, 138, 272; *Missi see entry*; oath formulas *see Oaths*

Charles Martel, mayor of the palace 23–24, 28–29, 39–43, 81, 84, 87; banishment of Rigobert 36; death of 18, 82; genealogies of 172–174, 176

Charles the Bald 21–22, 29–30, 46–47, 136–137; *court of* 204–206; genealogies of *see entry*; oaths to 193; psalters for 138–140; and the *Synod of Pîtres* 211

Charles the Fat, king and emperor 3, 171, 175–176

Charles III (the Simple), king of West Francia 170, 174–175, 191, 222

Childebert II, king of Austrasia and Burgundy 36, 38

Christ 17–18, 135, 143, 145, 179, 210; church of 289; disciples of 26; genealogy of 167; image of 141; incarnation of 21

Church property 30, 38, 41, 59, 225, 227; inalienability of 24–25; lay appropriation of 47–48; sacrosanctity of 28

Clement, pope 25–27

Clovis II, king of Neustria and Burgundy 25, 28

Codex Laureshamensis 178, 180

Cologne *Synod at* 222

conciliar *acta* 29–30, 272, 283, 293

Conrad II, king and emperor 178, 189

Constantine, emperor 18, 67–69, 79, 102, 213

consanguinity, claims of incest 20, 167–168, 179–181

conversion 18, 28, 79, 85

councils: Meaux-Paris 292; Nicaea 18; Paris 44, 283, 294; Ponthion 136; Rome 293; *see also* conciliar *acta*, synods

Cunigund, empress and wife of Henry II 170, 180

Danes, Danish identity 4, 46–47, 96–97, 207

decretals 43, 224–226, 293

deposition of bishops 36, 41–42, 47–49, 221–223

Dhuoda, duchess of Septimania 203–216

Domnolus, bishop of Le Mans 26

Drogo, son of Pippin II 173–174, 182

duchies, ducal and comital power 6, 144, 168–169, 190–192

Ebbo, archbishop of Reims 36–37, 45–49

Egbert, archbishop of Trier 83–85

Egidius, bishop of Reims 36, 38–39, 47, 49

Einhard 23, 63, 69, 95, 102

Emma, queen and wife of Lothar III 139–140

Emma, queen and wife of Louis the German 174

England 3–8, 96, 166, 292; Benedictine monasticism 262–263, 265–266, 268, 270–271; court of King Æthelstan 242; excommunication rites *see entry* historical martyrology 29

episcopal *gesta* 7, 23, 27–30, 37, 94

episcopal/archepiscopal: authority and power 6–7, 30, 222, 225–226, 230–232, 283, 286–287, 289–290, 294; capitularies and statutes 30–31, 226; histories and *gesta* 7, 23–31, 37–38, 42, 48–49, 94; solidarity and identity 222–233; succession 36–37, 43–46, 48–49, 67, 268

Ermengard, empress and wife of Lothar I 137, 142, 174, 176

Ermentrude, wife of Charles the Bald 137, 139, 174

Eucharius, bishop of Trier 79, 80, 85

Eucherius, bishop of Orléans 40–41

Eusebius 18–22

excommunication 9, 36–37, 41, 49, 282–295; *see also deposition*

exegesis 114–119, 253

faith/fidelity 191–195, 228; political, 20, 46, 48, 103, 191–195, 210–211, 226, 228; spiritual 7, 27–28, 138, 143

Farfa 59, 79

Fastrada, empress and wife of Charlemagne 133–135, 141, 143, 182

Felix of Urgell 113, 117–118

feudalism 4, 168, 193, 203, 215

Flodoard of Reims 8, 37–49, 232

Folcuin of Lobbes 42, 49, 232

Fontenelle, 23–24, 44

forgeries 7, 24, 38, 41, 44, 224; *Pseudo-Isidore* 44, 223–224

formulae 138, 140, 154–160, 283–295

Fortunatus, patriarch of Grado-Aquileia 101, 103

Franco, bishop of Le Mans 24–25

Franks, 137–138, 209–210, 269; and the papacy 23; changing historiography 26; conflicts amongst 205–206; successes of 15, 19–20; as foreigners 62–63, 69

fraternity, literal 174; spiritual 204–205, 210, 212–214, 221–230

Frechulf of Lisieux 16, 19–23

freemen 20, 193–195

Fulbert, bishop of Chartres 292–295

Fulk, archbishop of Reims 16, 40–41, 283, 285, 290–291

Fulk, count of Anjou 293–294

Gaul 18, 23, 27, 225, 230; its people 25–28, 62

fenealogies: narrative 166; noble 168–169; royal/imperial 169–173, 176–181; diagrams of 166–167, 169–173, 176–181

Gerald of Aurillac, saint 210, 214–215

Gerbert of Aurillac, later Pope Sylvester II 36, 49, 117, 245, 248; *Letters of* 292–295

God 17, 20–21, 25, 138, 142–145, 155, 157–158, 206–207, 210–211, 268, 270–272, 290–292; Church of 43–44, 225; command/intervention of 67, 190; invocation of 102; judgement/punishment of 63, 67; *Law of* 286; Old Testament people of 229–230; providential plan of 29; word of 27

Gontio/Gunzo 242–243

Goths 18, 62–63, 68

Gottschalk of Orbais 44–45, 291

Greek language 243, 245, 247–248

Gregory VII, pope 5, 36, 112, 172, 179, 193

Gregory I (the Great), pope 64–65, 68, 115, 224, 245

Gregory of Tours 38–39, 47, 80, 87

Grimoald II, ruler of Benevento 172–174

Hadrian, pope 40–42, 44, 135, 138, 291

Hadrian, archbishop of Canterbury 242

Hagarenes 63–64, 69

hagiography, martyrologies 29–31, 142; saints' *vitae* 7–8, 39–43, 77–88, 102, 209–210, 215, 246, 262, 267, 272; *Vita Agritii* 80, 83; *Vita Felicis* 80, 86–87; *Vita Hildulphi* 80, 82; *Vita Magnerici* 80, 82–83, 85, 87; *Vita Maximini* 79, 82, 87; *Vita Nicetii* 80, 87; *Vita Paulini* 80, 86; *Vita Rigoberti* 40–43

Hainmarus, bishop of Auxerre 28–29

Henry I, king of East Francia 83–85, 170, 191, 222

Henry II 94, 170, 248–250; ancestry of 181; court of 168, 180; death of 178; *see* at Bamberg 288

Henry II, duke of Bavaria 144–145

Henry III, king and emperor 178–179, 191, 251–252

Henry IV, king and emperor 172, 178–179, 181, 193

Henry, duke of Saxony 171, 177–178

heresies 28, 113, 117, 121

Heribert II, duke of Vermandois 41, 45

Hermann of Reichenau 95, 175

Hincmar, bishop of Laon 41–42

Hincmar, archbishop of Reims 15, 30, 208–209; Flodoard's memory of 37, 49; and forgery 41; letters of 41–42, 285–286

narrative history, biography 8, 39, 42, 96–100, 113, 169, 251, 266; *Gesta* (*see also* Episcopal *gesta*) 23, 44, 49, 191,

306 Index

194, 243, 245; universal/world histories 16, 21, 77, 97; writing 8, 15, 191, 196
homilies 64–65, 115, 245–247, 290; *Homily of Luculentius* 119–121
Hugh Capet, king of West Francia 36, 169–170
Hugh, king of Italy 221–222, 225, 228–233
Hugh of Parma 250–251, 253
Hugh, archbishop of Reims 36–37, 39, 41, 45, 48–49
Hungarians 65, 99, 207, 209, 214

identity: of bishops *see episcopal*; familial 168, 203; individual 211, 221; of local communities 78, 87–88, 203; new perspectives on 96–97, 100; of religious communities 26, 69, 113, 204–205, 208, 211–212, 263–265, 270–271, 273–274; Salian 178–179
Isidore of Seville 119, 167–168, 248
Islam, religion and traditions of 95, 118, 121, 155, 189

Jerome, saint 17, 21
Jewish faith, Jews 17, 121, 210
Johannes XVI (Philagatos), antipope 247–248
Judith, empress and wife of Charles the Bald 21–22, 137–138, 142
judicial inquest, inquests into property 25, 101–103, 194–195
Julian, emperor 18, 63, 67–68
Julian, bishop of of Le Mans 25–26

kissing, as act of binding 25, 155, 157, 159–160, 191; prohibitions against kissing 271
Konigsnähe 241, 247, 253

Lateran Palace 66, 138
law 209–210, 248–249, 295; Salic law 190; *see also entries under canon law and Roman law*
lay abbacy 77, 82–83, 268
Leo, bishop of Vercelli 248–249, 251
Life of John of Gorze 215, 267, 272
litanies/*laudes regiae* 134–145; alterations to 141–143; manuscripts of 138–143; performance of 143–145
liturgy 7, 119, 283; in Trier 78, 87–88; manuscripts 122, 138, 283
Liutprand/Liudprand of Cremona 246–247, 251, 253; on the Hungarians 207; and Rather of Verona 230, 232, 241

Lombardy 2–3, 245; its people 20, 62–63, 66–68
Lotharingia 2, 170–171, 190, 222; *Circulation of canons* 285–286, 295
Louis III, king of West Francia 173–175
Louis IV, king of West Francia 37, 48, 170, 267
Louis the Blind, king and emperor 15, 175–176
Louis the Child, king of East Francia 21, 95, 171, 173–175
Louis the German, king of East Francia 40, 47, 205, 208, 214; genealogy of 170, 174, 178
Louis the Pious, emperor 15, 213–215, 283; court of 21–23, 249; genealogy of 169–170, 176; Gerward, librarian of 59; as lawmaker 69; letters to 138; oaths to 193, *833* rebellion against 36, 45–47
Louis III (the Younger), king of East Francia 175–176, 178
Lothar I, emperor 15, 46–47, 142, 174, 205, 214–215; death of 15; genealogy of 170
Lothar II, emperor 15, 19, 174, 176
Lyon 18, 27, 29, 112

Magdeburg 48, 79, 94, 144
Magnericus, bishop of Trier 79–80, 83, 85–86
Mainz 83, 85, 248, 253, 283–284, 287; Cathedral 179
marriage 9, 29, 155, 167, 268; prohibition of 168
Martin, bishop of Tours and saint 26, 137, 212–213, 215; as inspiration 78–79; at Trier 85–88
martyrdom 17–19, 22–23, 27–28, 81
martyrologies 27–30, 142
Mary 46, 135, 137, 139
Maximinus, bishop of Trier 79, 80–82, 84, 87
Mediterranean 2, 5, 69, 121–122
Metz 38, 45–46, 135, 137, 206; cathedral of 265–266
Middle Rhine 3, 177–179, 190
miracles 85, 86, 215, 267
missi 23, 101, 103, 194, 208
monastic rules: *Regula S. Benedicti* 113–115, 271; and above under Benedictine monasticism, *Regularis Concordia* 262, 266; *Rule of St Augustine* 266
Monte Soratte 56–58, 67–69
Muslim armies 2, 45, 63–64, 115, 207

Narbonne 112, 114–115, 119–121
nationalism 4
Nazi Germany/Third Reich 99–100
Nonantola 144, 248
Normans 6, 207, 213
Novara 244–246

oaths 172, 189, 205, 207–209, 291; formulas of 191–192; rituals of 191; of Strasbourg 191
Odalric, provost of Reims 36–37
Odo, abbot of Cluny 161; author of saintly vita 214–215; on clothing 271–272; sermons 78
Orosius 19–22, 248
Otto I the Great, king and emperor 41, 94, 229, 231; conquest of Italy 247; court of 232, 241–245, 247; genealogy of 179; misappropriation of 99; prayers for 142–144; synods presided over 37, 47–49
Otto II, emperor 83–85, 87; conquest of Italy 66, 69; death of 144; diploma of 59; marriage to Theophanu 247–248
Otto III, emperor 1–2, 70, 94, 97–98, 144–145; chancery of 249; court of 292; education of 248–249; Gebetbuch 139–140; library of 249
Ottonian dynasty 2, 59, 70, 143, 169, 181, 192; capitularies of 193; patronage of 83–84, 250

pagans, paganism 25–27, 208, 229
Paris 139, 206, 243, 252, 294; Councils of 30, 44, 47 283, 294; siege of 171
Paul, saint 18, 118, 137, 142
Paul I, pope 68, 138
Paul the Deacon 23, 241
penance 19, 45–46, 176, 208, 283
perjury 190, 207
persecution 18, 27; of Christians 18, 27–29, 67, 230; as narrative device 22, 70, 222, 228, 230; political 22, 222, 228–229
Peter, Saint 17–18, 23, 25–27, 69, 79, 85–86, 138, 288, 290; disciple of 37; intercession of 142; throne of 251
Pippin II (of Herstal) 40, 82, 173–174, 178
Pippin III (the Short) 19, 28–29, 68–69, 138; genealogy of see entry; history writing in his reign 15; and the papacy 23–25; memory in Trier 81–82, 87
poetry 38, 97, 243, 249, 252
Poitou 101, 103

Poland 4, 122
prophecy 65, 69–70
Provence 2–3, 207, 232
providential history 19–20

Quedlinburg 77, 144–145
Quierzy 40, 208

Radbod, bishop of Utrecht 212–215
Rather, bishop of Verona 221–233, 267; on kingship/queenship 140–141; rebellion and exile 221–223, 225, 227–233; use of canon law 223–224, 226–227, 230
reform: canonical/clerical 44, 115–117, 227, 266, 268; Carolingian 30, 112–115, 117–118, 121–122, 265; discourse and rhetoric of 263–264, 266–267, 269–274; Gregorian 5, 112, 250; monastic 79, 83, 112–115, 160, 262–266, 269; problematic terminology of 262
Regensburg 134, 175, 194, 209, 273
Regino of Prüm 94–95, 207, 295; as abbot of Saint-Martin 85; his Chronicle 15–18, 21–23, 29, 77, 171, 176–178, 222; compiler of canon law 283–293; his Libri duo de synodalibus causis et ecclesiasticae disicplinae 22, 31; manuscript 174–178, 180–181
Reichenau 21, 177, 244, 253, 273
Reims 8, 36–49, 83, 262–269; formulae 283, 285; cathedral 263, 266, 268–269, 273–274, 292
relics 1, 69, 84, 206
Remigius, bishop of Reims 26, 37, 269
rhetoric 244–245, 251–253
Richildis, empress and wife of Charles the Bald 136, 176
Rigobert, bishop of Reims 36–37, 39–44
Ripoll 112, 114, 118, 121
Robert the Pious, king of West Francia 168, 294
Roman Empire 17, 20, 56; historiographical models of 15–23, 25, 27–29, 56, 63, 66–70
Roman law 5, 155–156, 161, 167, 252
Romans 62–68, 210
Rotgar, duke of Le Mans 24, 26
Royal Frankish Annals see Annales regni Francorum
royal women 9, and individual entries by name
Ruotger, biographer of Bruno of Cologne 262, 266, 269–272

308 Index

S. Andrea at Monte Soratte 56, 58–59, 68–70
Saint-Basle 39, 49, 267–268
Saint-Bertin 42, 274
Saint-Calais, monastery 25, 30
Sant Cugat de Vallès 114–115, 118, 120
St Gallen/Saint-Gallen/Sankt Gallen 21, 169, 244–245, 253
Saint-Martial in Limoges 154–156, 159–161, 242
Saint-Martin in Tours 85–86
Saint-Martin in Trier 82–83, 85, 87
St Maurice in Magdeburg 48, 79
St Maximinius, monastery 79, 82–84, 86–87
Saint-Michel de Cuxa 113, 121
Saint-Remi in Reims 49, 139–140, 263, 268
Saint-Vaast 47, 215, 274
Salian dynasty 3, 169, 178–181, 189–190
Saxony, 5–6, 47, 143–145, 205, 231; Saxons 6, 66, 205, 209–210
Scotland, Scots 4, 205
Sens 177, 291
Septimania 112–115, 120, 122, 205
Slavic march, Slavs 8, 145, 209
Smaragdus, abbot of St Mihiel 114, 120, 270, 272
Soissons 44–46, 177–178, 206, 291
solidarity *see faith/fidelity*
Spain 8, 29, 112, 117, 119
Spanish march 111–113, 115, 117–121
Stephen II, pope 23, 62
Stephen, grammarian 245–246
Strasbourg 39, 191
Sulpicius Severus 85–86
Sylvester I, pope 18, 67–69
Sylvester II, pope, *see* Gerbert of Aurillac
synods 31, 227, 270, 283; excommunication at 292–294; Synod of Aachen 271–272; Synod of Pîtres 211; Synod of Reims 262–264, 266–268, 273–274; synodal acts 46, 207; synodal judgement 40–41, 228

Tassilo III of Bavaria, duke 141–142, 176
Thegan 46–47, 166
Theophanu, empress, regent and wife of Otto II 139, 143–145, 248
Theuderic IV 39, 42
Thietmar, prince-bishop of Merseburg 77, 143–145, 273
Tilpin, bishop of Reims 40–45
Titus, emperor 17, 20–21
Tours 26, 112, 160, 212–213; formulae of 156–158, 160; Tours Bible 118
treason, conspiracy 38, 47–48, 63, 66, 192, 225
Trier 8, 273, 283–285; councils at 47; local memory and liturgy 79–88; scriptorium of St. Matthias 252

urbanity, towns 5, 44
Usuard's *Martyrology* 29–30
Utrecht 144, 212

Venantius Fortunatus 38–39
Verdun 45, 114
Verona 137, 142, 224, 227–228
Vespasian, emperor 17, 20, 167
Vic 112, 116–117, 120–121
Vienne 29, 232
vikings 30, 177, 206, 211–215; modern historiography of 95
visions 40–41, 81, 267

West Francia 2–3, 6, 40, 168, 170, 205, 222, 268, 283–284, 290, 292, 294–295
Widukind of Corvey 143, 205, 209–210
William V, duke of Aquitaine 101, 103
Wipo, royal chaplain 179, 189–196
Wulfstan, bishop of Worcester and archbishop of York 96, 288–290, 292, 295
Würzburg 177–178, 245–246

Zacharias, pope 42–44, 69
Zwentibald, king of Lotharingia 15–16, 171, 173, 175–176